World Politics
in an Age
of Revolution

$$R \begin{cases} \text{Direction} \\ \text{Control} \\ \text{Resources} \\ \text{Capacity} \end{cases}$$

Conflict likely when
(1) virulent ideological conflict
(2) chronic internal instability verging on mass society
(3) adequate relative resource base together with an absolute resource base which does not involve general, catastrophic risk
(4) regulative activity inadequate to cope with planned disturbance
(6) environmental capacity inadequate to neutralize the class of major inputs.

x

World Politics in an Age of Revolution

JOHN W. SPANIER

 FREDERICK A. PRAEGER, *Publishers*
New York • Washington • London

FREDERICK A. PRAEGER, PUBLISHERS
111 Fourth Avenue, New York, N.Y. 10003, U.S.A.
5, Cromwell Place, London S.W.7, England

Published in the United States of America in 1967
by Frederick A. Praeger, Inc., Publishers

Fourth Printing, 1968

Library of Congress Catalog Card Number: 66-18921

Printed in the United States of America

For
LISA
who sat and watched . . .

Introduction

As a teacher of international politics, I have long felt the need for a text which, by focusing on the contemporary state system, could provide the reader—primarily the college student—with a fuller understanding of the forces shaping the world in which he lives. It is my hope that this is such a text. I have deliberately limited my analysis to the three forces—the revolution in military technology, the nationalist and social revolution throughout the underdeveloped areas, and the "permanent revolution" of Communism—that, in my view, have profoundly transformed the nature of international politics since World War II. Each of these revolutions is dissected and its character clarified, the pattern of its interactions with the other two revolutions is demonstrated, and the impact of all three revolutions upon the nature of the present state system is assessed.

An additional purpose has been to present the reader with a framework within which he can analyze contemporary international politics. Many distinguished texts in the field suggest (or so it seems to me) that the essential determinants of state behavior remain fairly uniform, regardless of the context in which the system operates; for instance, it is assumed that all states at all times "seek power" or pursue their "national interest." Such analyses, by invoking either *a priori* explanations or nebulous concepts, seem to avoid explanation of the specific motives that determine state behavior. It is therefore necessary to examine the environment in which states actually conduct their relations in order to analyze why and how states do *in fact* behave and use the various instruments of foreign policy to achieve their ends. For example, the role of diplomacy and the manner of its employment, or the evaluation of a nation's power and its effective application, will depend upon the nature of the specific international system. Since state behavior varies with the characteristics of the system and since two of the three forces examined in this book are historically unique (nuclear technology and the post-colonial modernizing nationalism of the new nations), a study of the contemporary system is, of course, justified; but such an analysis also reminds us that international politics is the study of change and that we can avoid false generalizations about state behavior only if we analyze that behavior in the context of prevailing conditions. As Stanley Hoffman has stressed, only "historical sociology"—comparative historical systems analysis—can protect us from premature generalizations from the experience of one particular system, be it the pre-French Revolution dynastic system or the contemporary postwar system. Even the presence of one force not unique in this system (the revolutionary powers) underlines the need for a greater emphasis on historical research than has lately been fashionable in the discipline of international politics. Our revolutionary state system may not be the world's first, but we know all too little about the behavior of states, both revolutionary and traditional, in such a system. Certainly, it is clear that the traditional "power politics" concepts drawn from a relatively stable, nonrevolutionary context do not provide a sufficient guide for describing and explaining—let alone predicting—state actions and interactions in a revolutionary world.

My final reason for writing this book stems from a belief that while systems analysis has been a useful analytical tool, particularly in its emphasis on the impact of the system upon its actors and the limited choices nations confront in their policy alternatives, it has led to an underestimation of the degree of freedom that still remains open to states and it particularly neglects the influence of internal factors in determining their foreign policies. In a revolutionary state system in which the revolutionary powers' principal approach to foreign policy is premised on international civil war, in which the various problems of nation-building and modernization in the new nations mold their external policies, such a neglect must inevitably result in a distorted analysis of contemporary international politics. My own predisposition, as I started writing this book, was to weight the impact of domestic factors more heavily than that of international factors in the molding of a nation's foreign policy. But by the time I wrote the concluding chapter, I had—as the reader will note—come to qualify this earlier judgment. As qualified, my conviction can be stated as follows: that the study of international politics, certainly in our time, must be a two-level (international and domestic) analysis. Admittedly, scholars have explored a series of internal factors directly related to foreign policy: the organizational and motivational variables of decision-making; the composition, roles, and perception of different elites; and the impact of "political culture," "national style," and public opinion on policy. Nevertheless, very little research has yet been done to demonstrate how (and under what conditions) these internal determinants affect external policy—or how the domestic and internal variables interact.

This book, it should be quickly added, provides no definitive answers to these problems. What I have attempted is to suggest the need for a better "mix" in the analysis of the causal relationship between internal factors and the foreign relations of states. Certainly no theories of foreign policy comparable to the various theories of international politics can be developed unless we correct this present imbalance with its overemphasis on the external determinants of state behavior. It remains questionable whether the disappearing distinction between international and intranational politics will soon receive conceptual recognition. While scholars may recognize that it is difficult to draw a clear line between these two levels (in the real world), this distinction—intended to provide a focus for the description and analysis of international politics —is a venerable one that is reflected in the organization of studies in political science. Separate courses are offered in comparative government and international politics. The former concern themselves with national systems in which there is an "authoritative allocation of values" or a "legitimate physical compulsion"; the focus of analysis is on the patterns of interactions within the system. On the other hand, courses in international politics are concerned with the international system, in which there is obviously no structure of authority; the focus of analysis is therefore on the patterns of interaction among the members of the state system. The result is that the comparative specialist is uninterested in the foreign policy "spill-over" emanating from the national system, and the international expert remains largely uninterested in the internal origins of the foreign-policy "inputs" that create the patterns in the state system. Thus, because it falls between the national and international systems, a two-dimensional foreign-policy analysis incorporating both internal and external factors has been neglected—except in the area of supranational integration, an issue that has interested both comparative government and international relations specialists because of the impossibility of separating internal and external considerations.

It should be noted that throughout this book frequent references are made to American history and politics. It is hoped that this device of referring to the more familiar American scene may serve to help clarify certain aspects of international politics or nation-building and modernization. Indeed, an interest-group analysis of the American political system provides a useful model for an explanation of interstate politics; and since some of the models of development suggest that non-Western nations will pass through stages of development similar to those of Western states—and may mature to become industrialized, urbanized, affluent states with modern, Western-type, democratic political systems—I have found it useful to refer to the "first new nation" not only for domestic analogies (as Seymour Martin Lipset did in his book of that title) but also for foreign-policy similarities. The utility of these comparisons may be judged by the reader.

I should like to express my gratitude to Arnold Dolin, my very fine editor, whose efforts, in the face of my impatience and criticism, resulted in a more concise and polished manuscript. Mrs. Jackie Floyd, secretary in the Political Science Department at the University of Florida, also deserves my thanks for finding time to type large sections of the manuscript. Finally, the following authors and publishers were kind enough to allow me to quote from their books: Edmund Wilson, *To the Finland Station;* The RAND Corporation and Princeton University Press, Bernard Brodie's *Strategy in the Missile Age;* Viking Press, Ronald Steel's *End of Alliance;* Little, Brown and Company, George Kennan's *Russia and the West Under Lenin and Stalin;* Alfred A. Knopf, Hans Morgenthau's *Politics Among Nations* and A. F. K. Organski's *World Politics;* Harper & Row, Robert Heilbroner's *The Great Ascent;* The Council on Foreign Relations, Henry Kissinger's *Nuclear Weapons and Foreign Policy* and Eugene Staley's *The Future of the Underdeveloped Countries;* John Wiley and Sons, John Kautsky's *Political Change in Underdeveloped Countries;* and Harcourt, Brace & World, R. H. Tawney's *Religion and the Rise of Capitalism.*

J. W. S.

Gainesville, Florida
May, 1966

Contents

World Politics
in an Age
of Revolution

I

Revolutions and War

The Three Revolutions

The two decades since the end of World War II have aptly been called a "revolutionary age." For the entire world has been in a state of revolution. Indeed, it has experienced three concurrent revolutions: the revolution in military technology, which threatens the extermination of life itself; the "permanent revolution" of Communism, which aims at the establishment of a new world order; and the "revolution of rising expectations," which seeks national independence and a better life for the peoples of the underdeveloped areas. Thus, the postwar era has been one of constant change, accompanied by ferment, turmoil, and violence.

Peace, quiet, and orderly progress—these are only memories of a past long dead. Crisis seems to have become almost a daily feature of international life—in fact, the very word "crisis," defined by Webster's as the "decisive moment, turning point, a crucial time," has been robbed of its meaning. So many moments that were decisive and crucial have come and gone that the observing citizen has become almost immune to the shocks of these recurring "turning points." He watches helplessly, for what can he do to influence events—except perhaps to retreat into a nostalgic quest for formerly quieter times, for simple and easy answers to the complex and seemingly overwhelming problems of the world in which he lives. But these problems cannot be wished away. They are here to stay. We must therefore first learn to understand them. It is the purpose of this book to try to aid in this understanding by: (1) briefly sketching the nature of the three revolutions and their historical

3

backgrounds; (2) analyzing each of the revolutions in some detail; and (3) examining the interactions among them in order to comprehend the ways in which they shape the universe around us.

The most dramatic of the revolutions is, of course, the military one. From the moment the first atomic bomb was exploded, the question was posed as to whether this "absolute" weapon was compatible with the continued existence of man organized in nation-states.[1] Could man control this power he had unleashed, or had science rendered traditional political and social patterns obsolete? If nations were unwilling to relinquish their sovereign rights, might not some future quarrel spark a global conflagration that would leave the world in ruins, its smoldering ashes a monument to man's scientific genius and his ill-will toward other men? Ortega y Gasset wrote that man was "lord of all things, but he is not lord of himself." The bomb underlined the obviousness of this contradiction and revealed another paradox: On the one hand, man had gained the knowledge that would permit him for the first time in history to obliterate himself and all he had created. On the other hand, he was committed to his nationalistic patterns of behavior and loyalties, as well as to international rivalry and conflict. Shaw's Devil, in *Man and Superman*, asked the vital question long before Hiroshima:

And is Man any the less destroying himself for all this boasted brain of his? Have you walked up and down upon the earth lately? I have; and I have examined Man's wonderful inventions. And I tell you that in the arts of life man invents nothing but in the arts of death he outdoes Nature herself, and produces by chemistry and machinery all the slaughter of plague, pestilence, and famine. The peasant I tempt today eats and drinks what was eaten and drunk by peasants 10,000 years ago; and the house he lives in has not altered as much in a thousand centuries as the fashion of a lady's bonnet in a score of weeks. But when he goes out to slay, he carries a marvel of mechanism that lets loose at the touch of his finger all the hidden molecular energies, and leaves the javelin, the arrow, the blowpipe of his fathers far behind. In the arts of peace Man is a bungler. I have seen his cotton factories and the like, with machinery that a greedy dog could have invented if it had wanted money instead of food. I know his clumsy typewriters and bungling locomotives and tedious bicycles: they are toys compared to the Maxim gun, the submarine, torpedo boat. There is nothing in Man's industrial machinery but his greed and sloth: his heart is in his weapons. This marvelous force of life of which you boast is a force of Death: Man measures his strength by his destructiveness.[2]

---

[1] See John H. Herz, *International Politics in the Atomic Age*. [EDITOR'S NOTE: See Bibliography for publication data, which have been omitted from all footnote citations of titles listed in the Bibliography.]

[2] George Bernard Shaw, *Man and Superman* (Baltimore, Md.: Penguin Books, 1952), p. 145.

The atomic bomb, and later the even more destructive hydrogen bomb, reinforced this ominous conclusion and made it plain that total war could no longer be regarded as a rational instrument of national policy. In prenuclear times, a nation unable to attain its objectives or defend its possessions by peaceful means might well resort to war if the possible gains seemed to outweigh the costs or if the interests to be defended were worth the price that would have to be paid. War under such circumstances could well be regarded as a continuation of diplomacy by other means. Indeed, war "has been the instrument by which most of the great facts of political national history have been established and maintained. . . . The map of the world today has been largely determined upon the battlefield. The maintenance of civilization itself has been, and still continues to be, underwritten by the insurance of an army and navy ready to strike at any time where danger threatens."[3] Our own history abounds in examples: Wars among the European colonial powers largely determined the territory each acquired on the North American continent. The United States established its independence by war. The Louisiana Purchase was possible because France was deeply involved in a European war and expected to lose the territory anyway. It was the fear of war with the new republic that induced Spain to open up the Mississippi and surrender the Floridas. The threat of war was also used to resolve the Oregon boundary dispute; and a war with Mexico ensued after the annexation of Texas, leading to the acquisition of the entire Southwest territory. Force was employed to dislodge the Indians when they blocked the Westward expansion or were settled on land the frontiersmen sought. Puerto Rico and the Philippines were taken during the Spanish-American War. Hawaii was annexed after the American settlers had overthrown the Hawaiian government. The War of 1812 was fought to preserve American independence and security. And the Civil War was fought to preserve the union. American history would therefore suggest that wars have traditionally played a crucial role in giving birth to new states, defining their frontiers, and preserving political independence and territorial integrity.

But nuclear weapons changed this traditional relationship between military means and political ends once and for all. Rather than helping to preserve civilization, the new instruments of violence threatened to destroy it. What possible goal would be "worth" the cost of self-immolation? How could a nation defend its political independence and territorial integrity if in the very act of defense it might well sacrifice the life of its nation? Nuclear technology did not allow for discrimination between victor and vanquished. It obliterated this historical distinction. In short, if states were going to continue playing the age-old game of

[3] James T. Shotwell, *War as an Instrument of National Policy* (New York: Harcourt, Brace and Co., 1929), p. 15.

"power politics," they might well end up incinerating themselves. Nuclear weapons were the means *par excellence* to realize what Freud identified as man's instinct for self-destruction. Any nation that wished to commit suicide could now do so very quickly. The strategists had a name for it—a "spasm war," an orgiastic exchange of millions of tons of explosive force guaranteed to transform any large urban, industrial state into a smoking and radioactive wasteland in a matter of hours, if not minutes.

And the possibility that mankind might commit suicide, whether deliberately or accidentally, was enhanced by the postwar emergence of the Soviet Union as a powerful revolutionary state—a state that rejected the international order because it considered the member states responsible for all social injustice in the world. This attitude is characteristic of a revolutionary state, whether it is Communist Russia or, in the late eighteenth and early nineteenth centuries, democratic France. For the revolutionary state's leaders pose the same two basic questions. First, why do the mass of men live in poverty, ill-health, and ignorance? And second, why must mankind be constantly cursed by war? In answer, these leaders point to the *ancien régime*. The majority of men are destitute because they are exploited by a privileged minority. Wars are fought because they pay dividends in the form of enhanced prestige, territorial conquest, or economic gains; and while the few profit, it is the masses who are compelled to do most of the fighting and the dying. Thus man can be freed from economic exploitation, political subjection, and frequent interstate violence only by the destruction of the existing social order. Only after the overthrow of the ruling class in all states can man achieve freedom from want, despotism, and war. It is the revolutionary state that assumes this responsibility for the liberation of mankind from its present bondage.

Thus the revolutionary state clearly considers itself a "universal state." The very nature of its belief commits it to the "permanent revolution" —that is, the total defeat of the prevailing political, economic, and cultural system, which condemns man to eternal slavery. Only a world-wide victory of the "new order" can lead to the establishment of a universal society in which man will for the first time in history be truly free from oppression and need. Indeed, since the old order is the cause of all social injustice and war, it is in fact the *duty*, as well as the *right*, of the revolutionary state to extend the revolution beyond its frontiers to all other states. The revolutionary state is therefore a messianic power engaged in a "just war" whose purpose it is to establish once and for all domestic social justice and international peace for all men. Thus, after the French Revolution, the National Convention of the Republic could proclaim: "The French Nation declares that it will treat as enemies every people who, refusing liberty and equality or renouncing them, may wish to maintain, recall, or treat with the prince and the privileged classes; on the other hand, it engages not to subscribe to any treaty and not to lay down its arms until the sovereignty and independence of the people whose territory the troops of the Republic shall have entered shall be established, and until the people shall have adopted the principles of equality and founded a free and democratic government."[4]

A revolutionary state is universal also because it asserts an identity of interest with the exploited masses in other states. The French Revolution consequently felt that it represented the underprivileged majority in all other aristocratic states. Just as the nobility wherever it ruled in Europe was the Revolution's enemy, so its subjects—especially the middle classes —were the Revolution's allies; indeed, France, as the torchbearer of liberty, equality, and fraternity, embodied their "real" will. Similarly, the Soviet Union, as the only major Communist power in 1945, equated its interests with those of the world proletariat. Revolutionary France and Russia thus appealed to their followers in all states to overthrow the governing nobility or bourgeoisie. From their viewpoints, vertical divisions *between* states were replaced by horizontal divisions cutting *across* state frontiers. Men were divided not by nationality but by class *within* each nation. The foreign policy of a revolutionary power is thus essentially one of *international civil war*. As De Tocqueville noted of the French Revolution: "All political and civil revolutions have been confined to a single country. The French Revolution had no country; one of its leading effects appeared to be to efface national boundaries from the map. It united and divided men, in spite of law, tradition, characters, language; converted enemies into fellow-countrymen, and brothers into foes; or, rather, to speak more precisely, it created, far above particular nationalities, an intellectual country that was common to all, and in which every human creature could obtain rights of citizenship."[5]

De Tocqueville astutely observed that the fundamental reason for this was that the French Revolution was similar to a religious revolution, for it also spread "by preaching and propagandism."

A political revolution, which inspired proselytism, and whose doctrines were preached abroad with as much warmth as they were practiced at home, was certainly a new spectacle. . . .

The French Revolution acted, with regard to things of this world, precisely as religious revolutions have acted with regard to things of the other. It dealt with the citizen in the abstract, independent of particular social organizations, just as religions deal with mankind in general, independent of time and place. It inquired, not what were the particular rights of

[4] Quoted in Carlton J. H. Hayes, *The Historical Evolution of Modern Nationalism* (New York: The Macmillan Co., 1950), p. 40.
[5] Alexis de Tocqueville, *The Old Regime and the French Revolution* (New York: Harper & Brothers, 1856), p. 24.

French citizens, but what were the general rights and duties of mankind in reference to political concern. . . .

By seeming to tend rather to the regeneration of the human race than to the reform of France alone, it roused passions such as the most violent political revolutions have been incapable of awakening. It inspired proselytism, and gave birth to propagandism; and hence assumed that quasi religious character which so terrified those who saw it.[6]

In 1945, the Soviet Union sought to regenerate not only the Russian people but all people—and again, to the consternation of contemporary observers. For Communism was a secular religion of damnation and salvation which, like any religious movement that believes it knows how to save man from sin, committed its believers—the Soviet rulers—to a missionary crusade to free all men everywhere from the tyranny of capitalism and bourgeois rule. More specifically, this meant the Western proletariat and the non-Western peoples, who, according to the Communists, were being exploited by capitalist colonialism.

The third revolution was the anticolonial one that raged throughout the underdeveloped areas of Asia, Middle East, Africa, and Latin America. For 400 years, the relationship between the West and the so-called non-Western world had been one of master and servant. All the great Western powers—Portugal, Spain, France, Belgium, the Netherlands, Germany, and England—had at one time or another been colonial powers. So had one major non-European nation, formerly a colony herself, the United States. Each of these nations exercised its colonial control in one of two ways: by direct control, as did England in India, France in Indochina, and the United States in the Philippines; or by indirect rule through native leadership, as England controlled some of the areas of the Middle East through the local sheiks and pashas. But the form of control was less important than was the fact that in both instances a colonial relationship existed—that is, the areas were governed by foreign powers. Self-determination and self-government consequently were denied to the natives.

The key to the colonial relationship lies in the fact that it is a relationship between superiors and inferiors. The inferiority of the colony is most obvious in the realm of political rights, but it extends to economic and social spheres as well. Not only the political institutions, but also the major economic enterprises within a colony are controlled by foreigners.

Europeans, particularly Northwestern Europeans, also have a practice of considering the non-European inhabitants of their colonies as socially, culturally, and racially inferior. Coming into contact with people whose race and culture were different from his own, the European took it for granted that his own ways were superior. If the natives did not share his religion, they were "heathens," if they did not have his sex complexes and taboos,

[6] *Ibid.*, pp. 41–43, 24, 25–27.

they were "immoral," if they did not have his compulsion to work, they were "lazy," if they did not share his opinions or possessed a different kind of knowledge, they were "stupid," if they behaved in ways that he could not predict because of his own ignorance of their culture, they were "child-like." In short, the European judged the natives as if they were Europeans who were misbehaving. Accepting his own standards as absolute, he judged every departure from the European way of life in negative terms, with never a thought that the natives might have different standards of their own.

Cultural relativism and tolerance for the ways of others are more wide-spread today than they were in the heyday of colonialism, but even today the average European or American considers himself superior to non-Europeans in general. This attitude is an essential part of the colonial frame of mind. Without it, colonialism would probably never have existed, for one does not hold in permanent subjugation and exploit people whom one considers equals.[7]

It was this same sense of superiority, however, that helped to bring the colonial era to a close. For colonial subjection gave rise to resentment against the foreigner and a new sense of nationalism. The drive for independence and self-government was therefore a logical reaction to colonial control. But it was not the only consequence. Conquest by the West also produced the desire among the conquered peoples to transform their traditional, agrarian, and economically backward societies into modern, urban, industrialized states. They had been easily conquered because the colonial powers were culturally, politically, and economically more advanced—and thus militarily stronger. As a result, the prestige of the traditional society, its rules, values, and institutions were placed in doubt. They had failed to protect the society from invasion and occupation. In these circumstances, the colonized state strove not only for independence: it also sought to "modernize" itself, to become a "twentieth-century" nation that would possess the national strength and status requisite to give its people a sense of self-esteem, as well as to gain the respect of the older and more established nations. This "modernizing nationalism" would, however, yield more than power and prestige. It would also result in a higher standard of living. The colonial subjects were keenly aware not only of the Western power's far greater strength, but of its far higher standard of living. Everywhere around them, the Westerner built his "little Europes"[8]—the great cities like Bombay, Singapore, and Hong Kong. They could therefore hardly avoid seeing how much better he fared. And again, they ascribed their own abysmally low standard to the traditional organization of their society. Thus, just as Western control spurred their nationalism, so the Western presence inspired the "revolu-

[7] A. F. K. Organski, *World Politics* (New York: Alfred A. Knopf, 1958), p. 224.
[8] This appropriate term was coined by Theodore H. Von Laue, in *Why Lenin? Why Stalin?*, p. 23.

tion of rising expectations." The anticolonial revolution was therefore twofold, both a nationalistic and a social revolution, whose aim was to convert each colonized nation into a modern and progressive welfare state. Karl Marx, in fact, had foreseen this desire of the traditional societies to "Westernize" over a century earlier in the *Communist Manifesto*: "The bourgeoisie, by the rapid improvement of all instruments of production, by the immensely facilitated means of communication, draws all, even the most barbarian, nations into civilization. . . . It compels all nations, on pain of extinction, to adopt the bourgeois [read "Western"] mode of production; it compels them to introduce what it calls civilization into their midst, i.e., to become bourgeois [i.e., Western] themselves. In one word, it creates a world after its own image."[9] An astute contemporary observer referred to this anticolonial revolution as the "world democratic revolution":

> We in the West talk a great deal, and rightly so, about the world Communist revolution. However, we are hardly aware of, and only partially understand, what might be called the world democratic revolution that we ourselves have been, and still are, creating. In a sense, this is not surprising. Our revolutionary impact upon the world has been, to a very large extent, unplanned, undirected, and even unconscious. But it is essential that we recognize that not only our government representatives, and armed forces, but also our businessmen, missionaries, educators, and all other elements of our society that come into contact with the non-Western world are actually powerful agents and instruments of revolutionary change. Almost everywhere in the non-Western world . . . we have unwittingly helped to break down the fabric of traditional societies and to set in motion strong forces of change.[10]

Western civilization, in brief, has been the greatest subversive influence in all of world history. By undermining the traditional cultures of the colonial countries, it fathered the anticolonial revolution.

Yet the term "anticolonial revolution" hardly reveals the true dimensions of this revolt. To state the issue succinctly and dramatically: the anticolonial revolution signaled the end of the old Western-dominated —more specifically, European-dominated—international order. "The core [of this order] was the European political system created by the Vienna settlement in 1815. . . . What gave this intra-European political order global significance was the fact that Europe in the nineteenth century, together with the United States, brought most of the rest of the world within its political and economic orbit of control or influence."[11] Europe and European culture reigned supreme throughout the world in 1900.

[9] Arthur P. Mendel (ed.), *Essential Works of Marxism*, p. 17.
[10] A. Doak Barnett, *Communist China in Perspective* (New York: Frederick A. Praeger, 1962), pp. 24–25.
[11] Robert C. Tucker, *The Soviet Political Mind*, p. 186.

European power and values had spread to all continents, and European prestige stood at its pinnacle—even in the colonized areas. Many of the sons of the wealthier natives attended Western schools, usually in the metropolitan country, and adopted Western clothes, manners, habits, and values. They became, in Macaulay's words, Englishmen or Frenchmen or Dutchmen "in taste, in opinion, in morals, and in intellect"— in everything but the color of their skins. Their commitment to Western values of self-determination and self-government and their resentment against Western attitudes of white supremacy finally led these Westernized natives to organize the revolt against colonial subjection. Europe had thus taught only too well, for Westernization ensured both the emulation and the rejection of the West. Europe's very success in extending its power to all parts of the globe stimulated the anti-Western revolt and thus the end of the international order it had controlled.

The crisis for the West, however, stemmed not merely from its declining global influence, but also from the fact that the anticolonial and Communist revolutions coincided. From the moment of their assumption of power, the Communist leaders in Russia saw their revolution as the beginning of the end of the old capitalist order and the first step toward the establishment of a new and superior Communist world system. The "defection of Soviet Russia from the European system signalized most dramatically and consequentially the collapse of the old order. And instead of treating this initial great defection as a fluke or reparable accident, [Leninist] theory construed it to be the momentous beginning of a long process of further decline and eventual total fall of the European-centered order in the world. It projected the departure of Russia from the European system in 1917 as an augury of the shape of things to come." The old order, centered upon Europe, would be replaced by a new order, centered upon Soviet Russia. The *ancien régime* was based upon capitalism's exploitation of all non-Western areas, which served as the profitable "reservoirs of capitalist imperialism." The new order would be founded upon Russia as the nucleus around which Europe's "former provinces" would cluster when they had revolted against the European and capitalist domination of their countries. "In short, the underlying theoretical postulate of the Soviet thinkers is that what was formerly a huge 'reserve of imperialism'—the Eastern hinterlands of Europe—shall in time become a reserve of sovietism, that a partnership shall take shape between the Soviet bloc and the remainder of the non-Western world *against* the West, that the great Afro-Asian-Arab zone will become increasingly oriented toward the Soviet bloc as it is emptied of what remains of Western influence. Nor, in this thinking, does the anti-Western bloc exclude certain states that geographically belong to the 'West,' such as the Latin American countries."[12] Soviet expectations about such a

[12] *Ibid.*, pp. 186–88, 194.

partnership and eventual new Communist world order depended, however, upon the anticolonial revolution.

While this nationalist revolution, like the revolution in military technology and the permanent revolution of Communism, registered its powerful impact in the wake of Europe's second "civil war" of the twentieth century, the fact remains that each of these three revolutions emerged from the fires of World War I. It was the series of defeats suffered by the Russian armies that precipitated the collapse of the Czarist Empire in 1917. It was the weakening of Europe during the Great War that led to the loosening of her grip on the colonies. And even strategic bombing of the enemy's cities and industries with the maximum explosive tonnage was a legacy of World War I.

World War I: Catalyst of Revolution

World War I was a cataclysmic experience for Europe. It was the first total war—with the exception of the French Revolution—Europe had experienced since the Treaty of Westphalia in 1648 had ended the slaughter of the Thirty Years' War. While Europe had, to be sure, witnessed a number of wars during the nineteenth century, these had been minor and of brief duration. Thus, after the almost 100 years of relative peace since the Congress of Vienna in 1815 had brought to a close the war with Napoleon, Europe suffered the shock of another major war and a terrible blood-letting. Once the initial German offensive into France was halted, the war on the Western Front bogged down in the trenches. First one side, then the other tried to break through the opponent's lines—neither successfully. The successive lines of barbed wire protected the enemy's trenches. The murderous machine-gun and rapid-rifle fire mowed down row after row of the advancing infantry. Breakthroughs became impossible.

Yet the offensives continued. The generals had, after all, learned that the only defense was the offense—*l'attaque à outrance*, as the French said. So headquarters continued to hurl their armies into battles. The artillery first laid down a barrage—sometimes lasting a week or longer—on the enemy's trenches. This was supposed to pulverize his position and shatter the morale of the troops. It was a simple idea that should have worked, but it never did. So killing *per se* became the objective. If his lines could not be ruptured, the enemy could at least be worn down by the various offensives. Sooner or later, these constant blows would emasculate the enemy's manpower reserves, and his morale would collapse. World War I was not a war of mobility and maneuver, but a war of attrition—an organized, four-year-long attempt by both sides to gain victory simply by bleeding each other to death. It was an unsophisticated strategy.

In an age that accepts man's inhumanity to man as a matter of course and has invented weapons of unprecedented destructiveness, World War I may not seem especially shocking. But this was not true for its contemporaries. Churchill described it eloquently:

The Great War differed from all ancient wars in the immense power of the combatants and their fearful agencies of destruction, and from all modern wars in the utter ruthlessness with which it was fought. All the horrors of all the ages were brought together, and not only armies but whole populations were thrust into the midst of them. The mighty educated States involved conceived with reason that their very existence was at stake. Germany having let Hell loose kept well in the van of terror; but she was followed step by step by the desperate and ultimately avenging nations she had assailed. Every outrage against humanity or international law was repaid by reprisals often on a greater scale and of longer duration. No truce or parley mitigated the strife of the armies. The wounded died between the lines: the dead mouldered into the soil. Merchant ships and neutral ships and hospital ships were sunk on the seas and all on board left to their fate, or killed as they swam. Every effort was made to starve whole nations into submission without regard to age or sex. Cities and monuments were cast down indiscriminately. Poison gas in many forms stifled or seared the soldiers. Liquid fire was projected upon their bodies. Men fell from the air in flames, or were smothered, often slowly, in the dark recesses of the sea. The fighting strength of armies was limited only by the manhood of their countries. Europe and large parts of Asia and Africa became one vast battlefield on which after years of struggle not armies but nations broke and ran. When all was over, Torture and Cannibalism were the only two expedients that the civilized, scientific, Christian States had been able to deny themselves: and these were of doubtful utility.[13]

The French alone lost 955,000 men in 5 months of 1914—more than 200,000 of them during the first month; in 1915, 1,430,000 men; and in 1916, 900,000 men. The losses for single battles were staggering. The German attempt to bleed the French at Verdun led to a 10-month battle costing France 535,000 casualties and Germany 427,000—almost a million men altogether! An English attempt to pierce German lines in the same year, 1916, resulted in the 5-month Battle of the Somme. Although they pounded the German lines for 8 days with artillery before the troops were even sent into battle, the British gained only 120 square miles—at the cost of 420,000 men, or 3,500 per square mile; German losses were even greater: 445,000 men. Some estimates place the total Somme casualties even higher—at 1.2 million, the highest for any battle in history. At Ypres in 1917, the British bombardment lasted 19 days;

[13] Winston S. Churchill, *The World Crisis*, 1911–1918 (London: Landsborough Publications, 1960), p. 8.

321 trainloads of shells were fired, the equivalent of a year's production by 55,000 war workers. This time the English forces captured 45 square miles—at the cost of 370,000 men, or 8,222 per square mile.[14] By comparison, total British Empire casualties during the 6-year-long World War II were almost 1.25 million, including 350,000 dead and 91,000 missing. Approximately 9 million men in uniform were killed during the 4 years of the Great War, and the number of dead civilians totaled an additional several million.

But the impact of war cannot be measured merely by citing statistics of the dead. The real impact can only be understood psychologically. Losses are not just quantitative; they are qualitative as well. A nation can ill afford to lose millions of her men. She can even less afford to lose almost her entire youth. Is it to be wondered that the nations of Europe who lost so many of their men—and especially their young men and the unborn children they would have fathered—also lost their *élan*, their self-confidence, their hope for the future? For the men who would have supplied this vigor and optimism—had they grown up and become the leaders of government, business, labor, and science—lay dead in Flanders Field. And those who returned from the battlefields, where they had left the corpses of their comrades-in-arms, were haunted by the war. In the interwar period, they remained politically passive, withdrawing into their private worlds, avoiding any public involvement. Erich Maria Remarque dedicated his famous novel *All Quiet on the Western Front* to this "generation of men who, even though they may have escaped its shells, were destroyed by the war." One of Remarque's German soldiers expressed the disillusionment of this generation:

Had we returned home in 1916 [he said just before the armistice ending the war], out of the suffering and the strength of our experiences we might have unleashed a storm. Now if we go back we will be weary, broken, burnt out, rootless, and without hope. We will not be able to find our way any more.

And men will not understand us—for the generation that grew up before us, though it has passed these years with us here, already had a home and a calling; now it will return to its old occupations, and the war will be forgotten—and the generation that has grown up after us will be strange to us and push us aside. We will be superfluous even to ourselves, we will grow older, a few will adapt themselves, some others will merely submit, and most will be bewildered;—the years will pass by and in the end we shall fall into ruin. . . .

[14] On the slaughter of World War I, see Theodore Ropp, *War in the Modern World* (rev. ed.; New York: Collier Books, 1962); Hanson W. Baldwin, *World War I: An Outline History* (New York: Harper & Row, 1962); and particularly the dramatic book by Alistair Horne, *The Price of Glory: Verdun 1916* (New York: St Martin's Press, 1962).

I am very quiet. Let the months and years come, they bring me nothing more, they can bring me nothing more.[15]

For Europe, then, the Great War was the Great Divide. The nineteenth century had been one of confidence. Democracy was spreading in Europe and was expected to spread to all other continents, too—as soon as colonialism had prepared the natives of Asia and Africa for self-government. The future would belong to the common man; his rights and freedom would supplant the traditional privileges of the few. For the first time in history, men would join together in human brotherhood across national boundaries, in a new world of mutual understanding and good will. Peace would be both inevitable and permanent. And science and technology would improve everyone's standard of living; the age-old economies of scarcity would be transformed into economies of abundance and affluence. Poverty and misery would be ended forever. This optimism and faith in progress was aptly voiced by an American, Andrew Carnegie, in his instructions to the Trustees of the Carnegie Endowment for International Peace: "When . . . war is discarded as disgraceful to civilized man, the trustees will please then consider what is the next most degrading evil or evils whose banishment . . . would most advance the progress, elevation and happiness of man."[16] It was just a matter of time, then, until war would be eliminated. It would have been contrary to the spirit of the age to ask whether this abolition of war could indeed be achieved.

The Great War changed this optimism to pessimism, this confidence to doubt and fear. The West's utter certainty of its own greatness and future lay shattered on the battlefields among the decaying corpses. For the first time, Western scholars talked of the "decline of the West." Abroad, Europe's imperial control was weakened, and at home the expected trend toward democracy was halted, if not reversed. Fascism took over in Italy, Nazism gained power in Germany, and Mussolini and Hitler together helped Franco seize control of Spain; in Eastern Europe, only Czechoslovakia could be considered a democratic country. The nineteenth century had believed in the supremacy of reason and its ability to make the world a safer and better place in which to live. In the interwar period, demagoguery and the manipulation of hysterical crowds, totalitarianism and its warlike spirit seemed to be the wave of the future.

As the structure and hopes of the previous 100 years began to crash all around them, the leaders of France and England became concerned above all with avoiding another war. "No more war, no more war" became their cry. And who could blame them? These men were not con-

---

[15] Erich Maria Remarque, *All Quiet on the Western Front*, translated by A. W. Wheen (Boston: Little, Brown and Co., 1929), pp. 289–90, 291.

[16] Quoted in Kenneth W. Thompson, *Political Realism and the Crisis of World Politics* (Princeton, N.J.: Princeton University Press, 1960), p. 18.

cerned merely with their personal survival. They were men of honorable intentions and decent motives, greatly concerned for the welfare of their fellow men and repelled by the horror and senselessness of modern war. It is easy today to sneer at the appeasement of Hitler, but to the survivors of World War I, another war could mean only the slaughter and seemingly wasteful sacrifices of Verdun and the Somme. They still heard the "soldiers marching, all to die." And they remembered that the strain of that war had collapsed four of Europe's great empires: Austria-Hungary, Ottoman Turkey, Imperial Russia, and Imperial Germany. They also recalled that despite Germany's grievous losses, her opponents had suffered twice as many losses—and their populations were smaller than Germany's. If fighting another war would involve another such blood bath, surely they would be signing their nations' death warrants. Their social structures and morale could not absorb such losses for the second time in two generations. To most men who had lived through the tragic war years, peace thus became a supreme value. The appeasement of Hitler during the 1930's was to them not just the only policy—it was an absolute necessity. Surely it was "saner" to resolve differences with reason than with guns. Would it not be better to understand each other's legitimate grievances and settle differences in a spirit of good will rather than by war? Was it not preferable to make mutual concessions, thereby diminishing distrust and fear, and building the mutual confidence that could be the only basis of a firm peace? To ask these questions was to answer them for most of the men who had survived 1914–18. Between the alternatives of appeasement and war, no man of good will and humanity had a choice.

Thus Munich happened because the predominant mood and policies of the political and military leaders of France and Britain were defensive. War was to be avoided at almost any cost. It was to be fought only if the enemy—and the only possible enemy was Germany—left them with no alternative by directly attacking their countries. Moreover, if and when this happened there would be no more Western offensives. Let the Germans launch the offensives if they expected to win. The French would await them in their impregnable Maginot Line. German assaults would be defeated with such heavy loss of life that sooner or later the Germans would desist and call for peace on the basis of the prewar *status quo*. This plan in effect presupposed that the next war would be a repetition of World War I: a static trench war in which offensives were planned either to rupture the opponent's lines or to decimate his troops and break his morale. Since men tend to think of the future in terms of the past—for past experience provides them with their principal guidelines—the French conception of the next war and preparation for it seemed quite logical.

There was, however, a second reaction to the experience of World

War I. The Germans, too, rethought their approach to war. Indeed, the
military clauses of the Versailles Peace Treaty compelled them to do so.
For the German Army was to be limited to 100,000 men; it was to have
only 40,000 officers, who were to serve 25 years, and the length of service
for all others was 12 years. These stipulations were to ensure against the
Germans continuously recruiting new men, training them for a year or
two, and then discharging them, thereby building up a large army. The
army was to have no heavy weapons, such as aircraft, tanks, and large-
bore guns. Consequently, the German military had to answer the question of how such a small army could fight against larger enemy forces.
Beyond that question loomed the still larger one of how a second
slaughter could be avoided if another war were to be fought. The answer
was the *Blitzkrieg*—that is, a war conducted with lightning speed. Mobile land forces—meaning largely *Panzer* or tank divisions—in combination with tactical air power would smash the enemy's lines and break
through into the open and undefended areas in his rear. The infantry
would advance in the wake of this one-two punch and mop up the enemy's broken and confused forces. In short, the German military leaders, unlike their French and British—and, indeed, American—counterparts, were able to comprehend the impact on military tactics of the
airplanes and tanks which had appeared late in the previous war. They
realized their possibilities and thought of a unique manner in which a
combination of the two could restore to warfare the mobility that had
been lost during the Great War at such an enormous cost of life.

Both these reactions to World War I, different as they were, nevertheless shared one fundamental assumption: that the decisive engagements
of a future war would be fought on land. The third view of the conduct
of warfare rejected this assumption, maintaining that the key battles
would be fought in the air. Thus the interwar years witnessed the birth
of the concept of strategic air power. In a sense, this new concept of
warfare was the counterpart of the French Maginot Line psychology. If,
as World War I had shown, the defensive forces had gained a seemingly
lasting superiority over the offensive forces, then the only quick and effective way of breaking the stalemate on land and of achieving victory was
to attack the enemy's home front from the air. The target would be
his cities, and if these were heavily bombed, two objectives would be
achieved: first, the industrial strength that sustained his armies in the
field would be smashed; and second, the morale of the civilians—presumably less hardened to the rigors of war than the front-line soldiers—
would be broken. General Douhet, the Italian "founder" and theorist of
strategic air power described it as follows:

Take the center of a large city and imagine what would happen among
the civilian population during a single attack by a single bombing unit. For

my part, I have no doubt that its impact upon the people would be terrible. . . .

What could happen to a single city in a single day could also happen to ten, twenty, fifty cities. And, since news travels fast, even without telegraph, telephone, or radio, what, I ask you, would be the effect upon civilians of other cities, not yet stricken but equally subject to bombing attacks? What civil or military authority could keep order, public services functioning, and production going under such a threat? And even if a semblance of order was maintained and some work done, would not the sight of a single enemy plane be enough to stampede the population into panic? In short, normal life would be impossible in this constant nightmare of imminent death and destruction. And if on the second day another ten, twenty, or fifty cities were bombed, who could keep all those lost, panic-stricken people from fleeing to the open countryside to escape this terror from the air?

A complete breakdown of the social structure cannot but take place in a country subjected to this kind of merciless pounding from the air.[17]

The role of the army and navy was to be strictly subsidiary: to perform a holding operation on the ground while the air force pulverized the enemy's urban and industrial centers and compelled him to surrender. The development of big bombers and bombs was inherent in this line of thinking; the greater the explosive power of the bombs, the more destructive would be the impact. The first large-scale strategic bombing was carried out during World War II, but it was not until Hiroshima and Nagasaki that the decisiveness of strategic air power in a general war was dramatically illustrated.

World War I also acted as a catalyst to the Bolshevik Revolution in Russia. Czarist Russia was not the only country exhausted by the Great War. But Russia—a country composed of many nationalities, a diversity of religions, a huge population of 170 million, and immense territory— had already been in a state of potential revolution. The strain of the war so weakened the Russian state—previously weakened by its defeat at the hands of Japan in 1904–5—that it could no longer contain the political and social ferment stirring within it. The state simply collapsed under the hammer-like blows of the German forces, and the domestic ferment thereupon burst into revolution. The defeats the Russian armies suffered on the battlefield were, indeed, a clear symptom of Russia's decline and disintegration.

Czarist Russia was an autocratic state that imposed unity on its people from above. The Czars considered themselves as paternalistic and absolute rulers. The duty of the people was to obey, for the "Little Father" ruled them by divine right. All authority was vested in the

---

[17] Quoted by Edward Warner, "Douhet, Mitchell, Seversky: Theories of Air Warfare," in Edward Meade Earle (ed.), *Makers of Modern Strategy* (Princeton, N.J.: Princeton University Press, 1943), p. 491.

Czars, and they exercised this authority through the imperial bureaucracy, staffed by the nobility. This aristocracy was essentially a servant class, for the Czars made and unmade the nobility as they extended their authority. The Russian nobility, administering the civilian and military levers of power through which the Czars maintained their dominion, therefore never attained a degree of independence from the Crown, as did the nobility in most Western states. It never acquired a sense of its own rights, or the accompanying sense of class security which derives from the knowledge of its standing and authority in society. It would have been inconceivable for the Russian aristocracy to rebel against the Crown and compel a Czar to sign a Russian Magna Charta, as the British nobility had done when King John violated their historic and accustomed rights. The Russian nobles did receive some rewards for their faithful service. They held a pre-eminent social position and they were able to acquire economic wealth, consisting of both land and serfs. The autocracy was further bolstered by the Orthodox Church. The Czars were not only the secular rulers of the state, but the heads of the Church. Unlike the West, Russia never experienced the division of authority between state and church, with each tending to keep the other in check and preventing either from exercising absolute control over society. The Russian Orthodox Church was the bulwark of the autocracy. Both the aristocracy and the Church, in brief, identified their interests with the autocracy, which was committed to the preservation of the *status quo.*

This commitment to stability was to prove to be the autocracy's fatal weakness. For in a society that cannot change peacefully, the social forces that demand change have no alternative but to turn to violence and revolution to achieve rectification of their grievances. Czarist Russia contained three such social forces—more accurately, classes—each one of which felt increasingly alienated from the state. The first, and most prominent, was the peasantry, which constituted nine-tenths of the total population.[18] Originally owned by the nobility, the peasants still lived in a condition of virtual servitude after the Emancipation Edict of 1861, which had not greatly altered their circumstances. The land granted to the peasant under the Edict was not enough; and the high redemption payments for this land proved to be too burdensome for him to pay off. His methods of cultivation were primitive, and the resulting yield from his small plot of land was not enough to feed his growing family. In addition, the peasants went deeply into debt during the long agricultural depression from 1875 to 1895, when the price of wheat on the international market was low. None of the government's measures to ameliorate the peasants' lot were effective. In the wake of Russia's de-

---

[18] Hugh Seton-Watson, *The Decline of Imperial Russia, 1855–1914* (New York: Frederick A. Praeger, 1956), pp. 41–47, 109–14, 272–80.

feat in 1905, peasant dissatisfactions led to widespread spontaneous uprisings during 1905-6. The government's cruel suppression of these uprisings, and the accompanying looting and seizures of land—without any serious attempt to improve the conditions that had precipitated this turmoil—resulted in a dilution of peasant loyalty to the state. Here was a clear demonstration of the very shaky foundation upon which the Czarist autocracy rested—and of how little pressure was needed to collapse that foundation.

While Russia was predominantly an agrarian society, she had also begun to industrialize during the second half of the nineteenth century. The development of the 1860's and 1870's was followed by an even greater industrializing surge during the period from 1890 to 1914. But Russia's industrialization lagged far behind that of the West, and the rising middle class was relatively small. Thus, unlike its stronger and larger Western counterparts, it could not exert much pressure on the government to meet its demands for parliamentary government and free enterprise. It was, in fact, in no position to bargain at all. The state sponsored the industrialization, and industry received most of its orders from the government. The Russian bourgeoisie consequently never managed to establish its independence from the autocracy. Quite the contrary: the bourgeoisie remained dependent on the autocracy, and the latter was determined to preserve this dependence and squash any demands by the rising bourgeoisie for a share of its political power and control over the economy. The Russian middle class therefore also became increasingly hostile to the Czarist regime. If the regime was the bourgeoisie's best customer, it also stood in the way of the development of a large domestic market. In fact, the aristocrats who staffed the government were, with some few exceptions, generally hostile to business and hampered its growth; for extensive industrialization would have undermined the foundations of the Czarist state and society.

The third dissatisfied class was the proletariat, composed primarily of peasants recently arrived in the industrial cities. Very long working hours, subsistence wages, unsafe and unsanitary working conditions were this peasant-proletariat's sources of grievances. Attempts to correct these grievances were too little and came, in any case, too late. Furthermore, once concessions had been granted, the tendency was all too often to withdraw them at a later date when critical periods of strikes and demonstrations had passed. When trade unions were finally legalized at the beginning of the century, they were closely watched by the police and frequently suppressed. Not surprisingly, the workers began to feel that the government was not concerned with their miserable lot. They, too, became disenchanted with the Czarist regime, and their loyalty, like that of the families they had left behind in the country, was questionable.

Russia in 1914 was thus truly a giant with feet of clay. Every major segment of society was hostile to the Czarist regime—and had become so because of the short-sightedness and inflexible attitude of rulers who seemed unwilling to adjust to the changes transforming the very nature of Russian society. "State policy barricaded the road to reform and opened the flood gates to revolutionary upheaval."[19] The tragedy of the Czarist government and social order was that it was too strong for its own good; its ability to preserve the political and social *status quo* was to be its downfall. Conversely, the classes that might have transformed Russia into a constitutional monarchy were too weak. Perhaps if the war had not intervened, and the peasant dissatisfactions had grown more intense, and if the middle class and working class had grown in numbers and strength as industrialization proceeded, the Czar might have awakened to the plain conclusion that if the autocracy was not to be overthrown by bloody revolution he would have to satisfy the grievances of the people he ruled. But the war did intervene, and the attention and energy of the government became focused on the prosecution of the war. The subsequent defeats and retreats, and the huge manpower losses inflicted upon the Russian Army, further lowered the prestige of the regime. Finally, in March, 1917, bread riots and strikes in St. Petersburg sparked a general strike. The Czarist regime simply collapsed. In the final crisis, it was unable to rely upon even the army to suppress the disorder—hardly surprising, however, since the army was, after all, composed of the very same dissatisfied masses.

The First Revolution established a Provisional Government composed of liberals and moderate conservatives, led by Alexander Kerensky. If the war had been concluded immediately, the government might have been able to consolidate its position and Russia would then have been able to evolve in a democratic direction. But Kerensky's government felt honor-bound not to break the Czar's pledge to the Western powers that Russia would not sign a separate peace treaty with Germany. And the Western Allies would not release Russia from that pledge, because they were fearful that if Russia left the war, Germany would be able to transfer her forces from the Eastern Front to the West and thereby gain a possibly decisive advantage. Yet a conclusion of the war for Russia was a prerequisite for any possible stabilization of the domestic turmoil. The Russian people were weary of fighting. Above all else, they wanted peace. The army had already declared its desire for an end to the massacre by "voting with its feet": large numbers of soldiers had simply left the front lines and returned home. Even more important, the Provisional Government could not implement a land-reform program while simultaneously trying to conduct a war. The government was therefore unable to rally popular support. Lenin exploited this situation by promising that when the Communists assumed power they would end hostilities and

[19] Merle Fainsod, *How Russia Is Ruled*, p. 30.

grant every peasant his own piece of land. In November, 1917, the Communist Party seized power in the Second Revolution. Russia's continued participation in the war had been fatal for Kerensky's Provisional Government. The incompatibility between Allied war aims and Russia's own domestic needs was thereby resolved in the Communists' favor.

Once the Communists were in control, it was only a question of time until the Soviet Union would pursue its revolutionary and expansionist foreign policy. The opportunity to do so was denied it during the interwar period, when the Soviet leaders were far too preoccupied with domestic matters: conclusion of the civil war with the forces of the *ancien régime*; restoration of the economy to its prewar production level; elimination of all opposition parties and consolidation of their own hold on the reins of government; Stalin's succession to Lenin's leadership after the latter's death; the resultant elimination of all opposition to the new leader within the party; and the launching of the collectivization and industrialization programs to transform the Soviet Union from a backward, largely agrarian society into an urban and industrialized power of the first rank. As a weak state, the Soviet Union was hardly in a position to expand during the 1920's and 1930's. This opportunity came only in the wake of the retreating German armies during World War II as the Red Army moved into Eastern and Central Europe and cut Europe into two.

The Europe it advanced into and threatened was defeated, a weary, hungry, and demoralized land whose economy lay shattered and whose passions had been spent in the bloody slaughter of the continent's second Thirty Years' War. It was a Europe that above all else desperately wanted peace, after experiencing a "bellyful of history."[20] Europe was no longer considered master of its own fate. The European optimist, it was said, learned "Americanese," the pessimist Russian. History apparently had condemned Europe to impotence, and her future depended upon the actions of two non-European nations. This sudden fall from power was perhaps most dramatically symbolized by the European states' loss of their colonies. This "end of empire" was not always, to be sure, accepted with grace. France tried until the late 1950's to hold on to some of its colonies, especially Indochina and Algeria. Immediately after World War II, the Netherlands fought to retain the wealthy East Indies; but it lost, and the new nation of Indonesia emerged from this struggle. Even then, the Dutch clung for years to the economically valueless territory of New Guinea. Belgium held on to the riches of the Congo until 1960; indeed, the Belgians were so confident the Congo would not seek independence in the foreseeable future that they did not even prepare any plans for such a contingency or train the native political, military, and economic leadership the Congo would need to become

[20] Theodore H. White, *Fire in the Ashes*, p. 10.

self-governing. Portugal, too, refused to recognize that the age of colonialism was over; in the mid-1960's, she still tenaciously holds on to her African possessions.

Nevertheless, few colonies remain today. Even some of the economically least viable and politically most unstable states, like Rwanda and Burundi, have become self-governing. In the late 1950's, one African state after another became independent—most of them with populations of only 1–5 million, and several with fewer than 1 million. Moreover, most of the new states that have emerged since 1945 have done so without violence. Britain's record of voluntarily relinquishing colonial control was undoubtedly best, except in certain areas of Africa where the white settlers held firm control of the local government and the problem was thereby considerably complicated. France also acquitted herself well: In the mid 1950's, she granted freedom to Tunisia and Morocco; and after De Gaulle assumed power in 1958, he rapidly granted independence to the "overseas territories" of French Black Africa; there then remained only Algeria, which finally won independence in 1962.

The fact that violence did not play a more significant role in the retreat from colonialism is perhaps more surprising when it is recalled that the colonies served a number of vital purposes for the mother countries. First of all, they were international status symbols. A great nation, or one that wished to think of itself as great, had to possess a colony— just as today, in order to qualify as a great power, a nation must acquire the latest symbol, an atomic bomb. Britain, the world's greatest power during the nineteenth century, also possessed the largest empire. France, her prestige lowered by Germany's victory over her in 1870, turned to colonialism in Africa to recoup her status; her acquisitions there were second only to those of Britain. After achieving her national unification, Germany also sought colonies—not as a substitute for declining prestige, but as reinforcement of her new standing as a great world power. Of the traditional first-rank European states, only Austria-Hungary possessed no empire outside Europe—a sign of her decline and forthcoming disintegration. For a Western, but non-European power, the United States, the non-possession of any colonies meant that she had not yet "arrived." During the Spanish-American War, which heralded the entry of the United States onto the world scene as a great power, she picked up the Philippines, Puerto Rico, and Guam. She had already annexed Hawaii and was soon to add Samoa. National greatness also demanded a large navy; this seemed obvious from the fact that Britain, the world's greatest empire, possessed the largest navy. So the small American Navy, which ranked behind that of Chile, was expanded into the second largest in the world.

For most of the colonial powers, however, their empires meant more than status; they also indicated power. The colonies contributed to the power of the mother country by increasing her territory, population, and economic resources. A France of 100 million men was obviously a stronger and greater nation than a France of 40 million. Colonial troops from French Africa or British India, for example, could be employed to bolster the home armies against a numerically superior enemy. Europe's colonial expansion overseas was, in fact, not unlike America's westward expansion. A United States limited to the Eastern seaboard could never have become more than a second-rank power. Because the land she acquired was mostly contiguous rather than overseas, the United States never had to suffer a loss of colonial territory on the scale the European powers did. It was the consciousness of what this loss involved—becoming a small, insignificant, second- or third-rate nation—that made France cling to Indochina and Algeria for so long, and Holland hold on to the Dutch East Indies. America, even if confined to her North American continental boundaries, was a "superpower." She peopled her new and empty lands with successive waves of immigrants who became loyal citizens. But the French, the Dutch, and the English imposed their control on millions of people of other races whose nationalism, aroused by foreign conquest and rule, turned them against the colonizers and led them to seek freedom. The European powers' conception of their own greatness was thus at stake.

Finally, many colonies, though by no means all, served as a source of profit. They provided the mother country with cheap raw materials, which could be processed, turned into manufactured goods, and sold on the domestic and international markets. Colonies were a source of food as well. England, for instance, depended to a large extent upon Canada, Australia, and New Zealand for her wheat, meat, and dairy products. Protected colonial markets were also an assured outlet for English, French, or Dutch producers. In brief, colonies provided the nations of Europe with natural resources they usually lacked at home and additional markets in which to sell some of their goods. Both these factors contributed to the well-being of the mother country. In this respect, Europe's colonial expansion again resembled our own Westward expansion. The latter, too, provided vast tracts of land for the growth of food, raw materials for Eastern industry, and new markets as the West became settled. Our "colonialism," in brief, was primarily continental. Nor were the "colonials" always satisfied. Indeed, what else did the Populist movement of the late nineteenth century think it was protesting against but Eastern industrial and financial "colonial exploitation" of Western agrarian interests?

The major difference, however, was that the American "colonials" did not harbor any secessionist aims, while the colonial subjects of the European nations did, of course, wish to establish their own nation-states.

Their pressure for national independence could not, moreover, have come at a more appropriate time, coinciding as it did with Europe's postwar collapse. Britain's consciousness of its weakness made it more sympathetic to the cause of colonial freedom. The Dutch soon discovered how great the cost would be—in terms of manpower, money, and lost international prestige—to hold on to the East Indies. The French were to learn this lesson equally well. The nationalist movements had grown strong by the end of the war. And as the new states emerged one by one, and in large numbers after 1955, they pressed for the independence of their fellow colonials. In an age in which men increasingly recognized that colonial rule—no matter how benevolent—was no longer a proper justification for governing a foreign people, and that each nation had the right to govern itself, no matter how ineffectively or tyranically, the United Nations provided the young countries with an effective forum. Even Western opinion had to come to recognize the incompatibility between democratic government at home and the practice of authoritarian rule in the colonies.

The West's first twinge of conscience had, indeed, come after World War I, when Britain and France agreed to divide up the German and Turkish dependencies as part of the war booty. But because of its own anticolonial tradition, the United States insisted that these dependencies should not be treated as colonies. Thus the League of Nations established a mandate system that permitted Britain and France to govern Germany's and Turkey's former territories. Their own colonies were not, of course, placed under the League. It has been said therefore that this mandate system changed nothing, that it in effect continued the old-fashioned colonial rule under a new guise. "The old hag of colonialization," as Salvador de Madariaga has remarked, "put on a fig leaf and called itself mandate." What was significant, however, was that colonialism had to be called by a new name. Colonialism was becoming a "dirty" word, in apparent recognition that it was no longer a sufficient justification for governing another people. Under the mandate system, the mandate powers were to some degree to be held responsible for their administration. They were considered accountable for the well-being of their mandate subjects and were supposed to prepare them for eventual independence. The mandate authorities were to govern their newly acquired subjects as "a sacred trust of civilization." Each had to submit annual reports, and the people of the territories were granted the right to petition the League if they had grievances, although admittedly such a petition had to be channeled through the mandate authorities. Nevertheless, the mandate system for the first time stated that a colonial power did not have the right to rule its colonies as it pleased; and it sought to assure the colonial peoples that their interests and rights would also be considered. The mandate system thus represented a compromise between the "old hag" of colonialism and the national independence the colonies were to gain after World War II.

It was the United States that urged its Allies to relinquish their colonial holdings during the war. After one such urging by President Roosevelt, Churchill made his famous remark that he had not become the King's First Minister in order to liquidate the British Empire. Yet the very principles Churchill was fighting for were the principles of national independence and self-government. For the British Prime Minister, these principles, embodied in the Atlantic Charter, were limited to the European states conquered by Hitler. But they could not be thus limited. For Europe had itself spread them to the world, and the colonial peoples were by then beginning to demand their application. Did the Western leaders not regard these principles as the only basis for a legitimate government? Then they could hardly be in a position to deny the demands of their colonies; the colonial powers were only being asked to practice in their colonies what they practiced at home and often preached abroad. Europe's own weakness, the colonial peoples' agitation for freedom in terms of the West's own political principles, and the increasingly widespread feeling in the West itself that colonial rule was incompatible with Western democracy thus combined to end the era of Western colonialism. And with this end, the old European-centered international order collapsed.

War and Human Nature

The twentieth century has been one of almost incessant conflict. World War I was the "war to end all wars," but the Treaty of Versailles inaugurated only a twenty-year truce. At the conclusion of World War II, the victors could not even agree on peace treaties ending the hostilities with Germany and Japan. The American-Soviet conflict had already erupted. Called a Cold War, despite some rather warm moments, it was nevertheless a war. For war is essentially a struggle of wills that may or may not express itself in physical violence. Thus the conflict and warfare of this century, which have already helped to unleash the vast forces remolding our world, continues.

In these circumstances, it might well be asked why nations engage in "struggles of will"? Should not their leaders, acting as reasonable men, be able to resolve international problems peacefully? Has it not become imperative in the nuclear age for man to discover and eliminate the causes of war before nuclear war annihilates mankind?

Freud, however, asserted

> . . . that men are not gentle, friendly creatures wishing for love, who simply defend themselves if they are attacked, but that a powerful measure

of desire for aggression has to be reckoned as part of their instinctual endowment. . . . *Homo homini lupus;* who has the courage to dispute it in the face of all the evidence in his own life and in history? This aggressive cruelty usually lies in wait for some provocation. . . . In circumstances that favour it . . . [it] manifests itself spontaneously and reveals men as savage beasts to whom the thought of sparing their own kind is alien. Anyone who calls to mind the atrocities of the early migrations, of the invasion by the Huns or by the so-called Mongols under Jenghiz Khan and Tamurlane, of the sack of Jerusalem by the pious Crusaders, even indeed the horror of the last world-war, will have to bow his head humbly before the truth of this view of man.

Furthermore, Freud claimed:

This instinct of aggression is the derivative and main representative of the death instinct we have found alongside of Eros (which aims at binding together single human individuals, then families, then tribes, races, nations into one great unity, that of humanity), sharing his rule over the earth. And now, it seems to me, the meaning of the evolution of culture is no longer a riddle to us. It must present to us the struggle between Eros and Death, between the instincts of life and the instincts of destruction, as it works itself out in the human species. This struggle is what all life essentially consists of and so the evolution of civilization may be simply described as the struggle of the human species for existence. And it is this battle of the Titans that our nurses and governesses try to compose with their lullaby-song of Heaven![21]

While Freud ascribed conflict and war to man's inherent aggressiveness, others have attributed it to man's desire for power. Hans Morgenthau, the foremost proponent of "realism" among American political scientists, states that this "lust for power" is as basic a human drive as the drive to live and propagate. The "struggle for power," he says, "is universal in time and space."

The tendency to dominate, in particular, is an element of all human associations, from the family through fraternal and professional associations and local political organizations, to the state. On the family level, the typical conflict between the mother-in-law and her child's spouse is in its essence a struggle for power, the defense of an established power position against the attempt to establish a new one. As such it foreshadows the conflict on the international scene between the policies of the status quo and the policies of imperialism (expansion). Social clubs, fraternities, faculties, and business organizations are scenes of continuous struggles for power between groups that either want to keep what power they already have or seek to attain greater power. Competitive contests between business enterprises as well as labor disputes between employers and employees are frequently fought not only, and sometimes not even primarily, for eco-

[21] Sigmund Freud, *Civilization and Its Discontents*, translated by Joan Riviere (Garden City, N.Y.: Doubleday & Co., 1951), pp. 60–61, 75.

nomic advantages, but for influence over each other and over others; that is, for power. Finally, the whole political life of a nation, particularly of a democratic nation, from the local to the national level, is a continuous struggle for power. In periodic elections, in voting in legislative assemblies, in lawsuits before courts, in administrative decisions and executive measures—in all these activities men try to maintain or to establish their power over other men. The processes by which legislative, judicial, executive, and administrative decisions are reached are subject to pressures and counterpressures by "pressure groups" trying to defend and expand their positions of power.[22]

Furthermore, this lust for power knows no limits. It "manifests itself as the desire to maintain the range of one's own person with regard to others, to increase it, or to demonstrate it . . . the selfishness of man has limits; his will to power has none." Morgenthau quotes Cecil Rhodes as saying, "These stars that you see overhead at night, these vast worlds which we can never reach. I would annex the planets if I could. I often think of that. It makes me sad to see them so clear and so far away."[23] Power, whether for individual man or for man organized into nation-states, is thus an end in itself.

Can the causes of conflict and war, however, be ascribed so simply and directly to "human nature"? Undoubtedly, man's actions reflect man's nature.

But the importance of human nature as a factor in causal analysis of social events is reduced by the fact that the same nature, however defined, has to explain an infinite variety of social events. Anyone can "prove" that man is bad simply by pointing to evidence of his viciousness and stupidity. To relate unwanted events, such as crime and war, to this viciousness and stupidity is then a simple task. . . . Do such evidences of man's behavior as rapes, murders, and thefts prove that he is bad? What about the counterevidence provided by acts of charity, love, and self-sacrifice? Is the amount of crime in a given society proof that the men in it are bad? Or is it amazing that under the circumstances there is not more crime? Maybe we have so *little* crime and so *few* wars because men, being good, adjust so amazingly well to circumstances that are inherently difficult! To say, then, that certain things happen because men are stupid or bad is a hypothesis that is accepted or rejected according to the mood of the writer.[24]

If man were constantly at war, this state of affairs might well be attributed to his "nature." But men do not always fight; they also enjoy peace, although perhaps less so in this century than some previous centuries. If man's nature causes war, then his "propensity for peace" must

[22] Hans J. Morgenthau, *Politics Among Nations*, pp. 33, 34.
[23] Hans J. Morgenthau, *Scientific Man vs. Power Politics* (Chicago: University of Chicago Press, 1946), pp. 192, 193, 194.
[24] Kenneth N. Waltz, *Man, the State and War*, pp. 27–28.

be the cause of the periods of peace he experiences. To attribute war *and* peace, however, to man's nature is thus hardly helpful in analyzing why nations are sometimes at peace and other times engaged in conflict. Human nature is, in fact, too broad an explanation. By explaining everything, it explains nothing. The factors that produce conflict and warfare among states must therefore be found elsewhere—in man's social and political behavior.

II

International Politics in a Revolutionary Political System

The Sources of Politics: Interests and Groups

It has been said that man is born into blurred, buzzing confusion, and that he spends the remainder of his life imposing order upon this confusion. In order to function effectively, man must reduce the ambiguity of experience to coherence by structuring the world, endowing events and objects with meaning, and deducing the relevance of experience to himself. All individuals do this in varying degrees. Each, out of his confrontation with reality, builds a "picture" of reality for himself, a picture that is never quite the same as that of any other human being. This picture of reality is generally referred to as a "frame of reference"—or technically, as our perception of reality.

It is important to note the practical significance of these perceptions in our lives. Opinions differ in large part because we perceive the world differently and consequently respond to experience from different premises concerning what is "real." Equally important, our perceptions of reality are formed by abstracting from the totality of experience only those parts which we consider relevant. Obviously, no man sees every aspect of reality; the world is too complicated and confusing, and one is forced to simplify it to avoid being paralyzed by indecision and ambiguity. Most significant, however, is the fact that our perceptions of reality are actually models of the real world. We have *assumed* certain things to be true, we have *abstracted* certain principles, we have *hypothesized*

30

certain relationships to guide our behavior. We know intuitively that our perceptual model of reality is inaccurate and incomplete, so we constantly modify it. Nonetheless, in an unpremeditated and largely unconscious manner, we have created a crude model of reality and are engaged in testing it throughout our lives. Indeed, without this model, we could make no sense of experience, could never modify our behavior or evaluate the truth of competing interpretations of experience. In brief, we must have some model of reality in order to understand it.

Once one comprehends the instrumental nature of a model, the purpose it can serve in the study of international politics becomes apparent. For such a model, which attempts to structure and to explain the political interaction of nations, is a device for imposing order and meaning on the complexities of international affairs. However, unlike our perceptual models of reality, a conceptual model in international affairs is created deliberately, explicitly, and logically; in fact, one purpose of the model is to create propositions with which to test whether our *perceptions* of reality are accurate. Just as our own experience teaches us that our perceptions of events and people can be erroneous, so a conceptual model in international relations is an attempt to verify or to reformulate propositions that might not otherwise be identified as fallacious.

The first function of such a model is to *describe* reality. Thus, one can observe that, under certain conditions, states repeatedly behave in a similar manner. One can see these uniformities in state behavior just as one can see them in our own behavior. For example, we stop our cars when the traffic light is red and we wear coats on a cold day. To be sure, not everyone may do these things, but the probability is high enough that we can say they constitute a recurrent pattern of behavior. We can describe these patterns.

A second function of a model is to *explain* why a particular pattern of behavior tends to recur. We do this by generalizing and saying that a certain set of conditions will tend to produce this type of behavior. Again, this generalization may not hold true 100 per cent of the time, and we therefore do not refer to it as a "law" of social or individual behavior. We call it a hypothesis whose accuracy we then test by observation and experimentation. A model is in this sense a creative act, for its purpose is to construct a framework that the mind can handle in such a manner as to be able to perceive relationships in the form of hypotheses that can then be tested for their validity. For example, an increasing number of high-school graduates go on to college. This is a descriptive generalization. An explanatory generalization would be that these students realize that a college training and the acquisition of greater skills "pays off" in terms of better professional positions, higher salaries, and social status.

Finally, a model should offer a capacity for qualified *prediction* of future behavior. This is not necessarily as difficult as it might seem. Much depends on our ability to state accurately the conditions under which certain events will occur. We can certainly predict that if people suddenly notice the building they are in is on fire, they will scramble for the exits; or that if a state is attacked, it will fight back. Of course, not all predictions are this easy. Policy-makers who wish to know how other states may react to certain acts of their own might at times even doubt a model's predictive value. Nevertheless, prediction is one of the possible utilities of a model, although the model-builder should always be mindful that prediction in this instance means that he is stating not certainties but probabilities.

Now that the utility of models in the interpretation of international relations has been established, it becomes necessary to suggest a specific model that will provide the reader with a framework in which to organize the complexities of international relations. This has been done by abstracting certain political processes and situations that will be familiar to the reader from his knowledge of American politics, and making these components of the model. Of course, the total configuration of American politics is unique, and the reader should be warned not to attempt to generalize indiscriminately from the American system to international politics. Care has been taken here to select only those aspects of American politics which can be identified by analogy in international relations. Indeed, many aspects of American politics—as, for example, competition for authority and conflict of interest—are actually characteristic of any political system.[1]

It would not be an exaggeration to say that in the United States the word "politics" has come to have a rather unsavory connotation. The politician is—ironically—constantly denounced for "playing politics." When he publicly pronounces a proposal, he is accused of "seeking votes," and the implication is that he is not really concerned with the welfare of his constituents. He is "out for himself," and his professed desire to help those who vote for him is insincere. Politics and the welfare of the community are thus frequently considered incompatible. This popular impression of politics as a profession that corrupts its practitioners is reinforced by the belief that the politician constantly compromises his principles—if, indeed, he has *any*. And how can one compromise principles without losing one's virtue and morality? Compromise, in short, is immoral, and the person who "wheels and deals" is "expedient."

This attitude ignores the very nature of politics and refuses to acknowledge the function of the politician in American life. It is interesting that while the role of the politician is widely suspect, criticism of the businessman is rather limited and peripheral. The Great Depression

[1] Robert A. Dahl, *Modern Political Analysis* (Englewood Cliffs, N.J.: Prentice-Hall, 1963), pp. 14–25.

is now history. America is, as John K. Galbraith has called it, the "afflu-ent society"—or, in W. W. Rostow's almost equally felicitous phrase, in the "beyond high mass-consumption stage." Since business has pro-vided the average middle-class American with the goods that form the basis of his high standard of living, the businessman's socially useful role is both widely recognized and praised. No one accuses him of "play-ing business." When he produces and markets a new product, no one condemns him for "seeking profits." He would, in fact, be considered somewhat abnormal if he abjured profit; of course, he is "out for him-self," "to make a buck." No one really expects him to be genuinely concerned with the welfare of all consumers. It is simply assumed that his desire for profit will lead him to make and sell a product or service consumers want. If they do not want it—and if a sufficient "need" can-not be created by advertising—he will "go broke."

It is, to put the matter plainly, the businessman's personal and "self-ish" desire for gain that leads him nonaltruistically to concern himself with the wants and needs of the consuming public. Economic textbooks usually refer to this as the "law" of the market; the motivating force is normally described as "enlightened self-interest." How American society meets the problem of the production and distribution of goods and services is thus generally described in terms of the actual operational be-havior of the economic market. No one questions the "sincerity" of the businessman who is not selflessly interested in the welfare of the con-sumers. And no one proclaims that he should be "above profit." Indeed, to make such an assertion would be tantamount to demanding that the Pope be "above religion."

Just as the businessman's social role can be analyzed in the context of his response to the interests of his potential customers, the elected poli-tician's role can be understood only in the context of a response to the interests of his voters. Just as consumers can use the businessman's desire for profit to compel him to produce the goods and services they want, so the voters can utilize their Congressman's or Senator's desire for votes to elicit a response to their needs. He is their "representative," and what he represents is their various wants and needs—or, in a word, their "inter-ests." In a sense, this explanation of politics in terms of interests is popu-larly recognized, which is precisely why politics is so lowly regarded. The word "interest" implies both materialism and selfishness. For in a society that generally considers itself democratic and Christian—that is, com-mitted to such nonmaterialistic values as individual dignity, equality, and a consequent unselfish concern for the lot of one's fellow beings— men are bound to feel somewhat ill at ease when energetically pursuing individualistic and secular goals. Such pursuit strongly implies a lack of concern with the good of society, and is therefore a matter for social disapproval. Nevertheless, man by his very nature is bound to have a multitude of needs and wants. Quite apart from the fact that interests are not necessarily always either materialistic or self-centered, they are human and natural. The word "interest" encompasses three things: a *need or want* that seeks a degree of satisfaction, be it partial or total; a *conscious act of recognition* of this objective; and an *attempt to realize* it. By defining "interest" as the *disposition to act in order to achieve some goal*,[2] we in fact focus on the two principal aspects of politics—the ends to be fulfilled and the means employed to seek their realization.

The interests man harbors naturally reflect the entire range of his needs and wants; and they do not all involve politics. Yet, it is hardly surprising that many of them do. One need not look beyond the confines of American society.[3] Economic interests, for instance, have always played a significant role in American politics. The Founding Fathers were certainly very much aware of this fact; after all, the protection of their property interest was not completely absent from their desire to replace the confederation with a federal union. Indeed, in his famous chapter "The Federalist No. 10," Madison emphasized considerably ahead of Marx that historically "the most common and durable source of factions [in societies] has been the various and unequal distribution of property. Those who hold and those who are without property have ever formed distinct interests in society. Those who are creditors, and those who are debtors, fall under a like discrimination. A landed interest, a manufacturing interest, a moneyed interest, with many lesser interests, grow up of necessity in civilized nations, and divide them into different classes, actuated by different sentiments and views."[4]

One can divide contemporary American economic interests into three parts: labor, business, and agriculture. Labor, for instance, clearly shares many interests. From the latter part of the nineteenth century through the Depression of the 1930's, the labor movement had certain well-defined goals: to raise wages from the so-called subsistence level to a decent living wage; to reduce the six-day week, twelve-to-fifteen–hour work day to a more reasonable schedule; to improve working conditions (proper sanitation, safe machinery, etc.); to acquire overtime pay, a regular annual vacation, and retirement benefits; and finally, to eliminate such abuses as child labor and the company store. Labor, business, and agricultural interests can be broken down even further. Business, for example, can be divided into big business and small business, export and import business, steel and aluminum industries, etc.

[2] Samuel H. Beer *et al.*, *Patterns of Government: The Major Political Systems of Europe* (rev. ed.; New York: Random House, 1962), p. 52.
[3] For a detailed, comprehensive analysis of the American political process in terms of interest-group behavior, see David B. Truman, *The Governmental Process: Political Interests and Public Opinion* (New York: Alfred A. Knopf, 1951).
[4] Alexander Hamilton, John Jay, and James Madison, *The Federalist* (New York: Modern Library, 1941), p. 56.

If such economic interests play a vital, if not the key, role in American society, they do not, however, constitute the only significant interests. Ethnic interests, for instance, have always occupied a prominent place; in fact, it would have been unnatural if national origin had been discounted in a "melting pot" society like the United States. The country was originally settled by immigrants from Northwest Europe—primarily England and Germany—but after the Civil War, the flood of immigrants came from Southern and Eastern Europe. Swarthier of skin, unable to speak the English language, and unfamiliar with Anglo-Saxon concepts of democracy and self-government, they were considered real "foreigners" by the American "natives." Settling down in the cities, they supplied the cheap labor for industry, just as the Negroes in the South provided the cheap labor on the plantation. Looked down upon by the "old," self-styled culturally superior American stock of North European descent, which controlled the economic and political life of the country, they had to work hard to gain recognition. Italian-Americans, Polish-Americans, and other national minorities all had to struggle to achieve the level of American respectability—that is, middle-class status. Since the Republican Party was largely the party of the old stocks, the Democratic Party—the party of urban labor—became the instrument through which these new waves of immigrants sought this acceptance and respectability.[5]

There is, moreover, considerable overlapping of ethnic and religious interests. Indeed, it was symbolic of the times that Al Smith, the Democratic Presidential candidate in 1928, should have been a Catholic. For the Southern and Eastern European immigrants were largely Catholic (along with a large Jewish minority). Smith's candidacy represented the revolt of the non-Anglo-Saxon, non-Teutonic, non-Protestant urban (largely labor and "wet") voters against the older English, German, and Scandinavian stock which had settled the farms of New England and the West. The year 1928 was witness to the political rise of the city and the decline of the rural predominance in the political leadership of both parties.[6] It also represented a rejection by the city masses of the rural, fundamentalist Protestant morality embodied in the prohibitionist movement and the Ku Klux Klan. Much of the traditional rural-urban cultural cleavage in American society can indeed be traced back to these ethnic and religious conflicts.[7] To most farmers and small-town Americans, the city was the "root of all evil." It was the home of those inferior foreigners—sweaty workers, Catholics whose first loyalty was to a Pope

[5] For an analysis of the relationship between ethnic politics and American isolationism, see Samuel Lubell, *The Future of American Politics* (New York: Anchor Books, 1956), pp. 136–67.

[6] Lubell, *op. cit.*, pp. 29–43.

[7] Richard Hofstadter, *The Age of Reform: From Bryan to F.D.R.* (New York: Alfred A. Knopf, 1955), pp. 287–300.

in far-off Rome. The city was a place where people drank, danced the Charleston, played golf on Sundays instead of going to church, and blithely ignored their marriage vows. The city also bred "intellectuals" with "European" (that is, "un-American") habits and patterns of thought.

These stereotyped views still persist to some extent in the 1960's. And certainly religion has continued to be a significant factor in American politics. Following Al Smith's defeat in 1928, it was not until 1960 that another Catholic, John F. Kennedy, was nominated for the Presidency —and then only after he had first proved to his own party leaders in several primaries that a Catholic could win.

Finally, it seems almost too obvious to add that racial interests also play an important role in American life. The entire regional interest of the South is organically related to the issue of white supremacy. After the Civil War and Reconstruction, it was the Democratic Party that became the chief instrument for the oppression of the Negro in the South. Deprived of his right to vote, the Negro had no one to represent his interests, such as his desire for a decent education as a means to a good job and middle-class status. Because of the color of his skin, he was denied the rights granted to whites. Because he was black, he was deprived of the opportunities to better himself economically and socially. White Southerners voted almost solidly Democratic to preserve segregation.

The reaction was bound to come. In a democratic country, it was only a matter of time before the Negro would claim his birthright. If all men were "created equal" and possessed "certain inalienable rights," why were these rights denied to Negroes? Did the American credo apply only to the white man? In World War II, Negroes fought alongside whites against the Nazi racist tyranny. Having fought for democracy abroad, he expected to claim his democratic heritage at home. The postwar colonial liberation movement, which claimed racial and national equality for the yellow man and the brown man, reaffirmed his own determination to gain equality for himself within the United States. As Negroes moved out of the South to work in the factories of the North and received better pay, as some of them received a better education or sent their children to college to learn a profession, an articulate Negro middle class grew up and began to voice the Negro's aspirations for equal treatment and opportunity, and his resentments against the social, economic, and political discrimination and humiliation he had so long suffered. Just as the Italian, Polish, and Irish middle-class leaders had once led their peoples' fight for equality, so this Negro middle class became the champion of its race's struggle for its place in the American sun.

These, then, are the principal interests in American society. Such interests need not be organized: Madison, as we saw, spoke of a "landed interest" without the benefit of a National Grange, and of a "manufacturing interest" before the existence of a National Association of Manufacturers. In the same manner, we have talked of economic, ethnic, religious, and racial interests—as well as businessmen, workers, and farmers —in terms of broad groups sharing certain characteristics or functions. These interests, while they may be unorganized, tend to be represented by the two major political parties. For a Congressman or Senator, who serves his constituents, represents their various interests. Consequently, the American political party is essentially a coalition of interests. The Democratic Party, by and large, encompasses Southern rural Protestants and segregationists, the Northern urban working class (lower-income, non-college-educated, heavily Catholic—at least the white workers—and Negro), and Jews. The Republican party, on the other hand, has its strongholds primarily in rural and suburban areas: that is, among farmers, small-town residents, and especially the "organization men" (professional, business managerial, and sales personnel, who tend to be high-income, college-educated, Protestant, and old-stock American).[8]

But interests can be organized, and most in fact are highly organized. Again, this is quite natural since man is essentially a social being, and the individual lives his entire life in groups:

> [He] is literally conducted from the cradle to the grave by groups, for he is born in a family, goes to school in organized classes, goes to church, perhaps, plays with boyhood gangs, joins fraternities, works for a corporation, belongs to various associations, cultural, civic, professional and social, and is carried off to his immortal reward by a business enterpriser with the solemnity appropriate to such ceremonies. . . . Many organized groups operate out of the direct public gaze, like religious organizations, which tend to have a low degree of visibility. Others, like many trade union organizations, have a high degree of visibility, to the point where the average newspaper reader may easily see the selfishness of the prominent labor leader but not the selfishness of employer groups who comprise the other half of the collective bargaining relationship. The high visibility of national groups diverts the eye from the great number which stand at the elbow of the citizen of every small town.[9]

Another reason why interests are organized is that men with common needs and wants are more likely to accomplish their goals if they combine. The isolated individual may be impotent; the organized group possesses strength. Consequently, interests have organized themselves for action at every level of society. They run the gamut, from the Podunk Toastmaster Society to the American Legion. Those who speak on be-

---

[8] Clinton L. Rossiter, *Parties and Politics in America* (Ithaca, N.Y.: Cornell University Press, 1960), pp. 66–106.

[9] Earl Latham, *The Group Basis of Politics* (Ithaca, N.Y.: Cornell University Press, 1952), pp. 1–2.

half of each interest are the leaders of the organizations in their respective field of interest. Thus, among the most influential spokesmen for the business community are the leaders of the National Association of Manufacturers and the Chamber of Commerce. Labor spokesmen are made up of the leaders of the AFL-CIO, the United Mine Workers, the United Auto Workers, and other unions. The leaders of the National Grange, the American Farm Bureau Federation, and the Farmers' Union speak for the farmers. The list could go on and on—for Negroes and the segregationists, for kosher butchers and for cotton farmers, for teachers of political science and for public-relations men. The purpose of all these groups—as of all interests—is to protect and/or advance their particular interests.

The Conduct of Politics: Conflict, Change, and Power

Once the existence of these multiple interests in an organized society such as America is recognized, it becomes obvious that the resulting conflict of interests will be reflected in the political system. While man's wants and needs remain so varied, his interests are bound to clash and the resulting struggles will continue to occur. Modern Western society, precisely because it is pluralistic, is in a condition of constant *conflict* and *change*. Groups are continuously either defending the *status quo* or seeking to realize their aims more fully—that is, change the *status quo* in their favor.

A good example of such conflict in the United States was the late-nineteenth-century Populist movement. With the opening of the West and the application of modern technology to cultivation of the land, the farmer turned from subsistence farming (primarily growing enough food to feed himself and his family) to cash farming.[10] He could now specialize, raise a lot of wheat or cattle, sell his product, and use part of the cash to buy the food and other necessities of life he needed. In brief, he became a businessman, dependent on the demands of the market. But he faced a number of difficulties. First, he had to transport his goods to market, but the railroads were often a monopoly and charged the farmer excessive rates. He could, of course, choose not to ship his crop to town; but then it would rot and he would be unable to earn any money. When he arrived in town, he not infrequently found that the buyers had already decided what to pay him—usually a nice low price. He had little choice except to take the minimum price. And even when, say, the millers had not rigged the price beforehand, the farmer remained at a disadvantage. If he refused to accept a low bid from the miller, the latter could wait and buy the wheat from another farmer who would accept his price. But the farmer could not wait. He had to sell in order to live; and if he

[10] See Hofstadter, *op. cit.*, pp. 36–81.

waited too long, the price might be lowered even further as the millers bought almost all the wheat they wanted. The single farmer simply had no bargaining power. The farmer was also at a disadvantage in buying machinery. International Harvester was America's first monopoly. If the farmer did not buy a tractor, he would be unable to grow enough wheat and thus could be ruined. So he bought the tractor, even if he could not afford its high price. The result: he went further and further into debt. Finally, since the farmer wished to maximize his earnings—which often meant barely a "living wage," considering the low prices he was paid— he naturally planted as much wheat as possible. Since every other wheat farmer did the same, this meant the market was glutted and the price fell even lower.

The Populist movement grew out of the farmers' frustration and resentment. The Western farmer saw himself as David battling the Eastern Goliath, the big trusts, utilities, and corporations, who, he felt, exploited him at every turn and by keeping him in constant debt ruined him. He therefore wanted business to be regulated by the government —the rates of the railroads fixed at a fair level, monopolies broken up, and large corporations supervised. The farmers sought these objectives through two means: the vote and organization. They first established their own Populist Party. When this party showed its strength by electing a number of governors and state legislators, the two major parties, eager for their votes, responded to their calls for help. They also founded several farm organizations to influence both parties' selection of candidates, bring pressure to bear on Congressmen, and, more generally, present their case to the public in order to create an environment more favorable for the realization of their goals.

Other interests have followed the farmers' example—workers and Negroes, for example. The unskilled workers had no spokesmen for their grievances until 1932. The Republican Party was the majority party after the Civil War, and it paid little attention to urban labor. The Democrats, as the out party, were eager for the workers' votes, which Franklin Roosevelt won during the Depression. His New Deal then recognized labor's right to organize itself and bargain collectively with industry. The AFL already existed, but it was the CIO that in the 1930's organized the crucial segment of the economy, heavy industry, and used its resulting strength for collective bargaining as well as for electioneering, lobbying, and propaganda purposes.

The conclusion is clear: In order to realize its purposes, any interest must first become strong—that is, develop a sufficient capability. Neither good intentions nor a just cause alone will suffice. A group will gain its goals only to the degree that it becomes strong and exercises its capability effectively. If business is powerful and the farmers or workers are weak, the latter's grievances will not be met. When power meets weakness, it will exploit that weakness. Only when power is met by power can a previously weaker group secure some of its demands. The domination of one group over another group can be offset only by a more equitable distribution of power. The previous *dis*proportion of power can be corrected only by a *balance of power*. In the former condition, the stronger group can be certain of victory; in the latter, victory is less certain and will, in any case, be more costly. The previously stronger group will therefore possess an incentive to compromise peacefully and avoid a test of strength.

Actually, such a balance is unlikely to be exact. Power is composed of many factors—some tangible, some intangible. The real problem is to "add" up these factors and calculate one's own strength, as well as that of one's opponent. At best, taking into account the size of the opponent's membership, its economic strength, social standing, and morale, the quality of its leadership, and the nature of its political strategy and tactics, one can only hope to approximate its total power. This in turn makes it difficult to know precisely when a "balance" exists. Consequently, each group tends to strive for a little more than a balance in order to gain the extra insurance; each feels more able to protect or secure its interests if it is somewhat stronger than the other group. But an approximate balance results. "Equilibrium is balanced power, and balanced power is neutralized power. A society in political equilibrium is a society in which force is useless."[11] Group struggle thus gives rise to the rule that *power begets countervailing power*. Or, to put it slightly differently: The balancing-of-power process is inherent in any pluralistic system; and even if it does not result in an exact balance, it does produce a counterbalancing tendency.

The basic assumptions of this constant balancing process are twofold: that the many interest groups in society all have the right to exist and preserve their independence; and that they would lose their independence and ability to pursue their interests if one of the groups were to gain a clear superiority of power and impose its will upon the other groups. The balance is thus intended to maintain the stability of the political system *and* the existence of all the interest groups within it. Both functions must be emphasized since the stability of the political system could also be gained by permitting one group to achieve a dominant status. The balance is to prevent any group from attaining this position. "Power politics" is thus a constant factor in domestic and international life.

[11] Nicholas J. Spykman, *America's Strategy in World Politics: The United States and the Balance of Power* (New York: Harcourt, Brace and Co., 1942), p. 21. For a more extensive discussion of the various ways the term "balance of power" is used by analysts, see Ernst B. Haas, "The Balance of Power: Prescription, Concept, or Propaganda," in *World Politics*, July, 1953, pp. 442–77; and Inis L. Claude, Jr., *Power and International Relations*, pp. 11–39.

However, despite the fact that the balance of power has been formally incorporated into the structure of the American Federal Government:

> It has long been fashionable, particularly in America, to denounce power as some sort of evil and to consider "power politics" a noxious practice. We prefer to speak of morality and principles, of legality and justice, not of power. Somehow we assume that those who have power have no principles and that those with principles have no power, but why should this be so? Cynics declare that God is on the side of the largest battalions, and we reject this. But is it any more reasonable to assume that the smallest battalions always fight for the right? Are the powerful really so wicked? "Power corrupts," they say, but is this true or is it merely that corruption is more conspicuous when it is practiced on a large scale? Certainly it would be difficult to prove that powerful governments are more corrupt than weak ones, or that rich men are any more dishonest than the poor, or that small nations are any less selfish than the great powers.
>
> It is true, of course, that the powerful can wreak their evil on a larger scale, but their good deeds are also larger. In short, power in itself is neither good nor evil, and 'the men who wield it may be either virtuous or filled with vice.[12]

This is true because power is not an end itself but the means used by groups to realize their goals. Power might therefore be appropriately defined as the ability to influence the behavior of others in accordance with one's own ends. Power *as* power is consequently morally neutral. The morality or immorality of its use depends on the nature of the ends sought and the manner in which it is exercised. Indeed, in order to emphasize the instrumental nature of power, it would be more correct to speak of "purpose politics" than power politics. Furthermore, while power is the ability to make one's will prevail, whether it does or not— and if so, to what degree—depends on the power ratio between conflicting groups. Power is thus also relative. The outcome of a power struggle depends not on how strong each group is but on their comparative strengths; the quantity of power each group has is not the decisive factor. All group relations are power relationships, and it is the ratio of power that is significant. The term "power politics" is thus redundant since all politics are rooted in power. The very existence of two groups presupposes a power relationship.

The most obvious and dramatic exercise of power is, of course, violence. Usually, violence is an instrument of last resort, employed when a group cannot defend or gain its interests by peaceful means. If a group's leaders feel that what they seek to protect or hope to gain is of greater value than the cost to be paid—death, destruction, loss of prestige, etc.— then they are likely to invoke violence. At the other extreme stands nonviolence. While nonviolence is not normally thought of as a form of

[12] A. F. K. Organski, *World Politics* (New York: Alfred A. Knopf, 1958), pp. 93–94.

coercion, it is in fact because it is basically a technique for noncoopera-
tion. A group, unable or unwilling to use force, will withhold its participation from the daily process of life in the community. Negroes in the
South, for instance, have refused to obey laws that preserve segregation
or to buy at stores that will not hire Negroes for positions other than
menial labor or serve Negroes in their restaurants. Civil disobedience
and economic boycotts are, indeed, two of the most powerful forms of
nonviolent resistance that the weak can employ. And their use is especially effective because they place upon the group preserving the *status
quo* the moral onus of justifying that situation. This is difficult enough
(whether it is segregation in the United States or British colonial control
of India), and it is even more difficult if those trying to maintain the
status quo respond with disorder, violence, and destruction of life and
property.

Most intergroup conflicts, however, fall between these extremes.
Rather, they require a mixture of pressures and incentives for their resolution. A typical situation is an industry–trade-union dispute over wages
and hours. It is not insignificant that such talks are called "collective bargaining." Each group is organized, and the representatives who conduct
the talks are the appointed "diplomats" of the two groups; these diplomats then "negotiate" with each other, just as two sovereign nations do
in international politics. On the one hand, the union possesses a "stick"
since it can call a strike and stop work: this decreases the industry's income and could possibly bankrupt some firms. On the other hand, the
union holds up a "carrot": if a strike is avoided, and its men continue
to work, management will reap its corporate profits. Management, too,
can apply certain pressure and incentives. If the industry's income is reduced because it loses a part of its market during a strike, workers will
have to be laid off. Furthermore, weekly pay checks are higher than
unemployment insurance, which, in any case, is paid only for a limited
period. The negotiations therefore take place between two parties with
simultaneously conflicting *and* common interests. They may argue over
the terms of work. But they also share an interest in not closing down
the assembly lines, for functionally they need each other. Without cooperation, neither management nor labor can continue production, by
which profits and wages are earned. In this context, the negotiating tactics represent a mixture of sanctions and incentives, pressures and counterpressures, which after some tough bargaining may result in a compromise agreement.

When such group conflict and bargaining is channeled through the
formal institutions of government, it is described as the "legislative
process." But the difference from management-labor negotiation is
largely semantic. The process by which such negotiation settles on a
minimum wage is quite similar to that by which a minimum wage law

is passed by a legislature: group bargaining and the adjustment of differences by compromise. For a legislature referees

> . . . the group struggle, ratifies the victories of the successful coalitions, and records the terms of the surrenders, compromises, and conquests in the form of statutes. Every statute tends to represent compromise because the process of accommodating conflicts of group interest is one of deliberation and consent. The legislative vote on any issue tends to represent the composition of strength, i.e., the balance of power, among the contending groups at the moment of voting. What may be called public policy is the equilibrium reached in this struggle at any given moment and it represents a balance which the contending factions or groups constantly strive to weight in their favor.[13]

Finally, whether a decision as to the minimum wage is the outcome of group conflict within or outside the context of governmental institutions, the final accord is policy, and in each instance, the final settlement is incorporated in a formal written document—in international politics, it would be called a treaty—embodying the new terms.

Power, then, plays a vital role in the "peaceful resolution" of issues, or "peaceful change." The fact that it is there and that it can be applied as a sanction is indeed a principal incentive—and occasionally even the sole incentive—to conciliation. The "big stick" certainly augments the attractiveness of any preferred "carrot," which in many negotiations is the only visible part. But the fact that power is often kept hidden just below the surface does not mean that it has played no role in the negotiations. As Salvador de Madariaga has said in connection with international negotiations, "the normal wielders of armaments are not the soldiers, but the diplomats. The gun that does not shoot is more eloquent than the gun that has to shoot and above all the gun which has shot."[14] The domestic diplomats are the politicians, who act as both the representatives of interests and the negotiators who seek to resolve the constant and inevitable clashing of interests in the pluralistic system. They are their constituencies' ambassadors who seek to protect their constituents' varied needs and wants through bargaining. Politics thus plays an essential role in society, for without politics the "peaceful coexistence" of the multiplicity of interest groups would not be feasible.

Consensus: The Containment of Conflict

Three points about the American political process are evident by now: (1) it is an activity centering around the quest for advantage; (2) it occurs under conditions of change; and (3) the pursuit of this advantage affects the political system as a whole. What is still unclear is why

[13] Latham, *op. cit.*, pp. 35–36.
[14] Salvador de Madariaga, *Disarmament*, p. 57.

this continuous conflict does not normally erupt into violence. If the willingness to compromise is a principal characteristic of American politics, why is this willingness so widespread? What fosters such a condition of "pragmatic" and "unideological" politics? To put the question another way, why does one usually describe American politics not as a war but as a "game"?

One reason derives from the pluralistic nature of American society, in which most individuals play various roles and possess a number of interests. These interests may or may not be consistent with one another. Consider the businessman who wants lower Federal taxes and at the same time, as a property-owner, lower local property taxes; at the same time, because he is a veteran, he may favor greater defense expenditures, and as a father he is concerned with improvement in the standard of public education. His final position is likely to be some form of compromise between these various interests. The position he would advocate if he had only a single interest is balanced by an opposing interest; this individual is, in short, an object of cross-pressures. Overlapping interests therefore favor moderation.[15]

American society thus provides its own social checks and balances. This is revealed particularly clearly by the nature of the two parties. Each is a coalition of incompatible interests. The American political party, it has been well said, is "a powerful magnet, which draws together, in constantly colliding coalition, a bewildering variety of conflicting interests."[16] Each party is split between rural conservatives (Southern Democrats or Midwestern Republicans) and urban liberals from the Northeast. The surprising fact is that in these circumstances the party does act as a powerful magnet. That "these elements can continue in alliance seems to defy every law of logic."[17] But it is not really so surprising since the component interest groups cannot achieve their purposes singly. They need each other's help. They must form an alliance, and they are held together by the hope of winning the Presidential prize. Both parties hope that the coalition of interests they represent will attract a majority vote for their candidate. The party that wins the election and captures the control of the government can then use this political power to defend or advance all, or at least some, of the interests it encompasses. With this power as an incentive, the various interest groups within the party tend to resolve most of their internal differences by compromise. No single interest achieves everything it wants, but each attains something. Intergroup cooperation compels them to moderate their own claims, for if they refused to do so they would alienate some allied interests in the party and weaken the coalition.

[15] Truman, *op. cit.*, pp. 508–10.
[16] Lubell, *op. cit.*, p. 215.
[17] *Ibid.*

The fundamental reason for the willingness to compromise, however, is the presence of an ideological consensus—a basic agreement on the values of the society. Whatever the differences among the competing interest groups, most Americans are united by certain principles upon which they are in agreement. More specifically, this consensus means agreement on two things: the purposes for which society supposedly exists and, even more important, the "rules" by which the political "game" ought to be conducted.[18] The consensus thus comprises both substantive and procedural values; and these twin aspects are organically linked.

The basic values on which Americans generally agree are those "self-evident" truths of the Declaration of Independence which, above all else, emphasize the pre-eminence of the individual: "all men are created equal," with the right to equal opportunities and equality before the law; and all men possess "certain inalienable rights," including those to life, liberty, and the pursuit of happiness. Man was not created to serve government; the government was established to be the servant of the people, to protect and fulfill their rights. Social justice was to be ensured by the fact that the government had the consent of the governed.

The impact of these values on American politics is obvious. The Negro revolution has defined its very aims in the context of these values: It wishes to achieve the same freedoms and equality of opportunity that white Americans enjoy. In previous eras, these were the demands of the minorities that immigrated after the Civil War: the Italians, Irish, Jews, etc. In short, values affected the very definition of "interests." Nor is this surprising. It would indeed be strange if the values of the society—whether they were freedom or success—did not shape men's thinking and attitudes about what is important and desirable. The political system and its values, in short, play a major role in defining the behavior of its members.

Of at least equal importance with agreement on what government should do is *how* government should be conducted. For democracy is essentially a way of governing, a method of making political decisions. Even the Soviet Union, after all, proclaims the same value goals as the United States. The essential difference between the two systems is in their operational behavior. It is for this reason that procedural rules are so vital. In the United States, interest groups can organize to defend or advance their aims, and they have access to government at the state and national levels; it is particularly at the latter level that they seek to influence the legislative process and the administration of policy. Even more

[18] The significance of the rules of the game is stressed by Truman, *op. cit.*, pp. 510–16; Henry B. Mayo, *An Introduction to Democratic Theory* (London and New York: Oxford University Press, 1960), pp. 30–34; Beer *et al.*, *op. cit.*, pp. 33–38; and Herbert J. Spiro, *Government by Constitution* (New York: Random House, 1959), pp. 363–68.

fundamentally, there must be regular and free elections in which the electorate has the right to choose between the party in power and an opposition party that is free to criticize. The majority's voice at the polls determines who will enact and implement the laws. But the minority's right must also be protected. These two points—majority rule and minority dissent—are the principal tenets of democratic politics. The significance of such "mere methods," whose importance is all too frequently overlooked, would be only too evident if decisions were not made "according to the rules." Such policies embodied in the law either would be disobeyed or, if obeyed, would lack moral sanction. The system, in other words, also sets the "rules of the game."

Nowhere is this more clearly demonstrated than in the cardinal democratic principle that once a law has been passed, it must be obeyed by all, including those citizens who disagree with its content. The latter obey because they recognize that the law was made after a free election, debate in Congress, and majority decision, or Supreme Court interpretation of specific statutes and the Constitution. Or, to state it another way: People obey the law because they agree that the government has the right to govern, not because the government has at its command superior power and the individual is fearful of punishment. "For, if force creates right," Rousseau wrote, "the effect changes with the cause: Every force that is greater than the first succeeds to its right. As soon as it is possible to disobey with impunity, disobedience is legitimate and the strongest being always in the right, the only thing that matters is to act so as to become the strongest." But, Rousseau continued, "the strongest is never strong enough to be always the master, unless he transforms strength into right, and obedience into duty."[19] It is the almost universal agreement on the basic values of a political system that makes that system *legitimate*. And it is, in particular, the agreement on procedures that legitimatizes the power of the government (or, more appropriately, the coalition of interests that constitute the government) and accords it the right, first, to govern and to determine authoritatively the policies for the entire society, and, second, to crush anyone with force who seeks to oppose these policies—"the law of the land"—by a resort to violence. For a political system—and now it can be defined—is a structure that produces legitimate policy decisions as its "output." (The interests are the "input.") This consensus is in turn reinforced by the deep emotional commitment it inspires, embodied in nationalism and its various symbols: the flag, the national monuments, the national anthem.

It may perhaps be clear by now, from our brief analysis of the American system, how intimately the balance of power is related to the pre-

[19] Quoted in William Ebenstein, *Great Political Thinkers: Plato to the Present* (3d ed.; New York: Holt, Rinehart and Winston, 1960), p. 441.

vailing consensus. The basic assumption of the balance, as we saw earlier, is to maintain the stability of that system *and* preserve the independence and security of each of its component interest groups. The balancing process, in short, presumes that the political system should be preserved because it is *legitimate,* and that all the groups living in that system have the *right* to exist. It follows logically that if groups do not seek to destroy each other, they must resolve their differences. It is inherent in their decision to coexist. When the representatives of groups therefore sit down to negotiate with one another, they have in fact already tacitly accepted a compromise solution.

At issue are the terms of coexistence, not coexistence itself. The terms are the product of the particular "balance." Adjustments of competing interests are possible within a common consensual framework and social order because the political system and the values it incorporates are not themselves the subject of controversy and dispute. The resulting style of politics is pragmatic and empirical; and it is unideological precisely because all parties to a dispute share the same values or ideology. Consensus thus does not eliminate conflict, but it does limit the scope of that conflict.

"Dissensus," however, dissolves these restraints on conflict. For values embody concepts of "good" and "bad." Instead of politics being conducted with a common concept of what is "good," it must be carried out amid conflicting interpretations of what is "moral" and "immoral." Interest politics then becomes "ideologized," and ideological conflict is intensely emotional. For values cannot be compromised. One cannot "split the difference" among competing values. A group that considers its values as superior and exclusive will give priority to the realization of these values. Attaining them will take precedence over following the rules of the game. Indeed, a group that believes it is the bearer of the only true or moral values will consider itself committed to an ideological mission to erase "immorality," eliminate "sin," destroy "heresy," and convert the "heathens" to the "true faith." Thus, the Christians once sought to convert the infidels during the Crusades; similarly, Catholics and Protestants, each condemning the other as representatives of Satan, slaughtered each other for thirty bloody years—thereby proving that in the name of God and justice men could kill enthusiastically and in vast numbers. "True believers" everywhere have always been able to burn the heretic—that is, anyone who disagreed with the "true faith"—at the stake. Moreover, and what is equally significant, they have done so convinced that they were doing the heretic a favor. For by killing him and shortening the time he could live in sin, they were reducing the term he would have to spend in hell to atone for his sins. This attitude is just as typical in what are basically secular religious or revolutionary movements: *fiat justitia, pereat mundu*—let justice be done, though the world perish.

Once conflicting values are superimposed on competing interests, the conflict has a tendency to become total. This is true for two reasons: first, because revolutionaries are dedicated to the destruction of the political system they condemn as heretical, immoral, sinful, and evil. For not only do "true believers" assume that they are the representatives of the "true faith"; they are also passionately convinced that they have been selected by God or history or nature to bring the blessings of their faith to all men. They condemn the prevailing order as "illegitimate" because it is committed to "false beliefs." It is their destiny—their holy duty, in fact—to destroy the "old order." The new order must be established everywhere. The infidel has no *right* to exist. The second reason is that this kind of situation creates intense insecurity. When groups share a common set of values, they coexist in mutual confidence and trust. No group feels absolutely secure; this would be impossible in a pluralistic society. But, by the same token, no group feels so totally insecure that it becomes preoccupied with the issue of its own survival. Politics can thus be of a limited and pragmatic nature, for the balance of power is acceptable to all participating groups. But when groups lack this common set of values, the conflict becomes total since *the issues are the values themselves and the political system that incorporates them.* Revolutionaries dedicated to the system's demise are thus not interested in maintaining a balance; they must destroy the balance and seek a monopoly of power. Then, and only then, will they be in a position to kill the heathen, convert the misguided, and, above all, change the environment in which man lives so that future generations will never again be corrupted; then, and then only, can they eradicate sin, purify the world, bring it social justice, establish eternal peace, and, in general, create the "society of the true and the beautiful."

Coexistence, in these circumstances, becomes coexistence in mutual fear and suspicion; and groups tend to act as if they existed in a Hobbesian state of nature. Like Hobbesian man, they live in fear of violent death. Without a consensus, Hobbes points out, groups live

> . . . in that condition which is called war; and such a war as is of every man against every man. For *war* consists not in battle only, or the act of fighting, but in a tract of time; wherein the will to contend by battle is sufficiently known; and therefore the notion of *time* is to be considered in the nature of war, as it is in the nature of weather. For as the nature of foul weather lies not in a shower or two or rain, but in an inclination thereto of many days together, so the nature of war consists not in actual fighting, but in the known disposition thereto, during all the time there is no assurance to the contrary. All other time is *peace*.
>
> Whatsoever therefore is consequent to a time of war, where every man is enemy to every man, the same is consequent to the time wherein men

live without other security than what their own strength . . . shall furnish them. . . .

To this war of every man against every man this also is consequent; that nothing can be unjust. The notions of right and wrong, justice and injustice, have there no place. Where there is no common power, there is no law; where no law, no justice. Force and fraud are in war the two cardinal virtues.[20]

Or, to state it as simply as possible: a political system without consensus is a system in the grip of civil war. Politics is no longer a "game." When the issue is the organization of the system, its social structure, its political and economic order, and the values by which it will live, politics becomes war and domestic politics takes on the appearance of international politics.

The "National Interest" in a Revolutionary International System

International politics is often described in terms of war or potential war because of the high expectation of violence—that is, as a situation of conflict among interest groups without the limiting influence of a consensus.[21] The principal actor is the largest interest group of all, the nation-state, and the political order within which all the nations act is the state system. Every state in this system pursues its "national interest," and, because of the absence of a consensus or of a world government that could make legitimate policy decisions, each state's principal concern is the preservation of its national security. Each state can rely upon itself, and only upon itself, for the protection of its territorial integrity and political independence—that is, its way of life, its "core values." How does each protect itself? By increasing its capabilities or seeking power, for all policy-makers charged with the responsibility for safeguarding their nation know that in order to deter a possible attack their nation must be a little stronger than the neighboring state; but the neighboring state, because it also fears an attack, seeks to enhance its strength as well. The insecurity of all states in the system, in short, compels each to acquire greater security by engaging in a constant scramble for increased power. In turn, as each state watches its neighbor's power grow, its own sense of insecurity recurs; it then tries all the harder to gain even greater strength.

The nation-state system thus condemns each state to an eternal struggle for power because each faces a security dilemma. Nations seek power not because the maximization of power is their goal; they seek it because

[20] *Ibid.*, p. 368.
[21] See Stanley Hoffmann, *The State of War*.

they wish to guard their security. To forget this simple maxim, or relax in its observance, is to invite attack, if not defeat.

> Politically active groups and individuals are concerned about their security from being attacked, subjected, dominated, or annihilated by other groups and individuals. Because they strive to attain security from such attack, and yet can never feel entirely secure in a world of competing units, they are driven toward acquiring more and more power for themselves, in order to escape the impact of the superior power of others. . . . This very realization that his own brother may play the role of a Cain makes his fellow men appear to him as potential foes. Realization of this fact by others, in turn, makes him appear to them as their potential mortal enemy. Thus there arises a fundamental social constellation, a mutual suspicion and a mutual dilemma: the dilemma of "kill or perish," of attacking first or running the risk of being destroyed. There is apparently no escape from this vicious circle. Whether man is "by nature" peaceful and cooperative, or aggressive and domineering, is not the question.[22]

Each nation is thus transformed into a potential, if not actual, enemy of all other nations.

> Under these conditions the expectation of violence and even of annihilation is ever-present. To forget this and thus fail in the concern for enhanced power spells the doom of a state. This does not mean constant open warfare; expansion of power at the expense of others will not take place if there is enough counterpower to deter or to stop states from undertaking it. Although no state is interested in a mere balance of power, the efforts of all states to maximize power may lead to equilibrium. If and when that happens, there is "peace" or, more exactly, a condition of stalemate or truce. Under the conditions described here, this balancing of power process is the only available "peace" strategy.[23]

More specifically, the nature of the balance becomes the deciding factor in determining whether the state system will be wracked by war or continue to exist in peace. The significant distinction is usually made between what are called a "multiple and flexible balance" and a "bipolar and rigid balance." The former is characterized by the presence of three or more states classified as "great powers," although they may differ somewhat in their power. At the start of World War I, for instance, there were eight such powers: Austria-Hungary, Britain, France, Germany, Italy, Japan, Russia, and the United States. At the beginning of World War II, there were seven: all of the above with the exception of Austria-Hungary. The general rule is simple:

[22] John H. Herz, *Political Realism and Political Idealism* (Chicago: University of Chicago Press, 1951), pp. 14,3.
[23] Arnold Wolfers, *Discord and Collaboration: Essays on International Politics* (Baltimore, Md.: The Johns Hopkins Press, 1962), p. 83.

The greater the number of active players, the greater the number of possible combinations and the greater also the uncertainty as to the combinations that will actually oppose each other and as to the role the individual players will actually perform in them. . . . Whenever coalitions of nations comparable in power confront each other, calculations of this kind will of necessity be close, since the defection of one prospective member or the addition of an unexpected one cannot fail to affect the balance of power considerably, if not decisively. . . . In consequence, the extreme flexibility of the balance of power resulting from the utter unreliability of alliances made it imperative for all players to be cautious in their moves on the chessboard of international politics and, since risks were hard to calculate, compelled them to take as small risks as possible.[24]

In short, the greater the number of "players," the more possible combinations, the greater the opportunity for defection of a player from an alliance, the more cautious each player must be. This rule was noted earlier in our discussion of the American party system. Each party is composed of a coalition of interests, none of which is strong enough by itself to achieve its ends but must seek allies. No one interest can achieve its ends fully, since some of them might antagonize other members of the coalition. Thus, each interest must moderate its demands to avoid alienating its allies. By and large, then, a flexible balance tends to favor the adjustment of conflicting interests, thereby preserving the peace.

On the other hand, a bipolar division of power in which each of the two coalitions is dominated by a superpower increases international tension and the possibility of war. Without the shifting and countershifting of positions, there is less need for intra- and inter-alliance compromise. The superpower occupying the pinnacle position in a hierarchical alliance might take a stand that its allies consider dangerous and might even precipitate a war. But they cannot compel the superpower to "stand down" by threatening to pull out of the alliance, since they are dependent upon the superpower for their protection.[25] In this kind of rigid balance of power, a crisis—and particularly a succession of crises—could well result in a military conflict. Hans Morgenthau has commented on the rigidity inherent in the postwar bipolar distribution of power:

> These two blocs [the Communist and Western] face each other like two fighters in a short and narrow lane. They can advance and meet in what is likely to be combat, or they can retreat and allow the other side to advance into what to them is precious ground. Those manifold and varie-

[24] Hans J. Morgenthau, *Politics Among Nations*, p. 349.
[25] A smaller power can, of course, take a firm stand, then refuse to retreat, and thereby raise tensions and perhaps precipitate a war. Austria-Hungary did exactly that in 1914, but the fault lay with Germany for giving her weaker ally a free hand. In contrast, the United States has held a tight rein over Nationalist China for over a decade, preventing Chiang Kai-shek from landing troops on the mainland and thus involving the United States in a war with Communist China.

gated maneuvers through which the masters of the balance of power tried either to stave off armed conflicts altogether or at least to make them brief and decisive yet limited in scope—the alliances and counteralliances, the shifting of alliances according to whence the greater threat or the better opportunity might come, the side-stepping and postponement of issues, the deflection of rivalries from the exposed front yard into the colonial back yard—these are things of the past. With them have gone into oblivion the peculiar finesse and subtlety of mind, the calculating and versatile intelligence and bold yet circumspect decisions, which were required from the players in that game. And with those modes of action and intellectual attitudes there has disappeared that self-regulating flexibility, that automatic tendency . . . of disturbed power relations either to revert to their old equilibrium or to establish a new one.

For the two giants [the Soviet Union and the United States] that today determine the course of world affairs only one policy seems to be left; that is, to increase their own strength and that of their allies. All the players that count have taken sides, and in the foreseeable future no switch from one side to the other is likely to take place. Since the issues everywhere boil down to retreat from, or advance into, areas that both sides regard as of vital interest to themselves, positions must be held, and the give and take of compromise becomes a weakness neither side is able to afford.

While formerly war was regarded, according to the classic definition of the German philosopher of war Clausewitz, as the continuation of diplomacy by other means, the art of diplomacy is now transformed into a variety of the art of warfare. That is to say, we live in the period of Cold War where the aims of warfare are being pursued, for the time being, with other than violent means. In such a situation the peculiar qualities of the diplomatic mind are useless, for they have nothing to operate with and are consequently superseded by the military type of thinking. The balance of power, once disturbed, can be restored only, if at all, by an increase in the weaker side's military strength. Yet, since there are no important variables in the picture aside from the inherent strength of the two giants themselves, either side must fear that the temporarily stronger contestant will use its superiority to eliminate the threat from the other side by shattering military and economic pressure or by a war of annihilation.

Thus the international situation is reduced to the primitive spectacle of two giants eyeing each other with watchful suspicion. They bend every effort to increase their military potential to the utmost, since this is all they have to count on. Both prepare to strike the first decisive blow, for if one does not strike it the other might. Thus, contain or be contained, conquer or be conquered, destroy or be destroyed, become the watchwords of the new diplomacy.[26]

How accurate a descriptive, predictive, and explanatory model is this concept of the state system in international politics? Descriptively, it certainly has much in its favor. First of all, it encompasses all states and

[26] *Ibid.*, pp. 361–62.

does therefore possess the virtue of comprehensiveness. Second, it emphasizes the interactions among the system's members rather than being a straightforward historical account of individual state actions—particularly those of the great powers—as if these occurred in vacuum. This focusing on the system enables us "to study the patterns of interaction which the system reveals, and to generalize about such phenomena as the creation and dissolution of coalitions, the frequency and duration of specific power configurations, modifications in its stability, its responsiveness to changes in formal political institutions, and the norms and folklore which it manifests as a societal system. In other words, the systemic level of analysis, and only this level, permits us to examine international relations in the whole, with a comprehensiveness that is of necessity lost when our focus is shifted to a lower, and more partial, level."[27]

The real problem, however, arises from this model's lack of predictive value. According to the model, nations react to any shifts of power in the system; any shift away from the equilibrium results in a counteracting shift re-establishing the equilibrium and the stability of the system. This balance-of-power mode of analysis can therefore explain why, given Europe's state of collapse after World War II, once the Soviet threat had become clear, the United States sought to contain Soviet expansionism. It would have allowed us to predict that the United States would not tolerate the Soviet-backed aggression of the North Koreans against South Korea aimed at shifting the balance in the Pacific. Even earlier, it should have enabled us to predict British and French policy toward Germany in the 1930's; yet, in fact, neither nation acted as it *should* have acted. Similarly, because World War I had all too clearly revealed that Britain and France were too weak by themselves to contain German power, the United States *should* have committed itself to the preservation of the European balance of power against Germany; instead, it retreated into its traditional isolationist shell. The result was that instead of attempting to deter World War II, the United States had to fight another war to help restore the equilibrium after it had been upset. Thus the balance-of-power analysis again fails to account for a nation's behavior. A model that cannot explain the actions of a great power like the United States for a period of almost twenty years is one that obviously suffers some serious shortcomings. U. S. foreign policy during the interwar period indeed can hardly be explained in terms of the balance of power. Until the fall of France in 1940, in fact, the growing menace of Nazi Germany only made America cling to her posture of isolationism all the more tenaciously. And once engaged in the war, the United States did not foresee and prepare for the possibility of hostile postwar relations with the Soviet Union, although it should have been clear that the defeat

[27] J. David Singer, "The Level of Analysis Problem in International Relations," *World Politics*, October, 1961, p. 80.

of Nazi Germany woud leave a power vacuum in the center of Europe, that Soviet power would flow into this vacuum and threaten Western Europe if the United States did not take preventive measures, and that the European balance of power would thereby be upset. It would appear in retrospect that the two wartime allies were bound to clash. Yet American policy-makers during the war were hardly concerned with the emerging postwar balance, their overwhelming concern being the military defeat of Germany. On the whole, they expected future relations with the Soviet Union to be friendly and cooperative. Not until early 1947 were these expectations completely laid aside in the face of the harsh realities of the Cold War.

This predictive weakness in the model of the state system in turn reflects certain shortcomings of its explanatory capability. In the first place, nations have other interests besides security—e.g., national prestige and wealth. Admittedly, prestige is closely related to the possession of power. The quest for empire in the nineteenth century, for instance, was in good measure motivated by the drive for prestige. Thus, although Germany, the continent's most powerful nation after 1870, hardly needed colonies to add to her strength, all other great powers possessed them. Today, nations who wish to continue thinking of themselves as great powers despite their postwar decline (Britain and France, for example) and others who wish to achieve first-rank standing (Communist China) strive to develop their own nuclear bomb. Similarly, the "space race" between the United States and the Soviet Union is greatly influenced by the factor of prestige. Technological achievement is generally linked with a nation's political and social institutions. Western pre-eminence throughout the underdeveloped areas of the world in the nineteenth century may have been built largely on military strength, but this demonstration of Western power and technology reflected upon the whole Western way of life. The non-Western peoples were made to feel that Western culture, society, and government were superior. Hence, the great goal of the revolution of rising expectations became "Westernization," the creation of advanced, industrial, urban, affluent, Western-type societies. But prestige is not just a reflection of the quest for power. Smaller nations with no significant power potential seek it out of concern for their pride and self-respect. New nations, whose statehood and self-identity are barely established, are particularly concerned with asserting themselves and acquiring a sense of identity. They tend, in fact, to be hypersensitive—one might even be tempted to say "pathological"—about their prestige.

As with prestige, it is often difficult to distinguish wealth from power, since wealth has always meant power. A wealthy state can generally afford to support large military forces. But a higher standard of living can be a goal in its own right. No nation likes to live at a subsistence level. National prosperity has always been an American goal, and millions of immigrants were attracted to these shores by the dream of a better life. The "American promise" includes affluence as well as liberty, and the national commitment was to both purposes. Today, America's standard of living has become the envy of the world. Even the Soviet Union, with its claims of a superior social system, talks of catching up and surpassing the United States! On the other hand, one of the great attractions of Communism to the new nations is precisely its apparent ability to spur rapid modernization. As they see it, Communism has transformed the Soviet Union from an underdeveloped, agrarian country into the second industrial nation in the world within a record four decades. Since their highest-priority national goal is to satisfy the revolution of rising expectations, each seeks to achieve the miracle of rapid industrialization. "Economic development" has thus become a world-wide phenomenon. Virtually all peoples—including those of the Soviet Union—yearn for a higher standard of living. The "have-nots" are no longer resigned to their accustomed poverty and misery; they are determined to become "haves."

A final significant interest motivating nations is the desire for peace— that is, an absence of war, especially total war. The two world wars of the twentieth century were so destructive that peace now seems to be of overriding importance. Before the fury of World War I toppled some of Europe's greatest empires and left others exhausted, nations had been willing to sacrifice peace and fight for what they deemed to be their vital interests. Their security was the paramount objective, and they were always willing to go to war when this security was endangered. They wanted peace, but not "at any price." But as the costs of war rocketed, peace became more precious. And when, with the dawn of the atomic age, war threatened to exterminate all nations, there seemed to be, in President Eisenhower's words, "no alternative to peace." The preservation of peace thus became a primary aim. Nations still might not accept "peace at any price," but precisely because war had become "unthinkable," it was easy to identify the preservation of security with peace.

Clearly, then, nations pursue other goals besides security. Nevertheless, as the state-system model stresses, security does remain the most important national interest. Yet—and this is the state system's second shortcoming in its explanatory capacity—this concern does not result in a constant and inescapable struggle for power among all members of the system. Some nations hardly seem concerned with power at all—Switzerland and Sweden, for instance. And on the other hand, although the United States, as a great power, may be more concerned with considerations of power, it did not, for example, seek to maximize its power by destroying Russia and imposing a *Pax Americana* upon the world after the war—despite its monopoly of atomic power at the time. Futhermore, nations do not all face the same degree of insecurity, and only those engaged in a rivalry in which they think their *survival* is at stake tend to be preoccupied continuously with the enhancement of their power and thus act in a Hobbesian manner. Others are less concerned: "In international politics, the house is not always, nor everywhere, on fire although the temperature may not be comfortable, even under the best circumstances! This means that danger as well as opportunity for gain, and fear as well as appetite, are not constants but important variables. . . . Where less than national survival is at stake, there is far less compulsion and therefore a less uniform reaction."[28] In addition, there is also a difference between the degree of insecurity a nation actually confronts and the degree it *thinks* it confronts—that is, between the objectively measured threat and the subjectively perceived threat. The United States thought she was perfectly secure during the interwar period, but American security had actually begun to diminish the day Germany started to rearmass its tremendous power for foreign conquest. Because she did not perceive this threat, though, the United States refused to concern herself with the preservation of the balance of power—until forced to by the war. On the other hand, Israel in 1956 was not really as threatened by Egypt and the other Arab states as it thought. The Arab states were unable to unite in much more than formal communiqués. Their armies were composed mostly of peasants, and the Egyptians could hardly use the modern weapons the Soviet Union had supplied. But Israel—observing that states dedicated to her destruction were establishing a unified command, issuing threats, and receiving heavy weapons—felt gravely threatened and therefore attacked.

Finally, states react differently to a threat to their security because security is only one among various competing values—peace, for instance. Britain and France in the 1930's were concerned for their security. But they also feared a repetition of the Great War which could bring about their collapse. Security in these circumstances seemed to depend not upon going to war but upon preserving the peace. But security and peace were incompatible goals. Britain and France forgot this and identified the two, making peace an absolute value, and thus ended up appeasing Hitler and helping him upset the balance against themselves.

Security can also conflict with economic objectives. The more guns a nation buys, the less butter it can afford. The more it spends on maintaining military forces, the less it can spend on foreign aid, on construction of schools, hospitals, and roads, on education, vocational training, and a "war on poverty." The more taxes it needs to buy bombs, the less the taxpayer has left to buy a new house or car, to purchase family insurance, to go to Europe on vacation, or to send his children to college. Nations must make choices, and the choice is not usually either-or but

[28] Wolfers, *op. cit.*, p. 15. See also his more detailed critique of the power model, pp. 147–65.

how many guns and how much butter. Most nations realize that absolute security is not achievable because it would require world domination. Consequently, since they are condemned to "live dangerously" anyway, the question really is: How many more guns will yield how much of an increase in relative security—taking into account the fact that the opponent is also likely to increase the number of his guns? And how much *less* butter is a possibly small additional increase in security worth, assuming it *is* an increase?

Let us consider how such a conflict of values might operate in a democratic society. If a democratic nation really sought to maximize its security, it could start at home by establishing a "garrison state": The young would be drafted into military service and the older people into work in factories producing war material; all would be subjected to a strict discipline and orthodoxy that would squash diversity of opinion, and those who differed with the official viewpoint would be sent to prison camps as security and loyalty risks; all resources, except those used in producing the necessities of life, would be channeled into military production; and the power of the government would be centralized in the hands of a few leaders. Democratic values, competing political parties and opinions, the entire way of life would fall victim to the organization of the nation for maximum military security. But is a nation's concern only for its physical security or also for its way of life? This raises an obvious—but by no means easily resolvable—issue of priorities. For the means of securing a nation's territorial integrity may be incompatible with the values by which it lives. Should a nation root out all possible "security" risks at home, even if under the broad criteria established for a security program innocent people may be hurt, and if the resulting fear of expressing any criticism of governmental actions leads to a stifling of free speech, which could be followed by such other measures as the censorship of books and the banning of debates on "controversial" topics? Should the nation ally itself abroad with patently undemocratic countries in order to maximize its strength? Is its security increased thereby, or is it weakened because doubt is cast on the meaningfulness of its democratic credentials, which are an important element in its claim for world leadership? Or can a democratic state, for instance, launch a preventive war or fire the first shot?

It is these factors—the multiplicity of national interests, the differing degrees of security threats, the gaps between objectively existing and subjectively felt threats, and the conflict of competing values—that make it so difficult for the state-system model to predict a nation's actions; conversely, these factors explain the nation's actions when they do not conform to the expected behavior. The fundamental weakness of the model, therefore, is its attempt to analyze the behavior of states in terms of purely *external* causes: The foreign policy of states is determined by the state system; if states wish to preserve their independence, they are compelled to seek power; otherwise, they risk being attacked. Individual states are thus viewed as monolithic units, identical to all other states in interests, motivation, and behavior. The balance of power, in turn, becomes the central organizing concept, for it specifically determines how states *ought* to—and *must*—behave. The constant struggle among states leads the weak to combine against the strong; as the latter are checked, and other states in their turn threaten to upset the balance, the counter-alliances seeking to preserve the equilibrium shift as well. International politics thus becomes a matter of ever-changing alliances and counter-alliances, and the only issue among nations is which balance-of-power technique should be used to isolate the potential "troublemaker" and keep the balance flexible. International relations, in this view, might be likened to a "formalized ballet" whose steps fall into a continuously repeating pattern but tell no story.[29] All nations are constantly performing this balance-of-power ballet, with the balance dictating the direction in which each nation dances. War or peace, stability or instability in the system, is thus a matter of good choreography.

This mechanistic, if not deterministic, mode of analysis exaggerates the impact of the system upon individual states and conversely underestimates the impact of the states upon the system. A model that tells states they *must* behave as they *ought* to behave clearly implies that states frequently do *not* act as they should. Obviously, states—or more accurately, national decision-makers—do possess a choice in what they do. They do have some independence to decide their policies, since states do not just seek to "maximize power" and there is no single, permanent, and objectively determinable "national interest." Indeed, to tell policy-makers to act in accordance with the national or security interest of the state is to tell them nothing because these terms are so vague and broad as to be meaningless. Naturally, they wish to protect the national interest. They, like everyone else, are, of course, *for* the national interest, and in fact every interest group identifies its claims with the national interest. But what *is* the "national interest"?

This cannot be determined solely by the system to the complete exclusion of a nation's domestic politics. What does a nation see as its role in international affairs? How does it perceive its relations with other nations? How does it, as a result, define its interests, and *who* defines them? A nation's cultural values, social structure, economic system, political organization, public opinion, and especially its leadership and the views of this leadership—these are at least of equal if not greater significance in determining national behavior. Systems analysis has not usually consid-

[29] Stanley Hoffmann, *Contemporary Theory in International Relations*, p. 35.

ered these internal factors; by and large, it divorces international from internal politics.[30] A nation's domestic makeup is not considered important since its behavior will be dictated by the shifting balance of power. Thus, it apparently would not have mattered in 1945 whether the United States was capitalist or socialist, a democracy or a dictatorship, led by Democrats or Republicans. The Soviet threat would have compelled its leaders, no matter what their political or economic convictions, to react with a counterbalancing policy; the realities of international life would have left them no other choice. But the fact is that the United States might have reacted in various other ways. Still, even if the state-system model could predict why and how nations would react to an expansionist power, it could not tell us why that power was seeking to expand and what its purposes were. Yet it is most vital that we understand the ends nations seek, for international politics, like all politics, is not simply a struggle for power but the interplay of power and purpose.

And these ends are defined by those who govern the nation at the time. One of them may be security, but why does one group of policy-makers define this security in terms of preserving the *status quo* and another in terms of an expansionism that might be local, continental, or global? The national interest, to repeat, is *not* a constant, the sum of the geographic, political, and economic elements that have historically been associated with the security of the state.[31] Different policy-makers will stress different elements, give them different priorities, or completely re-

[30] Domestic considerations are only cited to show that they interfere with the implementation of a proper balance-of-power policy. That is, they are cited as being responsible for states not following the policy they should. Thus, in a backhanded fashion, their importance is acknowledged, but, instead of leading to a reassessment of the state-system model, this only reinforces the determination not to consider domestic politics. See, for example, Hans J. Morgenthau, *In Defense of the National Interest* (New York: Alfred A. Knopf, 1951).

The reasons given for this neglect are succinctly stated by another theorist of international politics:

> Foreign-policy analysis may and often has to start where domestic politics ends, that is to say, at the watershed. There are two major reasons. First, international politics of the state system has its conventions, techniques, and requirements which, embedded in tradition and existing conditions, are relatively independent of the internal political system of any one participant nation. . . . The second and related reason for drawing a line, however thin, between domestic and foreign politics is the persistence of national "self-preservation" and "survival" as the necessary and in themselves sufficient goals of foreign policy. . . . The irreducible minimum objective of foreign policy is precisely to safeguard the integrity of the state so that the values of the surviving society can be determined by domestic political processes independently of external pressures. (George Liska, *International Equilibrium: A Theoretical Essay on the Politics and Organization of Security* [Cambridge, Mass.: Harvard University Press, 1957], pp. 200–201.)

[31] The only major textbook to emphasize the internal dynamics of foreign policy is Ernst B. Haas and Allen S. Whiting, *Dynamics of International Relations* (New York: McGraw-Hill, 1956). See especially chapters 2–4.

interpret them. The substance of the national interest is thus a changing one, its definition depending on the internal structure of the state, its leaders, and their aims.

Thus state behavior—especially of states that seek to change the status quo—is, to paraphrase Clausewitz, essentially a continuation of domestic politics by other means; this is particularly true in a revolutionary state system, in which the revolutionary power's concept of foreign policy is one of international civil war. This has tended to be forgotten in stable periods—as in the Europe of the seventeenth and eighteenth centuries, when the states shared a set of common values deriving from the fact that they were all dynastic in structure and shared an aristocratic consensus. In these circumstances, it was all too easy to overlook the consensus and the role it played in limiting conflict. It simply existed, and because it was not a subject of great controversy, it remained virtually unnoticed; attention was focused instead on the everyday balancing of power, and it was this process that seemed to be the most important determinant of state behavior.[32] The significance of the internal social structures of the states, whose values were reflected in the consensus, was overlooked. Yet it was these structures that determined the international behavior of the states of the European system—and thus the stability of the system—during this period. Europe was, in a real sense, a single political community—a family of nations—bound together by an aristocracy whose allegiance transcended any single state. This was the age before nationalism, and the aristocracy was, so to speak, an "international set." Its members mixed socially, intermarried, sent their sons to the same schools, where they gained common cultural values, learned the same language (French), and, above all, were imbued with a sense of personal honor (what a gentleman did and did not do). They also mixed professionally by serving in each other's armies and diplomatic corps, for aristocrats had a virtual monopoly on commissions in the army and diplomatic posts. A Prussian officer, for instance, might serve the Czar of Russia at a time when Russia was at war with Prussia. No moral stigma was attached to such professional crossing of frontiers. An aristo-

---

[32] In this connection, see particularly Morton A. Kaplan, *System and Process in International Politics*, pp. 22–36. Kaplan states that the six rules national actors obey are:

1. Act to increase capabilities but negotiate rather than fight.
2. Fight rather than pass up an opportunity to increase capabilities.
3. Stop fighting rather than eliminate an essential national actor.
4. Act to oppose any coalition or single actor which tends to assume a position of predominance with respect to the rest of the system.
5. Act to constrain actors who subscribe to supranational organizing principles.
6. Permit defeated or constrained essential national actors to re-enter the system as acceptable role partners or act to bring some previously inessential actor within the essential actor classification. Treat all essential actors as acceptable role partners.

crat fought because soldiering was his profession, not because of any nationalistic hatred of the enemy. More often than not, he had at one time fought together with the officers now on the opposing side. If this sounds ludicrous in a nationalistic age, it might be well to recall that the wars of this period were limited and were fought for relatively short periods, over small pieces of territory, with relatively small losses—all quite unlike our bloody twentieth-century wars.

It was precisely because the members of the aristocracy had so much in common and were so far removed from the lowly peasants whom they ruled that interstate relations could be carried on in such a moderate political climate. All the states shared the same type of social structure and set of values; all wished to preserve the state system. No state was interested in destroying any other state. While each naturally concerned itself with its own security, none had to be concerned with its survival, for each recognized the other's right to existence. All conflict in the system was thus of a limited nature for the obvious and logical reason that once states abjure mutual destruction and decide to coexist, compromise becomes the only rule of conduct. Diplomacy as an instrument of compromise and conciliation served that function well; and wars of the period were similarly limited in aim. The idea of totally defeating an opponent and eliminating him was virtually unknown.[33] Indeed, each state was concerned with securing its own interests *and* the preservation of the European dynastic system. The balance of power operated within this consensual framework and achieved both aims.

The French Revolution represented the beginning of the end for this international system. For the Revolution, by overthrowing the dynastic social structure at home, also repudiated the aristocratic base upon which the European political system was founded. France thus became a revolutionary power—that is, a power that rejects the international order because it rejects the internal order and values of the great powers who are its members. France, proclaiming democracy and nationalism, repudiated the *ancien régime* domestically and internationally. For the first time in history, the forgotten masses were to participate in the political process. Government was no longer to be dominated by the few. During the dynastic era, the "common man" had not identified himself with the state; his loyalty had been limited to his family, village, and region. He shared neither a common language with his fellows nor a loyalty to a common set of state symbols. The French Revolution changed all this radically. The age of democracy was to be the age of the people and popular sovereignty. France was no longer to be divided into classes. France was to be one and indivisible, and all Frenchmen were to be bound to each other by fraternal ties of liberty and equality. The individ-

---

[33] This is, of course, in accordance with Kaplan's rules 3 and 6, but he attributes it to the balance-of-power system, not to a shared consensus.

ual citizen now began to identify himself with his nation and *its* set of values. And this identification was in turn reinforced by the new national language, national symbols, and universal education.

But the Revolution not only resulted in a domestic shift of loyalties; it also produced external expansion. The old regime was viewed as the embodiment of all injustice: domestically, the rule and exploitation of the many by the few; internationally, wars fought for the personal advantage of the aristocratic rulers, but with the common people suffering—and dying. The conclusion was clear: that social harmony and justice at home and international peace and good will among men could only be realized if the old order were swept into the dustbins of history. Once people elected their rulers, they would no longer be exploited or sent off to wars, for governments that were held popularly responsible would serve the public welfare and preserve the peace. It was therefore imperative to export the revolution to other states, where men still lived in bondage. Men were finally to be liberated from social tyranny and the scourge of war, to live together in human brotherhood and peace. In short, democratic and nationalistic France denied the legitimacy of the prevailing European state system. Indeed, she condemned it as heretical and denied the right of nondemocratic states to exist. She did not therefore favor a balance of power that would preserve the system. France's aim was total: the destruction of the European order and the international consensus. Democracy and nationalism thus eliminated the very factor that had previously limited the scope of interest conflict. As a self-appointed agent of history and humanity, France sought to remake the international system in her own image by democratizing it. The result was an ideological crusade.

France was eventually to be defeated, and the other great powers of Europe did restore the equilibrium. Their actions could be explained in terms of the balance of power, but the way in which revolutionary France defined her national interests could not be explained by systems analysis. Even the actions of the other European states could not be viewed as merely an effort to restore the balance. After the war, they restored the monarchy in order to re-create the old European order; the balance and the monarchical order were functionally interdependent. Obviously, to the practitioners of foreign policy, foreign and domestic politics were not two separate entities but were inextricably intertwined.[34]

An analysis of international politics must therefore focus on two levels. The first is the level of the system. We saw earlier that the behavior of group actors in the United States is shaped by the system. The values of the system and the distribution of the power within it help to de-

[34] For a theoretical analysis of international politics that successfully combines internal and external causes, see Kenneth N. Waltz, *Man, the State, and War.*

fine the objectives certain groups seek. And the institutional structure (freedom of association, elections, federalism, and separation of power) then largely determines how they will press their claims. Similarly, in international politics, the nature of the system (whether it is traditional or revolutionary), the distribution of power within the system (multipolar or bipolar), as well as within the opposing coalitions, and the type of weapons are bound to influence and shape the behavior of the members of the system. It has been said that one state's behavior is determined by that of others; for this reason systems analysis focuses first on the international environment in which states act and then on the interactions among states. Yet it is also true that while a state's choices are limited by the behavior of other states, the degree of these limitations should not be exaggerated.

> Imagine a number of individuals, varying widely in their predispositions, who find themselves inside a house on fire. It would be perfectly realistic to expect that these individuals, with rare exceptions, would feel compelled to run toward exits. General fears of losing the cherished possession of life, coupled with the stark external threat to life, would produce the same reaction, whatever the psychological peculiarities of the actors. Surely, therefore, for an explanation of the rush for the exits, there is no need to analyze the individual decisions that produced it. The situation would be different if one or several members of the group had not joined the stampede, but had remained unmoved after the fire was discovered or had even failed to perceive it. Such "deviationist" behavior, running counter to expectation, would justify and require intensive psychological inquiry.
>
> A different situation would arise if, instead of being on fire, the house in question merely were overheated. In such a case, the second prerequisite of compulsion—serious external danger—would be absent. The reactions of different inhabitants might range all the way from hurried window-opening and loud complaints to complete indifference. To formulate expectations concerning behavior in an overheated house, one would need intimate knowledge of the varying individual predispositions and of the symptoms by which they could be recognized.[35]

It is precisely because the house within which international politics is played is not on fire most of the time that we must also—and this takes on primary importance—focus on the level of the individual actor and analyze how he defines his national objectives. The state system provides the framework within which international politics occurs, and the foreign policies of the individual states constitute the "input." While the system can explain the reaction of states to a disturbance of the equilibrium, only the "internal determinants" can explain the actions of those states who are seeking to change the *status quo* (and this is, of course, true as well for the *status quo* states who do not react when the

[35] Wolfers, *op. cit.*, pp. 13–14.

balance is upset). Here the focus must be on the states' official policy-makers, their values and criteria of judgment, and their perception of their interests. How do they "see" the world? What conditions do they consider desirable or undesirable? Whom do they regard as their actual or potential opponents, why, and what do they consider the nature of the conflict? Attention must also be paid to the relationship of the decision-makers to those whom they govern. What is the impact upon them of public opinion or particular segments of opinion—that is, of the politically most active interest groups? In a democratic state, public opinion at times tends to set very definite limits to the policy-makers' freedom of choice in defining national objectives and the means to be employed in their achievement.

By contrast, in a totalitarian state, public opinion plays a minimal role and the starting point of any analysis of its foreign policy must be the party leaders and their particular *Weltanschauung*, or way of viewing the world.

III

Communism:
The Politics of
Permanent Warfare

The Revolutionary Strategy of Conquest

A revolutionary state—such as the Soviet Union after World War II —is a state at war. It rejects the social and economic structure of the traditional states who dominate the state system because it views this prevailing order as the source of injustice and war. The self-appointed agent of history, it is committed to the "permanent revolution" until the system has been liquidated and mankind converted to the "true faith." The revolutionary state has therefore, by the very nature of its ideological outlook, "declared war" on the old order. The nonrevolutionary states and their traditional international system have no right to exist. If man is to be absolved of sin, if the world is to be purified, the heretic must be eliminated. If man is to live in happiness and harmony, justice must triumph and the enemy must be vanquished. The "true believer," to save man from himself, must impose his faith on all men, not just those of his own nation. His victory must therefore be global. The war must be prosecuted with vigor and persistence until this aim is achieved. To relax from the historical struggle—let alone to desist—would be a betrayal of the revolutionary mission. An ideologically oriented movement is thus a movement permanently at war. Its *raison d'être* is its final goal. Since its leaders' sole claim to power is their ideological mission, there is constant pressure toward the fulfillment of the ideologically defined goal. The dynamic of the revolutionary state is thus continuous and boundless. It can never rest short of conquest of the world—the prerequisite for global conversion.

The issue for the traditional power thus becomes its survival. Yet, ironically enough, it often has difficulty in recognizing the seriousness of the challenge it confronts. The traditional power has always lived in the legitimate state system, and its attitudes and ways of thinking have been fashioned by this system. This means above all that its political outlook will be pragmatic. Since all states accept the social and economic order, their approach to politics will be empirical. The very fact that they all share a common ideology means, somewhat paradoxically, that this ideology fades into the background. It is simply there, and because it is not a matter of dispute, it is not a conscious concern. Constant conflicts of interests there are, to be sure, but these are always adjustable and reconcilable. A "practical" attitude is all that is required.[1]

This is why the traditional state has difficulty in coping with a revolutionary power. All its instincts will lead it to minimize the importance —if not, indeed, the relevance—of the latter's ideological pronouncements. After all, the leaders of the traditional power will tend to think, all politicians make speeches appealing to their constituents. So it is understandable that a Hitler or Khrushchev should deliver speeches denouncing other nations and promising his countrymen that they will rule the world. This seems little different from the behavior of politicians within their own countries, who constantly denounce each other, promise their constituents everything, and generally present themselves as the "good guys" battling for their country against the wicked opposition. But they are all participants in a great political game, and once the election is over, attacks and counterattacks are forgotten. Why then should political leaders raised in the traditional order really give credence to the grandiose plans of the revolutionary states? Do they not know from experience the gap between what politicians *say* for public consumption and what they actually *do*? As "practical" men who have all their lives been able to resolve domestic and international issues by com-

---

[1] On this "practical," or empirical, approach to international politics at a time of revolution—an attitude Americans share with Englishmen—the following comments seem appropriate: "In this story [of British appeasement of Germany] we see the decadence of British empiricism, empiricism carried beyond all rhyme or reason. In general I am in sympathy with empiricism in politics; I must prefer it to doctrinairism. The practical way of looking at things, not looking too far in advance, not rocking the boat, and other cliches that do duty for thinking ahead, may serve well enough in ordinary, normal times. But our times are not 'normal' in the good old Victorian sense, and never will be again. And this habit of mind in politics will certainly not serve in times of revolution, perpetual stress and conflict, war, the reshaping of the world. This conventional British way of looking at things was simply not equal to the times, and it caught these men [Britain's leaders in the 1930's] out badly." (A. L. Rowse, *Appeasement* [New York: W. W. Norton & Co., 1963], p. 116.)

promise, why should they now not be able to settle international issues in the same manner?

Traditional states are in this respect like individuals: they believe what they want to believe. They do not really relish an all-out challenge, and the dangers and arduous efforts required to meet such a challenge. They would much rather believe that the revolutionary leaders are not really revolutionary, that their pronouncements merely reflect limited grievances that can be resolved by "business as usual." The traditional statesmen, in short, by the very nature of their experience, will seek to belittle the nature of the challenge, believing that by satisfying the grievances of the allegedly revolutionary state they can "derevolutionize" it and transform it into a supporter of the *status quo*.

This belief of the traditional states that their opponent can in this manner be reconciled to the traditional system is reinforced by the way the revolutionary state approaches concrete international issues. Its aim is total, but it presents each specific issue as a limited one; moreover, each is cleverly disguised in the symbols and language of the old order. Since, in the traditional order, each issue has been limited and distinct, settled on the basis of its specific merit, why should the traditional states assume that this customary way of handling issues has now changed? On the surface, everything looks the same. Moreover, each challenge is accompanied by words the traditional statesmen recognize as their own. Would it not be unjust of them to oppose claims made in the name of peace or national self-determination or social justice?

Thus, by using the preconceptions of the traditional states and system against them, the revolutionary state gains a significant psychological advantage. It seeks the total destruction of the traditional states, but it does not want to provoke a military clash before it is ready: for a preventive war by the traditional states would endanger the "base of the world revolution." The revolutionary state's adoption of "salami tactics" meets this problem: One slice is cut off after another, as each is digested. This tactic conveys the impression that only the momentary issue is at stake; but each step is actually linked to the next step on the road toward the final goal—part of a "chain reaction," so to speak. Thus the balance of power is bit by bit turned against the traditional states, who meanwhile remain paralyzed because they are unwilling to precipitate war unless they are quite certain that the balance is endangered and their cause is just. But since none of the specific challenges by itself threatens to upset the balance, and since each issue is, moreover, presented as a redress for a justified grievance caused by the traditional states' violation of their own principles, they cannot be certain that their opponent is not sincere. The traditional powers are thus not only placed on the defensive, but made to feel guilty about defending their interests. If, at any time along the way to their destruction, they realize what is happening and decide to stand firm, there will always be those—in the government and, even more, among the public—who will denounce their country's stand because its cause is not just, because the opponent's claim is not totally unjustified, and because one should fight only on an issue whose morality is unquestionable. It is such doubts about the justness of an issue, hesitations about its defense, and fears of war that the revolutionary state seeks to exploit in order to paralyze the will of the traditional powers to protect themselves. The result is likely to be either inaction or ineffective action.

Until the postwar challenge posed by the Soviet Union, nothing illustrated as well the psychological advantage of the revolutionary state and the self-imposed handicap of the defenders of the old order as did the experience with Nazi Germany in the 1930's. Hitler's global ambitions were influenced by the English geopolitician Halford MacKinder, who, after World War I, had written: "Who rules East Europe commands the Heartland [largely Russia and China, plus Iran and Afghanistan]: Who rules the Heartland commands the World-Island [Eurasia and Africa]: Who rules the World-Island commands the World." His eastward expansion depended, however, on breaking or nullifying the alliances that had been established to contain Germany: the French alliances with Poland and the Little Entente (Czechoslovakia, Yugoslavia, Romania) and the British commitment to the defense of the Franco-German frontier. Hitler achieved this goal by a number of challenges, none of which by itself ever confronted France and England with a major change in the balance of power: the reintroduction of conscription—the German forces had been limited to 200,000 men by the Treaty of Versailles; the occupation of the Rhineland—an area neutralized at Versailles because Germany had twice launched her attacks on France from there; the demand for the return of the Sudetenland—a mountainous area which, despite its sizable German population, was at Versailles given to the new state of Czechoslovakia so that she could better defend herself against her large German neighbor; and finally, the demand for the return of the famous Polish Corridor. Each of these was a move toward changing the distribution of power in Europe in Germany's favor: Conscription would rebuild Germany's military strength; the militarization of the Rhineland would permit Germany to build the Siegfried Line, hold the Western front against France with minimal strength, and concentrate German power against the countries of Eastern Europe to blackmail them into submission once they could no longer count on their French ally. And the first prize of this policy—the acquisition of the Sudetenland in 1938—dismembered Czechoslovakia, left the rest of that unhappy country for Germany to swallow a few months later, and strengthened the vise around Poland that was to pressure her into submission.

Each of these moves was taken in terms of a justified grievance or a Western symbol. For instance, the Allies had said at Versailles that Germany's military limitation was only the first step toward a more general reduction of armaments. But after two wars with Germany, France was actually concerned with maintaining her military strength. Hitler could therefore pose as the spokesman for an aggrieved Germany which had in good faith "accepted" a large measure of disarmament, while its former enemies, despite their avowals, had not followed suit. A great power and the equal of France and England, Germany was being treated as a second-class state; all she asked was to be treated fairly. Hitler's other claims were advanced in the context of the most Western of Western democratic principles: national self-determination, which had been the basis of the Treaty of Versailles. This principle had been violated in the Rhineland, the Sudetenland, and the Polish Corridor, primarily for security reasons. Hitler could thus exploit a fundamental Western principle against the West in order to undermine the post–World War I settlement.

On what basis could France and England deny him any of these claims? Were equality and national self-determination all right for themselves but not for anyone else? Hitler's claims were recognized as just.[2] Who could really say that he was insincere and that he was using the Versailles principles cynically? Had the West not in fact—as Hitler repeatedly pointed out—violated its own principles? Was the German leader therefore not justified in demanding that the two Western powers correct the inequalities they had written into the peace treaty? The West, because of these tactics, began to feel guilty about Versailles. It had preached one thing and practiced another; and it had thereby placed the moral validity of the Versailles settlement in jeopardy. Increasingly, Hitler began to appear only as the spokesman for justified German grievances. And his frantic speeches were explained away in terms of the vigor of German resentment at the unjust treatment dealt her by France and England.

Hitler thus shrewdly disguised his aim and paralyzed the will of his opponents to act against him. Each challenge confronted them with the

[2] Of course, none of Britain's policy-makers had read *Mein Kampf* (see Rowse, *op. cit.*, pp. 31, 117). Thus, when Hitler marched into the Rhineland, Lord Lothian could say: "What has it got to do with us? It's none of our business, is it? It's their own back-garden they are walking into." And earlier, he had said that Hitler "said explicitly to me, as he has also said publicly, that what Germany wants is equality, not war; that she is prepared absolutely to renounce war; that he has signed a treaty with Poland removing by far the most dangerous and bitter element of the Treaty of Versailles—the corridor—from the region of war for ten years . . . and finally, and most vital, that he will pledge Germany not to interfere in his beloved Austria by force. . . . He will sign pacts of non-aggression with all Germany's neighbours, to prove the sincerity of his desire for peace, and in armaments he asks no more than 'equality' for Germany." (Quoted in *ibid.*, pp. 32–33, 40.)

question of whether they wanted to fight to preserve a morally dubious *status quo*. After the horrors of World War I, the answer was obvious. Why should a war be fought to defend unjust positions when it could be avoided? If Hitler was a nationalist who only wanted the return of German territory, would not the satisfaction of his demand for national self-determination end his claims and gain his support for the preservation of the European balance and peace? Was Hitler not as concerned as French and English leaders with maintaining the peace? It was upon this word "peace" above all others that Hitler relied for his successes. Revolutionaries seem to possess an uncanny ability to utilize the word, and all its implications, with great insight into the *status quo* powers' yearnings. Thus Hitler could announce Germany's rearmament while pledging Germany's willingness to renounce all offensive weapons or disband its entire military establishment—if only other nations would pledge to do the same. He could denounce a treaty with a neighbor while simultaneously issuing assurances that it was his own fondest hope to sign a nonaggression pact with that same neighbor. He "solemnly" guaranteed other countries' frontiers, promising not to interfere in their internal affairs, and never tired of declaring that his present claim was the last one he would ever make. Ironically, Hitler became the most effective spokesman for "peace" in the 1930's. An age that has almost forgotten him—or remembers him primarily as a raving maniac—has also forgotten that to his contemporaries Hitler often appeared to be sincerely and honestly dedicated to resolving all problems that might stand in the way of peace in Europe. His constant refrain was that Germany would never break the peace:

> At no moment of my struggle on behalf of the German people have I ever forgotten the duty incumbent on me and on us all firmly to uphold European culture and European civilization. . . . Why should it not be possible to put an end to this useless strife [between France and Germany] which has lasted for centuries and which has never been and never will be finally decided by either of the two nations concerned? Why not replace it by the rule of reason? The German people have no interest in seeing the French people suffer. And what advantage can come to France when Germany is in misery? . . . Why should it not be possible to lift the general problem of conflicting interests between the European states above the sphere of passion and unreason and consider it in the calm light of a higher vision?

On another occasion, Hitler said:

> All of us and all peoples have the feeling that we are at the turning point of an age. . . . Not we alone, the conquered of yesterday, but also the victors have the inner conviction that something was not as it should be, that reason seemed to have deserted men. . . . Peoples must find a new

relation to each other, some new form must be created. . . . But over this new order which must be set up stand the words: Reason and Logic, Understanding and Mutual Consideration. It is in the interests of all that present-day problems should be solved in a reasonable and peaceful manner. . . . The application of violence of any kind in Europe could have no favorable effect upon the political and economic position. . . . The outbreak of such unlimited madness would necessarily cause the collapse of the present social and political order.[3]

In the face of such statements, how could any national leader with the terrible responsibility of deciding whether to fight be certain of Hitler's insincerity and lack of devotion to peace? Confronted with the possibility of averting war and possibly gaining a convert for peace, and the *certainty* of a long and bloody war, was the "sane" man's choice not clear? Surely, to be opposed to a relaxation of tensions (which is what the word "appeasement" used to mean) was to be for war—a "warmonger"!

Not until after Hitler had taken over the whole of Czechoslovakia did England's leaders see the true Hitler and decide that he could not be allowed to go any further. Hitler, believing however that England's announced support of Poland was meaningless, and that his latest challenge would go unmet as before, attacked Poland. England then declared war on Germany, as did France. World War II thus began under the worst of all circumstances: after Germany's rearmament, the building of the Siegfried Line, the loss of Czechoslovakia, and the demoralization of France's other allies in Eastern Europe—in short, when Germany was no longer the weak power she had been at the time of Hitler's first expansionist moves, in the mid-1930's.

The responsibility for this war must go in large measure to the English and French leaders who, as traditional statesmen, did not believe that Hitler's ideological pronouncements had ever been seriously intended. Not surprisingly, they considered Hitler essentially "one of them," statesmen born and bred in a system founded upon nationalism. They could even cite a precedent, for Bismarck, after Germany's unification, had declared that Germany was satisfied and would henceforth support the new European *status quo*. Since Hitler talked in terms of national self-determination, why should they not now believe that the new German leader was merely a cruder version of the Prussian aristocrat, and that he, too, would be satiated once he had achieved his apparently nationalistic aims? This was indeed their tragedy: the ability of the revolutionary leader skillfully to exploit their preconceptions without their recognizing until too late what he was doing. But then, men's atti-

[3] Alan Bullock, *Hitler: A Study in Tyranny* (New York: Harper & Brothers, 1953), pp. 314, 315. See also G. F. Hudson, "Hitler and Khrushchev," *The New Leader*, October 2, 1961, p. 20.

tudes reflect their experience, and a revolutionary power was simply not part of their experience.

If it had been, they might have met the challenge of Nazi Germany. Conversely, if Nazi Germany had been merely a traditional national state, the differences between it and France and England could in all probability have been resolved without precipitating a war. But Hitler's Germany was a revolutionary state and therefore not interested in any settlement. Short of total dominion, no *status quo* could satisfy it. So the war that had in fact been declared on the bourgeois world upon Hitler's assumption of power, in 1933, was transformed from a cold war to a hot war six years later. The lesson the 1930's had taught was a crucial one: that revolutionary regimes are ideologically oriented; that their aim is total and global; and that while their tactics and vocabulary resemble those of the traditional states, the similarities end there. Traditional states can coexist. But just as a revolutionary party seeks total dominion within a nation, the revolutionary state seeks global domination externally; it cannot coexist with the old order either at home or abroad.

The Nazi experience—Europe's first encounter with a revolutionary state since the French Revolution—was too fresh to be absorbed rapidly. American leaders during World War II therefore repeated the earlier errors of their British and French colleagues. In their view, despite the major difference that it now flew the Communist flag, Russia remained primarily a Czarist state. Various factors influenced this assessment: the apparent identity of Soviet and traditional Russian foreign-policy objectives (concern for the security of Eastern Europe, the search for a warm-water port); the Soviets' stress on the "Great Fatherland war," exploiting Russian nationalism; conversely, the dissolution of the Comintern, the replacement of the "International" by a Russian national anthem, and the relaxation of restrictions upon the church; and the West's own hope that the wartime cooperation would mitigate, if not remove, Soviet suspicions of the West—particularly, if the West proved its sincerity by recognizing Russia's historic security interests. The impact of Communist ideology on Soviet policy was considered as largely irrelevant in the formulation of American wartime policy. Even Churchill talked of the postwar peace being guarded by the "Four Policemen" (the United States, Britain, Russia, and China): "I wished to meet the Russian grievance, because the government of the world must be entrusted to satisfied nations, who wished nothing more for themselves than what they had. If the world-government were in the hands of hungry nations, there would always be danger."[4] If they were jointly to preserve the peace, all four states would have to be satisfied; otherwise they would quarrel and fall out with one another. None of them should be "hungry." The assumption was

[4] Winston S. Churchill, *The Second World War*. Vol. V: *Closing the Ring* (Boston: Houghton Mifflin Co., 1951), pp. 363, 382.

that while Stalin might be hungry, his appetite was limited and an appropriate meal could therefore be served. At Yalta, when Stalin demanded certain concessions in the Far East in return for entering the war against Japan after the defeat of Germany, he appeared to do so not as a Communist revolutionary, but as an heir to Nicholas II, who had lost these possessions during the Russo-Japanese war, at the beginning of the twentieth century. The Yalta promise to return these to the Soviet Union was introduced by the following sentence: "The former rights of Russia violated by the treacherous attack of Japan in 1904 shall be restored." President Roosevelt's closest adviser described the mood at the end of the conference, after the Big Three had reached a number of agreements, some of which were expected to settle the major issues of postwar Europe: "We really believed in our hearts that this was the dawn of the new day we had all been praying for and talking about for so many years. We were absolutely certain that we had won the first great victory of the peace—and, by 'we,' I mean *all* of us, the whole civilized human race. The Russians had proved that they could be reasonable and far-seeing, and there wasn't any doubt in the minds of the President or any of us that we could live with them and get along with them peacefully for as far into the future as any of us could imagine."[5] Russian security needs in Europe and the Far East had been met, and no major conflict of interests with the Western powers was expected to mar the amicable relations established by the wartime cooperation. It was not recognized that the Soviet Union was a revolutionary power with unlimited aims, because American policy-makers interpreted Russia's "national interest" as divorced from the ideological source of its conduct.

This evaluation was not even reassessed when, toward the end of the war and immediately after Japan's defeat, the Soviet Union became increasingly intransigent, imposed Communist-controlled governments in Eastern Europe, and began to exert pressures on Iran, Greece, and Turkey. American officials recognized, of course, that serious differences had arisen between Russia and her former allies; but these differences did not lead to a fundamental change in the American perception of Soviet foreign policy. The United States, it was believed, overzealous in its efforts to win Stalin's friendship, had not always been firm enough, and the Soviet leader was now trying to take advantage of our good will. A firmer American line therefore had to be followed on issues on which the two powers differed. The assumption was that if the United States took a tougher bargaining stance and no longer seemed in a hurry to resolve particular points of tension, the Soviet rulers would see the pointlessness

[5] Quoted in Robert E. Sherwood, *Roosevelt and Hopkins: An Intimate History* (rev. ed.; New York: Bantam Books, 1950), II, 516. See also Churchill, *op. cit.*, VI, 362 (who seemed to share this expectation); Herbert Feis, *Roosevelt-Churchill-Stalin: The War they Waged and the Peace they Sought* (Princeton, N.J.: Princeton University Press, 1957), p. 558.

of their obduracy and agree to fair compromise solutions. In short, American firmness would make the Russians "reasonable." For they were regarded as "unreasonable" merely on particular issues; that this "un-reasonableness" might stem from the very nature of the Communist regime had not yet occurred to American policy-makers. The new American position, as one group of political analysts aptly summed it up, "meant to most of its exponents that the Soviet Union had to be induced by firmness to play the game in the American way. There was no consistent official suggestion that the United States should begin to play a different game."[6] Before such a suggestion could be made, American policy-makers had to recognize the revolutionary nature of the Soviet regime. This they began to do in 1947.

But men do not readily stop viewing the world in the former, more familiar way. Since the older states accept the traditional state system as the natural one, their disposition is to continue attempting to integrate the revolutionary state into the prevailing system. Every shift in the revolutionary state's tactics is eagerly examined for a change in the basic ideology. The fact that such a change is constantly expected shows how lightly the ideology is regarded. The altering tactics and the accompanying ideological justifications are, indeed, cited as evidence that the ideology is actually meaningless. The manipulation of this ideology to justify any and every change of foreign and domestic policy only "proves" that it is too flexible to be a guide to action. Rather, it is claimed, the ideology provides a rationalization for what would have been done even in its absence. The logical conclusion is that the Soviet leaders think in terms of the same "national interest" that motivates the behavior of other nation-states. Ideology, it is said, has not led Moscow to adopt any policy that Russian national interest did not demand. Apparently, this interest can be objectively discovered; the ideology is merely a means for promoting that interest.

All debates on Soviet policy, and on Western policy toward the Soviet Union, inevitably return to this fundamental issue of ideology (defined as "a comprehensive, consistent, closed system of knowledge, to which its adherents turn to get answers to all questions, solutions to all their problems").[7] Are the Soviet leaders really motivated by Communist ideology, or do they merely use it to justify and expand their power? Are they really bent on fomenting a world revolution, or are they only trying to increase the strength of Russia as a nation? In short, are the men in the Kremlin revolutionaries or nationalists? The answer is that the ideology cannot be divorced from the concept of Russian national

[6] William Reitzel, Morton A. Kaplan, and Constance C. Coblenz, *United States Foreign Policy, 1945–1955* (Washington, D.C.: The Brookings Institution, 1956), p. 89.

[7] Herbert J. Spiro, *Government by Constitution* (New York: Random House, 1959), p. 180.

interest, for this interest can be interpreted only in terms of its leaders' ideological beliefs. For they see the world through their ideological lenses.

To deny this and to assert that the Soviet leaders act nonideologically is to assume that "power politics" is merely a method of handling the day-to-day relations of nations on a pragmatic basis. Yet, an "empirical *Realpolitik* without ideological preconceptions can exist as little as can 'empirical science' without categories and hypotheses based on theoretical speculation."[8] Clearly, the manner in which the daily affairs of state are conducted, the judgments involved in choosing between alternative courses of action, will be determined largely by the way the issues are perceived. The crucial question has been posed, and answered, as follows:

> Do the leaders of ideologically oriented movements in the final analysis behave differently from other power-oriented individuals placed in a similar context? The answer to that is yes, with the added stipulation that there is no such thing as a "similar context." A political context is nothing more than the evaluation of the nature of the factors at play, of the relationships between other factors, and of the discernible trends in the situation. A political leader's evaluation of the situation determines his context and also his choice of alternatives. To be in a truly similar context to a Communist is in effect to be a Communist. . . .
>
> To dismiss ideology as an irrelevant criterion to an understanding of the political conduct of Soviet or Nazi leaders . . . would be to assume that it is possible to build up a large organization ostensibly dedicated to certain explicit objectives, in which individuals are promoted on the basis both of their professional ability and their demonstrable ideological dedication, but in which an inner sanctum operates, makes decisions with a complete disregard of the ideological principles of the movement, indeed remains immune to the constant pressures for ideological justification, and cynically disregards the official creed. However, it is a matter of historical record that many of the Soviet leaders suffered personal hardship in the name of their ideological commitment, were educated through the absorption of well-defined concepts, in turn contributed to their further elaboration, and subsequently educated others in the arcana of the ideological thinking. Once in power, they tended to view the world, particularly the outside world, in categories of thought shaped by the ideology and made political decisions on the basis of information forwarded to them by bureaucrats who were either indoctrinated with that ideology or who knew well that their leaders subscribed to it. As a result, the information flowing to the leaders in itself contained interpretations bound to reinforce the doctrine. These leaders, in turn, being intensely concerned with the use of power for the sake of pursuing their ends, made ideological faith a basic criterion of membership within the movement, and subsequently of advancement within it.[9]

[8] Richard Lowenthal, "The Logic of One-Party Rule," in Abraham Brumberg (ed.), *Russia Under Khrushchev*, p. 27. For a contrary view, see Samuel L. Sharp, "National Interest: Key to Soviet Politics," *ibid.*, pp. 15–26.

[9] Zbigniew K. Brzezinski, *The Soviet Bloc*, pp. 390, 388–89.

This stress on ideology as the key factor in the determination of the Soviet Union's foreign and domestic policies obviously does *not* mean that, in a specific situation, the Soviet leaders go to the library and find a statement of what to do clearly spelled out in Marx's *Das Kapital*. But it is the ideology that provides Communist leaders with a way of perceiving and interpreting "reality"—with their "model" of the world.

Nor does the fact that aspects of this ideology alter with changing circumstances indicate that the ideology is so elastic as to be valueless. As one political analyst has emphasized, the *doctrine*—the philosophical assumptions and historical laws that the ideology incorporates—never changes. It is the *action program* that is dynamic, changing with concrete circumstances, and it is precisely this organic relationship between doctrine and action that accounts for the permanent war and continuing dynamic of a revolutionary regime:

> Doctrine linked with action program gives modern ideology its religious fervor, its sense of constant direction, as well as its freedom of maneuver in the use of political power to achieve that which must be.
>
> Ideologically motivated power, while forcing occasional practical adjustments, also creates pressures for the fulfillment of the ideology. The maintenance of political power precludes static situations and continuously requires action and policy. . . . Since an important ingredient of the movement's power is the element of explicit and proclaimed purpose which furthers its seizure of political power, the fulfillment of major portions of the ideologically stated objectives becomes a necessity dictated by power, by the inner dynamic of the movement itself . . . a mere "power analysis," postulating that the maximization of power is the basic political impulse of [the Nazi and Soviet] regimes, would be inadequate to an understanding of German and Soviet developments. They only become meaningful when ideology, while considered an element of that power, is at the same time seen as a substantive and residual element in its own right. Purpose and policy thus constantly interact and are inseparable.[10]

Communist ideology thus serves four specific functions. First, it is a means of viewing "reality" and a tool for analyzing world events. Second, it is a total critique of contemporary society, which is condemned as utterly evil and beyond redemption. Third, it defines the historically appointed purpose the revolutionary movement seeks to achieve—namely, the destruction of the old order and the universal creation of the perfect society. And finally, ideology legitimatizes the authority of the leaders of the movement and sanctions the actions they take in seek-

[10] *Ibid.*, pp. 387–88. The "creative" adaptation of Communist ideology to socio-economic and geographic circumstances surely does not betray a lack of belief in Communist ideology any more than the changing concepts of "social justice" in the United States during the last century—on the racial issue, for instance—indicate that the basic democratic values of the Declaration of Independence and the Constitution are meaningless.

ing these objectives. Communism is, in short, a secular ideology of damnation and salvation.

Marxism: The Class Struggle and the Gravediggers

Marxism arose as part of a general protest movement—including everything from Utopian Socialism and Christian Socialism to Tory Democracy—against nineteenth-century industrial capitalism. While industrialization was eventually to lead to rapidly rising standards of living for the masses, the principal concern in its early stages was sustained economic growth. The reason for this is inherent in the process of industrialization itself. For industrialization seeks basically to accumulate capital (or, as economists term it, capital goods)—i.e., factories, machinery, and other equipment. This, of course, oversimplifies the nature of industrialization. If it is basically a process of economic growth, it is also vastly more than that; without an accompanying cultural, political, and social revolution uprooting the old rural and static society, no Industrial Revolution can occur. In short, the industrialization of a society is more than a "technical" problem. Nevertheless, the essence of industrialization remains the increase of a society's industrial capital. For it is this capital which, when combined with human labor, permits a society to increase its productivity. The machine allows the worker to raise his industrial output, producing in a day what he might otherwise have produced in a week. This higher productivity can then more adequately meet the people's demands for whatever goods they require. The result is better living conditions.

Ironically, though, capital can be accumulated only if consumption is postponed. In order to build a factory, expand an already existing factory, or buy more machinery, a businessman must invest money. But where does he obtain this money? The answer to this crucial question is that the sum he invests comes primarily out of his profit. Although he could simply save this money, his desire for more profit leads him to re-invest it. And how does he acquire the maximum degree of profit? By paying his workers as little as possible and making them work as long as possible. Otherwise, his profit margin would be lower, and he would not be able to invest as much money. This in turn would slow down the speed of industrialization. The industrial working class thus pays a large share of the price of industrialization. The farmer, too, pays a price, for if industrial wages are to be kept low, the cost of bread must also be kept to a minimum. This process of industrialization is essentially the same, no matter what the nature of the economic system. Even a Communist society accumulates capital in this manner; only, it is the state that accumulates the capital and squeezes it out of the general population.

The terrible effects of industrialization on the workers in the nineteenth

century have been vividly described by Edmund Wilson in his narration
of the arrival of Friedrich Engels, Karl Marx's colleague, in Manchester:

> He saw the working people living like rats in the wretched little dens of
> their dwellings, whole families, sometimes more than one family, swarm-
> ing in a single room, well and diseased, adults and children, close relations
> sleeping together, sometimes even without beds to sleep on when all the
> furniture had been sold for firewood, sometimes in damp, underground
> cellars which had to be bailed out when the weather was wet, sometimes
> living in the same room with the pigs; ill nourished on flour mixed with
> gypsum and cocoa mixed with dirt, and their wailing children with lau-
> danum; spending their lives, without a sewage system, among the piles of
> their excrement and garbage; spreading epidemics of typhus and cholera
> which even made inroads into the well-to-do sections.

The increasing demand for women and children at the factories was
throwing the fathers of families permanently out of work, arresting the
physical development of the girls, letting the women in for illegitimate
motherhood and yet compelling them to come to work when they were
pregnant or before they had recovered from having their babies, and ultimately turning a good many of them into prostitutes; while the children,
fed into the factories at the age of five or six, receiving little care from
mothers who were themselves at the factory all day and no education at
all from a community which wanted them only to perform mechanical
operations, would drop exhausted when they were let out of their prisons,
too tired to wash or eat, let alone study or play, sometimes too tired to
get home at all. In the iron and coal mines, also, women and children as
well as men spent the better part of their lives crawling underground in
narrow tunnels, and, emerging, found themselves caught in the meshes of
the company cottage and the company store and of the two-week postponement of wages. They were being killed off at the rate of fourteen hundred a year through the breaking of rotten ropes, the caving-in of workings
due to overexcavated seams and the explosions due to bad ventilation and
to the negligence of tired children; if they escaped catastrophic accidents,
the lung diseases eventually got them. The agricultural population, for its
part, deprived by the industrial development of their old status of handi-
craftsmen and yeomen who either owned their own land and homes or
were taken care of with more or less certainty by a landlord on whose
estate they were tenants, had been transformed into wandering day la-
borers, for whom nobody took responsibility and who were punished by
jail or transportation if they ventured in times of need to steal and eat the
landlord's game.

It seemed to Engels that the medieval serf, who had at least been attached to the land and had a definite position in society, had had an advantage over the factory worker. At that period when legislation for the
protection of labor had hardly seriously gotten under way, the old peasantry and hand-workers of England, and even old petty middle class, were
being shoveled into the mines and the mills like so much raw material for
the prices their finished products would bring, with no attempt even to

dispose of the waste. In years of depression the surplus people, so useful in years of good business, were turned out upon the town to become peddlers, crossing-sweepers, scavengers or simply beggars—sometimes whole families were seen begging in the streets—and, almost as frequently, whores and thieves.[11]

Marxism was one legacy of this Industrial Revolution. Specifically, it was a moral protest movement against the cruelties and miseries suffered by the workers. Such exploitation of man by man had to be ended, for it violated the whole Western humanitarian tradition from its Judaic-Christian beginnings to the French Revolution. The equality of man was meaningless in a society deeply divided, a society of the privileged few and the underprivileged many. The dignity and freedom of the individual possessed little reality when the majority of men were paid only subsistence wages, if they found any employment at all. Capitalism had enslaved man in economic bondage.

A system based on production for the "profit of the few" had to be changed to production for the "use of the many." To be sure, capitalism had brought mankind great benefits. And no one praised its success more than its greatest critic: "The bourgeoisie, during its rule of scarce one hundred years," Marx wrote in *The Communist Manifesto*, "has created more massive and more colossal productive forces than have all preceding generations together. Subjection of nature's forces to man, machinery, application of chemistry to industry and agriculture, steam-navigation, railways, electric telegraphs, clearing of whole continents for cultivation, canalisation of rivers, whole populations conjured out of the ground—what earlier century had even a presentiment that such productive forces slumbered in the lap of social labour?"[12] But now that the bourgeoisie had created the industrial machinery, the bourgeoisie itself was the greatest obstacle to mass production for the benefit of society. The assumption was that industry could abolish poverty once and for all by providing man with his basic necessities. But an economic system based upon the profit motive could only result in an inequitable distribution of the income. It was the desire for profit, then, that was seen as the cause of the workers' poverty and degradation. Marx tended to view the profit motive in much the same manner as had the medieval Church, which had equated profit with the sin of greed, and greed, in turn, with the un-Christian exploitation of man by his fellow man. To Marx, too, profit was a sin; moreover, it was the principal cause of the widespread misery industrialization had left in its wake. Capitalism therefore had to be replaced by socialism. The "acquisitive society" needed to be transformed into a society that concerned itself with social justice for the under-

[11] Edmund Wilson, *To the Finland Station*, pp. 134–36.
[12] Arthur P. Mendel, *Essential Works of Marxism*, pp. 17–18.

privileged. In a socialist society, the working class would receive a fair share of the national income.

But Marxian Socialism was more than a moral protest movement; it was also "scientific." Indeed, Marxism could be defined as that school of socialism which seeks to prove that the coming of socialism is inevitable.[13] Marxism was in that respect a product of the general Western belief in the inevitability of progress—the general view that human history is on an "onward and upward" path. This optimistic faith in continuous improvement—largely shattered in Europe by World War I, but still deeply ingrained in the "American way of life"—was an offspring of the eighteenth-century Age of Reason and the nineteenth-century Age of Progress, themselves reactions to medieval society and philosophy. In feudal times, man was a creature of custom and tradition. Religion dominated his life, and earthly existence was merely a short prelude to the life hereafter. Man's principal goal was not profit or a comfortable life, but salvation. Worldly activities were therefore subordinated to this spiritual pursuit. Man's existence—indeed, the universe, its creation, rules prescribing man's conduct on earth, and the very purpose of life—were all explained in religious or extrasecular terms.

The Enlightenment substituted reason for God. The material world became man's chief concern because he wanted to create a better life for himself while he was still living. The perfect society was no longer in the next life, but was to be created here and now. Man's condition resulted not from his sin, but from his ignorance. Not grace but reason was therefore the appointed instrument of his salvation. If man did not like his environment, he could change it in any manner he pleased. The master of his own fate, man could create the kind of world he wanted because God had given him the reason with which he could build a paradise on earth. Humanism replaced religious faith, and secular rather than spiritual activities became the chief focus of man's strivings.

Man could now master the universe through knowledge. For just as God had given man reason, He had created for man a rational world. He had constructed a perfect mechanism that operated in accordance with a number of rationally comprehensible laws. Once man discovered these laws, all problems of human existence could be solved. Just as scientists were already discovering the laws of the physical universe through rational inquiry, empirical research could yield knowledge of the laws of human behavior. Once these were known, man could be guided by them to create a better life for himself. The Age of the Enlightenment was thus also the Age of Reason—of "materialism," defined in this context simply as "realism" (i.e., rational inquiry into man's secular universe in order to discover the laws of the universe, composed of matter).

It was as a realist that Marx claimed the capitalist system was histori-

13 Alfred G. Meyer, *Communism* (New York: Random House, 1960), p. 10.

cally doomed. Capitalism asserted that the individual man responded to economic self-interest in the same way an individual atom responded to gravity. As Adam Smith, the great philosopher of laissez-faire capitalism, wrote: "It is not from the benevolence of the butcher, the brewer, or the baker that we expect our dinners but from their regard to their self-interest. We address ourselves not to their humanity but to their self-love, and never talk to them of our necessities, but of their advantages." Given this self-interest as man's basic motivation, the "economic laws" that would maximize society's economic benefits were the laws of supply and demand operating through the free market.

The capitalist argument was simple. The individual wishes to augment his wealth; his desire for profit therefore leads him to produce whatever product consumers demand. Naturally, he will try to charge as much as possible. But since others, in their search for profit, may produce the same item, his price must be competitive. If he charges more than they, no one will buy his product. And what price can he get? Each producer, hoping for increased sales, will try to undersell his competitors. But no producer can sell at less than cost and still stay in business. The market's free competition thus has three results: the supply of the products the consumers demand, the sale of these goods at a minimal cost to the consumers, and profit for the producers. Thus the "economic laws" channel each individual's self-interest in socially beneficial directions. The competitive mechanism of the market provides for the "greatest good of the greatest number." The free market thus ensures a harmony of interest between producers and consumers. But the market is not really "free." For the individual must conform to the laws of the market. If the demand is for one product rather than another, he cannot continue to produce the former; if competition sets a certain price level, he cannot charge a higher price. If man is to maximize his wealth and society is to maximize its welfare, men must obey the laws of economics.

Marx accepted this description of the capitalist market and focused his criticism on what he considered the market's central feature: namely, that it transformed all relationships between individuals into exchange or monetary relationships. In a market society, it seemed to him that this was the only meaningful bond between individuals. The consumer, in order to obtain the goods he wants, offers a cash incentive; the producer, in order to make a profit, responds to the consumer's demand. Men are thus linked to each other as buyers and sellers through money. However, men must earn the money. Consequently, the employer-employee relationship is also a monetary one. The employer buys labor power, sold by the worker in order to obtain a job. For Marx, this was the distinguishing feature of capitalism: the fact that not only goods but men were sold on the market. Indeed, human labor was sold like any other product. The bourgeoisie, as Marx bitterly said, "has left no other bond

between man and man than naked self-interest, than callous 'cash payment.' . . . It has resolved personal worth into exchange value, and in
place of the numberless indefeasible chartered freedoms, has set up that
single, unconscionable freedom—Free Trade. In one word, for exploitation, veiled by religious and political illusions (under patriarchal feudalism), it has substituted naked, shameless, direct brutal exploitation."[14]

The exploitation of the workers resulted from this sale of men as commodities. Like laissez-faire economists, Marx maintained that the value
of a product was equivalent to the amount of labor expended in its production. How then, he asked, did one derive profit? If the exchange value
of a product equaled its labor cost, then profit could be gained only by
paying the worker less. And this, he maintained, was precisely the case.
The worker received only a subsistence wage; his labor, when sold to the
employer on the market, was worth no more than the amount it took to
keep him alive. The difference between what he should have been paid
and what he was actually paid represented the profit, or "surplus value."

The significance of Marx's theory of value lies in its sociological implications. His analysis of the free market emphasizes not just the production and exchange of commodities, but the *social organization* for
production. The capitalists and proletariat need each other; both classes
are compelled to cooperate. Each contributes a specific function: one
the capital goods, or what Marx called the "means of production," the
other the labor power. But if the two classes are functionally interdependent, they are also mutually antagonistic. The capitalists exploit the
proletariat because the market transforms all human relationships—
whether buyer-seller or employer-employee—into exchange, or monetary,
relationships. The capitalists, to maximize their profit, will squeeze as
much surplus value out of labor as possible; and although they constitute
only a minority of the population, they can continue their exploitation
of the majority because they own and control the means of production
and the power of the state.

Political philosophers from Aristotle to Madison had already shown
that any group would organize to protect itself and advance its interests
politically. Marx was reasserting this interpretation when he stated that
the bourgeoisie controlled not only economic but political power. The
state was, in Marx's words, nothing but the "executive committee of the
bourgeoisie." It could therefore perpetuate its exploitation of the proletariat. The result was the class struggle between the exploiter and exploited. Nor was this class struggle, according to Marx, unique to capitalism. In every economic system, he said, the "forces of production"
produced a corresponding "relations of production," or social structure.
In the Greek and Roman slave system, which succeeded the stage of
"primitive communism" (primitive society, in which all production and

[14] Quoted in Mendel, *op. cit.*, p. 15.

appropriation had been communal), there were the slave owners and the slaves; in medieval feudalism, the landowners and the serfs; and in industrial capitalism, the capitalists and the proletarians. Every economic system was divided between the "haves" and the "have-nots," and wracked by the consequent class struggle.[15]

This class struggle could not be resolved politically; nor could capitalism be improved by political means. The members of the bourgeoisie, controlling the forces of production and the power of the state, were hardly likely to permit reforms that would cut into their profits and might ultimately lead to their overthrow. The political process, to Marx, was impotent:

> [His] views on liberalism and democracy, more particularly, which he considered to be nothing but veils for the dictatorship of the bourgeoisie, furnished an interpretation of the social situation of his time which appeared to fit only too well, corroborated as it was by sad experience. For Marx lived, especially in his younger years, in a period of the most shameless and cruel exploitation. And this shameless exploitation was cynically defended by hypocritical apologists who appealed to the principle of human freedom, to the right of man to determine his own fate, and to enter freely into any contract he considers favorable to his interests.
>
> Using the slogan "equal and free competition for all," the unrestrained capitalism of this period resisted successfully all labor legislation until the year 1833, and its practical execution for many years more. The consequence was a life of desolation and misery which can hardly be imagined in our day.[16]

But if a political solution of the class struggle was foreclosed, would the worker ever achieve abundance and freedom from his "economic slavery"? The answer was that the "laws of economics" assured his liberation. The class struggle was merely a manifestation of the underlying economic forces, which were the key to human happiness. If man wished to improve his society, he should above all gain a knowledge of the economic laws governing the world. Capitalism with its emphasis on laissez-faire laws was, in fact, symbolic of the nineteenth century's conviction of the pervasiveness and dominating influence of economic forces. Or, as Marx put it, economics was the substructure of any society. Everything else—social and political systems, law, philosophy, religion, and art—was the superstructure. And it was the substructure that molded the nature of the superstructure. Such stress on economic determinism was hardly surprising, since this was the era of industrialization, an era preoccupied with capital accumulation. To the businessman, wealth, profit, and success were synonymous. To the worker, who eked out a bare existence by laboring fifteen hours or more a day, economics was even more vital

[15] Quoted in *ibid.*, pp. 13–14.
[16] Karl R. Popper, *The Open Society and Its Enemies*, Part 2, pp. 311–12.

—a matter of survival. In an age in which the masses were still desperately poor but were beginning to see that such poverty could be ended, the economic causes of conflict seemed obvious.

The bourgeoisie and the proletariat were not fated thus to face each other eternally. "Judgment day" for the capitalist class would come, Marx said, for the proletarian revolution was *historically inevitable*. The economic forces that had earlier caused the death of the slave and feudal systems were destined to do the same for capitalism. From the theory of surplus value, which according to Marx was the axle around which the capitalist wheel revolved, Marx derived three economic laws. These laws explained the behavior of the system—and doomed it. The first was the law of "capitalist accumulation." Each capitalist, seeking to maximize profit, expands his output in order to sell more than his competitors. To do this, each must hire more workers, but as the labor supply diminishes, labor costs will rise and, in turn, cut into profits. Each employer must therefore install labor-saving machinery to reduce costs and preserve his profit margin. Thus he accumulates capital. But he is simultaneously working against himself. His source of surplus value is the very worker whom he must now replace. The increasing proportion of machinery to labor therefore produces the very thing the introduction of machinery was supposed to prevent: a decline in profits. The second law—the "concentration of capital"—follows logically. The competitive process that results from the struggle for profits drives the weaker capitalists into bankruptcy, thereby concentrating capital in fewer and fewer hands. Eventually, this process ends in the establishment of monopolies. Together, these two laws produce the third, the law of "increasing misery." On the one hand, as the capitalists are driven out of business and the workers are displaced by machinery, there is large-scale unemployment. On the other hand, the capitalist, compelled to compensate for his falling profits, must intensify his exploitation of the workers by further decreasing their subsistence wages. Since the unemployed—Marx called them the "industrial reserve army"—have no other means of existence, they have little choice; they must accept work at any price. Thus the wage level is driven down for all workers. Surplus value again increases, but only for a time. The competitive process begins again, further decreasing profit, concentrating capital, and increasing the proletariat's size and misery. And by a series of recurring crises, each more severe than the preceding one, capitalism arrives at the final stage of its development—the proletarian revolution. "The expropriators are expropriated."

Capitalism, Marx says, will thus be its own gravedigger—for through industrialization it fathered the very class that is to overthrow it when capitalism reaches economic maturity. The laws of the free market, ironically, will result in the overthrow of its advocates. The forces of production will then no longer be privately owned. The exploitation of man by man will be ended forever, since society will no longer be divided into "haves" and "have-nots." Industry, now publicly owned by the "dictatorship of the proletariat," will be used for the maximization of the proletariat's benefit. The rule of the dictatorship will, however, be only temporary. Once its principal purpose, the liquidation of the bourgeoisie, is accomplished, and private property—the source of class formation and the class struggle—eliminated, the state will "wither away" and a new period of history begin. Man will then be able to live in harmony, and the classless society will finally fulfill the ideals of fraternity, liberty, equality—and affluence—for the vast majority.

Bourgeois Reformism, Democratic Socialism, and the People's Capitalism

The fundamental error committed by Marx was that he confused capitalism with democracy. Because the state was the "executive committee" of the bourgeoisie, he said, capitalism could not reform itself; the parliamentary institutions of capitalist states were merely the façade for the "dictatorship of the bourgeoisie." According to Marx, the bourgeois minority would continue to use the power of the state—the police and the army—to preserve its dominance over and exploitation of the proletariat, and to quell any worker disturbances or riots. This state of affairs would end only on the day the proletariat rose up to overthrow its exploiters; since reform was impossible, revolution was the only means of changing the system. This conclusion was perhaps natural at the time Marx wrote, for the bourgeoisie was politically powerful and the reform movement very weak. Moreover, historically, ruling groups or classes have not willingly surrendered their power. The French Revolution, exemplifying a bourgeois revolution against the traditional order, seemed to be good evidence to support this contention. Marx, to emphasize this important point once more, "saw in parliamentary democracy nothing but a veiled dictatorship of the bourgeoisie. And it was easy for him to interpret these facts as supporting his analysis of the relationship between the legal and the social system. According to the legal system, equality and freedom were established, at least approximately. But what did this mean in reality! Indeed, we must not blame Marx for insisting that the economic facts alone are 'real' and that the legal system may be a mere superstructure, a cloak for this reality, and an instrument of class domination."[17]

Marx was mistaken, though, for democracy and capitalism, while closely related, are not identical. His mistake stemmed from his failure to distinguish between democratic ends and means. Certainly, in his own mind, he was committed to democratic ends: the inalienable rights of the individual and social justice for all men. Indeed, his basic charge

[17] *Ibid.*, p. 312.

against capitalism was that it frustrated the realization of the aims proclaimed by the French Revolution, that it was unjust, indeed inhuman; nourished by the greed of the few, it led to the exploitation of the many. Democracy could flourish only in the post-capitalist stage of socialism, after private property had been abolished. Marx's attack on capitalism was basically, therefore, a moral attack, "an anguished protest against the materialist spirit of capitalism, against the profit motive, against the mechanization and dehumanization of all classes of people in the service of industrial production."[18] Because political power was controlled exclusively by the ruling bourgeoisie, Marx did not hold out any promise of popular relief and amelioration. Consequently, he resorted to an economic interpretation of history to "prove" the "inevitability" of socialism. The "laws of economics" had already determined the doom of capitalism and heralded a new day of earthly paradise. In taking this view, Marx not only underestimated the importance of politics, but failed to grasp the essential relationship between democratic ends and the democratic process. For an essential corollary of the commitment to the rights of the individual, to individual liberty and equality, is that individuals sharing common values and interests have the right to organize to advance their goals. A society in which men can thus express their interests—whether organized as interest groups or social classes—is pluralistic. Democracy can therefore be seen largely as a *method:* It provides for the adjustment and accommodation of the constantly conflicting interests inherent in any multi-interest political system.

What is, above all, obvious about "democracy as a method of self-government" is that it rejects the claim that man is a prisoner of fate, that his life is determined by forces or "laws" beyond his control. Rather, democracy assumes that man is a reasonable, free agent who can to a large degree—although perhaps not to the degree supposed by the Enlightenment—determine the kind of society in which he lives. If purportedly historical or economic laws produce results he does not like, he can change the results. If, for instance, the *laissez-faire* market results in monopolies, unemployment, and low wages, man can remedy this by altering the manner in which the market operates. He is not the victim of the laws of the market. Once he determines the purposes an economy should serve in terms of his value preferences, he can then seek their realization through the political process.

This was exactly what happened in the late nineteenth century as the free market became increasingly less free, while capital concentrated, just as Marx had foreseen. Competition had resulted in industrial and commercial monopolies that dominated the market and controlled the levers of government. There was bound to be a political reaction. Any group holding a monopoly of power will use that power for its own purposes;

---

[18] Robert V. Daniels, *The Nature of Communism*, pp. 12–13.

unrestrained by the countervailing power, which is the basis of democratic freedom, it will abuse that power. Not only will other interests be neglected, but the dominant group will be in a position to exploit the interests of other groups—e.g., workers' wages and farmers' food prices (which can both be kept low), and consumers' needs (for which prices can be kept high). All these groups, having no means of effective protest, will seek to organize politically to gain satisfaction of their grievances. In Marx's age, big business was the dominant force in politics, and he thus believed that the bourgeoisie controlled the state and reform would be impossible. But he failed to recognize the "political law" that power begets counterbalancing power. As other interests—farmers, labor, etc.—now began to organize to avoid being controlled by business, democratic governments, reacting to the votes and needs of their citizens, began increasingly to interfere with the laws of the market—*not* in order to destroy capitalism, but to make it *responsive* to the needs of all groups. Democracy, in short, began to "socialize" capitalism—that is, to make it socially responsible.

Thus democracy avoided the violent revolution Marx had forecast for it. Monopoly-capitalism might well have precipitated such a revolution if it had been left unreformed. Too many social groups felt exploited. If a democratic reform movement had not responded to their grievances and needs, there would have been no alternative left to them but to seek satisfaction by nondemocratic means. Capitalism, if it was to survive, therefore had no choice but to accept democratic reforms. By accepting them, indeed, it consolidated its position, for its response to popular needs won it popular allegiance. Thus, by meeting the aspirations of the workers, it "de-revolutionized" them. As labor's economic situation improved, it began to have a vested interest in the *preservation* of capitalism. Industry obviously also played a vital role in this process, not only by accepting political reforms but by the rise in real wages which followed the early phase of industrialization. Industrialists ultimately realized that more profit could be earned if goods were mass-produced and reasonably priced so that workers with sufficiently high income could buy them. Thus democracy and industry were gradually able to satisfy labor's demands. As a result, the labor parties in Central and Western Europe abandoned the concept of the proletarian revolution. Revolution was replaced by democratic gradualism and peaceful change via the ballot box. And revolutionary Marxism became evolutionary socialism.

The word "socialism" has, of course, taken on unsavory overtones in the United States, and is popularly equated with "anti-capitalism" and "un-Americanism." This confusion stems in part from political semantics, but it also reflects pride in the role that "free enterprise" has played in producing the American standard of living. Nevertheless, even America, as a democratic nation, has to a large extent "socialized" its economy so that the market produces socially acceptable results. Actually, the same types of reforms of the market structure that have been introduced in Europe under the socialist label have been instituted in the United States. One merely has to substitute the term "social progress" for socialism.

The Populist and Progressive movements, the New Nationalism, the New Freedom, the New Deal, the New Frontier, and the Great Society have all advanced their programs in the name of social progress. And President Eisenhower, who considered himself both a conservative liberal and a liberal conservative, once suggested that American capitalism be renamed "people's capitalism"! Whether our "socialism" is known as the welfare state, welfare capitalism, or even "people's capitalism" is largely irrelevant. What is significant is that most Americans have come to accept in practice many of the ideas that Europeans consider socialist. For example, some students attending a state university may condemn "socialism" without stopping to think that they are receiving their education in a tax-supported, "socialistic" institution. Yet many of them would not have access to higher education—a prerequisite for economic opportunity and social advancement—if they could not attend such a low-tuition school. State universities, which are indeed socialist in nature, are a logical outgrowth of the democratic dedication to equal opportunity for all individuals.

Democratic socialism and welfare capitalism have in general resorted to three types of measures to make the market more socially responsible. First, they have redistributed income through such measures as minimum-wage laws, legalization of collective bargaining, social security, farm price support, and, above all, the income tax. Second, primarily through indirect planning—monetary controls, tax adjustments, and deficit financing—they have sought to control business cycles, particularly the downswings with their recurring unemployment. Third, they have established some supervisory control over the major sectors of industry by antitrust legislation, regulatory commissions, and—in the case of self-styled socialist governments (postwar Britain)—nationalization. But even the nationalization effected by Britain was hardly revolutionary. Far from expropriating all private property, the government nationalized only a small segment of industry; while this included such a strategically important area as steel, it was generally composed of economically decaying industries—such as coal, whose nationalization had been recommended not by the Labour but by the Conservative Party! Nationalization, in brief, has served basically as a utilitarian measure. It has done so little to change management-labor relations that European trade unions have become disenchanted with it. The German Democratic Socialists have dropped the idea from their party platform, and the right wing of the British Labour Party wants to drop it, too. European socialist parties have become essentially pragmatic and peaceful progressive parties committed to the welfare state for all classes. The proletarian revolution and the proletarian state have long been forgotten.

Lenin: The Politics of National Liberation and Totalitarianism

It was inevitable that Marxists would question the failure of the proletarian revolution to occur. Democratic reform was the one answer they would not accept. Something that was evil could not be made less evil by "reform." Perhaps its outward appearance could be altered, but basically it would remain unchanged. If capitalism was still evil, then, if it remained an exploitative order, why had it not collapsed as Marx had predicted? The usual explanation for the failure of the revolution was that the workers' rising living standards gave them a vested interest in the capitalist system. That was the principal reason why democratic socialists had given up their plans to overthrow capitalism. In Lenin's view, however, a movement that abandoned the revolution and sought to acquire a larger share of the capitalist pie was no longer Marxist. Lenin naturally recognized that the higher wages of the workers had undermined their proletarian consciousness and made them reform-minded in terms of improving their material standards; they had developed what he called a trade-union consciousness. The crucial question posed by this development was: What had made it possible for the capitalists to raise paychecks rather than decrease them further?

Since the ability of capitalism to reform itself had already been excluded, the answer had to be found in external circumstances. Colonialism, or imperialism, provided the key.[19] The "internal contradiction" of capitalism—the class struggle between the bourgeoisie and the proletariat —had been resolved by capitalism's indulgence in imperialism. It was imperialism that had changed the first and third laws of capitalism. The second law remained correct: capital was concentrated in fewer and fewer hands. The era of imperialism was, indeed, the era of monopoly-capitalism. But the law of capital accumulation, which forecast the declining rate of profits, had been reversed. Imperialism was the source of huge profits—so huge, in fact, that Lenin called them "superprofits." Colonies provided inexpensive raw materials and cheap labor. They also augmented the market to which goods produced in the metropolitan country could be sold and provided greater investment opportunities for surplus capital.

It was now clear why the European workers' living standards had risen, despite the law of increasing misery. For the proletariat had shared in the society's enormous increase of wealth. In the age of imperialism, capitalism could afford economic concessions to its laboring class in order

[19] V. I. Lenin, *Imperialism, The Highest Stage of Capitalism* (rev. ed.; New York: International Publishers, 1939).

to gain its support. It could even permit political concessions. Once the workers' allegiance to the capitalist system had been won, they could even be allowed to vote. After all, voting was meaningless when the choice was between two parties representing the capitalist class. Their only choice was which group of capitalists should exploit them, not whether by means of a free vote capitalism could be abolished. Nevertheless, the working class became increasingly "embourgeoisied," lost its revolutionary drive and spirit, and gained a vested interest in the preservation of capitalism. This commitment to capitalism was reinforced by the proletariat's new and intense nationalistic feeling. Hostile to the capitalist class in the pre-imperialist phase, the proletariat acquired this nationalism as it came to identify its interests with capitalist imperialism.

Lenin's explanation for the failure of the proletarian revolution implied pessimism about the future. While imperialism continued, the capitalists would reap sufficient superprofits with which to "buy" the support of the working class. Only if these profits were eliminated would the capitalists have to resume their pre-imperialist domestic exploitation. Then the class struggle would resume and finally result in the proletarian revolution. This was exactly what Lenin predicted would happen. For, through imperialism, the "inner contradiction" of capitalism had been projected on a global scale. Just as the capitalist class had exploited the proletarian class for profit, the capitalist countries now exploited the proletarian (colonial) countries for "surplus value." Imperialism had, by its conquest of most non-Western areas, transformed the fight against capitalism into a global conflict. The domestic class struggle was now an international class struggle. Indeed, since the workers' uprising in developed capitalist nations now depended upon the elimination of colonial holdings—and their source of markets, opportunities for the investment of surplus capital, natural resources, and cheap labor—the prerequisite for the proletarian revolution in capitalist countries now became the anti-imperialist revolution of the pre-capitalist colonial countries. "National liberation" became Communism's most immediate task.

Thus, Lenin turned Marx upside down. The proletarian revolution would now begin in nonproletarian societies. The workers' revolution would arise in lands whose economies were basically agrarian, where peasants (not workers) constituted the vast majority of the population. Marx had said that the proletarian revolution would occur spontaneously when the capitalist economy became mature. Lenin now observed that when the economy had become mature, the capitalists had avoided the revolution by the policy of imperialism. The consciousness of the proletariat was in these circumstances transformed from revolutionary to reformist. Conversely, the proletarian mood—the awareness of people that, being poor and miserable, they are exploited—became most highly developed in the colonial countries. Thus, where Marx had stated that

economic maturity *and* political consciousness were parallel developments that would precipitate the proletarian revolution, Lenin now asserted that they were *inversely* related in the age of imperialism. The
contrast was stark: Marx had stressed *economic* maturity as the prerequisite for the revolution. Lenin now emphasized *political* consciousness.
As Stalin later said, in his lectures on Leninism:

> Where will the revolution begin? Where, in what country, can the front
> of capital be pierced first?
>
> Where industry is more developed, where the proletariat constitutes the
> majority, where there is more culture, where there is more democracy—that
> was the reply usually given formerly.
>
> No, objects the Leninist theory of revolution; *not necessarily where in-
> dustry is more developed*, and so forth. The front of capital will be pierced
> where the chain of imperialism is weakest, for the proletarian revolution
> is the result of the breaking of the chain of the world imperialist which has
> started the revolution, which has made a breach in the front of capital, is
> less developed in a capitalist sense than other, more developed, countries,
> which have, however, remained within the framework of capitalism.[20]

This shift of the first phase of the proletarian revolution from economically advanced capitalist countries to economically underdeveloped,
pre-capitalist, feudal societies had a profound impact upon Communism.
The working class could no longer be trusted because its consciousness
had become corrupted by "bourgeois reformism." It was unreliable and
could no longer be expected to fulfill its historically appointed task.
Since the proletariat had, therefore, in effect betrayed the revolution, the
responsibility of carrying out the revolution would have to be assigned
to the "vanguard of the proletariat," a small party of professional revolutionaries.[21] Completely different from a democratic party, whose basic
function is to aggregate the nation's various interest groups, this was a
party of "true believers," of men like Lenin who had remained loyal to
the cause. It was they who were now the "defenders of the faith," the
sole guardians of the proletariat's consciousness. Dedicated and incor-
ruptible, they became the self-appointed instrument of history to implement the revolution and destroy the world bourgeoisie. Communism, a
self-proclaimed majority movement, thus transformed itself into a minority movement. A revolution that was to have been spontaneous and
inevitable as capitalism matured economically became a revolution

[20] Joseph Stalin, *The Foundations of Leninism*, quoted in Mendel, *op. cit.*, pp.
228–29.
[21] V. I. Lenin, *What Is To Be Done? Burning Questions of Our Movement* (New
York: International Publishers, 1929). On the development of the party before 1917,
see Bertram Wolfe, *Three Who Made a Revolution: A Biographical History* (New
York: The Dial Press, 1948); and on the party's development until just after Stalin's
death, see the definitive volume by Leonard Schapiro, *The Communist Party of the
Soviet Union*.

engineered by a highly conscious vanguard in an economically backward country whose working class constituted a small minority.

Political consciousness and will had obviously prevailed over economic determinism. Equally clear was the fact that the reason they had prevailed was that Communism was wracked with intense and constant self-doubt as to whether the revolution would occur. History might be predestined, but one had to help it along—because in fact it was *not* following its natural course. The revolution would not be the result of material conditions but the product of a few men's faith plus works. A small group of the elect—in the Calvinist sense—would make sure the revolution occurred. Just as the Calvinists knew the "will of God," so the Leninist revolutionaries knew the "objective laws of history." Each set of leaders knew "the truth," and because this truth would save man from sin and damnation, each had the right—even the duty—to impose its rule in order to rescue man from his wicked ways and ensure his salvation. Conversely, each movement distrusted the very mankind to whose service it claimed dedication. Man was weak and corruptible. He had to be protected from Satan or capitalism. Therefore, force had to be used to "save" him.[22]

Given this elitist, antidemocratic attitude, it was "inevitable" (in the best Marxist sense) that the vanguard of the proletariat should in these circumstances become a totalitarian party. As a minority party, it could never win power legitimately, but had to seize it by revolution. The campaign to seize the reins of government required the organization of this professional revolutionary vanguard as a general staff. Centralized leadership, hierarchical organization, strict discipline, and obedience all the way down the chain of command were absolutely necessary. Moreover, everything had to be subordinated to the objective of winning power. Disagreement or factionalism within this military-like elite was intolerable. The generals could not plan and implement a campaign if the colonels and majors—and even other generals—were constantly dissenting. The generals, especially the chief of staff, had to decide policy and be obeyed without question. The "Party line" was absolute for all members. To gain outside support—a general staff without an army is impotent—the Communist Party had to learn to exploit all resentments of different groups or classes directed against the government; all aspirations blocked by the government were to be manipulated in order to bring it down. Alliances could be made with any group or class if they brought the final goal nearer. Such alliances must also be broken when they no longer served their purpose. The main point was flexibility of tactics, since the end—power—justified the means. As the capture of power would destroy the heretical old society and supposedly usher in the new and

[22] This comparison of Calvinism and Communism is elaborated by Meyer, *op. cit.*, pp. 4–7.

better society—a truly moral society in which all men would for the first time in history be really free and equal—all means could be used to achieve this goal. If the means were immoral, the morality of the end provided the justification:

> The revolution was a life or death struggle, in which any and every means whatsoever had to be employed. Violence, deceit, demagogy, and betrayal became political virtues; humanitarian scruple was cast to the winds. This is not to say that the Communists abandoned the objectives of human welfare and social justice, they thought themselves devoted to these ends, but in an abstract fashion which did not preclude present violations of the ideal in the name of the future. "Morality," Lenin declared in 1920, "for us is subordinated to the interests of the class struggle of the proletariat." Everything hung on the success of the revolution; once it succeeded, it would supposedly guarantee the kingdom of righteousness on earth. . . . There could be no guarantee of the goodness of the coming society—it would be what its progenitors and their tactics made it. The violence, deceit, and authoritarianism employed to bring the revolution about had an epochal effect. The new order was indelibly stamped with the methods of its begetting: the Bolsheviks reaped as they had sown.[23]

In brief, the Party stamped the totalitarian character it had acquired in its struggle to win power upon the nation it had conquered. Moreover, these totalitarian features were to be reinforced by the Party's post-revolutionary efforts to impose its proletarian class-consciousness upon the unrevolutionary working class and tradition-bound peasantry "from without."

By establishing a totalitarian government, the Communists were in fact introducing a unique form of government that differed greatly not only from democracies, but also from the traditional dictatorships or autocracies of the past.[24] A constitutional democratic system—the United States, for example—places three kinds of restraints on political power: formal (as defined by the Constitution, Bill of Rights, and the law); informal (stemming from the pluralistic nature of the society); and cultural (resulting from the behavior patterns of the society). Traditional dictatorships or autocratic governments remove the formal restraints, and therefore, like totalitarian systems, they have arbitrary rule and lack political and civil rights—although even in this respect autocracies, while frequently oppressive, are still not so arbitrary as totalitarian governments. Autocracies do not select a whole part of their population accord-

---

[23] Daniels, *op. cit.*, pp. 92–93.
[24] The uniqueness of twentieth-century totalitarianism is analyzed by Carl J. Friedrich (ed.), *Totalitarianism: Proceedings of a Conference Held at the American Academy of Arts and Sciences, March, 1953* (Cambridge, Mass.: Harvard University Press, 1954); Carl J. Friedrich and Zbigniew K. Brzezinski, *Totalitarian Dictatorship and Autocracy*; Brzezinski, *Ideology and Power in Soviet Politics*; and William Ebenstein, *Totalitarianism*.

ing to class or racial criteria and then systematically liquidate them.[25] They do not generally eliminate all freedoms[26] or execute most of the opposition leaders.[27] In any case, autocracies do not generally eliminate the informal restraints. Indeed, they tend to be based on a coalition of groups or classes—for example, an alliance of the landed nobility, army, and church. Only if a group resists is it likely to be subjected to pressure and some of its leaders arrested. But they do not generally possess a government party that can reach down into society and organize, control, and manipulate the people. They are primarily interested in controlling their citizens' political activities. The pluralistic nature of the society is by and large left alone. The basic aim is to preserve the domestic political *status quo.* Family life, professional and business activities, and religious affiliations are considered private affairs—if they do not spill over into the political arena.

In vivid contrast, the very first act of a totalitarian regime after it has assumed power and suspended all constitutional limitations on governmental power is to destroy this social pluralism. All political parties and professional associations are declared illegal; not even the Boy Scouts or the local stamp club are exempted. The old society is completely atomized. All organizations are pulverized to permit the party's power to be applied directly to all individuals. Possessing none of the customary moral or religious scruples of autocracies, the party permits no restraints whatsoever on its power to achieve this atomization. Totalitarianism

[25] Thus, the Soviets shipped off to Siberia at least 5 million kulaks (prosperous peasants) as part of a policy aiming at the "liquidation of the kulaks as a class." About a million perished, and many of the remainder died during the next years because of the hardships resulting from forced labor. (Hugh Seton-Watson, *From Lenin to Khrushchev,* pp. 156–59.)

[26] "In tsarist Russia there was no freedom of the press in the Western sense. But antigovernment books and papers did circulate. Russian was the first language into which Marx's *Das Kapital* was translated from the German and, in 1912, *Pravda,* the organ of Lenin's Bolshevik group, was openly published in tsarist Russia. The editors were harassed but *Pravda* continued to be published with few interruptions from 1912 to 1914, carrying virtually all of Lenin's writings during that period. If the government allowed such revolutionary materials to be circulated, it goes without saying that liberal and democratic doctrines in books and periodicals were widely circulated without much official hindrance. In sharp contrast, only one viewpoint is allowed expression in the Soviet Union today—the 'party line' as stated by the leadership at a given moment." (Ebenstein, *op. cit.,* p. 25.)

[27] "Lenin's own experience as a political exile in Siberia (1897–1900) illustrates the difference. He was not imprisoned behind barbed wire, and he did no forced labor. He could move about freely within a prescribed area, he played chess regularly with police officials, he practiced law for the benefit of poor peasants. He even finished his book *Development of Capitalism in Russia* while in exile. Furthermore, he maintained excellent health during his stay in Siberia, married there, and was able to think and plot for the future. His main complaint, like that of other political exiles, was not cruelty or hard labor, but boredom. For Lenin, living in Siberia meant living in 'the sticks.' Like Lenin, Stalin also was banished to Siberia. Again the relative mildness of tsarist political repression is illustrated by the fact that Stalin managed to escape on three occasions, a feat unthinkable today." (*Ibid.,* p. 24.)

also seeks to destroy the cultural restraints in order to isolate the individual and control him more tightly.

The society is then rebuilt, with organizations created and controlled by the revolutionary party. No single group is left outside the scope of party control. Old social norms are destroyed to enable the party to mold the society in accordance with its own ideological norms. Unlike the old-fashioned autocracy, with its interest in maintaining the domestic *status quo*, totalitarianism is future-oriented. Its very essence is a continuous dynamics resulting from its commitment to a universal social revolution. From this determination to transform society itself follows the total control of every aspect of the individual's life. A militant and exclusive faith is bound by its very nature to politicize all phases of life. A movement that seeks to convert man to the true faith cannot exempt any facet of his life from its supervision. A monopoly of truth, wisdom, and virtue must produce a monopoly of political control over all economic, social, cultural, scientific, and spiritual matters. The distinction between a man's private and public lives is eliminated. It is not enough, as in an autocracy, if the citizen does not break the law, or engage in opposition political activities, or read forbidden books and newspapers. He cannot merely obey the Party's orders while not believing in its mission. No church with an exclusive faith allows the right to disbelieve. And the Communist Party, as a revolutionary totalitarian party, is comparable to a "church in the very obvious sense that it is the institutionalization of belief. It is the organization which bears and propagates the faith. In power, it assumes the exclusive right to teach belief. Within the Party one belief—the official version of Marxism-Leninism—has a doctrinal monopoly: one church, one faith."[28] Under traditional authoritarian governments, such an exclusive and demanding faith was unknown. Ideally, every citizen becomes the "new Soviet man," who internalizes the Party's line and therefore responds in exactly the same manner to his environment as if the Party had commanded him. He, too, in short, becomes a true believer and thinks and acts in the "right" way. Just as there are only friends and enemies in politics, so there are only the correct and incorrect ways of thought and behavior in all non-political areas. Even the Boy Scouts, for example, become the Young Pioneers and later the Komsomols (or in Hitler's Germany, the Nazi Youth Movement). They may still go camping and parading, but their principal function is the ideological indoctrination and training of the boys from whom future leaders will be selected. Similarly, art and literature must reflect the

---

[28] Daniels, *op. cit.*, p. 331. Thus Trotsky defended his oppositionist position with a declaration of loyalty: "My party—right or wrong. . . . I know one cannot be right against the party . . . for history has not created other ways for the realization of what is right." (Quoted by Schapiro, *op. cit.*, p. 284.) See also the brilliant fictional account of how one Old Bolshevik leader is finally led to confess in Arthur Koestler, *Darkness at Noon* (New York: New American Library, 1948).

revolutionary spirit of "socialist realism"; abstract art or dissonant music are denounced as "bougeois decadence."

Once the Communist revolution has smashed the old society, stamped out heresy, and remolded the society—and man, if possible—in accordance with its ideological tenets (or revealed "truths"), its second function is to organize and concentrate the society's entire resources toward industrialization. It has won power in an economically backward nation and must therefore industrialize, not only so that the nation can become stronger and wealthier, but so that the Party can legitimatize its power. The Party must create the proletariat in whose name it made the revolution. It must therefore organize the same capital accumulation it so harshly criticized under capitalist guidance. But capital accumulation, even when it is called "socialist construction," is by its very nature a cruel process. The Communist leaders can no more avoid squeezing the masses, including the proletariat, for savings than their capitalist predecessors. In fact, their means of capital accumulation are far crueler. Capitalism in the West was tempered by democracy. The political process provided a channel through which the workers' social protests could be heard; with the acquisition of the vote, they could gain satisfaction of their major grievances. But in an underdeveloped country industrializing under Communist Party control, there is no independent political channel through which the masses can seek amelioration. The Party is committed to industrialization, and rapid industrialization at that; it intends to drive the population toward that end as rapidly as possible. Incentives, controls, terror, propaganda are all employed to speed up the industrialization or at least to maintain its speed. At the same time, the subsistence, or near-subsistence, wages of the worker and peasants assure high "surplus values." The government's monopoly of political power, mass communications, and instruments of force, which make this quick industrialization possible, also allow it to control popular dissatisfaction. By an ironic quirk of history, a Communist state thus ends up fashioning itself in Marx's image of capitalism and becomes transformed into state capitalism.[29] And it is the Party leaders, rather than the capitalists, who

[29] The fact that the Communists had captured power in an economically backward nation, and that they would now have to carry out the industrialization program, meant of course that Leninism was skipping one of Marx's prescribed historical phases, namely, of bourgeois capitalism. Lenin recognized early that the Party would now have to tread the "road to state capitalism":

In reality, state capitalism would be a step forward for us. If we were capable of attaining state capitalism in Russia within a short time, this would be a victory. . . . I said that state capitalism would be our savior. If we would have it in Russia, then the transition to full socialism would be easy and certain. For state capitalism is a system of centralization, integration, control, and socialization. And this is precisely what we lack.

(Quoted by Herbert Marcuse, Soviet Marxism: A Critical Analysis [New York: Columbia University Press, 1958], p. 44.)

become the new ruling class.[30] This very political development also disproves Marx in his fundamental criticism that private ownership of the means of production and private profit are the basic causes of the workers' miseries during the era of bourgeois industrialization. Actually, the exploitation of the masses is not the product of capitalism at all, but of the early phase of industrialization. Paradoxically, Communism has by "historical necessity" thereby become a technique for the rapid industrialization of underdeveloped economies.

The third and final task of the totalitarian government is to harness the society's strength, particularly once it has become industrialized, to "export" the revolution. Remolding the nation in its own image is not enough; nor is economic development. The truth must enlighten false believers everywhere. "Socialist construction" at home and abroad is the two-fold mission. The same "passion for unanimity" that leads the party to squash all domestic disagreement compels it to smash all international opposition. An international crusade whose aim is global domination is the result of this commitment to "permanent revolution."

Soviet Conflict Doctrine: The Politics of "Who-Whom"

It should be clear by now that the national interest of the Soviet Union, which emerged as one of the two superpowers after World War II, could not be divorced from the ideological orientation of its leaders. Her leaders tended to view the world in the context of the class struggle. Every economic system produced a particular class structure, and the national interest of any country reflected the interests of the dominant class.[31] Soviet foreign policy, as defined by the vanguard of the proletariat, claimed to reflect the interests of the proletariat. Moreover, since Marxism stressed the community of interests that bound the proletariat of all nations, Soviet foreign policy asserted that it mirrored the interests of the world proletariat.

The Soviet concept of "national interest" therefore transcended the traditional definition of the term because it was not "national." Nation-state conflicts have historically occurred between two or more states; they

[30] Milovan Djilas, *The New Class*, pp. 37–69.

[31] "Ideology thus infuses Soviet foreign policy with a keen appreciation of the close relationship between international affairs and domestic developments. Rejecting the conception that international affairs involve principally the interplay of various nation-states attempting to promote their national objectives, the Soviets view the world as a continuing struggle among a variety of interests—domestic, social, economic, political, as well as national. The interplay between nation-states is merely one, and often only a formal, aspect of international affairs. In the Soviet view, for true understanding, one must seek to establish the correlation of the various forces that are dynamically coexisting within a given society and chart their likely pattern of behavior as well as their likely influence in the future." (Brzezinski, *Ideology and Power in Soviet Politics*, p. 105.)

have been vertical conflicts. In revolutionary periods, the conflict has been between classes (middle class against aristocracy, proletariat against bourgeoisie) or races (Aryan versus non-Aryan). These class or racial categories cut across national boundary lines, and the conflicts have consequently been horizontal because the revolutionary state transformed the conflict into an *international civil war*. Its purpose was missionary, for its revolutionary ideology was tantamount to a secular religion; and its aim was the abolition of evil and the conversion of mankind to the new religion. The Soviet Union was, in this sense, an ideological state without permanent geographic boundaries. Marxism-Leninism gave it aims Czarist Russia never possessed. To be sure, the Soviet rulers were as concerned with Russia's frontiers and national security as were their Czarist predecessors. This accounted for some of the similarities in foreign-policy objectives—for instance, the continuing search for security in Eastern Europe. But unlike the Czars, the Soviet Communists conceived of their security in global terms and felt that they could not gain lasting national security while non-Communist states—which were, by definition, anti-Communist—remained. Soviet Russia was therefore the base for a world revolution and the nucleus of a future proletarian world order. Until that goal had been achieved, the permanent revolution would continue. The capitalist states had no right to exist, and the traditional international order was illegitimate. Soviet foreign policy could therefore not be satisfied with a balance of power which would preserve all non-Communist states and the non-Communist international system. Only when Soviet Communism had achieved total power and control internationally could it —as it had done domestically, where it had total control—eliminate heretics and seek to remold the environment so that men could be brought up to live in the true faith.

In a brilliant and eloquent passage, George Kennan has described how this revolutionary approach to foreign policy made a "mockery of the entire Western theory of international relationships, as it evolved in the period from the seventeenth to the nineteenth centuries":

The national state of modern Europe, bitterly as it might feud with its neighbors over the questions of *relative* advantage, was distinguished from the older forms of state power by its abandonment of universalistic and messianic pretensions, by its general readiness to recognize the equality of existence of other sovereign authorities, to accept their legitimacy and independence, and to concede the principle of live and let live as a basic rule in the determination of international relationships. This did not, I reiterate, eliminate wars and struggles over limited objectives; but it did mean as a general rule that once another state had been recognized as a sovereign entity, one did not attempt to extinguish it entirely, or to deny to it the basic right to order its own internal affairs in accordance with its own traditions and ideals.

It was this theory that the Bolsheviki challenged on their assumption of power in Russia. They challenged it by the universality of their own ideological pretensions—by the claim, that is, to an unlimited universal validity of their own ideas as to how society ought to be socially and politically organized. They challenged it by their insistence that the laws governing the operation of human society demanded the violent overthrow everywhere of governments which did not accept the ideological tenets of Russian Communism, and the replacement of these governments by ones that did. . . .

The significance of this situation has been somewhat obscured by those Western historians and commentators who have been unable to perceive any difference in principle between the attitude of the Soviet Union toward the Western countries and that of the Western countries toward the Soviet Union. After all, they have said, were not the Western governments equally hostile to Russia? Did they not attempt to overthrow the Soviet regime by their intervention in 1918–1919? Could the challenge to existing concepts of international relations properly be laid only at the Soviet door? Was not the Western rejection of socialism as a conceivable governmental system just as important in the breakdown of the established theory of international life as the Soviet rejection of capitalism?

It is my belief that the answer to these questions is "No." Any unclarity on this point can lead to a grievous misunderstanding of some of the basic elements of Soviet-Western relations. There were, in those initial years of Soviet power, some very significant differences between anti-Sovietism in the West and the hostility which the Soviet leaders entertained for the Western powers. This hostility from the Communist side is preconceived, ideological, deductive. In the minds of the Soviet leaders, it long predated the Communist seizure of power in Russia. Anti-Sovietism in the West, on the other hand, was largely a confused, astonished, and indignant reaction to the first acts of the Soviet regime. Many people in the Western governments came to hate the Soviet leaders for what they *did*. The Communists, on the other hand, hated the Western governments for what they *were*, regardless of what they did. They entertained this feeling long before there was even any socialistic state for the capitalists to do anything to. Their hatred did not vary according to the complexion or policies or actions of the individual non-Communist governments. It never has. The government of Hitler was not more wicked or more repugnant in Moscow's eyes than that of Great Britain. The British Labour governments were in no respect superior, as seen from Moscow, to those of the Conservatives. The Swedish and Norwegian governments have realized general socialist aims to a very high degree; yet no greater merit could be conceded to them from the Soviet standpoint than, let us say, to the government of General Franco. The Baltic governments were not given any credit in Moscow for being the first to order their relations with the Soviet Union; they were, on the contrary, the first to be swallowed up by Moscow as a consequence of the agreement with Hitler in 1939.

What better proof could there be that it was not the manifestations of the *behavior* of the non-Communist states to which Moscow took exception, but their very nature, as Moscow saw it? In Moscow's view, non-Communist statesmen were regarded as incapable of doing good intentionally. If by chance they did something that was in Moscow's interest, it was because circumstances and their own shortsightedness forced them into it. In thirty years' experience with Soviet official literature, I cannot recall an instance of a non-Communist government being credited with a single generous or worthy impulse. All actions of such governments favorable to Soviet interests or even responsive to Soviet desiderata are invariably attributed to motives less than creditable: as a bowing to necessity, a belated yielding to the demands of outraged opinion, or the accidental subsidiary product of some sinister ulterior motive. Even during the common struggle of World War II the Soviet government meticulously refrained from endorsing the wartime motives and purposes of its Western allies. Since the war came to an end it has not hesitated to portray these motives and purposes to its own people as sinister and reprehensible in the extreme, not markedly superior, in fact, to those of Hitler. . . .

Surely, this approach cannot be equated with that of the pragmatic West, where for forty years the argument over the attitude to be taken toward Soviet power has revolved around the questions of interpretation of the behavior of the Soviet regime. There have undoubtedly been individuals here and there in the Western countries whose hatred of what they understood to be socialism has been so great that they have felt it should be rooted out with fire and sword, on straight ideological grounds, wherever it raised its head. But such people, surely, have been few; and I do not think that their views have ever been dominant in any of the major Western governments. I recall no suggestions in the Western chanceries that the initial government of the Weimar Republic, for example, ought to be overthrown on grounds of its socialist complexion. I have yet to know an American who thinks it our duty to overthrow the governments of Sweden and Norway for ideological reasons. Had the Soviet leaders contented themselves from the outset with saying that they felt that they knew what was good for Russia, and refrained from taking positions on what was good for other countries, Western hostility to the Soviet Union would never have been what it has been. The issue has never been, and is not today, the right of the Russian people to have a socialistic ordering of society if they so wish; the issue is how a government which happens to be socialistic is going to behave in relation to its world environment.[32]

The point is that the Soviets considered their relationship with the non-Soviet world to be one of conflict. While this might not be a "hot war," is was nevertheless deadly. Lenin agreed with Clausewitz that war was the continuation of politics by other means. "The Marxists," he said, "have considered this axiom as the theoretical foundation for the meaning of every war." The Communists also reversed Clausewitz. Peace, to them, was the continuation of the last war by other means. The whole outlook, organization, and language of the Communist movement was,

[32] George F. Kennan, *Russia and the West Under Lenin and Stalin*, pp. 179–83.

in fact, "military." The struggle between the Soviets and the non-Communist world was irreconcilable and unending—until the moment of victory. The basic "fact" of history was the existence of a state of war between classes or between states controlled by antagonistic classes. Politics was therefore not a means of reconciliation. The Communists, like all extremists, knew that they were right. How could they possibly resolve differences with the enemy by compromise? Only unconditional surrender could end the conflict. Politics was thus an unending series of "campaigns" whose aim was to defeat the capitalist enemy. The only question was "who-whom?" or "who-beats-whom?"—*kto-kovo*.[33] The entire world was the battlefield, and it was, in fact, divided between the "war zone" (the non-Communist world) and "peace zone" (Communist nations).[34] The Communists constantly sought to push the borders of the war zone back. As President Kennedy was to express the Soviet position later: "What is mine is mine; what is yours is negotiable." Each Communist victory, as in Indochina or Cuba, shrank the area of this zone. Western victories, by contrast, were limited to the successful defense of the *status quo*, to defeating further efforts at Communist incursions into the war zone. The Soviet Union in such instances accepted the dams built by the West, for "Its political action is a fluid stream which moves constantly, wherever it is permitted to move, toward a given goal. Its main concern is to make sure it has filled every nook and cranny available to it in the basin of world power. But if it finds unassailable barriers in its path, it accepts these philosophically and accommodates itself to them. The main thing is that there should always be pressure, increasing constant pressure, toward the desired goal."[35]

The Party was the military organization that led the proletarian army into battle in the class war. It was the vanguard of the proletariat, its officer corps, the "general staff of the revolution." Moreover, after it had seized power, its totalitarian organization of the nation permitted it to harness all resources for the international struggle. Just as centralized command, organizational hierarchy, and discipline were the bases of military victory in a hot war, so the same principles operated in the war against capitalism. The totalitarian society, in short, was organized for "permanent warfare." As Sigmund Neumann wrote long ago, totalitarian dictatorships were "governments for war. The analysis of their inner structure . . . has proved conclusively that the permanent revolution of perpetual motion is the driving force of totalitarianism. Expansion is of its essence. The rise, development, and survival of modern dictatorships are inextricably tied up with continuous dynamics.[36] There was always an enemy—inside the nation as well as outside—who must be defeated. If

[33] Nathan Leites, *A Study of Bolshevism*, pp. 27–63.
[34] Robert Strausz-Hupé *et al.*, *Protracted Conflict*, pp. 21–22.
[35] George F. Kennan, *American Diplomacy, 1900–1950*, p. 118.
[36] Sigmund Neumann, *Permanent Revolution*, p. 257.

no such enemy existed, and consequently no external and internal war could be waged, he would have to be invented to justify the militancy of the society. Ideology and organization were thus interrelated, the former defining the purpose that demanded the totalitarian organization, the latter requiring for its maintenance a "fighting" ideology. In the relationship between the Communist states and the outside world, "doctrine has been of central importance. The militaristic pattern and spirit of Communist organization require for their effective functioning a sense of conflict—there has to be an enemy somewhere. As it becomes more difficult or less expedient to find enemies at home, they must be sought abroad. . . . Discipline and belief mutually reinforce one another, and each is required to maintain the rigid strength of the other."[37]

It was thus unrealistic to expect the Soviet leaders to end the conflict with capitalism short of victory. To accept a permanent *status quo* would have been to deny their *raison d'être*. Any "normalization" or stabilization of relations with non-Communist states was only temporary and effected for tactical reasons. A particular balance of power may produce a *détente*, but a revolutionary state did not surrender its revolutionary purposes. It could not accept a long-term static position while the "enemy" still existed. To have done so would have been to accept the international social order—the very antithesis of its revolutionary ideology. Thus the struggle between Communism and capitalism could be resolved only by the latter's defeat. Until that point, the international civil war had to continue. Nor was the victor in question, for history had already decided that issue.

In these circumstances, the Cold War could hardly be resolved by diplomacy, although it has so often been proposed by Western statesmen and international political observers as the chief means of settling the basic issues between the Soviet Union and the United States. Great hope has generally attended the various "summit" conferences held since 1955. The feeling has been that once the Soviet and Western statesmen came to know and like each other, international tensions could be reduced, and possibly some or all of the political issues creating these tensions could be eliminated. As President Eisenhower emphasized before the 1955 Geneva Conference: "Our many postwar conferences have been characterized too much by attention to detail, by an effort apparently to work on specific problems rather than to establish the spirit and the attitude in which we shall approach them."[38]

The failure of the summit conferences to accomplish their aims, however, did not—it was claimed—invalidate the utility of diplomacy in a revolutionary situation. Rather, the failures were blamed on the conditions in which summit diplomacy had been conducted. Summit confer-

---

[37] Daniels, *op. cit.*, p. 352.
[38] *The New York Times*, July 16, 1955.

ences, it was contended, were hardly the place to arrive at compromise agreements. Any kind of "open diplomacy, openly arrived at" was bound to fail. Diplomacy, like any good horse-trading, begins with each side asking for more than it knows it can get. In this way, one may get more than was originally expected. At the same time, by maximizing its demands, the proposing side also may not have to give away as much as it decided at the beginning of the negotiations it could safely give up without compromising its vital interests. Once positions have been set forth, the bargaining begins. The final agreement must, of course, be publicly debated at the time of national ratification of the projected treaty. The objection is not to "open diplomacy," but to "openly arrived at," for "open diplomacy" is "frozen diplomacy." Each side's first position would be its final position if negotiations were conducted publicly. Once a country has taken a public stand, it cannot retreat. If the original proposal was in the national interest, how could it be compromised without endangering the national interest? Compromise thus becomes appeasement, and the leader who appeases will give his opposition—whether an opposition party in a democratic state or an opposing faction within a totalitarian state—the lever with which to pry him loose from power. Thus, instead of encouraging conciliation, open diplomacy fosters obstinacy, inertia, unyielding positions, and propaganda. Private and quiet diplomacy is the prerequisite for effective problem-solving bargaining.[39]

This well-argued plea for "open diplomacy, privately arrived at" is not persuasive, however. In the first place, the Cold War is not the outgrowth of simple mutual distrust between Soviet and American leaders, and therefore it cannot be resolved by bonhomie and the establishment of good personal relations.[40] Post–World War II summit conferences, even if they had been held without any publicity, could no more have bridged the gap between what the Communists refer to as the "two camps" than did the wartime meetings, where all negotiations were "privately arrived at." Whether Stalin liked Roosevelt or Khrushchev liked Eisenhower is of little import, for the Soviet leaders knew that the American Presidents were merely puppets of the objective laws of capitalism. The two social systems remained irreconcilable. The "basic (global) contradiction" could not be overcome by the "spirit of Camp David." The Cold War, according to the Communists, was fostered by the West, and only the demise of capitalism would establish a secure and lasting peace.

[39] See, particularly, Hans J. Morgenthau, *Politics Among Nations*, pp. 539–70.

[40] For an incisive critique of Western diplomacy vis-à-vis the Soviet Union, see Henry A. Kissinger, *The Necessity for Choice*, pp. 169–209 (on summit conferences, pp. 180–91). On a more general level, a balanced evaluation of the arguments for a restoration of "private diplomacy" may be found in A. F. K. Organski, *World Politics* (New York: Alfred A. Knopf, 1958), pp. 339–67. Indeed, Organski makes the good point that diplomacy has never been kept secret from those whose support was necessary for diplomacy—that is, the kings and courts.

This is also another reason why private diplomacy cannot end the Cold War. The argument that it can divorces the technique from the character of the social and political order in which diplomacy functions and then gives the technique absolute priority. Unfortunately, diplomacy is not a magic wand whose touch can resolve all problems. In a traditional order, where the economic and social basis is not in dispute, conflicts are generally resolvable; interest conflicts tend to be of a limited nature and can be settled pragmatically. When such an international consensus exists, the issue is not *whether* problems can be resolved, but *how*. At such times, it is the technique of diplomacy that is credited with the solution of problems. What is forgotten, because it is taken for granted, is that the diplomacy functioned effectively because it was conducted in a consensus situation. The issue of "open diplomacy" versus "quiet diplomacy" is therefore secondary to the fundamental issue of whether the states negotiating share a common agreement on the nature of the international system in the first place.

If there is no consensus, they will not even be able to communicate with each other properly. They may use the same words, but these words can mean diametrically opposed things to each side. Yalta was the last "real" negotiation with the Soviet Union, an attempt to adjust interests, formalize an understanding, and create an acceptable basis upon which the Soviet Union and the West could cooperate—all according to the best traditional diplomatic methods. The Allies agreed at Yalta that the countries of Eastern Europe would determine their own future. There were to be "free elections" in which all but the "fascist" parties would participate. "Self-government" would ensure "democracy" in these nations. This agreement looked fine on paper, but since it was the Red Army that drove the Germans out of these countries, the Russians implemented the agreement. It soon became clear that they used words in a quite different context. Claiming that they represented the majority of the population, the Communist parties in these countries asserted that they were the only democratic party. All other parties obviously represented the privileged; they were "reactionary" or "fascist." In a free election, they said, only a Communist Party runs; and self-government is rule by the Communist Party, which is the spokesman for all the exploited. Communism is thus synonymous with democracy. The Soviet occupation of Eastern Europe is not colonialism, for a proletarian state cannot be colonial by definition; only a capitalist state exercises imperial domination.

Thus the war of the Communist world against the non-Communist world continued. Negotiations were merely part of the unremitting struggle:

As long as the question "who-whom?" has not been decided by the con-

solidation of world Communism—and it cannot be decided short of that—
the world is, basically, in a state of high tension. If the Party were to forget this, it would not reduce the tension but merely render certain its own
annihilation in the further course of the conflict. To Bolsheviks, high tension is the normal state of politics. They do not experience it as something
that just cannot go on, but rather as something that will necessarily persist.
What Westerners call a "real agreement" seems to Bolsheviks inconceivable. It is often predicted in the West that if particular issues . . . could
be settled with the Politburo, an easing of over-all tension might ensue.
For Bolsheviks, this does not follow. There might be less "noise," but the
basic situation—the presence of two blocs attempting to annihilate each
other—would be unchanged. The only "real settlement" is that by which
one of the contestants is utterly destroyed; before this end is reached all
apparent "solutions" . . . are but weapons in the continuing conflict.
What a Western statesman called "local and limited settlements of outstanding issues" are usually possible and even required; but a "general agreement to live and let live"—"towards" which this statesman proposed to
"work" by "local and limited settlements"—is inconceivable. The Party is
obligated to strive for the annihilation of its enemies, a necessary condition for the fulfillment of its mission. . . . There are only two stable
situations: being dead and being all-powerful.

Whenever there is no "hot" war between the Party and the world, there
is always a cold war, in which it may or may not be practicable and useful to distract attention from the fact that it is only by the political death
of one of the contestants that the situation can really be changed.[41]

If the "political death" of capitalism remained the goal of the Soviets,
would not the continuing struggle some day spark a global conflagration? Was the world not moving inexorably toward the day when the
Cold War would be transformed into a hot war that would incinerate
both the major contestants? Had it not, indeed, been prophesied that
"the day of the Lord will come as a thief in the night; in which the
heavens shall pass away with a great noise, and the elements shall melt
with fervent heat, the earth also and the works that are therein shall be
burned up"?

[41] Leites, *op. cit.*, pp. 29–30.

IV

The Revolution in War

The Ascendancy of Strategic Bombing

It is ironic that democracy, which was expected to abolish war, actually created conditions in which a new kind of "total" war became possible. One of democracy's assumptions was that only irresponsible rulers were belligerent, that wars were for them merely an enjoyable—and quite profitable—"blood sport." It was the people who paid the price for wars with their lives and taxes. Thus, if the peace-loving people could hold their rulers accountable, wars would be eliminated and peace secured.[1] Democracy would bring an era of good will—of individual freedom and social justice at home, of peace and harmony abroad. The world would be safe for democracy—because it would be democratic. Government by the people, of the people, and for the people would ensure perpetual peace.

Instead, democracy gave birth to the "nation in arms." Once men were freed from feudal bondage and granted the right to self-government, they were, for the first time in history, able to identify with their nation. And if men now equated their well-being with that of their nation, if they were deeply attached to the fatherland, it was only reasonable that the nation should be able to call on them—its citizens—for its defense. The French Revolution, which inspired love of *la patrie*, symbolized by the *tricolore* and the *Marseillaise*, produced the first form of universal military service. If men's supreme loyalty was to the nation, the "nation in arms" followed logically. Democracy thus enabled France to

---

[1] See, for example, Immanuel Kant, *Perpetual Peace*, translated by Carl J. Friedrich and added as an appendix to his book *Inevitable Peace* (Cambridge, Mass.: Harvard University Press, 1948), pp. 251–52.

mobilize itself fully for total war—and to fight a war to destroy its opponent completely.

This was one reason the Congress of Vienna reacted with such horror to the Revolution, for it unleashed mass passions and all-out war. War had previously been restrained by the European aristocratic consensus, and this restraint had been reinforced by the internal structure of the dynastic state. Socially, men had not identified themselves with the nation. The mass army, fired by nationalism, was unknown. Napoleon's victories, then, were hardly surprising. The armies of the *ancien régime* were composed largely of mercenaries and such low elements of society as debtors, vagrants, and criminals—men who were animated neither by love of country nor by hatred of enemy, but fought because they were paid or compelled to do so. The states lacked sufficient economic resources to maintain sizable armies. Indeed, their tactics were determined by the need to limit expenses; thus, the emphasis was on maneuver rather than pitched battle, to keep casualties low. But the Revolution enlisted popular support, and soldiers began to fight in defense of their country: "A new era in military history now opened, the era of cannon fodder."[2]

If total war was a result of the disintegration of the European consensus and the rise of democracy and nationalism, it was the Industrial Revolution that produced the instruments enabling men to kill each other in greater numbers. Modern military technology thus brought total war to its fullest realization.[3] Mass armies could be equipped with ever more destructive arms, and nations could therefore inflict progressively more damage on each other in shorter and shorter periods. It took thirty years for the states of Europe to slaughter half the population of Central Europe in the seventeenth century. It took only four years in the second decade of the twentieth century for the European nations to bleed each other into a state of exhaustion and, in some cases, collapse. "Mankind," Churchill wrote after 1918, "has got into its hands for the first time the tools by which it can unfailingly accomplish its own extermination. . . . Death stands at attention, obedient, expectant, ready, if called on, to pulverise, without hope of repair, what is left of civilisation. He awaits only the word of command. He awaits it from a frail, bewildered being, long his victim, now—for one occasion only—his Master."[4]

[2] Bertrand de Jouvenel, *On Power*, translated by J. F. Huntington (Boston, Mass.: Beacon Press, 1962), p. 148.

[3] The interrelationship between war and industrial power is well treated in John U. Nef, *War and Human Progress* (Cambridge, Mass.: Harvard University Press, 1950) and Richard A. Preston, Sidney F. Wise, and Herman O. Werner, *Men in Arms: A History of Warfare and Its Interrelationships with Western Society* (rev. ed.; New York: Frederick A. Praeger, 1962), pp. 176 ff. For the impact of democratization and industrialization on American military performance, see Walter Millis, *Arms and Men* (New York: New American Library, 1956).

[4] Winston Churchill, *The Second World War*. Vol. I: *The Gathering Storm* (Boston: Houghton Mifflin Co., 1948), p. 40.

But it was not until the ascendancy of strategic air power—and ultimately, the development of atomic weapons—that man could accomplish his own extermination. If, as World War I seemed to prove, the defense had gained a decisive and apparently permanent superiority over the offense, the only way of winning victory was through the air. If ground forces found it virtually impossible to effect a breakthrough, only a bomber force could—according to General Douhet, the Italian Clausewitz of air warfare—impose defeat on the enemy. After the initial destruction of the opponent's air force through surprise attack, the bombers would attack his cities, eliminating the industries that supplied weapons to his troops and undermining the morale of his civilian population. Once the army in the front line had been deprived of sufficient weapons and ammunition, morale on the home front had collapsed, and the cities lay in rubble, defeat was certain. Douhet was thus convinced that air attacks on cities would play the decisive role in any future warfare, and that victory in such an air war would result from the virtual annihilation of the enemy. The assumptions upon which these convictions were based were that air power could in fact destroy the opponent's urban and industrial centers, and that air attacks could collapse civilian morale.[5]

As it happened, though, Douhet's theory did not "prove out" in World War II.[6] The key to victory was the combination of mobile ground power with tactical air support: i.e., armored divisions—essentially tanks, with some mobile infantry and artillery—cooperating closely with fighter aircraft. This tank-fighter combination restored the mobility to warfare that the trench warfare of World War I had lost; and because the thrust and speed of the attack led to quicker victories on the battlefield, casualty rates were reduced. The Germans called it *Blitzkrieg* (lightning war) and succeeded brilliantly with this tactic in 1940 on the Western Front.[7] In 1941, they almost achieved the defeat of the Soviet Union with the same tactic, but the Red Army held out and finally turned the tide against Germany at Stalingrad in 1942. The British and American forces, after their invasion of France in 1944, also used this combination of mobile land forces and tactical air power with great success. It was not accidental that most of the best-known generals of World War II were "tank generals." Such dashing figures as Rommel, Guderian, and Patton gained their fame not because they were first-rate strategists but because of their brilliant tactical handling of the tank and the spectacular results they achieved.

By contrast, strategic air power proved largely ineffective until the

[5] Bernard Brodie, *Strategy in the Missile Age*, p. 98. See also Edward Warner, "Douhet, Mitchell, Seversky: Theories of Air Warfare," in Edward Meade Earle (ed.), *Makers of Modern Strategy* (Princeton, N.J.: Princeton University Press, 1943).

[6] See Millis, *op. cit.*, pp. 253–55.

[7] Telford Taylor, *The March of Conquest* (New York: Simon and Schuster, 1958).

final phase of the war, when the outcome had already been decided. There were several reasons for this. Germany—like Russia—was a land power whose senior service was the army. It was thus natural that the Germans should think of war as land warfare—and that air power should be assigned to support ground operations. Air power was therefore not thought of in Douhet's terms, as a service operating independently of the army and navy.[8] Consequently, while the Germans did build up a bomber force, it was not sufficiently large at the beginning of the war, or by the fall of Dunkirk in May, 1940, to knock England out of the war. There was no invasion of England because the Luftwaffe had failed to establish command of the air over the Channel and southern England.[9]

This brings us to the second reason for the failure of strategic air power. According to Douhet, a bomber equipped with guns to ward off possible attacking fighters would always get through; he had not foreseen that fighters, guided by radar, would be extremely effective in finding their quarry and shooting it down. By the time of the Battle of Britain, the RAF possessed the famous Spitfires and Hurricanes, which proved the vulnerability of bombers. This was equally true for British and American bombers in their attacks upon Germany. The U.S. Army Air Force, whose officers were followers of Douhet, learned this lesson soon after American bombers started operations against Germany from English bases, in late 1942. The British had by this time already started bomber operations against Germany. Because British four-engine bombers were heavier and did not therefore carry as many guns for their protection as American bombers, they operated largely at night. The Army Air Force was confident, however, that it could "do the job" by day: the Flying Fortresses and Liberators were heavily armed and could fly high. After its air power in England had been built up and it had gained some bombing experience, the Air Force decided to prove Douhet's theory by attacking a single target, the city of Schweinfurt, where the Germans had concentrated their ball-bearing production. If the factories producing these bearings could be destroyed, the German military machine would be disastrously—and probably fatally—wounded. But the attacks on Schweinfurt proved to be disastrous only for the attackers. The losses of planes against the defense—especially air defense—were very high. The lesson was clear. Repeated attacks against such well-guarded targets could only lead to heroic suicide for the bombers and their crews. Schweinfurt was a grim reminder that fighter defenses could be effective and that even armed bombers needed fighter protection. The Flying Fortress—the name itself a symptom of the overweening confidence of Douhet's American pupils that the bomber would always get through—

[8] *Ibid.*, pp. 24–25, 366.
[9] Millis, *op. cit.*, pp. 255–56; see also Peter Fleming, *Operation Sea Lion* (New York: Simon and Schuster, 1957).

was not, in fact, self-sufficient.[10] After Schweinfurt, the Air Force ordered the production of long-range Thunderbolt fighters. Until they were ready to escort the bombers in early 1944, sustained, long-range, daylight precision bombing against military targets in Germany was called off. Only the British continued heavy night raids, which turned out to be largely indiscriminate city bombings, attacks on civilian population and industry.

In any case, in the four years from the German victory in France to the Allied invasion of France, independent strategic bombing did not produce spectacular results, let alone win the war. City bombing, admittedly, destroyed large sections of big cities, but it did not seriously affect essential war production. The reasons: most bombing was directed at centers of cities, while the industries—at least in Germany—were on the outskirts; even when factories were hit, more damage was done to the buildings than to the machinery inside—as, for instance, at Schweinfurt; and the Germans were quick to restore needed factory buildings to maximum working capacity. Indeed, the postwar U.S. Strategic Bombing Survey found that German war production—for instance, of fighters—increased until late 1944! And one reason for this was that Allied bombing, by destroying nonvital factories and services, allowed the Germans to channel labor and resources to the war industries. (Other important factors included the enlistment of female labor and the postponement of the retirement age.) Nor did German morale suffer critically. The civilians—"the soldiers on the home front"—proved to be tough and resilient; indeed, the aerial attacks tended to unify the population. And even though there was, inevitably, some decline in civilian morale, this had no vital impact on the behavior of the working population, which still went to work as usual. (No doubt the threat of reprisals by the Nazis against those workers who failed to show up exerted a strong influence.)[11]

It is true that strategic air power did play a more important role in the war against Japan. But by the time heavy attacks began in spring of 1945, Japan had already lost the war: her navy and merchant marine no longer existed, and her troops on continental Asia were cut off. Even if every Japanese war firm were still producing, the troops could not be properly supplied; as it was, the raw materials Japanese factories needed could not even be imported any longer. What was needed was to bring home to Japan's leaders the simple fact that the war was lost and there was no point in further resistance. The city bombing of Japan, climaxed by the atomic attacks on Hiroshima and Nagasaki, was intended to help make this clear.[12] Even after the vast damage inflicted by this bombing and

---

[10] Millis, *op. cit.*, pp. 259–60; Brodie, *op. cit.*, p. 115.

[11] See Brodie, *op. cit.*, pp. 120–24, 131–38.

[12] See *ibid.*, pp. 127–31, 138–43; also Herbert Feis, *Japan Subdued* (Princeton, N.J.: Princeton University Press, 1961), p. 185.

the resulting suffering of the Japanese population, Japan's military leaders still did not want to surrender, but were prepared to fight to the
death against the coming invasion. It was the Emperor who, having opposed the war from the beginning, finally stepped in and ordered the
military to surrender after the Soviet entry into the war had doomed all
hopes for Soviet mediation efforts to relax Washington's surrender terms.
Thus, without the Emperor's intervention, even the two atomic bombs—
and the United States had only two—might not have brought the war
to an end.[13] Indeed, it is questionable whether, in a totalitarian system,
a loss of morale can be transformed into a demand for surrender. How
can popular feeling be organized and who can be its spokesmen against
a fanatical regime?

What, then, of Douhet's theory? The results of city bombing were not
rewarding. The predicted collapse of war production and civilian morale
did not occur. The evidence of the period prior to the 1944 invasion
would therefore seem to be negative. During the last phase of the war in
Europe, however, strategic air power came into its own, and its impact
was devastating. Interestingly enough, though, its primary use was no
longer in city bombing. Rather, the targets the Allied air forces—by now
very large and escorted by fighters—selected were transportation complexes and centers of the chemical–synthetic oil industry, both of
which proved extremely vulnerable. Road, railroad, and canal transportation were brought to a virtual standstill. For a highly developed, interdependent economy, this turned out to be fatal. How could the coal that
stoked the furnaces be brought to the factories? And how could more
weapons and ammunition be brought to the front? Moreover, the attacks on the oil industry reduced oil production drastically, and production of aviation and motor gasoline was even more seriously affected.
Thus, while fighter-aircraft production rose, there was less and less gasoline available for flight training or combat flying. Similarly, on the
ground, German tanks lacked sufficient fuel, and their effectiveness in
battle was thereby severely hampered.[14] Thus strategic air power did
achieve, in the final stage of the war in Europe, the kind of impact predicted by Douhet. Douhet had provided a theory that was to guide action, but strategic bombing had never been practiced, and aspects of
the theory needed to be changed with circumstances and experience.
The switch from general city bombing to selective target bombing demonstrated how effective bombers could be in collapsing a modern economy and halting a military machine—provided the right targets were
chosen. Douhet, then, had not really been wrong. Indeed, in the opinion
of a leading military analyst, Bernard Brodie, Douhet's ideas have "fared

[13] Paul Kecskemeti, *Strategic Surrender: Politics of Victory and Defeat* (Stanford,
Calif.: Stanford University Press, 1958), pp. 199–206; Louis Morton, "The Decision
To Use the Atomic Bomb," *Foreign Affairs*, January, 1957, pp. 352–53.

[14] See Brodie, *op. cit.*, pp. 109–20; Georges Blond, *The Death of Hitler's Germany*
(New York: The Macmillan Co., 1954), pp. 105–6.

better than those of most of his critics. Strategic bombing did pay large military dividends, and . . . could have paid much larger ones if its limitations as well as its real capabilities had been more adequately understood. Douhet provided a framework for such understanding. It is not altogether his fault that his followers were too content with what he gave them to develop and refine his insights further."[15]

What Douhet's students failed to appreciate until rather late was that a modern economy, being highly specialized and interdependent, is an extremely sensitive structure. The denial of one essential element can cripple it *if* there is no substitute for that one element—a necessary qualification since advanced technology can usually produce a substitute in a highly industrialized economy. It has been said that a nation's industry is not like a building, to be destroyed, but like a tree which can grow new branches when old ones die. An economy is less a structure than a process or set of activities and purposes that can be undertaken in a variety of ways; the loss of one element in this process is seldom irreparable. But what substitute is there for destroyed railroad lines— when barges and road transportation are also under continuous heavy attack? Or for a synthetic-oil industry—itself already a substitute? Where is the substitute for the substitute?

Certainly, whatever the shortcomings of strategic bombing during World War II, Douhet was proved prophetically correct with the development of the atom and hydrogen bombs, though even he, in his advocacy of air warfare, had never dreamt of such enormous destructive power. But surely it was clear now that air power would play the decisive role in any future total war. Cities—indeed, whole nations—could be laid waste in a matter of hours, if not minutes. The effectiveness of strategic air power was no longer a matter of dispute. Nuclear bombs had the capacity to impose a degree of destruction that would make World War II bombing attacks appear trivial by comparison. The atom bombs dropped on Hiroshima and Nagasaki (20 kilotons, or 20 thousand tons of TNT) were within a few years surpassed in their destructive power by both the United States and the Soviet Union. Kilotons were replaced by megatons (1 million tons of TNT). A single U.S. Strategic Air Command B-52 bomber carries an average of 25 megatons of explosive power— which represents 12.5 times the entire explosive power of all bombs dropped during World War II, including the two atomic bombs![16] (The B-52 could carry a 50-megaton bomb, if the United States possessed one.[17])

The total estimated American nuclear stockpile by 1962 was approximately 35 kilomegatons (35 *billion* tons of TNT)—"enough bang to

15 Brodie, *op. cit.*, p. 105.
16 Arthur T. Hadley, *The Nation's Safety and Arms Control*, p. 4.
17 *The New York Times*, August 14, 1963.

provide 10 tons of explosive power for everyone in the world. In the form of TNT this much explosive power would fill a string of freight cars stretching from the earth to the moon and back 15 times (approximately 240,000 miles each way)." The estimated Soviet stockpile in 1962 was 20 kilomegatons.[18] The Soviets have tested the world's largest bomb —58 megatons—and claim that their stockpile includes 100-megaton bombs. Actually, a bomb can be made as large or as small as desired— up to 1,000 megatons, or a "gigaton." Moreover, it is cheap to increase the yield of a bomb. It costs $750,000 for a 100-kiloton atom bomb, $1 million for a 1-megaton hydrogen bomb, $1.1 million for a 10-megaton bomb, and $1.2 million for a 100-megaton bomb; above 10 megatons, each additional ton of explosive costs about a penny. In short, bombs come in true economy sizes.[19] However, it is not necessarily true that the larger the bomb, the more effective it is; while a larger bomb may cause greater damage, the amount of damage does not increase proportionally with the size of the bomb. A 10-megaton bomb is sufficient to incinerate any large city, and two 25-megaton bombs dropped several miles apart will cause more extensive damage than one 50-megaton bomb.

A nuclear explosion has three effects: blast, thermal, and radiation. The blast, or shock wave—the almost solid wall of air pressure produced by an explosion—resulting from a bomb exploding in a city will collapse all wooden buildings within 6 miles of ground zero for a low-altitude 1-megaton bomb, 14 miles for a 10-megaton bomb, and 30 miles for a 100-megaton bomb. For brick buildings, the comparative figures for the same bombs are 4, 9, and 18 miles; and for sturdier buildings, the distance ranges from 3 to 12 miles.

The thermal impact is even more devastating. The heat generated by a 1-megaton bomb is tremendous, producing second-degree burns of the skin up to 9 miles from ground zero; a 10-megaton bomb has the same effect up to 24 miles, a 100-megaton bomb up to 70 miles.[20] Moreover, the heat would in most cases ignite wooden houses—as, for instance, those in many suburbs—and other combustible objectives over about the same range. World War II demonstrated that the real danger from fire, even when started with ordinary incendiary bombs, is the resulting "fire storm."[21] The intense heat from the fire rises, producing hot air. Fresh

---

[18] Hadley, *op. cit.*, pp. 3, 4. The American stockpile was so large that in January, 1964, President Johnson ordered a 25 per cent cutback in the production of enriched uranium and closed four of the fourteen American reactors producing plutonium. This was followed by a further cutback of 15 per cent in April, 1964.

[19] Ralph E. Lapp, *Kill and Overkill*, p. 37.

[20] *Ibid.*, pp. 51–52; Scientists' Committee for Radiation Information, "Effects of Nuclear Explosives," in Seymour Melman (ed.), *No Place to Hide*, pp. 98–107.

[21] A vivid account of the fire storm is given in Martin Caidin, *The Night Hamburg Died* (New York: Ballantine Books, 1960), pp. 80–105, 129–41. The German estimate of those killed in Hamburg was 60,000 people. The American B-29 attack on Tokyo on March 9–10, 1945, burned up 16 square miles and killed 84,000 peo-

oxygen is needed to replace the burned-up oxygen, and the pressure differential between the hot and colder air sucks in fresh oxygen to feed the hungry flames. Faster and faster, the air rushes in; the wind velocity surpasses gale force. The flames, fed further by the gas, oil, and other incendiary materials of the homes and streets of the burning city, leap upward, stabbing high into the air, enveloping the stricken area. Everything burns in this womb of heat and flame. There is no escape. Those who have not yet been crushed in their shelters will be asphyxiated by a lack of oxygen or carbon monoxide; if they seek to escape into the burning streets, they will expose their lungs and bodies to the intense heat and suddenly burst into flame. (During the World War II attack on Hamburg, the fire storm caused a ground temperature of 1400° F. Indeed, near the center of the fire storm, the temperature exceeded 2200° F.) A 100-megaton bomb could cause fire storms up to 75 miles from the point of explosion: woods, trash, dry leaves, all provide good kindling fuel.

The third effect of a nuclear explosion, the radiation impact, can be maximized by a ground burst of low-altitude explosion. The resulting fireball—the large, rapidly expanding sphere of hot gases which produces high and intense heat—scoops up the debris and converts it into radioactive material. The fireball of a 10-megaton bomb has a six-mile diameter. The heavier particles of debris fall back to earth within the first few hours. The lighter particles "fall-out" during the following days over an area whose size depends on the size of the explosion, the surface over which the explosion occurs, and the meteorological conditions. The American 15-megaton thermonuclear explosion of 1954 in the Pacific caused substantial contamination over an area of 7,000 square miles (equivalent to the size of New Jersey). Under more "favorable" conditions, the fallout could have covered an area of 100,000 square miles (equivalent to New Jersey plus New York plus Pennsylvania). Such fallout, moreover, can emit radiation for days, months, or even years. The ability of this radiation to kill depends on the number of roentgens a human being absorbs. A dosage of 100–200 roentgens causes radiation sickness, a combination of weakness, nausea, and vomiting; this is not fatal, although it can result in disability. At 200 roentgens, the radiation becomes dangerous: disability is certain, and death can come within a month. Above 300 roentgens, the possibility of death increases until at 500 roentgens, death is certain for 50 per cent of those exposed to the ra-

---

ple, most of whom were burned to death or died from wounds caused by fire. By contrast, the Hiroshima atom bomb killed 72,000 people. The most destructive attack ever, however, was the two-day Anglo-American bombing of Dresden in February, 1945, in which 135,000 people were killed.

[22] Lapp, *op. cit.*, pp. 53–54.

diation. Above 600 roentgens, the number of deaths goes up and they occur more rapidly.[23] Radiation also has two other effects: it can cause cancer and genetic transmutations that may affect following generations.

Three conclusions would seem to follow from this description of the impact of nuclear weapons. First, the World War II problem of failing to hit a target industry or only damaging the buildings but not the machinery they house no longer exists. An entire city can now be eliminated with a single bomb. Even the smallest strategic warhead—600 kilotons mounted on a Polaris missile—is 30 times more powerful than the bomb dropped on Hiroshima; the warhead of the solid-fuel Minuteman has the same yield. Both missiles will eventually receive warheads of approximately 1 megaton. (The quick-firing liquid fuel Titan 2 has a yield of 4–5 megatons.) The Polaris will indeed eventually be replaced by the Poseidon, which will have a warhead of about 2 megatons. With a more powerful booster, the United States may place even more powerful warheads on its missiles. The yield of Soviet missiles ranges from 1 to 20 megatons.[23] Any of these warheads is powerful enough to destroy a city. Thus a coordinated nuclear attack on a nation's major urban and industrial centers would be catastrophic, reducing everything to rubble and leaving the population dead or injured and with little hope of help. Most hospitals, doctors, nurses, drugs, and blood plasma would be destroyed; so would the machinery for the processing and refrigeration of food and purification of water. There would be no transportation left to take survivors out of the smoldering ruins and into the countryside; most, if not all, of the fuel would also have burned up. Estimates of those killed in such a coordinated strike on a modern industrial nation range from 30 to 90 per cent of the population, depending upon the yield, the heights of the explosions, weather conditions, and preparations made to cope with the aftermath of such an attack. It has, for instance, been estimated that a Soviet attack employing 260 H-bombs with a yield of 1,500 megatons against 224 American strategic targets would in the first day result in a minimum of 50 million dead and another 20 million injured. The estimate of those killed in a Soviet 20,000-megaton attack is 95 per cent of the country's population.[24] This capacity to destroy the opponent's society is termed "assured destruction."

To be sure, it has been suggested that such devastation need not occur if both sides avoided striking at cities. A counterforce strategy—as opposed to a countereconomy strategy—would spare cities; the strategic forces of both sides would strike only at each other. Warfare would thus again be conducted in accordance with the classic military rules. The destruction of the opponent's military forces would once more become

<hr />

[23] *Ibid.*, p. 77.

[24] Harrison Scott Brown and James Real, *Community of Fear* (Santa Barbara, Calif.: Center for the Study of Democratic Institutions, 1960), pp. 20–23.

the aim of the war. As Secretary of Defense McNamara explained in 1962:

> The United States has come to the conclusion that, to the extent feasible, basic military strategy in a possible general nuclear war should be approached in much the same way that more conventional military operations have been regarded in the past. That is to say, principal military objectives, in the event of a nuclear war stemming from a major attack on the alliance, should be the destruction of the enemy's military forces, not of his civilian population.
>
> The very strength and nature of the alliance forces make it possible for us to retain even in the face of a massive surprise attack, sufficient reserve striking power to destroy an enemy society if driven to it. In other words, we are giving a possible opponent the strongest imaginable incentive to refrain from striking our own cities.[25]

A no-city strategy would in this manner save civilization from inflicting mortal wounds upon itself. Indeed, the provision of shelters to protect civilians from fallout could minimize the deaths resulting from an attack on air bases and missile pads—perhaps to the level of 3 to 5 million. At the same time, such a strategy would allow the side that succeeded in eliminating most of the other side's strategic forces to "prevail" in the war (rather oddly, advocates of counterforce strategy rarely use the word "win"). The loser might still possess some bombers or missiles. But he would surrender rather than dare to retaliate against his opponent's cities. The logic is clear. Side A would have utilized only part of its striking power to destroy the heart of B's forces. After delivering its blow, A would tell B that if it used the remnants of its forces in a mission against A's cities, A would use the rest of its bombers and missiles to wipe out B's cities. B would then have no choice but to surrender. B is already defeated because it has lost almost all of its striking forces. It cannot destroy A's remaining forces in a retaliatory blow; thus, to avenge itself against a few of A's cities would be to commit suicide. It is far more sensible for B to surrender and save its population from virtual extinction than to seal its death warrant in a futile attempt at vengeance.

But despite all these persuasive arguments, a counterforce strategy does not actually seem to be a feasible policy. Deterrence depends for its effectiveness upon its ability to threaten the opponent with massive devastation and death. A strategy that spares cities and thereby minimizes casualties may also perhaps reduce its deterrent value. Furthermore, a counterforce strategy is basically a first-strike strategy. The purpose is to hit the enemy's forces before he launches them to destroy your own. Consequently, in each political crisis, both sides would constantly be tempted to strike pre-emptively, particularly since the penalty

[25] Robert S. McNamara, "Defense Arrangements of the North Atlantic Community," *Department of State Bulletin*, July 9, 1962, pp. 64–69. See also William W. Kaufmann, *The McNamara Strategy*.

for initiating hostilities is purportedly no longer fatal. The possibility of an outbreak of war thereby increases. But the validity of counterforce strategy is even further undermined by the fact that it would not necessarily spare cities. For instance, if the Soviets limited their attacks to SAC bases, they would in all probability also hit nearby cities (e.g., Savannah, Georgia); since SAC, in a crisis, would also seek to reduce the possibility of a successful surprise attack by dispersing its bombers to civilian airports, the cities served by these airports would suffer, too. If the Soviets sought to hit missiles, they would have no choice but to eliminate Tucson, Arizona, which is ringed by missiles. If they attempted to hit Polaris submarines in their bases, Charleston, South Carolina, would be devastated. SAC headquarters at Omaha, Nebraska, and the North American Defense Command headquarters at Colorado Springs, Colorado, are also obvious targets.

In any case, even if most cities were not hit, they would still remain unprotected against the fallout resulting from Soviet attacks on military targets. The very basic requirement for a counterforce strategy—enough public shelters to protect America's urban and suburban population—does not exist. Finally, technological change is increasingly outmoding any possible counterforce strategy. Even if the United States were able to destroy all Soviet bombers and stationary missiles, it would not be able to hit Soviet submarines. As both sides rely more and more on hardened and mobile underwater missiles, or even missiles on surface vessels, the possibility of knowing the location of an opponent's striking forces will be drastically diminished. Missiles can be zeroed in on stationary targets; they cannot find moving targets whose whereabouts are unknown. Thus, in the long run, a counterforce strategy is not an answer to the nuclear dilemma. Secretary McNamara has himself testified that the United States "could not have any realistic prospect of being able to destroy the major part of a Soviet submarine missile force in one quick first strike. Neither could we count, with any reasonable degree of assurance, on destroying all or almost all of the Soviet's hardened missile sites, even if we were to double or triple our forces." A resulting nuclear exchange in which the United States would also be protected by bomber and missile defenses and civil-defense measures would "even under the most favorable circumstances to us . . . do enormous damage to both sides." Fatalities would run "into tens of millions."[26] The Defense Department estimated in 1965 that fatalities would be 129 million Americans if they were sheltered—and 149 million if they were unprotected. Under these circumstances, a counterforce strategy—now renamed a "damage-limiting" strategy since it could not destroy all of Russia's nuclear striking forces—was hardly an answer to the nuclear dilemma.

[26] See McNamara's statement in *The New York Times*, January 28, 1964.

This does not mean that bombers and missiles would not be targets in a nuclear war. But it does mean that cities may not be spared from attack. The Soviet superbombs are, in fact, countercity rather than counterforce weapons. In any case, a purportedly counterforce exchange that could kill 300 million or more Americans, Europeans, and Russians would seem to differ little from a countereconomy strategy. Indeed, it was precisely a threat of such magnitude that was supposed to be the very basis of deterrence. Each superpower was to hold his opponent's population hostage to ensure his good behavior. It was the threat of having his entire population virtually wiped out and his cities laid waste that was to restrain him from launching an attack.

If cities should be targets of an attack, the psychological impact upon the survivors rather than the vast material destruction would be the crucial consequence. The elimination of a nation's larger cities, the deaths of tens of millions, the wrecking of its industries, communication, and transportation systems—all would be bound to undermine the self-confidence of those who remained alive. A nation in ruins is not likely to retain its *élan vital* or entertain any optimistic expectations. It has taken Europe, and especially France, over forty years to recover from the psychological wounds of World War I and the loss of its younger generation on the bloody battlefields. Moreover, the European nations received American economic aid on a vast scale after World War II to help rebuild their ravaged societies. Yet their wounds and losses were minor compared with those a nation would suffer during a nuclear attack. For the result would be not only the destruction of cities but the disorganization of social life:

Any society operates through confidence in an orderly succession of events, either natural or social. A catastrophe is an interruption in what has come to be considered natural. The panic it often produces is the reflection of an inability to react to an unexpected situation and attempt to flee as rapidly as possible into a familiar and, therefore, predictable environment. If a familiar environment remains, some confidence can be restored. Most natural catastrophes can be dealt with, because they affect only a very small geographic area or a very small proportion of the population. The remainder of the society can utilize its machinery or cooperative effort to come to the assistance of the stricken area. Indeed, such action tends to reinforce the cohesiveness of a society, because it becomes a symbol of its value and efficiency. The essence of the catastrophe produced by an all-out thermonuclear war, however, is the depth of the dislocation it produces and the consequent impossibility of escaping into familiar relationships. When all relationships, or even most relationships, have to be reconstituted, society as we know it today will have been fundamentally transformed.[27]

[27] Henry A. Kissinger, *Nuclear Weapons and Foreign Policy*, p. 79.

One must logically conclude that modern nuclear warfare is irrational. Nuclear technology has so vastly augmented the scope of violence and destruction that total war can destroy the very nation that wages it. A nation may possess large nuclear forces with which to defend itself, but it is at the same time very vulnerable. It is thus both powerful and prone to destruction. In the more familiar analogy of the "father" of the atom bomb, Robert Oppenheimer, nations possessing nuclear weapons live like scorpions in a bottle. Total nuclear war, in short, can know no victors; all the contestants must be losers.

Escapes from Nuclear Reality:
Complete Disarmament and World Government

How could the ultimate disaster of nuclear war be avoided? This was the central question posed by the new technology in the early years of the Cold War. Two things seemed certain to all too many people: one, that the political conflict would be accompanied by an arms race; and two, that at some point, this arms race would erupt into a nuclear war. Such wars could perhaps be tolerated in pre-nuclear times when weapons, destructive as they were, at least were not capable of destroying entire societies. But warring nations in the nuclear era could be sure that they themselves would be devoured in the hellfire of the nuclear flames they had lit. Would it not therefore be safer for all nations to disarm? If nations maintained their arms, was war not inevitable sooner or later? Had not all arms races sparked wars? The answer seemed as obvious as did disarmament as a solution. Armaments were no longer a means of protecting nations, and only disarmament could guarantee national security. An arms race was bound to produce a war; disarmament was therefore the prerequisite for the preservation of peace. Failure to disarm would leave the nuclear powers with no recourse but to fight. The goal had to be total disarmament—nothing less.

Actually, though, it can be seen that complete and general disarmament is not the answer to the dilemma of nuclear weapons in a world of political conflict. In the first place, there can be no such thing as *total* disarmament. But this is more than merely a semantic problem. In assessing a nation's strength and capacity to wage war, one must take into account—along with the number of men under arms and the weapons they possess—geographic position, population, natural resources, productive capacity, and scientific ability, all of which are equally important. Moreover, no disarmament treaty could eradicate man's knowledge of nuclear physics and his ability to reconstruct an atom or hydrogen bomb if needed. Military power is only one aspect of a nation's over-all strength, and it cannot be artificially eliminated. Even total disarmament would leave a nation with a "war potential" that could be mobilized *after* a declaration of war rather than, as formerly, before the outbreak of hostilities. International quarrels would not be discontinued by the abolition of armaments.

The belief that disarmament is the solution to the nuclear dilemma is based on the assumption that arms races cause wars: A nation, in order to protect itself, increases its military strength; another nation, seeing this, builds up its military power to guard against a possible attack; the ensuing arms race develops its own momentum and creates a war psychology; at a favorable moment, therefore, when one country feels that it is stronger than the other—or believes that the other side is beginning to pull ahead—it will attack. The interactions among the contestants is thus seen to produce an arms spiral which, when it reaches a critical point, automatically precipitates hostilities. But why, then, have some arms races ended in war and others not? The answer is that to attribute wars to arms is to confuse cause and effect. An arms race does not obey a logic of its own. It cannot be seen as an autonomous process divorced from the political context in which it occurs. Capabilities cannot be artificially separated from intentions. History does not move along predetermined paths on which men tread like puppets. An arms race reflects political tensions between nations; it does not cause these tensions. Armaments are needed by states to protect what they consider to be their interests. Nations do not fight because they possess arms. Rather, they possess arms because they believe it might some day be necessary to fight. Military power serves the political ends of the state.[28]

Indeed, when nations involved in political quarrels fail to arm themselves, they only invite aggression. World War II was not caused by the presence of armaments. Exactly the opposite: it was the lack of Western arms that tempted Hitler. If France and Britain had possessed sufficient military power, Nazi Germany might have been deterred. While it is true that when power confronts power, there may be danger, it is certain that when power meets weakness, aggression is invited. It is all too easy to point to conflicts and attribute them falsely to arms races. It is much more difficult to point to wars that were prevented because nations guarded themselves.

In any case, since arms are a symptom of interstate political conflict, it is an illusion to expect nations to disarm. The prerequisite for disarmament would be political agreement on the issues separating the nations involved in the arms race.[29] How can nations be expected to agree to the elimination or reduction of the instruments with which they seek to pro-

[28] See Samuel P. Huntington, "Arms Races: Prerequisites and Results," in Carl J. Friedrich and Seymour E. Harris (eds.), *Public Policy*, pp. 41–86; Hedley Bull, *The Control of the Arms Race*, pp. 6–12.
[29] Merze Tate, in *The United States and Armaments*, makes this point very well in analyzing the only reasonably successful disarmament agreement, the Washington Naval Conference of 1921–22.

tect themselves or gain their ends? If nations cannot settle their political differences, they cannot end the arms race. If these differences could have been resolved, the arms race would never have started. But in the absence of political agreement, the distrust, suspicion, and fear among states, which precipitated the arms race, are bound to color their disarmament proposals. If a nation is already stronger than its opponent, it will want to preserve and even enhance this superiority, and its disarmament plans will contain this built-in bias. If a nation is weaker, it will want to catch up with and, if possible, surpass its opponent, and its disarmament proposals will reflect these objectives. Disarmament negotiations in these circumstances become merely another form of the arms race itself, the aim of each nation being an increase in its relative power position.

It could not be otherwise. In the state system, each nation must defend itself in case of attack. The possibility of war being inherent in the conflict of national wills, each state must pay attention to its armed strength. As Salvador de Madariaga has remarked: "All disarmament conferences are bound to degenerate into armament conferences. In all of them discussion is based on the assumption of war, and they all reveal the inevitable conflict between the ardent endeavors of the delegations present, each of which has for its main aim to secure the highest possible increase of its relative armaments in a general reduction of absolute forces, if such a reduction there must be."[30] A parable of a disarmament conference held by animals illustrates this point. The animals, according to the story, having decided to disarm, convene in order to discuss the matter. The eagle, looking at the bull, suggests that all horns be razed. The bull, looking at the tiger, says that all claws should be cut short. The tiger, looking at the elephant, is of the opinion that tusks should be either pulled out or shortened. The elephant, looking at the eagle, thinks that all wings should be clipped. Whereupon the bear, with a circular glance at all his brethren, says in a tone of sweet reasonableness: "Comrades, why all these halfway measures? Let us abolish everything—everything but a fraternal, all-embracing hug."

If the very nature of the state system is the principal obstacle to disarmament, the nature of the Soviet system provides another insuperable obstacle. The technological revolution in weapons has made it mandatory that any disarmament accord be accompanied by the establishment of international controls. Nuclear fuel intended for peaceful purposes could also be employed for the manufacture of nuclear bombs. If states remained in control of their own atomic-energy production for what they claimed were nonmilitary ends, it would be impossible to detect and prevent such diversions of atomic fuel for military purposes. No disarma-

---

[30] Salvador de Madariaga, *Disarmament*, pp. 62–63. For an account of the disarmament negotiations as part of the postwar arms race, see John W. Spanier and Joseph L. Nogee, *The Politics of Disarmament*.

ment agreement involving the abolition of nuclear weapons could rest on promises alone; compliance would have to be assured. In pre–World War II days, such extensive controls were not necessary because no armaments were able to inflict an initial blow that could be fatal to a nation's existence. Mobilization took place largely after the commencement of hostilities. If it began earlier, other nations would notice since it was impossible to disguise such movement. They could then take remedial action and try to maintain a balance of strength.

The difference today is that a few H-bombs could be decisive. Consequently, a treaty outlawing nuclear warfare, but with no provisions for international controls, would not suffice because it would fail to eliminate the temptation to an aggressor to build a number of bombs. And this temptation would be extremely strong because a successful evasion could mean the acquisition of a monopoly of nuclear bombs and could possibly result in world domination. In order to remove this temptation, the United States has insisted that controls be built into any disarmament agreement to which we are a party. For the United States, therefore, control is a substitute for trust in Soviet promises to honor a disarmament accord.

But the Soviet Union opposes any inspection of her territory. Inspection is condemned as a means for the West to pierce the Iron Curtain and gather industrial and military information. In a sense, this charge of "espionage" is quite correct. Obviously, inspectors can "control" a disarmament agreement—ensuring against possible violation and assuring proper implementation—only while simultaneously "mapping" a nation by gathering intelligence about the strength and location of its military forces and keeping a vigilant eye on its factories and transportation and communication systems. And undoubtedly, the "inspectors could scarcely fulfil their functions without undermining the whole character of Soviet society. Though the business of inspection concerns the examination of material objects, this is not possible without interference in social and political arrangements. Unlimited rights of access, the immunity of citizens volunteering information from police control, their duty not to withhold information, appear to undermine the secrecy endemic in Soviet society and to set the authority of the inspectorate above that of the government."[31]

Even more fundamental is the Soviet opposition to inspection that stems from the Communist assumption that the Communist and capitalist systems are irreconcilably opposed to each other.[32] The basic social and economic conflict is not between nations, but between classes. More

---

[31] Hedley Bull, *op. cit.*, p. 101.

[32] A good analysis of the manner in which Soviet hostility to capitalism influences her opposition to any international controls or inspection may be found in Joseph L. Nogee, *Soviet Policy Toward the International Control of Atomic Energy.*

specifically, the conflict is between Western states controlled by the bourgeoisie and Communist states controlled by the "vanguard" of the proletariat (as the Communist Party styles itself). Westerners therefore could hardly be permitted to inspect the Soviet Union. The Soviet leaders do not question the moral character or personal integrity of Western representatives who would be assigned to such inspection duties. But they do question whether they could rely upon the fairness of men whose education and values have been conditioned by a hostile political system. For these men would have to render daily decisions that would involve above all their political judgments. Reflecting their capitalistic upbringing, these decisions would have to be anti-Communist. There is not one world, but two—the Soviet world and the non-Soviet world—and only angels could be "independent" or politically neutral between them. Statesmen, on the other hand, reflect the points of view of the classes to which they belong, and can hardly be expected to be "above politics." Western inspectors, in short, are inherently anti-Soviet; they are "spies" *by definition*. Moreover, even inspectors from neutral or nonaligned nations are not, from the Communist point of view, unbiased and objective. There simply are no "neutral" men. One is either Communist or anti-Communist. In these circumstances, inspection cannot be substituted for trust. For it is precisely this missing trust that leads the West to insist on controls; and it is the same distrust that compels the Soviet leaders to reject any controls.

This fundamental Communist hostility to non-Communist systems not only blocks any inspection, but also minimizes the possibility that any political agreements will be followed by any large-scale disarmament. The traditional view is that if the political tensions that precipitated the arms race were resolved, the arms race would subside. But this would assume a situation in which states at least did not consider their very existence at stake:

> Is there any basis for confidence that the prospects for disarmament will improve with the resolution of specific controversies? Are the specific points of conflict around the globe where American and Soviet power contend the real source of the tension that has led to the arms race? Or put differently, if all the particular political crises of major importance were resolved, would the Soviet-American rivalry end?
>
> If Russia were a typical imperialist power, one might confidently give an affirmative answer. For example, the disputes of the colonial powers before World War I involved limited objectives, and national survival was seldom at stake. But the situation is quite different today. The differences between Russia and the United States are not causes but manifestations of a deeper rivalry. Neither side needs nor wants for its own use any real estate now in issue. Neither side is primarily interested in securing economic advantages outside its borders at the expense of the other. Com-

mercial rivalry is not a major source of contention. What divides the two super-powers is the very question of coexistence: Can a dynamic state with a revolutionary ideology and apparently unlimited ambition live side by side with an equally powerful state that resists its encroachments? The specific issues dividing the Communist and non-Communist world in 1960 are not the same as in 1946. Iran, Greece, Korea, and Indochina are quiescent. Berlin and Formosa have taken their place. As Mao Tse-tung describes it, Communist strategy is one of "protracted war." The pressure points change, but the conflict continues. If the Chinese leader has accurately described the character of the struggle between the two worlds, then it is clear that the liquidation of particular controversies is not an occasion for disarming.[33]

This conclusion, based on the nature of the state system and the revolutionary nature of the Soviet regime, has been challenged by a rather ingenious scheme known as "graduated reciprocation in tension reduction" (GRIT). Advocates of GRIT recognize that, in the state system, contestants find it impossible to end an arms race because they bring to the negotiating table the distrust, suspicion, and fears they have acquired as opponents. As antagonists, each has come to believe that it represents wisdom, virtue, and morality, and that the other side is not only the embodiment of evil but seeks its destruction. Thus, the United States views the Soviet Union as a Communist dictatorship that exploits its masses at home and is bent on a global crusade for Communism. The Soviet Union is equally convinced that the United States is a dictatorship of the bourgeoisie that has enslaved its proletarian majority at home and seeks to export capitalism abroad by force. We, of course, know how false this image of the United States is. At the same time, the Soviets would contend that they do not exploit their masses, that the austerity of the period of intensive industrialization is being replaced by increasing attention to the welfare of Soviet citizens, and that in international politics, they seek only to be left alone to complete their industrial revolution; their large armies and powerful rockets are needed only because of the threat of an American attack (paralleling the U.S. claim that our military forces are needed only to deter a Soviet attack).

In short, according to the GRIT proponents, each side has a false image of the other, and it is on the basis of these distorted, "bogey-man" views that both act belligerently, thereby bringing the world to the precipice of utter destruction—and for no "sane" reason! As Erich Fromm has said, each side views the other "pathologically"—in terms of paranoia, projection, fanaticism, and Orwellian "double-think." This "Cold War mentality" presents a formidable impediment to a resolution of the arms race.

It is claimed that the only way of changing these "insane" attitudes

[33] Richard J. Barnet, *Who Wants Disarmament?*, pp. 53–54.

and reversing the "arms spiral" before it detonates into a cataclysmic holocaust is through "graduated reciprocation in tension reduction." Only GRIT, says its creator, psychologist Charles Osgood, can restore to each side a sense of perspective, a realization that neither side is all good or all bad, and thereby gradually replace pathological with "sane" thinking:

> Perhaps the most general characterization of my proposal would be that it asks for a deliberate "peace offensive" designed to induce reciprocation by an enemy. It is an offensive in deeds rather than words, but the deeds are carefully graduated in magnitude of risk so as to maintain tolerable levels of dignity and security. . . . The goal is reversal of the tensions/arms-race spiral and creation of an atmosphere in which steps toward a more permanent solution of the problem of survival in the nuclear age can be taken.[34]

Such a "peace offensive" would require the United States to take a number of minor, unilateral steps of such a nature that they would be perceived by the Soviet Union as reducing the external threat to its security. Each step, moreover, is to be accompanied by an invitation for Soviet reciprocation. If the first step is not answered by reciprocal action but is denounced instead as propaganda or a "trick," the next steps would deny this and assure the Soviets that the United States is sincere in seeking the reduction of tensions and preserving the peace. This would lessen Soviet suspicions of American intentions and induce Soviet reciprocation. In her turn, the United States could now respond with a more important unilateral step in order to accelerate the downward spiral to disarmament and the concurrent upward spiral to the establishment of mutual confidence and good will.

GRIT—which might more simply be called a minus tit-for-tat system—is of course correct in one respect: that the mutual distrust, fear, and suspicion existing between the Soviet Union and the United States does hamper Soviet-American negotiations. Its error lies in the assumption that these attitudes, while a product of the conflict inherent in the state system, are the symptoms of a conflict that has no "real" causes. Not all individuals who feel persecuted are, after all, necessarily paranoids. Some of them may indeed be persecuted. There is little reason to believe that American policy-makers have since World War II had a seriously distorted view of Soviet society and behavior. They have received constant reminders from the Soviet leaders themselves that this is the era of the West's decline. And Soviet actions have constantly sought to accelerate this decline and move history along its predetermined path to the "world socialist system." No doubt the Soviet leaders do harbor a false image of the Western world. But the point is that they consider theirs to be the

[34] Charles E. Osgood, "Reciprocal Initiative," in James Roosevelt (ed.), *The Liberal Papers*, p. 195.

correct view of capitalism, and it is upon this perception that they act. One cannot therefore simply dismiss Communist ideology as meaningless and state that the Soviet Union as a "have" power is now committed only to a conservative *status quo* policy. Nor can one accept the Soviet leaders' characterization of themselves as the apostles of "peaceful coexistence" at face value; neither Lenin nor Stalin were advocates of all-out military attacks upon the West. Communists, unlike Nazis, have never worshiped force and gloried in its use; ideological revolutionaries they have been, but they have also always been military conservatives.[35] Disarmament is no doubt a desirable goal, but its desirability should not obscure the nature of Soviet totalitarianism and Soviet objectives.[36] Certainly it is unpleasant to acknowledge that disarmament may be impossible, since this means that the world will continue to "live dangerously." On the other hand, to interpret the nature of the Soviet political system so that disarmament seems an attainable goal is poor logic and dangerous politics.

American policy toward Russia during World War II proved this danger rather conclusively. The desire to get along with the Soviet Union in the postwar period was taken for granted. How then could continued Soviet suspicions of the United States and Britain be explained? American leaders sought to do so by assessing Soviet foreign policy not in terms of the internal dynamics of the regime and its enmity toward all non-Communist nations, but in terms of Russian reactions to Western policies. The Soviet attitude was thus viewed against a Western pattern of prewar anti-Soviet acts: the Allied intervention in Russia at the end of World War I for the alleged purpose of overthrowing the Soviet regime and, after the failure of that attempt, the establishment by France of the *cordon sanitaire* in Eastern Europe to keep the Soviet virus from infecting the healthy European body politic; the West's appeasement of Hitler, which, by satisfying the Nazi dictator's appetite on the Western front, permitted him to turn eastward to realize his ambitions in Eastern Europe; and particularly, the Munich agreement of 1938, which, by destroying Czechoslovakia, in effect invited Hitler to march toward Russia via the Polish gateway. Thus Western efforts to ostracize the Soviet Union, and the alleged attempts to turn Hitler from the West and toward Russia, were considered the primary causes of Soviet hostility.

Western demonstrations of peaceful intentions were therefore thought to be necessary to dissolve Soviet distrust. Western actions must prove the falsity of the Soviet image of the West and demonstrate that the West harbored no aggressive aims. Thus reassured, the Soviets would then be freed of their sense of insecurity and their fear, and mutual good

---

[35] See below for an elaboration of this theme, pp. 145–48.

[36] For a discussion of the meaning of post-Stalin changes within the Soviet Union, see Ch. IX.

will and tolerance would be able to resolve all differences of national interest. In the interests of gaining a lasting peace, nothing was done to arouse Soviet fears and suspicions of the West's intentions—or, to the extent that they already existed, to reinforce these feelings. Thus, during the last months of the war in Europe, when signs of Soviet hostility were increasing, no counteractions were taken to establish an effective balance of power on the Continent.[37] American forces were not sent to capture Berlin. They were withdrawn from Czechoslovakia before they could enter Prague; and their withdrawal was not used as a bargaining tool to urge the Soviet Union to uphold her Yalta pledge to hold free elections in Eastern Europe. Above all, American forces were quickly transferred to the Pacific after V-E Day—before the Yalta settlement on Europe had been implemented by the Soviets—and the United States thereby lost its principal instrument to exert pressure upon the Soviet Union.

An additional explanation for Soviet wartime behavior was to minimize any possible danger of the Soviet Union's expansionist activities during the late stages of the war. It would, after all, take her ten to twenty years to reconstruct the vast damage she had suffered,[38] and her attention and energies would thus be absorbed internally. Her imposition of pro-Soviet governments in Eastern Europe only gave evidence of traditional Russian security interests in that area. Stalin—affectionately known as Uncle Joe in the United States during the war—was acting as any pre-Revolutionary Czar would have. Indeed, his dissolution of the Comintern and his view of the war as the "Great Fatherland War" were merely two of several indications that Stalin and the other Soviet leaders were Russian nationalists rather than Soviet revolutionaries. Ideology no longer mattered. Stalin was obviously responding to American tension-reducing steps, and any false image he might have harbored of an aggressive capitalist West was clearly being dissolved in a spirit of growing mutual amity and trust.

The failure of this "GRIT approach" to the Soviet Union during the war should not have been surprising. For whatever Americans and their leaders hoped—and have continued to hope—would be the results of attempts to eliminate Soviet suspicions of Western intentions, the real issue is how the Kremlin judges these attempts. The Soviet leaders believe in the innate hostility of the capitalist world; their relationship with it is one of war. Concessions offered by the capitalists are usually dismissed either as tricks designed to lull the Soviet Union into relaxing its vigilance while the enemy prepares to "put something over" on them, or as concessions they were compelled to make anyway because the "bal-

[37] Churchill, *op. cit.*, pp. 463–501, and see pp. 572–74 for Churchill's famous Iron Curtain telegram to President Truman, May 12, 1945; see also Feis, *op. cit.*, pp. 600–12, 633–38.
[38] Henry A. Kissinger, *The Necessity for Choice*, pp. 196–99.

ance of forces" left them no choice—in which case, they are hardly concessions. Conversely, why should the Communists grant concessions to gain the nonexisting good will of an enemy who seeks their destruction as they seek his total defeat? Such concessions could only weaken the Soviet Union's international position. In fact, no matter what the West does, the Soviets will only be confirmed in their viewpoint. If the West is tough, it only "proves" that the West is hostile; if the West holds out the "olive branch," it is only because the West seeks to deceive the Soviet Union or is weak and fearful. Thus Western proposals must be either resisted or exploited for greater gains. The assumption of Western enmity is, however, a constant. Western acts only reaffirm this fundamental Communist assumption, and no Western policies will change it. All efforts to overcome the Soviet Union's suspicion of the West have ended in failure precisely because to the Soviet leaders it has never been the behavior of Western states but the very nature of their governments —and the economic and social systems these governments represented— which has been decisive. Communist hostility has always been preconceived and ideological.

It seems clear that, in these circumstances, no tension-reducing steps will change the Communist viewpoint that non-Communist states do not have the right to exist. Therefore, GRIT can hardly be relied upon to lead the two superpowers into an era of good will and mutual trust. Nor do the Soviet-American agreements of the early 1960's—the limited test-ban treaty, the establishment of the "hot line" between Moscow and Washington, and the agreement in principle to ban nuclear weapons in space, as well as the Soviet and American arms budget reductions of 1964–65, the American cutback in nuclear-material production, and the Soviet promise to match these cutbacks—contradict this conclusion. Neither Washington nor Moscow expected these agreements to produce large-scale disarmament. What both did expect was to reduce the possibilities of nuclear war by slowing down the proliferation of nuclear weapons and minimizing the opportunities for accidental warfare, as well as barring the extension of the arms race—for the time being, at least— into outer space.[39] There were other motivations, too. America's nuclear stockpile, for example, was so huge by 1964 that it was rated as possessing an "overkill" capacity—that is, a capacity to nuclearize the Soviet Union several times over, even though once would be quite sufficient. The United States could therefore easily afford to cut back its annual production by 40 per cent without affecting its ability to destroy its op-

---

[39] Still—just to be on the safe side—the United States went ahead and developed two anti-satellite systems and proceeded to construct a two-man orbiting laboratory to help determine the military usefulness of space. (*The New York Times,* September 18, 1964, and August 26, 1965.)

ponents in an all-out nuclear war. Similarly, it could reduce military budgets because the strategic and limited-war arms buildup of the preceding years had ended. Further increases in strategic delivery systems promised little added military advantage; and the limited-war forces had been brought up to what was considered necessary strength.[40] Consequently, President Johnson's nuclear cutbacks and budget reductions were shrewd propaganda moves, as well as good economy, for the United States. Both sides were, in fact, interested in saving some of the enormous funds spent each year on the arms race. If the tax burden was high for the relatively well-off American taxpayer, the armaments burden was even higher for the smaller Soviet economy. If the Soviet Union already possessed the strength to deter an American attack, the Soviet leaders may have asked themselves, why spend billions of rubles annually to test and produce new weapons? Why not invest some of these funds in agriculture or in consumer-goods industries? The CIA estimated a sharp drop in the average annual increase of the Soviet gross national product during 1962–63 to approximately 2.5 per cent. Under the circumstances, a letup in the arms race was clearly desirable for the Soviets. Finally, the limited test ban—signed *after* each side had concluded a set of tests —was testimony not only to the American and Russian desire to relax tensions, but also to their desire to retain dominance within their respective alliances by preserving their nuclear monopoly (in the American case, a virtual monopoly since Britain too possessed a small nuclear force). Each power also expected to retain certain military advantages: The United States believed it had acquired superiority in the quantity, quality, and variety of strategic and tactical nuclear weapons. The Soviets, on the other hand, had tested their "superbomb" of 58 megatons, and may have felt they were ahead in building and testing bombs of such an enormous yield.[41]

These various agreements and moves therefore hardly add up to the replacement of the spiral of mutual fear with a spiral of increasing trust that will render disarmament feasible. As the Soviets have themselves stated, disarmament will probably have to await the demise of capitalism and a global Communist victory. "Only after the proletariat has disarmed the bourgeois," Lenin said long ago, "can it . . . scrap arms of all kinds. The proletariat will doubtless do this, but only after disarming

[40] Roswell L. Gilpatric, "Our Defense Needs," *Foreign Affairs*, April, 1964, pp. 370–71.

[41] The Soviets may also have thought they knew more about anti-missile missile techniques of neutralizing the fissionable material in an incoming warhead. And they may have had more data on the effects of a bomb's blast and radioactivity in blacking out the radar communication systems and electrical connections controlling missile-launching facilities. (See Hanson W. Baldwin, *The New York Times*, July 26 and August 13, 1963.)

the bourgeoisie and no earlier."[42] Yet, significantly, GRIT advocates prefer to minimize the political obstacles to disarmament, sometimes even ignoring their existence entirely—reflecting the attitude that there *is* a solution to the arms race, and that its implementation is barred only by "politics" and "politicians" (be they Presidents, diplomats, or generals). The overriding issue, in short, is the objective: disarmament, the absolute prerequisite for survival; otherwise, to use another shorthand term of the strategists, DOE (death of earth) is a certainty. Since the problem of the arms race *must* be resolved, GRIT proponents say, the problem has to be resolvable. To admit that it might not be possible to disarm would be "too negative" or "too pessimistic," and would discourage further efforts to seek agreements and encourage instead a complacency that could only end in disaster. Obstacles blocking the way to disarmament are not recognized as insurmountable, but only as incentives to be overcome.[43] If the problem of nuclear fission was solvable, why couldn't human ingenuity—applied to the abolition of weapons rather than the production of ever more destructive ones—solve the problem of disarmament? Why should man not apply his reason for once to constructive rather than destructive purposes? All that is really required, according to the spokesmen for GRIT, is a change in attitude: the diplomats must become "peace seekers" and "turn toward peace." If they genuinely desire to end the Cold War and to achieve a "disarmed world under the rule of law," they can by "creative methods"—to be revealed through "peace research"—attain their objective.[44]

Since disarmament is theoretically feasible, GRIT advocates conclude that it is also technically possible. Disarmament may not be the usual way to resolve conflicts, and "politicians" may reject the idea outright as "impractical and impossible," but the uniqueness of our times demands bold solutions. The search for disarmament is therefore not an idealistic but a highly realistic policy; the admonition to "Love thy neighbor" becomes "Love thy neighbor if you love yourself."[45] However impossible disarmament may have been in the past, there is no alternative to it today. No great power can afford *not* to love its neighbor if it values its own life. The world cannot destroy itself because the leaders of these

[42] Quoted in Barnet, *op. cit.*, p. 6. See also Robert A. Levine, "Unilateral Initiative: A Cynic's View," *Bulletin of Atomic Scientists*, January, 1963, pp. 22–24; he stresses that it is those who have a healthy distrust of the Kremlin—and not the advocates of GRIT, who should judge the Kremlin's initiatives or reciprocal moves.

[43] See, for example, Philip Noel-Baker, *The Arms Race*, pp. 8–11.

[44] See Charles E. Osgood, *An Alternative to War or Surrender*; Erich Fromm, *May Man Prevail?*; Amitai Etzioni, *The Hard Way to Peace*; and John W. Burton, *Peace Theory* (New York: Alfred A. Knopf, 1962).

[45] John H. Herz, *Inernational Politics in the Atomic Age*, p. 333. For an interesting examination of some nuclear scientists who share the opinion that disarmament is technically feasible, and therefore politically possible if only "politicians" would not interfere, see Robert Gilpin, *American Scientists and Nuclear Weapons Policy*.

powers still think in terms of "national interests" rather than the "common interests of mankind" in preserving peace. What the world needs is not more traditional diplomacy—which inevitably leads to war—but imaginative and radical solutions. Nuclear bombs make it mandatory for statesmen to change habits and ways of thinking inherited from a pre-nuclear age. If the world is not to be engulfed in nuclear flames, statesmen must be objectively concerned with the needs of humanity, regardless of their own subjective prejudices and national ideologies, which pale into insignificance beside the overwhelming central issue of survival. Implicit in this line of thinking is a clear-cut division between those who have a vested interest in the preservation of the nation-state—after all, what jobs would there be for soldiers or diplomats if the nation-state were abolished?—and "humanity." The former obviously oppose disarmament, and they cannot successfully participate in negotiations since their pattern of thought is a reflection of the state system. But the future of the world demands that statesmen think as though the state system has *already* been transcended.

Thus the argument for disarmament often spills over into an argument for world government. If disarmament is defeated by the existence of the state system, would not the abolition of that system safeguard the future existence of mankind? Governments preserve peace and maintain law and order on the domestic scene. If a government could be created that would supersede the governments of sovereign nations, could it not, like national governments in their spheres, ensure global peace once and for all?[46] Under the American Articles of Confederation, the states retained their sovereignty and continued their quarrels. But under the Constitution, the states were reduced in status to nonsovereign members of a new Federal system in which the Federal Government was supreme and applied the Federal law directly to individuals. This gave to the Federal Government the responsibility and the authority to ensure domestic tranquility. Could one not then argue, as advocates for world government do, that the American Constitutional Convention was the great rehearsal for a global convention that would transfer all nations' sovereignty to a world government whose purpose would be to ensure global peace through the establishment of the "rule of law"? These partisans seem to believe that wherever a "legal order" is established—that is, where government applies the law directly to its citizens—government can be a peace-keeping institution. What leads them to this conclusion? One analyst has answered as follows:

A clue may perhaps be found in the intimate association between the idea of world government and the fashionable theme of the world rule of law. *Law* is a key word in the vocabulary of world government. One reacts

[46] Hans J. Morgenthau, *Politics Among Nations*, p. 502; see also Emery Reves, *The Anatomy of Peace* (New York: Harper & Brothers, 1945), pp. 253–70.

against anarchy—disorder, insecurity, violence, injustice visited by the strong upon the weak. In contrast, one postulates law—the symbol of the happy opposites to those distasteful and dangerous evils. Law suggests properly constituted authority and effectively implemented control; it symbolizes the supreme will of the community, the will to maintain justice and public order. This abstract concept is all too readily transformed, by worshipful contemplation, from one of the devices by which societies seek to order internal relationships, into a symbolic key to the good society. As this transformation takes place, law becomes a magic word for those who advocate world government and those who share with them the ideological bond of dedication to the rule of law—not necessarily in the sense that they expect it to produce magical effects upon the world, but at least in the sense that it works its magic upon them. Most significantly, it leads them to forget about *politics*, to play down the role of the political process in the management of human affairs, and to imagine that somehow *law*, in all its purity, can displace the soiled devices of politics.

Inexorably, the emphasis upon law which is characteristic of advocates of world government carries with it a tendency to focus upon the relationship of individuals to government; thinking in legal terms, one visualizes the individual apprehended by the police and brought before the judge.[47]

This argument for world government suggests that peace in a society relies primarily upon the superiority of the government's power and the enforcement of the law upon the individuals. This, in fact, not only exaggerates the coercion needed to maintain law and order, but shows that world-government advocates misunderstand the function of government. Admittedly, a government's power does play a role in preserving peace. At the same time, though, this power is not the principal force for peace in democratic societies. Rather, peace results from two other factors: the compromises struck by the conflicting interests and the consensus reached on fundamental values. The government's domestic function in a pluralistic society is primarily concerned with the adjustment and accommodation of conflicting interests. It is not the application of the laws to individuals and their imprisonment if they disobey the laws that are primarily responsible for peace; it is the political negotiations and compromises required by the constantly changing internal balance of power. It is not the policeman or judge who plays the principal role in preserving peace; it is the politician:

> The tributes which are regularly paid to the "rule of law" should more realistically be paid to the "rule of politics." In a society of contending groups, law is *not* the only effective way of preventing violence, or even the most important method; instead, politics is the device which has proved most useful. The American Civil War was the result of a failure of political adjustment among sectional forces, not of a breakdown of law enforcement against individuals. . . . It would indeed be ironical if men

[47] Inis L. Claude, Jr., *Power and International Relations*, pp. 260–61.

passionately devoted to the rule of law should define their ideal pattern of order-keeping as one which is realized only, or best, in totalitarian systems. The sort of national government which champions of world government propose to emulate is best exemplified by liberal regimes which depend primarily upon processes of political adjustment for maintaining social order.[48]

In short, world government is not acceptable even as a *theoretical* answer to the problem of our time—and cannot be until a global consensus exists. Only then can the conflicts among national interests be resolved more peacefully. Only then will a world government acquire the legitimacy necessary for the obedience of its laws—laws that are the product of political rather than judicial decisions. It is precisely the absence of such a consensus today that explains the survival of sovereign states and the high expectation of violence.

In the final analysis, both total disarmament and world government have much in common. Both assume that the alternative to either "common sense" solution is for the world to perish in nuclear flames. Since the conventional balance-of-power politics has "never" been able to preserve peace, nuclear warfare is a certainty sooner or later. Radically new methods to prevent such a holocaust must therefore be found and tried. The abolition of all weapons or the transformation of the state system may involve risks, but nuclear warfare is an unthinkable disaster. And no "sane" man hesitates between a risk and a certainty. It's a simple "either-or" problem, and the solution is just as simple. All men have to do is to realize the peril of their existence, the stark alternatives, and the urgency of implementing the remedy.

Unfortunately, though, the fact that a goal seems necessary does not render it attainable. The search for total security—whether for nations or individuals—is bound to be frustrating precisely because it cannot be achieved. Such a state of bliss may be desirable, but it is also an illusion. Few individuals expect to eliminate the problems and risks of their own lives. They accept them, however reluctantly, and learn to cope with them by isolating, moderating, conciliating, and containing them as much as possible. Yet many people expect to eliminate all insecurities and risks from international life. Their answers for the problems of national existence are all-encompassing, complete solutions for all problems for all time: e.g., total disarmament or world government.

Neither "solution" is, in fact, the quick and easy remedy that each claims to be. For each avoids the real problem: i.e., how to resolve conflicts without sparking a nuclear war. One cannot answer this by refusing to "think about the unthinkable." To avoid confronting reality by escaping into a dream world of utopian solutions is merely to evade respon-

[48] *Ibid.*, pp. 265, 268.

sibility. To think about nuclear strategy is not to invite a nuclear war or to favor one (and it is certainly not to be less moral or concerned for the survival of one's fellow men). If one buys automobile insurance, this hardly indicates that one wants to have an accident; nor is the captain who has lifeboats on his ship necessarily a reckless navigator. In both instances, though, the possibility of an accident has been confronted; naturally, having safeguarded oneself, one still hopes that an accident will be avoidable, particularly if one drives or navigates with due caution and does not transgress the rules of the road or sea. "Thinking about the unthinkable" is thus clearly seen as the beginning of wisdom and sanity because it leads one to devise the necessary prophylactic or deterrent measures.[49]

The Stabilization of Mutual Deterrence

In the absence of total disarmament or world government, the security and independence of nations remain dependent on the balance of power. Moreover, the military component of national power will remain vital to this balance. Yet, nuclear technology has fundamentally changed the manner in which this military strength can be used to attain an approximate equilibrium to prevent an expansionist power from dominating the international system.[50] Traditionally, military power has sought to do this in two ways: to deter war, and more important, once it erupted, to win the war. But nuclear weapons now assure that any total war will risk the very substance of national life. Thus, *total wars may be in accord with weapons of limited destructive capacity, but they are incompatible with "absolute weapons."* The first conclusion to be drawn from this general principle is that the principal function of strategic military strength in the nuclear age becomes the *deterrence* of an all-out attack. In other words, its chief purpose now is to prevent any attack from occurring, rather than to defend the nation after it has become engaged in hostilities. The opponent is threatened with such massive retaliation that he dare not attack. The assumption is that, faced with the risk of virtual suicide if he attacks, he will desist, since the price he would have to pay for any possible gains would be far too high. "It is sometimes stated," writes Herman Kahn, "that even an adequate . . . deterrent would not deter an irrational enemy. This might be true if irrationality were an all-or-nothing proposition. Actually, irrationality is a matter of degree and if the irrationality is sufficiently bizarre, the irrational decision-maker's subordinates are likely to step in. As a result, we should want a safety

[49] See particularly Herman Kahn, *Thinking About the Unthinkable*, pp. 17–37 (the chapter entitled "In Defense of Thinking").

[50] Glen H. Snyder, "Balance of Power in the Missile Age," *Journal of International Affairs*, 1960, pp. 21–34.

factor in . . . deterrence systems so large as to impress even the irrational and irresponsible with the degree of their irrationality and therefore the need for caution."[51] Such a condition of mutual deterrence—or
what Churchill called the "balance of terror," and a German author
"the interdependence of doom"[52]—provides the best hope for peace.
Both the Soviet Union and the United States possess hydrogen bombs
with which each can destroy the other. But since each wishes to survive,
neither is likely to initiate a nuclear exchange. In Churchill's famous
words, the world may "by a process of sublime irony, have reached a
stage in this story where safety will be the sturdy child of terror, and
survival the twin brother of annihilation." States will, on the one hand,
possess overwhelming and devastating power; on the other hand, they
will be completely vulnerable to attack and destruction. Nuclear technology and national rivalry, not religion and good will among men, may
thus bring mankind peace on earth: a *pax atomica*—perpetual deterrence
for perpetual peace!

It is unnecessary to explain why, in the nuclear age, this deterrence
must be perpetual. Obviously, there can be no margin for error. In previous periods of history, if a deterrent did not perform its assigned function, war resulted. But since no weapon was so destructive that failure
spelled extinction, such mistakes were not irreparable. The crucial problem for the military was not so much whether it could prevent the
outbreak of hostilities, but whether it could win the war once the country was mobilized. This is no longer true, since an all-out nuclear war
would surely be fatal. The decisive test of military policy is therefore no
longer to vanquish in war, but to deter the enemy from even precipitating a nuclear attack. This extraordinary situation is paradoxical: military
capacity must be strong, but the stronger it is, the less the chance it will
ever have to be used. Its most important role is in its peacetime impact;
if war erupts, it will have failed. In short, its effect will be not so much
physical as *psychological*. For its principal function is to dissuade the
potential aggressor from attacking, and this it seeks to do by convincing
the opponent that the risks of such an attack far outweigh any possible
rewards. The opposing nation must know before launching a strike that
it may, in fact, be signing its own death warrant.

Thus the "two scorpions in a bottle" may after all provide the best
hope for the prevention of all-out war. It has even been suggested that
such a state of mutual deterrence is in accord with a "law of nature."[53]

---

[51] Kahn, *op. cit.*, pp. 111–12.

[52] W. W. Schütz, quoted in Herz, *op. cit.*, p. 304.

[53] While fighting between members of the same species is almost universal among
vertebrates—because they compete for the same food, nesting sites, and mates—it almost never ends in death and even rarely in serious injury to either combatant. If this
were not the case, such fighting would eventually lead to the extinction of the species.
All-out fighting does occur, but usually only among species that possess no weapons

For animals who possess "absolute" weapons do not engage in a "total war"; if they act this way instinctively to preserve the species, they also act "rationally." Most of their fighting is indeed highly ritualistic. Often their contests begin and end with a duel of threats—posturings, movements, and noises—designed to intimidate the opponent without any physical contact at all; and where physical contact does occur, they usually fight without seriously injuring each other. In short, they act not unlike the two superpowers with their nuclear weapons. Nations demonstrate the same instinct for survival, and deterrence is the rational expression of this instinct.

Yet the "balance of terror" is *not* automatic. Strategic bombing may well be decisive in the nuclear age, and the American-Soviet capacity to inflict mutually mortal wounds may give each side a vested interest in not *wanting* to fight a total war. But this desire to avoid war will not suffice of itself. The crucial prerequisite for the *pax atomica* is not "the bomb" but the delivery system. If deterrence is to function effectively, the opponent must never have any doubt that the bombs can be delivered on the target. He must always fear that any attack he will launch will result in his own atomization. Nuclear stockpiles thus demand the development of effective delivery systems. The offense must remain superior to the defense. Since defensive measures are constantly being improved, the maintenance of this offensive edge requires continuing and unrelaxing effort.

The result has been an intensive effort to design carriers with high performance characteristics. Because of the rapidity of technological change in delivery systems, this has required constant attention. Thus the bomber, which came into its own during World War II, was already on the way out less than two decades after the end of the war. No sooner had one bomber been designed, produced, placed in service, and the crews trained than it became obsolescent. The Flying Fortress, the workhorse of the U.S. Army Air Command, was flying before the nation entered World War II, and it was still flying by the end of the war in Europe. Only in the last stage of the air war against Japan did the Superfortress come into service. In the nuclear age, it was soon outmoded as the need was for an intercontinental bomber. The B-36, with its six piston motors and four jet engines, and a range of 10,000 miles, answered this need. But its slow top speed of only just over 400 mph soon made it

---

with which to inflict mortal injury. Rattlesnakes, for instance, could kill each other with a single bite; yet, when they fight, they never bite. Instead, they glide alongside each other, each with its forward third raised in the air. In this posture, they push head against head, each seeking to force the other sideways and to the ground, quite reminiscent of the strict rules of "Indian wrestling." The successful snake pins the loser for a moment with the weight of his body and then lets the loser escape. (See Irenaus Eibl-Eibesfeldt, "The Fighting Behavior of Animals," *Scientific American*, December, 1961, pp. 112–23.)

vulnerable to fighter attack, and it had to be replaced by the B-47, a pure jet bomber with a speed of over 600 mph. Because the B-47 was a medium-range bomber, it could operate from the United States only if it were refueled in the air, so it flew mostly from overseas bases in Europe, North Africa, the Middle East, and the Far East. Consequently, another intercontinental bomber was still necessary. Overseas bases were within range of the Soviet Union's sizable force of medium-range bombers; continental American bases were still beyond the range of Soviet bombers in the early and middle 1950's. The United States therefore developed the B-52, whose eight jet engines gave the bomber a speed of over 650 mph and a range exceeding 6,000 miles. This bomber subsequently became the backbone of the Strategic Air Command.

It was precisely this ever-increasing speed of bombers, however, that destabilized the balance of terror from the mid-1950's to the early 1960's. Even before the development of high-speed bombers, surprise attack had been possible. The Germans had achieved it against the Russians in 1941, despite the large-scale movement of troops to Poland; and the Japanese had been highly successful at Pearl Harbor a few months later. The speed of postwar bombers made such an attack even more feasible, particularly since it would no longer have to be preceded by massive troop or ship movements. Since bombers constantly flew training missions, the potential victim's first knowledge of an impending attack was not likely to come before they approached very near to or crossed into his territory. Thus, while the United States, for instance, sought to deter a Soviet attack by threatening to drop enough bombs virtually to wipe the Soviet Union off the map, it might not be able to deter war if most American bombers were destroyed in a surprise attack. The surviving bombers might not be able to retaliate with sufficient destructive power. Not all of them would have enough fuel to reach their targets. Soviet fighters and ground-to-air missiles, alerted for the arrival of the bombers that did reach Soviet territory, would be able to shoot down many, if not most, of the bombers. The few bombers that managed to penetrate the Soviet defenses might no longer be able to impose catastrophic damage.[54] The resulting damage might, indeed, have been acceptable to the Soviet leaders if it would have meant once and for all the elimination of their deadliest enemy and his ability to destroy the Soviet Union. Thus, instead of deterring the Soviets, the very horror of nuclear war might in fact have tempted them to launch a surprise attack on SAC's vulnerable bombers. After all, in the one year 1941, the Soviet Union had lost control of more than 40 per cent of its population, 40 per cent of its grain production, approximately 60 per cent of its coal, iron, steel, and aluminum output, and 95 per cent or more of certain key military indus-

[54] Albert Wohlstetter, "The Delicate Balance of Terror," *Foreign Affairs*, January, 1959.

tries, such as ball-bearing production; it had also lost 4 million soldiers (dead, wounded, and prisoners) and more than two-thirds of its tanks and aircraft.[55] Since it had withstood such losses, perhaps comparable losses would be considered a "fair" price for ridding itself of the world's leading capitalist power and the only real threat to its survival.

The vulnerability of bombers to a nuclear Pearl Harbor, in short, rendered mutual deterrence very unstable because of the high dividend their destruction would pay to the side striking the initial blow. The possibility of eliminating the opponent's retaliatory bombers—bombers above ground being "soft" targets—therefore became a powerful *incentive* to attack. The balance of terror was described as "delicate." What conditions might instigate an opponent's first strike against one's retaliatory force? And what could be done to "stabilize" mutual deterrence? These were the questions to which students of "arms control" addressed themselves in the late 1950's. Arms control from the beginning rejected the feasibility of general disarmament. It was understood that conflicts among states could not be abolished "by fiat," that nuclear weapons were here to stay, and that man's best hope for earthly salvation lay in the "control" of armaments. The all-or-nothing attitude—disarm or perish—was rejected, and the competition inherent in the state system was accepted. Deterrence was therefore recognized as necessary; but it had to be improved, to be made "safe." The purpose of arms control, then, was to devise feasible ways to save a world armed with nuclear weapons from the agony of nuclear war by stabilizing Soviet-American deterrence. In this sense, arms control was intended to supplement defense policies, since its aim was identical: to protect the national security by deterring war. Whereas disarmament stressed the reduction of a nation's military *capability*, arms control emphasized the elimination of American and Soviet *incentives* to strike first. Two assumptions underlay arms control: one, that despite the continuation of their political conflict, both nuclear powers shared a common interest in avoiding nuclear war; and two, that although the basic tensions were due to political antagonism, the nature of the delivery systems increased tensions even more because they provided a strong and *independent* incentive for a first strike. This incentive was simply the paramount importance of hitting first, for to come in second was to lose; to be caught off-guard could be fatal; policy-makers thus seemed to have no choice but to initiate a strike.

If the *only* defense was indeed the offense, then pre-emptive war was a particular danger during crisis periods. Such a war differs from a preventive war, in which the aggressor coolly calculates beforehand to strike at his opponent in the belief that he possesses the capacity to obliterate him; the attacker picks a specific date and then sends his force on its way, irrespective of any possible provocation. But in a pre-emptive war,

[55] Raymond L. Garthoff, *Soviet Strategy in the Missile Age*, pp. 90–91.

the attack is launched in order to forestall the enemy's initial blow. The aggressor in this instance believes that his opponent is about to hit him; he therefore launches his strike in order to destroy the enemy's forces before they take off. The attack occurs as a result of the other side's measures. This urge for an "anticipatory strike" has been aptly compared to the Western gunfighter's dilemma:

> The "equalizer" of the Old West (the pistol) made is possible for *either* member of the hostile pair to kill the other; it did not assure that *both* could kill each other. If one is face to face with a potential enemy and both are armed with pistols, the advantage of the first shot aggravates any incentive to shoot. The survivor can argue, "He was about to kill me in self-defense, so I had to kill him in self-defense." Or, "He, thinking that I was about to kill him in self-defense, was about to kill me in self-defense, so I had to kill him in self-defense." But if everyone who was shot were assured of living long enough to shoot back with unimpaired aim, there would be no advantage in jumping the gun and no reason to expect the other to try it.[56]

It was exactly this inability of most of the retaliatory bomber force to survive that provided the incentive for a first strike. The role accident might play in precipitating such a strike thus became clear. The sign that an opponent was about to launch an attack was likely to be ambiguous. He might be taking measures not to attack but to render his strategic force less vulnerable and thereby to enhance his deterrent stance. For instance, he might send many of his bombers into the air in order to avoid having them caught on the ground; by rendering them less prone to sudden destruction, he was trying to caution the other side against launching an attack. But his action could easily be misinterpreted as a possible prelude to attack. In a situation of mutual vulnerability in which the "nice guy" finishes last, delay could prove fatal. Offensive action was therefore the only wise course: " 'Self-defense' becomes peculiarly compounded if we have to worry about his striking us to keep us from striking him to keep him from striking us."[57] What was important, therefore, was not what A *intended* to do, but the other side's *interpretation* of A's actions and intentions. And in this type of hair-trigger situation, the interpretation would not be conservative. Since the survival of the nation would be at stake, the worst had to be assumed. The strategic bombers of both sides were, of course, ready at all times to take off on their mission. When one side placed a sizable number of them in the air, the possibility of a sudden attack increased. Even defensive actions intended merely to enhance one's deterrent power might thus have served to intensify international tensions and perhaps touch off a nuclear conflagration.

[56] Thomas C. Schelling, *The Strategy of Conflict*, pp. 232–33.
[57] *Ibid.*, p. 231.

The crucial problem which arms control had to answer in these circumstances was how a pre-emptive strike could be forestalled—or, in an extreme situation, a preventive war, if one side ever felt it could "get away with it." The remedy was to render each side's retaliatory forces *invulnerable*. And this could be achieved in two ways. First, a second-strike force had to be developed. The vulnerable bomber deterrent was a first-strike force. If it were surprised on its bases, most of it could be wiped out; the fact that it had to be used first created the dangerous situation of mutual trigger-happiness. A second-strike force is one that can absorb an initial blow and *still* effectively perform its retaliatory task. The deterrent force that matters is, in brief, that part of the force left after an enemy attack, not the size of the force that existed before the attack. Second, such a retaliatory force had to be so well safeguarded that the antagonist could not possibly cripple most of it. The principle was simple: "Known ability to defend our retaliatory force constitutes the only unilaterally attainable situation that provides potentially a perfect defense of our home land. Conversely, a conspicuous inability or unreadiness to defend our retaliatory force must tend to provoke the opponent to destroy it; in other words, it tempts him to an aggression he might not otherwise contemplate."[58] The best method of developing a well-protected retaliatory force was to disperse it, harden it, and make it mobile. Solid-fuel missiles, which could be fired instantly, met these requirements. They could be dispersed more easily than bombers, which are generally concentrated on a relatively small number of bases whose location is easily discernible. Missiles could also be hardened or buried underground in concrete silos which could withstand great pressure. Finally, and most important, missiles could be constantly moved around so that the enemy would never know their exact location. Even underground missiles would become increasingly vulnerable to destruction with the improvement of guidance systems. (The United States is developing a guidance system to ensure that two Minutemen can destroy a hardened Soviet missile. On the other hand, it is estimated that one of the Soviet Union's huge 50–100-megaton warheads could destroy two hardened American missiles. With smaller warheads, the Pentagon estimates that it would take from three to eight attacking Soviet missiles to hit an American missile.) But mobile missiles, such as the Polaris, which are carried under water on nuclear-powered submarines, are virtually impossible to hit. To the extent that an enemy in a first strike would seek to destroy such mobile missiles, an oceanic system would have the advantage of moving an initial strike—or at least a good part of that strike—away from the land or the Zone of the Interior.[59] In the words of the Navy jingle:

58 Brodie, *op. cit.*, p. 185.
59 Oskar Morgenstern, *The Question of National Defense*, pp. 81–98.

Move deterrence out to sea
Where real estate is free
And where it's far away from me.

The importance of the dispersal, hardening, and mobility of missiles lay in the fact that they deprived a surprise attack of its rationale. The entire justification for a first strike had been to surprise the enemy's "soft" bombers on the ground and destroy them. But when the opponent's retaliatory power consists entirely or primarily of mobile, solid-fuel, long-range missiles, it is impossible to know where to hit him in order to destroy this retaliatory capacity. Obliterating his cities would benefit the aggressor very little if his opponent still retained this capacity. Surprise, therefore, no longer confers any significant advantage to the side that hits first. Conversely, since missiles are invulnerable, there is no longer any incentive for a pre-emptive blow. The enemy's first strike could be absorbed; there would always be enough time after his attack to launch the counterblow. The fact that a second-strike retaliatory force remained would be the best guarantee against war. Invulnerable deterrents thus stabilized mutual deterrence because each side knew that the advantage of a first strike had been outweighed by the almost suicidal cost. In other words, once the advantage of the initial attack has been greatly reduced, if not eliminated, the incentive to strike at all, and therefore the possibility of war, also disappears. "There is a difference between a balance of terror in which either side can obliterate the other and one in which both sides can do it no matter who strikes first. It is not the 'balance'—the sheer equality or symmetry in the situation—that constitutes mutual deterrence; it is the stability of the balance. The balance is stable only when neither, in striking first, can destroy the other's ability to strike back."[60]

The question is, of course, whether future advances in technology will not undermine this nuclear stalemate (or balance):

Many see in this balance, this system of mutual deterrence, the hope for the continued security of the world. The United States and the Soviet Union will both be able to destroy each other's populations but not each other's weapons. In effect, we are back in the barbarian world where hostages are exchanged. America's population is hostage to the Soviet Union for the behavior of American leaders. And the Russian population is hostage to America for the behavior of their leaders. No matter who starts the war, the hostages may be destroyed. This is a sobering thought. But even in international relations, a field where there aren't many strong reeds, it is a weak reed on which to build hope for continuing peace. Left to itself, the balance of terror is not a stable balance.[61]

[60] Schelling, *op. cit.*, p. 232.
[61] Hadley, *op. cit.*, p. 23.

If, for instance, one side were to develop an anti-missile missile—an "active defense" weapon—before the other, the balance would immediately collapse, and an unquestioned superiority would be conferred on the side that could shoot down all retaliatory missiles.

Nevertheless, the danger of such a major technological breakthrough by one side long before the other is probably less likely than is usually believed. Throughout the twentieth century, the great powers have produced new weapons at approximately the same time. After all, their cultural levels are about the same, and their scientific knowledge is at roughly the same stage of development; men ask themselves similar questions and come up with similar answers. The period after World War II, when the United States held an atomic monopoly until the Soviets exploded their bomb in 1949, stands out as a major exception. But both tested their first hydrogen devices within a few months of each other. The American development of the ICBM has not lagged far behind that of the Soviets.[62] Thus, a Soviet first in developing an anti-missile missile would not be likely to upset the nuclear stalemate the moment it was successfully tested. First of all, the Soviets would not be developing, manufacturing, and deploying a sufficiently large number of AICBM's overnight; it would take at least three to five years to build up a stockpile. Second, Soviet AICBM's could not stop a massive American attack of ICBM's and IRBM's from penetrating the Soviet defenses and reaching their targets. The attacker would be using decoys ejected from a missile's nose cone to saturate enemy radar with what would look like incoming warheads. The AICBM's would then have to be aimed at all the blips on the radar screen in order to hit the real warhead, and they would be used up quickly, with most of them probably being wasted. Thus, not only would a Soviet first in AICBM's not overturn the balance of military power immediately, but it could not even do so over a longer-run period, for the United States could counter the Soviet AICBM by augmenting its attacking forces. In any case, the United States would not be far behind the Soviet Union in obtaining its own AICBM.[63] In the meantime, the Soviet Union would hardly launch a first strike. No conceivable technological breakthrough would be likely to upset the deterrent balance overnight. For the key factor is not who is first with a new weapons system; rather, it is whether this weapons system can render a completely successful surprise attack feasible or shoot down virtually all of an attacker's bombers and missiles. A blow that destroys "only" 80 per cent of the enemy's force is not good enough; the other 20 per cent

[62] Huntington, *op. cit.*, pp. 72–73; Jerome B. Wiesner, "Introduction," in Donald G. Brennan (ed.), *Arms Control, Disarmament, and National Security*, p. 14.

[63] For American efforts to produce devices to penetrate an anti-missile defense, see *The New York Times*, November 9, 1963. The immense difficulty of inventing an AICBM—"a bullet to hit a bullet"—is discussed by Hanson W. Baldwin, "Race for the Anti-Missile Missile," *The New York Times*, April 15, 1962.

can still obliterate the nation that initiated the strike. A decisive technological breakthrough upsetting the stability of the nuclear stalemate is therefore a more remote possibility than it might at first seem.

One final point should be noted about this stable deterrent arrangement: It is mutual. Each side takes similar steps. In a sense, therefore, a "treaty" committing each of the two powers to a particular type of arms-control arrangement has to exist. It is based upon the mutual desire to avoid false alarms or misunderstandings that might trigger an accidental war. Its sanction against violation is self-interest. And although the treaty in this instance is not formal, it does exist by tacit understanding or informal agreement. Mutual restraints achieved without specific diplomatic negotiations are no less valuable because of the informal approach. Communication with the enemy—who in this form of negotiation is a potential partner—is established and implemented by action. What matters is what is done: for instance, how strategic forces are equipped and the manner in which they are deployed. Behavior is the key to this kind of indirect and informal negotiation, for it conveys to the opponent one's intentions and way of thinking. His self-interest is then expected to compel him to reciprocate. Instead of *"arguing* about what we should do, we will simply do it and dare the other side to do likewise, or do it and quietly suggest that we would like to keep it up, but only if they find in their interest to do something comparable."[64] Not that words are no longer necessary. They supplement the actions taken and explain the meaning of these actions, in case these are not in themselves sufficiently clear. Together, they constitute the diplomacy of arms control.

The "Nuclear Stalemate" and the International Civil War

The vital question posed by the nuclear stalemate has been what would be the impact of this mutual deterrence upon the Cold War. Since 1956, the Soviet leaders have repeatedly declared that war between capitalism and socialism was no longer "fatally inevitable."[65] The present era of history, Khrushchev said at the Twentieth CPSU Congress, was one of "peaceful coexistence." Since the alternatives posed by the devastating power of nuclear weapons seemed to be coexistence or coextinction, did this mean that the possibility of a nuclear holocaust had led the Soviet Union to recognize that if the two social orders were not to destroy each other, they had to learn to live together? Did the Soviet

[64] Thomas C. Schelling, "Reciprocal Measures for Arms Stabilization," in Brennan, *op. cit.*, p. 174; see also Morton H. Halperin, *Limited War in the Nuclear Age* (New York: John Wiley and Sons, 1963), pp. 77–86.

[65] See Khrushchev's Twentieth Party Congress speech in G. F. Hudson, Richard Lowenthal, and Roderick MacFarquhar, *The Sino-Soviet Dispute*, pp. 42–44. Frederic S. Barin, "The Communist Doctrine of the Inevitability of War," *American Political Science Review*, June, 1963, pp. 334–354, traces the development of the Communist doctrine on war.

Union's renunciation of total war as an instrument of policy indicate that it had given up its drive to destroy the bourgeois West? Since war risked suicide, and it was the Soviet Union's determination to change the *status quo* which raised the specter of war, might one conclude that the Kremlin was prepared to accept the post–World War II *status quo*, seek a *modus vivendi* with the West, and negotiate outstanding differences?

The answer to these questions was "No." For the Soviets place the emphasis on the word "coexistence" rather than "peaceful"; coexistence today is, after all, either peaceful or no existence at all. However, before two nations can genuinely agree to coexist, they must first recognize each other's right to exist. And it is exactly this that the Soviets deny. They are not willing to coexist permanently with states outside the "true faith." History has, they say, doomed capitalism; the end of the bourgeois system has already been ordained. Coexistence in this dissensus situation is strictly temporary. "Peaceful coexistence" is, then, the very opposite of a long-term policy of live-and-let-live. "Peaceful coexistence of states," declared the statement issued after the 1960 meeting of the Communist leaders of eighty-one countries, "does not imply renunciation of the class struggle, as the revisionists claim. The coexistence of states with different social systems is a form of class struggle between socialism and capitalism. . . . Peaceful coexistence of countries with different social systems does not mean conciliation of the socialist and bourgeois ideologies. On the contrary, it implies intensification of the struggle of the working class, of all the Communist parties, for the triumph of socialist ideas."[66] Nor is the transitory nature of this coexistence likely to change; no consensus will develop between capitalism and Communism. As one Soviet writer has noted:

The idea of peaceful coexistence is wrongly interpreted at times. Specifically, attempts are being made artificially to tie up the task of improving international relations with problems of an ideological nature; expectations of "concessions" by Communists in the Marxist-Leninist ideology are associated with peaceful coexistence . . . that there will be an "inevitable smoothing over" of differences between the socialist and capitalist states . . . as a result of some kind of fundamental "changes" in the social and economic system, political structure and ideology in the socialist countries . . . (or) that a slackening of the class struggle within capitalist countries is possible. . . . The idea of the gradual "elimination" of the basic differences between states with contrary social and economic systems is being preached more vigorously now that world tensions are easing. . . . Another no less important aspect is . . . the reactionary Utopian thesis that an "approximation" of the social purposes of communism and capitalism is possible, and to support the false idea that the Soviet system is "draw-

[66] Washington Center of Foreign Policy Research, *Two Communist Manifestoes*, p. 61.

ing closer" to the "Western pattern." It goes without saying that there is not much logic to such a twist. Why, in fact, should the . . . socialist countries strive for the notorious "Western pattern"? After all, if, as is generally recognized, socialism is scoring ever new successes, including victories in the "battle for the minds of the people," in the international arena . . . is it not natural to assume that an opposite process is inevitable?[67]

The "who-whom" conflict thus continues until the final and complete collapse of capitalism and imperialism, which does not necessarily have to be achieved by total war. Lenin at one time, to be sure, did predict such a war between capitalism and Communism. "We are living," he said, "not merely in a state but in a system of states and the existence of the Soviet Republic side by side with imperalist states for a long time is unthinkable. One or the other must triumph in the end. And before that end supervenes, a series of frightful collisions between the Soviet Republic and the bourgeois states will be inevitable."[68] These "inevitable" clashes would occur because the capitalist powers, sensing their own decline, would try to reverse their historically appointed demise by attacking the Soviet Union. However, since the mid-1950's, the Soviet leaders have emphasized that although the aggressive nature of capitalism persisted, war could be deterred by three principal forces: the military strength of the Soviet Union, the power of the entire "socialist camp," and the "peace-loving" anticolonial countries. Consequently, while "war is the constant companion of capitalism," the combined strength of the "zone of peace"—the Sino-Soviet bloc plus the anti-imperialist nations— "will make it actually possible to banish world war from the life of society even before the complete victory of socialism on earth."[69] Implicit in this statement voicing confidence in Soviet deterrent strength is a renunciation of a possible Soviet preventive strike against the United States.

It would, however, be wrong to take this renunciation of total war as an offensive instrument of Soviet policy as an indication that the Soviet leadership has become "sincerely" converted to the cause of peace. It means only that it sincerely wishes to avoid risking the liquidation of the Soviet base of the world revolution. This is in firm accord with the longstanding Communist "operational code," which specifically warns against any "adventurism" or "romanticism" that might result in a military clash and defeat. Above all else, the base of operations must be kept safe. Khrushchev's rejection of a quick and strictly military solution of the

[67] T. Timofeyev, quoted by Vernon V. Aspaturian, "Dialectics and Duplicity in Soviet Diplomacy," *Journal of International Affairs*, XVII, No. 1 (1963), 55.

[68] Quoted by Joseph Stalin, *Problems of Leninism* (Moscow, 1940), p. 156.

[69] *Two Communist Manifestoes*, pp. 47–48, 59; "The New Program of the Communist Party of the Soviet Union," in Arthur P. Mendel (ed.), *The Essential Works of Marxism*, p. 417.

Cold War thus stemmed more from "caution" than from peaceful intent.

His "moderation" differed little in this respect from that of his predecessors. Neither Lenin nor Stalin was ever willing to endanger the base of the revolution and the survival of the movement. Soviet foreign policy, revolutionary as it has been in its over-all purpose, has *never* been revolutionary in its military aspect. Lenin demonstrated this dramatically when, a few months after the Bolsheviks had seized power, he signed the German-dictated Treaty of Brest-Litovsk despite the opposition of most of his colleagues, who argued that the new Communist state should launch a revolutionary crusade to defeat the German armies and liberate the proletariat of all of Europe. The chances of successfully accomplishing these goals were dim since the new state had virtually no effective and reliable military forces. But, most of Lenin's colleagues argued, it was better to be faithful to the Communist mission and die in the process than to betray their mission and remain in power. Nevertheless, Lenin remained unwilling to export the revolution militarily and thus risk the first base of power the Bolsheviks had captured. Guarding the citadel of the revolution was to be the primary imperative.

Stalin's foreign policy also refused to risk the security of this citadel. The Red Army was used to impose Soviet control over Eastern Europe, but Soviet expansion into this area occurred during World War II as the Red Army compelled the Germans to retreat. Stalin then tried to exploit the misery of postwar Europe, but the Marshall plan forestalled this by making possible the recovery and reconstruction of Western Europe. He also sought to keep West Germany from allying herself with the Western powers and, indeed, to show Europe that America would not protect it. The Berlin airlift and the formation of NATO defeated these attempts. His moves to take over Iran, to pressure Turkey into submission, and to capture power in Greece by means of a guerrilla war were also defeated. Stalin knew he had been checked and that further attempts to expand would have to await the growth of Soviet economic and military (especially nuclear) power. After the failure of the Berlin Blockade, Stalin relaxed Soviet pressure on Europe and launched an intensive "world peace movement" condemning nuclear weapons. The intention was to exploit the non-Soviet world's horror and fear of nuclear war in order to inhibit any possible American use of nuclear weapons against the Soviet Union—while concentrating Soviet research on the development and production of an atomic stockpile. Only in Korea was force used, and this was limited force employed by a satellite army —apparently in the expectation that South Korea was a "power vacuum," since American troops had been withdrawn and South Korea had been declared outside of the American "defense perimeter" in the Pacific.[70]

---

[70] John W. Spanier, *The Truman-MacArthur Controversy and the Korean War*, pp. 15–23.

The point, in any case, is that Stalin, however brutal and savage and arbitrary he may personally have been, acted rationally, not rashly, in his foreign policy.[71] Like Lenin, he was sufficiently cautious not to endanger the Soviet Union's security. Militarily, both leaders were "conservatives." Indeed, it was not Khrushchev but Stalin who first stated that war was no longer inevitable between the capitalist and socialist worlds! In 1952, Stalin declared that the "socialist camp" was strong enough to deter a Western attack.[72]

But Lenin's willingness to sign the Brest-Litovsk Treaty and Stalin's interwar policy of rapidly building "socialism in one country," plus his failure to employ the large and powerful Red Army at any time between 1945 and his death in 1953, did not indicate that either Soviet leader ever renounced the ultimate aim of world revolution or that the struggle to realize this aim would be permanently relaxed. Militarily conservative, they remained ideologically revolutionary and willing to advance the cause of Communism by economic, political, and psychological means when the opportunity presented itself. But Stalin had few such opportunities. Russia was the only Communist state in the world prior to World War II, and a weak one at that. He therefore concentrated his efforts on industrializing the Soviet Union as rapidly as he could. After the war, he was preoccupied with economic recovery, consolidation of his hold on Eastern Europe, and the production of an atom bomb. It was, in fact, Khrushchev, the de-Stalinizer, who benefited from Stalinism because he was heir to the great strength built up under Stalin and was able to exploit it internationally to advance the cause of Communism. The opportunity to weaken "capitalism" effectively did not really present itself until 1955 with the increasingly rapid emergence of the former colonized areas and the Soviets' acquisition of a long-range delivery system for their nuclear stockpile. The point, in brief, is that after the unexpected failure of the Bolshevik Revolution of 1917 to spread spontaneously to Germany and the rest of industrial Western Europe, victory over capitalism was not renounced, but was no longer expected to occur overnight. The struggle would be a protracted conflict. According to George Kennan: "The Kremlin is under no ideological compulsion to accomplish its purposes in a hurry. Like the Church, it is dealing in ideological concepts which are of long-term validity, and it can afford to be patient."[73] In the resulting conflict, setbacks are considered as merely temporary. No specific defeat is ever regarded as a defeat of the Communist movement as a whole. A battle may be lost, but not the war. Just as there are advances, there are bound to be "strategic retreats"

[71] Marshall D. Shulman, *Stalin's Foreign Policy Reappraised*; see also Philip E. Mosely, "Is It Peaceful? Is It Coexistence?," *The New York Times Magazine*, September 1, 1963.

[72] Marcuse, *Soviet Marxism*, pp. 146–48.

[73] George F. Kennan, *American Diplomacy*, 1900–1950, p. 118.

—as Lenin used to say, two steps forward, one step backward. Stalin talked of a "succession of ebbs and flows in the revolutionary tide."

If peaceful coexistence, then, becomes the most effective tactic of waging this protracted struggle at a time when the Soviet leaders have every vested interest in thinking of war as not being inevitable, one feature of this struggle remains permanent—namely, the Soviet political interest in Europe. The reason for the constancy of this drive is clear: The orientation of Europe, with its high degree of industrialization and its technical and scientific skills, can decisively affect the global balance of power. Separating Europe from the United States would isolate the United States and gravely weaken her. "The principal target of the Soviet offensive has been NATO," one Soviet expert has said, "not because the alliance is the easiest prey, but because, next to the United States itself, it represents the most valuable prize in the global struggle. Western Europe is of overriding importance to the Soviet Union because of its economic and political strength and its military potential." Nor does it seek Europe's immediate Communization: "The surest way for the Soviet Union to capture the economic resources of Western Europe and to keep its military potential from being fulfilled would be its Communization, but this seems to be out of the question in the foreseeable future. More promising is a strategy aimed at reducing the commitments of various countries to NATO and pushing them toward neutralism."[74] Indeed, even the close Soviet attention to underdeveloped nations is indirectly aimed at Europe. While the long-run purpose of Soviet concern for the new nations is to Communize them, the short-term goal is to establish friendly political and economic ties with them in order to break their economic ties with their former European masters. For the Communists believe that if Europe is denied raw materials and markets for its industry, it can be brought to the point of economic and political collapse. The loss of the capitalists' "super-profits" would trigger a renewed class struggle, and the proletariat would emerge triumphant. The Soviet emphasis on the non-Western areas is thus, in a manner of speaking, an attempt to outflank Europe. If successful, the strategic blow struck at the United States would outweigh the acquisition of the new underdeveloped nations. They can be brought under Communist control at a later stage.

Soviet tactics to achieve these goals in Europe and the underdeveloped areas can easily be kept below the threshhold of nuclear war. Challenges remain limited, and power is judiciously exercised. The Soviet power that is applied, it must be noted, moreover, *cannot* be evaluated solely in terms of the traditional criteria: that is, the simple quantitative additions of population, guns, industrial production, and the like. Even the

[74] Herbert S. Dinerstein, "Soviet Goals and Military Force," *Orbis*, Winter, 1962, p. 427.

inclusion of less tangible factors such as national character or morale will not suffice, although they do result in more accurate and sophisticated power calculations, if properly assessed. It is precisely this manner of "adding" power that has so frequently led Westerners to see the Soviet threat as uni-dimensional, in terms of sheer military power and expansion —and also led them to wonder how the Soviets can be so successful in foreign policy despite the fact that the United States possesses greater over-all power. The Soviet conception of power is neither purely quantitative nor primarily military, but highly *qualitative*, or *political*. The normal categories of power, such as military strength, are carefully related to fundamental attitudes and social forces—for instance, the desire for peace, the dread of nuclear war, the appeal of nationalism, and the desire for speedy modernization, social changes, and economic progress. It is by exploiting these emotions and forces that Soviet foreign-policy-makers expect to achieve their revolutionary aims. These forces would exist even if there had never been an international Communist movement. They were not created by a "Communist conspiracy"; but the Soviet Union uses them as multipliers of its own efforts.

Thus, in Europe, the Soviet Union cleverly uses military force to threaten total war. On the one hand, the intention is to frighten the Europeans, who, after two long wars and great suffering, are naturally averse to the thought of an even more devastating war. On the other hand, nuclear blackmail is also meant to show them that the United States, fearful of committing nuclear suicide in defense of Europe, will not protect them. These two fears—of war and of being left undefended —which Soviet tactics attempt to instill in the Europeans are shrewdly alternated with sirens of peace: If the Europeans wish to escape the constant fear of nuclear war shadowing their lives, they need only accept the "reasonable" Soviet solutions for European problems; these will "normalize" Soviet-European relations and provide greater security for both parties; everyone can then coexist peacefully ever after. These threats of war and messages of peace are managed in such a manner that defenders of the *status quo* are likely to seek relief from tensions by concessions. At no point is force ever openly used. The effects are strictly political and psychological: to encourage popular fear and hope and to exert pressure on the Western governments to incline them more favorably toward Soviet policies.

And in the new nations of the world, the Soviets need merely to exploit the internal struggle of the "national bourgeoisie" against the Western-oriented ruling classes where these still exist or the external struggle of the new governments to preserve their independence by reducing, if not completely eliminating, Western power and influence in their regions. The determination of the underdeveloped states to modernize themselves—a complex process involving a political, social, and cultural revolution—is also tailor-made for a movement that first of all views, analyzes, and understands political dynamics in terms of class struggle, and second, believes that it knows the formula for speedy modernization and industrialization of a backward nation.

The "nuclear stalemate" does not therefore mean the freezing of the territorial *status quo*. Rather, it shifts the struggle from the military and diplomatic to the political and psychological arena—precisely the arena in which the revolutionary power excels. For international *civil* war is psychopolitical war. The traditional powers' orthodox military doctrines —which stem from *inter*nation conflicts—provide them with little guide to action in *intra*nation conflicts. It is characteristic that the American approach to power is in terms of military power and that the United States has throughout the Cold War emphasized the military aspect of the struggle—and hoped for the type of relatively speedy ending of the Cold War that it had experienced in its pre-nuclear wars. It is equally characteristic that the Soviet Union thinks of the Cold War in terms of a protracted political conflict and of power in political terms.

Because, in addition, it believes that the social forces in the world favor the inevitable Communist victory, the Soviet Union also approaches the international conflict in a mood of pronounced self-confidence. Capitalism has allegedly entered the period of its decline and collapse. World War I witnessed its first general crisis with the birth of the Soviet Union. The first socialist state—as the Communists define "socialism"—spelled the beginning of the end for world capitalism. The post–World War II rise of new socialist states in Europe and Asia, the disintegration of colonialism, and the intensification of the class struggle within the capitalist states are all seen as symptoms of the decay of world capitalism and the approaching victory of the "world socialist system." The interwar "capitalist encirclement" of the Soviet Union has been replaced by the "socialist encirclement" of capitalism. Communism is no longer, as Marx said in his opening words of *The Communist Manifesto*, "a specter haunting Europe." At present, it is a political and economic system embracing one-third of mankind. Tomorrow, say the Communists, it will embrace the world. Global victory, even in a bipolar and nuclear world, is certain, they say—and without a global holocaust. History is moving toward its prescribed end, and the Soviet task is to hurry it along, to shorten the present period of history—the era the Communists define as one of "transition from capitalism to Communism." And there is no better place to hurry history along toward its predestined end than in the new nations of the world.

V

The Revolution of Non-Western Nationalism and Modernization

The Westernization of the Intelligentsia

The right of national self-determination, born in the West but denied by the Western powers in their overseas territories, became a key issue in the postwar world. Throughout Asia and Africa, former colonies sought national independence and most of them gained it. And the Latin American nations, long overshadowed (and sometimes dominated) by their powerful neighbor to the north, began to assert the formal independence they had acquired over a century earlier. The common denominator of this global nationalist revolution is thus a fundamental assertion to be "free *from*" the control of the former colonial power. At the same time, it is a drive for equality and respect, both national and individual. In this sense, it is only the latest manifestation of the drive for secular equality that began in Europe with the French Revolution. Indeed, the paradox of Western colonialism is that its disintegration testifies to its efficacy as a carrier of nationalist sentiment and activity. For most of the Western powers, including the United States in the Philippines, justified their imperial domination in terms of bringing the backward peoples of the earth the benefits of Western democracy, medical science, and technology. It was the "white man's burden," or duty, to educate the natives so that one day they could govern themselves. To be sure, some states were more sincere in this aim than others. The British record of training native leaders in the art of government is superior to that of, say, the Dutch or the Belgians.[1] But even the British timetable for independence seemed too gradual for Africans dominated by white settlers. The colonial powers taught their lesson only too well. They ruled their colonies autocratically, while simultaneously propagating the virtues of democracy. But democracy and national self-government were obviously incompatible with foreign rule.

Thus, from the beginning, colonialism held the seeds of its own destruction. The humiliation and resentment of foreign domination stirred a "reactive nationalism" that asserted itself in a search for national identity, dignity, and equality. Past impotence and subordination led to a drive for national power, prestige, and respect. The nation would be master of its own destiny; no one would ever dominate it again or treat it condescendingly as a "second-class" nation. The determination of the new, underdeveloped countries to modernize has been strongly motivated by this desire for state power. "Power is of more importance than wealth," said a nineteenth-century German nationalist, "because the reverse of power—namely feebleness—leads to the relinquishment of all that we possess, not of acquired wealth alone, but of our powers of production, of our civilization, of our freedom, nay, even of our national independence."[2]

This desire for power as the means of guarding national independence and gaining a status equal to that of other nations is implicitly also a demand for respect on the one ground on which the West has always denied it—race. A famous sign said to have hung over the entrance of a European club in Shanghai, "Chinamen and dogs not allowed to enter," was symptomatic of the Western attitude. The very basis on which colonialism was justified was that the nonwhite people were simply inferior—"childish," "immoral," "lazy," "dirty," and "heathen." Therefore, they had to be ruled by the paternal and superior white man, who would "civilize" them by teaching them the virtues of hard work, religion, and sanitation. Although many of these same inferior characteristics were in the last century also attributed by the European ruling classes to their own "common people" at home, and by the Anglo-Saxons and Teutons to Southern and Eastern Europeans, it was all the more rankling and humiliating when such judgments were based merely on color—and were made by white men who, in their arrogance, condemned all colored peoples to the lower scales of humanity.

---

[1] The French were the major exception. The 1944 imperial conference rejected the idea of any autonomy outside the French Empire. The English word "self-government" was even used in the final communiqué rather than French. French policy was one of assimilation. The natives were part of a "greater France." Once they had matured, they were to be awarded French citizenship.

[2] Friedrich List, quoted by Edward Meade Earle, "Adam Smith, Alexander Hamilton, Friedrich List: The Economic Foundations of Military Power," in Earle, *Makers of Modern Strategy* (Princeton, N.J.: Princeton University Press, 1943), p. 118.

The urge among backward, agrarian countries to transform themselves into modern urban-industrial states stems not only from the desire for strength, but also from the determination to achieve a higher standard of living. Industry spells both power and welfare. Without power, the new nations cannot really be free, and certainly cannot gain respect. Without welfare, they cannot abolish the abject poverty and misery of past centuries. Colonialism taught them that modern technology was the basis of the West's strength and wealth. It was industrialization that had made the West strong enough to conquer and colonize; and it was science that permitted the North Americans and West Europeans to live so much longer and better than non-Western man.

In the economically underdeveloped countries, however, man continued to live basically on subsistence agriculture because he did not possess the modern tools—the factories, the machinery, the dams, etc.—with which to increase his productivity. Even more important, he lacked the cultural values, the social structure, and the political order that are necessary for industrialization. The hallmark of a developed society is its capacity for *continued* economic growth. But there is little, if any, possibility of sustaining the savings required to augment national production in an economically backward nation. The dividing line between developed and underdeveloped (or developing, in recognition of the progress being made) societies is an average annual income per person of $500. In most of the new nations, the per capita income figure is far lower—more often, about $100. In such circumstances, the standard of existence (hardly a standard of living) verges literally on starvation. Disease is rampant amid such grinding poverty. Many people suffer from malaria, tuberculosis, trachoma, hookworm, or venereal disease because of a lack of the most elementary sanitation and medical care, and the omnipresence of such problems as contaminated water, insects, malnutrition, and sheer ignorance. Illiteracy is also widespread. The impact of such conditions on an economy is obvious. When a large percentage of the population are ill, crops may not be sown or harvested. Life expectancy is short, and the young are a burden because they consume part of the already far too low level of production.

By contrast, the annual average per capita incomes in Western Europe and the United States are astronomical—three to six times respectively the $500 figure that qualifies an economy as "developed." Moreover, these incomes are constantly on the rise, while those of the underdeveloped nations are at a virtual standstill. The industrial West has the capital for further growth; the new nations suffer from a lack of capital. For the affluent white middle-class American, who has forgotten what it is like to be poor—and who spends a minimum of $100 per year on recreation, as well as about $500 on tobacco and food—it is impossible to conceive of the life led by a typical family in a developing nation. Robert

Heilbroner has graphically conveyed what such an existence would mean to a suburban family living on a $6,000–$7,000 income.

We begin by invading the house of our imaginary American family to strip it of its furniture. Everything goes: beds, chairs, tables, television set, lamps. We leave the family with a few old blankets, a kitchen table, a wooden chair. Along with the bureaus go the clothes. Each member of the family may keep in his "wardrobe" his oldest suit or dress, a shirt or blouse. We will permit a pair of shoes to the head of the family, but none for the wife or children.

We move into the kitchen. The appliances have already been taken out, so we turn to the cupboards and larder. The box of matches may stay, a small bag of flour, some sugar and salt. A few moldy potatoes, already in the garbage can, must be hastily rescued, for they will provide much of tonight's meal. We will leave a handful of onions, and a dish of dried beans. All the rest we take away: the meat, the fresh vegetables, the canned goods, the crackers, the candy.

Now we have stripped the house: the bathroom has been dismantled, the running water shut off, the electric wires taken out. Next we take away the house. The family can move to the toolshed. It is crowded, but much better than the situation in Hong Kong, where (a United Nations report tells us) "it is not uncommon for a family of four or more to live in a bedspace, that is, on a bunk bed and the space it occupies—sometimes in two or three tiers—their only privacy provided by curtains."

But we have only begun. All the other houses in the neighborhood have also been removed; our suburb has become a shantytown. Still, our family is fortunate to have a shelter; 250,000 people in Calcutta have none at all and simply live in the streets. Our family is now about on a par with the city of Cali in Colombia, where, an official of the World Bank writes, "on one hillside alone, the slum population is estimated at 40,000—without water, sanitation, or electric lights. And not all the poor of Cali are as fortunate as that. Others have built their shacks near the city on land which lies beneath the flood mark. To these people, the immediate environment is the open sewer of the city, a sewer which flows through their huts when the river rises."

And still we have not reduced our American family to the level at which life is lived in the greatest part of the globe. Communication must go next. No more newspapers, magazines, books—not that they are missed, since we must take away our family's literacy as well. Instead, in our shantytown we will allow one radio. In India the national average of radio ownership is one per 250 people, but since the majority of radios is owned by city dwellers, our allowance is fairly generous.

Now government services must go. No more postman, no more fireman. There is a school, but it is three miles away and consists of two classrooms. They are not too overcrowded since only half the children in the neighborhood go to school. There are, of course, no hospitals or doctors nearby. The nearest clinic is ten miles away and is tended by a midwife. It can be reached by bicycle, provided that the family has a bicycle, which is unlikely. Or one can go by bus—not always inside, but there is usually room on top.

Finally, money. We will allow our family a cash hoard of five dollars. This will prevent our breadwinner from experiencing the tragedy of an Iranian peasant who went blind because he could not raise the $3.94 which he mistakenly thought he needed to secure admission to a hospital where he could have been cured.

Meanwhile the head of our family must earn his keep. As a peasant cultivator with three acres to tend, he may raise the equivalent of $100 to $300 worth of crops a year. If he is a tenant farmer, which is more than likely, a third or so of his crop will go to his landlord, and probably another 10 per cent to the local money lender. But there will be enough to eat. Or almost enough. The human body requires an input of at least 2,000 calories to replenish the energy consumed by its living cells. If our displaced American fares no better than an Indian peasant, he will average a replenishment of no more than 1,700–1,900 calories. His body, like any insufficiently fueled machine, will run down. That is one reason why life expectancy at birth in India today averages less than forty years.

But the children may help. If they are fortunate, they may find work and thus earn some cash to supplement the family's income. For example, they may be employed as are children in Hyderabad, Pakistan, sealing the ends of bangles over a small kerosene flame, a simple task which can be done at home. To be sure, the pay is small: eight annas—about ten cents—for sealing bangles. That is, eight annas per gross of bangles. And if they cannot find work? Well, they can scavenge, as do the children of Iran who in times of hunger search for the undigested oats in the droppings of horses.[3]

The developing countries generally tend to blame Western capitalism for these conditions and for the vast disparity between themselves and the West. This should not, however, divert attention from the role played by the West in forging their nationhood. For it was the "territorialization" by the colonial powers that defined the present frontiers of these nations. The Western powers drew arbitrary lines on a map, often straight through tribal or ethnic boundaries, and then imposed a single administrative and legal structure upon the territory. All who lived within this structure were treated as if they belonged to a single nation. A graphic example of the impact of this on the new nations is seen in the case of Indonesia. When Indonesia received its freedom, it did not receive as part of its territory Dutch New Guinea, or West Irian. The Dutch claimed that the people of New Guinea were ethnically, racially, and culturally distinct from Indonesia. Nevertheless, Indonesia persisted until it acquired the territory in 1963. New Guinea had been part of the old Dutch East Indies empire, and Indonesia defined its territorial limits in terms of the former imperial frontiers. Similarly, India, in her quarrel

[3] Robert L. Heilbroner, *The Great Ascent*, pp. 33–36.

with China over precisely where the Sino-Indian boundary lies in the Himalayas, defined her claim to Indian territory in the context of the line drawn by the British colonizers.

Another by-product of colonialism was the construction of harbors, roads, railroads, airports, telephone and telegraph lines, and factories, and the development of natural resources. These provided what economists call the infrastructure, or capital overhead—the prerequisite for any major industrialization.[4] To be sure, the Europeans did not undertake these projects for the benefit of the natives. The roads and railroads carried the resources or crops from the interior to the harbors; they were also used for troop movements to quell uprisings and riots. Nevertheless, their impact upon the traditional native economy and society was disruptive. In the cities, the traditional patterns of life and expectations of the vast majority of the peasants who had migrated from the land were altered. The European-built centers of government, business, and communications offered the peasants who came there to work a new way of life and new values. Urban life provided what Barbara Ward has called the "demonstration effect."[5] The Europeans lived better and longer. Why, the natives wondered, could they not live as well and as long? They could hardly avoid awareness of the technical and scientific knowledge, tools, and skills that had given the Europeans their higher material standards, as well as their power. Why, the natives asked themselves, could they not learn these secrets of science? One thing was especially noteworthy. Europeans believed that one could improve life here on earth rather than accepting poverty as one's fate. The natives began to realize that even they could earn money and buy products to improve their way of living.

The urge to transform backward societies into modern societies and economies thus began with the European introduction of urbanization, industry, a wage labor force, an exchange economy, and secular ideas. Yet, the modern, productive segment of the colonial economy—that part involved in the extraction of natural resources for the industrial Western nations—remained an "alien enclave, a foreign island or oasis of modern industrialism . . . established within a pre-industrial country." The result was a dual society and economy:

> Everywhere there was ferment; everywhere there was the beginning of change; everywhere a profound sense that the old ways were becoming inadequate, were in some way no longer valid or viable for modern man . . .
> all these changes, introduced pell-mell by colonialism, did not really pro-

[4] The disruption of the traditional colonized society by Western economic behavior is analyzed by Max F. Millikan and Donald L. M. Blackmer (eds.), *The Emerging Nations*, pp. 3–17; Immanuel Wallerstein, *Africa, The Politics of Independence*, pp. 29–43.
[5] Barbara Ward, *The Rich Nations and the Poor Nations*, p. 54.

duce a new and coherent form of society, as they had done in the West. There was no "take-off," to use Professor Rostow's phrase, into a new kind of society. . . . Little economic activity could spread beyond the Westernized areas; for there were no markets, no savings, no initiative; only the dead weight of rural bankruptcy. . . . There was little general change among the people at large and, above all, no trace of change in the vast number—eighty or more per cent of the population—who lived on the land where the old, unchanged, subsistence agriculture went on as before. And so there came about what one can only call a kind of dual society, in which the scattered growing-points of a modern way of life were restrained almost to the pitch of immobility by enormous forces of inertia inherent in the old framework of society.[6]

At the same time, however, Western colonialism educated the social group that was determined to break through these "enormous forces of inertia," lead their shackled nations into freedom, and modernize their backward countries. A relatively small and youthful group, this nationalist intelligentsia has produced the leadership of revolutionary movements in the underdeveloped countries. The members of this intelligentsia may be doctors, journalists, civil servants, lawyers, etc.; what they have in common is their "Westernization." Educated in Europe or America, or in Western schools in their own countries, they have learned the Westerner's ways—his language, dress, and conduct. Even more significant, they have learned in the course of their professional training to think in characteristically Western rational and secular terms. But this "scientific" and "material" pattern of thought holds revolutionary implications. As it did for their eighteenth-century European *confrères*, it has provided an escape from the traditions, customs, and privileges that held their societies in the tight grip of economic, social, and political backwardness. Materialism, with its simple but powerful message that man is the master of his own destiny, is for them an exhilarating philosophy of intellectual liberation from religious superstition; it substitutes rationalism for obsolete traditions and institutions. It was the absence of just such a material attitude that was responsible for their nations' economic underdevelopment. The intelligentsia, thus, have tended to repudiate the traditional values of their societies and to seek to modernize —to secularize, industrialize, and urbanize.

There are certain features of the predicament of the modern-educated intellectual in an underdeveloped country which are common to them all. Its essence is the frustration caused by their awareness of the contrasts between their own cultural level and standards of life and those of their people; between the backwardness of their country's economy and the needs of the modern world; and between the political ideas they have

[6] *Ibid.*, pp. 56–57.

learned in their Western-type education and the tyrannical regime that rules their country.[7]

Education, then, was the chief means by which Western political and social thought was diffused to non-Western areas. As one political analyst has wisely observed: "The future will look back upon the overseas imperialism of recent centuries, less in terms of its sins of oppression, exploitation, and discrimination, than as the instrument by which the spiritual, scientific, and material revolution which began in Western Europe with the Renaissance was spread to the rest of the world."[8]

It is because of this very Westernization, then, that the members of the intelligentsia become leaders in the nationalist and modernizing movements of their countries. For it confronts them with a personal emotional and psychological dilemma that "politicizes" them intensely and turns them to revolutionary politics—which may be difficult for an American to understand, accustomed as we are to consider professional middle-class men solid, reliable, and satisfied burghers. But unlike his Western counterpart, the non-Western intellectual is not a product of his society's organic social development. As the "returned student," he is literally a stranger in his own country, an outcast who has broken with the ways of his society. A Westernized foreigner to his own people, he remains a native—with all that that word denotes—to the colonial power. He is, so to speak, born into one world, lives in another, and belongs to neither. He is an isolated and lonely figure with no sense of belonging. The profession he has learned and the way of thought he has acquired— modern, secular, and rational—compel him to live his life suspended between the foreign colonial rulers and his own custom-bound people.[9] That the intellectual, facing such an acute psychological crisis, should become rebellious is hardly surprising. Nor is it surprising that he should become politically oriented in his search for "something new." For only

[7] Hugh Seton-Watson, *Neither War Nor Peace: The Struggle for Power in the Postwar World* (New York: Frederick A. Praeger, 1960), p. 167.

[8] Rupert Emerson, *From Empire to Nation*, p. 6.

[9] "The term 'intelligentsia' is [thus] used to denote specifically those intellectuals who are experiencing internal conflict between allegiance to traditional cultures and the influence of the modern West. Within these terms of reference it is not the amount of knowledge or education that determines membership in the intelligentsia. . . . No man, no matter how learned, is classified as a member of the intelligentsia if he has retained his identity with his national background. As long as he remains integrated in his society and accepts the values of that society as his own, he is likely to remain essentially a conservative without that revolutionary spark which . . . would class him as a member of the intelligentsia. If, on the other hand, he is an intellectual who has felt the impact of Western civilization and has been drawn into the vortex of conflicting ideas, he enters the ranks of the intelligentsia. . . . Within the intelligentsia, however, rebelliousness is a common characteristic. Beset with doubts about traditional cultural values, its members have felt a driving need to search for something new." (Klaus Mehnert, "The Social and Political Role of the Intelligentsia in the New Countries," in Kurt London [ed.], *New Nations in a Divided World*, pp. 121–22.)

in revolutionary politics can he find a new home. Disoriented because he has been deprived of his old values, he finds in the "nation"—a modern, urban-industrial, Western-type nation in which his values are the accepted values—a new sense of belonging. He therefore becomes a member of the "party of national independence" in order to overthrow the Western colonizer and then to close the vast gap between his own backward nation and a "twentieth-century nation" by "Westernizing" it.

In addition, the non-Western intellectual, because he is cut off from his own society, is denied the recognition, social status, and respect a person of his attainments would expect from his community. To most of his countrymen, he is a stranger whose whole pattern of thinking and life is "foreign." Instead of acquiring status in the traditional manner—by age, family rank, or land ownership—he depends on his own achievements. If he were a Westerner, he would gain social recognition and advancement in terms of authority and financial rewards. But he lives in an economically backward nation where there are few outlets for his skills. What kind of a career can a journalist expect in a country of illiterates, or a doctor in a culture where the ignorant place their trust in witch doctors? He thus becomes an unemployed, frustrated intellectual. His education has raised his aspirations too high for a society in which his opportunities for a productive life and satisfaction of his ambitions are thwarted: "There is no more explosive political material than the doctor who knows what modern medicine can do but does not have the facilities to put his knowledge to work; or the teacher who must teach, if at all, without textbooks; or the engineer without access to capital equipment; or the businessman without a place of business; or the politician without a following that understands what he is talking about."[10]

Even if employed, however, he has another strike against him—the color of his skin. As Westernized as he has become in language, dress, manners, and thinking, he is still not accepted by Europeans as an equal. They have pre-empted all the top positions in Western-owned businesses, and in the Western-controlled government, police, and army. He can occupy only the lower positions, no matter how well-prepared he may be for more responsibility—and even then, he is rarely paid on the same wage scale as Europeans doing the same work. Despite his Westernization, he remains a native to the colonial power—an inferior being, a second-class citizen. He refuses to accept this inferior status, and is therefore driven to overthrow colonial rule. If he cannot be an Englishman or a Dutchman, he can be an Indian or an Indonesian. Denied the recognition his European education and professional training led him to expect, he turns in his frustration to a political movement seeking the end of white European rule with its lack of opportunities for employ-

[10] Eugene R. Black, *The Diplomacy of Economic Development*, p. 12.

ment, its racial discrimination, and its economic exploitation. In the "party of national independence," he will gain not only a sense of belonging, but a position of leadership suited to a man of his education. And in the nation that he and his fellow intellectuals will create, he can live a useful life. His skills can be fully utilized and properly rewarded in terms of position, power, and pay.

The intellectual's yearning for security and a sense of belonging, as well as status and a productive life, instills in him not only fervent nationalism, but also a powerful populist, or "socialist," concern for the people's welfare. His cultural isolation from the mass of his own countrymen, the very countrymen for whom he seeks national independence, feeds his need for communion with them and sense of service to them. Nehru expressed this feeling before India's independence:

> Indeed, I often wonder if I represent any one at all, and I am inclined to think that I do not, though many have kindly and friendly feelings toward me. I have become a queer mixture of the East and the West, out of place everywhere, at home nowhere. Perhaps my thought and approach to life are more akin to what is called Western than Eastern, but India clings to me, as she does to all her children, in innumerable ways; and behind me lie, somewhere in the subconscious, racial memories of a hundred, or whatever the number may be, generations of Brahmans. I cannot get rid of either that past inheritance or my recent acquisitions. They are both part of me, and, though they help me in both the East and West, they also create in me a feeling of spiritual loneliness not only in public activities but in life itself. I am a stranger and alien in the West. I cannot be of it. But in my own country also, sometimes, I have an exile's feelings.[11]

It is this feeling of alienation from his own people that is the final element compelling the intellectual to achieve independence for his country. Only then can he really belong and devote his energy and talent to alleviating the lot of "his people." Only by dedicating himself to their welfare can he regain his sense of identification with them and find an outlet for the genuine sense of compassion that their misery has stirred within him. "The people" become his standard; all that he does or wants to do he justifies with reference to "the people." They legitimatize his political activities. Nationalism cannot be limited to the intellectuals alone, but must encompass the entire nation.

> Thus, nationalism and socialism were the two outstanding dynamic forces at work within the intelligentsia of the new countries. These forces answered the need for a "cause" and gave the intellectuals the group feeling that they craved after breaking away from the traditional groups of their youth. It is in periods of crisis that individuals wish to submerge them-

[11] Jawaharlal Nehru, *Toward Freedom* (New York: The John Day Co., 1941), pp. 352–53.

selves in a group in order to find fellowship and security. The nation (politically and culturally) and the people (socially) were the two super-collectives from which the new intellectuals drew the longed-for feeling of warmth and community. The greater an individual's awareness—and acute awareness of life is characteristic of the intelligentsia—the greater is his need to find an ultimate meaning in existence, particularly in a period when values cannot be taken for granted but must be rationalized. It is such times as these that the thought of being superfluous is particularly painful.[12]

The two forces of nationalism and socialism together also represent a claim to public stewardship. The intellectual is dedicated to the people's welfare. He is at the same time the only one in the traditional society who knows the modern world and has absorbed its values and a few of its skills. Since the old ruling class or tribal chieftains, who usually collaborated with the colonial power, wish only to preserve the existing society, the intelligentsia proposes their overthrow and advances itself as the group that will lead the people out of the wilderness of servitude, backwardness, and destitution into the paradise of national independence and the twentieth-century welfare state. Thus it plays quite a different social and political role from that of its Western counterpart: "What distinguishes such non-Western intelligentsias from most intellectuals in Western societies is that they wield political power as it were independently, i.e., they wield it in their own right, *as* intelligentsias, rather than as spokesmen for entrenched social forces. In other words, these intelligentsias are a *ruling class,* or rather *the* ruling class *par excellence,* whereas elsewhere intellectuals do not as a rule constitute a socio-political class of their own so much as an adjunct to other classes or groups in society."[13] In the West, intellectuals have generally been spokesmen for a particular class or interest group, but it is the professional politician, the aristocrat, the businessman, or the trade-union leader who represents them. Thus the example of the intelligentsia as ruling class is unique. But the intelligentsia actually governs in the non-Western world because there is no one else who can perform this function. Moreover, while it was the capitalist who stoked the furnace of industrialism in the West, the intelligentsia has had to do this, too, in most underdeveloped countries.

As intensely aware as they are of the underdeveloped nature of their countries, and as determined as they are to initiate development, the ruling intelligentsias face almost insuperable obstacles which tend to hamper an economic "take-off" and self-sustaining economic growth: a lack of national cohesion, a far too rapidly growing population, a dearth of capi-

---

[12] Mehnert, in London (ed.), *op. cit.,* p. 130.
[13] Harry J. Benda, "Non-Western Intelligentsias and Political Elites," in John H. Kautsky (ed.), *Political Change in Underdeveloped Countries,* p. 237.

tal, and a traditional social structure and values. All of these impede the
modernization of their societies.

The Absence of National Unity

The Westernized intellectuals may have become rulers of a new nation, but few of their subjects share their nationalism. Concepts of a
nation, of national loyalty, of a national government that makes decisions for the benefit of the entire community, of national laws and regu-
lations that take precedence over local government and tradition are all
new and unique to most of the peoples of the underdeveloped areas.
The very first requirement of the leaders of the new nations is to construct the nation in whose name they have revolted against colonial
domination. They must be "nation-builders" in order to give reality to
the nation they have long felt inside themselves. But their masses have
never lived in a "nation." Their lives have been rooted in smaller communities and their first loyalty is to the tribe, to the region, or to religious, racial, or linguistic groups.[14] Loyalties are parochial and attitudes
are particularistic. These stand as formidable barriers to the formation of
a sense of national consciousness and a devotion to national symbols.
Men from other regions will be regarded not as fellow nationals with
whom one shares a certain loyalty to the nation, a language, historical
memories (beyond the one memory of colonial rule), and hopes for the
future, but as "strangers," "foreigners," "outsiders." Disunity rather than
unity is the spirit of the new nations. The communities created by the
colonial powers may have become "national" in the sense that the people living within these areas desired to rid themselves of the foreign
rulers. But their common resentment and aspiration to be free never
developed into a shared allegiance to the nations whose frontiers had
been artificially drawn in previous centuries by European statesmen in
Europe.

The crucial problem of integrating the diverse masses into the new
nation, of forming a national consensus, is therefore not an easy one.
Race is one element impeding this "integrative revolution." In Africa,
the issue of the natives' relations with the white men is obviously significant. The white settler has lived in Kenya and Southern Rhodesia
for a long time. Naturally, he took the best land tended by himself and
his "boys," and in time it became his land. He and succeeding generations lived on it and farmed on it. And the "nation" to which they had
emigrated became *their* nation; they were its citizens in the same sense

---

[14] See particularly Emerson, *op. cit.*, pp. 89–187, 295–359; Clifford Geertz, "The
Integrative Revolution," in Geertz (ed.), *Old Societies and New States*, pp. 105–57;
and James S. Coleman, "The Problem of Political Integration," *Western Political
Quarterly*, March, 1955, pp. 44–57.

that they had once been citizens of Holland, Belgium, or Britain. But the natives now want to determine their own fate and end the rule of the smug, superior white man. The European, though he has made the land "his own," remains the foreigner and colonizer. It is his political and economic power that must be broken and controlled by the "real" natives—"Africa for the Africans!" A racial problem of this sort hardly provides an auspicious opportunity for consensus formation. And in the extreme situation of South Africa, where the white government pursues a strict and harshly enforced policy of apartheid, the result can only be violence and a great bloodletting.

But the race issue is not always in terms of black and white. Many of the countries of Southeast Asia, for instance, contain sizable Chinese elements. Out of a population of almost 28 million in Thailand, 3 million are Chinese; of 7.5 million and 2 million in Malaya and Singapore, respectively, almost 2.8 million and 1.3 million are Chinese.[15] Many of these Chinese settlers have achieved great economic success. For example, while they constitute only 10 per cent of Thailand's population, they control almost its entire retail business and a very large share of the rice and export timber trade. Almost everywhere in Southeast Asia, the Chinese are the middlemen. They are the distributors of consumer goods, the bankers, the investors, the shopkeepers. At the same time that they virtually control Southeast Asia's economic life, the Chinese have retained their language and customs—and, for the most part, their loyalty to China. Having thus isolated themselves, they remain foreigners in the nations where they live. As a result, of course, they provoke jealousy, dislike, discrimination, and accusations of "alien exploitation" on the part of the natives. The danger here lies in the renewed pride of the Chinese in the new China—not because it is Communist but because it is a China that can no longer be humiliated by other nations. Consequently, they may look to Peking for protection against native restrictions, discrimination, and reprisals. Whether the Chinese can be assimilated and integrated into the national lives of the nations of Southeast Asia in time is an open question. The departure of Singapore from the Malaysia Federation in 1965 was a bad sign. Even without the menace of Communist China, this would be a long and difficult task. One principal obstacle to assimilation via intermarriage is religion. Marriage between heathen Chinese and practicing Moslems is unthinkable. Such religious obstacles to marriage are hardly unique.

Nor are religious animosities. But when they lead to the massive dislocation of millions of people and the slaughter of hundreds of thousands, they *are* unique—at least to a Western world that has long forgotten the

[15] See Richard Hughes, "I Am Chinese! I Live in the Southern Ocean," *The New York Times Magazine*, August 4, 1963, p. 61; and A. Doak Barnett, *Communist China and Asia*, pp. 172–210.

Thirty Years' War. This was what happened when India, upon gaining its independence, was partitioned into Hindu India and Moslem Pakistan because the Moslem minority wanted its own nation. In the words of Pakistan's founder, Mohammed Ali Jinnah, "To yoke together two such nations under a single state, one as a numerical minority and the other as a majority, must lead to growing discontent and final destruction of any fabric that may be so built up for the government of such a state."[16] Avoiding such a single state, however, resulted in a great bloodbath: In the Punjab, for instance, "Members of the minority fled from isolated villages to larger centers in the hope that numbers would provide a measure of security. Some were killed *en route*. . . . No quarter was given—torture, mutilation, assault, conversion by force. It was nothing less than a war of extermination. The battlefield was everywhere, in village, town, road, temple and mosque. Trains going between Lahore and Amritsar were considered fair prey. . . . The less fortunate began a trek by foot. . . . In sheer numbers it was the greatest in history, about twelve million, equally divided between Hindus and Sikhs fleeing from West Punjab and Muslims from the East. Before the year was out half a million people died, or were murdered."[17] Not all religiously divided nations, of course, experience such a bloody or even a nonviolent partition. But internal dissension that hampers "nation-building" does occur in a nation such as Lebanon, which is divided between Moslems and Christians, or Burma, with its religious differences between the Karens and the Moslem Arakanese.

Regional differences tend to be a further divisive factor, and this is particularly true if they are accompanied by uneven distribution of resources and wealth. Indonesia, for instance, is a nation of islands, the main ones being Java (on which the capital of Jakarta is located), Sumatra, Celebes, most of Borneo, and about half of West Irian. Sumatra is the source of Indonesia's oil and rubber wealth, and the Sumatrans have little use for the Javanese, whom they feel they are supporting. And the Menadonese on Celebes are suspicious of both the Javanese and the Sumatrans. Finally, the people of West Irian have little, if anything, in common with the people of the other islands. In 1957, before Indonesia's acquisition of West Irian, the outer islands revolted unsuccessfully against Java's domination. Interestingly enough, the centers of revolt were northern Sumatra and the Christian areas of the Celebes. As can be seen in Indonesia, as in some of the new African countries, "Regionalism is understandable because ethnic loyalties can usually find expression in geographical terms. Inevitably, some regions will be richer (less

---

[16] Quoted in Emerson, *op. cit.*, p. 348.
[17] Michael Brecher, *Nehru: A Political Biography* (London and New York: Oxford University Press, 1959), pp. 362–63.

poor) than others, and if the ethnic claim to power combines with relative wealth, the case for secession is strong."[18]

As if the three factors of disunity named thus far were not sufficient, there is yet a fourth—tribalism. Particularly in Africa, the tribe is still the psychological, economic, and political reality to many, for it is the social organization most familiar to them. The colonial powers, particularly the British, who ruled their colonies "indirectly"—via the traditional chiefs— helped to preserve the tribalism. The African tribes generally are not, as might be thought, small groups of a few hundred or thousand members. The larger tribes, if they lived in the United States, would be considered ethnic, or national minority, groups.[19] The Hausa, for instance, exceed 10 million, and the Bakongo number about 800,000; the approximately 2 million Somali live in an area the size of Texas. The problem is thus less the large numbers of tribes than it is the large size of some tribes. As a result, the cohesion of the new nation may be weakened by the desire of tribal chieftains to invoke the same claim of national self-determination that the intelligentsia has already invoked on behalf of the nation. Secondly, since the Europeans often split up tribal groups when they drew up their artificial boundary lines in the conference rooms of Berlin, London, and Paris, the new nations' frontiers tend to be unstable. Thus, depending on the season, there are 300,000 Somalis in southern Ethiopia, 70,000 in Kenya's Northern Frontier District, and 30,000 more in French Somaliland. This is so because the vast majority of Somalis survive as nomads—herding flocks of sheep, goats, and cattle —and in their search for water and grazing lands, they cross freely into Ethiopia and Kenya. They have been doing this for centuries, and international frontiers do not stop them. Somalia, in fact, claimed a third of Kenya, a sizable part of Ethiopia, plus French Somaliland—all in the name of tribal, or ethnic, unity and national self-determination. Thus Kenya, immediately upon gaining its independence, was confronted with the desire of its Somalis to break away—a desire encouraged by their "countrymen" across the border. Ethiopia and Kenya, in turn, became involved in serious frontier fighting, since neither was willing to see a part of the nation secede, thus weakening, if not disintegrating, the entire state. Such "tribal" conflicts occasionally still occur in the "developed" parts of the world as well: for instance, in Cyprus between the Greek majority, which seeks union with Greece, and the Turks, who are fearful of their minority rights; and in Belgium, between the Flemish and Walloons. And on the North American continent, the French-speaking Canadians in Quebec actually seek secession from the rest of Canada.

[18] Wallerstein, *op. cit.*, p. 88.
[19] See James S. Coleman, "The Character and Viability of African Political Systems," in Walter Goldschmidt (ed.), *The United States and Africa*, pp. 49–50.

The new nations' lack of political and cultural cohesiveness is nowhere more dramatically evident than in the language problem. For language is one of the most important factors in forming and preserving a sense of nationalism, and uniformity of language, by helping men to communicate with one another, promotes common attitudes and values. In turn, a feeling of group consciousness and common interests is stimulated; men learn to think in terms of "we," as opposed to the "they" who speak a different language and have different ideas.

But instead of one common language, India has at least 12 major languages, each of which is spoken by more than a million people.[20] In addition, there are 24 tribal languages or dialects, each spoken by more than 100,000 people, and 63 non-Indian languages, of which English is the most widely spoken. An Indian commission investigating this linguistic problem found that regional cultures, based on language communities, were more intelligible to the average Indian than Indian nationalism. The commission concluded that Indian nationalism must therefore "acquire a deeper content before it becomes ideologically adequate to withstand the gravitational pull of the traditional narrower loyalties."[21] Prime Minister Nehru put it more simply: "Integrate," he warned, "or perish." This lack of a common language is a problem in almost all the new nations. African nations are plagued by an even greater diversity of languages. For example, the 2 million people of Dahomey speak 6 different languages; and the half-million population of Gabon speak 40 different languages and dialects. The prospects for national cohesion in these circumstances are certainly not promising. And the question for the new nations, almost all of whom lack a common language, is less whether they will develop economically than whether they will survive as national entities.

Overpopulation and Economic Development

The second problem the modernizing intelligentsia confronts—again unique—is that of overpopulation. Not all underdeveloped nations, to be sure, have this problem—for instance, the continental nations of Southeast Asia and some of the new states in Africa—but for the many who do it places in question whether they can make any economic progress at all. Obviously, if there are always more mouths to feed, all or most of the increment in national income is likely to be eaten up. World population has already passed the 3 billion mark and is increasing at an annual rate of just over 2 per cent. Three children are born each second, 260,000 each day, and almost 2 million per week. But Northern and Western

---

[20] See Selig S. Harrison, "The Challenge to Indian Nationalism," *Foreign Affairs*, July, 1956, p. 624.
[21] Emerson, *op. cit.*, p. 142.

Europe average an increase of only 0.9 per cent, and the American rate is 1.6 per cent. It is in the underdeveloped areas that the rate is high: 2.8 per cent for Latin America (7 million people per year), 2.6 per cent for Southeast Asia. India's birth rate is enough to fill a city the size of New York every year; her total population is more than 400 million. China's new population would permit her to add another Canada annually; her population, already estimated at 700 million, is expected to reach the billion mark by the year 2000, if not earlier. In 1900, there was 1 European for every 2 Asians; in 2000, the ratio will probably be 1 to 4. It is also estimated that by 2000 there will be 2 Latin Americans for each North American—and this is based on a 300 million population for the United States.[22]

This is the "population explosion"—an explosion that, in its own way, is every bit as serious as the atomic explosion. Nearly half of the world's population today are under twenty! It was in 1830 that world population reached 1 billion. By 1930, it had doubled, and after that it took only 30 more years to add another billion for a total of 3 billion people. In less than forty more years, at the present rate of growth—that is, by the year 2000—it is expected to rise to 6.2 billion people. The birth rate increases with each decade.

The underdeveloped countries have thus come face to face with the elements of the Malthusian problem: the constant hunger and grinding poverty that result when the population grows faster than do the means of subsistence. More than 150 years ago, the Reverend Malthus, who was also an economist, predicted this fate for the Western world—unless the population growth was limited either by "positive checks," such as wars or epidemics, which result in a high death rate, or by "preventive checks," which result in a low birth rate. Yet, despite the huge population increase since 1800, the West has made great economic progress: agricultural production has provided a plentiful supply of food, and industrial production has raised the standard of living to new heights. The West's recent history would thus refute Malthus' gloomy prediction.

Unfortunately, the conditions that confront the underdeveloped nations are quite dissimilar from those experienced by the West. One of the chief differences is that the Western countries had far smaller populations when they began industrializing, and their subsequent population increase did not outdistance the economic gains. The pattern in the non-Western countries was actually significantly affected by the colonial pow-

[22] Between 1951 and 1961, the population of the 20 republics of Latin America rose from 163 million to approximately 206 million—an annual increase of about 4 million people to feed, house, educate, and employ. The 600 million population estimated for the year 2000 may even be conservative. Brazil's population rose from 52 to 66 million in the 10 years after 1945, and it exceeded 75 million in 1963. Venezuela's population during the last 10 years grew by 30 per cent, and tiny El Salvador's grew by 50 per cent. (Tad Szulc, *The Winds of Revolution,* pp. 17, 47.)

ers. In the pre-colonial period, the Malthusian "positive checks" had in their own cruel way maintained some sort of balance between population and resources. The typical, age-old pattern was simple: once a tribe had eaten up most of the available food in the area it inhabited and had overfarmed the land so that soil erosion had begun, it would invade the hunting preserves of neighboring tribes. The ensuing battles would kill off members of both tribes, decreasing the number left to be fed. Periodic famine and pestilence also helped to maintain a balance between births and deaths. This seemingly eternal cycle of peace and population growth, succeeded by violence and population decline, was broken by the colonial power's preservation of peace in the areas it ruled, and by its introduction of modern medicine. As a result, more of the newborn survived and people lived longer; populations began to increase at much greater rates.

The European nations were also aided by the New World and by their colonial empires, which provided them with outlets to relieve population pressures. About 60 million Europeans emigrated during the nineteenth and early twentieth centuries. The United States and Canada, rich in resources and fertile in land, absorbed millions of immigrants with ease and still were able to raise their living standards; Australia, New Zealand and South Africa experienced similar population and economic expansion, although on a smaller scale. If these millions had not emigrated and if the mother countries had not found many of their colonies profitable sources of cheap raw materials and labor, as well as markets for their products, the West might today face some of the same problems as the underdeveloped nations. The colonies thus served Europe as a frontier similar to the American West, which absorbed population that might otherwise have overcrowded the Eastern seaboard. But the underdeveloped countries can find no such relatively empty and rich spaces to absorb their surplus populations. The 50,000 Puerto Ricans who immigrate each year into the United States represent a unique situation that can hardly be duplicated elsewhere. At any rate, it is estimated that it would take the enormous number of 25 million annual emigrants from Asia to keep that area stable. An alternative in some countries might be internal migration. In Indonesia, for instance, three-quarters of the population live in the island of Java, while Sumatra remains largely jungle. But habit, inertia, and deep roots make such extensive internal migration very difficult, if not impossible.

Another advantage of the West was that the Industrial Revolution made it possible to apply machinery to agriculture, thus producing a great increase in the food supply. Efficient agriculture also meant that food could be produced by a smaller farm population. Excess labor on the land was thereby forced to go to the city, where it was used in the factories. This, in turn, accelerated the industrialization process. Moreover, quite apart from modern technology, Europe, being a temperate land with sufficient sunshine and rain, was more favorable to food production than are many of the underdeveloped countries which are in tropical and monsoon areas. Europe could thus grow sufficient food to feed its multiplying population, and what it could not produce it imported from the colonies and the New World in exchange for industrial products. By contrast, in the nonindustrialized nations, the majority of the population are still engaged in primitive agriculture. Moreover, there is generally not sufficient land for any major agricultural expansion; and more intensive farming of land already under cultivation—that is, using better seed, more chemical fertilizers, and insecticides—might perhaps yield only enough to keep pace with the population growth. During India's First Five-Year Plan for economic development, about half of the new product was needed to feed new mouths. "If our population continues to increase as rapidly as it is doing," the President of neighboring Pakistan has said, "we will soon have nothing to eat and will all become cannibals." Although this statement may perhaps be a slight exaggeration, it does dramatize the underdeveloped countries' problem of overpopulation. There are simply too many poor people. This might have been all right if the sleeping masses had not awakened, but had continued to accept their miserable lot as natural. Suddenly, though, they became aware that their fate was not ordained by God but was man-made. Having made this discovery, they demanded the chance to eat more and live better. It is this "revolution of rising expectations" that creates the problem, for it will be impossible to fulfill these expectations unless there is a reduction in birth rates. The population pressure keeps the masses living close to subsistence level; and such widespread poverty makes it very difficult, and perhaps unfeasible, to accumulate enough capital to stoke industrial growth. The countries of Asia must raise their aggregate product by 60 per cent by 1975, and an additional 75 per cent for the twenty-five years thereafter, merely to maintain their current standard of existence.[23]

The birth rate in the West declined after 1850. With industrialization and the growth of cities came the spread of literacy and knowledge of artificial birth-control techniques. Malthus was thus right even for the West because preventive checks were adopted. But Asia has not yet reached this level of economic development, and knowledge of birth-control methods is likely to spread only very slowly. This is true partly because of the opposition of the Roman Catholic Church, whose influence is strong in all of Latin America and in such Asian countries as the Philippines, Vietnam, and Ceylon. And although the Church is now beginning to re-examine its attitude toward birth control, the fact is that con-

[23] Robert L. Heilbroner, "Dynamics of Foreign Aid," *The New Leader*, September 18, 1961, p. 19.

traceptives are generally too expensive for those living in utter poverty. Nor do any of the alternatives—such as the rhythm method, sterilization, or self-control in marriage—seem feasible.

There is one more, and very powerful, reason why artificial birth control is not likely to meet with a large measure of success in the underdeveloped areas for a long time to come: Children in many of these countries are a religious, social, and even economic necessity.[24] In India, for instance, Moslems believe that children are a "gift of Allah," and the childless couple is pitied or despised; a woman does not even establish herself with her husband or his family until she has borne a son. A Hindu needs a son to perform certain rituals after his death, and during life he needs sons to fight in village feuds or in tribal warfare. Moreover, there is a fear of *too few* children because they may be needed to help work in the fields and support their parents as—and if—they grow older. Children are in this sense a substitute for the social-security payments or endowment policies common to the West. In any case, the family is the hub of life for the Indian villagers. Weddings and births are festive social occasions, important events in the village life. A woman's prestige may even be in direct proportion to the number of children, especially sons, she bears. A voluntary reduction in the size of her family would in these circumstances strike at the very basis of her life.

Still, there is a definite desire in most underdeveloped countries to lower the annual increase in population. The Indian Government has instituted a public education campaign in family planning, is financing research to discover a cheap and effective means of contraception that the untutored can use, and is even considering sponsoring a law permitting sterilization. The situation has become so desperate in Japan—which has a population of nearly 90 million, with 0.15 acres of arable land per person and a food supply below minimum—that the government has legalized abortion.

Yet, it is doubtful that the birth rate will decline significantly in most of these countries during the next crucial decade or two. This means that the pace of economic development must surpass the fast-rising populations. Economists seem to agree generally that an annual investment of 12 to 15 per cent of the national income is needed to transform a static agrarian economy into a modern, dynamic, industrialized economy in which capital accumulation begins to sustain itself. But these countries simply do not have that kind of capital. Even the United States has great difficulty creating the 1.25 million new jobs needed each year to keep pace with the rising labor force, to construct the additionally needed school and college buildings, let alone to furnish enough properly trained teachers and professors. For Egypt or India, obviously, the prob-

[24] See Peggy and Pierre Streit, "New Light on India's Large Worry," *The New York Times Magazine*, March 13, 1960.

lem is multiplied hundreds of times. The number of extra children to feed may jeopardize the nation's ability to lift itself "by its own sandal strap" even *with* Western foreign-aid funds. This dilemma has been neatly summed up as follows: "Industrial revolutions may be defeated by Malthusian counterrevolutions."[25]

The Lag in Capital Formation

As if the problems caused by the gap between themselves and the tradition-bound masses, and by overpopulation were not sufficient, the leaders of the new countries also face backward, if not stagnant, economies. It is upon such a base that they must build an industrial economy that they hopefully expect will banish the poverty of their peoples, bring them the material abundance of the West, end their economic dependence on the former colonial power, and give them international standing. Industrialization, to put it another way, is to them a symbol of being modern. It is also a means of escaping a past of need and humiliation, a past in which their countries were largely "raw-materials appendages" to the industrial colonial power. Yet, while they are vitally concerned with the economic "take-off" and the transition to a modern society, their first thoughts and efforts must go to an even more fundamental problem— that of simply "getting into position" for the "take-off." From where do they obtain the requisite capital for capital accumulation?

The underdeveloped nations are basically exporters of primary products or raw materials, such as coffee, tea, rubber, copper, tin, bananas, and cocoa. Most of them, moreover, possess only one major product for export. Theoretically, they should be able to earn sufficient capital from their exports to carry out large-scale industrialization. For, as Western nations continue to consume more, their demand for raw materials should rise correspondingly. In practice, however, things have not worked out so well.[26] It is precisely the fact of their dependence on raw-materials exports that limits the earning capacities of the underdeveloped countries. For their exports rise or fall with every fluctuation of the Western business cycle. A fall of just a few cents in coffee prices is a disaster to a country whose economy is based upon coffee exports. As the Mexicans used to say, "A sneeze in the American economy could lead to pneumonia in Mexico." Moreover—and this may hurt even more in the long run —advanced Western technology has made it both possible and profitable to develop synthetics or other substitutes. Producers are thereby released from their dependence on natural raw materials; in turn, demand de-

[25] Alexander Gerschenkron, *Economic Backwardness in Historical Perspective*, p. 28.
[26] For an example, see Susan and Peter Ritner, "No Time for Cocoa," *The New Leader*, April 14, 1961, pp. 17–20.

creases and prices are lowered. Finally, competition among underdeveloped countries exporting the same raw material drives down prices.

Thus the dilemma of underdeveloped countries is truly an agonizing one. They desperately need capital. They rely on their raw material exports to earn this capital. But the harder they work to enlarge their volume of exports to enhance their earnings, the more prices fall. At the same time, since they do not produce enough food for their rapidly growing populations, they must pay for the food they need and for the machinery required to start their industrialization—Western machinery whose prices are, on top of everything else, almost always rising. Exports, then, do not seem a likely escape for the underdeveloped countries from their poverty—a poverty that need not be but is enforced upon them by the "laws" of the "free" international market. It is the Western powers who are favored by this "structured poverty," but they have done little to meet the problem, such as agreeing to high and stable international commodity prices—high so that the underdeveloped countries could earn a clear profit to enable them to diversify their economies, and stable so that their earnings would not constantly fluctuate, thus making it virtually impossible for them to plan their program of industrialization. Yet such price stabilization is as essential to the livelihood of the underdeveloped countries as farm parity prices are to American farmers. When the laws of the *laissez-faire* market produce unacceptable results—when, in fact, they stabilize only hunger—they should be amended. This has been done in the United States to distribute the national income more equitably; but it has not yet been done internationally.

Nor can the underdeveloped countries rely on private foreign investments. In the past, the burden fell primarily upon private capital, although even during the nineteenth-century days of *laissez-faire* economics, governments lent much of the money needed for projects and services which, while quite necessary for economic development, did not produce immediate returns; included were services like education and such projects as construction of roads, railroads, and harbors. In its days as the world's leading power, Britain invested about 7 per cent of its national income outside the country each year. America's economic development, for instance, would have been neither as rapid nor as extensive without British investments. In order to match the British contribution today, the United States would need to invest approximately $28 billion per year—more than the underdeveloped countries could actually absorb. Private capital has, in any case, been in short supply for the kind of long-range development that the new nations need. Approximately two-thirds of private American investments outside the United States have been made by a small group of oil companies to build refineries and to discover and pump out oil fields in Latin America and the Middle East. Such investments may meet the needs of the Western industrialized nations, but they do not contribute much to the development of the backward economies. Rather, they perpetuate the "colonial" relationship, in which the principal function of the underdeveloped economy is to supply the raw materials to feed the advanced economy's industry.

The reasons for this lack of private Western—and especially American—capital for foreign investment are not hard to find. The American economy has, on the whole, been booming since the end of World War II. European capital has concentrated on the rebuilding, modernization, and expansion of its own capital plant. Indeed, the high rate of economic growth in Europe, particularly since the inauguration of the Common Market in 1957, has even attracted large-scale private American investments. Private capital is drawn to investments that will yield relatively good profits in a reasonable period of time. Such expectations cannot on the whole be realized in underdeveloped economies, for industrialization is a long-range process. Moreover, the basic prerequisite for economic growth is capital overhead: schools, roads, railroads, ports, hospitals, housing, and power. Education is fundamental, both to "nationalize" the people—to instill in them a sense of national consciousness and loyalty—and to teach them the skills necessary for the operation of a modern economy and society. Transportation systems return too low a profit and too slowly.[27] Even in nineteenth-century America, the private companies building railroads or turnpikes were usually encouraged by the government—national or state—through land grants, public credit, and direct financial support. Roads are still paid for almost entirely with public funds from the Federal Government. What private firm in an underdeveloped country would find it profitable to build the low-cost housing projects that will be needed by the peasants who will come to the cities seeking factory jobs? How could private enterprise build large dams when there might as yet be little industry that would consume the electricity? Education, housing, and public-health services would not yield rapid economic returns, but they are essentials whose contribution would, in the long run, pay off. Public funds are thus necessary in the early stages of economic development. Only when the infrastructure has been laid will private capital be attracted by the possibilities of more rapid economic growth in the future. Money is attracted to money, not to poverty.

In any case, many leaders of new nations are not particularly enthusiastic about attracting private capital, at least in the first stages. Colonialism and capitalism are in a sense synonymous to them, and consequently they tend to be hostile toward private enterprise. They are suspicious that private foreign investment might forge new economic chains for their enslavement. To them, national independence means more than

[27] See Millikan and Blackmer (eds.), *op. cit.*, pp. 46–53; and W. W. Rostow, *The Stages of Economic Growth*, pp. 21–26.

just a formal political independence granted by the colonial ruler. They know that a country can seem to be politically free, but actually be subject economically to a foreign power—as were Latin America's so-called "banana republics," for instance, because their governments were dependent on the United Fruit Company. "Real" political freedom is equated with economic independence. The new nations therefore constantly guard themselves against the possible re-establishment of economic control by what they call "neocolonialism." Capitalism is linked in their minds to a "dog-eat-dog" competition, high profits for a privileged few and exploitation and subsistence existence for the many. In other words, they view capitalism largely in terms of its nineteenth-century image rather than its twentieth-century behavior. This is understandable since the underdeveloped countries have not experienced Europe's and America's capital accumulation and social programs, through which the benefits of industrialization are spread to all sectors of the community. On the contrary, their experience with capitalism has been closer to that of Western workers during the Industrial Revolution.

Since most of the leaders of the new nations regard themselves as socialists, they believe particularly that heavy industry—steel, rubber, chemicals, etc., the backbone of an advanced economy—should be publicly rather than privately controlled. Thus, even where private capital might be attracted to underdeveloped nations, investors fear their firms might be expropriated and nationalized, or subjected to discriminatory taxes or to currency controls to prevent the withdrawal of profits; and, of course, the contingency of nationalist agitation is ever present.

Another source of capital formation is through internal savings. In the West, the capital was mobilized primarily by private businessmen, although governments always played an important role in their support of the business community—by such means as protective tariffs, permission of a high degree of industrial concentration, and pursuit of vigorous anti-labor policies. All this assured high profits, and thereby stimulated the process of accumulation, which required a vast inequality of income. Those with high incomes, because they could not consume all their earnings, saved and invested a considerable amount. In the mid-twentieth century, however, the idea of a small minority of businessmen earning large profits at the expense of their countrymen finds little favor. The egalitarianism of the West's democratic revolutions has spread too far for this not to smack of social injustice to the leaders of underdeveloped countries. More than that, even if this prejudice against private capital did not exist, from whom could one squeeze the savings? The overwhelming majority of the populations live on the land and are engaged in subsistence farming. It would be difficult to depress their primitive standards of existence further—at least without resorting to totalitarian techniques and imposing the cruelest sacrifices on the people. By contrast, the West possessed a wealthy class when industrialization began: the commercial bourgeoisie, which had grown prosperous during the mercantilist era, when Europe first expanded overseas to India and the New World.

To be sure, many of the underdeveloped countries, as in Latin America, do have a wealthy class—the large landowners who cooperated with the colonial power not only because it was profitable to do so, but because it guaranteed the stability of the traditional society and their own position at the top of the social hierarchy. While this class usually possesses great wealth, its members tend to spend it largely in ostentatious living and foreign travel, are generally quite content with their way of life, and are not by and large too concerned with the welfare of the peasants. Nor are they interested in industry, since it would destroy the existing society and, with it, their social position and their economic and social privileges. They thus have a vested interest in the *status quo*.

More generally, however, the whole concept of enterprise is alien to such a traditional society, which lacks the secular orientation that produces the idea of material progress, individual achievement and reward, including vertical social mobility. Yet, these are prerequisites for any sustained effort at saving and capital formation. In their absence, the few who possess wealth spend it extravagantly rather than investing; money-making is frowned upon as an ignoble and dishonorable profession; and the merchant remains a figure of reprobation. A very apt demonstration of the largely extrasecular nature of life in a traditional society is the fact that necessary functions involving trade and money had to be left to "outsiders," or "foreigners." Thus, in Southeast Asian countries, most of the commerce is in the hands of the Chinese minorities; and in sub-Sahara Africa, business is left largely to the Indians.

The same traditionalism of society and culture also handicaps the modernization of agriculture. Although the overwhelming majority of the underdeveloped nations' populations live on the land—and these populations are growing all too rapidly—the peasants in most countries cannot produce enough food. Java, for example, one of the most intensively cultivated regions in the world, was once a rice exporter, but today it is dependent on food imports. The overriding concern of the leaders of underdeveloped countries with industrialization has too often led to an understandable neglect of agriculture. Their nations are preponderantly agrarian—normally more than 75 per cent of their people are engaged in agricultural pursuits—and to them agriculture means poverty; it also is a constant reminder of their past colonial subjection, of their former status as a supplier of raw materials. Industry, on the other hand, symbolizes modernization and equality. Nevertheless, agriculture remains vital, and food production must be raised drastically to feed the growing population, both rural and urban-industrial, and to earn foreign exchange with which to buy required goods and services—or, at least, to decrease the amount of foreign currency spent on food imports. Economic development, in short, refers to *both* industrial and agrarian development. Instead of being separate and distinct processes, they are intertwined. An industrial revolution cannot occur without the provision of extra food. This in turn requires the application of machinery and science to farming.

This is a far from simple task in traditional societies, where peasants have for centuries tilled the soil by the same methods. Unlike the Western farmer—who produces cash crops for a market and is therefore alert to technical innovation in order to increase his production and with his earnings buy the other goods he needs, including food items he does not grow himself—the peasant produces largely for his family, exchanging with his village neighbors any surplus he may have for things he needs. Usually, the peasant is the last person to be touched by the currents of modernization. Poorly educated and physically isolated from the growing urban centers, he lacks contact with the latest trends in politics, with the new intellectual and technical currents that sweep the cities. The peasant is subject mainly to conservative influences: to religion, which tells him that he must bear his lot patiently and prepare himself for the hereafter; and to the landowner, who is the local political leader and the man to whom the peasant traditionally pays deference as well as portions of his crop. It is therefore the city-dweller who is the activist and organizer of revolutionary movements, while the peasant tends to be politically passive.

This does not mean that the peasant lacks grievances which can be manipulated by revolutionary leaders in the attempt to break the power of the landowners and undermine the existing society. For the peasant has an intense "land hunger." He wants to own the land he tills. But most of the land that peasants hold by tenure is owned by a few wealthy landlords. In Latin America as a whole, for instance, 90 per cent of all land is owned by 10 per cent of the landowners. In Paraguay, 11 farms cover 35 per cent of the wealthier eastern region; 63 per cent of the arable land in Chile is held by big estates (while only 0.3 per cent of it is held by small farms); and in Peru's highlands, 1.3 per cent of the estates control more than 50 per cent of the land.[28] Moreover, land tenure systems are frequently subject to such abuses as excessive payments in kind (generally from 10 to over 50 per cent, and in some cases even 90 per cent) or work to be done on the landlord's estate. On the other hand, peasants who own their own land are handicapped by the small size of their holdings as well as their crude methods of work. The backward and impoverished peasants, compelled to borrow money in order to survive, can do so only by paying a moneylender, usually the local landowner,

[28] Szulc, *op. cit.*, pp. 54–55.

extremely high interest rates (ranging from 20 to 40 per cent, or even higher). The peasants are thereby condemned to live in a state of continual indebtedness.

Thus the technical backwardness of the peasant, his small holdings of land, and the concentration of land ownership all stand as formidable obstacles to agricultural development. Consequently, the overthrow of the old landowning class is not just a matter of social justice but a functional political and economic prerequisite for modernization: to bring to power men whose aim it is to industrialize; to destroy the traditional social structure, founded upon a grossly uneven distribution of wealth; and to channel savings into industrialization and permit agrarian reform.

Fundamentally, this means that the peasant must be granted his own land. But the redistribution of land is only the beginning. In most areas, the density of the population is likely to result in too many small farms —or what has been called "postage-stamp cultivation." Even if the peasant is taught more modern farming methods, receives proper credit facilities, and gains a market for which to produce, his crop production may continue to decline. A small farm is simply unproductive, and mechanical equipment is both too costly and inefficient for use on small farms. There are no easy solutions, then, even after the political and social barriers are overcome. Collectivization of the land has not been too successful where tried, largely because of bitter peasant opposition; after almost half a century, agriculture remains the weakest area in the Soviet economy. Perhaps the Japanese type of farmer-operated cooperatives for credit, processing, and marketing is a feasible way of permitting the farmer to maintain his own plot of land, even if relatively small, while extending to him the advantages of a larger unit.

In any case, whatever the size of the farm, if the peasant is to till his soil and produce a surplus that can be siphoned off to feed the city population, it is absolutely essential that a good part of the population be moved off the land. It is the population growth that has crowded the land with small, inefficient, subsistence farms. Thus, with fewer peasants on the land, it would be possible to concentrate land in larger farming units and thereby raise the over-all output. At the same time, such a shift of population could provide the necessary labor force for a growing industry. In these two ways, agriculture can produce capital. But such changes are not likely to come speedily or painlessly. For the peasant, whether he stays on the land or moves to the city, is a creature of habit. His whole way of living and his traditional values will change only gradually. Yet change there must be to meet the needs of commercial agriculture and the pattern of urban-industrial life. Basically, then, what is needed in the underdeveloped nations is a transformation in the people's modes of thought, beliefs, and perception—in short, a cultural revolution.

The Cultural and Political Transformation

It should be obvious by now that the term "economic development" presents a one-dimensional picture of the process involved when a traditional rural society undergoes the transition to an advanced modernized nation. For "economic development" implies that the only requirement is industry, that industrialization follows automatically from capital formation, and that mobilizing this capital is therefore the crucial problem. But this is a vast oversimplification—if indeed not a distortion—of the complex realities of modernizing a traditional society. Industrialization is more than simply building steel mills and constructing dams. It is *above all else* a change in people's values, aspirations, and expectations. The necessary changes are not just economic, but political, social, and cultural. Economic development is, in brief, multidimensional, aimed at the complete transformation of society.

Since the modernization that underdeveloped countries are currently launching is in many ways comparable to earlier Western development, it would perhaps be instructive to review briefly some of the principal changes involved in the transition from medieval feudalism to the more "modern," centralized monarchical states. It has been pointed out previously that the traditional societies do not regard economic activity as a prime concern of life. Surprising as it may be, even in Western history money-making was not always the chief pursuit. In the Middle Ages, religion was man's principal concern. His earthly existence was merely a short prelude to eternal life, for which he prepared himself by adherence to the moral code of the Church. Every aspect of his behavior was subjected to the spiritual authority of the Church. In the economic sphere the Church condemned the charging of interest rates—a basic necessity in a monetary economy—as usury. The usurer was stigmatized as a heretic; he could not receive a Christian burial, and his soul was consigned to hell. The desire for profit was equated with greed. The Church clearly recognized this greed as one of man's most powerful appetites, but for that very reason it had to be watched constantly to keep it in check and save man from indulging in one of the cardinal sins. Economic competition simply was not part of an accepted way of life.[29]

This attitude toward interests and profits was, of course, inimical to business. Economic competition, profits, savings, investments, and the whole concept of economic growth were alien ideas in the Middle Ages. The merchant and craft guilds, which existed in the towns that had grown up by the eleventh century, functioned to prevent competition and regulate the economic life of the town. Membership in a guild was a prerequisite to the establishment of oneself in "business" as a crafts-

[29] See R. H. Tawney, *Religion and the Rise of Capitalism* (Baltimore, Md.: Penguin Books, 1947), p. 35.

man, and it was no easy task to become a member. After an initial training period of several years as an apprentice, a young man had to spend
additional years as a journeyman to gain further experience. Only then
could he become a master craftsman. The guilds regulated the age at
which apprenticeship began, the cost and duration of training, and the
number of apprentices each guild master could have at any specific time.
Thus no master could acquire more helpers than his competitors and
thereby threaten their survival. Moreover, the guilds regulated prices—
which, according to the Church, had to be "just." A merchant was expected to be satisfied with a price that covered the cost of materials plus
labor.[30]

This anti-economic attitude was typical of the static nature of medieval economic organization. Economically, socially, and politically, the
aim of medieval life—apart from its overriding religious purpose—was
stability, security, and subsistence for everyone. Nowhere was this more
evident than in the countryside, where the vast majority lived. Here the
manor was the center of organized life and loyalties. Feudalism, which
lasted from approximately 850 to 1200, arose after the collapse of Rome
and, later, Charlemagne's empire. The dissolution of these larger political
units for the organization of social and economic life and the preservation of order had resulted in widespread chaos, disorder, and violence.
The resulting search for security led to the establishment of the manorial
system, whose function was not only to produce food for its inhabitants,
but to provide them with a government and protection. The lord of the
manor, whose title and position derived from his ownership of the land,
filled many functions. He was governor, judge, and military defender; no
one else could undertake these tasks in the absence of a central government. But the lord of the manor was not an entrepreneur. The manor
did not produce for a national market; agricultural methods and practices were dictated by custom, and only enough food for local subsistence
was grown.

The serfs owned no land; nor could they buy it. Land was inherited,
and it was the basis of the entire social order. The lords, precisely because of their ownership of the land, were the social, political, and military elite. There was no chance for the landless serf or his children to
acquire land and rise socially. The lord-and-serf relationship involved
mutual responsibilities and obligations. In return for the stability and
security provided by the lord, the serfs performed the manorial labor.
Bound to the land, they owed their master certain traditional services,
such as working in his fields and paying him taxes (these were paid in
kind with a part of the crop grown by the serf on the lord's land). There
was no exchange economy; the medieval economy was essentially a "natural" one.

Thus, in order to modernize at the end of the Middle Ages, Europe

[30] *Ibid.*, pp. 37, 38, 43.

had to shift some of the religious emphasis from the spiritual afterlife to the temporal, replace the landowning nobility with a class concerned with capital accumulation, achieve a more fluid social structure that permitted upward mobility on the basis of achievement, and, finally, create a larger framework of political, social, and economic organization. None of these changes came quickly. For instance, although the attitude toward wordly affairs and goods began to alter in the sixteenth century, the change was not fully realized until two hundred years later. The first thorough break with the medieval attitude came with Calvinism. The heart of Calvinist doctrine, predestination, stated that God had already selected the persons who would gain salvation. All others were condemned to damnation and could do nothing to redeem themselves. The Calvinists naturally believed that they were among the few slated for salvation in the hereafter. In the meantime, they would dedicate their life on earth to the glorification of God, demonstrating their spiritual devotion to Him—not just by prayer, but by action. Calvinism, in contrast to Catholicism, thus did not reject secular activities as unimportant; rather, it assigned priority to them. The vigor with which a person pursued his "calling" was a token of his dedication to God and his own spiritual worth.

As wealthy as a man might become, though, he could never forget that he was "ever in the great Taskmaster's eyes." He was not to spend his money frivolously, but exhorted to save it and use it to produce more and even greater "good works." Industriousness, profits, savings, and investments were thus legitimatized by religion. Thrift, character, and hard work represented the Calvinist's earthly trinity. A man's energy should be focused on pursuing the work to which God had called him. He was to shun luxury, leisure, entertainment, and sexual enjoyment. So he would not be tempted, and morally corrupted, he had to exercise stringent discipline over his weaknesses and emotions.

It is hardly surprising that the "Protestant ethic" and capitalism have become so closely identified, for Calvinism dictated a "new scale of moral values and a new ideal of social conduct." It was but a short way from Calvin to Adam Smith, whose theory of capitalism was based upon a recognition of the acquisitive passion the Church had earlier condemned. He accepted the desire for gain as a "fact" of life, calling it "enlightened self-interest." *Laissez-faire* capitalism was merely to harness this acquisitive instinct to the public welfare:

> Calvin did for the bourgeoisie of the sixteenth century what Marx did for the proletariat of the nineteenth. . . . He set their virtues at their best in sharp antithesis with the vices of the established order at its worst, taught them to feel that they were a chosen people, made them conscious of their great destiny in the Providential plan and resolute to realize it. The new law was graven on tablets of flesh; it not merely rehearsed a les-

son, but fashioned a soul. Compared with the quarrelsome, self-indulgent nobility of most European countries, or with the extravagant and half-bankrupt monarchies, the middle classes, in whom Calvinism took root most deeply, were a race of iron.[31]

This rise of capitalism and the bourgeoisie was, furthermore, accompanied by the centralization of political power in the state. The bourgeoisie settled in the new towns on or near rivers and roads, and were thus well located for the conduct of trade. They considered themselves to be free men, not subject to the control of the local lord. "City air makes men free" went a medieval German saying. Peasants escaped to the cities, or, with the introduction of money, they sought their freedom from their lords to go there and earn their living. The consequent town–country, feudal nobility–commercial middle-class conflict forged an alliance between the king and the bourgeoisie. Because of the decentralization of power in medieval Europe, the king had been the supreme lord largely in name only. Now, in order to consolidate power in his hands, he had to break the power of the nobility, upon whom he was dependent for his wealth and army. The bourgeoisie proved to be an alternative source of wealth for him. It was willing to furnish money and give the king its allegiance, for its aims coincided with his. First, it sought town charters specifying the citizens' freedom and their rights. Second, it wanted a larger area in which to trade. A powerful monarchy and the establishment of a sovereign state were thus in its interests. By the early sixteenth century, England, France, and Spain were already ruled by strong kings. The greater size, the single code of law, security of travel, a common set of weights and measures, and a common currency were all to the pecuniary advantage of the bourgeoisie.

The bourgeois particularly benefited from the king's desire to enhance the power and prestige of the new state. Since the index of power was wealth—with which the monarch could pay the bureaucracy administering the state, maintain a strong army, or build a sizable fleet—mercantilism aimed at the development of a more self-sufficient economy. State policy was to maximize exports and minimize imports. Governments subsidized everything from porcelain manufacturing to armaments production; and this ever-growing economy in turn provided the economic foundation for the increasing political and social cohesion of the state. Governments also sponsored the great voyages of exploration, which were now made possible by the development of the compass, quadrant, sextant, and navigational charts. And they granted charters to trading companies to exploit the wealth of the New World and the Orient. The result was a shift in trade from the Mediterranean to the Atlantic. Gold, silver, jewelry, spices, tobacco, ivory—and, of course, slaves—and many

[31] *Ibid.*, p. 39.

more items were transported to Europe from the new lands, most of which were colonized. This "commercial revolution" transformed Europe into the economic center of the globe, the cockpit of world power. But this result would not have been achievable without the prior change of values and social structure plus the establishment of a central government.

From Traditional to Modern Society

A number of conclusions seem fairly clear about the process of development and modernization. The first is that the conditions confronting the leaders of the new nations today are somewhat similar to those which once confronted Western leaders: the stagnant agrarian economy, with its low subsistence productivity; the traditional culture, with its fundamentally subsistence and barter economy; a rigid class structure based upon land ownership; a ruling class with a vested interest in preserving this structure and therefore hostile to social change; decentralized political power and parochial loyalties; an ignorant, superstitious, and illiterate population with little vitality; and isolated "modern economic" pockets in towns whose impact upon the vast "rural slum" surrounding them is not strong enough to effect the breakthrough needed for the economic "take-off" stage. The problems, too, are similar: to unify or integrate the people within the nation; to shift from a subsistence to an exchange economy; to induce the necessary capital from savings; to change the social structure and political leadership; to educate the masses; and to train men in the skills necessary for the operation of a modern economy. But the underdeveloped countries have additional problems as well. Unlike the West, they have no sizable native commercial bourgeoisie, and they are confronted with the overwhelming problem of overpopulation. These added features, especially the latter, may possibly defeat the arduous efforts by the underdeveloped countries to reach economic take-off. At the very least, the speed of development is likely to be seriously affected in most of the backward nations. Only very slowly will the infrastructure be laid for the take-off and the drive toward economic maturity, for this task can be completed only by postponing consumption.

A second conclusion is that economic development is not a matter merely of "reform" as Americans normally use that term. Rather, what is demanded is the complete transformation of society. This cannot be achieved smoothly, but is generally accompanied by considerable social upheaval, possibly including violence. A change in class structure is a fundamental prerequisite for economic progress. The landowners—with their disproportionate share of the income, leading social position, and political power—have a vested interest in preserving the traditional society; they must be displaced if the intelligentsia is to gain power and be able to effect modernization. But they are unlikely to surrender without a struggle, and pass the power, status, and property to another class or group as an act of grace.

Moreover, as modernization proceeds, tradition and customs collapse. The old ways of doing things no longer suffice. New ways must be adopted. The result for the masses of people is bewilderment and intense frustration. They find it difficult to adjust the behavior and attitudes of a lifetime to the changing environment. The peasant's sense of security (which stems from knowing his place in society) and his sense of belonging (which results from being part of an old way of life) collapse—particularly in the case of the peasant who is forced off the land and herded into the city and the new factory, where he must learn the values and habits of industrial civilization. He resents the factory with its discipline and monotony, long hours and low pay, and he hates the vast slums where he lives in filth, poverty, and disease, with tens of thousands of other uprooted peasants. He feels degraded. As a peasant, poor as he was, he at least felt that he had a status and a role in society; as a peasant-worker, torn loose from his traditional moorings and submerged in the anonymity of the labor force, he feels the denial of his individuality. He has become an isolated atom in a mass society.

Failing to understand the nature of the social forces that are responsible for the vast changes he is experiencing so painfully, he identifies his troubles with such symbols as the machinery he tends; or—where private enterprise plays a role—the object of his hatred becomes the bourgeoisie, who purportedly forced him to move off the land and into the impersonal cities and factories which exploit him to accumulate wealth for their owners. Marx, who confused capitalism as a mature economic system with the early phase of capital accumulation under any economic and political system, caught the essence of these peasant-laborers' protest. The bourgeoisie, he said, "has pitilessly torn asunder the motley feudal ties that bound man to his 'natural superiors,' and has left remaining no other nexus between man and man than naked self-interest, than callous 'cash payment.' . . . It has resolved personal worth into exchange value." Marx might more appropriately have used the words "Industrial Revolution" for "bourgeoisie." Indeed, he did say:

> Owing to the extensive use of machinery and to division of labor, work of the proletarians has lost all individual character, and, consequently, all charm for the workman. He becomes an appendage of the machine. . . . Modern industry has converted the little workshop of the patriarchal master into the great factory of the industrial capitalist. Masses of laborers, crowded into the factory, are organized like soldiers. . . . Not only are they slaves of the bourgeois class, and of the bourgeois state; they are daily and hourly enslaved by the machine, by the supervisor, and, above

all, by the individual bourgeois manufacturer himself. The more openly this despotism proclaims gain to be its end and aim, the more petty, the more hateful, and the more embittering it is.[32]

The peasant who stays on the land is subject to similar frustration, hostility, and impatience. His transformation is from a subsistence peasant producing for his family to a commercial farmer producing for a market. He now must learn to operate new farm machinery and try new methods. If herded into collectivized farms, he will also feel deprived of "his" piece of land and his personality. Furthermore, he is resentful because, with the exception of the crop he needs to feed his family, the state takes away his increased yield to feed people in the cities and to earn foreign exchange. His consumption therefore does not materially improve. His hopes for a better life remain unrealized, and his symbol of resentment becomes the city, the city-dwellers, and the "financial interests" who are allegedly exploiting him and destroying his way of life. Thus the peasant is torn in every direction. He wants to cling to his old and familiar ways, but he must change. He resents industrialization, and yet he harbors the hope that it will provide a better life for himself and his children. Thus, whether he lives on the land or in the city, the peasant has great expectations for almost immediate improvement, and he becomes bitter when his hopes are not fulfilled. In the past, he was constantly told by his leaders that once the bad colonial rulers were ousted, life would improve. But this better life cannot come for a long time since capital formation requires the postponement of consumption—and his level of consumption is already desperately low. The greater the gap between expectation and satisfaction becomes, the greater his frustration. Only a gradual closing of this gap, affecting him in terms of some improvement of his own life, can relieve this dissatisfaction. In any event, a society in transition is teeming with discontent, bewilderment, and insecurity—a condition that does not help to facilitate the task of modernization.

This frustration is not likely to be diminished in the near future since the task of "economic" development takes time. Despite an unprecedented volume of investments, public and private, during the 1950's, the underdeveloped countries practically stood still in per capita income. The Managing Director of the United Nations Special Fund summed it up this way:

Estimated income per person in the 100 [underdeveloped] countries and territories associated with the United Nations averaged approximately $90 in the year 1950. It probably reached slightly over $100 per person in 1959. National income grew at the rate of 3 per cent a year, but, because

[32] Quoted in Arthur P. Mendel (ed.), *The Essential Works of Marxism*, pp. 15, 19–20; see also Adam B. Ulam, *The New Face of Soviet Totalitarianism*, pp. 12–20.

there were two hundred million more mouths to feed in these countries in 1959 than there were in 1950, the net increase in income per person was only about 1 per cent, that is, about $1 a year. Over this same decade, income per person in the Netherlands increased by more than $300, in the United Kingdom, Western Germany and Switzerland by more than $400, and in the United States and Canada by more than $500. Now we all know that statistics about the less developed countries can hardly be more than educated guesses, and notably that dollar estimates of income are understated when compared with those of the advanced countries. But clearly, in both relative and absolute terms, the rate of increase in the poorer countries was too slow—dangerously too slow.[33]

To nations in a hurry, this conclusion appears, if anything, as an understatement.

Finally, the leading role in economic development, certainly in the early stages, will be played by the government rather than by private initiative. There are several reasons for this. Most obviously, the traditional societies did not breed enough entrepreneurs. There is no commercial middle class with capital, as there was when industrialization began in the West. Perhaps when the old society disappears, and men become more "secularized," more concerned with mastering the environment as well as with personal achievement, the capitalist spirit may grow. But this development still lies in the future. Moreover, the intelligentsia by and large harbors a hostility toward capitalism; memories of colonialism associate it with capitalism. It will be some time before the intelligentsia learns that Western capitalism has changed radically since the nineteenth century—or gains a perspective on capitalism's alleged "plundering of the poor" through its own experience with capital accumulation. Above all else, though, the state must take the political initiative in the early phases of economic development for functional reasons. This would be true even if the intelligentsia did not think of itself as "socialist"—as can be seen in American history.

To an age that often seems to believe that America was the home of *laissez-faire* capitalism before Franklin Roosevelt and the New Deal, it may be a surprise to learn that the Founding Fathers acted politically and economically very much like today's nationalist leaders. This was especially true of the Federalists; men of wealth, privilege, and education, these conservative gentlemen might now be dubbed "socialist planners." Nor did the Republicans, once they achieved power in 1800, behave very differently. Under both parties, the national and state governments played the leading role—a mercantilist role—in economic affairs for three main reasons: to unify the nation by knitting it together economically, to develop its strength so that it could defend its independence, and to provide the people with a better standard of living. These

[33] Quoted in Eugene Staley, *The Future of Underdeveloped Countries*, p. 404.

aims required that the political leadership lay down the economic infrastructure.

It may be useful to recall in this connection that although the United States had been united by the struggle against the colonial ruler, it returned to its pre-independence "tribalized" existence after the Revolutionary War was concluded. A man's loyalty was to his state. The first Union was a Confederation without an effective central government—a league in which each state remained sovereign, a compact of independent states. The central government possessed neither an executive nor an independent judiciary; the Congress represented the states, and each state cast one vote. Important decisions required nine votes, and even then the resulting laws depended for their execution upon the will of the state governments.

> Congress had no power to tax, to regulate commerce or to negotiate effectively with foreign countries or Indian tribes. In the enthusiasm of their newly won sovereignty the States carried on independent relations with foreign powers, issued their own currencies and, with an inherited mercantilism, constructed tariff walls at the expense of their neighbor. New York State not only prosecuted its ancient war with Connecticut over the Long Island trade, but even taxed the vegetables brought over for sale to the citizens of New York City from the New Jersey shore; and New Jersey retaliated by imposing a tax on Sandy Hook lighthouse at the entrance to New York harbour, which happened to be on Jersey soil.[34]

It soon became clear that the Articles of Confederation needed to be replaced by a national constitution and the "firm league of friendship" transformed into a "more perfect union" if the United States was to survive. Yet the strength of state loyalties over national loyalty remained very much in evidence even after this decision was made. One indication was the fight of the small states in the Constitutional Convention to preserve the Confederation, even though they intended to strengthen it somewhat. Another was the continuing attempts by states to thwart the Federal Government and minimize its authority by threats of secession. It was to be the South that actually tried to secede. And Lincoln's primary aim during the ensuing war, as he himself stated it, was not to free the slaves but to save the Union. Later, with the waves of non–Anglo-Saxon, non-Teutonic, and non-Protestant South and East European immigrants to the United States, massive efforts were required to integrate these people into the fabric of American life. But by that time, the bonds of union were no longer so tenuous as they had been when the nation was still "new"—a time when even Madison, a Founding Father, could be rebuked in the House of Representatives for using the word

[34] Frank Thistlethwaite, *The Great Experiment* (London and New York: Cambridge University Press, 1955), pp. 43–44.

"national," a term so suspect that it had *deliberately* been omitted from the Federal Constitution.[35]

It is economic development which, in such circumstances (then as today), can help strengthen the fragile bonds of national unity established by the state's founding fathers. An industrial economy, because of the specialization and division of labor, ties different sectors of a country together; men of different ethnic backgrounds and religious beliefs work together because of the imperative of economic interdependence. As these men interact economically, travel to other sections of the country, and communicate with people in different areas, they become more aware that they are all part of one nation and that unity is essential if their common hopes for the future are to be realized. An advancing economy also creates a new pattern of interests; the old farming interests are supplemented by a host of new economic and professional interests, from businessmen to doctors and lawyers. In this context, individuals define their roles less in terms of prior ethnic or religious allegiances than in terms of their "interests." This rise of interest groups and of new social classes (the urban middle and working classes) is of key significance. For such groups or classes tend to be nationwide rather than regional. Men thus become nationally self-conscious, and as they act together—primarily through political parties—to advance or protect their interests, the possibility of secession from the new union fades from their minds.

Unifying the nation was only one goal of the Founding Fathers. Another was to lay the basis for a high degree of economic self-sufficiency and strength. The United States needed to augment her power in order to defend herself, secure her independence, and ensure that other nations would respect her and treat her as an equal rather than an ex-colonial appendage. As Thomas Jefferson pointed out:

> Experience has shown that continued peace depends not merely on our own justice and prudence, but on that of others also; that when forced into war, the interception of exchanges which must be made across a wide ocean, becomes a powerful weapon in the hands of an enemy domineering over that element, and to the other distresses of war adds the want of all those necessaries for which we have permitted ourselves to be dependent on others, even arms and clothing. *This fact, therefore, solves the question by reducing it to its ultimate form, whether profit or preservation is the first interest of a State?* We are consequently become manufacturers to a degree incredible to those who do not see it.[36]

Economic development also produces a better life for the citizen; the significance of this is its *political* "pay-off." To the people of a new na-

---

[35] John C. Miller, *The Federalist Era, 1789–1801* (New York: Harper & Brothers, 1960), p. 3.
[36] Quoted in Earle (ed.), *op. cit.*, p. 137.

tion not yet solidly knitted together, the nationalist intelligentsia has to prove that what it is seeking to establish will be beneficial to them. Devising a governmental structure, however good, and writing a formal constitution, however democratic, is merely the beginning. Neither can, so to speak, be eaten. The people whose loyalty must be won and held must be shown the effectiveness of the political system—that is, "what's in it for them." To be sure, this pay-off is not exclusively economic. In nineteenth-century America, the people could enjoy security from wars, and they could also enjoy a higher degree of freedom than anywhere else on earth. Many came to this country for these very reasons. Yet security and liberty were not all. The millions of immigrants entering New York harbor in the late nineteenth and early twentieth centuries had left Europe to escape wars, oppression, *and* poverty. Their predecessors had felt the same way. The economic pay-off in terms of satisfying popular aspirations was thus crucial in winning the people's allegiance for the new nation. The United States could "deliver the goods."

In seeking these goals, the U.S. national and state governments implemented their mercantilist role in two principal ways. First, they built roads, turnpikes, canals, rivers, and railroads. Second, the national government, under Hamilton's guidance, encouraged manufacturing. Labor and capital were in short supply. A majority of immigrants had turned to farming. And the capital Americans earned abroad was being used to purchase consumer goods rather than machinery and tools. To induce businessmen into industry, the Federal Government established a Bank of the United States and then enticed them with high profits and generous government aid: protective tariffs; bounties for establishing new industries; premiums for improvement of quality; awards for inventions, particularly labor-saving machinery; and exemption from payment of duty on essential imported raw materials.

The transportation system and the growing manufacturing base achieved their objectives. The more perfect political union established by the Constitution rested on a more perfect economic base, and thus the country was bound together into a more cohesive unit. The national strength that was to bring the United States the respect and economic independence without which there could not have been any real political independence, was also increased. Thus, as with the new nations of today, early American economic-development programs sought power before profit. This was the reason for all the "government interference" and "socialistic-type measures."

Moreover—and this is particularly significant—it was precisely the government intervention that attracted the large-scale "foreign aid" funds that this country (wealthier at the time than any of today's underdeveloped countries) needed if it was to grow economically. British capital proved to be the chief source of these funds:

As in colonial days, Americans imported more manufactures than they could pay for by exporting raw materials. Until as late as 1873, the United States had an unfavourable balance of trade which neither the earnings of her merchant marine nor, after 1850, Californian gold were sufficient to make good. The deficit was, in the last analysis, made good by loans from abroad. In their drive across the continent, the American people still depended on the Old World, and especially on Britain, not only for manufactures but for credit to sustain them until they had subdued the wilderness. . . . Opportunities for investment in the young Republic were much sought after. The bonds of the Federal Government found a ready sale in London; but the greatest avenue of British investment was into the State-financed canals, railways and turnpikes, those "internal improvements" in transport which were so essential for the commercial development of what came to be called the Midwest. Between 1821 and 1837, foreign capital to the value of about 125 million dollars, most of it British, was invested in the United States. . . . During the 50's nearly 200 million dollars worth of new capital flowed into the United States, mostly into railways.[37]

Thus, without the political organization of the nation by America's "nationalist intelligentsia," and the national and state governments' economic initiative, the nation would never have become the cohesive unit that was the prerequisite for economic development. American power and wealth were the product of this political leadership. It was not until the 1850's that *laissez faire* became a part of the American creed. Moreover, the rise of the *laissez-faire* approach to capital development was the product of manufacturing. Protected in their infant days by tariffs, manufacturers did not press for greater freedom from governmental policies until the 1840's.[38] Their demand was a symptom of the mercantilist success in laying the foundation, or infrastructure, upon which private enterprise could build. Precisely because government can play such a leading role in economic development and nation-building, the leaders of many of today's new nations look to Communism and totalitarian techniques as a possible means of rapid modernization for their underdeveloped nations.

The Appeal of Communism

Among the dominant characteristics of the new nations' intelligentsia are the following three: its members govern; they seek accelerated modernization, largely through industrialization; and they are anti-Western in attitudes. Communism—more specifically, Leninism—makes its appeal to all three of these characteristics. First, it offers the men who make up the intelligentsia a leading, dynamic, constructive role in the

[37] Thistlethwaite, *op. cit.*, pp. 77–78.
[38] *Ibid.*, p. 86.

development of a better way of life for their peoples. Or, perhaps more accurately, Leninism offers them a justification for the role they have long felt they must assume—that of rulers. In the traditional society, they are the only group that wishes to modernize, and only they possess some of the required knowledge and skills. On this basis, they claim the political leadership that will satisfy their personal yearnings for power, status, and communion with the masses. Yet the intelligentsia's essentially "populist"—or, as they call it, "socialist"—attitude does not mean they are necessarily good democrats. The desire to create the "good society" for "the people" may confer legitimacy on the nationalist revolution and the post-independence government, but this legitimacy is quite compatible with elitism. The intelligentsia governs on behalf of the people; therefore, it embodies the national will.

> The gap in awareness of the modern world between the Western-oriented elite and the largely unreformed mass furnishes . . . [the] justification for the exclusion of the mass from any effective share in political life. Until the gap is greatly lessened the claim of the educated few to manage the affairs of the society is as good—and as bad—as that of the colonial administrators who preceded them, with the one great difference that they operate within and not outside the national fold. The white man's burden thus finds its counterpart in the contention that those who know best should be the custodians of power.[39]

This elitist attitude is akin to that of Leninism, except that the elite claims it embodies the people's rather than the proletariat's will.

Leninism also seems to offer the intelligentsia the solution to the problem of modernization. The example of the Soviet Union's rapid industrialization, particularly over the last two decades, is bound to be very attractive to the economically backward nations. Over-all Soviet industrial output rose from

> . . . the beginning of the five-year plans in 1928 through the 1930's at an average rate of about 15 per cent annually. The corresponding industrial growth rate in prerevolutionary Russia from 1885 to 1913 was 5.7 per cent annually, though in the decade of the 1890's it was 8 per cent. United States industrial output in the rapid expansion after the Civil War grew at rates which exceeded 10 per cent annually for some nondepression periods, but the over-all rate in the late nineteenth century was closer to 5 per cent. Germany's industrial growth rates in the decades of the nineteenth century were about 5 per cent, Sweden's 6 to nearly 10 per cent, and Japan's about 8.6 per cent from 1907 to 1913.
>
> Thus, Soviet industrial development has been extremely rapid by any standards, even allowing for the advantage of late-comers in taking over technology already developed elsewhere. It is especially impressive when

[39] Emerson, *op. cit.*, p. 281.

looked at from the perspective of underdeveloped countries that are striv-
ing to initiate industrial growth.[40]

It is significant to note that even as a technique of modernization,
Communism's real appeal to the intellectuals is not primarily economic,
but political: If political power can be concentrated in a disciplined
party that penetrates all geographic corners of the land and all social
activities, the new nation's leaders can tighten the bonds of unity and
mobilize the population for the task of industrialization. The party can
squeeze savings out of the peasant-workers' wages; facilitate the deposi-
tion of the old ruling class and the taxation or confiscation of their
wealth; enable the peasant to be collectivized, despite any resistance,
and siphon off his food production beyond his own minimum needs;
stifle the protests of the deprived masses and control them; and direct
and accelerate the cultural revolution. The intellectuals may well ask
themselves if this means of industrialization does not seem cruel. The
standard Communist rationalization is that the masses have always suffered; if, in the long run, they and their children can be assured of a
better life, surely they will be willing to sacrifice and suffer a little
longer? The point is that the tentative unity and the underdeveloped
economy of the new nations can be developed only if industrialization
occurs quickly and is implemented primarily on a "do-it-yourself" basis.
The Soviet technique of capital formation promises both these things.
In effect, Communism seeks to present itself as the most effective
twentieth-century means of nation-building; it promises to modernize
the new nations as nineteenth-century capitalism modernized the developing nations of Europe.

If the non-Western intelligentsia are drawn to Leninism as a means
of legitimatizing their power and of industrializing their underdeveloped
nations, it also offers them an outlet for their anti-Western, anti-capitalist feelings. Western colonialism accounts for these feelings, and Leninism provides a channel for their expression. It is not only a guide to
future action but a "scientific" explanation of past history. Lenin's
theory of imperialism, especially, is unquestioned. After all, it contains
enough half-truths to seem plausible even to Western non-Marxists, let
alone men made sensitive by their experience of Western colonial rule.
It is above all the cry for freedom inherent in this theory attributing
colonial enslavement to Western capitalism that is so appealing to

[40] Staley, *op. cit.*, pp. 161–62. In early 1963, the Central Intelligence Agency announced its conclusion that Soviet growth had dropped from annual rates of 6 to 10
per cent during the 1950's to less than 2.5 per cent in 1962–63. These figures were
released to tarnish the image of the Soviet Union as a nation that had discovered the
secret of rapid economic development. But the real issue is whether the Soviet experience of development is at all applicable to developing societies. See particularly
W. Donald Bowles, "Soviet Russia as a Model for Underdeveloped Areas," *World
Politics*, April, 1962, pp. 483–504.

them. Only freedom from the "foreign exploiters" and their native "lackeys" or "tools" can liberate the colonial countries from their cultural and economic backwardness. Only the overthrow of colonialism can achieve national self-determination and set the nation on the path of "socialist construction." In this respect, Communism represents itself as the twentieth-century descendant of the French Revolution, the defender of the "rights of man." Industrialization is a short-cut to a utopian society in which the state will wither away, the class struggle will end, and all men will live in freedom, equality, fraternal harmony, and affluence. Thus anti-Westernism is combined with a characteristically apocalyptic Western vision of paradise—a vision which Marxism-Leninism inherited from the eighteenth- and nineteenth-century secularization of the Judaeo-Christian interpretation of history. The appeal of such an all-encompassing view, promising deliverance from the toils of today and future salvation in a Communist state, is undeniable, and it augments the functionally attractive nature of Communism.

> Communism's most strategic export to underdeveloped countries is ideas. . . . The Communists themselves, despite their doctrines of economic determinism, do not act on the assumption that people are mainly interested in their own material advancement. . . . *In their attempts to influence the peoples of underdeveloped countries the Communists put great emphasis, even chief emphasis, on appeals not to the material wants of man but rather to the human desire for status, equality, freedom from domination or oppression, especially domination by foreigners.*[41]

It is clear that Communism no longer holds so great an attraction for the increasingly affluent workers in the West. Because of the higher wages of a mature industrial economy and the economic benefits distributed by democratic governments, these workers have been able to gain most of their original demands. Their vested interest in the welfare state has, if anything, turned them into self-satisfied, smug, and rather conservative citizens, bent primarily on maintaining and increasing their share of the national wealth. Nor does Communism have a mass appeal in underdeveloped countries where the traditional society is still functioning reasonably well. For it is not merely poverty that converts men to Communism. As Trotsky once wrote: "In reality, the mere existence of privations is not enough to cause an insurrection; if it were, the masses would always be in revolt."[42] Communism does, however, have an appeal in backward nations where the traditional society is being transformed by the initial impact of industrialization. When the old patterns are disintegrating, the society is in a state of flux, and conditions are beginning to improve, men suddenly realize that their misery can

---

[41] Staley, *op. cit.*, p. 181.
[42] Quoted in Crane Brinton, *The Anatomy of Revolution* (rev. ed.; Englewood Cliffs, N.J.: Prentice-Hall, 1952), p. 34.

be alleviated, and their aspirations are stirred. As Marx himself observed: "A house may be large or small; as long as the surrounding houses are equally small it satisfies all social demands for a dwelling. But if a palace arises beside the little house, the little house shrinks into a hut."[43] It is, then, in this transitional phase between the traditional society and the emergence of a self-sustaining industrial economy that Communism becomes attractive—and not to the embryonic labor force, or even to the peasants seeking land reform, but to the members of the Westernized intelligentsia who provide the organization and leadership for any existing social dissatisfaction. It is this group whose hopes and expectations of progress are the most intense.

Not surprisingly, the Soviets hope to exploit these various appeals that Leninism holds for the nationalist intelligentsia. The intelligentsia that has risen to leadership in Asia, Africa, the Middle East, and Latin America is not viewed as "socialist" by the Soviets; it is, in fact, overwhelmingly "bourgeois." Nevertheless, this "national bourgeoisie," as they call it, is anti-imperialist and anti-feudal; because it opposes the former foreign power and the domestic ruling class through which that power controlled its nation, the Soviet Union lends its support to these "bourgeois-democratic national-liberation movements" in the underdeveloped nations. The rise of this ex-colonial world between the capitalist and Communist worlds does not, however, alter the fundamental Soviet view that the globe is divided into two camps. Support for the national bourgeoisie does not indicate an abandonment of the international class struggle. But it does mean a tactical modification. In most cases, an attempt to overthrow the new government in order to put the local Communist Party into power would drive these nations back into Western arms. On the other hand, accepting their self-proclaimed neutrality in the Cold War, and supporting their drive for political and economic independence from the West, helps to deepen the gulf between the ex-colonial countries and the West.

Thus, for tactical reasons, the Soviet Union is willing temporarily to modify its two-camp doctrine verbally. This does not mean that the Soviet Union accepts the nonaligned stance of the new nations in the long run. Nonalignment, like coexistence, is seen as a temporary feature that will pass when the world becomes Communist. "National liberation" is still the ultimate objective. But the immediate Communist purpose is to deny the resources, territory, and population of the underdeveloped nations to the West. On the other hand, an intermediate stage, called "national democracy" has been introduced:

> The national-democratic tasks on the basis of which the progressive forces of the nation can and do unite in the countries which have won their

[43] Quoted in Seymour M. Lipset, *Political Man: The Social Bases of Politics* (New York: Doubleday & Co., 1959), p. 63.

freedom, are: the consolidation of political independence, the carrying out of agrarian reforms in the interest of the peasantry, elimination of the survivals of feudalism, the uprooting of imperialist economic domination, the restriction of foreign monopolies and their expulsion from the national economy, the creation and develoment of a national industry, improvement of the living standard, the democratization of social life, the pursuance of an independent and peaceful foreign policy, and the development of economic and cultural cooperation with the socialist and other friendly countries.[44]

The foregoing statement clearly reveals the purpose of Soviet support for the governments of newly independent states. The "consolidation of political independence" means cutting all political ties to the West; the "carrying out of agrarian reforms in the interest of the peasantry, elimination of the survivals of feudalism" refers to uprooting the social and economic basis of the old pro-Western ruling class; the "uprooting of imperialist economic domination, the restriction of foreign monopolies and their expulsion from the national economy" proposes the expropriation of Western-owned industry and especially the end of all economic relations with the West (since colonialism does not, according to the Communist doctrine—and many non-Communist nationalist leaders— end with a grant of political independence, but only when the capitalists' economic chains of subjugation are broken); the "democratization of social life" calls for the freedom of the Communist Party to organize itself for political purposes; and the "development of economic and cultural cooperation with the socialist and other friendly countries" means that the foreign political and economic relations of new nations should be oriented toward the Communist nations.

In turn, the purpose of establishing "national democracies" is to pave the way for the second stage of the revolution in the underdeveloped countries. The first anti-imperialist and anti-feudal stage will be superseded by the socialist stage. The national bourgeoisies, once having freed their countries from the West and prepared the way for their development, will have outlived their historic function. For the social and economic problems confronting their nations can be resolved only by Communist techniques of development. The national bourgeoisie opposes the accompanying Communist control this requires. In order to maintain itself in control, the bourgeoisie therefore compromises with "domestic reaction and imperialism." The Communists must in these new circumstances expose the now "reactionary bourgeoisie," denounce their demagogic use of "socialist slogans to disguise their class interests as nationally beneficial," and rally all "progressive forces in the struggle."

The promotion of the national-democratic state is thus a tactical de-

[44] Washington Center of Foreign Policy Research, *Two Communist Manifestoes*, p. 72.

vice by which the local Communist Party seeks to form a united national front with the nationalist leadership and then pressure the national bourgeoisie to eject Western power and influence and support pro-Communist domestic and foreign policies. It is, in brief, a transitional phase in which the bourgeoisie is supposed to become its own grave-digger. "The correct application of Marxist-Leninist theory in the newly independent countries," Khrushchev said, "consists precisely in seeking the forms that take cognizance of the peculiarities of the economic, political, and cultural life of the peoples to unite all the sound forces of the nation, *to ensure the leading role of the working class in the national front*, in the struggle completely to eradicate the roots of imperialism and the remnants of feudalism, and to clear the way for the ultimate advance toward socialism"[45] (synonymous in Communist language with control by the Party). Or, as it has been described by a noted political analyst: The national-democratic phase of development is "intended to put the country firmly on the 'noncapitalist road of development,' to create the precondition for the second 'socialist' phase. . . . *The struggle for 'national democracy' is a struggle for Communist leadership within the united national front*, for the extension of Communist influence on the nationalist government, and the Communist occupation of key positions in the political, military, and economic state machine; it is, however, conducted wherever possible within the framework of the existing nationalist regimes—without aiming at the overthrow of popular nationalist leaders at this stage . . . *the achievement of socialism in the ex-colonial countries* (as in all other countries) *will only be possible once state power is in the hands of a Communist Party.*[46]

[45] *Ibid.*, p. 75; italics added.
[46] Richard Lowenthal, " 'National Democracy' and the Post-Colonial Revolution," in London (ed.), *op. cit.*, pp. 56–74; see also William T. Shinn, Jr., "The 'National Democratic State,' " *World Politics*, April, 1963, pp. 376–89.

VI

Limited War
and Nuclear Diplomacy

The Key Challenge: The Limited Challenge

It is a major paradox of our age that, despite the devastating destructiveness of nuclear weapons, the dependence on military force to preserve the international balance of power is perhaps greater now than ever before in history because the traditionally nonmilitary means of maintaining that balance no longer exists. The fundamental consensus shared by the old ruling classes of Europe has vanished, and the new ideological struggle has transformed contemporary interstate relations into a total political-moral conflict. No longer is power equally distributed among a number of great powers; the postwar world has been essentially bipolar in terms of power. Thus the flexibility inherent in the old balance of power has been eliminated, for no major aligned nation voluntarily shifts from one ideological bloc to the other. Finally, the limitation on national power imposed by a pre-industrial economy has disappeared. Instead, modern industry and technology have unveiled weapons so powerful that man is afraid to use them lest he destroy himself.

On the one hand, then, the global balance today rests largely on military strength, but on the other hand total nuclear warfare threatens to destroy the very nations who would dare engage in it. This is why total war is now considered to be an "irrational" instrument of national policy. Nations do not generally defend their "national interests" by committing suicide. It is also why the emphasis in military strategy has shifted from fighting an all-out nuclear war to preventing the outbreak

196

of such a war. Such an outbreak would, indeed, signal the *failure* of military policy. For the aim of strategy is *deterrence*. The purpose of strategic forces and total war planning is to threaten the opponent with such devastation that he will be afraid to risk an actual "strategic nuclear exchange." At all times, the cost to be paid by the potential attacker if he attacks must remain excessive to the value of his potential gain.

This situation of mutual deterrence does not, however, mean a freezing of the political *status quo*. The very fact that the Strategic Air Command can dissuade a full-scale Soviet strike places a high premium on the limited political-military challenge. Total war may well be irrational for the Soviet Union; but it is equally irrational for the United States. Therefore, if the Soviets, as well as the Chinese Communists, can confront the West—and particularly the United States—with less than total challenges to which we can reply *only* with a total response, the so-called nuclear stalemate can be shifted in a piecemeal fashion against the West. All or nothing, war or peace, deterrence or self-destruction are not feasible alternatives. For if the United States and her allies cannot counter a limited challenge with an equally limited response, they face a simple but agonizing dilemma: Either they can answer the challenge with total force and risk suicide, or they can decide not to react at all, which would be tantamount to surrender or appeasement. In short, while the all-out use of violence is really irrational, it does not follow that the use of *any* violence is irrational. Indeed, in a condition of nuclear plenty for both principal contestants, the use of limited force—actual or potential, as a threat—is highly rational, and the key challenge becomes the limited challenge. A series of such limited challenges—and the military necessity for such challenges only reinforces what is in any case the essence of a revolutionary state's strategy—could thus undermine the West's global position.

The American capacity for "massive retaliation" may, in other words, forestall a resort to total war, but it lacks credibility for less than total challenges. The Kremlin, for example, knows that the United States would not respond to limited issues with an all-out attack upon the Soviet homeland. Even before the atomic age, no "rational" nation fought an all-out war to defend limited stakes. In 1936, for instance, the French were unable to respond to Hitler's march into the Rhineland—which had been "neutralized," or "demilitarized," at Versailles—because they had prepared war plans only for an all-out war with Germany. Moreover, the implementation of these plans was contingent upon a German attack on France.[1] Unprepared to meet Germany's limited challenge and unwilling to risk a total war (remembering how badly they

[1] See B. A. C. Parker, "The First Capitulation: France and the Rhineland Crisis of 1936," *World Politics*, April, 1956, pp. 355–73.

had suffered in World War I), the French did not react, even though
the Rhineland issue was crucial. Once Hitler had refortified the Rhineland—by building the famous Siegfried Line—and was in a position to
stop any possible French attack, he could concentrate his army and air
force on Germany's eastern frontier and pick off one after another of the
smaller nations, thereby gaining dominance of the continent. Thus the
inability of the French to fight less than a total war—and, admittedly,
they were reluctant to fight any kind of war—had a disastrous impact.
Instead of avoiding war, France ensured its inevitability, and at a time
when she was far weaker and Germany stronger.

Following World War II, the United States enjoyed virtual immunity
to attack until the mid-1950's, for the Soviets did not explode their first
atomic bomb until late 1949, and the Soviet long-range air force did not
begin its major development until 1954. Conversely, the Soviet Union
was vulnerable to SAC bombers, whose American bases were supplemented by a global string of bases around the periphery of the Sino-Soviet
bloc. However good the Soviet air defenses may have been, they were
not foolproof; even a 90 per cent "kill" rate would not have saved the
Soviet Union from devastation. Yet, even under such favorable conditions, the United States was unwilling to fight a total war in response to
limited provocation. There was no doubt about the U.S. commitment to
resistance against "aggression," but such aggression was generally thought
of in terms of an all-out attempt at world domination. Thus American
power would be unleashed only if the Soviets attacked first; short of
such a strike, it would not be invoked. This policy, as Henry Kissinger
has argued, held dangerous implications:

> In a society of "sovereign" states, a power can in the last resort vindicate
> its interpretation of justice or defend its "vital interests" only by the will-
> ingness to employ force. . . . The motive force behind international set-
> tlements has always been a combination of the belief in the advantages of
> harmony and the fear of the consequences of proving obdurate. A re-
> nunciation of force, by eliminating the penalty for intransigence, will
> therefore place the international order at the mercy of its most ruthless or
> its most irresponsible member.[2]

The truth of this observation and the lack of SAC's credibility to deter
limited Soviet probes were nowhere more clearly demonstrated than by
the North Korean attack on South Korea in June, 1950. The Soviets
were apparently quite willing to commit open aggression despite
America's overwhelming strategic superiority. Obviously, they did not
expect the United States to retaliate against Russia.

The debacle in Indochina in 1954 provided another such clear illustra-

[2] Henry A. Kissinger, *Nuclear Weapons and Foreign Policy*, pp. 4–5.

tion. The French had reoccupied their former colony after World War II. Refusing to grant any concessions to the nationalist demands for self-government, they soon found themselves engaged in a long guerrilla war with the Communist-controlled Viet-Minh.[3] After the end of the Korean War, the Chinese Communists augmented their assistance to the Viet-Minh. The French, attempting to fight a conventional war and unable to find their elusive opponents, occupied Dien Bien Phu, hoping the Viet-Minh would be lured into the open and be badly defeated in a battle. They were successful in enticing the Viet-Minh, but it was the latter who emerged as victors. This defeat confronted the United States with a serious dilemma. On the one hand, it recognized Indochina as the "gateway" to Southeast Asia. President Eisenhower described Indochina as being "of the most transcendent importance" to American security and compared the effect of the possible loss of the area upon the rest of Southeast Asia to a row of falling dominoes; the implication was that to prevent the dominoes from falling over, the first domino would have to be upheld. Secretary Dulles made a similar declaration:

> Under the conditions of today, the imposition on Southeast Asia of the political system of Communist Russia and its Chinese ally, by *whatever* means, would be a grave threat to the whole free community. The United States feels that that possibility should not be passively accepted, but should be met by united action. This might have serious risks, but these risks are far less than would face us in a few years from now if we are not resolute today.[4]

On the other hand, the Eisenhower Administration was firmly committed to a policy of "massive retaliation."[5] Secretary Dulles strongly believed that the Korean War would never have occurred if the Soviets had known beforehand that the invasion of South Korea would be met with a retaliatory strike against the Soviet Union itself. Future Koreas could therefore be deterred by warning the enemy that the United States would retaliate with an attack on his homeland. The Truman Administration had met the limited attack on South Korea locally; fortunately, the occupation troops in Japan had been available for deployment to Korea at the moment of crisis. During the course of the war, moreover, the armed forces had been built up. But the Eisenhower Administration had no intention of fighting another limited war. As a fiscally conservative administration, it was particularly concerned with balancing the budget. Therefore it cut heavily into the army's budget, and the defense

---

[3] The background to the Indochina War may be found in Ellen J. Hammer, *The Struggle for Indochina*, and Bernard B. Fall, *The Two Viet-Nams*.

[4] *U. S. Department of State Bulletin*, April 12, 1954, p. 540; italics added.

[5] On the formulation of the policy of massive retaliation, see Robert E. Osgood, *Limited War*, pp. 189–214; and John W. Spanier, *American Foreign Policy Since World War II* (2d rev. ed.; New York: Frederick A. Praeger, 1965), pp. 103–8.

budget was concentrated on increasing the strength of SAC as the "great deterrent" of both total war *and* limited challenges.

Dien Bien Phu was the test of this policy. The Eisenhower Administration had warned the Chinese Communists not to intervene; its warning had not been restricted to the contingency of open and direct intervention, but applied even to indirect Chinese help to the Viet-Minh in the form of military advisers, equipment, and training for its forces. The crucial issue was the strategic significance of Indochina. Logically, the United States should have attacked the China mainland after its repeated warnings had been ignored. But Eisenhower was no more willing to do this than Truman had been willing to bomb across the Yalu River after the Chinese intervened in Korea in late 1950. Clearly, the reason in each instance was the realization that an attack on China could precipitate Russian intervention, thereby triggering a world war. Neither North Korean nor Indochinese real estate seemed worth that high a price. Eisenhower's attempt to contain Communist expansion thus failed, and American power and prestige were badly bruised. The French were left to work out the best deal they could get. Surprisingly—and probably because the new post-Stalin government was trying to impress the world with its peacefulness and reasonableness—they managed to save Vietnam south of the 17th Parallel.

Several conclusions could be drawn from this disastrous experience of 1954. First, it revealed once more the lack of credibility of the total-war threat. The experience of the Korean War had already shown that containment of the Sino-Soviet bloc could be implemented militarily only if the United States possessed the capacity to fight limited wars. Reliance upon an all-or-nothing strategy paralyzed American foreign policy. The ability to drop atomic bombs on Moscow or Peking was less than useless in deterring or defeating limited incursions. Under the circumstances, the Communists could nibble away bit by bit and change the balance of power in their favor without ever confronting the United States with the one challenge that was "worth" a total war—an attack on this country. The lesson of Indochina was thus the need for a flexible strategy. Deterrence had to operate effectively against both total *and* limited wars; the basic necessity of an invulnerable retaliatory force had to be supplemented by the requirements of limited war—conventional army forces supported by tactical air elements and an airlift capacity to rush the troops to any needed area of the world, *plus* special forces trained in the techniques of unconventional or guerrilla war. Only then would attacks at any level of violence be unprofitable for an aggressor; and only then could an aggressor be deterred or, if not, deprived of any victories.

Second, Indochina showed that the capacity alone to meet limited challenges would not suffice. There also had to be a *willingness* to meet them. This, in turn, demanded a major change in the characteristic American attitude toward war and peace as two mutually exclusive states. To Americans, peace was the normal state of affairs, as it had in fact been for most of the nation's history. Men were concerned with earning their living and improving themselves economically and socially. Only when attacked would Americans turn from their individual, material preoccupations to fighting. War was considered an abnormal condition, a temporary interruption of international peace, a temporary diversion from domestic matters. Whoever was responsible for this interruption therefore had to be punished. As George Kennan has observed: "A democracy is peace-loving. It does not like to go to war. It is slow to rise to provocation. When it has once been provoked to the point where it must grasp the sword, it does not easily forgive its adversary for having produced this situation. The fact of the provocation then becomes itself the issue. Democracy fights in anger—it fights for the very reason that it was forced to go to war. It fights to punish the power that was rash enough and hostile enough to provoke it—to teach that power a lesson it will not forget, to prevent the thing from happening again. Such a war must be carried to the bitter end."[6] For Americans, the aim had to be total victory and the enemy's unconditional surrender. Maximum force had to be applied to the aggressor to punish him, to teach him that aggression was immoral and would not be rewarded. American wars, then, were total wars aimed at the enemy's total destruction.

The Korean War was therefore a new and unsatisfying experience after the two total wars of this century. There was no total defeat of the enemy. He did not surrender unconditionally. The war lasted for three long and bloody years, and at the end the battle lines were drawn approximately where the war had begun—at the 38th Parallel. General MacArthur, who had commanded the military operation in Korea, voiced his frustration openly. "War," he said, indicated that "you have exhausted all other potentialities of bringing the disagreements to an end," and once engaged, "there is no alternative than to apply every available means to bring it to a swift end. War's very objective is victory—not prolonged indecision. In war there is no substitute for victory." The very term "resisting aggression" indicated "that you can destroy the potentialities of the aggressor to continually hit you" and not "go on indefinitely, neither to win or lose." One cannot fight a "half war." The Administration's policy was based upon the assumption that "when you use force, you can limit that force." This introduced "a new concept into military operations—the concept of appeasement."[7] General MacArthur's fellow countrymen understood. No more Koreas—that was the popular reaction to Korea—no more "half wars." Eisenhower's policy of

---

[6] George F. Kennan, *American Diplomacy*, 1900–1950, pp. 56–60.

[7] Quoted in Spanier, *op. cit.*, p. 101.

massive retaliation was attuned to this demand. Rejecting the concept of limited war, massive retaliation reasserted the more traditional all-or-nothing American approach to war. Once attacked, the United States would fight a total war to eliminate the enemy completely—which could, of course, be achieved by nuclear bombs in a minimum of time with maximum efficiency. It did not matter whether the attack was limited or even whether it was launched by Soviet troops. Any aggression by a satellite would be met with the full force of America's great strength, and the aggressor—in this case, the chief aggressor—would be punished.

The third, and perhaps the most important, conclusion to be drawn from the Indochina experience follows logically. If the United States has neither the capacity nor the willingness to meet limited challenges, and seeks to deter them with words only, it may allow the Communists to miscalculate and blunder into a nuclear war. In the Indochina War, the United States repeatedly warned the Chinese Communists that they would suffer massive retaliation unless they desisted, and then at the moment of decision it demonstrated that its policy was merely a bluff. It was thus not only unable to respond to the particular challenge, but it gave the Chinese the impression that American declarations of intent are *always* bluffs. There is nothing more dangerous for the United States in this megaton age than to proclaim loudly that it will defend a particular position, and then fail to follow up its words with actions. The impression conveyed to an opponent is that the United States talks tough, but fails to support its vital interests with force in a crisis. In a given situation, then, the antagonist refuses to believe the statements emanating from Washington, feeling certain that, as in previous crises, the United States will back down. After all, the United States does not wish to invite suicide over a limited probe. Suppose, though, that this time he is wrong. Having suffered a series of setbacks and endangered its global position, the United States is determined to meet this issue. The threats of retaliation are repeated, but the enemy goes ahead. The result is nuclear war. The enemy has, of course, miscalculated American intentions. But his miscalculation resulted from earlier American policies. The responsibility for the war would belong to the United States. Ironically, Washington's policies would have precipitated the very nuclear war the "great deterrent" was meant to forestall.

It is perhaps instructive to recall that World War II began as a result of just such a miscalculation by Hitler. Not that Hitler did not want a war in order to establish his "new order." But in 1939, Germany had not yet reached the height of its strength. The German attack on Poland was to be merely another limited challenge. Although Britain had guaranteed Poland's frontiers by treaty, Hitler believed that Britain—and France—would meet his action with inaction. For they stood by silently while he rearmed, marched back into the Rhineland, annexed Austria.

seized Czechoslovakia's Sudetenland and then the rest of Czechoslovakia. Why should he now expect them to react? If they had wished to resist, surely they would have done so earlier when they were stronger and Germany weaker? Why should they fight now? In Hitler's view, there was no reason, but the point was that at least the British had by then realized that while Hitler's specific challenges were limited, his ultimate purpose was not. Therefore they determined to stand fast on Poland. Not until after his attack, when he discovered that the British meant to honor their commitment to Poland, did Hitler realize he had miscalculated.

The lesson for our age is clear, and it is one we must learn if we are to avoid an all-out nuclear war. The West, and especially the United States, must be able to respond to the crucial Communist political-military challenge in any of the three major forms in which the Soviets and the Chinese have posed it: limited war, guerrilla warfare, and "nuclear blackmail."

Limited Conventional and Guerrilla Warfare

The term "limited war" is defined as a war fought for limited political purposes. The aim of total war is generally the complete destruction of the enemy's military forces and the elimination of his government—in short, total victory, with the opponent's unconditional surrender. In limited hostilities, the objectives fall far short of these; perhaps the most obvious goal here is the capture of strategically located and/or economically important territory. Thus, in the Korean War—the first major limited war fought by the United States in the postwar era—if the North Korean army had captured South Korea, it would have established Communist control over the entire Korean peninsula, and thereby, in the deadly metaphor used by the Japanese, "pointed the Korean dagger straight at Japan's heart." It is significant to recall in this respect that the precipitating cause of the Russo-Japanese War of 1904–5 was Russia's penetration of Korea from the Russian sphere of influence in Manchuria. Japan at that time offered to divide Korea at the 38th Parallel, but the Czarist government refused. As a result of this refusal, Japan attacked Russia in Siberia. Japanese security demanded that the southern half of Korea remain free of Russian control. In 1950, when Japan served as a base for American forces, the U.S. reaction was similar: to resist the Soviet bid to take over South Korea.

But territory is not necessarily always the principal aim of a limited challenge. It is more likely to be to test the will and determination of the power defending the *status quo*. For the failure to meet such a challenge, and meet it effectively, can be grave—primarily because of the impact of such a failure upon the challenger himself. President Truman and his advisers were very much aware of this fact in Korea in June, 1950, for they compared the North Korean attack to the Nazi and Fascist aggressions of twenty years earlier. As one reporter summed up the opinion of sources close to leading American officials: They "were certain that the North Korean attack was being viewed [in Moscow] as a test of the countries, including the United States, that are standing up against Communist expansion. In such a light, the march across the North-South Korean border would appear similar to the attacks that Hitler used to make to feel out the opposition."[8] Thus the President and other top policy-makers viewed Korea as their "Rhineland." The analogy was decisive, for they believed that Stalin, like Hitler before him, would not be satiated if he were allowed to devour this single "situation of weakness" in peace. Rather, his appetite whetted, he would be tempted to devour other areas.[9]

Failure to meet the Soviet challenge was seen as affecting not only Soviet behavior but that of our allies as well. For if the United States did not measure up to the test, the leaders in the Kremlin would succeed in demonstrating their own strength and resolution, and, conversely, America's fear and unreliability. Thus, if the United States abandoned Korea under the threat of force, America's European allies might conclude that they, too, would be abandoned in a similar crisis. The recently signed NATO alliance would undoubtedly collapse. The Europeans might dismiss Washington's treaty pledge to protect them as valueless and turn to neutralism. In this condition, they would be subjected to increasing Soviet pressure and eventual domination. Virtually the entire length and breadth of Eurasia would then be under Sino-Soviet control. Japan, too, would have no choice but to turn to neutralism if the United States did not go to the defense of South Korea: Mainland China had just fallen to the Communists, and the United States wished to rearm Japan to create a new situation of strength in the Pacific. But the precondition of transforming Japan into an American ally was the protection of her security.

Finally, this test of will inherent in the limited challenge has a significant impact on the new nations also. Nonaligned at present, they may not necessarily remain so in the future. If they believe that the balance of power is turning in favor of the Communist powers, be it Russia or China, because the United States fails to react effectively to specific challenges and therefore cannot guard them, then their "neutralism" will increasingly lean toward the Communists. This need not indicate that they are pro-Communist—only that they cannot in these circumstances afford to appear hostile to the Communist states. As Russian or

[8] Jay Waltz, in *The New York Times*, June 26, 1950.
[9] See Harry S. Truman, *Memoirs* (New York: Doubleday and Co., 1956), II, 332–33; and Joseph Alsop, in the *New York Herald Tribune*, June 27, 1950.

Chinese power comes ever nearer to their borders, expediency dictates a policy of Russian or Chinese amity—and often anti-Americanism.

Thus, even if Korea had been geographically unimportant, the challenge posed by the North Korean attack upon South Korea would have required that a stand be taken. "Firmness now would be the only way to deter new actions in other portions of the world," said President Truman. "Not only in Asia, but in Europe, the Middle East, and elsewhere the confidence of peoples in countries adjacent to the Soviet Union would be very adversely affected, in our judgment, if we failed to take action to protect a country established under our auspices and confirmed in its freedom by action of the United Nations."[10]

Clearly, then, the political aims implicit in limited challenges—whether in Korea, Vietnam, or Quemoy-Matsu—usually extend far beyond the immediate area where these challenges occur. And the consequences are more intangible than tangible, related more to political-psychological aspects than, say, to strictly territorial ones. Yet they may well have wide-ranging effects on the global distribution of power in terms of influencing the Soviet or Chinese willingness to undertake limited probes, the cohesiveness of America's alliances around the Sino-Soviet periphery, and the position, present and future, of the nonaligned countries. Nevertheless, while affecting the long-range position of the major Cold War contestants, they avoid the terrible devastation that an all-out nuclear war would inflict.

It is, indeed, in this sense that the limited conflicts of the post-1945 era differ from those of past ages. Europe's wars between 1648 and 1914, with the exception of the French Revolution, also were fought for limited political ends. But they were restrained by an underlying consensus among the participants. Each European state recognized the other's right to exist; none wished to convert another state to its own ideological concepts. The absence of large-scale industrial strength and modern technological means of destruction had the effect of a further restraint (although this became less true in the nineteenth century). None of these restraints, however, operate today among the great powers. The present state of "peaceful coexistence" is based on mutual fear and suspicion stemming from the revolutionary states' proclaimed purpose of reforming the world and winning it for the "true faith." The right of other states to exist who do not share their revolutionary values is not recognized; coexistence is not permanent but temporary.

Thus the modern limited war is very different from anything in the past:

> We are talking about something quite new. If wars were limited in ages past, the reasons why they were so have little relevance for us today. Apart

[10] Truman, *op. cit.*, II, 339–40.

from the existence of moral, religious, and dynastic scruples, and the fact that anything as basic as national existence or even the survival of a dynasty was rarely at stake, wars were kept limited by the small margin of the national economic resources available for mobilization and by the small capability for destruction that could be purchased with that narrow margin. Today, on the contrary, we speak of limited war in a sense that connotes a deliberate hobbling of a tremendous power that is already mobilized and that must in any case be maintained at a very high pitch of effectiveness for the sake only of inducing the enemy to hobble himself to like degree.[11]

In brief, limitations on political objectives in specific conflicts today are dictated, of necessity, by the very fact of nuclear technology. "We should be willing to limit objectives *because* we want to keep the war limited, and not the other way round. And we want to keep the war limited simply because total war as it would be fought today and in the future against a well-armed enemy is simply too unthinkable, too irrational to be borne."[12] To be sure, as has sometimes been argued, a limited war may escalate into a total war. The great powers, whether they are directly or indirectly involved, do not apply all their power. It is therefore easy to assert that any restraints operating during a limited war are arbitrary, indeed silly, and that rather than suffer a defeat, the losing side may ignore these restraints and expand the scope of the war. Nevertheless, the very fact that a limited war is being fought indicates that the major participants do not wish to engage each other in a total war. Each possesses the power to expand hostilities, and the existence of this power strengthens the common interest of both in avoiding a nuclear holocaust. Certainly, the losing side has no incentive to expand the war all the way. Nations do not seek to escape a limited defeat by initiating a total war they might not survive at all. For example, the United States was unwilling to extend the air war to China after the Chinese intervention in Korea lest it escalate into a greater war; therefore it had to be willing to backtrack in its political aim of unifying Korea—decided upon after the defeat of the North Korean army—and settle once more for a Korea divided at the 38th Parallel. Similarly, it preferred to lose North Vietnam and, later, a part of Laos rather than intervene and risk a major conflict. It was only in South Vietnam that the United States drew the line. Likewise, the Soviets accepted the defeat of the Communist guerrillas in Greece, a divided Korea and Berlin. And the Chinese, in order not to provoke an American attack on China, accepted continuing American control over South Korea and Nationalist control of Quemoy and Matsu.

But if the losing side is willing *not* to escalate limited wars in order to

---

[11] Bernard Brodie, *Strategy in the Missile Age*, p. 311.
[12] *Ibid.*

avoid specific losses, the winning side must also surrender any thoughts of gaining a complete local victory. The winner on the battlefield is equally responsible for preserving the restraints on the war. Victory in a limited war does not mean the enemy's unconditional surrender, for the existence of his state cannot become the issue. Halting his violation of the other side's interests is the issue. The Korean War provides a good example of this. The United States first sought merely to restore the *status quo*. But once the North Korean forces had been beaten and driven back to the 38th Parallel, the United States, seeing an opportunity to unify all of Korea and destroy a Communist satellite government, enlarged its objective. By turning around the "dagger" once aimed at Japan, and endangering the political survival of the North Korean regime, the United States provoked Chinese intervention—just as the Soviets had originally provoked American intervention by aiming the "dagger" at Japan and threatening the existence of the South Korean Government.[13] China's entry into the conflict intensified the fighting and risked a major escalation of the war. But Washington, fearful that to strike back against China *in* China would bog the United States down in a full-scale war on the Asian mainland—if, indeed, it did not precipitate World War III —reverted to its original aim.

The conclusion seems clear that the winning side must also exercise caution. This does not mean his aim must be limited to the restoration of the *status quo*, although this is undoubtedly the simplest solution. But it does mean that his aim must fall short of the elimination of the opponent's regime. Indeed, this holds true for both sides. It was the North Vietnamese attempt (backed by the Chinese) to take over South Vietnam that led to American air attacks on North Vietnam, which demonstrated rather vividly the basic point: If either side fails to keep his political objectives limited, the other side is compelled to escalate the conflict. For only by imposing severer sanctions and exacting a greater price for "victory"—and also posing the greater possibility of a rapid escalation into a far larger, if not a total war—can the "escalator" hope that the opponent will back down and limit his objectives. Thus, on the one hand, the belligerents limit their aims in order to avoid a strategic nuclear war; on the other hand, if one of the belligerents goes beyond these bounds, some escalation may be required to force him once more to exercise self-restraint. The escalation, by taking the hostilities one step nearer to all-out war, underlines the fact that the price of a complete victory, even locally, is far too high.

> We cannot have limited war without settling for limited objectives, which in practice is likely to mean a negotiated peace based on compromise.

[13] See Spanier, *The Truman-MacArthur Controversy and the Korean War*, pp. 84–134; and Allen S. Whiting, *China Crosses the Yalu*.

Clausewitz's classic definition, that the object of war is to impose one's will on the enemy, must be modified, at least for any opponent who has a substantial nuclear capability behind him. Against such an opponent one's terms must be modest enough to permit him to accept them, without his being pushed by desperation into rejecting both those terms and the limitations on the fighting. This principle, if consistently pursued, should dispose of the hackneyed argument that limited war is impossible because the losing side will always be constrained to reject limitations rather than accept defeat. . . . We must be clear, however, that the curtailing of our taste for unequivocal victory is one of the prices we pay to keep the physical violence, and thus the costs and penalities, from going beyond the level of the tolerable. It is not the other way round.[14]

It is therefore vital to limit the political objectives and to restate these objectives frequently in order to impress the limitations upon one's own people—and this is particularly necessary in a democracy in order to control the rather natural wartime feelings that the aggressor must be punished—and to reassure the opponent that the restraints will be respected.

Thus the basic restraint that must be maintained during a limited war is the nonuse of strategic nuclear weapons, although at the same time these weapons serve as the best safeguard against escalation to total war. Almost equally important is the noninvolvement of American, Russian, and Chinese troops. Again, this is not to say that if these forces clashed, total war would be inevitable. But their involvement would increase the difficulty of preserving the limitations on the conflict. The great powers seem to be well aware of this second restraint, and the United States and the Soviet Union have been careful to avoid any embroilment in which they might confront each other directly. Indeed, one of the aims in stationing American troops in Europe was to let the Soviets know that any attack there would inevitably involve the United States in war. In the ground and air corridors to West Berlin, as well as in the city itself, incidents involving a direct clash between American and Russian forces have been scrupulously avoided. Significantly, the Soviets have thus far been willing to risk a conflict only in a situation where American forces had been withdrawn—South Korea. And even then, the initial fighting was done by their North Korean satellite. Even the Communist Chinese troops that later intervened in the Korean War were not sent *officially* by the Chinese Government. Peking never declared war, and it never accepted responsibility for the Chinese troops in Korea, which were declared to be "volunteers." Nor did the United States declare war on North Korea or Communist China. American troops were regarded as part of the United Nations forces fighting a U.N. "police action." The nondeclaration of war and the use of volunteers may well seem to be both minor and obvious disguises. Nevertheless, they play a significant

14 Brodie, *op. cit.*, pp. 313–14.

role in keeping wars limited. Again, despite the fact that the Soviet Union was the instigator of the Korean War and supplied both the North Koreans and Communist Chinese with military equipment and diplomatic support, it was no more officially involved than was the United States when she supplied weapons to the Nationalist Chinese on Quemoy and Matsu in 1958.

A further restraint required in limited war is geographical—i.e., limited wars have generally been confined to one nation. The Yalu River served as the frontier in the Korean War, and even after Peking's intervention, the war was not extended beyond it. Bombers were not sent to hit the factories, railroads, or military supply depots in Manchuria. In fact, even the bombing of the bridges crossing the Yalu into China was restricted to the North Korean side. Thus the Korean War was confined to Korea—and similarly the Indochina War to Indochina, and the Quemoy-Matsu crisis to the two islands and surrounding waters. This is not to say that if there had been an extension beyond these frontiers, total war would have resulted. It is doubtful that air attacks on Manchuria would have incurred Soviet intervention, for the Soviet Union at the time was strategically inferior to the United States. Indeed, the American air attacks on North Vietnam after 1965 have not precipitated all-out war. Yet boundaries do serve as clear lines of demarcation. Even such a line as the 38th Parallel, which had been intended to serve only as a temporary divider between the Soviet and American zones of occupation of Korea to disarm Japanese troops after Japan's defeat, grew into an unofficially recognized frontier between the Soviet and American spheres of influence. Territorial water lines serve the same purpose. During the Quemoy-Matsu crises of 1958, Peking proclaimed that its territorial waters extended 12 miles out to sea. The United States rejected this claim, recognizing only the traditional 3-mile limit. American supply ships stopped just short of this and then transferred their supplies to smaller Nationalist ships. The Chinese Communist guns on the mainland fired only at the Nationalist ones when they crossed within the 3-mile limit. They did not fire on American ships, and American naval guns and planes did not attack the Chinese Communist shore batteries and nearby airfields.

Thus, in a limited war, each side usually acknowledges that it must allow the other to possess "privileged sanctuaries"—inviolable areas in which are held reserve troops, supplies, and air and naval bases. To attack these areas is to remove one of the important restraints limiting the scope of the conflict. Manchuria was such a sanctuary for the Communists during the Korean War. While this was generally recognized in the United States, especially by those who demanded that Manchuria be bombed, there was little realization that the United States, too, possessed privileged sanctuaries—in Japan and Okinawa. Moreover, the Communists made no attacks on sea transports that supplied American, South Korean, and allied forces. There were even sanctuaries within the actual area of the fighting: The Communists launched no air attacks on either Pusan or Inchon, the two largest ports through which most of the supplies for the U.N. forces were channeled. If either port had been subject to frequent bombing, U.N. operations might have been seriously hampered. And it was precisely for that reason that bombing the ports would have been risky for the Chinese. For American planes might then have attacked Chinese cities in retaliation. Similarly, Chinese Communist jet fighters did not attack U.N. troops in the field, U.S. air bases in South Korea, or aircraft carriers lying off the coast; instead, they limited themselves to the Yalu River area, defending the bridges across the river.

A fifth, and final, restraint in limited wars is the nonuse of tactical nuclear weapons.[15] Use of these weapons, which did not become available until the mid-1950's, is often proposed because of the West's inferiority in manpower in relation to the Sino-Soviet bloc. If they are not employed, it is argued, the Communists could in a series of limited wars kill off the West's manpower. Actually, the United States and Western Europe together possess *more* manpower than the Soviet Union. The Chinese, to be sure, do outnumber us by far, but manpower has rarely been a decisive factor in war. In any event, the often-cited "hordes" of Russian and Chinese soldiers are a myth. The only soldiers that are important are the trained ones who can be well supplied once they have been committed to battle. The United States, with its enormous productive plant, could outproduce the Chinese and the Russians, and their economies would be far more strained by the maintenance of forces in the field during a long limited war than the United States. Indeed, resort to tactical nuclear weapons would impose much less strain on the Communist economies, and the use of tactical nuclear weapons would thus be to America's *dis*advantage. The United States also enjoys a superior logistical system. The Soviets and the Chinese might find it difficult to sustain a large supply system over a long period of time in areas not so well located as Korea, which was close to Manchuria's factories and Soviet supply lines. Even then, Chinese troops in Korea carried most of their supplies with them, and when these were depleted— usually after a few days—they broke off engagements. A sustained Western offensive against the larger Chinese armies therefore might well have been successful in effecting breakthroughs in the Chinese lines.

In any case, tactical nuclear weapons do not necessarily favor the defending side. A conventional defense is generally calculated to hold an

---

[15] Arguments to the contrary are presented by Kissinger, *op. cit.*, pp. 174–202 (although he changed his mind in *The Necessity for Choice*, pp. 75–86); Oskar Morgenstern, *The Question of National Defense*, pp. 145–54; and Osgood, *op. cit.*, pp. 251–59.

offense three times its size, but tactical nuclear weapons would eliminate this advantage. When both sides are equally matched in numbers, there is no innate reason why the defender should hold his ground, let alone advance. In these circumstances, tactical nuclear weapons are likely to favor the larger army. Their superior firepower does not really make them a substitute for manpower. In fact, precisely because they can impose a much higher casualty rate, an army must be larger in order to replace its high rate of killed and wounded. Moreover, if the use of tactical nuclear arms were a foregone conclusion, and the Communists therefore resorted to them from the beginning, they might completely overwhelm their victims and attain their political objectives before the United States could mobilize its forces and move them to the attacked area. If the North Koreans, for example, had possessed tactical nuclear weapons, it would have been impossible for the first American troops to fight an effective rear-guard action, reorganize the defeated South Korean Army, and defend themselves for weeks in a narrow beachhead perimeter while waiting to go on the offensive. In such an instance, the enemy's use of tactical nuclear arms and the extremely high casualty rates the United States would suffer if it responded to such an attack could actually prove a *deterrent* to an American response.

Most important of all, though, tactical nuclear weapons are a political liability. Few nations want to be "saved from Communism" by tactical nuclear weapons, which could devastate much of their nation. The average tactical nuclear weapon in the NATO stockpile, for example, has a yield five times greater than that of the bomb dropped on Hiroshima. Thus its tremendous destructive power is its chief political disadvantage. On the other hand, the principal advantage of the *non*use of tactical nuclear weapons is the distinction between them and conventional arms —a distinction as clear-cut as a boundary line, and as vital in preserving the limitations on war. For once this distinction has been erased, where can a new boundary line be drawn? Will the momentum of battle not lead to the employment of ever larger nuclear weapons until the escalation finally results in the use of strategic arms?

It is necessary to clarify one fact that seems to be confused not only among laymen but also among many scientists and even professional military officers. One frequently meets references to "tactical" nuclear weapons as distinct from "strategic" ones with the implication that there are marked intrinsic differences between them or the factors governing their use. The most common belief is that the former are necessarily of small yield and the latter of large. These ideas are completely erroneous.

The first A-bombs were tactical bombs as much as they were strategic; more so, in fact, since their yields were of a size now regarded as falling entirely inside the tactical range. But there is no *military* reason why tactical weapons should have to be of small yield. Usually, where a small weapon is good, a larger one is better; and the delivery of the latter is likely to be about as feasible and not much more expensive. . . . The argument that we *must* use nuclear weapons tactically but that only the smallest nuclear weapons should be so used seems to be somewhat wanting in consistency. If they must be very small, why not none at all? If they must be used, why not use large ones?[16]

To sum up: Limited wars are, in fact, another form of arms control, which seeks not only to stabilize mutual deterrence and thereby prevent a nuclear war, but also to preserve the restraints on less than total military conflicts in order to forestall escalation into total war. Like other arms-control measures, limited wars are based on tacit bargain between the participants to observe certain restrictions and not to exceed them. However ridiculous these restrictions may appear to be from the military point of view, their principal aim is to convey to the opponent the desire to abide by existing limitations and to provide the opponent with some incentive to show a similar restraint. The limitations must be clearly drawn: Because they are not formally negotiated but are, like other arms-control measures, tacitly agreed upon, it is necessary, above all, that the terms are qualitatively distinguishable from possible alternatives. This difference is more than one just of degree. It has been explained as follows:

> "Some gas" raises complicated questions of how much, where, under what circumstances: "no gas" is simple and unambiguous. Gas only on military personnel; gas used only by defending forces; gas only when carried by vehicle or projectile; no gas without warning—a variety of limits is conceivable; some may make sense, and many might have been more impartial to the outcome of the war. But there is a simplicity to "no gas" that makes it almost uniquely a focus for agreement when each side can only conjecture at what rules the other side would propose and when failure at coordination on the first try may spoil the chances for acquiescence in any limits at all.[17]

These, then, are the principal restraints that, if observed, keep limited wars limited. In addition, these restraints tend to reinforce one another; conversely, the more that are violated, the more tenuous the limitation. No single escalation will erupt immediately and automatically into total war. There are different gradations or levels of violence between a Lebanon landing, a Quemoy-Matsu, a Korea or Indochina, and an all-out nuclear conflict between the United States and the Soviet Union. Indeed, nuclear strategist Herman Kahn has constructed an "escalation ladder" that ascends from the lower rungs of an "ostensible crisis" to what he terms a "spasm or insensate war."[18] The very fact that each

[16] Brodie, *op. cit.*, pp. 325–26.
[17] Thomas C. Schelling, *Strategy of Conflict*, p. 75.
[18] See Herman Kahn, *On Escalation: Metaphors and Scenarios* (New York: Frederick A. Praeger, 1965).

restraint violated weakens the over-all capacity to limit the conflict means that when one side does escalate, the step must be taken carefully and slowly. The first U.S. air attack on North Vietnam was in response to a PT-boat attack on American destroyers in the Gulf of Tonkin; the target was the harbor from which the PT-boats had sailed. Later, several air attacks were launched to retaliate for Viet-Cong attacks on American servicemen and planes in South Vietnam. The next step was to hit North Vietnamese military targets, regardless of attacks on American personnel or equipment. These strikes, it was stressed, were aimed at halting Communist aggression against South Vietnam. Thus, the scope of the attacks, initially narrowly confined, was only gradually broadened—and never to the point of including general attacks on population centers like Hanoi.

But gradual escalation is a question not only of the nature and scope of the targets, but also of timing. After each step upward on the ladder, the escalator—if he is careful—stops to see if his opponent will desist as a result of the escalation and the fear this has induced of a greatly expanded, if not total, war. If he does, there will be no need for a further escalation; if not, it may be necessary. Thus the first U.S. air strikes against North Vietnam were north of the 17th Parallel but south of the 19th. When this produced no results, the strikes hit targets north of the 19th Parallel. The important point is that at each rung of the ladder there be time for either tacit or explicit bargaining to occur. The side against whom the escalation is directed must have time to evaluate its next move; and it can do this only after it has decided what the escalation signifies about the opponent's intentions.

These calculations and countercalculations are clearly complex and sensitive. And the Soviets have frequently questioned whether the various limitations could indeed confine hostilities. Khrushchev once said: "There is much talk in the imperialist camp today about local wars, and the imperialists are even making small-caliber atomic weapons to be used in such wars. There is even a special theory on local wars. Is this mere chance? Not at all. . . . There have been local wars in the past and they may break out again. But the chances of starting wars even of this kind are dwindling. A small-scale imperialist war, no matter which of the imperialists starts it, may develop into a world thermonuclear and missile war."[19] Denying the possibility of limited war, of course, serves Soviet purposes. The Soviets would like the United States to believe that it must continue to confront Communist challenges with an all-or-nothing response. But the Soviets themselves have fought limited hostilities, as with Japan in Siberia before World War II; and they triggered the Korean War and helped to keep it limited. They are, in any case, fully aware that nuclear bombs could destroy the principal base of the world revolution and are therefore unlikely to risk its loss by permitting

<hr />

[19] Washington Center of Foreign Policy Research, *Two Communist Manifestoes*, p. 50; see also Raymond L. Garthoff, *Soviet Strategy in the Nuclear Age*, pp. 107–15.

a limited war to escalate to such a point. To the degree that the Soviets are genuinely worried about the problem of keeping a limited war limited, however, their anxieties will deter them from precipitating such hostilities. During the Cuban missile crisis, in October, 1962, for instance, the Soviet ships carrying nonmilitary items respected the American naval blockade, and the others returned home before they neared the American destroyers. Moreover, the ships carrying the Soviet missiles back to Russia allowed their cargoes to be photographed. The Soviets were anxious to avoid any clash between their ships and American forces, thereby showing their aversion to any direct hostilities, however limited, with the United States.

But the Soviets—and certainly the Chinese—have shown no hesitation in favoring "wars of national liberation" in the non-Western areas of the world. Khrushchev made the following announcement in 1961:

> There will be liberation wars as long as imperialism exists, as long as colonialism exists. Wars of this kind are revolutionary wars. Such wars are not only justified, they are inevitable, for the colonialists do not freely bestow independence on the peoples. The peoples win freedom and independence only through struggle, including armed struggle. . . . These uprisings cannot be identified with wars between countries, with local wars, because the insurgent people are fighting for the right of self-determination, for their social and independent national development; these uprisings are directed against the corrupt reactionary regimes, against the colonialists.[20]

One advantage of these wars of national liberation—in effect, guerrilla wars—is that the Communists may, as Khrushchev stated, "support just wars of this kind wholeheartedly and without reservations and they march in the van of the peoples fighting for liberation,"[21] but at the same time such wars do not pose the issue of aggression as clearly as do conventional limited attacks. There is no single moment when a major attack across a well-defined frontier or line alerts the United States and her allies, let alone the nonaligned nations. "In the conventional war, the aggressor who has prepared for it within the confines of his national territory, channeling his resources into the preparation, has much to gain by attacking suddenly with all his forces. The transition from peace to war is as abrupt as the state of the art allows; the first shock may be decisive. This is hardly possible in the revolutionary war because the aggressor—the insurgent—lacks sufficient strength at the outset. Indeed, years may sometimes pass before he has built up significant political, let alone military, power. So there is usually little or no first shock, little or no surprise, no possibility of an early decisive battle. In fact, the insurgent has no interest in producing a shock until he feels fully able to

[20] *Two Communist Manifestoes*, pp. 51–52.
[21] *Ibid*.

withstand the enemy's expected reaction."[22] Furthermore, the guerrilla forces generally are preponderantly natives, not foreigners; thus a guerrilla war has the appearance of "domestic" conflict rather than an invasion from another nation. Finally, guerrilla wars tend to be lengthy. If the guerrillas were as strong as or stronger than their opponent, then they would seek to defeat him quickly in a conventional battle. But their very weakness compels them to whittle away at their enemy's strength bit by bit. This process of attrition can go almost unnoticed by the outside world until the last stage of the war, when the guerrillas are poised to achieve the defeat of their by now weakened and demoralized opponent. By then, it is usually too late for effective countermeasures. Waging guerrilla warfare is thus considerably safer than fighting a regular war in the nuclear age.

The ultimate aim of the guerrillas is, of course, the capture of state power. That is why guerrilla war is often referred to as a war of "internal conquest," or subversive warfare. In the initial phase of the war, the guerrillas, as the weaker side, are strategically on the defensive; tactically, though, they are always on the offensive. In order to wear the enemy down and weaken him gradually, they adopt hit-and-run tactics. Mobility, surprise, and rapid military decisions are characteristic of their operations. They fight only when there is a good chance of victory; otherwise, they do not attack or, if engaged, they quickly disengage. Their attacks are swift, sudden, and relentless. There is no front line in this war. The front is everywhere, and the guerrillas strike anywhere and everywhere. In the words of the man sometimes called the Clausewitz of guerrilla warfare, Communist Chinese leader Mao Tse-tung, the guerrillas "must move with the fluidity of water and the ease of the blowing wind. Their tactics must deceive, tempt, and confuse the enemy. They must lead the enemy to believe that they will attack him from the east and north, and they must then strike him from the west and the south. They must strike, then rapidly disperse. They must move at night."[23] The Viet-Minh (North Vietnamese Communist) manual states seven rules as governing the conduct of guerrilla warfare:

1. Make a feint attack on one point but actually attack somewhere else so that the enemy cannot protect himself. . . .
2. Make yourself alternatively visible and invisible so that the enemy does not know where we are and cannot attack. . . .
3. Avoid the enemy's strong points and attack only his weak points; in other words, do not insist on confronting a numerically superior or watchful enemy with our entire forces. Catch him at his weak points: rear-guard of marching troops, isolated soldiers who are resting or re-

---

[22] David Galula, *Counterinsurgency Warfare*, pp. 9–10.
[23] *Mao Tse-tung on Guerrilla Warfare*, pp. 103–4.

treating. If we attack an enemy formation or an enemy on his guard, we are bound to suffer losses.

4. Know when to advance and when to retreat; if a stronger enemy attacks us violently, withdraw in order to try to counterattack his weak points; for instance, wait until he is demoralized, tired, or overconfident. Never fight foolhardily or obstinately; . . .

5. Attack, destroy, and withdraw in such a way that the enemy cannot react, bring up reinforcements in order to encircle us or call upon his air-force. . . .

6. Do not fight unless success is certain, otherwise withdraw. One must not attack foolishly, or persist regardless of cost, nor must one show useless obstinacy. If one wants to give battle one must be certain of success. If victory is not assured one must resolutely refuse to attack, and wait for a more favourable opportunity. If success is assured during battle one must resolutely assault in order to annihilate the enemy; but otherwise one must hold on for a while and then withdraw without regret or hesitation.

7. One must not always use the same tactics. The constant use of the same tactics allows the enemy to defend himself more easily and to gain the initiative.[24]

Guerrilla tactical doctrine is perhaps most aptly summed up in Mao's well-known brief formula: "Enemy advances, we retreat; enemy halts, we harass; enemy tires, we attack; enemy retreats, we pursue."

Rather than imposing any major or severe defeats on the enemy, these tactics harass, confuse, and frustrate him. The guerrillas do not, in fact, engage in conventional battle until the last stage of the war; they are too weak throughout most of the hostilities. The violence at the physical level is important, but it is the violence at the *psychological* level that is decisive. If the enemy cannot be beaten physically, his *will to fight* can be worn away. And this can be achieved in two ways. Basically, his army can be demoralized. Suffering one minor defeat after another, rarely finding the enemy to engage and defeat him in battle, forced increasingly to the defensive by the guerrilla's tactics, the army loses its offensive spirit as it finds that Western conventional tactics are useless. The army's determination to stay and fight declines; its stamina is eroded.

Even more important in undermining the enemy's will to fight is to isolate him by capturing the support of the population. Popular support is essential if the guerrillas are to realize their objective of "internal conquest." The people provide them with recruits, food, shelter, and, above all else, intelligence. For if the guerrillas are to surprise the enemy, they must know where to strike and when. They must know all the opponent's moves in order to be able to fight at moments of their own choos-

[24] Otto Heilbrunn, *Partisan Warfare*, pp. 78–79.

ing, against smaller groups, and to escape if government reinforcements suddenly arrive.

Victories are naturally one way of impressing the people, just as they depress the enemy's army. A government that cannot provide its people with elemental security is bound to lose their allegiance. The village peasants, generally removed from any contact with their government, are most concerned to ensure their own future. If they think the guerrillas will win the war, they are unlikely to antagonize them, but instead will cooperate increasingly with them. Terror also plays a role in eliciting this cooperation. This terror is usually selective and its aim is to reaffirm the weakness of the government; thus it is applied mainly to government officials. (Obviously, wholesale terror would only alienate the very people whose support the guerrillas seek to win.) The guerrillas have made their point vividly when they can show the peasants that the government is not even able to protect its own officials.[25] Moreover, by eliminating these officials, the guerrillas break the link between the government and the majority of the people, thus limiting the government's authority mainly to the cities.

The guerrillas, then, enlist popular support because they appear to be the eventual winners and because of their intimidation of many villagers. However, they also gain support in more positive ways. To quote the Viet-Minh manual again:

Propaganda among the population [involves]:
—Forbidding the soldiers billeted in a private house to walk about disorderly, to sing or to make a loud noise, to take anything away without the owner's permission;
—Informing oneself about the regional customs and habits, the life of the people and their feelings towards the resistance; dispelling the uneasiness of the population, for the [Viet-Minh] government. Stay for choice with the poor peasants and people, try to understand their problems and help them in their daily work (in Vietnam, the peasants were grateful when the guerrillas assisted with the harvesting);
—Taking part in the meetings and activities of the groups and the popular guerrillas. If possible, organizing study groups together with the popular guerrillas [in this way troops and guerrillas can inform each other about their personal experiences and help each other in their studies];
—In case of differences with the population, immediately organizing a recapitulatory control meeting in order to maintain the spirit of unity.[26]

It is clear that each guerrilla is not just a soldier, but is also a propagandist—or what the Communists call an agitator. He is well indoctri-

[25] In South Vietnam, for instance, more than 15,000 village officials were murdered between 1957 and 1965. (Bernard B. Fall, *Viet-Nam Witness, 1953–66*, p. 203.)

[26] Heilbrunn, *op. cit.*, pp. 145–46; see also George K. Tanham, *Communist Revolutionary Warfare*, p. 143.

nated, which makes him, first of all, a loyal and highly motivated fighter. "I love you," wrote one Viet-Minh guerrilla to his girl, "almost as much as I love Ho Chi Minh." This soldier, dedicated to his cause, will also be capable of explaining that cause to the village population, and he will present it as the people's cause. This is the fundamental reason for the guerrillas' success: their ability to identify themselves with popular aspirations. Communist guerrillas do not present themselves as Communists; nor do the people support them because they are Communists or desire the establishment of a Communist state. The guerrillas present themselves simply as spokesmen for the people's existing grievances and aspirations. If the people are resentful of continued colonial rule or a despotic native government, the Communists take up their cries. If the people seek social and economic justice, the Communists demand it on their behalf. The Communists, in short, identify themselves as "liberators" and "reformers," promising that they can satisfy the revolution of rising expectations. Thus in South Vietnam, the Viet-Cong appealed to the peasants by pointing out that they were working in the landowners' rice fields for the landowners'—and not their own—benefit. Now that the landlords had fled to the cities, the peasants no longer needed to pay rents to them or taxes to the government, the Viet-Cong said. The peasants now owned the land—and the Viet-Cong would protect them if anyone sought to take it away from them. The result was a virtually complete schism between the government in Saigon and the peasantry.

Once the guerrillas have won popular support and the government army has become demoralized, only a final *coup de grâce* is needed to topple the government. This means resort to conventional battle—*unless* the guerrillas can, as in Cuba and South Vietnam, isolate the government and thereby contribute to the disintegration of the entire governmental structure and authority in the capital city. The guerrillas must, of course, be extremely careful in their timing. If they engage in conventional fighting too early, before the enemy army has lost most of its will to fight and before they themselves are properly trained and equipped, they may be badly defeated. On the other hand, if they have the patience and are able to calculate correctly the moment of transition, the war will end in their victory. The defeat of the French forces at Dien Bien Phu broke France's determination to hold onto her old colony. The French garrison there consisted of only one-fifteenth of the total number of French troops in Indochina. The French suffered 12,000 casualties, including prisoners, and the estimated Viet-Minh casualties were 15,000. Since their total force was not as large as that of the French, the Viet-Minh clearly had been badly hurt. Yet this single battle of Dien Bien Phu sapped France's will to resist.[27] While it was not militarily a decisive battle, it was certainly politically—and psychologically—decisive.

[27] See Tanham, *op. cit.*, pp. 32, 97.

The French determined to end the long and—for them—futile fighting.

It is in this final phase, according to some experts, that the guerrilla forces' need for a contiguous external source of support and supply becomes crucial:

> A siege-like battle on the scale of Dien Bien Phu, with its heavy requirement for artillery and manpower, would have been unthinkable without the constant supply line from Communist China and without the ease of access of personnel from one country to the other. Not for many years, if ever, could the Vietminh alone have manufactured the artillery necessary for the decisive battle against the French, and it needed the experience and expertise of the Chinese to train the Vietminh soldiery and military leadership, both in China and in Vietnam. In both respects, the advantage of contiguity was vital: Without a common border, the logistic problem of moving men and weapons would have been formidable so long as the French controlled both sea and air. There can be no doubt whatever that China's interest in supporting the revolutionaries, coupled with the common border, was a strong contributing—if not the decisive—factor in the success of the Vietminh.[28]

Perhaps the word "decisive" is a bit strong. Admittedly, the guerrilla war in Greece after World War II did not end in the guerrillas' defeat until after the Tito-Stalin break had deprived them of their sanctuary. No doubt, also, the Chinese Communist sanctuary did play a vital role in the French defeat at Dien Bien Phu. But the French had, in effect, already lost the war to the Viet-Minh by late 1950 since almost the entire half of North Vietnam had by then become a Viet-Minh stronghold. Moreover, the Viet-Minh received most of its weapons from the defeated French forces. Similarly, North Vietnam had by early 1966 infiltrated an estimated 14,000 troops—of the approximately 73,000 Viet-Cong hard core—into South Vietnam;[29] moreover, Hanoi's role in the direction of the war in the South was by then quite clear. But there could also be little doubt that the Viet-Cong had widespread support and that the Saigon government lacked popular roots. Castro, on the other hand, possessed no sanctuary. He won because the Batista regime had alienated the masses, particularly the urban middle class, and the army just disintegrated. Likewise, the Chinese Communists won because Chiang Kai-shek's regime had lost mass support after the defeat of Japan. To be sure, they greatly benefited from the arms they took without the Na-

---

[28] *Ibid.*, p. 144. Bernard Fall also believes that the external sanctuary is decisive: "The successive failure of *all* rebellions since World War II depended on whether the active sanctuary was willing and able to perform its expected role." Yet Fall himself admits that "the French were definitely the 'aliens' and the Communist-led Viet-Minh forces could count on the instinctive support of the native population." The French were therefore unable to create antiguerrilla forces and their intelligence was often faulty because they were isolated from the population. (See Fall, *Street Without Joy*, p. 16.)

[29] Fall, *Viet-Nam Witness*, p. 337.

tionalists' permission from the surrendering Japanese Army. Further-more, the Soviet troops in Manchuria supplemented this stock, and the Chinese Communists also captured great quantities of American arms from Nationalist forces whom they had defeated. But fundamentally, they were successful because they were able to exploit peasant dissatis-faction. In short, while the external sanctuary may play an important role in guerrilla warfare, as it does in conventional limited war, the "de-cisive" role continues to be played by the populace.[30]

Thus not only is guerrilla warfare a safer war in the sense that it does not carry the same risks of escalation as conventional limited war, but it is also the logical way for the Communists to exploit the vast wave of social, economic, and cultural change sweeping through the under-developed nations. This revolution would be occurring even if Com-munism did not exist. The Communists merely feed on the issues raised by the urge for change—the desires for national independence, land re-form, economic development, etc. In this sense, the Communists are truly, as they have been called, the "scavengers of the modernization process.[31] Guerrilla warfare may at times seem militarily primitive, for the rifle, the knife, and piano wire (for strangulation), for example, can-not begin to compare with the highly intricate weapons in Western ar-senals. But, as has been emphasized, guerrilla warfare is "in fact more sophisticated than nuclear war or atomic war or war as it was waged by conventional armies, navies, and air forces."[32] More than any other kind of war, it requires a high degree of political intelligence—as does counter-guerrilla or counterinsurgency warfare. "A successful response to the problem posed by the guerrilla is neither simple to plan nor easy, cheap, and quick to carry out. Guerrilla operations are as difficult to fight as the Cold War itself. . . . Basically, the problem is a political one; to at-tempt to understand it in purely military terms is the most dangerous kind of oversimplification. Guerrillas are a symptom rather than a cause. Lasting success requires a viable political settlement, and even opera-tional success over a period of time demands the proper political frame-work for effective military action.[33] But more succinctly, for a country such as the United States, which believes that a war is a strictly military contest, a counterguerrilla war is the most difficult one to fight—far more difficult than a total nuclear war or a limited conventional war.

The political and psychological effects of military actions are para-

---

[30] On the decisiveness of civilian loyalties rather than the external base, or terror, or military tactics, see Chalmers A. Johnson, "Civilian Loyalties and Guerrilla Con-flict," *World Politics*, July, 1962, pp. 646–61.

[31] W. W. Rostow, "Guerrilla Warfare in Underdeveloped Areas," in T. N. Greene (ed.), *The Guerrilla—And How To Fight Him*, pp. 54–61.

[32] Samuel B. Griffith, "Introduction," *Mao Tse-tung on Guerrilla Warfare*, p. 7.

[33] Peter Paret and John W. Shy, *Guerrillas in the 1960's*, pp. 71–72; see also Charles W. Thayer, *Guerrilla*, pp. 42–60.

mount in counterguerrilla warfare. The first requirement is, of course, to impose military defeats on the guerrilla forces. The guerrillas need victories to maintain their morale, discipline, and momentum, and constant defeats are bound to have a serious impact. Moreover, the civilian population, witnessing these defeats and no longer sure that the guerrillas will win, will tend to become less cooperative. Such defeats can best be won by the government if the counterguerrilla forces divide the country into a number of areas and flush the guerrillas area by area. In order to do this, it is necessary to counter the basic mobility and surprise principles of guerrilla warfare—that is, government forces must find the guerrillas, pin them down, and force them to stand and fight. Once an area has been cleared, garrison forces composed of regular troops and perhaps militia can be left to guard it. The striking forces must be highly professional, extremely tough, thoroughly trained in unconventional warfare, and mobile enough at all times to seek out the enemy. The British in Malaya, for instance, used squads and platoons who lived in the jungles for months, gathering their own intelligence, ambushing enemy patrols, and cutting supply lines. At the same time, they held out amnesties to guerrillas who surrendered; a number of guerrillas, feeling beaten, did accept these amnesties.[34] This tactic also proved relatively successful against the Mau Mau in Kenya.[35]

Counterguerrilla forces can avail themselves of modern methods of communications, such as radios or walkie-talkies, which allow troops in contact with the enemy to call in reinforcements in an attempt to cut off the guerrilla's retreat. The helicopter has proved to be particularly valuable as a means of searching for guerrillas; the guerrilla, for a change, feels hunted and is placed on the defensive. The helicopter can also be used to bring reinforcements quickly to the battlefields, thus forcing the guerrilla either to fight or to flee. But the helicopter is subject to certain limitations as well. It is virtually useless at night, and during the daytime its success in finding guerrillas depends on how bushy or jungle-covered the terrain is. Moreover, guerrillas have managed to devise anti-helicopter tactics by which they try to knock them out.[36] Yet the helicopter certainly makes it more difficult for the guerrillas to defeat piecemeal a well-equipped and mobile enemy, such as the United States, or to impose a conventional defeat upon him in the final phase of the war.

It may, of course, be questioned whether, in instances where the external sanctuary plays a vital role, these military measures will suffice if the supply lines from the sanctuary are not cut. Attacking the sanctuary

[34] For more on Britain's successful counterguerrilla war in Malaya, see Lucian Pye, *Guerrilla Communism in Malaya*; Rowland Mans, "Victory in Malaya," in Greene (ed.), *op. cit.*, pp. 115–43; and William J. Dederer, "Malaya: The Practice," *The New Leader*, April 16, 1962, pp. 11–14.

[35] Heilbrunn, *op. cit.*, pp. 148, 163–64.

[36] Fall, *The Two Viet-Nams*, p. 380.

may seem the "militarily necessary" thing to do, but it must also be remembered that guerrillas generally live off the land and capture many of their weapons from the enemy. Aerial bombardment of the sanctuary, as in the Vietnam war, can "succeed in wiping out all North Viet-Nam's conventional industrial and military targets, but it would probably have little immediate effect on its armed forces. After all, they successfully fought the French for eight years from hidden guerrilla bases and without making use of electric-power plants and railroads. . . . Lest it be forgotten, the United States Air Force was unable successfully to interdict Communist supply operations in Korea despite the fact that all conventional targets had been effectively destroyed."[37] In this connection, it is interesting to note that the air attacks on North Vietnam after 1965 were not launched primarily for military reasons—i.e., they were not expected to slow down appreciably, let alone halt, the supplies flowing southward. Rather, the attacks were intended to have a political impact —to punish North Vietnam for continuing its aggression. The hope was that North Vietnam, fearful of more air attacks of increasing destructiveness, would desist from its efforts to extend its rule to South Vietnam. The key question which arises in these circumstances is, of course, what should be done if this intensified pressure does not lead to a cessation of hostilities. One answer is to invade the sanctuary with a conventional army. This action could, however, result in a Korea-type war and, by its violation of the external sanctuary's immunity, eliminate one of the principal restraints upon a limited war, thus risking its escalation to a large-scale regional war involving Communist China. At the same time, such an invasion would not *guarantee* that the guerrillas would be defeated, at least any more quickly than by an intensive and effectively conducted war within the guerrilla-infested areas. One point is certainly clear. Whether the war is expanded or not, it remains a fact that no counterguerrilla war can be won by military means alone; a purely military solution is an illusion. It is interesting to note in this connection that the successful guerrilla and counterguerrilla leaders of the past two decades have largely been *non*military men. In China, Mao Tse-tung, a student and librarian, and subsequently a professionally trained revolutionary, defeated Chiang Kai-shek, a professionally trained soldier. In Indochina, Ho Chi Minh, a socialist agitator, and General Giap, a French-trained history teacher, defeated four of France's senior generals, including a marshal. Castro was a lawyer, and Magsaysay, a successful counterguerrilla, was an auto mechanic who became a politician.[38] In short, the orthodoxly trained military officer has by and large been unable to cope with the unorthodox nature of guerrilla warfare.

A second requirement in antiguerrilla warfare is to separate the guer-

[37] *Ibid.*, p. 402.
[38] Thayer, *op. cit.*, p. 69.

rillas from the population. One technique by which this can be accomplished is to resettle the latter in so-called "strategic hamlets."[39] Since people do not enjoy leaving their homes and villages, they rarely go freely. In Malaya, the Communists had been supplied by about a half-million Chinese "squatters" who lived near the edge of the jungle and worked in nearby mines and plantations. All of them were moved, and the Communist guerrillas, left without their source of food, then had to clear sections of the jungle and plant their own food. (British RAF planes subsequently searched for these spots and dropped poison on the crops.) Such a relocation of the population not only isolates the guerrillas, but also gives the government an opportunity to prove its ability to remedy the people's grievances and satisfy at least some of their aspirations. The resettled population must learn that they can live in safety and enjoy improved social conditions: some land of their own, electric light, health facilities, education for their children, and a voice in their own government. Otherwise, the people will remain hostile to the government and probably will continue to help the guerrillas as much as possible. If the people are made securer and happier, however, they are more likely to defend themselves against the guerrillas. Once this happens, the war is half won.

The problem here is that the remedy is easy to prescribe but difficult to implement. In Malaya, the resettlement program was relatively simple, despite its large scale. The Chinese, an ethnic minority in Malaya, were easily identifiable. Nor were all Chinese involved in supporting the guerrillas—only the poor squatters, and not the urban middle class. The squatters thus were visibly different from the rest of the population and, moreover, lived in a particular area. To find and remove them to areas away from the guerrilla war was therefore comparatively simple compared with the task in South Vietnam. Here no such distinct group exists. The strategic-hamlet program would have required moving almost 10 million people—obviously a colossal operation. All this effort would, in any case, be useless if the camps did not provide their inhabitants with better living conditions and security. The strategic hamlets must instill in the people a reason for supporting the government. Malaya's "new villages" provided such social services; moreover, the 8,000 Communist terrorists were too weak to attack the villages. South Vietnam's hamlets, before the overthrow of Ngo Dinh Diem in late 1963, failed in both respects. The regime was not concerned with its people's grievances or aspirations; and the Communist guerrillas were strong. The Communists frequently attacked the hamlets and destroyed them, thereby proving to the people that the government could not protect them, no matter what it did.

In the final analysis, the government can only win its war against the

[39] Paret and Shy, *op. cit.*, p. 46.

guerrillas if it alleviates the conditions that led the peasantry to support the guerrillas in the first place. This is the third requirement in counter-guerrilla warfare. The French refused to prepare Indochina for eventual independence; the people therefore supported the Viet-Minh as their national liberating force. In Malaya, the British granted independence during the fighting, thus giving the Malayans a stake in the struggle and at the same time depriving the Communists of their pose as liberators from colonialism. Clearly, whatever the popular grievances and aspira-tions, the government must show its genuine concern through both words and deeds. Popular confidence is the *indispensable* condition for successful antiguerrilla warfare. Military countermeasures alone can never be adequate; the troops trained in the tactics of unconventional warfare must be supported by political, social, and economic reform. It was this kind of combination that defeated the Communist-led Huks in the Philippines during the 1950's. The government won the alle-giance of the peasantry by instituting reforms to improve their lives; thus the Communist appeal was weakened and the Huks lost their support.[40] A British Colonel summed up the essence of counterguerrilla warfare when he said, "There has never been a successful guerrilla war conducted in an area where the populace is hostile to the guerrillas. . . . *The art of defeating the guerrillas is therefore the art of turning the populace against them."*[41]

The major task of antiguerrilla warfare is thus fundamentally a politi-cal one. Guerrillas are a barometer of discontent. This discontent must be ameliorated, for it is the decisive element that determines victory or failure. Guerrillas are not invincible, as the British proved in Malaya and Kenya; on the other hand, they did lose in Palestine and Cyprus. In all four of these counterguerrilla efforts, the British had support among the population; they also possessed great superiority in numbers of troops, and they utilized all the usual counterguerrilla techniques, such as popu-lation resettlement. Yet only in Malaya and Kenya did they win—and at a high cost. In Malaya, for instance, the British had no thoughts of grant-ing independence when the struggle began; this colony, which produced much of the world's tin and rubber, was too profitable. Granting Malaya independence therefore cost Britain much in rich revenues. In a sense, the British did not really win the war; the Communist terrorists lost it, as a result of the British grant of independence. The Communist insur-rections in Burma and Indonesia in the late 1940's failed because of sim-ilar lack of popular support. The French experience in Algeria reinforces

[40] See Frances L. Starner, *Magsaysay and the Philippine Peasantry: The Agrarian Impact on Philippine Politics, 1953–1956* (Berkeley, Calif.: University of California Press, 1961). For views of the contrasting situation in South Vietnam, see Fall, *The Two Viet-Nams,* and Denis Warner, *The Last Confucian* (New York: The Mac-millan Co., 1963).

[41] Quoted in Heilbrunn, *op. cit.,* p. 34 (italics added).

this basic point. The French actually won the military war against the guerrillas. By 1960, the Algerian National Liberation Army no longer possessed even a battalion-size unit. And by the end of the war in 1962, the Algerian guerrillas had, according to French Army sources, fewer than 4,000 troops left (10,000 according to other, more sympathetic French sources) out of a total of almost 60,000 three years earlier.[42] French military tactics were, in short, as effective in Algeria as they had been ineffective in Indochina. Nevertheless, the French lost the war because it was *politically* "unwinnable." The Algerian population was hostile; so were France's NATO allies and the nonaligned states. The suppression of a nationalist movement was politically unpalatable and unfeasible in an age when the legitimacy of all former colonial nations to rule themselves was almost universally recognized and asserted.

Perhaps the term "guerrilla warfare" is indeed too simple since it implies an emphasis on such tactics as ambush and sabotage, and neglects the pre-eminent political-psychological ingredient without which the military cannot win. The French have another name for it—revolutionary warfare. Expressing it in terms of an equation: guerrilla warfare plus psychological warfare equals revolutionary warfare.

> Revolutionary warfare is the result of the application of guerrilla-warfare methods and psychological-political operations for the purpose of establishing a competing ideological system or political structure. And this is basically where the Communists, in spite of their professed materialism, apparently have understood the rules of the game a great deal better than the United States, which professes to defend spiritual values: The Communists have correctly identified as the central objective of a revolutionary war—and, in fact, its only worthwhile prize—the *human beings* who make up the nation under attack. On our side, the securing of communication lines, the control of crops and industrial installations, and the protection of one particular power group seem·to be the overriding considerations. The population at large becomes an object that is manipulated, transferred, searched and seized, shoved out of the way when it impedes military operations, and, finally, strafed and napalm-bombed.[43]

The final requirement in waging counterguerrilla warfare is, simply, time. Such wars do not end in one or two or even three years. In Malaya, where the Communist terrorists had almost no outside help and little or no support from the Malays or wealthier Chinese, it took 80,000 British and Commonwealth troops, plus 180,000 Malayan special police, constables, and village-militia members, 12 years (from 1948 to 1960) to defeat only 8,000 guerrillas—and this despite the removal of the squatters! The minimum ratio of counterguerrillas to guerrillas would thus

[42] Fall, *The Two Viet-Nams*, pp. 346–47. The Algerian example also clearly demonstrates that the use of counterterror is not successful in ending guerrilla warfare.
[43] *Ibid.*, p. 349.

seem to be 10 to 1, and a better ratio might well be 15 to 1, or even 20 to 1. In the Philippines, it took 5 years (1947 to 1952) to defeat the Huks. And after President Magsaysay died, the corrupt Garcia Administration faced a revival of Huk activities; the new President, Macapagal, had to order mop-up operations in 1962. Unfortunately, Americans like to win their wars quickly. Viet-Minh General Giap's shrewd political estimate of the Western powers' determination to continue fighting an inconclusive war for so long may prove to be all too accurate: "The enemy will pass slowly from the offensive to the defensive. The blitzkrieg will transform itself into a war of long duration. Thus, the enemy will be caught in a dilemma: He has to drag out the war in order to win it and does not possess, on the other hand, the psychological and political means to fight a long-drawn-out war."[44] One need only recall the more direct challenge in Korea. By 1952, Americans were fed up with "Truman's war" and the continuation of the apparently futile loss of American lives; this mood undoubtedly contributed to their election of Eisenhower, who made a campaign promise to end the war. Americans want quick results, not long commitments without conclusive and "happy" endings. A long, drawn-out, indecisive engagement does not fit the traditional all-or-nothing approach. The guerrillas exploit this impatience.

In these circumstances, perhaps prevention remains the best part of the cure. The new nations suffering the growing pains of development appear to provide fertile ground for guerrilla wars. The Communists seek to exploit these conditions. Prevention thus demands that the West help the new nations modernize themselves politically, socially, culturally, and economically. But the problem is that the very process of development causes both economic hardships and psychological dislocation. Capital accumulation demands saving, which, in turn, imposes austerity. The collapse of traditional customs robs people of their sense of security. Modernization also means the overthrow of the long-established ruling class and thus social upheaval. All this creates fertile ground for Communist exploitation. Even in the absence of these conditions, discontent of some kind is likely to exist. National allegiance in most underdeveloped societies is nonexistent or, at best, fragile. The government is "they," not "we," for government has played little role in the lives of the rural population; its contact with the people has been mainly as a tax collector and as a recruiting sergeant. A well-organized minority, such as the Communists, can exploit this antigovernment attitude and the many social grievances harbored by the peasantry. Thus prevention may not be possible in some circumstances; as one writer has commented, it is rather like telling an insomniac to get plenty of sleep.[45] Guerrilla wars may indeed become the most frequently fought wars of the last half of the

[44] *Ibid.*, p. 113.
[45] Thayer, *op. cit.*, p. 55.

twentieth century. For this period is likely to remain one of political, economic, social, and psychological changes—and turmoil—throughout the underdeveloped areas. The Communists will continue to seek to exploit this "revolution of rising expectations," and their success will depend on the extent to which this revolution achieves satisfaction. And finally, in an age of nuclear weapons, guerrilla wars fought within a society are the safest way of "continuing politics by other means."

Nuclear Blackmail

The threat of war has historically been one of the most potent means employed by states to gain their political ends. As Salvador de Madariaga has said, "The normal wielders of armaments are not the soldiers but the diplomats." This remains true today, even though total war can no longer be considered as a rational instrument of national policy. It is precisely because nuclear war is so devastating that the very prospect of it can be used as a diplomatic tool. It is not the actual dropping of bombs, but the threat of dropping them, that provides the nation seeking to change the *status quo* with a powerful bargaining point. This nation makes limited demands. Knowing that he can deter an attack upon himself, he states that if his demands are not satisfied, he will unilaterally change the *status quo*, and that if his opponent resists this change, he will create a "grave situation." The maneuver is not unlike the limited-war challenge—only in this case there is no actual aggression. The defender of the *status quo*, however, faces the choice of suicide or surrender. The "incentive" held out to him is the avoidance of all-out war—but at the price of the demanded concessions. Nuclear blackmail, in short, is the test of will *par excellence*. A failure of nerve can not only result in the loss of the disputed territory or right, but it is also likely to have a grave impact upon the defender's allies and the nonaligned states. Again, it is the intangible, or psychological, impact that is vital: "For expectations about the circumstances and consequences of war in the minds of nations and statesmen—Americans, adversaries, allies, and the nonaligned —may affect the fortunes of the cold war no less decisively than war itself."[46]

Nuclear blackmail differs from limited-war challenges in one significant respect. Soviet forces have never been directly involved in these challenges; the actual fighting has been done by the Chinese or by a satellite of the Soviet Union or China. But the Soviets are directly involved in nuclear blackmail, and it is Soviet power itself that is the instrument. Berlin has been a dramatic example of the Soviets' application of this tactic.

[46] Robert E. Osgood, *NATO: The Entangling Alliance*, p. 16.

In Europe the cold war is a struggle for prestige and influence and a test of will and nerves waged against a background of beliefs about the relative military power of the participants, and about when and how they might use their power, and about what the results would be if they did. The Soviet objective is to so exploit Russian military power in conjunction with political threats and conciliatory gestures as to exacerbate the "contradictions" among allied states, stimulate neutralism and pacifism among their citizens, convince them that NATO cannot protect them but will only draw them into crises and war, induce them to abandon their collective efforts to build a "situation of strength," and persuade them to accept the Soviet terms of "peaceful coexistence." To these ends, Moscow tries to convince the Western nations that the military balance has shifted drastically against them in favor of the U.S.S.R., that they can maintain their "provocative" military bloc and sustain their "untenable" outposts like Berlin only at the risk of a catastrophic war, and that their only reasonable recourse is to accept Russia's conciliatory proposals to relieve international tensions—for example, by making West Berlin a "free city," recognizing East Germany, withdrawing foreign troops from the Continent, disbanding military bases, abandoning nuclear weapons, and, ultimately, dismantling the alliance. At the same time, they try to demonstrate NATO's impotence by maneuvering the West into tests of will that humiliate the most powerful allies and intimidate the others, while undermining the willingness of all members to support each other's interests at the risk of war.[47]

It was in 1958, the year after Sputnik and the first Soviet ICBM test, that the Soviets attempted to exploit politically what they considered to be a military advantage. At the very least, they felt they now possessed the strategic nuclear strength to deter any American attack; at best, they hoped to intimidate the United States. The Soviet Sputniks had greatly impressed Americans with their new vulnerability to nuclear attack. SAC was said to be particularly vulnerable to a surprise missile strike; its credibility even as the "great deterrent" was in some doubt. In these new circumstances, the Soviets demanded that West Berlin be "demilitarized" and become a "free city" by the withdrawal of Western troops.[48] If the Western powers did not comply by the end of a six-month period, the Soviet Union would turn the approaches to West Berlin over to the East German Government, with whom the Western allies would then have to negotiate the terms of access. If they refused—quite likely, since they did not even recognize the German Democratic Republic—and they attempted by force to break through a subsequent East German blockade, they were warned that Soviet troops would come to the aid of East Germany. On the other hand, if the allies did negotiate new terms of access, they would at the same time be jeopardizing their future in Berlin. Their presence in the city by right of occupation stemming from the defeat of

[47] *Ibid.*, pp. 16–17.
[48] *The New York Times*, November 28, 1958.

Nazi Germany—a right that depended on no other nation's consent—would be transformed into a presence by the consent of East Germany. One thing would then be certain: East Germany would, bit by bit, whittle away at Allied "rights" until there was none left. In brief, the only question being left for the United States and her allies to decide was the manner of their withdrawal.

The Soviet challenge was as obvious as it was crucial. If the West—in effect, the United States—were driven or squeezed out of West Berlin, the Soviets would demonstrate that America's NATO guarantee to defend Europe was meaningless. Faith in the United States as the "great protector" would thus be undermined, and West Germany and the other European allies, at least those on the Continent, would quickly realize that the United States was an unreliable ally and that each nation had better sound out Moscow to obtain the best possible bargain. NATO—and the new-born Common Market, the nucleus of a potentially united and powerful Europe—would disintegrate and its European members turn to "neutralism" and an increasing acceptance of the Soviet Union's terms of "peaceful coexistence." As President Kennedy stated the issue in 1961:

> The fulfillment of our pledge to that city is essential to the morale and the security of Western Germany, to the unity of Western Europe, and to the faith of the whole free world. Soviet strategy has long been aimed, not merely at Berlin, but at dividing and neutralizing all of Europe, forcing us back to our own shores. We must meet our oft-stated pledge to the free peoples of West Berlin—and maintain our rights and their safety, even in the face of force—in order to maintain the confidence of other free people in our word and our resolve. The strength of the alliance on which our security depends is dependent in turn on our willingness to meet these commitments.

West Berlin was therefore "the great testing place of Western courage and will, a focal point where our solemn commitments and Soviet ambitions now meet in basic confrontation."[49]

The difficulty, though, was how to contain these ambitions without precipitating a nuclear war. The Soviets could, of course, simply march into West Berlin. But this would constitute clear-cut military action that would unite the West and leave it no alternative but to react with force. The responsibility for the initiation of the use of force, and its possible escalation once Soviet and American troops clashed, would clearly point to the Russians. The Soviets therefore posed the issue in terms of a series of limited challenges to Western rights. If, on the one hand, these were not defended, the West's position in Berlin would be slowly eroded. On the other hand, by exerting pressure on the West to accede

[49] Quoted in *The New York Times*, July 26, 1961.

to their demands, the Soviets shrewdly placed on the West the burden of initiating the use of force. The Soviets merely made the demands. It was the Western powers who had to decide whether they would stand firm or not. The decision to stand firm at all times entailed the possibility of the need for the use of force to back up Western rights; in turn, this included the possibility of nuclear escalation. The essence of nuclear blackmail is thus that the powers defending the *status quo*, rather than the power demanding change, bear the responsibility for firing the first shot. This very clever maneuver put the West on the spot precisely because the fear of war was so great. If the Soviets could demonstrate the impotence of NATO, and American hesitancy and fear, they could deal the death blow to West Berlin without firing a shot. If the future of the city looked uncertain, West German businessmen, whose economic support was vital, would not risk investing their capital there. The effect would be to bring the economic life of the city to a standstill. Moreover, if the city appeared to be doomed, West Berliners—particularly the younger people—would leave for West Germany. The exit of Western troops was thus not the only means of "demilitarizing" West Berlin. Undermining the confidence of the city's citizens and, in general, of all West Germans in the United States would suffice. If this were achieved, the city would subsequently wither away, despite the continued presence of Western troops.

Thus, the manner in which the United States handled this situation, as well as the substance of the positions it took, were extremely significant. In both instances, the United States more often than not failed to impress the Kremlin with its determination to honor its commitments. There were, to be sure, constant proclamations by the West affirming its stance in the defense of West Berlin. But the real question was at what point the United States would resist Soviet intimidation. For instance, when the Soviet Union followed up its demand for the "demilitarization" of West Berlin with the proposal for a summit conference on a German peace treaty, the United States accepted on two conditions: that the six-month ultimatum be withdrawn and that a preliminary foreign ministers' conference yield fruitful results that would then merely be ratified at the later summit meeting. The Soviets deliberately turned down all Western plans at the foreign ministers' conference in order to keep up their pressure on the West, and President Eisenhower then invited Khrushchev to meet him in this country. The six-month deadline had, to be sure, been postponed, although the Soviets even denied that it had been an ultimatum; still the basic threat to West Berlin was maintained. Yet, rather than call off the negotiations and test whether the Soviet Union really intended to carry out its threat at the risk of nuclear warfare, the President reversed his previous position—and proved that Khrushchev had been right in not showing a conciliatory attitude toward the West. Indeed, the more bellicose Khrushchev sounded and the more firmly he stood by his demands, the more flexible the Western position became. His invitation to visit the United States was a major tactical victory. It also brought other rewards. It demonstrated his own equality with the President, and accorded the Soviet Union recognition as one of the two great superpowers, no longer militarily inferior in strength. It also deepened the fissures among the Western allies. The American conduct of the negotiations had already upset the West Germans and the French. Fearful that the United States might not stand firm, they were now worried that Khrushchev and Eisenhower would arrange a deal that would get the United States "off the hook" at Europe's expense—precisely the impression Khrushchev wished to convey.

The substance of the negotiations was handled in a similar manner. During the foreign ministers' conference, the West first offered the Soviet Union a "package plan" linking a West Berlin solution with German reunification. The Soviets immediately rejected this, as their concern was to expel the West from Berlin. The West then retreated to a five-year interim solution providing for free and unrestricted access to West Berlin for civilian and military traffic. In return, the West would not station nuclear weapons in Berlin—hardly a concession since there was no plan to do so anyway—would accept East Germans as Soviet "agents" for the control of traffic, and would curb propaganda and intelligence activities that "might either disturb public order or seriously affect the rights and interests, or amount to interference in the internal affairs, of others." The West, in short, was seeking to extricate itself from the risk of war by converting its permanent status to a temporary status based on Soviet consent. If, at the end of the five-year period, the Soviet Union refused to renew the agreement or would do so only on conditions unacceptable to the West, the city and the West's position would be in even greater jeopardy since the right of the West to be in Berlin at all would have been abrogated. While the Western powers did state that in the event of such disagreement, their old rights would be reinstated, it remains true, as has been observed, that the West, after a five-year interval, would hardly have been likely to defend rights it had not been prepared to defend when they had first been challenged and which had been specifically altered by the interim agreement.[50] It is also likely that the West's position would, in any case, have further eroded during this five-year period. For example, the West's offer to curb propaganda and intelligence activities in West Berlin was altered by the Soviet Union during the discussion to read that West Berlin was not to be used for "hostile propaganda" and "subversive activities against the Soviet Union, the German Democratic Republic, and other socialist states." Since the Soviet Union defines all ideological points of view different from its own as

[50] Kissinger, *The Necessity for Choice*, pp. 142–43.

hostile and all criticism of itself as subversive, virtually any political news or article, editorial, or radio and TV broadcasts in West Berlin would fall under these all-encompassing terms as defined by the Soviets. If the Soviets then, in displeasure, threatened to break the interim agreement, would the West impose censorship on all media of communication in West Berlin? If it did not, it would confront the very risk of war it had sought to avoid in the first place; and if it did—for would an editorial be "worth" fighting a nuclear war over?—the West would then have proven its lack of nerve and will to resist Soviet piecemeal encroachment. West Berliners would have been demoralized and the West's position badly undermined. This would especially have been the case if the West had also acceded to the Soviet demand for a reduction of the West's approximately 11,000-man garrison to a "symbolic" 3,000–4,000 men. This would have constituted a major withdrawal of the Western powers, and would have provided more evidence that at the end of five years the West would not oppose further Soviet demands, let alone reassert its former rights. If the Soviets did not accept the West's interim proposal, it was only in order to compel the West to continue negotiating under stress and to seek the immediate "de-Westernization" of Berlin.

Three aspects of the Soviet tactics were particularly interesting. First, the Soviets tended to pose each specific challenge in terms of minor points that seemed of little importance, particularly when viewed against the risk of nuclear war. Indeed, the issue of Western access and presence in West Berlin was already three years old by 1958. The Soviets had, in fact, after the failure of their earlier Berlin Blockade, resurrected this issue in 1955, when control of civilian German traffic and goods transportation was handed over to the East Germans. During the same year, East Berlin was declared to be the capital of the German Democratic Republic. Shortly thereafter, Berlin was declared to lie "in the territory of the G.D.R." This was, in fact, a challenge to Western authority in Berlin. But at no time was there any response, for each of the acts was so minor. The declarations could easily be shrugged off since the Western powers remained in Berlin and the city thus could not become East Germany's capital. Was it worth risking a war over whether Russians rather than East Germans handled traffic? And what matter that the East Germans unilaterally announced that Greater Berlin lay in their territory? Or, take one more "minor" example. Each year since 1955, the German Bundestag had opened its session with a week-long meeting in West Berlin as a reminder to all Germans that Berlin was Germany's capital. Ironically, it had been the Communist deputies in the West German Assembly who had first suggested these Berlin meetings. The Soviet Union was then still seeking to impress on the West Germans that it, and it only, stood for the reunification of Germany; and Berlin had been the capital of the old Germany. After 1958, however, the Russians reversed their position. The annual Bundestag meetings were denounced as "provocations" and "Cold War measures." In 1960, Khrushchev threatened that he might sign his separate peace treaty with East Germany if the annual meeting were held again. The Western powers yielded and the meeting was called off. After all, was this issue sufficiently important to resist Soviet pressure and take the risk of war? Obviously not.[51]

Second, it should be noted about Soviet tactics that each challenge, no matter how minor it seemed, was in fact important. Thus what appeared to the West to be relatively unimportant issues not worth the risk of war—supposedly this risk was to be accepted only on "major" issues—were vital from the Soviet point of view. For to them Western inaction and willingness not to resist minor demands and changes in the *status quo* meant that the West could perhaps be pressured into larger concessions. Thus, the Soviet reaction to Western inaction was not the desired relaxation of international tensions but a heightening of these tensions. A minor challenge unmet was followed by a greater challenge. If the West's will to resist was wanting on a small issue, its nerves might also fail on a more important issue as the pressures increased. An excellent example of the Soviet means of augmenting the scale of a challenge was seen in the aftermath of the tragic death of a young German boy, Peter Fechter, shot while seeking to escape from East Berlin over the Wall. For an hour the East German border guards left him to bleed to death—in front of American guards, who stood by passively. In reaction, outraged West Berliners stoned the Russian bus that each day carried Russian guards to the Soviet War Memorial in the British sector. Purportedly to safeguard their men from broken glass and stones, the Soviets then notified the Western allies that they would send their guards in three armored personnel carriers. Although the local American command apparently foresaw the harmful effect of Russian armor traveling through West Berlin, it also had received orders from Washington not to do anything that might further raise the already high tension. The Soviet armored cars were thus permitted to enter West Berlin. On the third day, the Russian soldiers during their trip threw open the turrets of their vehicles and stood at attention holding their submachine guns. On the fourth day, an American convoy leaving West Berlin was detained for almost seven hours. The two Russian colonels who supervised the detention frequently phoned their headquarters. Ostensibly, the issue was whether the soldiers would dismount to be counted, and they finally did; but the real point seems to have been that the Russians were serving notice that they now equated their own armored access to West Berlin with that of the Western powers. On the seventh day, when there was

[51] Hans Speier, *Divided Berlin: The Anatomy of Soviet Political Blackmail* (New York: Frederick A. Praeger, 1961), pp. 115–17.

no longer any danger of demonstrations, it was suggested to the Soviets that they return to the use of busses to transport their men. They replied that the busses were no longer available. Instead, the Soviets now began to build up their "military presence" in West Berlin. On the tenth day, they added two jeeps as escorts to their three armored cars, and the next day they switched from the four-wheel carriers they had been using to six-wheelers. At this point, Washington finally awoke to the danger of what was happening and took a firm stand. But this necessary, though belated action, could not undo all the damage that had been done.[52] One West Berliner, asked what the Americans would do in another similar situation, was quoted as saying, "Maybe they'll go on a hunger strike." The Soviets, in short, had scored another point.

Finally, each Soviet challenge was an act of definition of *Western* rights. Herein lay the importance of the initial "minor" demand and the subsequently enlarged demand. Each challenge not met established a more advanced position for the Soviets—and the basis for subsequent demands. The Soviets' demonstration of their armored access to West Berlin was typical. Another precedent was established in early 1962 when a Soviet officer at a checkpoint on the highway connecting West Germany and Berlin protested his inability to count the American soldiers in a convoy. He suggested that the soldiers dismount to facilitate his count, and they obliged. Again, the issue seemed minor, but the point scored by the Soviets was not, for they sought to convey that they, and not the allies, established the conditions for travel along the access routes to West Berlin. Afterward, the allies reasserted Western rights by allowing the soldiers to dismount for a count only when the convoy carried a certain number of soldiers. Dismounting was not called off, however; it had become "established procedure." Each challenge thus not only eroded the Western position, but defined Western rights on a descending scale. The most dramatic Soviet act of definition was, of course, the building of the Wall, which divides East and West Berlin. Overnight, the Four-Power Statute, under which the entire city had been ruled by wartime agreement—and which the Soviets had been undermining for years—was eliminated. Fearful of reacting and precipitating armed conflict—although the Wall was the type of "major" issue on which the allies had previously suggested that they would "react sharply"—the almost relieved allies quickly announced that they were now responsible only for their respective sectors. If the Soviets continued to define the West's rights in this manner—and the West continued to be blind to the psychological impact of its inactions or its half-hearted and timid reactions—there would someday be nothing left to defend.

The West has much to learn before it can counter these "salami tac-

[52] Daniel Schorr, "The Trojan Troika in Berlin," *The Reporter,* September 27, 1962, pp. 25–27.

tics," by which one Western right after another is sliced away. Above all, it should be clear that general commitments of defense, however eloquent and however often repeated, are not the answer to Soviet nuclear blackmail tactics. Such commitments are meaningless if there is no response to specific challenges. These tests cannot be met with formal diplomatic protests or solemn assurances of Western determination or threats of nuclear warfare; what is needed are speedy, effective, and continuous countermeasures against Soviet encroachment and pressure. Only when each specific challenge is resisted can one hope even to maintain the *status quo*. Upholding one's rights does not raise international tensions. Rather, it lowers them because the test of wills has been successfully met. The real danger in nuclear blackmail situations is not a war stemming from a determination to stand firm but a war of miscalculation resulting from weakness. Admittedly, the Soviets like to convey the impression that they are irrevocably committed to the fulfillment of their demands. But they are no more anxious to precipitate an all-out war than is the United States. They always leave openings through which they can retreat. The safety of the Soviet Union is their principal consideration. If their country is endangered, the Soviets will withdraw, irrespective of any possible humiliation. "One should not," Lenin once said, "be guided by the feeling of a participant in a duel who draws his sword and exclaims: I must die because I am compelled to sign a humiliating peace."[53] On the other hand, nothing will incite the Soviet Union more than a nation begging for negotiations under duress, retreats, however small, and frequent hesitations to make decisions that affirm previously stated commitments. Such actions can only increase the possibility of war through miscalculation. No "hot-line" communications between the White House and the Kremlin, no summit-meeting warning to the Russians[54] can possibly substitute for timely and effective countermeasures to any Soviet encroachment. In circumstances where the challenger thinks that he can erode the *status quo* with military threats, the following analysis may well be valid:

> A nation which has stopped at a certain point, far short of its goal, because it was afraid of a nuclear response that did not materialize, is likely to be just a little bit less timid when it must gauge the enemy's intentions at the next confrontation. Having stopped the first time at three paces from what it thought was the brink, it may well calculate that it can afford now to take another halfstep forward and still remain at a safe distance. If its calculation turns out to be correct, it may well be tempted at the third confrontation to take another halfstep forward, and so forth, so that either

[53] Quoted in Nathan Leites, *The Operational Code of the Politburo*, p. 84.
[54] Characteristically, Khrushchev renewed his pressure on West Berlin after his 1961 Vienna meeting with Kennedy, who had sought to impress the Soviet leader with American determination in Berlin and thereby forestall a Soviet miscalculation.

the margin of actuality will narrow with every confrontation or the likelihood of nuclear response will decrease with every retreat by the challenged nation.[55]

This was nowhere more clearly illustrated than in Cuba, in October, 1962, when Khrushchev tried to take another step forward by installing medium-range Soviet missiles. The Soviets had apparently become convinced that the United States would not use force to defend its vital interests, and Khrushchev talked openly of America's failure of nerve. In West Berlin, for instance, the Soviets had been quite successfully nibbling away at Western rights for years. The West's passive acceptance of the Wall was characteristic. So was its verbal reaction: "Negotiations are now more necessary than ever." The almost constant pressure on West German Chancellor Adenauer to accede to American diplomatic positions was to the Soviets another indication of American fear. So was Laos, where the Kennedy Administration had repeated Eisenhower's 1954 experience of first threatening intervention and then failing to act; in this case, the result was a "neutralized" nation in which the real power for a while lay with the Communist Pathet Lao. And there was the debacle of the Cuban invasion, an ill-fated venture in which the United States failed to provide sufficient support. The lesson Khrushchev had apparently drawn was that the United States talked loudly but carried a small stick. It did not appear, then, that the installation of Soviet missiles in Cuba would involve a great risk. The Soviet Union merely had to confront the United States with a *fait accompli*, and we would then retreat rather than face a test of wills. Past American inactions or ineffective reactions thus seem to have encouraged the Soviets to continue their probes—and this time the probe was to be 90 miles from the American shore. On this occasion, however, the United States did react. Passivity in the face of such a clear menace—underlined by both the stealthiness and the speed of the Soviet missile build-up—would have humiliated the United States. It would have lent credence to repeated Soviet claims that Communism was the wave of the future and that the Soviet Union had become the world's foremost power. It would also have demonstrated American impotence to a watching world. A United States unable or unwilling to prevent the installation of Soviet missiles so near the mainland would obviously also be thought too weak or fearful to defend vital Western interests farther away. The Soviet's MRBM's in Cuba would have enhanced the Soviet capacity for a first strike, its ability to strike at a larger portion of America's strategic forces, and its capability to do so without giving much warning, since the early warning lines were all positioned in the north to detect a strike across the North Pole. The result

[55] Hans J. Morgenthau, "The Four Paradoxes of Nuclear Strategy," *American Political Science Review*, March, 1964, p. 24.

would have been to reduce even further the credibility of SAC to deter limited Soviet challenges. In these circumstances, the Soviets would undoubtedly therefore have renewed their pressure on Berlin since they had already announced that they wished to resume "negotiations" on this subject after the American mid-term election in November. They would also have furnished "proof" that America's allies in Europe, the Middle East, and Asia could not rely upon the United States in any major crisis. The future existence of these alliances would thus have been seriously jeopardized. And in the Western Hemisphere, this evidence of American impotence would have greatly encouraged Castro and all other anti-American movements, sharply reducing the authority of the "colossus of the North" in Latin America.

The United States, then, had no choice but to react in Cuba and demand the withdrawal of Soviet missiles. The American reaction, however, also clearly showed the danger of permitting the opponent to miscalculate. If a nuclear holocaust is to be prevented, this danger must be avoided; and it can only be avoided by reacting early enough to prevent the escalation of the challenge to the level of the Cuban missile crisis. The decisive American victory, in fact, demonstrated that the Soviets were aware of the United States' superior strategic striking power. It also demonstrated Soviet unwillingness to risk *any* direct hostilities with the United States. Rather than take that risk, Premier Khrushchev quickly assumed a conciliatory tone and promised to dismantle the missiles in Cuba and ship them back to Russia. Nor did he, as some expected, take any retaliatory action in Berlin, where Soviet power dominated. Quite the reverse: Khrushchev followed his Cuban surrender by sounding reasonable about Berlin, too. "Indeed, Soviet quiescence in Berlin during and immediately after the Cuban missile crisis demonstrates the severe limitations of even overwhelming local military superiority in the hands of a strategically inferior power when the issue at stake is of central, not peripheral, importance to the opponent."[56] Thus the Soviet Union's nuclear blackmail tactics had finally brought defeat—but only after the challenge had been transferred from Berlin to Cuba, where no American government could avoid so obvious a test. The Soviets had badly miscalculated and had thus precipitated a dangerous crisis. But was the United States not largely responsible for this miscalculation that set it and the Soviet Union on a "collision course"? Would French President de Gaulle's approach not have been wiser? De Gaulle, who withheld French participation in the various negotiations over Berlin from the beginning, had declared that there was nothing to negotiate about in West Berlin: Any Western compromises and concessions would only erode Western rights that were theirs by right of conquest. If the West did not imme-

[56] Arnold L. Horelick, "The Cuban Missile Crisis: An Analysis of Soviet Calculations and Behavior," *World Politics*, April, 1964, pp. 363–89.

diately and forthrightly reject Soviet demands that the West leave Berlin, it would only demonstrate Western fear and weakness. The West would not be able to prove to Khrushchev its determination to stay in Berlin by showing its great reluctance to confront Soviet power in a Soviet-initiated test of wills. Moscow would only be encouraged in its belligerency and step up its pressure. Washington disagreed with De Gaulle's analysis. Moscow did not—and, as a result, almost miscalculated.

United Nations Preventive Diplomacy

Although the possibility of nuclear war has obligated the United States and the Soviet Union to limit the scope of their specific challenges, there remains one set of conflicts that might spark a war between the superpowers—i.e., conflicts between the newly independent nations and their former colonial rulers. Arising on the periphery of the Cold War, these conflicts tend to be drawn into the world-wide confrontation of the two superpowers. Since any shift in a regional distribution of power will affect the global distribution, one of the powers is likely to take advantage of an opportunity to shift a regional "balance" in its favor, while the other will wish to prevent it.

The Suez crisis of 1956 provides a good illustration of this tendency of conflicts emanating essentially from the end of colonialism to spill over into the Cold War zone. Egypt had been a British protectorate from 1881 to 1936, when she was granted her independence. Britain retained control of the Suez Canal, though, and in effect maintained her dominant position. But mounting Egyptian nationalism and a corresponding rise in anti-British feelings afterward eventually led Britain to relinquish her Suez military base in 1954, although not her control of the Canal. The moment British troops had withdrawn, President Nasser launched an energetic anti-Western campaign to eliminate all "colonial" governments in the Middle East and North Africa. Success would, of course, make him the leader of all Arabs and give him control of most of the Arabian oil. Once Egypt became the strongest Arab state, it would have tremendous bargaining power since Europe, especially Britain, was dependent on Middle Eastern oil. The United States and Britain were alarmed by these attempts to eliminate Western power and influence in the economically and strategically vital Middle East, particularly since Nasser leaned increasingly toward the Soviet bloc. Shortly after he extended diplomatic recognition to Communist China, the United States withdrew its offer to finance the Aswan Dam, which was to irrigate much of Egypt's weather-beaten soil and thus help her economic development. Nasser's reaction was to nationalize the Suez Canal, claiming that he would use its income to build the dam.

Britain now felt compelled to act. If Nasser were allowed to seize Suez with impunity, other Arab governments would appropriate Western property—particularly oil property; nor would any pro-Western Arab government be safe from overthrow by pro-Nasser elements within their countries. Britain—joined by France, which wished to stop Egyptian shipments of arms to the Algerian nationalists—gained the opportunity when Israel attacked Egypt. This moment occurred after Nasser's famous arms deal with Russia, made with the stated purpose of driving Israel into the sea. The consequent hostilities threatened to develop into a major war as the Soviet Union, which shared Egypt's interest in eliminating the West from the Middle East, threatened to send volunteers to Egypt and even to rain atomic rockets on London and Paris. The possibility of Soviet intervention naturally brought forth an American response. The United States disapproved of her allies' attack on Egypt, feeling that it smacked of nineteenth-century colonialism and would alienate the new nations. U.S. support for the British and French action would have allowed the Soviet Union to pose as the friend and defender of the new nations. The United States therefore voted with the Soviet Union in the Security Council to condemn Britain and France's aggression and to call upon them to desist. At the same time, she could not stand by and let the Soviet Union send volunteers into the Middle East, let alone attack Britain and France, so a warning note was sent to Moscow. Yet, could the Soviet Union, posing as Egypt's protector, really remain inactive in the event of American intervention without endangering her good relations with the other nonaligned states? At the very least, then, the situation was dangerous.

Another, and even more dramatic, illustration is provided by the Congo crisis. The Congo became an independent state in 1960. But the Belgians, unlike the British and the French in most of their colonies, had not trained native leaders to take over for them. Complete disorder soon broke out when the native army rioted. The Belgian settlers fled, and to protect them Belgium flew in troops. The Congolese Prime Minister, Patrice Lumumba, interpreted the Belgian action as an attempt to restore its colonial rule. He appealed to the United Nations to compel the Belgians to withdraw. The Soviets immediately supported his appeal and condemned Belgium, accusing her of acting as the front for "NATO imperialism." An even more serious situation developed when the province of Katanga seceded. Katanga's rich copper mines were the Congo's major source of revenue, and the secession thus threatened the survival of the entire nation. But the Katanga mines were owned by the powerful Union Minière du Haute-Katange, which supported the secession. This company, representing Belgian and British capital, helped the provincial President Moise Tshombe build up a large army led by Belgian and other European officers. Lumumba demanded that the United Nations crush Tshombe's mercenary army and help him restore Congolese unity.

When his demand went unheeded, Lumumba appealed to the Soviet Union to help him against the "colonialists." He received both Russian diplomatic support and military supplies, and the danger of Soviet influence in Africa now became a grim reality. Nor was this danger diminished when Lumumba was dismissed from office by the Congo's President, a moderate whom the United States supported in its efforts to prevent the establishment of a Soviet foothold in Central Africa. The Soviets refused to recognize his successor, contending that only Parliament had the right to dismiss Lumumba and that since it had not, he was still the Congo's legitimate Prime Minister and must be restored to his office. Lumumba's subsequent murder exacerbated the situation. The national coalition government formed in early 1961 faced a major crisis from its beginning—a crisis that could only benefit the Soviet Union unless a solution was found. The government, committed to a policy of nonalignment in foreign policy, had as its first objective national reunification. Failure to achieve this goal would undermine its authority and lead to its collapse through political failure and financial weakness. The transfer of power to a more radical pro-Communist government would then be a certainty. Lumumba's successor, Antoine Gizenga, might in these circumstances become Prime Minister. Or the central government, to head off its own collapse, might itself turn toward Russia, just as Lumumba had done earlier. In either case, there would be a Soviet-American confrontation in the Congo. Belgium, Britain, and France supported Katanga's independence. In fact, Tshombe was dependent upon his Belgian advisers and European officers. Without them and the revenues of the Union Minière, Katanga could not have preserved its independence. All attempts to restore the unity of the Congo by peaceful means therefore proved futile. Indeed, Tshombe used the negotiations with the central government to delay any possible use of force against him. The longer the delay, the nearer the collapse of the central government, and the sooner could the left-wing takeover occur. Katanga, with its anti-Communist pose, would then be the only government the United States could support against Soviet influence in the Congo.

It is in such situations outside the Cold War zone, where the two superpowers are drawn in and threaten the peace of the world, that the United Nations plays its most important role. It might perhaps be stressed that this role is not that of the "great solver" of all problems. The United Nations is not a superstate, usurping its members' sovereignty and imposing its will on them. Nor is the United Nations independent of "politics." Its decisions are not made according to some impartial, nonpolitical, and therefore purportedly morally superior standard of justice. The United Nations is not above politics because it does not exist and act independently of the politics of its members. Rather, the United Nations reflects the political interests, attitudes, and problems of its member states. It does not possess independent authority, but is merely the channel through which the power and purposes of its members flows. In short, the United Nations is not a substitute for power politics; it only registers the power politics of the state system. It is a mirror, not a panacea; it has no magic wand by which it can resolve all of man's international problems. It cannot transcend the Cold War or the anticolonial struggles. It must function in the world as it exists, and it cannot solve any problems that its members, because of conflicting interests, are not prepared to resolve. Its failures indicate only its members' inability to reach agreement.

If then, the United Nations reflects the world in which it exists, its functions can only be understood in terms of the changing conditions of the postwar world. When it was formed, the United Nations reflected the wartime hopes for continued great-power cooperation and peace after the victory over Germany had been won. Primary authority for the preservation of peace and security was vested in the Security Council, composed of eleven members, six of them on a rotating basis. The real authority, however, was to be exercised by the United States, the Soviet Union, Britain, France, and China. If they voted unanimously to take enforcement action against aggression, their decision had to be followed by all U.N. members. Thus, through an oligarchical organization, which reflected the global distribution of power, the great powers were the masters of the United Nations. Indeed, the United States and the Soviet Union, actually the only two great powers remaining in 1945, were the real masters. Britain was exhausted, France still recovering from her defeat and German occupation, and China a weak country embroiled in civil war. So long as the two superpowers could maintain harmony, peace would be preserved.

The security system was thus directed only against the smaller nations; if they disturbed the peace, and the great powers agreed to take punitive action, they could be squashed. In short, the United Nations was, in the words of one delegate at its first conference, "engaged in establishing a world order in which the mice could be stamped out but in which the lions would not be restrained."[57] The veto was to prevent one of the great powers from mobilizing the United Nations against another great power. The United Nations was never intended to be a collective-security organization, since going to war to punish a great power's aggression would precipitate another global war. The "insertion of the veto provision in the decision-making circuit of the Security Council reflected the clear conviction that in cases of sharp conflict among the great powers the Council ought, for safety's sake, to be incapacitated—to be rendered incapable of being used to precipitate a showdown, or to mobilize collective action against the recalcitrant power. The philosophy of the veto

[57] Quoted in Inis L. Claude, Jr., *Power and International Relations*, p. 59.

is that it is better to have the Security Council stalemated than to have that body used by a majority to take action so strongly opposed by a dissident great power that a world war is likely to ensue."[58] Great-power conflicts were to be handled *outside* the United Nations under collective self-defense arrangements which did not require prior Security Council authorization to take individual or joint military action against an attack.

As the two superpowers assumed opposing sides at the beginning of the Cold War, the United States sought to mobilize the support of the United Nations and thereby associate its policies with the organization's humanitarian, peaceful, and democratic values. This was most dramatically illustrated in Korea. The United States had no choice but to oppose the Soviet Union, but it acted under U.N. auspices. The Soviet absence from the Security Council enabled it to act. But such an absence was not likely to occur a second time. The United States therefore introduced the "Uniting for Peace" resolution in November, 1950, the purpose of which was to transfer primary responsibility for the preservation of peace and security to the General Assembly if the Security Council was paralyzed by the veto. Constitutionally, this transfer of authority should not have been possible. The General Assembly was granted authority only to debate, investigate, and recommend in issues concerning international peace and security. Even then, it could offer no recommendations that were on the Security Council's agenda; by placing an issue on the agenda, then, the Council could reduce the Assembly to a mere debating society. Moreover, the architects of the United Nations had specifically provided the veto power for the great powers so that none could employ the United Nations against another in military actions.

The American argument was, however, that the U.N. responsibility for the preservation of international peace and security could not be abandoned just because the Security Council was stymied. If the Council could not fulfill its "primary responsibility" for this function, the Assembly would have to assume this task. It need hardly be added that in the Assembly the United States could easily muster the two-thirds majorities needed for important resolutions from the NATO countries, the older British dominions, the Latin American republics, and one or two Asian states. The Soviet Union, with no veto in the Assembly, was of course constantly outvoted. Yet she was still able to use the Assembly at least to give vent to her own point of view.

The attempt to use the Assembly to support American anti-Communist policies did not last long. Just as the configuration of power underlying the original Security Council—the wartime alliance—was to be changed shortly after the establishment of the United Nations, so the political alignment at the outbreak of the Korean War was a fleeting one not destined to survive even the war, despite the "Uniting for Peace"

[58] *Ibid.*, p. 160, and Claude, *Swords Into Plowshares*, pp. 80–86.

resolution. The United States had received U.N. support at the beginning of the war for two reasons. First, an overwhelming number of its members, including the nonaligned states,[59] saw in the North Korean aggression a test of the United Nations itself. If the organization failed to respond, it would follow the League of Nations into the dustbin of history. Second, the smaller powers saw in the transfer of authority on security matters to the Assembly an opportunity to play the enlarged role in U.N. affairs that they had originally been denied by the "lions," much to their resentment. But Communist China's intervention in late 1950 changed this American-sponsored role of the United Nations as an instrument of collective enforcement against the Communist bloc. The involvement of a major Communist power, and the possibility that the U.S. Government might accede to strong domestic pressures to extend the war to China by air bombardment, naval blockade, and the landing of Nationalist forces on the mainland, dramatized the wisdom of the U.N. architects' original intent to avoid the organization's involvement in the military conflicts of the great powers. The danger of world war was simply too great.

In addition, the then twelve Arab-Asian members of the General Assembly were determined to remain nonaligned in the Cold War. Their earlier support for American intervention in Korea had been motivated by their concern for the United Nations as an institution. It was essential that North Korea's aggression be met, and since the United States had the strength to take the appropriate measures, they had approved of the original American reaction. But they had no desire to participate in taking collective measures against one side or the other, thus in effect becoming allied to one of the Cold War blocs through the mechanism of the U.N. voting procedure. The problem was to prevent military clash between the great powers and simultaneously avoid becoming aligned in the Cold War themselves. The answer was to shift the function of the United Nations from enforcement to conciliation.[60] The United Nations was to serve as an instrument of mediation in conflict situations between the great powers. The original assumption that peace could be preserved by having the five lions—headed by the two biggest lions—act as the world's guardians now was replaced with the recognition of the imperative need to keep the lions from mauling each other to death—and trampling the mice while they were at it.

A third United Nations was thus born. The first one had been dedicated to preserving the wartime Grand Alliance; the second one, which succeeded it, had been, so to speak, a wing of the State Department.

[59] Egypt, because her feeling that the United Nations had not supported her in the war against Israel in 1947–48, was an exception.

[60] Ernst Haas, "Types of Collective Security: An Examination of Operational Concepts," *American Political Science Review*, March, 1955, pp. 40–62, examines this transition from "permissive enforcement" to "balancing."

This United Nations began to die during the Korean War. By exerting great pressure, the United States could still, in the spring of 1951, obtain the two-thirds majority needed in the General Assembly for the condemnation of Communist China. Already though, she had to make concessions to collect these votes—the price being that she not follow the condemnation with additional military or economic measures. Instead, she was to give primary emphasis to the conciliatory efforts of the Arab-Asian bloc—supported by most of her NATO allies, who were also concerned about a possible escalation of the conflict—to end the war. By 1955, the third United Nations—born in 1950 when the six Arab and six Asian members of the United Nations began to consult each other regularly about the positions they adopted during the Korean War—had reached adolescence; and as the number of newly independent members, especially African ones, grew rapidly after 1955, it matured quickly. In 1955 and 1956 respectively, six and four new Asian and North African states were admitted to the United Nations; in 1960 the number of new states admitted was seventeen, mainly from Sub-Saharan Africa. If both the American and the Soviet blocs had previously used the United Nations for their own Cold War purposes, the neutral bloc now employed the organization to erase the vestiges of Western colonialism as soon as possible. The Assembly was a particularly good forum in which to voice anticolonial sentiments and to keep the pressure on the West by passing, or trying to pass, with the help of the Communist bloc, resolutions in favor of national self-determination.

The new United Nations could not, however, help but become involved in the Cold War. The United States and the Soviet Union, to be sure, did not allow the organization to interfere in *their* clashes. The Soviets had no intention of permitting the United Nations to intervene in Hungary. Nor would the United States permit the United Nations to become involved in the post-1958 Berlin crises or the 1962 Cuban crisis.[61] East-West issues were only debated; no action was taken. The superpowers handled their own direct confrontations. But on the periphery of the Cold War the United States and the Soviet Union were constantly tempted to interfere in the conflicts stemming from the end of colonialism. Such interference, by threatening the peace and involving the neutrals in the Cold War, was bound to lead the nonaligned nations to take protective action. The United Nations to them was more than a political platform. It was also a shelter in which they sought refuge from great-power pressure. They thought of this third United Nations as *theirs*, and they were determined to use it to remain nonaligned. The chief

[61] Only after the Cuban missile crisis had already been resolved was the organization to be used—and then it was to check that all Soviet missiles were removed from Cuba. But since Castro refused to submit to international inspection and the United States had no doubts that all the missiles had been shipped back to Russia, the United Nations remained uninvolved.

function of the United Nations thus became one of "preventive diplomacy"—that is, the stabilization of local conflicts *before* either of the superpowers could become involved and thereby provoke its antagonist's intervention as well. Or, to state it negatively, preventive diplomacy was intended to prevent the extension of American-Soviet clashes beyond the Cold War zone. At the same time, by containing the Cold War, it would safeguard the new nations' independence and permit them control over their own future. The chief means of stabilization was the establishment of a "United Nations presence" in these peripheral quarrels. The United Nations, in short, became a fire brigade. In a highly combustible world, it rushed to potential fire-hazard areas to contain the initial flames and douse them.

As the Security Council had been intended to be the focus of authority of the first United Nations, and the General Assembly the focus of the second, the Secretary General was to be the principal actor in this third United Nations. No longer merely the prime U.N. administrative officer, the Secretary General, in partnership with the nonaligned nations, became its leading political officer. Thus Dag Hammarskjöld assumed the role that has been described as "custodian of brushfire peace" by establishing the U.N. presence in troubled areas. The most dramatic form this presence has taken has been the "nonfighting international force," whose purpose is not so much military as political. The size of the force and its firepower is not as significant as its political presence, which forestalls the influx of Soviet or American forces. Thus, in the Suez crisis, the U.N. Emergency Force supervised the withdrawal of British, French, and Israeli troops from Egypt. It did not seek to compel their withdrawal through combat. The cease-fire agreement was the prerequisite for its use. Yet the fact that the force was available made it easier to obtain British, French, and Israeli agreement to withdrawal. Once the withdrawal had been completed, 5,000 men were left to guard the Israeli-Egyptian frontier and maintain the peace in that area. They are still there. In the Congo, Belgium agreed to pull its troops out only if a U.N. force replaced it to keep order and protect Belgian nationals. In both instances, then, the availability of U.N. forces facilitated the termination of military action, and thereby the pacification of each situation.

The members of these U.N. forces are not drawn from the great powers. Rather, the men come primarily from the smaller nations, most of whom are not participants in the East-West struggle, or if they are involved, generally are the smaller and less partisan states. The U.N. force in Suez, for example, had contingents from Brazil, Canada, Colombia, Denmark, Finland, India, Indonesia, Norway, Sweden, and Yugoslavia. And the initial Congo force consisted of 13,000 African troops from Ethiopia, Ghana, Guinea, Liberia, Mali, Morocco, Sudan, and Tunisia; Ireland and Sweden also sent 2,000 troops. The participation of these nonaligned, "third world" nations is thus a stabilizing factor in an inflammable situation. If not for their presence, each of the two superpowers might be tempted to send in his own forces to ensure a favorable outcome, or at least to prevent his antagonist from exploiting the situation in his favor.

At least two other conditions are imposed on such an international force. First, the nation upon whose territory the force is to show its "presence" must grant permission for its entry. The host nation thus has some control over the composition of the international force and can exclude troops from nations it considers undesirable. The second condition is that the U.N. force not intervene in any purely internal conflict. Thus, in Egypt, the force was not employed to impose a specific settlement on Nasser, or to replace him, in order to calm the international situation. It merely disentangled the combatants and then interposed itself between them. The U.N. presence was not intended to deal with the causes that precipitated the Suez crisis; it dealt only with the effects. This was also true in the Congo—although with a special twist. Initially, when the danger was that Lumumba would turn to the Soviets to eject the Belgian troops, the U.N. force was employed only to replace the Belgians. In fact, it was precisely the U.N. refusal to interfere in the domestic politics of the Congo that created most of the later difficulties. Lumumba insisted that the force must be employed to squash the Katanga secession, and only when the United Nations did not oblige did Lumumba request Soviet help. In the end, however, the international organization could not isolate itself from the Congolese civil war. The effect of the U.N. nonintervention was to freeze the Congolese schism in Katanga's favor. Since the Katanga secession was the chief cause of the trouble, the United Nations could hardly disengage itself until, hopefully, the Congo had been reunified. In this instance, the secession was clearly supported by Belgium and the Union Minière—that is, external factors impinged on domestic conditions, and vice-versa—with the result that the internal Congolese situation threatened to implicate the two superpowers. Consequently, after the formation of the Congolese coalition government, the United Nations sought the removal of Tshombe's political advisers and foreign mercenaries. Patience and negotiations, however, failed in the face of European intransigence, and force was therefore employed to resolve the issue of Katanga once and for all. The second condition, that of domestic nonintervention, must therefore remain a qualified one.

The Congo operation may, however, have jeopardized the vital peacekeeping role of the United Nations. The organization may belong to the nonaligned nations, and in order to preserve their newly gained independence and avoid losing their nonaligned status, these states may play an important role in limiting conflicts bordering on the Cold War zone. But they can perform this operation *only* if the superpowers permit them to do so. The fundamental assumption underlying the pacifying role of the nonaligned states is that both the United States and the Soviet Union wish to avoid adding new areas of conflict to the Cold War because of the high degree of risk. Their common desire in avoiding nuclear war gives them a vested interest in keeping peripheral conflicts limited and under control. Thus they will at least acquiesce in the establishment of a U.N. presence: "It cannot be done *against* the major parties; it cannot be done *by* them; it can only be done *for* them and by their leave."[62]

Four alternative courses of action are possible to implement preventive diplomacy. The United Nations may take pro-Western action, impartial neutralizing action, no action at all, or pro-Soviet action. The American preference is in this order, of course, and the Soviet preference is the exact reverse. Neither extreme is really feasible, but the difficulty is that the United States stresses the impartial, neutralizing action of the remaining alternatives, while the Soviet Union prefers inactivity. The reasons for this are obvious. The United States fears that inactivity will either produce a Soviet advantage or lead to a collapse requiring American intervention and Soviet counterintervention. It also hopes that impartial, neutralizing action will result in pro-American results. Conversely, the Soviets hope that inaction will produce pro-Soviet results while avoiding American intervention, and they fear that the course preferred by the United States might indeed produce results detrimental to Soviet interests. In terms of these calculations, preventive diplomacy serves American purposes both by limiting the scope of conflicts in marginal situations and by seeking to stabilize such situations. The Soviet Union, however, is frustrated and bitter when the U.N. presence stabilizes a situation and blocks what might otherwise have been her path to success. To the Soviet Union, this only proves that the Secretary General is an "imperialist tool" and that it must have a veto over his actions. The Soviets thus proposed a "troika" plan intended to achieve just this goal by the appointment of three Secretary Generals, each of whom would represent one of the major blocs in the world. By insisting that unanimity be the prerequisite for action, the Soviets would then possess an actual veto in the Security Council, a virtual veto in the General Assembly (where the Soviets can now usually find enough votes among the nonaligned states to prevent a two-thirds majority resolution being passed against them), and a hidden veto in the Secretary Generals' office. In this way, the United Nations could not be employed in any way detrimental to Soviet interests.

As a result, the Soviet attitude toward preventive diplomacy has been

---

[62] Claude, "Containment and Resolution of Disputes," in Francis O. Wilcox and H. Field Haviland, Jr. (eds.), *The U.S. and the U.N.,* pp. 101–28.

ambivalent. On the one hand, the Soviet Union wishes to avoid a total war. On the other hand, if the risks are not too high, it also would like to exploit situations outside the Cold War Zone (such as the Congo) for its own expansionist ambitions.

Thus the Kremlin's reaction to the U.N. intervention in the Congo was one of growing disenchantment with the international organization in its peace-keeping operations. (It refused to contribute any funds for these operations.) The nonaligned states have, however, shown no such disenchantment. They unanimously opposed the "troika" plan to hamstring the Secretary General, for they value the organization as the protector of their independence and "neutralist" position in the Cold War.

VII

Neutralism:
The Foreign Policy of
Nation-Building

The Domestic Sources of Foreign Policy

The new nations generally refer to their foreign policies as "neutralist," but a more accurate term would be "nationalist." Neutralism implies— as Americans often charge—a moral neutrality in the Cold War, but this implication of moral indifference is false. The leaders of the new countries simply view the East-West conflict from a different perspective. Their attitudes are bound to be influenced by their colonial experience. American statements that the global struggle is one between freedom and despotism—and therefore one in which all nations must "stand up and be counted"—may well be regarded with some skepticism by those once ruled autocratically by the West. But even if the leaders saw the Cold War in these terms, they would be unlikely to take sides in an alliance. Pakistan, for instance, might join SEATO in order to acquire arms in her conflict with India over Kashmir, but the majority of these states prefer to remain "nonaligned," even though some may recognize their moral stake in the outcome of the Cold War. The reason is simply that the Cold War is secondary to the new nations' preoccupation with their own development and modernization. In these circumstances, their foreign policies become essentially a reflection of their quest for national identity and cohesion. Reacting to past colonial domination, they cannot join the West in a coalition against the Soviet bloc.

Only by asserting their independence can they acquire a sense of nation-hood. "We find," Kenya's Tom Mboya has said, "that both Westerners and Russians look at Africans through the same pair of glasses: the one lens is marked pro-Western; the other pro-Communist. It is not surpris-ing that, looking at Africans in this way, most foreigners fail to under-stand the one great reality about our continent—that Africans are neither pro-West nor pro-Russian; they are pro-African."[1] Or, to put it another way, the foreign policies of the new nations, like their domestic policies, reflect their preoccupation with nation-building. Indeed, it has been said that for a "new state, foreign policy is domestic policy pursued by other means; it is domestic policy carried beyond the boundaries of the state."[2]

And what are the domestic conditions? The first is the intensely felt nationalism of the new leaders. Their memories of colonialism and the long—and sometimes bloody—colonial struggle were not erased on the day they achieved national independence. For them, the past *is* the present, and their vivid memories make them jealous guardians of their nations' newly won independence—the prerequisite, as they see it, for national self-respect and equality, as well as social and economic development to create better lives for their peoples. Their relations with their former metropoles cannot therefore be characterized by words such as "friendly" or "unfriendly."

> [Such] words lack rigor. They define the normal spectrum of relations be-tween sovereign states which vary from amity to tension. The striking thing about relations between the postcolonial states and their erstwhile mother countries is that often, these relations are *not* "normal" during the first years following independence. . . . Their relations with the former colo-nial power are in transition from what is held to be excessive dependence, to that degree of independence regarded as consistent with the principles of reciprocity and juridic equality. There is a useful analogy with the be-havior of a state immediately following defeat in war. Foreign policy is then directed toward "normalizing" relations with the victor—disentan-gling itself from the harassment of alien garrisons and from the restraints imposed on its freedom of action, and overcoming the complexes that arise from impotence, inferiority, and insecurity. The foreign policies of many new states toward their former metropoles may be regarded in much the same way. The postcolonial states pursue this transition to "normality" in an atmosphere that varies from relative amity to relative antagonism.[3]

But the nationalism of the new states is not merely the product of past subjugation. Even more, it is a reflection of their future hopes. Far

---

[1] Quoted in Colin Legum, *Pan-Africanism*, p. 13.

[2] Robert C. Good, "State-Building as a Determinant of Foreign Policy in the New States," in Laurence W. Martin (ed.), *Neutralism and Nonalignment*, p. 3.

[3] Robert C. Good, "Changing Patterns of African International Relations," *Ameri-can Political Science Review*, September, 1964, p. 638.

more significant than the memories of colonialism is the problem of achieving post-independence national cohesion. The new nation has shared only one experience—that of colonial rule—and it was this that enabled the various groups that constituted the colonized "nation" to cooperate for the single purpose of gaining national freedom. But once the colonial power has been ejected or has voluntarily withdrawn, these groups have little sense of belonging to a distinct cultural entity with certain shared expectations about its future. Quite the contrary. They may have neither a common language nor a similar culture. Tribes are generally opposed to one another and regions are in conflict. Once independence has been gained, these centrifugal forces begin to exert their pulls. The opponent who united them is gone, and there is little else to hold them together as a political, economic, and administrative entity. Ironically, since most of the new states are composed of several nationality or ethnic groups, the resulting disintegration is given impetus by the very principle of national self-determination in whose name the anti-colonial revolution was carried out.

The central question is how this fragmentation can be halted. The obvious answer is to "nationalize" the people—to inculcate in them a sense of national consciousness and loyalty, recognition of the national government as *their* government, of its laws as the laws of the nation reflecting *their* will and requiring *their* adherence. The majority must acknowledge that they are citizens of one nation and that the national government has the legitimate authority to make decisions on behalf of the entire population. Such a popular consciousness cannot be developed overnight. But it will occur during the transformation of the traditional, agricultural society into a modern urban-industrial civilization. An entire people must, in a sense, go to school—to learn their nation's language and history (most of it mythical anyway, but devised nevertheless for the purpose of fostering a sense of national identification) and to be brought into the mainstream of national life. Only then will the national symbols stimulate deeply felt emotion; only then will a truly national community emerge.

In the meantime, if the nation is to hold together, a substitute must be found—the "hero," the single person who more than anyone else symbolizes in his person the new nation.[4] Generally, this is the leader of the pre-independence nationalist movement—the man who for years agitated for freedom, propagated its mythology, and went to jail for it. The forces supporting the *status quo* jailed him for breaking the "law and order" of the community; but by doing so, they conferred upon him a badge of honor. For his supporters, jail represented his willingness to speak and act on behalf of his oppressed people to demand their freedom. Once independence has been achieved, the heroic leader becomes

[4] Immanuel Wallerstein, *Africa, The Politics of Independence*, p. 98.

the national leader. He and the nation are in a very real sense identical. As the long-time spokesman and militant champion of the nation he now leads, he has come to embody its aspirations. As the "founder of the nation," he can say, *"La Nation, c'est moi."* For without his symbolic presence, the unity of the new nation would erode. Loyalty can usually be felt more keenly for an individual who incorporates an idea—such as the "nation"—than for the idea itself. One is flesh and blood, the other an abstraction. The hero in a new nation is a transitional figure in a transitional society. He serves the indispensable function of encouraging a shift from the traditional, parochial loyalty to the tribe or region to the broader loyalty of the still abstract nation-state. The hero possesses charisma—"a quality of extraordinary spiritual power attributed to a person . . . capable of eliciting popular support in the direction of human affairs." Whether he is a Bourguiba, a Sékou Touré, a Nasser, a Nehru, or a Sukarno, he is, in fact, a *substitute* for the real nation, for the national institutions which have not yet captured the popular allegiance—in short, a substitute for the still nonexistent consensus. "The charismatic justification for authority ('do it because I, your leader, say so') can be seen as a way of transition, an interim measure which gets people to observe the requirements of the nation out of loyalty to the leader while they (or their children) learn to do it for its own sake. In short, the hero helps to bridge the gap to a modern state. The citizens can feel an affection for the hero which they may not have at first for the nation."[5] Thus the charismatic hero confers legitimacy upon the new nation and its government.

This hero is usually supported by a single party, which is the principal instrument of national integration. Unlike Western political parties, whose primary function is to represent the various interests within the nation, the one party in a developing country seeks to integrate the traditionally "tribalized" people on a national basis. Organizing the masses in the towns and countryside into members of provincial and local cells, it tries to instill in them a sense of identification as citizens of a distinct national community by drawing them into contact with national political life. Just as the charismatic hero replaces the traditional chieftain, the nation is supposed to replace the tribe. For the party claims that it represents the nation.

Thus, by 1965, only five of the thirty-six independent African states still had some form of parliamentary democracy.[6] And opposition to the hero and the party is generally considered tantamount to treason. This may seem undemocratic by contemporary American standards, but such standards hardly apply in an underdeveloped country lacking national

[5] *Ibid.*, p. 99.
[6] Colin Legum, "What Kind of Radicalism for Africa?," *Foreign Affairs*, January, 1965, p. 239.

unity and cohesion. In the United States, the opposition is a loyal opposition whose allegiance is to the same nation and values as the governing party. But in a new African nation, the opposition's allegiance is often regional and tribal, and it thus represents the centrifugal forces in the society. In these circumstances, a democratic change of government could result in the disintegration of the state. The hero may well appear to be dictatorial for considering differences with him synonymous with disloyalty to the state, but that is frequently the case. The choice is *not* democracy or dictatorship, but nationhood or disintegration.[7] It is interesting in this connection to recall that American democracy also began its life with a charismatic figure—George Washington. As the first President, Washington was the hero who symbolized the infant nation and who sought to win loyalty to the nation through loyalty to his person.

An aloof and solemn figure, he was hardly a "man of the people," but he was quite aware of the "nationalizing" role he played. He vigorously opposed the "baneful effects of the spirit of party," lest it divide the country. When he nevertheless identified himself with one of the political parties—the Federalists—he described the opposition Republicans, or Jeffersonians, as a band of villains; his own party, though, he considered to be made up of men of sense and patriotism. The Republicans were "not *the* opposition but 'opposition' in the sense of obstruction, misconduct, disloyalty." In his Farewell Address, written by Hamilton, Washington condemned party division and strife. "The unity of government," he said, "which constitutes you one people . . . is a main pillar in the edifice of your real independence, the support of your tranquillity at home, your peace abroad, of your safety, of your prosperity, of that very liberty which you so highly prize." Parties would, however, endanger this unity. Factionalism, he said, "serves always to distract the public councils and enfeeble the public administration. It agitates the community with ill-founded jealousies and false alarms; kindles the animosity of one part against another; foments occasionally riot and corruption, which find a facilitated access to the government itself through the channels of party passion. Thus the policy and the will of one country are subjected to the policy and will of another. . . . A fire not to be quenched, it [factionalism] demands a uniform vigilance to prevent its bursting into a flame, lest, instead of warming, it should consume."[8]

Washington's strictures against parties certainly would be considered undemocratic by present American standards, for the very essence of democracy is a choice among competing parties. Yet it is the very same identification of nation and nationalist party—as the Federalists conceived of themselves—that is found in so many of the contemporary new na-

---

[7] Wallerstein, *op. cit.*, p. 96.
[8] Quoted in J. N. Larned, *The New Larned History* (Springfield, Mass.: C. A. Nichols Publishing Co., 1851), X, 8677–79.

tions. Washington's condemnation of an opposition party, and his equation of opposition with obstructionism and disloyalty, are echoed by most of today's nationalist leaders. The common fear, then as now, is that the opposition party threatens the new nation's cohesiveness because it represents largely the "locals." The Federalists, as the government party composed of the "nationalist intelligentsia," regarded the Republicans essentially as "locals" for they were fundamentally a "state's rights" party committed to minimizing the authority of the national government. Characteristically, therefore, when the Federalists felt that the nation and they themselves were threatened by Americans who were supposedly in league with "foreign agents" (the French), they sought to squash the opposition party. The Alien and Sedition Act of 1789—making it a criminal offense to organize in order to oppose government policies or to speak ill of the President or Congress—was the instrument with which this objective was to be achieved.

In America's early days, then, the distinction between loyalty to the nation and loyalty to the government was not too firm either. And certainly democratic concepts were more deeply implanted then in the United States than they are in any of the new nations today! It was the defeat of the Federalist Party in the Presidential election of 1800 that contributed to the survival and institutionalization of a two-party system. For three decades after the decline of the Federalists, furthermore, the nation was governed by Jefferson, Madison, Monroe, and John Quincy Adams, the first three of whom had the prestige of having been Founding Fathers. Not until such decisive issues as the Louisiana Purchase, the War of 1812, and the Missouri Compromise had been resolved did an opposition party, under Jackson, win power. "The almost unchallenged rule of the Virginia Dynasty and the Democratic-Republican Party served to legitimate national authority and democratic rights. By the time the nation divided again into two broad warring factions which appealed for mass support, it had existed for forty years, the Constitution had been glorified, and the authority of the courts had been accepted as definitive."[9]

It is significant, in any case, that the hero and the party in the new nations, in their attempts to "nationalize" their people, tend to invoke anticolonial nationalism. The fact is that the only force that has ever united the people is generally the former colonial power; their nationalism stemmed from their resentment and determination to end colonial rule. Since this nationalism tends to lose its force as a socially cohesive factor after independence, the only way of arousing the people and keeping them united is to continue the struggle against European colonialism or "imperialism" in general. The more tenuous the bonds uniting the members of the society, the more ardent a campaign against the "ves-

[9] Seymour M. Lipset, *The First New Nation*, p. 45.

tiges of imperialism" is waged. By asserting that the nation is once more threatened by the Dutch or the French or the British—if not by all the Western states acting jointly as "NATO imperialism"—the heroes again seek to arouse their people and unite them against a common external danger. Thus anticolonialism does not end with the achievement of national freedom. The struggle for independence must be waged until a measure of national integration has occurred. Nationalism serves as a substitute for the missing consensus. It is not surprising then that the foreign policy of the developing nations becomes a quest for national identity and cohesion.

Two further factors intensify this nationalism and reinforce the need for the new nations to assert themselves internationally—and in both respects the new states differ from the early America. First, the Westernized nationalist leader of a contemporary developing society has in the past been a stranger in his own land, for his acquired Western values alienated him from his own culture. The assertion of nationalism therefore not only enables the masses to identify themselves with the hero— and thus with the nation—but also allows the hero to identify himself with his people. The hero-leader, as a Westernized man, knows that he has more in common with his former rulers than with the people in whose name he speaks. Before independence, he achieved identification through his leadership of the nationalist movement. After independence has been gained for "his" people, he cannot relax this nationalist stance. His need to identify with the people is stronger than ever. A nationalist foreign policy is thus a psychological imperative for him. Without nationalism, he lacks personal roots, security, and communication with his people. By contrast, the leaders of the American Republic shared a common language and Western culture with the majority of their countrymen.

The second factor concerns economic development. For all the new nations, it is the response to the revolution of rising expectations that will be decisive. The degree to which these expectations are satisfied will be proof of the effectiveness of the new national government to the "tribalized" populace. It is for this reason that the government must play the leading role in this early phase of economic growth. This was true in capitalist America as it is today in the developing socialist societies. But the United States possessed a far greater capacity for economic take-off than any of the contemporary new nations. Her greatest advantage was the fact that she had never passed through a feudal stage. Thus the United States was never handicapped or held back by the influences of the traditional society, with its emphasis on a rigid social hierarchy and status based on birth and the consequent inability of a man to better himself; by an antibusiness attitude stemming from the political domination of a land-owning aristocracy and the spiritual domination of the

Church, with its emphasis on the life hereafter; or by the restrictive or monopolistic practices of guild organizations. Moreover, she was rich in resources and was not burdened with an excessive population. She possessed a fairly sizable and wealthy commercial bourgeoisie, as well as a large class of land-owning farmers. No one-party system could long have survived amid this social pluralism. Born into the post-feudal era, the United States grew up as a democratic, Protestant, capitalist, middle-class society in which the Horatio Alger entrepreneur whose efforts were rewarded with wealth, power, and social position was the cultural hero. In short, she had all the noneconomic prerequisites for economic development—and the young republic made rapid economic progress.[10]

This could hardly be less true for today's developing nations. Burdened by tradition, a multitude of languages and ethnic groups, the absence of an entrepreneurial class, a very low per capita annual income, a much too high birth rate, and a dearth of almost all the skills required for modernization, they tend to have difficulty even taxiing into position for the economic take-off. Indeed, the nationalist leaders confront problems so vast that they may prefer to project their heroic roles on the international stage. Their resort to nationalism is thus reinforced. At home, only painfully slow progress can be realized; the task is bound to be a long and arduous one. At the same time, the masses tend to become increasingly restless and dissatisfied. The gap between their rising expectations and satisfaction seems unbridgeable, particularly during the initial capital-accumulation phase. The increased movement from the country to the impersonal and unfamiliar cities disrupts the traditional loyalties and ties of the people; unable to find substitutes, they live isolated in a mass society.[11] Thus the pressure on the national leaders resulting from the continuing need to improve living conditions and build the new nation is unrelenting. Unable to satisfy popular demands, the leaders and their governments suffer a decline of prestige. In order to preserve or recapture the people's support, stay in power, and stabilize the government, the leaders assert themselves in foreign policy. In these circumstances of economic stagnation, cultural alienation, and governmental insecurity, nationalism proves to be a useful tool. It can be used to manipulate the masses since they can find a new home only in the nation; and it can enable the leaders to maintain their position and buttress their claim as indispensable stewards. They can blame the West not only "for its real sins, which they inevitably magnify, but [by] making it the scapegoat for their own failures."[12] But this is hardly surprising, as has been explained with regard to African leaders:

[10] See Louis Hartz, *The Liberal Tradition in America* (New York: Harcourt, Brace and Co., 1955); and Daniel J. Boorstein, *The Genius of American Politics* (Chicago: University of Chicago Press, 1953).

[11] See W. Kornhauser, *The Politics of Mass Society* (Chicago: The Free Press, 1959).

[12] Hugh Seton-Watson, *Neither War Nor Peace* (New York: Frederick A. Praeger, 1960), p. 182.

Africa's economic dependence on, and heavy involvement with, the West make it inevitable that economic and governmental failures at home should be attributed, at least in part, to the West. The West becomes the scapegoat for failures at home. It is blamed for not doing enough; for not responding in the right way; for not being sufficiently understanding of African needs; and not caring enough—beyond the protection of its own economic and strategic interests. These attitudes are shared by leaders one would readily identify as being well disposed to the West. . . . Frustrated and impotent, government leaders become anxious and defensive. They begin to feel that their survival is at stake; and because they are the leaders who brought their countries to independence, they tend to equate their own survival with the survival of their country's independence. In this anxious mood they turn on their friends who they feel are letting them down. The more a government feels beholden to the West, or economically tied to one of the Western countries, the more strongly it reacts.[13]

The Characteristics of a Neutralist Foreign Policy

Basic to the new nations' anticolonial nationalism is their nonalignment (once referred to in the United States as nonentanglement, or isolationism).[14] The new nation seeks to discover and enhance its personality, and, in so doing, refuses to ally itself with the former colonial ruler and, in fact, abstains from involvement in the quarrels of the great powers. Indeed, it gains self-recognition by asserting itself—at the very minimum on a verbal plane—against the great powers. Having gained independence, it must preserve its separate identity. Consequently, the speeches of a Nehru or a Nasser have echoed John Adams and George Washington. Turning to Washington's Farewell Address, for instance, one reads:

The great rule of conduct for us in regard to foreign nations is, in extending our commercial relations to have with them as little *political* connection as possible. [Italics added.] . . .

Europe has a set of primary interests which to us have none or a very remote relation. Hence she must be engaged in frequent controversies, the causes of which are essentially foreign to our concerns. Hence, therefore, it must be unwise in us to implicate ourselves by artificial ties in the ordinary vicissitudes of her politics or the ordinary combinations and collisions of her friendships or enmities. . . .

Why forego the advantages of so peculiar a situation? Why quit our own to stand upon foreign ground? Why, by interweaving our destiny with that of any part of Europe, entangle our peace and prosperity in the toils of European ambition, rivalship, interest, humor, or caprice?[15]

[13] Legum, "What Kind of Radicalism for Africa?," pp. 242–43.
[14] This section owes much to the suggestive article by Alan F. Westin, "We, Too, Were Once a 'New Nation,' " *The New York Times Magazine*, August 19, 1962.
[15] Quoted in Larned, *op. cit.*, pp. 8680–81.

Jefferson summed it up succinctly when he said simply: "Peace, commerce and honest friendship with all nations—entangling alliances with none."

The War of 1812 illuminates dramatically this relationship between the search for national identity and anticolonial nationalism. British impressment of American sailors was considered an insult to the nation: it appeared that the American flag could not protect those who served it; moreover, Britain continued to treat this country as though she were still a colony. In a sense, the issue was "neocolonialism." Not surprisingly, the War of 1812 came to be known as the "second war of independence." Britain was still challenging American sovereignty, and she thus had to be shown once and for all that the United States was an independent and a proud nation, demanding treatment as an equal. Jackson's defeat of the British at New Orleans—the only American victory of the war, and it came two weeks after the signing of the peace treaty!—proved to Americans that the United States need not tamely submit to the indignities imposed upon her by her former colonial ruler. American dignity and honor had been saved, and the superiority of the American militiaman, especially the Western rifleman, over the British soldier had been demonstrated. Albert Gallatin, Jefferson's Secretary of the Treasury, said, the war "has renewed . . . the national feelings and character which the Revolution had given. . . . The people have now more general objects of attachment. . . . They are more Americans; they feel and act more as a nation." And according to the September, 1815, issue of the *Niles' Register*, the first to be "printed on beautiful new type of *American* manufacture," "The people begin to assume, more and more, a NATIONAL CHARACTER; and to look at home for the only means, under divine goodness, of preserving their religion and liberty."[16]

The best example of nation-building through the rejection of the European "father," however, was the Monroe Doctrine. The Doctrine formalized the rejection and demonstrated explicitly that American nationalism—or anticolonialism—was directed not merely at Britain, the former ruler, but at all of Europe. The New World would stand apart from the Old. Interestingly enough, this formal step of separation was taken at a time when American security was threatened by a possible attempt of the Holy Alliance to help Spain restore control over its ex-colonies in South America. Despite this menace to her safety, the United States refused to ally herself with Britain, the only power capable of protecting her from the Holy Alliance. Because Britain, too, opposed the Alliance, she proposed to the United States that the two countries form a common front against the monarchical reaction it represented—against what was a threat not only to American security but also to constitutional government anywhere. The British approached the United States not because

[16] Quoted in Marcus Cunliffe, *A Nation Takes Shape, 1789–1837* (Chicago: University of Chicago Press, 1959), p. 132.

the American Navy and Army were strong, but because they sought the kind of moral support that American diplomats today seek from India. Yet, despite the fact that U.S. interests coincided with those of Britain in this instance, Washington refused. The American policy remained one of nonalignment—of not becoming involved in Europe's conflicts. The United States refused, as Secretary of State John Quincy Adams put it, to become "a cockboat in the wake of the British man of war."

Instead, she unilaterally proclaimed the Monroe Doctrine. Significantly, instead of informing the European powers privately that this hemisphere was no longer to be regarded as a preserve for European colonialism, the President resorted to "open diplomacy." Clearly, such a public pronouncement was more gratifying to national pride and more insulting to Europe. Here stood the young United States, without much of an army or navy, defying the great powers of the Old World. It was an exhilarating experience for the new nation, and American confidence and self-satisfaction were raised to a new pitch.

This separation between the New and Old Worlds lasted well into the twentieth century. It was only as British power declined and Britain was no longer able to preserve the European balance of power by herself that the United States was "called in" to restore the balance. Thus American power was needed in World War I to defeat Germany. Yet, even then, the United States did not consider herself an "ally" of Britain and France; rather, she called herself an "associated" power. And after the war, the long-time deep distrust of colonial Europe showed up again. The United States, it was claimed, should never have become involved in Europe's war. Indeed, she could have abstained from the conflict had not certain forces sympathetic to the Allies tricked her: shrewd and unscrupulous British propaganda; American munitions makers and financiers —the so-called "merchants of death"—who had an economic stake in an Allied victory; and a pro-British President. Implicit in this view was the traditional assumption that the United States had no stake in Europe's affairs. Potential German hegemony over continental Europe posed no threat to American security. The United States could therefore have avoided involvement had she only possessed the will to stay out of Europe's affairs. Failing to ratify the Treaty of Versailles, America retreated once more into her isolationist shell. The 1929 Kellogg-Briand Pact outlawing war was intended to ensure that no country would ever attack the United States. And, to complete this withdrawal, the U.S. Congress in the 1930's passed a series of neutrality laws designed to keep the country out of war even if the Kellogg-Briand Pact were violated. The first of these laws was appropriately dubbed by the *New York Herald Tribune* as "An Act to Preserve the United States from Intervention in the War of 1917–1918."[17]

[17] Quoted in Alexander DeConde, *A History of American Foreign Policy* (New York: Charles Scribner & Sons, 1963), p. 570.

If the United States was still rejecting Europe only 30 years ago—that is, 150 years after she had won her independence—it is hardly surprising that this is the basis for the foreign policies of most of today's new nations. For example, Nasser of Egypt has been particularly successful in awakening Egyptian—indeed Arab—nationalism through a foreign policy that hinges on the rejection of the colonial father. His seizure of the Suez Canal in 1956 in response to what he felt was America's neocolonial treatment of Egypt was characteristic. The United States had withdrawn funds pledged for the Aswan Dam after Egypt had signed her famous arms agreement with the Soviet Union in late 1955, stepped up her campaign to overthrow the pro-Western governments of Iraq and Jordan, recognized Communist China, and intensified the virulence of her verbal onslaught against the West in general. Already acclaimed the new Saladin of the Arab world for his Soviet arms deal—"this one bold stroke [with which] he declared his independence of the West and proclaimed his leadership of the Arabs."[18]—Nasser now nationalized the Suez Canal and announced that Egypt would build the Dam with the money earned by the Canal. It would be the symbol of an Egypt freed from colonial humiliation and servility:

> Citizens, we shall never allow the imperialists or the oppressors to have a hold over us. We shall never allow history to repeat itself. We have marched forward to build Egypt strongly and surely. We march forward to political and economic independence, we march forward towards a strong national economy for the masses of the people. We march forward to work. If we look back, we do so only to demolish the relics of the past, to demolish the relics of oppression, servility, exploitation and domination. We look back at the past only to put an end to its effects. No, O citizens, as the rights revert to their owners, now that our rights in the Suez Canal have reverted to us after 100 years, we are building the real foundations of sovereignty and the real edifice of grandeur and dignity.[19]

It can well be said of Nasser that "His power and influence rest on his ability to symbolize Arab nationalism as an idea and as a practical force. As he walks on the world stage, millions of Arabs see him playing the role they would like to play and doing the things they would like to do. . . . When he challenges the great powers and takes daring risks in the name of Arab 'rights and dignity,' and gets away with it, the Arab masses feel an emotional lift and a satisfaction that no Arab leader has given them within memory."[20]

If nonalignment in the East-West conflict is the basic principle of the new nation's foreign policy in its search for self-recognition, opposition

[18] John C. Campbell, *Defense of the Middle East*, p. 73.
[19] Quoted in The Royal Institute of International Affairs, *Documents on International Affairs, 1956* (London: Oxford University Press, 1959), pp. 111–12.
[20] Charles D. Cremeans, *The Arabs and the World*, p. 25.

to great-power bases or involvement in its area is a second aspect of its quest for national identity. To return to the American analogy, the leaders of the young republic could well recall that during the seventeenth and eighteenth centuries, four wars had involved the colonies,[21] and they were determined to avoid such a repetition. No more wars were to be fought in the New World by the European powers. The Monroe Doctrine made it unmistakably clear that this hemisphere was no longer an arena for European colonization or intervention. While the Doctrine was, to be sure, specifically aimed at colonial reimposition, the general principle was clear: opposition to the presence of the European powers in the area. Clearly, America feared "neocolonial" control, as well as the possibility that she might become involved in Europe's quarrels and wars. Similarly, today's new nations fear that the continued presence of a former colonial power might enable it to keep them so weak that they would once more become dependent semi-colonies. They define neocolonialism as a relationship between a superior and inferior power in which the former uses its greater strength to subject the latter to its will.

The same kind of fear was evident at the time the United States was considering the annexation of Texas. Unwilling to recognize American hegemony of the North American continent, Britain and France set out to contain her influence and power. They urged Texas to remain independent, and even at one time thought of guaranteeing her independence. If this had occurred, an additional sizable and strong state might have been established in North America. Indeed, during the 1840's, Americans feared—although falsely—that the two great European powers were seeking to establish an independent "California" (an area that included the present states of California, Nevada, Utah, Arizona, New Mexico, and parts of Wyoming and Colorado) and perhaps even an independent "Oregon" (composed of the present states of Oregon, Washington, Idaho, and small parts of Montana and Wyoming). The expansion of this period was therefore in good part motivated by the determination to forestall European encroachment,[22] which could have splintered the continent into three or more nations. In that event, the European states would have been able to exploit divisions and quarrels among these nations for their own purposes. Such purported "divide-and-rule" tactics by the European colonial powers, aimed at the preservation of their own power and influence by keeping the young America as weak and helpless as possible, led to strong condemnation. President Polk, for instance, wrote in 1844 before he was even a candidate for office: "Let

[21] King William's War, 1689–97 (War of the League of Augsburg); Queen Anne's War, 1702–13 (War of the Spanish succession); King George's War, 1744–48 (War of the Austrian succession); and the Seven Years' War, 1756–63 (French and Indian War).

[22] Albert K. Weinberg, *Manifest Destiny* (Baltimore, Md.: The John Hopkins Press, 1935), pp. 109–10.

the fixed principle of our Government be, not to permit Great Britain, or any other foreign power, to plant a colony or hold dominion over any portion of the people or territory of either [continent]." As President, he set forth the following thoughts:

> Jealousy among the different sovereigns of Europe . . . has caused them anxiously to desire the establishment of what they term the "balance of power." It cannot be permitted to have any application on the North American continent, and especially to the United States. We must ever maintain that people of this continent alone have a right to decide their own destiny. Should any portion of them, constituting an independent state, propose to unite themselves with our Confederacy, this will be a question for them and us to determine without any foreign interposition. We can never consent that European powers shall interfere to prevent such a union because it might disturb the "balance of power" which they may desire to maintain upon this continent.[23]

The opposition by today's new states to great-power presence in their areas remains as vehement as it was when the United States entered the international arena. The establishment under U.S. sponsorship of the Middle Eastern Treaty Organization (the Baghdad Pact) in the 1950's —comprising Britain, Turkey, Iraq, Iran, and Pakistan as a "northern tier" to contain possible Soviet expansion along a 3,000-mile frontier— provides a revealing example. Nasser saw the alliance as an attempt by the Western powers to preserve their former colonial domination of the Middle East. Britain, he said, having lost her controlling influence in Egypt, had now merely shifted her base of control to Iraq. Thus he denounced the Baghdad Pact, which had tied Iraq to two NATO members, as an instrument of neocolonialism forged in the name of anti-Communism. The difference in perspective here is clear. The West thought of METO in terms of the need to preserve the global balance of power. But to the leading new nation of the area, the alliance between a weak Arab state, Iraq, and England—a close ally of the world's mightiest nation, the United States—seemed an attempt by the West to preserve Iraq as a colony and to maintain its control of the Middle East.

To Egypt, the primary concern was not Communism but Western "colonialism." Egypt's reaction was to try to undermine the alliance and drive "colonialism" from the Arab world. Since Western colonialism, Egypt said, attempted to maintain its position by keeping the Arab world divided, it could be countered only by a Pan-Arab policy whose aim was to unite all Arab nations. But here Egypt met a problem the United States had never confronted in its Westward expansion—already existing nations who carefully safeguarded their independence. And the union of Egypt and Syria as the United Arab Republic did not long survive Syrian

[23] Quoted in Dexter Perkins, *The Monroe Doctrine* (Boston: Little, Brown and Co., 1941), p. 79.

resentment of Egyptian "colonialism"! But Nasser's Pan-Arab policy had some success in the toppling of the pro-Western monarchical Iraqi government; the new nationalist government of Iraq withdrew its participation in the pact named after its own capital city.

In Africa, too, the advocacy of a Pan-Africa, based on concepts such as the "African Personality" and *Négritude,* stems in large measure from the fear that Europeans will seek to preserve their influence through tactics that will keep the continent divided and weak. Said Julius Nyerere, now President of Tanzania:

> We know that even after our independence has been achieved that *African Personality* which we would build up will depend upon the consolidation of our *unity,* not only in sentiment but in fact. We know that a *Balkanised* Africa however loudly it might proclaim to the world its independence and all that, will in fact be an easy prey to the forces of neo-imperialism (*neo-colonialism*). The weak and divided can never hope to maintain a *dignified independence* however much they may proclaim their desire to be strong and united; for the desire to unite is a very different thing from actual unity. One can foresee the forces of neo-imperialism manipulating these little states in Africa, making them complacently smug in this mere sentimental desire to be one, and at the same time doing everything possible to prevent the realisation of that unity.[24]

And former Foreign Minister of Ghana Ako Adjei:

> As the former colonial territories become independent, new dangers await us. The European colonial powers, although they are now being compelled by the force of African nationalism to grant independence, are nonetheless planning to continue to dominate Africa by a new system of foreign domination, namely the *Balkanisation* of Africa. They are ready to grant independence, but under certain conditions, such as the negotiation of defence agreements and the guarantee of economic advantages such as would satisfy the demands of African nationalism. By this means, they expect to be able to create a large number of small independent States, but which shall continue to be dependent upon the former colonial powers perpetually for their economic, technological, social and cultural development.[25]

Without unity, in short, there can be no true African independence, strength, or prestige.

A third feature of the new nation's foreign policy is usually a propensity toward lecturing the colonial powers about their international manners—that is, to moralize. It is almost as though the developing nations seem to compensate for their sense of inferiority, their long subjection and humiliation, as well as their lack of strength with a pose of "spiritual superiority." Not that the new nations are not sincere. The younger gen-

[24] Quoted in Legum, *Pan-Africanism,* p. 111.
[25] *Ibid.,* p. 120.

eration always tends to criticize and reject the ways of its elders. This was certainly true of the young United States. The new republic was a democracy, not a monarchy. It stood for the rights of all, not for the privileges of the few. In a world of aristocratic, hierarchical, conservative societies, America proclaimed the virtues of egalitarianism and liberalism. The rulers were responsible to the ruled. America was to be the beacon of liberty to the world. It was to be the first nation to devote itself to the common man, to grant him a voice in the government and an opportunity to improve himself socially and economically. This did not mean that the American Revolution was to be exported by force or political subversion, for the United States recognized the right of other states to exist. Her task was only to create a democratic society that would be an example for other nations to follow if they wished. In the meantime, the republic would isolate itself from Europe's nondemocratic ways and thereby remain uncorrupted in thought and deed. Self-abstinence, not the conversion of others, would be the guardian of her purity. Let the Europeans do what they pleased in Europe—but their political patterns and morals were not wanted in this hemisphere. The New World would do things better. It was precisely the contrast between a Europe of poverty and exploitation and an America of opportunity and democracy that subsequently attracted millions of immigrants to these shores. America's appeal should be noted for precisely what it was—a "leftist," even "socialist" appeal.

Just as the new nations call themselves socialists in the general sense that their societies are committed to the welfare of all their citizens, so the new United States proclaimed what *in its time*, too, was a "left-wing" ideology—that all men were equal, that they possessed certain inalienable rights, and that government should be by consent of the governed (and the governed were hardly likely to favor a government of privileges only for the few, which was precisely why Hamilton's Federalist Party was soon to die in the nonaristocratic American political environment). However, the young republic, like most of today's new states, did not limit the rejection of the colonial order to its political structure and values. The economic system was repudiated as well. Thus, just as "capitalism" is rejected today because it is held responsible for colonial "exploitation," so the United States reacted against the British mercantilist system, which had assigned her to the status of supplier of raw materials (sugar, indigo, rice, cotton, molasses, and tobacco) to be shipped to Britain, there turned into finished products, and then shipped back to be sold on the American market. While American merchants flourished, they were also restricted: they could not manufacture the final products themselves, export to and import directly from Europe, or compete with English goods. In any case, the opportunities for economic development were far too great for the United States to be politically subordinated, economically regulated, and taxed for another nation's benefit. America wanted to govern herself and develop the economy for her own benefit.

The repudiation of the Old World's social, political, and economic order was, furthermore, paralleled by the renunciation of power politics. Nonentanglement was a policy by which America would quarantine herself not only from Europe's social structures but also from its "old-fashioned" international habits. The two were thought to be organically linked. Power politics—considered equivalent to war—was the "sport" of princes unrestrained by democratic public opinion. Only democratic nations, whose leaders were responsible to the people, could be peaceful. European conflicts were thus seen largely as products of mutual jealousies and rivalries of princes, rather than real or meaningful conflicts of national interests. Moreover, it was assumed that if the parties to the dispute would forget their obstinacy, pride, and prestige long enough to allow for a relaxation of tension or settlement of the issue, wars could be avoided. Reason, patience, and good will—not the careful manipulation of the balance of power—were considered the necessary ingredients of peaceful resolution. As Jefferson said, diplomacy was "the pest of the peace of the world, as the workshop in which nearly all the wars of Europe are manufactured."[26] America's distance from Europe had enabled this country to remain at peace during most of the nineteenth century, which only seemed to prove that democracy and peace were synonymous and that the Founding Fathers had been wise to dissociate the United States from the Old World's power politics. That this peace may actually have been the result of the balance of power maintained by Britain was hardly noticed, let alone admitted. Americans could therefore enjoy the luxury of feeling superior and lecturing the Europeans on their poor political manners. Naturally, the Europeans returned these compliments, calling the United States arrogant, naive, and hypocritical: arrogant because, as in the Monroe Doctrine, she addressed the powers of Europe as an equal; naive because, as a young republic, she had yet to learn the facts of life; and hypocritical because, as a self-proclaimed beacon of the virtues of the democratic way of life, the "land of liberty" was the last to outlaw slave traffic, denied its Negroes their "inalienable" human rights, practised lynching, ruthlessly removed her Indians from fertile lands to make room for white settlers, and was not loath to use a little "power politics" in order to win further territory in the Southwest and West.

In recent years, of course, a nation like India, under Nehru—posing as spiritually superior, as the shining example of the virtue of practising nonviolence in international affairs—lectured the United States on power politics and the immoral use of force, and attributed the Cold War to

---

[26] Quoted in Felix Gilbert, *To the Farewell Address: Ideas of Early American Foreign Policy* (Princeton, N.J.: Princeton University Press, 1961), p. 72.

mere rivalry and jealousy. Meanwhile, at home (where another form of segregation, the caste system, has been part of her traditional culture for centuries) she had some second thoughts about trying her own hand at power politics, even resorting to the use of force in Kashmir and Goa.

The three characteristics of the new nation's foreign policy named thus far—nonalignment, opposition to regional great-power involvement, and a predisposition to moralize—have stressed the formation of national identity through rejection of and opposition to the former colonial powers. The fourth—and most important—characteristic emphasizes the opposite side of this nationalistic coin: the new nation's desire to be left alone in order to concentrate its energies on nation-building. While this is basically an internal task, its external manifestation is the attention paid to claims made on what is considered national territory. Thus Indonesia sought Dutch New Guinea, which had been a part of the Dutch East Indies. No Indonesian nation existed before Dutch rule, but by centralizing the administration of the various islands of the Indies the Dutch defined the outlines of Indonesia and stimulated a common anti-Dutch nationalism. Similarly, India claimed the Portuguese enclave of Goa, finally taking it by force after years of preaching to the world's great powers against violence. (The Indonesians never had to go that far; they only threatened to use force and the Dutch, under American pressure, succumbed.)

The United States, too, once confronted this problem of her territoriality. Early in her history, she indicated that she believed it her "manifest destiny" to become the dominant power in North America despite specific claims by France, Spain, Britain, and Mexico. American isolationism was in this sense merely another name for American continentalism. Even before the Louisiana Purchase of 1803, there had existed a feeling of "our rising empire," a belief that the United States would reach from the Atlantic to the Pacific. By the time of the War of 1812, the spirit of "manifest destiny" was strong, and it was "North America for the North Americans." To acquire the continent Providence had provided for the American children, the United States—as the world's foremost preacher against the evils of power politics—demonstrated that she had little to learn of that art so near home. She pressured Spain into opening up the Mississippi—and thus moving the frontier westward—and surrendering the Floridas; eyed Canada as it went to war in 1812 to defend the national honor and dignity; provoked a war with Mexico in order to add Texas, California, and New Mexico to the Union; and threatened Britain to gain the Oregon Territory. Within the Union, moreover, the Indians were driven off their land—sometimes even when they possessed treaties guaranteeing their reservations. American nation-building thus spilled over into what Egypt's Nasser or Ghana's Nkrumah might have called Pan-Americanism.

But the essential task of nation-building remains internal. If the nation

is ever to become a cohesive unit, if it is to "nationalize" the consciousness of its people and win their allegiance, the principal focus of attention must remain on "economic development." It is ironically the Cold
War and the bipolar distribution of power within the state system that
in these circumstances come to the rescue. First, by remaining nonaligned, the new state maximizes its attractiveness to the Soviet and
Western blocs, both of which woo the neutral nation. Particularly the
Soviet Union and the United States act like suitors hoping to win the
hand of the beautiful, but still unattached maiden. By occasionally seeming to promise herself without ever actually making a commitment, the
new nation in turn makes the most of her bargaining strength. For each
suitor is thereby compelled to show his ardor and "prove his love"—with
his pocketbook. This tends to maximize the economic aid the new nation will receive. Second, such aid diminishes the nation's economic and
political dependence on the West. And the further a nation moves away
from the West, the more eagerly will the Communists offer it a loan. On
the other hand, the more resistance it shows to Communist seduction,
the quicker will the United States promise largesse. In fact, such neutrals
as Tunisia, who have generally taken pro-Western stands, have at times
expressed their bitterness that nonaligned leaders who are hardly friends
of the West or who are highly critical of the West have received propor-
tionately more American aid than they have. The middle position in the
Cold War is thus politically and economically a very useful one:

> The possibility of "blackmail" is built into the very structure of Cold War
> competition. But from the point of view of the excessively dependent, rela-
> tively impotent new state, this is not blackmail. It is the equally ancient
> but more honorable art of maintaining political equilibrium through the
> diversification of dependence, the balancing of weakness—in short, the
> creation of an "alternative" lest the influence of one side or the other be-
> come too imposing. The attraction of Communist aid is enhanced for radi-
> cal governments whose wariness of the intentions of the former metropole
> extends to the "capitalist-imperialist West" in general. Yet [even] . . .
> conservative governments—Morocco and Ethiopia, for example—are recep-
> tive to Communist aid. They want it partly to placate their radical opposi-
> tions and to hasten development, but also, one suspects, to pursue the first
> requirement of operational independence—the creation of a rough equilib-
> rium among foreign influences in the life of the country. Conversely, radi-
> cal governments that have developed extensive relations with the Com-
> munist bloc may seek the re-establishment of compensatory links with the
> West, as in the case of Guinea and the U.A.R.[27]

Nor is this surprising, for nonalignment depends in the final analysis for
its maintenance upon the approximately equal distribution of power between the two nuclear giants.

[27] Good, in Martin (ed.), *op. cit.*, p. 11.

Economic Aid, Military Rule, and Political Development

It is in the developing areas of the world that the Communist powers and the Western alliance are in direct competition. And it is there that the nuclear stalemate may be broken. Militarily, neither of the great contestants is likely to achieve a sufficiently decisive technological break-through that would so upset the present balance of power that either side would believe it could strike the opponent with relative impunity. Politically, despite dissension within both camps, no major power in either can be expected to change sides and align itself with its former enemies against its erstwhile friends, thereby drastically altering the rela-tive strength of each. The Soviet Union and the United States, and their respective allies, can achieve a *political* breakthrough only in the develop-ing areas. The maximum objective of each bloc is to enhance its strength by adding to its side the territory, population, and resources of the new nations (or at least the potentially stronger and politically more im-portant states); the minimum goal is to keep these nations from joining the other side. Unwilling to risk total war, each of the two superpowers hopes to defeat its opponent in the developing areas. The resulting con-test is a deadly one that is at least as significant as the arms race. Foreign aid as an instrument of policy in this contest may, indeed, be considered a substitute for arms: "In our times, economic activities are not an al-ternative [to war]; they are a substitute. They are no longer a preferable alternative to clearly feasible war and to equally despicable but appar-ently dispensable power politics. They are instead a substitute for prac-tically self-defeating major war, and they are more than ever an instru-ment of the again respectable politics of power."[28] In short, foreign aid has become an instrument of economic warfare.

For the United States, the foreign-aid program is a matter of security. Many of the new states are located around the periphery of the Sino-So-viet bloc. If they should " go Communist," the entire Eurasian continent, with the exception of the relatively small European peninsula, would be under Communist control. And it is questionable how long Europe could preserve its independence in these circumstances. There is no ques-tion that the weak states of Africa would not be able to withstand the overwhelming Communist pressure. The policy of containment was specifically intended as a means of maintaining control of the Eurasian rimland, or periphery, to prevent any further expansion that would lead to Communist domination of what MacKinder called the World-Island. But most of the nations along this periphery face the same problems as the other underdeveloped areas: lack of national cohesion, political sta-bility, capital, modern skills, sufficient natural resources, and population control. And they are critically handicapped by the institutions, customs,

[28] George Liska, *The New Statecraft*, p. 3.

and values (generally anti-economic and secular) of the traditional society. If, as a result, these new states cannot achieve self-sustaining economic growth and corresponding modernization, they may, out of frustration and desperation, turn to Communism.

For Communism permits them to express anti-Western national grievances and at the same time offers them a totalitarian political organization for a supposedly rapid transformation of the traditional community into an urban, industrialized society. It is the transitional period between these two stages of development that is the most dangerous. In terms of Rostow's five stages of economic growth—the pre–take-off, the take-off, the drive to maturity, the age of mass consumption, and beyond high-mass consumption[29]—this period lies between the two initial stages, as the old society breaks down and approaches the point for the actual "take-off." Can it, in fact, ready itself to take off, and, if it does, can it continue to climb upward? Although the rate of economic growth is obviously important, it is not the speed with which the society climbs that is of primary importance, but the fact that it does climb and that it climbs steadily. For it is vital that all members of the society see changes and that some of their expectations are met. While improvements are gradually occurring, and hopes for continued improvements remain high, all sectors of the community will be willing to give the new state at least the benefit of their doubts. It is when there is no noticeable betterment that trouble and turmoil will occur. The members of the intelligentsia are likely to despair, the displaced and often bewildered peasant-workers in the cities will grow increasingly restless, and peasant grievances will remain dissatisfied. It is thus imperative that the United States and the West in general, help the recently emerged states to achieve self-sustaining growth—that is, help them build their nations.

If this challenge is not met, the Western countries will witness on the international scene the same division between the rich and the poor that in an earlier time they experienced domestically. But this time the division will be between the minority of "bourgeois" nations and the majority of "proletarian" nations. It was the nineteenth-century Western society of the few wealthy and privileged and the many destitute and needy that Marx wrote about in *The Communist Manifesto*. He merely projected this actual social division into the future when he prophesied the demise of capitalism. However, most of the Western nations managed to avoid the "inevitable" proletarian revolution by redistributing their national incomes, stabilizing their economies, and regulating their large industrial corporations. Democracy, by reforming capitalism, de-revolutionized labor and gained its allegiance for a form of welfare capitalism, or social democracy, in which labor shared in the general improvement of living standards.

The same kind of maldistribution of income now plagues the world

[29] W. W. Rostow, *Stages of Economic Growth.*

for a second time—and this time the inequities exist between nations. Again, the rich are getting richer, and the poor poorer. Again, the "iron laws" of wages—the money the developing countries can earn with their exports—seem to condemn the proletariat to everlasting poverty and misery. One wonders whether the specter of Communism has been defeated domestically only to reappear now and defeat the bourgeois West internationally.

There is, however, a major difference between then and now. Within the Western countries, the aspirations of the poor were generally met because democratic governments responded to their votes (except in Germany, where the welfare measures were adopted by a monarchical and semi-absolutist government to avoid revolution and win working-class support). But there is no democratic world government today. At the same time, Western self-interest dictates that the "revolution of rising expectations" be satisfied. In the final analysis, it was this same self-interest that compelled the Western ruling classes to respond to working-class grievances. A failure of self-interest in the second half of the twentieth century—especially by the United States—would gravely jeopardize Western security. Minimum American security interests require that the new states become self-sufficient and develop their sense of nationalism, resisting attempts by both the West *and* the Communist bloc to dominate them.

The United States also has an economic stake in preserving the freedom of the developing states. With only 6 per cent of the world's population, she produces nearly 50 per cent of the world's goods. Yet, despite her own great fund of resources, the United States is dependent on other nations, especially in the developing areas, for certain vital resources. She imports 100 per cent of the natural rubber needed, 100 per cent of the tin, 100 per cent of the stagnite, 100 per cent of the industrial diamonds, 98 per cent of the platinum, 95 per cent of the manganese (needed for steel manufacture), and 72 per cent of the tungsten. If imports like these were cut off, both the military strength and the living standards of the United States would suffer seriously. A commercial jet liner, to cite merely one example, depends for its construction on chromium (92 per cent imported), nickel (97 per cent imported), and cobalt (88 per cent imported). Conversely, as developing countries succeed in building up their economies, they will need the type of goods in which American industry excels—from heavy machinery and trucks to refrigerators, television sets, and washing machines. Or to state the proposition negatively: Poverty anywhere is a threat to prosperity everywhere. The less developed a society, the less it is likely to buy from other nations. Thus an English or Dutch citizen may buy, say, $50–200 worth of American goods per year, while an Indian or Egyptian may purchase only $1–5 worth of the same goods.

Economic aid by the United States—and also by its allies—is therefore *at least* as important as the money spent to maintain American military strength. Military expenditures obviously make an indispensable contribution to national security. But at best, military power can hold the line. The United States could continue to build up her military forces and increase her nuclear capability. Still, the balance of world power could be turned against the West in the developing areas. Clearly, economic aid is an indispensable instrument of U.S., and Western, foreign policy in this world-wide struggle.

The term "economic aid" is actually something of a misnomer since it incorporates several different kinds of aid.[30] The giant portion of American aid since the Korean War, for instance, has been *military aid* to support the armies of allied nations around the Sino-Soviet periphery—particularly Nationalist China, South Korea, South Vietnam, Pakistan, and Turkey. To be sure, such military assistance is a form of economic aid. For if its army is being supported, the recipient nation spends less of its own money on its military forces and can instead invest more heavily in its economic development. Another form of aid might—for want of a better term—be called *"bribery" aid.* Much of the aid extended to Latin American republics before the Alliance for Progress could be included in this category. Dollars, as well as military equipment, sent to these countries under the guise of economic development or hemispheric collective self-defense were actually intended to "buy" the support of the ruling classes and the military, neither of which was particularly interested in modernization. The United States was preoccupied in Europe, Asia, and the Middle East—that is, anywhere but Latin America, whose grave social, political, and economic problems were ignored until Castro suddenly and dramatically drew attention to the vulnerability of the United States in her own backyard. Up to that point, the United States had been interested primarily in preserving hemispheric stability and securing votes in the United Nations. Latin American armies, hardly threatened by the Russian or Chinese military, and useless as fighting machines anyway, could nevertheless be strengthened to deal with unrest at home. A third form of economic aid might be termed *"prestige" aid.* In this category one finds such highly visible items as a state-owned commercial airline, a few jet fighters, a concrete road, or a modern factory. This kind of aid allows the recipient nation to feel it is making strides toward modernization. The factory may not serve an economic purpose, and the recipient may not possess sufficient skill to run it, but its construction serves important political and psychological purposes. This kind of aid has, on the whole, had good results; it has pleased the beneficiaries while also raising the prestige of the donor.

But the most vital form of aid—in view of the almost global scope of

---

[30] For the classification of aid generally followed below, see the excellent article by Hans J. Morgenthau, "A Political Theory of Foreign Aid," *American Political Science Review*, June, 1962, pp. 301–9.

the "revolution of rising expectations," the persistence of this revolution, and the fact that its frustrations represent a "clear and present danger" —is that given for *capital development*. By its very nature, this aid must be accompanied by fundamental social and political reforms in order to achieve its purpose; unfortunately, this had not always been the case.

> The economic interests which tend to prevent foreign aid from being used for economic development are typically identified with the ruling groups in underdeveloped societies, which derive their political power in good measure from the economic *status quo*. The ownership and control of arable land, in particular, is in many of the underdeveloped societies the foundation of political power. Land reform and industrialization are in consequence an attack upon the political *status quo*. In the measure that they succeed, they are bound to affect drastically the distribution of economic and political power alike. Yet the beneficiaries of both the economic and political *status quo* are the typical recipients of foreign aid given for the purpose of changing the *status quo*. To ask them to use foreign aid for this purpose is to require a readiness for self-sacrifice and a sense of social responsibility which few ruling groups have shown throughout history. Foreign aid proffered under such circumstances is likely to fail in its ostensible purpose and, performing the function of a bribe to the ruling group, to strengthen the economic and political *status quo*. It is more likely to accentuate unsolved social and political problems than to bring them closer to solution.[31]

Moreover, capital-development aid has suffered from a lack of public understanding—indeed, a generally unsympathetic attitude. Specifically, this has significantly affected the program's scope and long-term commitment. America's annual aid cost is less than one-tenth of its military spending. And relative to the nation's increasing ability to pay as national income rises, the aid "burden" is declining. In the late 1940's, Marshall Plan aid for the recovery of Western Europe took 2 cents out of every dollar the United States produced; by 1962, our total aid bill accounted for two-thirds of a cent out of each dollar. Yet foreign aid actually constitutes one more subsidy for the domestic American economy, for the largest portion of the aid funds are spent in this country, thereby creating jobs and helping business. The public attitude toward foreign aid has also impeded the kind of long-range planning—over two or three decades —needed to achieve a program equal to the magnitude of the task. "The annual debate on the continuation of foreign assistance is both absurd and misleading. It only confuses our purposes, increases impatience, obscures the issues, and inhibits success. We might as well have an annual review of the wisdom of having a public school system."[32]

Yet President Johnson, in 1966, proposed a major change in develop-

[31] *Ibid.*, p. 305.
[32] James A. Perkins, in *The New York Times*, March 28, 1966.

mental programs that would, in effect, constitute a further reduction in the size of our aid. What he suggested was a shift from industrialization to the areas of health, education, and food production—in short, to a "bare-bones" *technical assistance* program. Clearly, what is still needed is a public decision for the kind of action in the international sphere that was taken domestically to defeat the inevitability of the Marxist proletarian revolution. Numerous proposals have been put forth for a more equitable sharing of aid costs by the Western nations—including one for a progressive international income tax according to which nations with per capita earnings above a certain level would contribute 1-2 per cent of their national income to the development of the new nations. The various American and European aid programs have already moved in this direction, as is testified by the Alliance for Progress, Point Four, The British Colombo Plan, and a number of bilateral French and West German programs. But all efforts to date have fallen short of fully recognizing the political necessity for a long-range international sharing of the wealth.

If this imperative is not yet apparent, Soviet foreign aid may clarify the need. For the Soviet Union attempts to exploit the anticolonial feelings and aspirations for modernization in the developing countries. Thus, although the bourgeoisie remains the class enemy, she supports the "national bourgeois" leaders in the new states. Her aim is to utilize their anti-Western nationalism to cut the political and economic ties between the newly independent countries and the former colonial powers, and by so doing, to isolate the West and bring about its collapse. Then the task of Communizing the developing nations will hardly present any problems. But the Soviet Union does not rely solely on the exploitation of the new states' anti-Western nationalism. She expects the national bourgeoisie to be overthrown eventually because the bourgeoisie will not be able to modernize as quickly as the people demand. Clearly, only Communism can perform this task effectively. So the Soviets grant aid to remind the recipient peoples of the Soviet Union's rapid industrialization and of their need for Communist political techniques of capital mobilization. Indeed, some measure of improvement in living conditions increases the possibility of a Communist takeover, for it sharpens popular awareness of the gap between achievements and aspirations—and whets the appetite for even greater improvements.

Are these Soviet expectations realistic? American critics of foreign aid, cited earlier—reacting to developing nations' apparent anti-American, pro-Soviet attitudes, as well as their one-party governments and "socialism"—tend to think so. Soviet aid, they fear, will only reinforce a strongly "pro-Communist" predisposition. If Soviet foreign-aid programs usually give the impression of being successful, however, it also needs to be understood that such "successes" have little, if anything, to do with the aid as such. The Soviet Union would be admired by the leaders of the new nations even if no aid were being offered. For she offers them a channel for expression of their anti-Western feelings; furnishes them with a model for rapid industrialization; and represents herself as a supporter of their aspirations for political and economic independence, racial equality, and national dignity and equality. Soviet aid merely reinforces this image. In short, the important factor is the political-ideological-psychological context in which Soviet aid is extended.[33] It is one of the ironies of our age that the Soviet Union, a totalitarian and expansionist state, has managed to present itself so effectively to the underdeveloped areas of the world as a nation that not only knows the secrets of quick modernization but is dedicated to national self-determination and social justice for all men. And it is at the same time a tragedy that the United States, a democracy and capitalist welfare state genuinely concerned with the right of all peoples to govern themselves, has all too often managed to present itself as a supporter of colonialism, racialism, and nineteenth-century "free enterprise," a system that to the new nations means only social irresponsibility and exploitation.

It also must be remembered, in any evaluation of the effectiveness of Soviet and American aid, that the two are really not comparable because their aims are different. The Soviet Union, as a revolutionary state, is determined to destroy the existing world order and thus has a vested interest in social and political instability:

> One of the great advantages which the Soviet Union possesses in confronting the underdeveloped countries outside its own orbit is its almost total lack of entanglement with, and responsibility for, the existing world order that it encounters there. [Italics added.] The Soviet leaders are in the enviable position of being able to look in from the outside, so to speak, on a dangerously unbalanced, imperfectly functioning, conflict-ridden system of international relationships, in the stability of which they have no stake and from the disturbances of which they are themselves effectively insulated. While they hold no brief for the system's survival, they also bear no blame for its troubles.[34]

The Soviets have therefore concentrated most of their aid in just a few countries that are either politically vital, such as India, are strategically located, such as Afghanistan, or possess both these qualities and are (or were) also troublemakers, such as the United Arab Republic, Iraq, Indonesia, Algeria, and Cuba. Moreover, the Soviets do not necessarily ask for the economic justification of a project as a condition for a loan. Thus they furnish aid to build projects like the Aswan Dam for the United

[33] See Joseph S. Berliner, *Soviet Economic Aid*, pp. 179–80; and Hans Heymann, Jr., "Soviet Foreign Aid as a Problem for U.S. Policy," *World Politics*, July, 1960, pp. 525–40.
[34] Heymann, *op. cit.*, p. 528.

Arab Republic or a steel mill for India if the host country asks them for such support and if it happens to serve their purpose. But since they are not particularly concerned with how a particular project fits into an over-all plan for development, the Soviets also will spend their money on such highly visible projects as paving Kabul's main street and supplying the Afghani with busses, or building sports stadiums in Rangoon and Jakarta. Finally, they are quite willing to send the new states modern weapons, which provide the recipient with the symbols of a modern nation and the illusion of national strength.

American aid, by contrast, has different objectives:

> Whether wisely or not, *the task we have assumed adds up to nothing less than an attempt to preserve the whole precarious system of international order with which we are intimately identified and on which we critically depend.* We feel called upon to keep this system of world order function-ing in a manner compatible with our own continued development as the kind of nation we are, and we seek to keep it sufficiently flexible and dy-namic to accommodate the infinitely diverse interests and demands of the rest of the non-Communist world. Given such ambitious aims, we soon dis-cover that a crisis anywhere becomes our crisis, and failure at any point re-flects on us. *Our responsibilities, accordingly, are pervasive, the claims on our resources heavy, and our involvements interminable.* [Italics added.][35]

The contrasting Soviet and American purposes also affect the means by which the respective aid programs are administered. The Soviet Union has relied almost exclusively on credits, while the United States has relied largely on grants. It is often argued that the former has a distinct psy-chological advantage over the latter. Unlike grants, which supposedly have a tendency to make the recipient feel he is accepting charity, credits are claimed to permit the borrower to retain his dignity; since he is pay-ing for the loan, he will feel that he is engaged in a normal business transaction of mutual benefit to both parties. Moreover, the Soviet loans have been extended at an interest rate of 2–2.5 per cent, while American loans have generally carried a 4–5 per cent charge. Their lower rate has allowed the Russians to accuse the West of exploiting the developing countries in typical capitalist fashion, and to stress the mutual advantage of Soviet aid to a developing country. On top of this, the Soviets have seemed more willing to accept repayment of their loans in local currency or in the form of the recipient country's exports, which often helps to relieve a surplus of cotton, rice, fish, or sugar and to preserve the slim dollar or sterling reserves.[36] Yet, while the Soviet loan policy may appear to have many advantages, it cannot be adopted in the same form by the United States for it fits specific Soviet purposes, which actually have little

[35] *Ibid.,* p. 529. It should be noted, though, that U.S. recognition of this has not always been reflected in the amount of funds appropriated.
[36] The terms of Soviet aid are discussed in Berliner, *op. cit.,* pp. 144–67.

to do with the recipient's sense of self-respect. The most obvious reason for a loan program is that it is less expensive than a grant program. Since loans must be repaid, the number of applications is limited. Equally important, loans establish bilateral trading relationships with the recipients, and the Soviet Union may thus obtain commodities it needs.

All indications to the contrary, however, the Soviet Union's aid program has not really been so successful as one might have thought.[37] The results speak for themselves. Soviet aid to a particular country has often been initiated at a point when relations between the recipient and the West were poor. Aid to Iraq was begun after that nation's pro-Western government had been overthrown by a new nationalist government which denounced Western "imperialism" and withdrew from METO. When Guinea opted to leave the newly formed French Commonwealth and France accordingly withdrew all her aid, Soviet rubles began to pour into the country. As Egypt grew increasingly anti-Western in the mid-1950's, opposed METO, and sought to overthrow pro-Western governments throughout the Arab world, the Soviet bloc offered Egypt a huge supply of modern weapons. When the United States then retracted her offer to build the Aswan Dam, partly because of Egypt's new close ties with the Soviet Union, the Soviets took over financing of the project. Yet Iraq did not go Communist, and General Kassim finally arrested the the Iraqi Communist leaders. Sékou Touré of Guinea sent the Russian Ambassador home for allegedly plotting to overthrow his government, and then began to re-establish his relations with France. And Nasser also arrested Egyptian Communists, and even denounced Khrushchev on several occasions. In no developing nation has Soviet aid yet resulted in the acceptance by local leaders of Soviet dictation on domestic or foreign policy—except in Cuba, where the Communists were already in power *before* the Soviet aid program began, and possibly in Ghana under Nkrumah. In fact, when the positions of the Soviet bloc and the new nations coincide on certain international issues—as they do on colonialism—it may be more appropriate to assign the reason to Soviet support of the new nations rather than to the "pro-Communism," "gullibility," or "naïveté" of the leaders. Even in the absence of Soviet aid, their positions would be identical; one would expect the Soviet Union to support Egypt during the Suez crisis, or India when she siezed Goa.

Why, then, has Soviet aid been relatively unsuccessful in exploiting the new states' anti-Western emotions? One reason is certainly the Soviet performance. The Soviets have at times failed to deliver the quantity of goods promised, engaged in questionable practices (such as reselling Egyptian cotton at lower than world market prices and thereby both competing with and underselling Egypt's own cotton), delivered their

---

[37] For a well-balanced analysis, see Barbara Ward, "The Other Foreign Aid Program," *The New York Times Magazine*, June 17, 1962.

supplies late or irregularly, and sent goods of shoddy quality (e.g., the poor-quality crude oil, wormy wheat, and unsatisfactory machinery occasionally sent to Egypt).[38] Some of these failures might, indeed, have been expected. The Soviets generally perform best in the area of heavy industry, where they have considerable experience, rather than in light industry or the production of consumer items. Soviet experience in agriculture, the proverbial Achilles heel of the Soviet economy, has little applicability to the tropical farming of most of the underdeveloped areas. Yet these defects of the Soviet aid program should not be overstressed. Not only has the American program suffered its own failures—such as the dumping of surplus American rice on the world market, thus undercutting a surplus-producing Burma in a year when it otherwise could have been self-sufficient—but the Soviet program also has certain advantages over its American counterpart.[39] The Soviets, not needing anything like Congressional approval of annual foreign-aid appropriations, can commit themselves for years in advance, thus allowing the recipient nation to plan a long-range economic program. They have the flexibility to exploit favorable new situations as they arise, since no Congress assigns their aid money for specific projects. The Soviet Government can also mobilize its best engineers and technicians if it so desires, for there are no private Russian corporations whose higher wages would attract top talent away from government-sponsored aid projects. Finally, no citizen or official, ethnic group, or farm lobby in the Soviet Union is likely to embarrass the government by denouncing the aided country or attempt to block an aided nation's efforts to pay its debts through the sale of farm goods of which the Soviet Union already possesses a surplus.

But Soviet aid has not been successful principally because its political aims do not in the long run coincide with the aspirations of the developing countries. Short-range Soviet goals may well be compatible with their aims of national independence and nonalignment in foreign policy. Indeed, one of the attractions of Soviet aid is that it strengthens the newly independent nation by lessening its otherwise exclusive dependence on the former mother country or the United States. But Communism's eventual aims diverge sharply from the objectives of the new states. On the other hand, the United States, as a pluralistic society, can live in a pluralistic world and is willing to accept the desire of the nonaligned to remain nonaligned. Although at one time she would have preferred to

[38] Berliner, *op. cit.*, pp. 171–77. Other instances that might be cited are: the establishment on Java of an East German sugar mill designed for beet sugar and not suitable for Indonesia's cane sugar; the supply for inter-island transportation of twenty-four small ships that rocked fearfully, despite the installation of "permanent ballast," and whose engines were impossible to maintain because the parts came from all areas of the Communist world; and Soviet submarines with air conditioning that was inadequate in tropical waters. (See *U.S. News & World Report*, September 30, 1963, p. 80.)

[39] Heymann, *op. cit.*, pp. 538–39.

make aid dependent upon the recipient becoming an American ally, she learned several essential lessons about the new nations: that they cannot be bought, that their leaders are not quite so susceptible to Communist promises or so naive about Communism as had been thought, and that they are intensely nationalistic. This last point is especially important, for these nations have keen memories of their long colonial subjugation, and they are not about to substitute Communist colonialism for Western colonialism. Their nationalism is directed against any foreign control. This satisfies American interests since it means that they will not align themselves with the Soviet bloc, but it poses a real dilemma for the Soviets. Wherever the Soviets have not interfered in its domestic politics they have enjoyed good relations with the recipient nation—as, for instance, with India. But where the Soviets have sought to apply pressure to a government to support Communist positions or even gone so far as to attempt to overthrow the government, it has resulted in local Communists being sent to jail, the Soviet ambassador being sent home, or Communist technicians who supervise the aid programs being carefully watched. Yet, if the Communists have been unsuccessful up to now in converting aid into pressure on a local government to support Communist positions in world affairs, it has not yet convinced them to discontinue their aid program. For they cannot vacate the foreign-aid field completely to Western programs. Moreover, they remain confident that the new countries cannot achieve development without Communist political organization. Thus, until the present nationalist leaders are replaced by a Communist government, they use their aid to help establish and foster good relations with the new states.

The essential problem remains for the United States: Will the developing countries *develop?* Moreover, the United States is interested not merely in these nations' economic development but also in their political—that is, democratic—development. Indeed, foreign aid is usually justified by the argument that economic development leads to democratic development. Rostow's "mass consumption stage" occurs in a highly urbanized and industrialized society—in short, a pluralistic society. It is certainly true that democracy cannot develop amid conditions of poverty. As Aristotle pointed out, "Poverty is the parent of revolution and crime," and "when there is no middle class, and the poor greatly exceed in number, troubles arise, and the state soon comes to an end." Aristotle believed that political stability depended upon the absence of extremes of wealth and poverty: "Thus it is manifest that the best political community is formed by citizens of the middle class, and that those states that are well-administered, in which the middle class is large, and stronger if possible than both the other classes, or at any rate than either singly; for the addition of the middle class turns the scale, and prevents either of the extremes from being dominant."[40] In other words,

[40] In W. Ebenstein, *Great Political Thinkers* (New York, 1960), p. 105.

widespread affluence is a prerequisite for democratic government. When the majority of men live in dire need—and are aware that a better life is possible, but see no signs of any improvement—democratic government will not be able to establish roots. A higher national income, and a more equitable distribution of that income, are more likely in a developed economy, and these will tend to promote democracy. The society that can afford to "deal everyone in" can afford to be democratic.[41]

Because of this purported relationship between economic and political development, the United States has tended to concentrate its nonmilitary aid efforts in the economic area—capital accumulation, technical assistance, economic efficiency, and financial stability. But unfortunately, economic growth does *not* automatically produce a democratic society— Germany and Japan in the 1930's and the Soviet Union today being obvious examples to the contrary. In each of these cases, an economically developed nation has been controlled by an authoritarian or totalitarian regime bent on regional or global expansion. The values of freedom and democracy are not the necessary result of economic development. Economic development may be a *necessary condition*, but it is not *sufficient* of itself to ensure the development of a democratic society.[42]

It is already becoming all too clear that—with a few possible exceptions, such as India and some Latin American republics—successful modernization will not occur under democratic auspices, if, indeed, it occurs at all. Almost everywhere else in the developing areas, democracy has failed. Nor is this surprising. There are numerous reasons for this trend in the developing nations toward authoritarianism, stemming from their colonial legacy, from the problems they confront, and from the attitudes of their leaders as they begin the task of nation-building. Certainly, the colonial government was not democratic; political and economic affairs were generally administered by the bureaucracy in the capital city. The experience of colonialism also left the new states with a view of capitalism as a system of exploitation; at the same time, it produced a predisposition toward "socialism"—that is, toward government ownership and operation of the major sectors of industry, for the benefit of all the people. But even for those nations more favorably disposed toward capitalism, the process of development generally includes a "mercantilist" phase, in which the government plays the leading role in laying down the economic infrastructure. Moreover, since the new states are in a hurry, they tend to look upon the Soviet Union's rapid economic development as an example for themselves. In any case, authoritarian or totalitarian governments may be more suitable forms of government than democracy during the early phases of industrialization because they can

[41] David M. Potter, *People of Plenty* (Chicago: University of Chicago Press, 1954), pp. 118–19.

[42] See Eugene R. Black, *The Diplomacy of Economic Development*, pp. 19, 23. For a general analysis of the conditions necessary for democracy to flourish, see Seymour M. Lipset, *Political Man* (New York: Doubleday & Co., 1959), pp. 45–67.

deal more effectively with the social dissatisfaction involved in modernizing entire societies. For example, economic growth demands savings for investment. Yet the accumulation of capital is incompatible with the rapid rise of real wages, a relatively equitable distribution of the national income, or major welfare programs. The requirement is for austerity or postponing the satisfaction of the revolution of rising expectations. In addition, the social stresses and strains resulting from the disintegration of the traditional society and values are likely to produce great instability; in these circumstances, an authoritarian government may be able to preserve law and order more easily than a democratic one, and the leader, particularly a charismatic figure, is someone with whom the people can identify. Finally, the new states lack the prerequisite for the conduct of a democratic government: a relatively high standard of living, mass literacy, a sizable and stable middle class, a sense of social equality, and a tradition of tolerance and individual self-reliance. A Western political analyst has put it as follows:

> The peoples of the West advanced toward democracy by very slow and gradual stages which included long periods of rule by absolute monarchs and despots, benevolent or otherwise. The achievement of ordered societies, reasonably in agreement on those basic elements of social cohesion necessary for the functioning of democracy and well started on the path of economic development, was in good part the product of the firm authoritarian rule which bridged the transition from the Middle Ages to the contemporary world.
>
> For a backward people precariously moving out from under colonialism into independence with all the problems of economic development still ahead of them, it is highly doubtful that the sovereign remedy is a full-scale installment of democracy as the latter has evolved in advanced and prosperous Western societies. Democracy implies far-reaching freedoms, and an opposition; but the prime requirement is not for more freedoms but for discipline and hard work, not for opposition but for a national consolidation of all forces and talents. This is all the more true in countries such as Nigeria or Malaya where the opposition is likely to be made up of parties formed on tribal, racial, or religious lines, deepening inner divisions at a time when the essential need is strong and unified managment. The achievement of coherent national unity can properly be set as the first goal since it is an indispensable condition for internal order and security and for representative government as well.[43]

And an African leader thus:

> Once the first free government is formed, its supreme task lies ahead—the building up of the country's economy, so as to raise the living standards of the people, to eradicate disease, to banish ignorance and superstition. This, no less than the struggle against colonialism, calls for the maximum united

---

[43] Rupert Emerson, *From Empire to Nation*, pp. 289–90.

effort by the whole country if it is to succeed. *There can be no room for difference or division*. In Western democracies, it is an accepted practice in times of emergency for opposition parties to sink their differences and join together in forming a national government. *This is our time of emergency*, and until our war against poverty, ignorance, and disease has been won, we should not let our unity be destroyed by a desire to follow somebody else's "book of rules."[44]

Authoritarian government, then, seems to be the order of the day in the developing areas. Sukarno of Indonesia has called it "guided democracy" in his country; other terms used include "tutelary democracy" and "modernizing oligarchy." It is important to note that despite the similarity in form of the single-party state to a Communist-dominated state, the two are not alike in substance. The nationalist party is not a messianic totalitarian movement that seeks to build a particular kind of society at home and abroad. While it is opposed to the traditional society with its land-owning ruling class or tribal chieftains, its opposition is based on the fact that these forces impede the modernization of the society. But its aim is not modernization according to ideologically preconceived notions of social change. The party may believe in governmental ownership of heavy industry and banking, but its socialism is less a matter of a particular economic structure than it is an issue of moral behavior. Actually, to most of the leaders of the new nations, socialism means something like what democracy means to Americans—that is, a system that provides not only political rights but economic benefits for all. The party is generally a mass party, nationally organized, whose aim is to instill the people with a national consciousness and awareness, as well as to industrialize the country. It is the party of "modernizing nationalism."

> Marxism-Leninism is not the only ideology appropriate to this process. . . . In fact, the modernizing nationalists have developed an alternative set of ideological assumptions and propositions that shares some elements of the Marxist-Leninist model, but differs significantly from it in other respects. Moreover, this ideology is in many ways superior to Marxism-Leninism, since it is more pragmatic and more related to the problem of modernization than are the simplistic dogmas derived from the experience of nineteenth- and early twentieth-century Europe which comprise the Marxist-Leninist solution.
>
> From the Marxist analysis, the modernizing nationalists have accepted certain elements and rejected others. While recognizing the central importance of economic motivation, they do not accept Marxist economic determinism. In nationalist thinking, political forces are capable of subduing and controlling economic forces, and the state is not destined to wither away. Moreover, Marxist materialism is specifically rejected in favor

[44] Julius Nyerere, quoted in Paul E. Sigmund, Jr. (ed.), *The Ideologies of the Developing Nations*, p. 199.

of the recognition of the importance of the spiritual aspects of life. Marxist class analysis is also regarded as inadequate. History involves more than the struggle of the proletariat and bourgeoisie. Other groups in society are also significant, among them the rural elements, the intellectuals, and perhaps the military men as well. The nation as a whole is the primary unit of loyalty, not the class, and in the case of the African nationalists, it is denied that class divisions even exist in the new nations. . . .

Undoubtedly, there are strong authoritarian tendencies in the desire of the nationalist leaders to remold their societies by government action, but thus far there is little evidence of the characteristic totalitarian attempts at thought control, absolute unanimity, and the establishment of the infalli- bility of leader and party. The emphasis is on persuasion, negotiation, and conciliation, while the threat or use of violence that has typically accom- panied the totalitarian attempts to transform society is largely absent. Moreover, with the exception perhaps of Ghana's version of Pan-African- ism, the ideology itself is limited in its goals to national independence and development and does not have the universality or inherent expansionism of the totalitarian doctrines.[45]

The real danger may be that these parties are not *sufficiently* disci- plined or well led to organize and mobilize their populations for the hard task of modernization. Thus far, the failure of civilian government has led to military rule in a number of developing states: the Sudan, Iraq, Jordan, Lebanon, the United Arab Republic, South Korea, Pakis- tan, Burma, Indonesia, the Central African Republic, the Congo, Da- homey, Upper Volta, Nigeria, and Ghana. Indeed, where disciplined one-party governments do not exist, military rule may perhaps be the most appropriate substitute, for it may be able to organize the nation for the economic take-off and surmount the dangerous transition period be- tween the traditional society and the industrial society. There are several reasons why armies, even including some Latin American ones, may play such a key developmental role. First, civilian leadership, overwhelmed by the massive problems confronting it, has often proved inept, indeci- sive, if not outright inefficient and corrupt. Political instability, national humiliation, and deteriorating living standards all undermine faith in the politicians, political institutions, and "politics," and the people auto- matically turn to the army, the symbol of the nation it is sworn to de- fend, the guardian of the "national interest." The army is founded on centralized command, hierarchy, and discipline—the very characteristics which, the Communist Party claims, would allow only it to modernize an underdeveloped nation successfully and rapidly. The army may, in fact, be the only organization that can compete with the Communists in their capacity to break the power of the landowning classes, carry out land reforms, organize the nation's human and natural resources for

[45] Sigmund (ed.), *op. cit.*, pp. 38–39.

development, and control the unhappy masses from whom the capital savings must be collected. Second, the real power in most Asian or Arab armies lies with the younger, highly nationalistic officers, who are dedicated personally and institutionally to the modernization of their nations. In the past, their senior officers came from the landed upper class, which had a vested interest in preserving the traditional society; this is still by and large the case in Latin America. But today it is not the generals but the captains who play the key role in control of the army. As sons of small landowners and low-grade civil servants, they consider themselves true "sons of the land" and despise the ruling class. They are aware of the comparative weakness of their army—a weakness reflecting not merely the absence of modern weapons but also the pre-industrial nature of their society; for a strong army cannot exist apart from an urban-industrial nation. Thus, these younger military leaders share the nationalistic and modernizing desires of the Westernized secular intelligentsia; indeed, they are usually referred to as the "military intelligentsia," or "intelligentsia-in-uniform." Third, the skills necessary for the functioning of a modern society—to the extent that they exist at all—tend to be concentrated in the armies of developing nations. Colonial rulers have often left behind them first-rate fighting units—for example, the Indian Army, the Malaya Regiments, the Philippine Scouts, the Arab Legion, the Gurkha Regiments, and the King's Own African Rifles. These more than any other institution in backward societies embody the spirit of the future nation.

Indeed, these armies are microcosms of modern, industrialized societies. They are technically and rationally oriented in their occupational activities. They cannot function without engineers, mechanics, communication specialists, etc.; even the operation of jeeps, tanks, guns, and other military equipment by the ordinary soldier demands elementary "industrial" skills. Military units have, in fact, on occasions been used for such tasks as the construction of roads, bridges, and harbors—recalling the role of U.S. Corps of Engineers in the West's development. Armies, despite their hierarchical organization, are in some ways "democratic," or revolutionary, organizations. In a traditional society, where a man's status in society was decided at birth, it was only in the Westernized institution of the army that personal advancement was possible. For this reason, young and ambitious lower-class men, whose prospects of social advancement and economic reward were cut off in a highly stratified civilian society, often entered the army, where their status was determined not just on the basis of birth and family, but also by ability and hard work. Yet the fact that there was a relationship between effort and reward in the military also served to point up the injustice of the surrounding civilian society.

Finally, the army can be a nationalizing instrument in countries where large numbers of young men have to serve. It not only trains the recruit in certain basic technical skills, but more important, it transforms him from a tradition-bound illiterate villager with unsanitary habits and a parochial loyalty to a man equipped to be a citizen of a modern nation. Above all, it brings him in contact with a new world beyond that of his village or tribe—the nation, national symbols, and national values. The army can thus be a modernizing experience for the young soldier who, after his term of service, will return to civilian society—and will probably want to have a hand in changing it.

But if some military governments should be more successful than civilian governments in organizing their societies for economic take-off —and it is by no means certain that they will succeed—the problem of *democratic* political development would still remain.[46] Even if the controlling party or army should voluntarily relinquish power—which again, may not necessarily occur—its stewardship would already have tended to strengthen the authoritarian tradition the new nation had inherited from the colonial period, a tradition reinforced by the nation's economic development. Consequently, foreign aid must be accompanied by *social technology*. It is a mistake to concentrate on strictly economic growth, in accordance with the economically determinist view that such growth will "inevitably" produce political democracy.

If democratic societies are to be developed, Western aid programs should emphasize a number of means, among which public education ought to rank especially high. Probably no other type of investment, public or private, could in the long run produce a greater return, since democracy cannot flourish amid illiteracy. The very minimum requirement is that citizens read and write and have some understanding of their civic and political rights and obligations. Average income, stages of industrialization and urbanization, and levels of education are usually much higher in democratic than in nondemocratic countries. "If we cannot say that a 'high' level of education is a *sufficient* condition for democracy, the available evidence suggests that it comes close to being a necessary one."[47] Education must, however, extend itself beyond this fundamental need of literacy. Great emphasis should be placed on vocational training. For the new nations suffer from a dearth of well-trained personnel—be they peasants acquainted with modern techniques of farming or civil servants with the requisite qualities of nonpartisanship, bureaucratic efficiency, incorruptibility, and technical skills. Business and labor also lack trained managerial personnel and trade-union organizers (with the exception, of course, of the Communists, who may as a result

[46] The lack of emphasis on political development in American foreign aid and the reasons for this are analyzed in Robert A. Packenham, "Developmental Doctrines in Foreign Aid," *World Politics*, January, 1966, pp. 194–225.

[47] Lipset, *op. cit.*, p. 57.

gain leadership of the labor movements by default). Above all, the need is for leaders in these various fields who not only have the professional skills but also are democratically inclined. This is by far the most difficult task facing the educational systems.

Instilling democratic values will not, however, suffice alone. There must also be a dispersion of power. In the initial phase of development, the government tends to concentrate power in its hands. But in the long run, the government cannot direct virtually the entire economy without inhibiting the evolution of a pluralistic society.

> From the political and social point of view, a vigorous growth of private business enterprise—provided it is widespread, and not concentrated in a few hands—broadens the bases of political power, helps to create an independent middle class, promotes decentralization of authority and leadership, and helps to separate economic power from political and other forms of power. These are among the fundamental requirements . . . for development of democratic, free societies.[48]

In brief, to favor government leadership in economic development is not to oppose private enterprise and a free market.

Nor is such a development to be achieved by removing what is popularly called "government interference." Just as there must be a change in educational philosophy, so there is needed a change in economic philosophy. This will be difficult in a cultural environment that is as hostile to "business" as was medieval Europe. It will be even more difficult where governments must play a major economic role and the nationalist leaders distrust private enterprise. Yet, while it may be necessary for governments to own and direct public utilities or railroads, for instance, it does not follow that once the country is well on the way to development, it also needs to control the "commanding heights" of heavy industry. The present cultural antipathy toward profit-making may perhaps decline in the future. Already, some of the new nations are showing signs that their socialism is more pragmatic than doctrinaire. In Africa, for example, one of the principal targets of "African socialism" has been the trade union! The reason for this is quite simple (and capitalistic): Wages cannot be permitted to outstrip productivity, and strikes cannot be allowed to endanger "business confidence," if the new nations are to attract—as many of their leaders increasingly realize they must—foreign private capital for their economic growth. More and more, African leaders, including self-styled socialists, have been proclaiming in a most un-Marxian fashion that they are prepared to give the guarantees that private foreign investors usually require, such as tax exemption for the first years, tariff protection for the young industries, and fair compensation in case of later nationalization. To the extent that the private sector of the economy is

---

[48] Eugene Staley, *The Future of Underdeveloped Countries*, p. 239.

encouraged and broadened, it may also produce needed native entrepreneurs. Men must first, however, see that efforts will be rewarded and that opportunities for economic and social advancement do exist. The ambitious young men, once attracted to the military, will then also be attracted to business. If the private sector remained restricted, trained and talented civil servants would be needed to operate the large-scale industries. There is no reason why in these circumstances the same ability cannot be discovered in, or shifted to, the private sector once opportunities in business broaden and the status of business rises to or beyond that of government service. What is particularly needed is an extensive training program. "Private enterprise fails to function effectively in most underdeveloped countries not so much because it is repressed or interfered with as because it does not yet exist in the modern sense in which Americans automatically think of it. The problem is not merely to 'release' it but to cultivate it."[49]

The significance of developing a large private sector, then, is not primarily economic, but political and social. For it will result in the rise of various nationwide business interest groups and professional organizations—lawyers, accountants, etc.—who will express themselves politically. The reason for training trade-union leaders is the same expectation that the workers will express their grievances and aspirations through political channels. The point is not whether one is for or against business or labor or agriculture. The point is the necessity to broaden the base of political power—or, more specifically, to include more people in the processes of government and to achieve a greater diffusion of political and economic power in the society. And this can occur only

> . . . when more people outside the hitherto privileged groups acquire the means of making their influence felt in government, in economic affairs, and in society generally. These means include education, energy (health), skills, money, experience in management or group leadership, self-confidence, initiative, and some degree of economic independence (in the sense of not being completely dependent for the opportunity to make a living on the will of a landowner, or the group in control of the government, or any particular employer) . . . all who favor the democratic path to development should prefer, on political and social grounds, types of economic development that tend to diffuse skills, opportunities, wealth, initiative, self-confidence—and therefore political power—more widely. This is a necessary part of the process of building an economic and social base on which responsible, democratic citizenship can rest.
>
> The same idea is often expressed by saying that it is necessary to develop a "middle class." . . . Broadening the bases of political power also means lowering the barriers of custom, caste, and prejudice and the barriers of educational and economic opportunity which prevent talented individuals from working their way upward into the elite, that is, into positions of lead-

[49] *Ibid.*

ership. There must also be *different*, though overlapping elites in the major areas of social life—economic, political, educational, religious, artistic, and so on. Those who control the wealth should not also control the government and the educational system. Those who direct the police should not also direct the farms and factories and the artistic life of the country. Such a "separation of powers" distinguishes a healthy democratic society from that of some underdeveloped countries where privileges and power are concentrated in relatively few families. It also distinguishes democratic society from totalitarianisms of the left or right in which a party elite control everything.

For these political and social reasons (aside from the question of efficiency in production) it is important to encourage a wide area of private initiative and enterprise.[50]

Such developments will also produce another requirement for a democracy—an opposition party or parties. As economic development integrates all sectors of the nation and unites the people, as an intricate division of labor is created, and as new interest groups and social classes rise, political parties reflecting their needs and wants will also grow.

Perhaps, then, one-party or military governments will some day evolve into democratic, urban, industrialized nations. But, as must be clear by now, such a democratic development of the new states is by no means certain. The one-party "tutelary democracy" may remain tutelary, and the democracy may become nothing more than a façade hiding the reality of an authoritarian civilian or military regime. One result is certain, though—namely, that the bipolar age of the immediate postwar years is slowly passing. As some of the new nations who "count"—such as India, Brazil, and Nigeria—slowly modernize and become major powers, the world will become increasingly pluralistic. Indeed, this trend away from bipolarity to pluralism in the state system began *within* the two Cold War blocs. The French challenge of the United States in NATO and the Chinese Communist challenge of the Soviet leadership of the Communist bloc during the late 1950's signaled the end of the "good old days," when America and Russia reigned virtually supreme within their respective alliances.

[50] *Ibid.*, pp. 223–24. On the role of private enterprise in India, see, for example, John P. Lewis, *Quiet Crisis in India* (New York: Doubleday and Co., 1964), pp. 219–49.

VIII

The Rise of Europe
as the Third Superpower

The Recovery of Postwar Europe

Western Europe's growing assertion of political independence of the United States by the early 1960's was, ironically, a tribute to the success of American foreign policy in helping to rebuild the nations of the Old World. In the immediate years after the defeat of Germany, few would have prophesied that in less than two decades Europe would not only have regained, but surpassed, her prewar economic strength and political vigor. For two long world wars between 1914 and 1945—a period some referred to as the "Second Thirty Years' War"—had drained her of all her energies. History, it seemed, had written *finis* to Europe's glorious and long dominant role on the world stage. She had had "a bellyful of history."[1]

Twice already during this century, Britain's growing weakness had compelled the United States to intervene in Europe's wars in order to preserve the European equilibrium. For without the counterweight of American power, Germany would undoubtedly have emerged as the master of the Continent, if not as the victor. She would then have been in a good position to defeat England, and since it was the British Navy that guarded the Atlantic approaches to the Western Hemisphere, U.S. security would then have been jeopardized. During most of the nineteenth century, Britain had successfully maintained the European bal-

[1] Theodore H. White, *Fire in the Ashes*, p. 10.

ance. She had fought Napoleon for twenty-five years to prevent his dominion of Europe. She had opposed the ambitions and pretensions of the Holy Alliance. Only from 1870 to 1890 had Britain neglected Europe, paying principal attention to Asia and Africa; she was able to do this because Bismarck was committed to the European *status quo*. After Bismarck's fall, however, British attention became focused once more on Europe as Germany began to view her neighbors with increasing ambition.

Thus, following World War II, Britain's responsibility for securing the European balance was transferred across the Atlantic to the United States. Britain had long protected the United States; indeed, British power had allowed the infant country to grow to maturity and full strength. It was now America's turn to protect Britain and Western Europe in their hour of desolation and need—and for the sake of her own security.

For Europe's and America's security were inextricably intertwined, even in the age of the atom bomb and long-range bombers. Soviet troops could not be allowed to march to the English Channel or sail across it. If Europe had been permitted to fall under Soviet domination, almost the entire Eurasian continent would have been under Communist control after Chiang Kai-shek's defeat by the Chinese Communists in 1949. The new nations of the Middle East and Africa would not under these circumstances have been able to maintain their independence. The Western Hemisphere would have been isolated as a single "island" floating in a Communist sea. Democracy, extinguished in Europe, would have had great difficulty surviving in the United States; only as a "garrison state," with all men, women, and resources organized to provide the nation with a maximum of military strength, could the United States temporarily have staved off her slow strangulation. Thus, America had to defend postwar Europe not only to ensure her security as a nation, but also to keep democracy alive.

In 1949, therefore, the United States established the North Atlantic Treaty Organization and extended its protection to Belgium, Canada, Denmark, France, Great Britain, Iceland, Italy, Luxembourg, the Netherlands, Norway, and Portugal. The principal means of protection—often referred to as NATO's "sword"—was SAC. And to ensure that the Soviets would be left in no doubt that the United States meant what she said—that she would defend the nations of Europe—several American divisions were sent to the Continent in 1950 to beef up the occupation troops in Germany. If the Russians attacked, they would then face American forces, which would ensure a retaliatory American atomic attack on Russia. The American land forces, part of a larger force composed of contingents from other NATO countries, thus served the function of a "trip wire." They also served as a "shield" whose purpose was to hold the

Red Army at the point of attack, the Elbe River, while SAC pounded
the Soviet Union into submission, if not nonexistence. The Red Army
could not be allowed to advance. The Europeans wanted no part of a
strategy that called for a withdrawal—for instance, from the West German plains to the more defensible Rhine River—and would thereby
bring the Soviets to their frontiers, or even into their countries. They had
no desire to suffer Communist invasion and occupation while the United
States conducted an air war against the Soviet Union. A "forward strategy" was thus a political necessity.

But it was in the economic area that American policy was particularly
imaginative. Defense policies were intended to protect Europe until she
could look after her own security. The prerequisite for this, however, was
Europe's economic recovery. For what remained at war's end was a badly
battered and destroyed Europe:

> . . . a curiosity unique in all time. Here was a community of 300,000,000
> men who had developed a civilization so unbalanced that they could not
> possibly survive as a civilization on their own resources. The vital margin
> of their food supply, almost all the fibers they used to clothe themselves,
> the tea at breakfast, the evening coffee, rubber sheathing and copper wires,
> liquid fuels—all of these products that Europeans not only enjoyed but
> could not live without came from overseas on the cycling tides of trade.
> . . . For a century the community had unthinkingly relied on invisible
> strands of trade which brought these necessities to the home ports in return
> for what Europe could ship out; these strands had seemed once as rugged
> and strong as bonds of iron. Now they were cut. With the strands cut, Eu-
> rope threatened to sink, or rather to plummet, directly out of modern
> civilization.[2]

England, for example, depended on international trade for her livelihood.
Fewer than 5 per cent of her population were engaged in agriculture,
which meant that she had to import much of her food. Before World
War II, she had bought 55 per cent of her meat, 75 per cent of her
wheat, 85 per cent of her butter, all her tea, cocoa, and coffee, and 75
per cent of her sugar. Except for coal, Britain also had to import most of
the raw materials needed by her industries: cotton, rubber, wool, iron
ore, timber, and the oil she was becoming increasingly dependent upon
for the fueling of her factories.

The problem was how Europe could pay for the food and raw materials she needed for her recovery and reconstruction. There were basically
three ways for the European nations to earn the money: first, they could
export; second, they could provide services such as shipping; and third,
they could use the interest payments on their foreign investments. The
trouble was that none of these traditional means could be used extensively in the late 1940's. Many of Europe's factories lay in ruins, and

[2] *Ibid.*, pp. 46–47.

much of the remaining machinery in the factories still standing was obsolescent. Many of Europe's prewar customers had, during the war, either started to produce those goods they had previously imported from Europe for themselves, or found an alternative and generally cheaper source of supply in the United States. Europe's merchant fleet had been largely sunk and destroyed. And her overseas investments had been either heavily reduced or liquidated in paying for two world wars. On top of all this, the empires the Europeans had once held began to disintegrate. One of the results was that the new emerging nations, with their desire to industrialize, began to compete with their former rulers for the same resources, thereby further raising the prices of the goods the Europeans needed. In short, the Europeans were basically in a position of being unable to earn sufficient funds, particularly in dollars, to buy the commodities they needed for their recovery. There was little chance of competing extensively against mass-produced American goods. Yet the United States possessed most of the items Europe needed for her reconstruction—wheat, cotton, sulphur, sugar, machinery, trucks, and coal. At the same time, the United States was so well supplied with everything that she had little need to buy much from abroad. Europe was therefore confronted with an ominous "dollar gap"—and her fate seemed to be hunger and cold and loss of hope.

The American response was both generous and self-interested. Under the Marshall Plan, Europe was granted a massive program of economic aid. As the doctor to an economically sick Europe, the United States prescribed a $17 billion injection as the main part of the cure (the patient recovered with $12 billion). Only in this manner could Europe restore, and even surpass, her prewar agricultural and industrial production, earn her way in the world, and regain her political vitality and military strength. Most significant, American aid was made conditional upon economic cooperation among the European states. In this respect, the United States clearly held herself up as a model for the Europeans. The Economic Cooperation Act of 1948 called specifically for European economic integration, which was considered both the prerequisite for Europe's recovery and the necessary basis for Europe's long-range economic prosperity. It is not difficult to see why American policy-makers, with their belief in low-cost mass production, should have felt that Europe's economic recovery and health depended on the creation of a mass market. For decades, the European nations, living together on a continent one-fourth the size of the United States, had divided their markets from one another with tariff walls, quota systems, and import and export licenses. By this means, manufacturers assured themselves of the lion's share of their national markets. Sheltered from external competition, they had little incentive to modernize their equipment or techniques, for they minimized domestic competition by dividing their relatively small domestic markets among themselves. The different sectors of the national economies were thus controlled by monopolies. Furthermore, many of these firms, particularly in France, were small family-owned and managed businesses which were, on the whole, economically inefficient. Nevertheless, the American pressure for European economic integration was not aimed primarily at converting Europe to mass production and economic efficiency. Its chief purpose was to create a politically unified and militarily powerful Europe which, combined with American strength within the NATO framework, could contain Soviet expansionist pressure. By launching this experiment in supranation-building, the United States may have initiated a new revolution; for if the experiment should prove successful, this attempt to integrate nation-states into a larger "security community"[3] may become the example for other nations to follow as they someday become pluralistic and industrialized societies with compatible value systems.

In Europe, in any case, France quickly realized the benefits of European integration and became its leading advocate. One reason for her advocacy was that by 1947 French expectations of keeping Germany weak had failed. As after World War I, France in 1945 had hoped to forestall another revival of German power by such measures as detaching the Ruhr and Rhine provinces, imposing heavy reparations, and controlling German industrial production. But the French found little support for their policy. As the Cold War grew more intense, the Soviet Union—to whom a policy of dismembering Germany might otherwise have been appealing—presented itself as the champion of German unification. So did the United States. Each of the two superpowers hoped that someday a united and powerful Germany might be on *its* side. Therefore the United States was not favorably disposed toward exacting reparations or limiting production—which would also have been incompatible with the objective of restoring Western Europe's economy, of which West Germany's economy was an integral part. What was needed was stimulation, not economic bleeding. There was little point in investing Marshall Plan funds in Europe, including West Germany, if France was going to drain the German economy. In short, the fear of Germany's economic revival, fed by apprehensions of renewed German power, did not last beyond the onset of the Soviet threat to European and American security.

The rebirth of West German power was naturally not a welcome prospect to a nation that had fought three wars against Germany in seventy years—and been defeated twice by her. Battered as she was, West Germany remained potentially stronger than France. What, then, could France do? How could West Germany—Europe's greatest potential power next to the Soviet Union—be held in check? In the nineteenth

[3] Karl W. Deutsch *et al.*, *Political Community and the North Atlantic Area.*

century, after Germany's unification, France had formed alliances with Germany's neighbors. Before World War I, the ally had been Russia, and between the two wars she had found partners in Poland, Czechoslovakia, Romania, and Yugoslavia. None of these alliances had saved France, however; in both wars, British and American power had been the decisive factors in defeating Germany (and, of course, Russian power in World War II). But once saved, the French again responded in terms of their traditional reflex—despite the extension of Soviet power into the heart of Europe. For France, Germany was still *the* enemy, and in December, 1944, the French signed a Treaty of Mutual Assistance with the Russians, thus forming an alliance they considered a prerequisite for France's security. (Britain also signed such a treaty.) Soviet hostility soon disillusioned the French and deprived the treaty of any meaning, however, and made it necessary in fact to add Germany's power to that of the West.

The failure of the traditional balance-of-power technique, by which an inferior power had generally sought to balance a stronger nation, led France to seek a new way of exerting some control over Germany's growing power. French statesmen found a novel means in European integration. It was through the creation of a supranational community, to which Germany would transfer certain sovereign rights, that German power could be controlled. Only in this manner could German strength be prevented from again causing harm to all of Europe, and simultaneously be employed for Europe's welfare and security.

Another reason why they supported European integration was that the French also quickly realized that small nations—and even nations the size of France or West Germany were small nations after 1945—could no longer play an important role in world affairs. Rather, they would become virtually completely dependent upon their protecting superpower, with a status less that of allies than of wards. It was the superpower that possessed the real power and responsibility and, in the final analysis, that defined *their* interests as well. If it decided, for example, to rearm West Germany—as the United States did after the Korean War erupted—that became allied policy. If France or any other country objected—and virtually every one of our European allies did—there was little they could do. They could, to be sure, scream in anger and thereby delay the "inevitable." But in the end they would have no choice but to accept Washington's policy decision.

The French were particularly conscious of their "satellite" status. Britain, with her linguistic and cultural ties to the United States, as well as the recent close wartime cooperation, felt it less keenly. The special relationship between the two English-speaking peoples—from frequent consultations on foreign policy to American help in developing a British atomic bomb—served Britain as a psychological buffer against the realization that her days as a great and independent power were past. Her appearance as a major world power was further bolstered by her leadership of the Commonwealth. Not until the Suez invasion did the British fully realize how complete was their reliance on American support; without it she could not even defeat Egypt. Before 1956, Britain could therefore simply postpone what France went through in the late 1940's —a reassessment of her role in Europe.[4] Until that year Britain never seriously confronted the basic question of whether she could continue to isolate herself from the Continental integration into a larger and more powerful community that would some day rival the United States and the Soviet Union. For the French, by contrast, their lack of importance within NATO was further emphasized by the resurgence of West Germany. The latter's recovery would only reinforce France's subordinate status within the Western alliance. For Washington would undoubtedly pay more attention to Bonn than to Paris since West Germany was the stronger of the two powers. Thus France would find herself well behind Britain and West Germany, and just a step ahead of Italy and the small Low Countries. On the other hand, a united Europe based upon Franco-German reconciliation and unity was an alternative to remaining subservient to the United States and without influence either in NATO or on the world stage. It was the means by which France could gain sufficient strength to acquire an equal voice with the "Anglo-Saxons" in NATO and the nations of Europe could re-exert their prestige and influence in the postwar age of superpowers. In short, an anti-American bias was present from the very beginning of the movement to create a United States of Europe.

The Atlantic Alliance is imposed upon Western Europe by factors outside its control. This circumstance is the major obstacle to harmonious relations between the United States and the principal European nations, who until lately were masters of their destiny and free to contract whatever alliances they considered suitable. In the measure that these nations . . . retain memories of this recent past, they are bound to view the United States as a temporary overlord, whose sudden elevation to the rank of *primus inter pares* corresponds neither to innate virtues nor to the long-range interests of the Western world as a whole. . . . If the U.S.S.R. ceased to appear as a constant threat to the independent existence of all European countries and their democratic freedoms, it is fairly certain that this underlying impatience would soon translate itself into a determination to have done with

[4] French and British foreign policies seemed almost reversed. French policy in Europe was highly imaginative while in the French colonies it was almost reactionary, seeking to hold overseas territories even at the cost of long, bloody, expensive—and, in the end, unwinnable—guerrilla wars. British policy, in contrast, was shortsighted in Europe, with its view of the Channel as an ocean barrier, while in the Empire it was imaginative and flexible. It is a tribute to Britain that most of her colonies stayed within the Commonwealth, although the Commonwealth by the late 1950's was of declining importance to Britain.

America's physical presence in Europe. Conversely, the certainty that Soviet pressure is likely to endure, probably for a generation, helps to cement the Alliance, but also tends to make Europeans more conscious of the need to attain a greater measure of political unity among themselves.[5]

European Economic Integration and Supranation-Building

But how could this unity be achieved? The French rejected the most obvious approach—the idealistic appeal. They were well aware that the Little Europe—the Europe of the Inner Six (France, West Germany, Italy, and the Benelux countries)—which they were seeking to build could not be constructed solely upon a vision of a united Europe. Even such a vision would not fire imaginations to the degree that nations would suddenly discard their nationalism for a wider European allegiance. The only sure basis, according to Jean Monnet, the French master planner of the New Europe, would be individual and group "self-interest." There had to be "something in it for everyone." European integration had therefore to be built upon an economic foundation. The principal instrument of economic action was the elimination of all trade barriers, import quotas, and other restrictions between the participating nations, and the formation of a single Common Market among them. Industry would then have a potential market of more than 150 million people. Efficient and energetic enterprises presumably would expand and modernize their plants to take advantage of this enlarged market. By the same token, inefficient plants unable to compete—and unwilling to make the effort—would be closed. But business in general would profit —and thus European integration would be in its interest. Labor would acquire a similar stake in this New Europe as production rose and the level of employment and real wages followed suit. To be sure, workers in the more inefficient industries would lose their jobs, and they might have to be moved to other areas in search of new employment. But generally, the Common Market would produce more jobs. The consumer would also benefit from the expanding economy. As he saw national economic barriers tumbling and witnessed industry increasingly converting to the principles of mass production—large-scale production at reasonable cost and sufficiently high wages so that the consumer could buy in volume—he, too, would recognize the pocketbook advantages of the Common Market. Political integration was thus a continuing process that depended for its realization upon the interest calculations of the participating groups and individuals in a pluralistic society.[6]

The French shrewdly chose to approach the question of integration step by step. Rather than attempting immediate integration of the en-

---

[5] George Lichtheim, *The New Europe*, p. 217.
[6] Ernst B. Haas, *The Uniting of Europe*, p. 13.

tire economy—which would have been politically impossible to implement—they selected the coal and steel sector. In 1950, Foreign Minister
Robert Schuman proposed that the Six, Little Europe, pool their coal and
steel industries in the European Coal and Steel Community. The Schuman Plan, as it was also known, sought first of all to interweave German
and French heavy industry to such an extent that it would become impossible to separate them. Germany would never again be able to utilize
her coal and steel industries for nationalistic and militaristic purposes.
The political and military power of the Ruhr would no longer be acces-
sible for purely German purposes. War between Germany and France
would become not only unthinkable but impossible under these circumstances. The choice of coal and steel as the sector to be integrated first
was particularly astute since it forms the basis of the entire industrial
structure. It is the one functional sector that cannot possibly be separated
from an industrial economy. The separation created by the establishment
of ECSC was therefore artificial, but it was for this very reason that it
would have an economic "spill-over" effect. ECSC would exert pressure
on the unintegrated sectors of the economy; and as the benefits of the
pooling of heavy industry became clearly observable, these sectors would
follow suit. The Coal and Steel Community was thus seen as the first
stage of an attempt to create a wider market in one particular area of the
economy. It was expected that this approach would be gradually extended to other functional areas of the economy, such as agriculture,
transportation, and electricity, with the eventual creation of a federal
European state with a huge market and a highly developed mass-produc-
tion system.

This was, of course, precisely what occurred in 1958 when the Six
established the European Economic Community, or the Common Market. Their aim was the formation of an economic union over a twelve-to-
fifteen-year period. During this time, all tariffs, quotas, and other restrictions hampering trade among themselves would be completely
eliminated; in turn, they would establish a common tariff on imports
from outside the EEC. Furthermore, they would gradually abolish restrictions on the movement of labor, capital, and services within the
Community and set up three funds to help realize the Common Market.
First, there was the European Investment Bank as a supplement to private capital within each member state to make loans for the development
of backward areas, to help inefficient firms modernize to meet competition or convert to a different type of production. Second, there was the
European Social Fund, to be used for such tasks as helping any member
to meet the expenses in retraining workers for different kinds of labor,
resettling them in new areas, or, in certain instances, providing them
with unemployment benefits. The third was the Development Fund, to
be used for the economic development of the members' overseas terri-

tories, especially France's North African territories, which were also to be linked to the Common Market. Duties on imports to the Common Market from the overseas areas were to be abolished, but the territories would be allowed to charge customs duties on imports from the Six in order to gain funds for their own development.

Finally, the Six established a third community, Euratom, for the generation of industrial nuclear energy. Together, ECSC, EEC, and Euratom constituted the European Political Community.

Fundamentally, Monnet's theory of integration thus rested on Adam Smith's theory of free trade. Each nation would specialize in those commodities it could produce best, and the resulting trade would maximize consumer choice and national prosperity for all the concerned nations. It was in the results of this free trade, however, that the significant ingredients of integration were to be found. The first was the economic spill-over from one sector of the economy to another. The second, and even more important effect, was the political spill-over. If there was to be a Common Market, and it was to be more than just a customs union, there had to be a uniform set of rules to govern economic and social policies.[7] For example, if one nation should adopt a deflationary policy, its industries would be able to undersell those of its five partners and capture their markets. Clearly, this kind of development had to be guarded against. Or, if a nation, while abolishing its tariffs for a specific industry, then subsidized that industry's production or imposed an internal tax on competitive foreign goods, it would gain an obvious advantage for its own industry. Such discrimination by a government therefore had to be forbidden. Uniform rules could not be established, however, simply by preventing deviant behavior; they required affirmative action. Since prices reflect production costs, which in turn reflect (in part) national regulation of wages, hours, working conditions, and social welfare programs, the industries of a nation with lower standards would possess a major advantage over competitors in the neighboring states. A single set of standards in such areas as minimum wages, maximum hours, and welfare programs was thus a necessity. In addition, since workers would be able to move from one country to another in their search for employment and better jobs, there had to be a single social-security program for all six nations. If labor was to be mobile, its welfare programs had to be Community-wide.

Furthermore, as the economies became increasingly integrated, other problems would arise. What would happen if one nation should experience a major recession? Would a program limited to that country alone

---

[7] The best analysis of the harmonization of national policies may be found in Michael Shanks and John Lambert, *The Common Market Today—and Tomorrow*, pp. 56–105; see also Emile Benoit, *Europe at Sixes and Sevens*, pp. 28–66; and U. W. Kitzinger, *The Politics and Economics of European Integration*, pp. 21–59.

remedy the situation, or would a Community-wide program have to be instituted? The answer, again, was clear. If Texas suffered a serious economic crisis, it would not be able to resolve the problem alone, since Texas industry is part of a nationwide industrial structure; the remedy would thus have to be nationwide. Similarly, the Common Market would be compelled to take Community-wide action to stabilize the business cycle. In the long run, the Six would also no doubt have to create a single banking system with a common currency.

In any case, the significant point is that just as national policies in the United States required central decision-making, so the increasing need to harmonize the social and economic policies of the Six would demand a single center for policy formulation in Continental Europe. Common policies would require common institutions with supranational authority (which "starts to come into play when a state agrees that it is willing to carry out decisions to which it is itself opposed. Most obviously, such a situation arises when it has agreed to be outvoted if necessary by other states—either by a simple or by some weighted or qualified majority"[8]). Such institutions would, moreover, play a central role in furthering the larger political community.

> If economic integration merely implied the removal of barriers to trade and fails to be accompanied by new centrally made fiscal, labor, welfare, and investment measures, the relation to political integration is not established. If, however, the integration of a specific section (e.g., coal and steel), or of economics generally (e.g., the "General Common Market") goes hand in hand with the gradual extension of the scope of central decision-making to take in economic pursuits not initially "federated," the relation to the growth of political community is clear.[9]

In a developed economy, those whose interests were affected by the decision-making institution, adversely or otherwise, would organize to lobby at the supranational level in order to influence particular decisions. Again, one is reminded of the United States, where various interests lobby at the state level and especially at the national level. Whenever the Federal Government becomes involved in new areas of policy-making, such groups seek to influence its decisions—in the formulation of policy, as well as in the legislative and executive stages. For in a free, pluralistic society, interest groups and political parties (as aggregates of interest groups) will normally tend to act at whatever level of government important political policies are decided. It was this interaction between the decision-making institution and the lobbying of the multitude of interest groups, then, that was of vital importance to the integration of the Six.[10]

All three European associations—ECSC, EEC, and Euratom—possess

[8] Kitzinger, *op. cit.*, pp. 60–61.
[9] Haas, *op. cit.*, pp. 12–13.
[10] *Ibid.*, p. xiii.

such supranational institutions. Each has an executive—called, respectively, the High Authority, the European Economic Commission, and the Euratom Commission. The members of the executive, although chosen by the governments of the member states—no more than two members can be of the same nationality—are independent of their control. The governments can refuse to re-appoint a man after his term of service has expired, but they cannot dismiss him during his tenure. Collectively, each executive is responsible to the European Parliament, which is composed of members of the Six's national parliaments. All parties except the Communist Party are represented in proportion to their strength in those bodies. Moreover, as it has happened, members of the same or similar parties tend to sit together, regardless of their nationality. Voting patterns, too, have developed according to party rather than national origin. The High Authority must submit an annual report to the Parliament, and a two-thirds vote of censure can force the Authority to resign. The two Commissions could also be censured and compelled to resign. But this is not likely to occur often, if ever. The influence of Parliament rests primarily on moral suasion and on public opinion within the Six. The third supranational organ is the Court of Justice, which, acting as a kind of constitutional court, adjudicates disputes that arise over the meaning of the three Community Treaties and ensures that the organs of the Communities do not exceed the authority granted to them by the Treaties.

Finally, the High Authority has two committees which act in an advisory capacity: the Consultative Committee and the Economic and Social Committee. The latter is of special importance since it is composed of "representatives of producers, farmers, transport operators, workers, merchants, artisans, the professions, and representatives of the general interest." Between these interests

> a tripartite division was agreed upon in practice whereby the trade unions, the employers, and the rest of the community are each assigned a third of seats: Each of these thirds is then split up among different organizations in each sector, after elaborate calculations and consultations. In fact, the interest groups have been taking the Committee so seriously that some three-quarters of its members are the general secretaries or the chairmen of the national trade-union councils, employers' federations, and other professional associations. . . . The Rome Treaties frequently stipulate that the Committee must be consulted before a decision is reached. . . . In fact, the Commission and Council have repeatedly thought it politically advisable to consult the Committee even where the Treaty does not oblige them to do so, as in the case of restrictive business practices and the common commercial policy.
>
> It has indeed been argued that the Economic and Social Committee, representing the interest groups, has a greater influence on the details of economic and social policy than the Parliamentary Assembly, representing

political parties, can exert. If this is so, it is due not least to the positions and influence of its members back home and to the expert knowledge which they have or on which they can draw through their organizations. The Economic and Social Committee thus constitutes an institutionaliza- tion of the two-way flow of information and views between the Commis- sions and the interest groups. These groups are in fact more and more forming committees on a European basis, working out their Community policy, opening offices in Brussels (unless, like the free trade unions, they had them there already), and lobbying the Commission as they would a national government.[11]

None of these European institutions, however, is yet so completely supranational as might appear. In each Community, the executive co- operates closely with the Council of Ministers representing the national governments. The relationship between ECSC's High Authority and the Council is, to be sure, somewhat different from that between the EEC Commission and the Council. In the former, the High Authority was to be the leader. Although the Authority's jurisdiction was carefully con- fined to its particular sector of the economy, it was quite strong within this sector, being empowered to tax, to abolish monopolistic arrange- ments, to eliminate all quotas and tariffs, and to suppress subsidies and discriminatory pricing practices and transportation rates. The Author- ity's directives were to be binding on both states and private enterprises; it could fine business firms for violations and call upon member states to enforce its orders. The Authority was thus not merely an executive agency, but—like the American Presidency—an executive and legislative agency. It was not merely to administer policy; it was also to formulate that policy. And the European Parliament, rather than serving as a legis- lative organ, had as its principal function to hold the Authority respon- sible. In short, the Authority was to have the power of initiative, decision, and execution. On the other hand, within EEC, the Council of Ministers was to be the decision-maker. The Commission would formulate pro- posals and execute the policy, but the decision whether to adopt these proposals or not belonged to the Council as the *de facto* legislative organ of the Community. The Parliament in this instance therefore controls only the institution that draws up policy and implements it, but not the actual decision-making authority.[12] This separation of executive and legis- lative functions in EEC thus does not allow even theoretical parliamen- tary control.

These executive-Council relationships are more the formal than the actual ones, though before taking action, the High Authority has gen- erally consulted the Council of Ministers and, through them, the na- tional governments of the Six. It has not actively sought to accelerate

11 Kitzinger, *op. cit.*, pp. 83–84.
12 *Ibid.*, pp. 68–69.

the spill-over effect because it has been unwilling to risk governmental opposition by taking the leadership in speeding the integrative process. Yet, considering that Europe is still in its early phase, this cautious role is probably wiser than it is harmful for the future strengthening of the supranational institutions. It may well be the path of virtue to make haste slowly, to consult the governments along the way rather than offend them or arouse their opposition by taking an energetic role, which might jeopardize the future development of integration. By contrast, in the EEC, the Council may make the decisions, but it does not choose the agenda. Both the agenda and the proposals submitted to it are drawn up by the Commission, which views matters not in terms of national interests but in terms of the Community interests of all the members. The Council, moreover, can only accept or reject these proposals: It cannot modify them, except by unanimous vote. The initiative is thus held by the supranational organ, and it does therefore control a high degree of legislative authority. By the same token, the Council does *not* compromise different national interests. Rather, it must argue with a solution proposed for the common good of the entire Community.

This last point is most significant. The three Community institutions, rather than being either completely supranational or subordinate to national governments, actually stand somewhere between the federal and national levels. Policy results from executive-Council interactions, since the two are interdependent. The Council, composed of representatives from the various national governments, is theoretically either the watchdog or the formal decision-maker. Obviously, it appears to be a brake to restrain the supranational institutions. Yet, the Council acts virtually as if it were an organ of the Commission. Its decision-making process is essentially different from traditional diplomatic bargaining because the member nations generally feel—at least they did before De Gaulle—committed to the process of integration. They are "engaged."[13] Thus they begin their considerations on the basis of drafts prepared by the Commission. Consequently, even if at times one government, for instance, disagrees with a majority decision, it will in all likelihood usually accept the decision. For it shares with its partners the desire for success in their goal of a fully integrated Common Market. It could, of course, oppose the wishes and interests of its partners, but this would tend to isolate it and expose it as "anti-European" (as De Gaulle's France was considered in the mid-1960's—and only a De Gaulle could really have survived the resulting reputation for being "against progress"). Conversely, the majority will not impose its decision on the dissenting country, for each

[13] "The concept of 'engagement' postulates that if parties to a conference enjoy a specific and well-articulated sense of participation, if they identify themselves completely with the procedures and codes within which their decisions are made, they consider themselves completely 'engaged' by the results even if they do not fully concur in them." (Haas, *op. cit.*, pp. 522–23.)

member state realizes that someday it may be in this minority position. Consequently, both sides will seek a decision acceptable to all. Thus the spill-over has affected the Council of Ministers—just as it has the interest groups.

There are plans for the further consolidation of this institutional framework.[14] The first is to triple the size of the present Parliament to more than 400 members, two-thirds of whom would be elected by universal suffrage, with all citizens over twenty-one eligible to vote. The other one-third would temporarily continue to be elected by the national parliaments, but after a transitional period, all members of the European Parliament would be elected. This development would clearly give the Parliament real authority. As a popularly elected assembly, it could demand the right to exercise budgetary control over the three Communities; the right to have a voice in appointing individual members to the executives, rather than just the power to dismiss them collectively; and the right to introduce legislation. A second proposal is the fusion of the High Authority and the two Commissions into a single High Commission, slated someday to develop into a federal cabinet. In the meantime, its status as the one and only "federal" executive would probably enhance its prestige and popular support.

If these plans are ever realized, it will be clear that the New Europe will have been built on a solid foundation. But in the long run, the self-interest of the various groups will not suffice. A truly federal Europe must have popular support. The spill-over is supposed to achieve this as well.

As the process of integration proceeds, it is assumed that values will undergo change, that interests will be redefined in terms of a regional rather than a purely national orientation and that the erstwhile set of separate national group values will gradually be superseded by a new and geographically larger set of beliefs. . . .

As the beliefs and aspirations of groups undergo change due to the necessity of working in a transnational institutional framework, mergers in values and doctrine are expected to come about, uniting groups across former frontiers. The expected overlapping of these group aspirations is finally thought to result in an accepted body of "national" doctrine, in effect heralding the advent of a new nationalism. Implied in this development, of course, is a proportional diminution of loyalty to and expectations from the former separate national governments. Shifts in the focus of loyalty need not necessarily imply the immediate repudiation of the national state or government. Multiple loyalties have been empirically demonstrated to exist. . . .

New loyalties may come into existence as end values, i.e., the new order is desired as an end in itself. Secondly, new loyalties may develop merely

[14] Kitzinger, *op. cit.*, pp. 88–96.

in response to a pressure for conformity exercised by the new center of power. Thirdly—and most importantly for the study of political integration in a framework of consensus—new loyalties are thought to grow haphazardly in their function as intermediary means to some ultimate end, perhaps the same end also fought for in the context of the established national loyalties. Groups and individuals uncertain of their ability to realize political or economic values in the national framework may thus turn to supranational agencies and procedures, without being attracted by "Europeanism" as such.[15]

The three Communities are thus the means to realize a United States of Europe. Based upon "the logic of integration," EEC is designed to develop through three stages: the first stage was a customs union; the second an economic union; and the final stage will be the political union. Yet the "logic of integration" has underestimated one factor—the degree of *political will* required if the spill-over is to occur from the economic into the political realm. ECSC, EEC, and Euratom are, after all, the deliberate creations of the Six. The very procedure by which the Council of Ministers reaches decisions is less a testimony to the impact of the spill-over than to the prior political decision made by the Six to integrate politically. The spill-over, in brief, is not so much cause as it is effect.

Some theists have envisaged a world living under its own laws—those of physics and those of men—once God had given the push that set the world on its course. Political integration is not so cosmically self-generating. What launched the European integration movement was neither the common climate nor the common ideological and social structure, but the initiative of political leaders (Schuman, Adenauer, de Gasperi) at a time when the Western European political constellation was unique. And what governments have done they can still undo or at least twist or halt. Consequently, any theory that exaggerates the "automaticity" of the spill-over process in integration must be rejected. As long as the process is not completed, we must analyze the building of the political community both as an *incipient* instance of "interest group politics," of "domestic politics of the community," and as a *continuing* example of traditional interstate politics.[16]

It was President de Gaulle who was determined that the European construction that occurred would be a "continuing example of traditional interstate politics." His conception of Europe was that of an association of states—a "Europe of fatherlands." He proposed that the Six extend the scope of their cooperation to foreign affairs and defense via inter-

[15] Haas, *op. cit.*, pp. 13–14.
[16] Stanley Hoffmann, "Discord in Community: The North Atlantic Area as a Partial International System," in Francis O. Wilcox and H. Field Haviland, Jr. (eds.), *The Atlantic Community*, p. 11. See also Raymond Aron, "Old Nations, New Europe," *Daedalus*, Winter, 1964, pp. 54–55.

governmental organs. The heads of state or governments should meet regularly to discuss these, as well as cultural and economic issues. In this way, all states would retain their particular identities. What was clear from De Gaulle's opposition to an integrated Europe was that the transition from several nation-states to a single European state could result only from an act of political will by all participating members. Such a qualitative political transition could not be produced by the mere quantitative growth of economic agencies. The contrary belief was the offspring of two fundamental functionalist assumptions: first, that economic and social matters could be separated from political problems; and second, that cooperation could be transferred from the former area to the political level. De Gaulle effectively demonstrated the weakness of these assumptions. On the other hand, a unified Europe cannot be built without the common material base that the functionalists have supplied; political will alone is not enough. The question that, of course, remained unsettled is what kind of Europe—federal or confederal—would be erected upon this base.

One thing did, however, seem certain—namely, that this "New Europe" would assert itself against the United States:

> Some strain on Atlantic solidarity was almost inevitable as a result of any progress toward European political unity. After all, what the "Europeans" are engaged in is an attempt at "nation-building," though in this instance on a scale transcending the boundaries of the old nation-states which, if the "Europeans" and their American backers have their way, are eventually to merge into a single sovereign federal unit. The strongest motivation for such an attempt is the desire to overcome compartmentalization, considered to be the source of European impotence in a world of continental superpowers. Without a considerable dose of European "nationalism" to accompany and assist the birth of a new "nation" called Europe, the chances of overcoming the deep-seated primary loyalties to the traditional nations would be slim indeed. Yet, it would run counter to historical experience if such "nationalism" did not presuppose and stimulate a spirit of "national" pride and self-assertion as well as some antagonism against outsiders. How are Germans, Italians, Frenchmen, and others to come to identify themselves with a "nation" embracing them all except by becoming aware of what they have in common and wherein their interests differ from those of others? Some may have hoped that the Soviet Union would become the target of such "Europeanism" rather than the United States. If this is not happening, it is because, in their confrontation with the Soviets, the Europeans cannot identify themselves with the larger Atlantic Community and defense system. The only way to make themselves conscious of their special European destiny is, therefore, to set themselves off against their ally, the United States.[17]

[17] Arnold Wolfers, "Integration in the West: The Conflict of Perspectives," in Wilcox and Haviland (eds.), *op. cit.*, pp. 244–45.

Nuclear Diffusion and NATO Dissension

When the Marshall Plan was launched and the NATO alliance formed, the European states were weak and exhausted. The transatlantic "harmony" and NATO "unity" of the first few years were therefore based on an unequal power relationship. The nations of Europe were America's friends; they were also her client states. They had little choice but to acquiesce in the general outlines of American foreign policy, even where they disagreed. Therefore, while there was frequently genuine harmony and unity, what often passed for that was actually acquiescence and grudging acceptance.[18] As by far the strongest NATO power, the United States had to exercise her leadership, of course; no one else in the alliance could. Her European allies, once mighty, no longer had the power to lead.

> For Europeans the signing of the Atlantic treaty was a moment not of pride but of resignation. They were quite aware that the alliance was not a partnership of equals, but a covenant by which the powerful agreed to defend the weak. And, as Machiavelli had recognized four centuries earlier in warning weak nations against signing alliances with strong ones except by necessity, there can be no equality among those who are unequal in power. . . . We learned to take this dependence for granted without ever testing its assumptions or questioning its abnormality. . . . It came to seem perfectly proper that American strategists should have sole responsibility for the way in which Europe would be defended, and that the political future of Europe should be decided in Washington.[19]

But it was only a question of time before we could expect to face the rebellion of Europe. It was in the nature of things that the states of Europe would again seek to play a major role in the world as they regained their great-power status. De Gaulle's assertive posture toward the United States is in this sense primarily an expression of confidence in a Europe that will again someday be the master of its own destiny: "In his exasperating arrogance he has become a self-appointed spokesman for the new nationalism that has come in the wake of European union."[20]

More specifically, Europe's demand for equality meant first of all that it would no longer allow itself to be treated as a satellite. Somewhat ironically, it was America's closest ally, Britain, that was subjected to the most humiliating treatment, in 1962; and because of the "special relationship" existing between the two English-speaking peoples, the exam-

---

[18] This point, generally glossed over in all talk of the harmony of the alliance, the spirit of unity, and the formally acknowledged equality, is well made by Ronald Steel in *The End of Alliance*; see especially pp. 10–14, 80–82.

[19] *Ibid.*, p. 30.

[20] *Ibid.*

ple was the more vivid and the lesson the clearer. For a number of reasons—prestige among others—Britain had maintained an independent national deterrent, and thus continued to believe in her great-power status. Her 170-odd bombers at least permitted the appearance of that status, if not perhaps its substance. At the same time, though, the British found it increasingly prohibitive to keep up with evolving nuclear technology in the key item, the delivery system. In 1957, they began to develop their own missile, the Blue Streak, but it proved too burdensome economically and was therefore scrapped in 1960. Instead, the British decided to buy the Skybolt air-to-ground missile from the United States when it became available. The development of Skybolt was seen as a way of prolonging the life of Britain's bombers, because the missiles could be attached under their wings; if the bombers were unable to penetrate Soviet defenses, the Skybolts could still be shot at their targets. British prestige, and the Conservative Government's political future, therefore seemed to depend on American delivery of the Skybolt. Failure to deliver, thus eliminating Britain's national deterrent, would humiliate America's closest ally and undermine the Conservatives' self-proclaimed position as the best guardians of British security, whose voice—and therefore Britain's voice—was always listened to in the White House.

Yet, in an abrupt decision, the Kennedy Administration decided to halt the Skybolt development program because the missile had failed several tests. Further research and development was deemed too costly in terms of Skybolt's ultimate value since bombers would be increasingly phased out as they were replaced with Minutemen and Polaris missiles. However sound these reasons may have been technically, the decision clearly seemed to have been made without regard to the political impact upon the Conservative Government or British sensitivity. On the other hand, if the technical reasons were merely a disguise for a fundamental political decision to compel Britain to surrender its national deterrent (a Skybolt was successfully tested after the program's cancellation, and the Kennedy Administration's opposition to any independent allied national deterrents that it could not command and control was well known), the cancellation of Skybolt only showed more clearly the disregard with which the United States at times treated its allies. At any rate, this politically significant step had been taken without any consultation. Washington's edict was simply assumed to be law for the alliance; the United States unilaterally determined the political and military future of its partners.

Nor was Skybolt an isolated instance in which an American decision adversely affected the vital interests of its allies. Suez was an even more dramatic example. The British view was that if Egypt's Nasser was allowed to seize the Suez Canal with impunity, his action would compel other pro-Western Arab rulers to seize Western property—above all, oil wells—or risk being overthrown themselves by Nasser's followers. The British, in short, saw not only their influence but all Western influence in the Middle East at stake. But the United States, while generally agreeing with the British evaluation of Nasser's anti-Western influence and actions—and having, indeed, been at least partially responsible for Nasser's seizure of the Canal because of its withdrawal of a previous offer to help finance the Aswan Dam—refused to sanction military action. When the British and French invaded Egypt after Israel's preventive invasion, the United States opposed their action and pulled the rug out from under them by withholding alternative supplies of oil until they desisted. Whether the British and French were right or wrong in invading Egypt is debatable. What is not debatable is the general question it posed—that is, whether American policy meant that "the alliance will be expected to work in matters that the United States deems important, but not in matters that Britain and France deem important, and even perhaps vital to their existence."[21]

This is indeed the crucial question. If it is applicable to Britain, which, despite the two cited examples, has had a special relationship with the United States, it is even more to the point for the Continental nations. No longer willing to be treated as wards who have little choice but to accept the decisions of their guardian, the European states want to share in the formulation of general NATO policy and the military strategy supporting this policy. They can no longer stand by while vital decisions affecting their future are taken by Washington alone. Perhaps the most important of these since the early 1960's has concerned the problem of limited warfare in Europe. Originally, as we have seen, NATO ground forces had been assigned two functions—as "tripwire" for the SAC "sword" and as "shield" for Western Europe during the presumably short period during which SAC would atomize the Soviet Union into submission.

As the existence of a nuclear stalemate became increasingly clear in the late 1950's, however, the possibility of limited Soviet challenges in Europe suggested that the ground forces should be as ready to fight limited wars on the Continent as outside Europe.[22] And if limited-war forces were needed to avoid the dilemma of suicide or surrender in responding to such challenges, they also had to be conventionally armed. For an army equipped with tactical nuclear weapons was not thought to be a credible deterrent. In the first place, a limited war fought with tactical nuclear arms would be as devastating for Europe as would an all-out strategic nuclear war for the United States. Therefore, just as the threat

---

[21] Geoffrey Crowther, "Reconstruction of an Alliance," *Foreign Affairs*, January, 1957, pp. 180–81.

[22] Alastair Buchan, *NATO in the 1960's*, p. 35; see also Malcom W. Hoag, "The Place of Limited Warfare in NATO Strategy," in Klaus Knorr (ed.), *NATO and American Security*, pp. 98–126.

of all-out war by the United States was not a sufficient deterrent to a limited Soviet probe, the threat of fighting a tactical nuclear war might not deter the Soviets. Indeed, since they were well aware that the Europeans had no desire to see their lands laid waste for a third time, the Soviets might be tempted to attack in the gamble that America's European partners might prefer to surrender rather than commit virtual suicide. A second reason for conventional arms was that once tactical nuclear weapons were employed, the clear-cut distinction between nonnuclear and nuclear tactical arms would have been erased, and the possibility of an escalation to strategic nuclear war increased; the pressure from field commanders to use weapons of larger and larger yields would be great once the original nuclear-conventional distinctions had been eliminated.

From the American point of view—where the concern was to meet limited Soviet challenges *without* precipitating total war—this emphasis on conventionally equipped limited-war forces was, then, an arms-control measure. It permitted the NATO alliance to defend Europe—*after* a limited attack had occurred. The Continental countries were, however, less concerned with defense than deterrence.

> There is an inevitable difference of perspective between ourselves and some of our allies. If the NATO area is looked on as a unit, a strategy that exposes a limited territory to the fluctuations of conventional combat may seem eminently sensible. To the allies on whose territory such a war would be fought, however, a Soviet penetration of even a hundred miles might well spell the end of their national existence. They have compelling incentive to strive for a strategy that poses the threat of maximum devastation for the Soviets. Europeans are almost inevitably more concerned with deterrence than with defense. They will prefer a strategy that seems to magnify the risks of the aggressor rather than reduce the losses of the defender.[23]

Accordingly, the Europeans have generally argued that ground forces should be equipped with tactical nuclear weapons—not in order to fight *after* an attack has been launched, but to *deter* the attack. If the danger of employing tactical nuclear weapons is indeed the possibility of escalation, then this very danger constitutes a deterrent. For the Soviets will be as fearful of an escalation into a strategic exchange as the Western powers. The danger of escalation, in brief, would protect Europe from local attack. If the fear of total war is a deterrent because all-out nuclear war has become "unthinkable," then the fear that a tactical nuclear war might ignite a thermonuclear war would also render a war in Europe unthinkable.

[23] Henry A. Kissinger, "NATO's Nuclear Dilemma," *The Reporter*, March 28, 1963, pp. 26–27.

The Europeans, in short, want to settle for deterrence on the tactical level as well as the strategic. It is not true that they eagerly accept tactical nuclear weapons out of ignorance of the terrible implications of their use. They accept them in the same way and for the same reasons that Americans accept nuclear strategic deterrence. In fact, deterrence on the tactical level means for them exactly what deterrence on the strategic level means for us.[24]

Whatever the merits of this controversy, the point is clear: Washington decides alliance strategy and Washington decides how to meet Soviet challenges.[25] The Europeans feel that they are merely pawns of a strategy that may not be in their interests, but their protests are dismissed. It is precisely against such unilateral American decisions—decisions affecting political and military issues of vital significance to the Europeans—that Europe is protesting and rebelling. Whatever the validity of the strategy, it is poor alliance politics.

Europe wants to share in the formulation of basic political and military alliance policy not only because of its resurgent strength, pride, and sense of equality, but also because of fear—fear that it will at some future date, perhaps, be left undefended by the United States. The original American monopoly of atomic weapons—which had never been placed under NATO control—had protected Europe from a Soviet attack. Deterrence had worked because the United States had been immune to attack. But this situation has changed drastically. The United States can still respond to a Soviet challenge in Europe with an attack upon Russia, but the Soviets can now reply by launching their bombers and missiles against the continental United States. In these circumstances, the Europeans not surprisingly see the American emphasis on conventional limited war as a form of "nuclear disengagement" by the United States from Europe. Above all, they see the emphasis on conventional warfare as a reversal of the concept of the sword and the shield. SAC, formerly NATO's sword, had now become the nuclear shield deterring an attack *only* upon the United States, while the defense of Europe depended primarily upon the former shield, which was now the nonnuclear sword. To the Continental countries, this reversal seemed tantamount to a tacit "deal" between the United States and the Soviet Union that Europe could be a battleground while their respective homelands remained out of bounds, protected by their strategic nuclear forces.

It is not that the Europeans do not understand the American dilemma. They fully realize that any American President, confronted by Soviet challenges in Europe, constantly faces the agonizing choices of

[24] Bernard Brodie, "What Price Conventional Capabilities in Europe," *The Reporter*, May 23, 1963, p. 33.

[25] For the most detailed historical analysis of NATO and presentation of Washington's point of view on this matter, see Robert E. Osgood, *NATO: The Entangling Alliance*, pp. 31–32.

suicide or surrender. They know that before the atom bomb, nations could pledge themselves to come to one another's rescue in the event of an attack and expect, at worst, to lose the war, pay reparations, and possibly lose some territory. They also know that nuclear weapons have changed this situation radically. No one nation can be expected to commit suicide for an ally, no matter how close the relationship.

Perhaps the United States can still be relied upon to honor its commitments today. But will it do so five, ten, or twenty years from now? Can the NATO allies *always* depend upon America—whatever the circumstances? In 1959, Christian Herter—successor to John Foster Dulles as Secretary of State—had stated, "I cannot conceive of any President engaging in an all-out nuclear war unless *we* were in danger of all-out devastation *ourselves* [italics added]." Herter thus said what the Europeans already suspected. More specifically, they, as nonnuclear powers, feared that the United States, as the principal nuclear power upon whose strength and determination the defense of Western Europe rested, would make a tacit or actual deal at their cost in order to avoid a test of wills that might incur the risk of nuclear war.

Ironically, it was the Soviets whose actions bore out the Europeans' worst fears during the Cuban crisis of 1962. Confronted for once with the kind of dilemma in which she had usually placed the United States —suicide or surrender—the Soviets surrendered to the American demand to withdraw their missiles and permit U.N. inspection of the withdrawal. Castro refused to accede to such inspection. But what was instructive was the fact that one of the great nuclear powers, in its "moment of truth," was quite willing to make a deal at the cost of nonnuclear Cuba, despite the humiliation this deal inflicted upon its ally. Castro could do nothing to stop the Soviets from shipping the missiles back to Russia. His opposition was simply ignored. In the "dialogue" between the United States and the Soviet Union, Cuba was helpless and impotent, and its interests were ignored in order to call off the challenge before it sparked a nuclear war.

If European apprehensions that this might occur to them one day seem to cast a slur upon American honor, Americans need only ask themselves how sure they would feel of assistance if circumstances were reversed—if, for instance, France provided the great deterrent for a NATO that included a nonnuclear America? How would France react when the Soviets demanded the return of Alaska on the grounds that it had been sold by a "capitalist" regime whose acts the Soviet Government did not recognize? Would Alaska be a "vital interest" to Paris? Would it be worth risking suicide for, or was it merely of secondary importance, an area whose loss would not significantly alter the Franco-Soviet balance of power as seen from Paris? What would American editorials and American Congressmen say as Paris announced that while it would defend Alaska if an attack upon that territory occurred, the problem ought to be dealt with by negotiations? And what would be their reactions when the foreign ministers' conference called to discuss this matter failed and the French Prime Minister invited the Soviet Premier to come to Paris to talk matters over with him? Would they feel, in the resulting "spirit of Paris," that the French Government could be depended upon to defend Alaska on the assumption that American and French interests coincided because both countries were members of the same alliance? And even if they felt that, in this instance, they could rely on Paris' word, would they feel just as sure that Paris would come to their defense in the future? Since France would be anxious to avoid its own destruction if at all possible, would Americans not feel anxious lest Moscow and Paris someday strike a bargain at their expense? More specifically, could every American President simply place the existence and well-being of the United States in the hands of *every* future French Prime Minister, no matter who he might be or whatever the circumstances, and still feel that he, the President, was fulfilling his constitutional duty to protect the United States? The answer is self-evident. Even if the French suddenly claimed—as the United States did during the Kennedy Administration —that they had adopted a counterforce strategy which, because it would allegedly spare cities and therefore avoid the risk of nuclear suicide, would continue to permit France to meet all Soviet challenges, faith in the credibility of the French deterrent would not be restored, particularly if the Prime Minister and Minister of Defense on several occasions stated that in a nuclear war Central and Western Europe, including France, could expect to lose 100 million people!

Such are the changes in the original conditions under which NATO was established that have slowly been eroding the bonds of "entangling alliance." Both Europe's drive for equality and her fears have led first Britain and then France to develop their own national nuclear deterrents. These deterrents were expected to realize three aims. The first was prestige. Nuclear weapons are status symbols. Just as a great power once demonstrated its primary status by acquiring colonies, so after World War II it acquired nuclear weapons. For nations who were once great powers and continued to think of themselves as such, or saw themselves once more becoming great powers, nuclear weapons were symbols that they had to acquire. In their view, not to possess them would be a retreat from greatness, an abandonment of power, and a loss of international respect—and indeed self-respect. For in the nuclear age, was a nation not impotent if it did not own such arms? Could a nation still claim to be a sovereign and independent nation if it had in effect surrendered its authority to make decisions on the vital issues of life and death to a nuclear protector? National pride is, in short, a powerful incentive to the development of nuclear deterrents.

Second, nuclear arms were to gain for the allies a voice in Washington so that they could influence its policy decisions. At the very least, they wished to prevent actions they deemed detrimental to their interests. Why would the possession of nuclear weapons gain them such influence?

> Obviously, the members of NATO have special as well as common political interests. . . . A great deal of their effort to promote and safeguard their interests must be transmitted through their influence on the alliance. This influence is, in large measure, a function of their strategic role, which is, in turn, a product of the strategy of the alliance and the terms of allied collaboration. Therefore, by granting or withholding their commitments and contributions in order to get the most favorable strategy and terms of collaboration, the allies try to secure an advantageous strategic role and, through that role, effective political influence.[26]

Since American strategy had for most of the period since the end of World War II relied primarily upon massive retaliation to deter a Soviet attack, the allies soon realized that their influence within the alliance would be proportional to their contribution to this strategy. Britain's early development of a nuclear force was thus not merely a means of satisfying national pride; it was even more a means of continuing and strengthening the special relationship with the United States which had emerged from World War II. As former Prime Minister Macmillan explained it: "The independent contribution gives us a better position in the world with respect to the United States. It puts us where we ought to be, in the position of a great power. The fact that we have it makes the United States pay a greater regard to our point of view."[27] Not surprisingly, the French soon began to realize the value of both European integration and the development of a French bomb as a means of regaining their great-power status and influence in Washington. Both programs were launched *before* De Gaulle became President of France, in 1958. France, like Britain before it, intended to be one of the NATO "equals" who were, in George Orwell's words, "more equal than the others."

The third goal in the development of national deterrents was to protect the nations' vital interests in those instances when the United States might feel that a particular interest was not worth the risk of all-out war. To the degree that, in the nuclear age, the superpower might not risk its existence for the defense of its protectorates' interests, a national deterrent becomes the substitute for an alliance. The question, of course, was whether such a *force de frappe*, whose striking capacity would only be about 5 per cent of that of the United States, could constitute an effective *force de dissuasion*? Were small independent national deterrents composed primarily of bombers not useless *even* as first-strike forces (the

[26] *Ibid.*, pp. 349–50.
[27] *The Times* (London), February 24, 1958.

only way they could be employed since they are not strong enough to survive a Soviet first-strike and hit as second-strike forces)? How could they deter a Soviet challenge when the Soviet Union was in fact virtually invulnerable because the British or French strategic forces could knock out only a fraction of the Soviet bomber and missile force? Were these allied deterrents therefore any more likely to be used than the far larger and more powerful American deterrent? Indeed, were these forces not a wasteful and useless duplication? President de Gaulle has answered this in the negative.

> "The atomic force with which France intends to equip itself is and will remain," they [France's critics] say, "insignificant in relation to those of the U.S. and Russia. To build it up is thus to waste a lot of effort and money for nothing. And then, within the alliance, the U.S. has an overwhelming superiority, therefore no one should run counter to its strategy through any divergent action."
>
> It is quite true that the number of nuclear weapons with which we can equip ourselves will not equal, far from it, the mass of those of the two giants of today. But since when has it been proved that a people should remain deprived of the most effective weapons for the reason that its chief possible adversary and its chief friend have means far superior to its own?
>
> France, when formerly it was its turn to be a world colossus, often experienced the worth of, either the resistance of a less powerful but well equipped adversary, or the support of an ally lining up inferior but well-tempered and well-employed weapons.
>
> Moreover, the atomic force has a feature of its own, in that it has an efficacy that is certain and to an extent that is frightening even if it does not approach the conceivable maximum. . . . I only want to say that the French atomic force, from the very beginning of its establishment, will have the sombre and terrible capacity of destroying in a few seconds millions and millions of men. This fact cannot fail to have at least some bearing on the intents of any possible aggressor.[28]

Whatever the pros and cons of these arguments over the effectiveness of small deterrent forces, there can be no doubt that they posed a crisis for the alliance. No nation is willing to permit another to risk its survival on an issue it may not deem vital. The possibility that one member of the alliance might pull all its partners into war, even though none considered the particular issue at stake worth the risk, could weaken, if not dissolve, the bonds of cohesion. This would be particularly true if the French deterrent were to serve as an example to West Germany. The future emergence of a West German deterrent is not likely to be welcomed by the allies with open arms. One of the basic motivations that impelled France and the other nations who joined ECSC and EEC was, after all, distrust of Germany and the need to control the West German

[28] Press conference on January 14, 1963; quoted in *Major Addresses, Statements and Press Conferences of Charles de Gaulle* (French Embassy), pp. 216–17.

economy and military. One of their aims was to deprive West Germany of full national control over its economy so that its industrial strength could not again be used for purely German goals. Moreover, when West Germany was admitted to NATO, it became a member of the newly established Western European Union whose purpose was to impose a series of controls over West German military power. An independent and nationally controlled West German deterrent would therefore be bound to shatter allied unity into mutual fear and suspicion.

Even more serious, independent national deterrents would loosen U.S. ties with her European allies.

> On the one hand, nuclear diffusion might increase American suspicion, if not the actual likelihood, of some ally involving or threatening to involve the United States in nuclear war under circumstances in which she would not be willing to become involved. After all, to pose a more credible threat of nuclear war than the American threat, to threaten to act when the United States might not, was one of the primary justifications that the British and French presented for their nuclear programs. And, considering the limited nuclear capability that any ally was likely to achieve in the near future, the ability to trigger American nuclear power might appear to be its chief utility. . . . The effect would be to sever the vital entanglement of the United States and Europe, to drive the United States to do exactly what her allies have always feared: to diminish her obligation to come to the defense of Europe.[29]

Thus the birth of independent deterrents radically altered the previous situation, in which the United States possessed the exclusive authority to decide when to fight and over what issue. Now Britain and France had their fingers on the trigger as well. Thus the age when the United States alone could decide what issues Americans—and Englishmen and Frenchmen—would die for was past. Britain and France could now decide for what causes Americans would perish. For this country the risk was new, extraordinary—and unacceptable. Europeans had had no choice but to accept it. They did, of course, protest on occasions when they felt that the United States might act recklessly and involve them in all-out war. But the final decision rested in American hands. Thus the United States acted in Cuba in 1962 without even consulting its allies. Not that the Europeans opposed our action. De Gaulle was indeed the first European to announce his support—even before Britain, whose press was generally opposed and called for "negotiations." But by acting unilaterally when its vital interests were involved—and thereby risking a war that could incinerate tens of millions of Europeans—the United States was doing exactly what it does not want the Europeans to do. The very fact that the United States does not want to be triggered into war against its will, however, supports the European case for independent deterrents.

[29] Osgood, *op. cit.*, p. 272.

The United States has generally insisted that national deterrents are not needed since the alliance shares common interests, all of which will be defended by the American deterrent. Its opposition to these deterrents, however, is based on her refusal to be drawn into a war against her will —which could only occur on a particular issue that Britain or France might define as vital but which the United States does not itself deem vital. In effect, the opposition to national deterrents is a confession that the Europeans may be right when they state that they need deterrents in the event that issues arise over whose importance there may be serious conflict between the United States and its allies. Thus, to avoid being triggered into a war against its will, the United States had to retain its virtual nuclear monopoly and predominant position within NATO. For as De Gaulle has perceptively remarked, "Countries which do not have an atomic arsenal believe that they have to accept a strategic and consequently a political dependency in relation to that one of the two giants which is not threatening them."[30] For the giant this is, of course, the most desirable relationship since, as De Gaulle has said, "In politics and in strategy, as in the economy, monopoly naturally appears to the person who holds it to be the best possible system."[31]

The Collapse of the Atlantic Partnership

The question that therefore confronted the United States was how its pre-eminent position and virtual nuclear monopoly could be preserved. Washington's answer was that the United States and Europe should become *interdependent* by forming an Atlantic Community partnership. But as one close observer of American policy has noted, " 'Partnership' implies equality, and 'community' suggests common decisions, but nobody in Washington really means either thing. Washington, putting up most of the power, insists on being the 'senior partner' with the decisive vote and voice, and the 'Atlantic community' it has in mind could take 'common decisions' only if the United States agreed."[32]

Three links were to tie the European countries closer to the United States. The first was economic—specifically, mutual profit. Europe was to have access to the huge and affluent American market, and the United States was to gain similar access to the European market. The opportunities the Common Market presented to American industry were, of course, tremendous. EEC comprised 170 million people, almost as many as the population of the United States itself. Europeans in 1959 possessed one-seventh as many cars, one-fifth as many telephones, one-fourth as many radios, and one-sixth as many television sets as did Americans.

[30] *President de Gaulle Holds Tenth Press Conference* (French Embassy), p. 8.
[31] *Major Addresses* . . . , p. 217.
[32] James Reston, in *The New York Times*, December 9, 1964.

The Six, whose prosperity was rapidly rising, would thus stimulate the growth of the American economy by providing a large outlet for American consumer goods. Not that American exports to the Six would be limited to consumer items. The more advanced sectors of American business would be able to exploit their leadership in such areas as electronics, communications, and food processing. In addition, according to Labor Department estimates, each $1 billion of exports would generate about 150,000 jobs—and it was anticipated that American exports to the Common Market would rise by several billion dollars during the first half-dozen years.

There was, however, a rub. The Common Market countries had lifted the trade restrictions that existed among themselves, but at the same time they had erected a common trade wall around themselves. A uniform external tariff for each commodity was generally set at a level representing the average of the separate tariffs formerly charged by each of the Six. The obvious benefit provided by this common external tariff was that it gave the Six great bargaining power. If another nation, such as the United States, wished to import into the Six, it would have a difficult time paying the duty and still competing against similar European products, which would be produced in increasing volume by large-scale industries at a low production cost *behind* the tariff wall. Consequently, American exports faced a serious decline.

How then could American industry gain a foothold inside the Six? One way would be to jump over the tariff wall and build factories in Europe. In this case, however, American exports would still suffer, and since the export market was important to the health of the national economy, this would be a serious matter. In the late 1950's, the United States was selling $20 billion worth of goods abroad—that is, $1 out of every $25 of the GNP. It exported over half of its total output of tractors, locomotives, and industrial sewing machines, and over 40 per cent of its civilian aircraft and rolling mill machinery. It was also selling 35 per cent of its oil-field machinery, 25 per cent of its synthetic rubber, and approximately 20 per cent of its textile machinery, trucks, and buses overseas. The percentages were even higher for agricultural products: for rice, cotton, wheat, and soya beans, the respective figures were 60, 49, 45, and 42 per cent. Translated into jobs, these figures meant that 1 out of 5 or 6 factory workers—3 million workers all together—and 1 out of every 7 farm workers owed their jobs to export activities. While Europe was not the only export market, it did account for a large share. The United States clearly had an important stake in exports. An increase in the volume of exports would spur economic growth and prosperity, as well as help absorb some of the approximately 1 million new job-seekers entering the labor market each year. Any significant decline in foreign trade would have a serious impact on both factories and farms.

There was, however, an alternative method of entering the Common Market: instead of jumping over the tariff wall, one could attempt to lower it. But in order to obtain a reduction or elimination of tariffs, the United States would have to take reciprocal action—that is, it would have to lower its tariff barriers and permit the Six the same opportunity of selling in the American market that it sought in the Common Market. Under the 1934 Reciprocal Trade Agreement Act, the United States could only bargain item by item; moreover, since the early 1950's, the Act had become increasingly burdened with restrictive peril-point and escape clauses to prevent the President from granting concessions that threatened "injury" to domestic industries. What the Europeans wanted —and offered—however, was a 20 per cent across-the-board cut. The Kennedy Administration sought to meet this challenge with its Trade Expansion Act, which would give the President the authority over a five-year period to reduce existing tariffs by 50 per cent in reciprocal negotiations and to eliminate tariffs entirely on those products for which the United States and the Common Market accounted for 80 per cent of the world trade (this group includes the products we would most like to sell in Europe and vice-versa); an adjustment assistance program would provide retraining opportunities and unemployment and relocation allowances for workers and farmers who lost their jobs as a result of the tariff cuts, as well as tax benefits, loans, and technical advise to injured firms who wanted to open new businesses (the adjustment assistance, in short, would replace the peril-point and escape clauses formerly used to limit imports if they injured business or labor). The total number of workers who would be adversely affected was estimated at about 18,000 per year. While this seemed large, the figure had to be weighed against the much greater number—a million in 1959—engaged in transporting, distributing, and processing imports. Certainly, the argument that millions of Americans would be put out of work by an influx of cheaper European goods was not valid. For the decisive factor in the price of a product is not the actual wages of the workers but the labor cost per item; in other words, while an Italian worker may earn only a fifth of what his American counterpart earns, the latter probably produces seven times as many products.[33] Significantly, the highest-paid American industries have been most active in exporting; in 1960, for example, the ten industries paying the highest wages produced three-quarters of total U.S. exports.

[33] In any event, European wages have been rising faster than American wages since World War II; and the growing shortages of skilled labor in Western Europe will result in wages being pushed up even higher and faster in the future.

How well the United States, with its highly paid labor, competes can be illustrated by the example of the Volkswagen. When compact European cars were first imported into the United States, they sold well because the manufacture of such cars had been neglected by Detroit. Once Detroit began to produce compact cars, however, foreign sales declined for all compact cars except the VW. The VW continues to sell well precisely because no American car can compete with it in size and price.

International economic competition could thus be a boon to the United States. In the long run, indeed, there would seem to be little need for any tariffs since the United States and the Common Market would include virtually all the non-Communist industrialized nations. In the short-run, though, the zero-tariff clause was unlikely to be implemented. The external tariff is the heart of the Common Market. Behind it, the members lower their tariffs to one another not only as a means of increasing trade among themselves but as a step toward their unification.

> It is being said that the Six are threatening to create a rift between the Common Market countries and the other members of the Atlantic Community by directing their economic policies inward instead of toward liberal trade practices throughout the Atlantic area and beyond it. Some such inward orientation is indispensable, however, if even a start is to be made in the direction of the genuinely united Europe that the United States so eagerly desires. The growth and solidarity among the Six hinges on the experience of common benefits enjoyed as a result of integration. One such benefit is the more rapid growth in intra-Common Market trade compared to trade with outsiders. Thus, discrimination resulting from continued external tariffs is an essential part of the process of integration.[34]

Conversely, the elimination of these tariffs and the creation of an Atlantic Free Trade Area would halt European unification and dissolve the Six in a wider Atlantic Community in which the United States was economically and politically the leading power—in short, it would create a "partnership" between a giant and a number of dwarfs.[35] The first link forging the Atlantic partnership would thus remain a tenuous one for the immediate future.

The second link was to be Britain's membership in the Market. In one sense, of course, Britain's application in 1961 was an indication of the Market's success, for previously her attitude toward all postwar European integration schemes had been completely negative. She had been asked to join ECSC, but had refused. She had been invited to join EEC and Euratom, but had again refused. At no time between 1950 and 1961 had Britain seen any need to join her Continental allies in their efforts to integrate in a more powerful union. Ironically, this was, at least in part, a result of the fact that Britain had been neither defeated nor occupied during World War II. Emerging from the war as one of the Big Three powers, she retained her self-confidence, in strong contrast to the Continental states, all of whom had experienced invasion, conquest, foreign occupation, and postwar collapse. Their sense of impotence was reinforced by both the Soviet threat and the predominance of American power. But, "as British power ebbed, the symbols of power came to be

34 Wolfers, *op. cit.*, p. 245.
35 A characterization attributed to Dr. Walter Hallstein, President of the Common Market Commission. (Robert Kleiman, *Atlantic Crisis*, p. 111.)

prized above the reality. Like an aging actress, Britain's statesmen and people sought refuge from the harsh facts in an illusion of grandeur . . . [particularly] the Churchillian doctrine of the 'interlocking circles'—the theory that Britain was uniquely placed at the heart of three great blocs: the Atlantic alliance with America, the Commonwealth, and Western Europe. This doctrine carried the flattering implication that Britain really was 'at the still centre of the turning world,' buttressed and shielded by innumerable friends."[36]

Economically, too, Britain looked to the United States and the Commonwealth. She was almost completely dependent on American dollars for her recovery. The Commonwealth—what remained of the British Empire—had in the past served Britain as its own "common market," with an external tariff surrounding her and a multibillion-dollar free-trade area for every type of Commonwealth product, from Canadian wheat and New Zealand butter to Indian tea and textiles. In their turn, the Commonwealth countries had provided Britain with outlets for manufactured goods. Politically and economically, then, Europe hardly seemed important. The British Labour Party—in power at the time ECSC was launched—had further reasons for not joining the Six. Labour was devoted to the national planning of the economy, and this was incompatible with European integration. Not that the Conservative Party was any more disposed to integration. Member of Parliament Harold Macmillan said in May, 1950: "One thing is certain and we may as well face it. Our people are not going to hand to any supranational authority the right to close down our pits or steelworks. We will allow no supranational authority to put large masses of our people out of work."[37] Britain's traditional aloofness from the Continent plus her general distrust of the political stability and aptitude of her Continental neighbors intensified her negative attitude. The only European organizations Britain joined were those which committed American power to Europe.

Nevertheless, because of Britain's dependence on trade, it soon became evident to her that she could not afford to be shut out of the Common Market. To reap its advantages, Britain therefore proposed that the Common Market be included in a large free-trade area including Sweden, Norway, Denmark, Switzerland, Austria, and Portugal. Members would abolish the tariff barriers among themselves, but would establish no common tariffs against third parties. The British purpose was clear: to eliminate tariffs on industrial goods but not on agricultural commodities, which she received from the Commonwealth countries under preferential tariff arrangements. In short, she wanted to exploit the benefits of the Common Market, for which she was in a strong competitive position, while simultaneously maintaining the advantages she derived from her

[36] Shanks and Lambert, *op. cit.*, p. 26.
[37] Quoted in Nora Beloff, *The General Says No*, pp. 58–59.

Commonwealth association. Indeed, the proposed seventeen-nation Free Trade Area would have destroyed EEC before it even began, since it would have eliminated the common external tariff. But this did not matter to Britain since she remained unsympathetic to the political goals of the Common Market, viewing it exclusively in terms of trade and business. Yet the primary goal of EEC was political rather than commercial. Not surprisingly, therefore, Britain met with a rebuff. Still seeking admission, she decided to form a rival European Free Trade Association, or Outer Seven (herself plus the six countries she had earlier recommended as additional members of the Common Market), in an attempt to undermine the Inner Six. EFTA was to accomplish this by putting the squeeze on West Germany.[38] Almost one-third of the latter's exports were sent to EFTA, and nine-tenths of this went to Scandinavia and Switzerland. If Britain could push West Germany out of these markets, Bonn might in turn put pressure on her five partners to transform the Common Market into an enlarged EFTA. Since the Common Market could not succeed without Germany, her desire to admit the Outer Seven would be decisive. The British plan failed, however, partly because West German Chancellor Adenauer was determined to consolidate Franco-German ties and integrate West Germany into "Little Europe," and partly simply because the European Commission accelerated its timetable for tariff reduction. The Council of Ministers approved this speedup, and the effect was to improve West German business opportunities in the Common Market and demonstrate to Britain that the Six were not to be sidetracked from their movement toward unification.

Not until mid-1961 did Britain, unable to continue her fight against the obviously successful Common Market, announce that it wished to join. EFTA, which offered Britain about 40 million customers, was no substitute for EEC's 180 million. And for the time being, the confederationists had won out over the federationists. Britain, like De Gaulle's France, did not wish to lose its national identity or be governed by supranational institutions; it was just as vehemently committed to a "Europe of fatherlands." Moreover, Britain was suffering economically. The Commonwealth countries imported less and less from Britain, tending either to produce more of the goods they needed at home or to buy these goods from the United States, Japan, or Western Europe. In the late 1940's, Commonwealth trade accounted for 60 per cent of Britain's exports, while only 25 per cent went to Western Europe (including the Six). In 1956, the respective figures were 48 and 27 per cent. But by 1962, Britain was exporting more to Europe than to the Commonwealth: Her trade with the Six from 1960 to 1962 increased 30 per cent; and her total trade with the Six accounted for more than one-third of her total exports. Some of the Commonwealth countries—particularly Ghana, Malaya,

[38] Benoit, *op. cit.*, pp. 79–91.

Nigeria, Tanganyika, and Pakistan—were also becoming more dependent on their exports to the Six. Symbolic of this changing relationship was the Common Market countries' aid to several of the underdeveloped Commonwealth countries. For example, West Germany alone was investing more than Britain in the development of India and Pakistan. In investments, as in trade, Britain's links with the Commonwealth were weakening while the latter's bonds with the Six were strengthening. Europe was the largest and fastest growing importer in the world, and the second largest provider of development assistance. The Commonwealth's economic value was therefore declining—only 90 million of its 600–700 million citizens had any real purchasing power in any case—and Britain needed the Common Market's 180 million customers. Britain also needed competition to stimulate certain sectors of its industry to become more efficient, to improve designs, and to do a more aggressive sales job. British labor, too, needed to be shocked out of its general complacency.

In the final analysis, however, it was not economics but politics that proved to be the decisive factor in Britain's bid to join the Six. World War II had changed the nature of the Commonwealth. Until the war, the self-governing members—Britain, Australia, New Zealand, Canada, and South Africa—had been white or ruled by whites; except for South Africa, they were relatively developed (agriculturally or industrially) parliamentary democracies with populations largely of British stock, and the Empire was ruled from London. After 1945, almost all the members of the Commonwealth became independent, and the new nations were underdeveloped, non-British, and colored, with no deeply felt loyalty to Britain. Instead of parliamentary democracies, they were military and one-party dictatorships, monarchies and republics, and a half-dozen other political varieties. Thus the Commonwealth hardly presented a clear image of itself any more as standing for a particular system of government. Nor did the prewar coordination of foreign policy and military defense continue. Before 1939, Britain had been responsible for the defense of the Commonwealth. After the war, the United States assumed the major share of responsibility for defense of the entire free world, including the Commonwealth nations. In foreign affairs, most of the new nations pursued a policy of nonalignment and were often quite critical of British—and general Western—foreign policy toward the Communist world. Inevitably, the impact of this loosening of Commonwealth ties on Britain brought a decline in her power and status. By the early 1960's, therefore, Britain was compelled to re-evaluate her role. Former Secretary of State Dean Acheson stated the central issue bluntly when, in December, 1962, he said that Britain had "lost an empire and has not yet found a role." She was attempting, he said, to play a "role apart from Europe, a role based on a special relationship with the United States, a role based on being head of a commonwealth. . . . This role is about played out."[39] Britain had to face the prospect that as a single power she would be increasingly ignored. As her strength declined, so would her influence in Washington and Moscow, as well as in New Delhi and Peking. In a world in which continental-sized powers with populations of approximately 200 million or more would be the principal actors, more and more attention would be paid to the New Europe. Thus the advantages of joining the Common Market were clear: Britain would become a member of a potential superpower comprising nearly 224 million people (more than the United States or the Soviet Union), producing more coal and steel than either of the two present superpowers, and absorbing almost half of the world's exports.

Economic and political factors were, however, to block Britain's entry in the early 1960's. First, Britain had an obligation to the Commonwealth countries, whose exports now entered Britain duty-free, but against whom the common external tariff would apply once she was in the Common Market. This meant that particularly the temperate-zone producers—Australia, New Zealand, and Canada, Britain's biggest food suppliers—would suffer. New Zealand would be especially hard hit since over 60 per cent of its total exports, mainly dairy products and meats, went to Britain. Britain therefore wanted guarantees that these countries would find continuing markets for their grain, meat, and dairy products —as well as their industrial products. Second, Britain wanted to protect her own farmers. Dependent on exports, she had always kept food prices low—higher food prices would have required higher wages and resulted in higher production costs—to remain competitive in industrial and consumer goods. The problem with these British demands was that economically the Common Market was basically a bargain between German industry and French agriculture. The latter was being modernized and becoming very productive, and the Common Market enabled France to sell its basic foods—wheat and meat—protected from Canadian, Australian, New Zealand, Argentinian, and American products. In exchange, German industry could sell in the same protected market. (This relationship was thus comparable to the U.S. "common market" between the industrial North and the agrarian South and West.) French farmers, like their American counterparts, were beginning to overproduce and held political power; they saw in Britain a further market, and they were in favor neither of opening the Common Market to Commonwealth agriculture nor of protecting British agriculture, even though this might mean a 10 per cent increase in British food prices. Third, Britain, having used the EFTA members to break up the Common Market, was in no position to desert them unless she could also obtain for them favorable trade terms with the Six.

The British position proved incompatible with the Common Market.

[39] *The New York Times*, December 7, 1962.

Britain sought special arrangements that would grant Commonwealth products continued favorable access to the British and Continental markets. Yet, if many holes had been punched in the Common Market wall, the whole Common Market system might have broken down since the external tariff is the brick and mortar of the Common Market.[40] In short, if Britain wished to join the Common Market, she would have to adopt its common rules and not seek special privileges.

If the economic difficulties presented a barrier, the political difficulties were even more formidable. The former problems might have been resolvable if the political will existed. But it did not. First, British leaders too often talked of guiding the Community from within, and one import the Six felt they did not need was a British nanny.

> It is not surprising that French and Community officials feel that they have done sufficiently well without British guidance and against British opposition, and that guidance ill becomes those who have just landed themselves in an unenviable economic situation. Indeed, those who built the Community as a racing car to keep up with the Eastern bloc are unhappy that it may now be thumbed as an ambulance to pick up the "British invalid."[41]

The invalid's talk of leadership particularly worried President de Gaulle. For one thing, he was determined that the leader of the European Political Community would be France. And for another, he feared that Britain's entry would cause EEC to lose its European identity because Britain would be America's spokesman in the Community. Europe should, as far as possible, however, be master of its own destiny. Would Britain, as the price of entry, therefore surrender her special relationship with the United States and prove her conversion to "Europeaness"? Could she demonstrate this time that she really was sympathetic to the political unification of the New Europe, or were her interests in Europe purely commercial and would she continue to give primary emphasis to her relationship with Washington?

> It is not necessary to go so far as to assert that "the European idea has an anti-American flavour" . . . it is quite enough to realize that its unspoken premises include the belief that Europe has been unduly overshadowed in the system built up after 1945 under Anglo-U.S. auspices. . . . It is a notion oddly at variance with Washington's reputed hope that Britain will act as America's most reliable ally in Europe. . . . that, once inside Europe, the British will "manage" it—in the joint interest of the Anglo-Saxon powers. This is wishful thinking; the Europeans are in no mood to have their affairs run by people whom they regard as outsiders. If the British count on playing a leading role in the new Europe, they will have to

---

[40] On the partial package deal worked out between Britain and the EEC, see Kitzinger, *op. cit.*, pp. 205–9.

[41] Kitzinger, *op. cit.*, pp. 199–200.

demonstrate to their skeptical partners that in any serious conflict of inter-est between the two halves of the Atlantic world they can be counted on to come down on the European side.[42]

If a truly "European" Europe is ever to emerge, and if such a Europe is to control its fate, it will presumably control its own defense. It was in this field that, in late 1962, the crucial test of Britain's Europeanness came when the United States canceled the Skybolt program. Britain's choice was clear: "There was the possibility of going to America and asking for a substitute for Skybolt. There was the possibility of dropping the British deterrent completely. But there was—in De Gaulle's mind, at least—a third possibility. That was to go to the French and say: 'Let's produce ballistic missiles together.' "[43] Apparently De Gaulle had as-sumed that Britain would pay this price as the cost of admission to the European "club": an *entente nucleaire* between France and Britain. In June, 1962, in talks with Prime Minister Macmillan, De Gaulle report-edly intimated that the two countries should join in establishing an Anglo-French atomic force as the basis of a European deterrent that could redress the balance within NATO.[44]

Yet, at the decisive moment, despite her public humiliation by the United States, Britain signed the Nassau Pact. As a replacement for the Skybolt, she was to receive American Polaris missiles, and she would her-self provide the submarines and warheads. Britain thereby chose to re-main dependent on the United States for maintenance of her "independ-ent" deterrent. Moreover, her submarines were to be assigned to a NATO multinational Force, composed essentially of three American Polaris submarines that were to replace the MRBM's in Europe and Turkey, Britain's bombers, and several fighter-bomber squadrons from eight other NATO countries (including two from France). Since this nuclear force would be commanded by SACEUR—as were all forces as-signed to NATO—the British submarines would be controlled by the United States and during hostilities employed according to American

[42] Lichtheim, *op. cit.*, pp. 36–37.

[43] Raymond Aron, "Size-Up of de Gaulle," *U.S. News & World Report*, April 22, 1963.

[44] "After entry into the Common Market, Macmillan said, Britain looked forward to political union with the Six. That would mean close cooperation with France and the Six, not only in foreign policy but also in defense. He spoke for the first time of a European, rather than simply a NATO, defense policy. There was a mention of future Anglo-French cooperation in defense production and research. While no de-tails were discussed or engagements made, de Gaulle emerged with the impression that the door would be open to Anglo-French cooperation in the nuclear defense field after Britain entered the Common Market. There was no indication in the British minutes that cooperation in nuclear arms production, as such, had been discussed. But Macmillan, according to the French minutes, suggested that the two countries coordinate the plans of their nuclear forces for circumstances, should they arise, where the United States might be unwilling to employ its deterrent.

"De Gaulle's conviction, after Champs, was that the British 'had made their choice —for Europe.'" (Kleiman, *op. cit.*, pp. 69–70.)

war plans. Although Britain was to be permitted to use her deterrent uni-laterally whenever she decided that her "supreme national interests" were at stake, this qualification was essentially without value.[45]

Thus Nassau demonstrated clearly once again that Britain's first loyalty was to the United States, not to the Europeans with whom she was at that very time negotiating for economic and political integration. For fifteen months, the British stalled, haggling over the subsidies for bacon and eggs, and avoided a choice between the Commonwealth and Europe. But compelled to choose between the United States and Europe at Nassau, the British Government made the decision in forty-eight hours to hand over to the United States the one contribution she could have made to Europe. The French President reportedly considered that Britain had thereby disqualified itself as a European power by allowing one of the vital attributes of its national sovereignty—the deterrent force—to become dependent on the United States. This dependence, in turn, confirmed De Gaulle's suspicions that once inside the Common Market, London would play the role of a Trojan horse.[46] The result was a French veto of Britain's membership in the Common Market.

The third link in the Kennedy "Grand Design" was to be nuclear because Washington recognized the need for some way of sharing nuclear responsibility within NATO. In reality, however, American policy remained one of preserving the American nuclear monopoly—"with a British appendage that, it was hoped, would ultimately disappear"[47]—and of retaining the sole authority to decide when to fight. At first, the United States offered to "assign" five Polaris submarines to NATO. But this assignment was only symbolic since the submarine commander's orders to fire the Polaris missiles would ultimately come from the President. If France, for example, wanted to counter a Soviet threat over an issue the United States did not deem vital, it could not do so by threatening Moscow with the eighty missiles carried on the five American submarines, since the President retained his veto power over all nuclear weapons. A second proposal was for a multilateral NATO nuclear fleet (MLF) composed of twenty-five surface ships, each carrying eight Polaris missiles. The fleet was to be manned by interallied crews. The French soon dubbed the proposal a "multilateral farce" since, again, the United States retained the veto power. The only finger on the trigger

[45] See Kleiman, *op. cit.*, pp. 56–59. "Macmillan, back in London, stressed his right to withdraw Britain's Polaris submarines from NATO for national use and insisted that he had retained an independent deterrent. *Administration spokesmen, in Washington, emphasized the multilateral aspects of the agreement and described Britain's withdrawal rights as virtually useless.* . . . At Nassau, when Britain in return for Polaris agreed to commit its deterrent to NATO, it became possible for the first time to offer France equal treatment *without* accepting the concept of a completely independent French nuclear force [Italics added]."

[46] Edmund Taylor, "After Brussels," *The Reporter*, February 14, 1963.

[47] Kleiman, *op. cit.*, p. 114.

was to be the American finger. The French therefore refused to participate. The Europeans were in effect being asked to build a force which,
while costing several hundred million dollars, would not meet their political and military needs. Instead of resolving NATO's fundamental problem, it would merely accentuate it. For the American definition of
"interdependence" was a relationship in which the United States re-
served the right of independent action, while denying this right to its
"partners."

The MLF proposal, furthermore, came on top of the conventional
ground forces that the United States was already pressing the Europeans
to build. Even if the Continental nations were not opposed to such conventional armies, the MLF would stop their buildup since none of the
potential participants was likely to raise its defense budget beyond the
expenditures needed for the MLF. In addition, since the United States
was itself relying on submarines, it was assumed that the U.S. Navy had
already rejected the placement of Polaris missiles on American surface
craft because they were too easily detectable and were therefore vulnerable. The whole point of the underwater mobile deterrent was that the
Soviets could never be sure where the submarines were and thus could
not knock them out of action before they had fired their missiles. This
was the guarantee of the oceanic system as an effective deterrent. The
American reply that these surface ships would be disguised as merchant
ships and therefore would go undetected did not explain why, in that
case, the United States was relying exclusively on submarines.

There was another objection to the MLF. One of its aims was, by
granting the Germans a share in the "control" of the fleet, to prevent
West Germany from following France in seeking its own national deterrent. Indeed, West Germany was to provide 40 per cent of the manpower
and financing. The Germans naturally agreed. Unlike Britain or France,
West Germany was excluded by legal and political reasons from seeking
an independent national deterrent. Her influence within NATO therefore depended on tightening the political and military bonds of the alliance and then pressing for a more important role, including a larger share
of the control of nuclear weapons, within the alliance. But as an attempt
to isolate France by consolidating German-American bonds, MLF would
probably fail. For the West Germans, MLF might be an entry into the
nuclear field. If they were to become interested in acquiring a strategic
nuclear force of their own some day, the MLF would be the easiest way
to such an acquisition. And it was difficult to conceive that West Germany, considering herself an equal ally, would remain satisfied with second-class nuclear status. The West German Defense Minister had,
indeed, stated that the fleet could not become "a genuine military instrument" until the American veto was withdrawn.[48] Thus, for West
Germany, the fleet would in all probability be only an interim step and

[48] *The New York Times,* May 28, 1963.

the United States, instead of preventing nuclear weapons from being placed in West German hands, would make possible just what it was trying to avoid. Since a West German deterrent would create grave opposition in other NATO countries—if not, in fact, stimulate neutralism in Britain, Denmark, Norway, and the Benelux countries—the United States was creating a situation ready-made for Soviet exploitation. And without Britain and Italy, who were both unenthusiastic about the MLF, it would become basically an American-German device.

Finally, the MLF would probably weaken European unity. All plans for furthering this unity have to start with De Gaulle's proposal for regular meetings of the heads of government and their ministers to coordinate policies in the various fields of common concern. This is the fundamental De Gaullist prerequisite. The Community members are *first* to talk to each other, and only *then* to the United States. There could be no "Europe" if each Common Market member tried first to establish its own bilateral relations with Washington. It was on this issue that De Gaulle vetoed Britain's entry into the Six. London gave priority to its special relationship with Washington over its interests with the European Political Community. It was for the same reason that the French opposed German participation in the MLF. De Gaulle had offered West Germany a privileged position within his confederated Europe. If West Germany, however, preferred a special relationship with the United States —and played along with the American attempt to isolate France—the danger was that France might reconsider its membership in the Common Market and negotiate bilaterally with the Soviet Union over Germany.

Thus the Grand Design foundered soon after its launching on the twin problems of the resurgence of Europe and the nuclear stalemate. Clearly, the period of American dominance had come to an end with Europe's search for a more equitable role within NATO. American policy toward Europe was, however, contradictory. On the one hand, the United States had sought for twenty years to create a powerful and united Europe which could take care of its own defense. On the other hand, as Europe grew stronger and more unified, the United States began to balk at the logical conclusion of its policy. Fearful that such a Europe might have interests of its own, and increasingly apprehensive of the results of nuclear diffusion under these circumstances, the United States preferred to keep its allies in a state of nuclear and political dependency. This paradox was neatly summed up as follows: "We would like Europe to be united, but still under American direction; we would like it to be militarily strong, but to permit us a monopoly of the West's nuclear power. We speak of 'interdependence,' but by it we mean that the United States should be independent of Europe, while our allies should be dependent ones."[49] Because the integrated nature of NATO's organization was to him symbolic of this American hegemony and European

[49] Steel, *op. cit.*, p. 66.

subordination, President De Gaulle pulled France out of NATO's command structure and demanded the withdrawal of U.S. forces and the alliance headquarters out of France.

NATO, in short, can only survive if its organization reflects the balance of power as it has changed within the alliance since its formation, and if it rests on two equal—and therefore nuclear—pillars. A European deterrent, it has been suggested, would present several military and political advantages. First, it would be the obvious corollary of European unification. A European identity in nuclear arms is as logical as it is in economic and political affairs. Just as the Common Market is symptomatic of the Six's growing economic integration, so a European nuclear deterrent would symbolize the Six's political resurgence and new assertiveness. A European deterrent would consummate the entire unification movement and instill it with a new momentum by adding a new incentive for political cooperation, by supplementing EEC and the emerging European Political Community with a European Defense Community. Not only economic affairs, but military affairs, too, would then spill over into the unification process. Even Jean Monnet, a vehement critic of De Gaulle, has concluded that no genuine political community would be possible without common means of defense:

> It is difficult to conceive that the peoples of Europe will engage themselves toward a common economic destiny without engaging themselves toward a common political destiny, and, necessarily, that leads them to have a common defense. . . . This relationship of equal partners must be applied to the responsibilities of the common defense. It requires, among other things, the organization of a European atomic force, including England, and in partnership with the United States.[50]

There might also be an economic necessity for the European states to develop a nuclear weapons technology. Scientists and businessmen recognize that one of the byproducts of military manufacturing is cadres of trained experts and inventions that might not otherwise be developed.

> Governmental expenditures in the areas of advanced military technology generate national overhead capital in the development of several key industries: fuels, metals, plastics, engines, ceramics, electronics, chemicals, and others. In the absence of a significant effort to build a deterrent force, Europe's economic growth may lead to an excessively "soft" productive system in which investment capital will be attracted increasingly toward consumer-satisfaction industries and away from the producer durables on which continued growth depends, and also away from new industries on the technological frontier on which strategic power must be based.[51]

[50] Quoted in *The New York Times*, April 18 and May 9, 1963.
[51] James E. Daugherty, "European Deterrence and Atlantic Unity," *Orbis*, Fall, 1962, p. 415.

Third, just as ECSC and EEC were means of controlling West German economic power, so a European deterrent would allow West Germany to contribute to and participate in the nuclear field while simultaneously ensuring that she would never gain national control over the WEU deterrent or any other nuclear activities. The achievement of nuclear status by West Germany cannot be avoided forever—and it should be recognized that this is not just a matter of keeping up with France (or with Britain, for that matter), but that West Germany's acquisition of nuclear arms is the logical conclusion of the *American* policy of rearming the Germans.

A fourth advantage of the European deterrent is that both France and Britain could someday transfer their own deterrents to such a force. Indeed, just as the threat of a revived Germany was once an incentive to the other five Continental powers to control West German power and thus assure that it would be employed for the benefit of all Six, so the existence of the French deterrent is likely to be an incentive for France's partners to gain control over her nuclear force. And for Britain, such a transfer would finally indicate her acceptance as a European power ready to become a full-fledged member of the emerging European union.

The final advantage of the European deterrent is that it would promote transatlantic bonds:

> The real basis of our opposition to national nuclear forces . . . [is] that we do not want to be drawn into a war against our will. . . . We thus reach the heart of the issue raised by European nuclear forces. Does the interdependence of the Atlantic area have to be vindicated by a structure in which only one ally possesses the physical ability to engage in nuclear war? Is the test of Atlantic partnership really a "single strategic force"? . . . Or is it possible to have several centers of decision coordinated politically so that their power serves a common end? . . .
>
> The real problem is whether we are ready to face an independent European center for decision on nuclear matters, and rely on political consultations to relate European purposes to ours.
>
> So far, we have indicated a preference for continued hegemony. Terms like "multilateralism" and "interdependence" have hidden the reality of an attempt to maintain undivided physical control. . . . Given European pressures in the opposite direction, this policy has forced us to adopt remedies more dangerous than the ill they have sought to cure. . . . Almost every program that we have advanced in the name of our notion of multilateralism has had the practical consequence of accentuating rather than ameliorating NATO's nuclear dilemma, and therefore it has undermined the long-term political stability of the Atlantic Alliance.[52]

The difficulty is that however great might be the merit of a European deterrent in the long run—and in contrast to national deterrents, which

---

[52] Kissinger, *op. cit.*, p. 28.

may be politically divisive, and a NATO deterrent, which preserves American hegemony and creates European resentment, a European deterrent does possess great merit—no such deterrent will be born in the near future. While Europe has made impressive advances toward economic integration, its progress toward political integration lags far behind; and during De Gaulle's reign, it is likely to continue to lag. It will be a long time before the Six will coordinate their foreign policies—the prerequisite for a common military strategy and force.

Thus the dissensions within NATO seem sure to continue. Our European allies were bound at some time to reject American hegemony within NATO and seek what they consider to be their rightful share of the authority in formulating alliance policies. And it is on this issue—the sharing of authority within the Western alliance—that the conflict within NATO, especially over nuclear weapons, has focused. It remains to be seen whether in the long-run such sharing will be possible without the establishment of some form of North Atlantic political confederation; it may certainly require a major reorganization of the structure of the Western alliance.[53] The alternative course is that Europe, particularly France, increasingly dissatisfied with its subordinate status and role, will grow more and more rebellious and obstructive. A "split," similar to the Sino-Soviet split, might then plague the Western alliance. For in essence, the quarrels threatening to rend the American and Soviet alliances are similar: both center on the issue of leadership and the sharing of authority in alliance policy-making.

[53] De Gaulle has intimated that he intends to withdraw France from NATO when the North Atlantic Treaty expires in 1969 and renegotiate a less integrated alliance. For he identifies the present organization of NATO with U.S. domination over Europe.

The General thinks the Western alliance should be replaced by two alliances: one, a traditional nonintegrated treaty of alliance between all NATO members; and two, a "local" European alliance with a large measure of nonnuclear integration. In this way, De Gaulle seeks to reduce what he regards as the excessive role of the United States in NATO and keep West Germany from achieving military, and especially nuclear, independence. France would give West Germany a nuclear guarantee for its defense.

IX

The Socialist Camp: From Monolith to Fragmented Bloc

The De-Stalinization of the People's Democracies

With the death in 1953 of Stalin, who had ruled the Soviet Union for thirty years, one of the dominant figures of the twentieth century passed into history. Through his ruthless collectivization and industrialization programs, the Soviet dictator had proved himself to be the greatest "robber baron" of all time; a self-proclaimed Marxist-Leninist, he had in fact lived the life of a state-monopoly capitalist. By his pressure on postwar Europe, Stalin had in a sense also fathered the movement toward a more united Europe. And he had founded the Soviet Union's empire in Eastern Europe. The bayonets of the Red Army had transformed "socialism in one country" into "socialism in one zone," comprising the Soviet Union, Albania, Bulgaria, Czechoslovakia, East Germany, Hungary, Poland, Romania, and Yugoslavia (which later withdrew). After the Chinese Communist victory on the mainland, China became formally allied with the Soviet Union in a Treaty of Friendship, Alliance, and Mutual Assistance. The Communist world then ranged from the Elbe River to the Pacific Ocean, but beneath the monolithic structure there soon developed serious strains that threatened eventually to rend the surface unity and lead to the disintegration of the Sino-Soviet bloc. These deep built-in tensions stemmed largely from the Soviet Union's attempt to subordinate the states of Eastern Europe, and even China, to Soviet rule.

The Red Army's conquest of the states of Eastern Europe, while Soviet power advanced into the heart of Europe, had for the first time con-

fronted the Soviet Union with the new problem of how to organize a
Communist state system. Before World War II, to be sure, there had
been an international Communist movement known as the Comintern.
Just as Lenin had organized his professional revolutionaries into a hierarchical and disciplined Party along military lines to serve as the general
staff of the Russian Revolution, so Lenin had organized the Comintern
as the general staff for world revolution. It was natural that the Soviet
leaders considered theirs, the only Party that had captured state power,
as the leading Party; it was also natural that non-Soviet Communists
should tend to defer to them. The role of Moscow as leader of the international Communist movement was reinforced by two other considerations. First, there were the failures of the expected post–World War I
revolutions in Germany and Hungary. Moscow refused to believe that
these failures had anything to do with the different conditions in these
countries, but attributed them to a poor choice of tactics by the local
leaders, over whom the Kremlin felt it had little control. The implication was that with Lenin in control, these revolutions would have succeeded. Second, Lenin—as did Stalin and Khrushchev later—claimed that
he was the authentic disciple and successor of Marx. By setting himself
up as the source of Communist theological interpretation, he in fact asserted his—and therefore Moscow's—legitimate authority to govern not
only Russia but also the international Communist movement.

All Communist parties were thus subordinated to the Kremlin's leadership and expected to obey its orders unquestioningly. The Soviet
Union, as the only Communist state, was the bastion of the world revolution, and its preservation was therefore indispensable to the future of
the Communist movement. Soviet interests and those of the Comintern
thus became identical. As weak bastions in an allegedly hostile capitalist
world which was constantly seeking to destroy its "class enemy," foreign
Communist parties would have to follow Moscow's decisions unhesitat-
ingly to ensure the security of the "proletarian fatherland," even if it
involved great hardship, including the sacrifice of the local Party. For
instance, when British and French leaders at Munich sought to appease
Hitler by giving him the Sudetenland, thereby diverting Nazi pressure
from the West to the East, the Soviets reacted by turning the German
threat back to the West again. Just as some British and French leaders
hoped that Germany and Russia would fight it out and leave them in
the position of strength, so the Soviet leaders hoped that the Germans,
French, and British would exhaust themselves in a war, leaving the Soviet
Union to dictate the peace of Europe. The Nazi-Soviet Pact of 1939, a
result of this calculation, assured Hitler that he would only have to fight
a one-front war. The fact that the Soviet Union, which had for years
vigorously denounced Nazi Germany and tried to form an anti-Nazi
coalition, aligned itself with Hitler and proceeded to divide up Poland

with him shocked and gravely weakened Western Communist parties, which suddenly had to explain that Hitler was now a "friend of peace."

The twenty-year pattern of Soviet domination and subordination of all other Communist parties proved a hard habit to break after World War II when the Red Army installed the "People's Democracies" in Eastern Europe. The Soviet Union now no longer ruled just foreign Communist parties, but entire nations.

> The construction of the Soviet bloc . . . could not be carried on at a sacrifice to the Soviet state. In fact, since what harmed the Soviet state harmed socialism and what aided it could not help but aid socialism, the construction of the Soviet bloc was only meaningful if it strengthened the U.S.S.R. The strength of the Soviet state, in turn, was bound to aid the People's Democracies in their "construction of socialism." This meant, simply, that no conflict of interest was possible as long as a consistent policy of assigning priority to the interests of the Soviet state was pursued.[1]

Soviet control was assured at both the Party and governmental levels. The Party levers were the most important since the Party controlled the state machinery. First of all, the satellite leaders were appointed by Stalin, which meant that the men had proved their loyalty and devotion to Stalin. A strong incentive for them to remain loyal was the knowledge that the Soviet dictator could—and frequently did—purge them. Stalin usually held only bilateral "consultations" with his viceroys so that each set of Party leaders faced him alone. Assured that the other satellites had already given their support to whatever policy Stalin was discussing, they inevitably endorsed the policy, too. A second lever of control was the Soviet ambassador in each satellite, who maintained a close watch on the Party leadership and kept Moscow informed. Knowing that the ambassador's reports on their performance reached Moscow regularly, the satellite leaders generally checked their views and evaluations with the ambassador to ensure favorable reports. A more obvious instance of close supervision by the Soviet Government was found in the command of the People's Democracies' armies. The Polish Army was led by Russian General Rokossovsky; less open, and more typical, was the appointment of Russian officers to high command positions in the Czech Army. The Red Army itself remained in the background, but its presence was a constant reminder that it was there to be used—if necessary. There was also close cooperation between the Soviet and the satellite secret police. Just as the people's armies were for all practical purposes directed by Moscow, so the Soviets "liberated the police from [national] party control and made it a semi-autonomous agency subject, in the final analysis, only to Moscow itself."[2] In addition, the Soviet secret police maintained its own in-

[1] Zbigniew K. Brzezinski, *The Soviet Bloc*, p. 106.
[2] *Ibid.*, p. 120.

dependent structure in Eastern Europe. Whenever it considered Soviet security to be at stake, it could arrest any nationals of the People's Democracies. Finally, Soviet political and military domination was reinforced by economic control. Stalin established joint companies in which the shares and profits were to be divided on a fifty-fifty basis between the Soviet Union and each satellite nation. In reality, however, these joint companies were merely vehicles for Soviet exploitation of the economy. Another economic institution, the Council for Mutual Economic Aid (Comecon) was to be the economic equivalent of the Cominform (the postwar successor to the Comintern, abolished after Stalin's death). The principal concern of Comecon was to coordinate trade among the states of the socialist camp. The treaties governing these trade relations specified what goods the satellites had to deliver to the Soviet Union and at what prices. Thus Comecon served as another instrument of Soviet exploitation. All phases of the satellites' lives, then, were subject to close Soviet supervision. Their foreign affairs, particularly relations with the West, were "guided" by Moscow. They were told what their foreign policies should be, and that was that. Discussion, let alone disagreement, was futile and could well be dangerous for them.

Naturally, such complete subordination and exploitation led to strong popular resentment and anti-Russian feeling, although these remained hidden underneath the surface harmony and comradeship of "proletarian internationalism." Only one state opposed the Stalinist pattern of imperial control—ironically, Yugoslavia, once the most Stalinist of all Stalin's states. Its leader, Tito, had denounced the West in the harshest terms. He had shot down American planes and encouraged the Greek civil war. He had collectivized agriculture and industry at a rapid pace. Nevertheless, there were a number of reasons why a Stalin-Tito conflict was inevitable. First, Tito had gained international fame during the war as the leader of the Yugoslav partisans who resisted the German occupation forces and liberated their country with little or no help from the Red Army. Second, since Tito had built up his own party and army, he resisted Soviet attempts to penetrate them and remained in full control of all the instruments he needed to govern Yugoslavia. Third, Tito's ambitions were not compatible with Soviet control of Eastern Europe. He envisaged a Balkan federation composed of Yugoslavia, Albania, Greece, Romania, and Bulgaria, stretching from the Black Sea to the Adriatic (if he contemplated Poland's membership, as he apparently did, the federation would border the Baltic as well). In short, Tito was emerging as a serious contender to Stalin and his conception of a monolithic empire. If Tito were successful in presenting himself as a rival leader who, while also a Marxist-Leninist, would permit members of his federation greater independence in their internal affairs—plus refuge from Moscow's pervasive control and exploitation—Soviet leadership of Eastern Europe would be threatened. Stalin had no intention of permitting the members of his empire to travel their own domestic roads to socialism; each had to travel the Soviet road. And this could only be assured by Soviet supremacy. In order to discourage any other potential challengers of Soviet primacy, Stalin expelled Tito from the Cominform in 1949, and at the same time actual and potential leaders throughout Eastern Europe were dismissed from office, publicly tried, and in many cases executed. But the issue dramatized by the Tito-Stalin conflict—how to organize the new socialist camp—remained. According to the Soviet point of view:

> Communism was one and indivisible, a single, monolithic bloc, tightly bound together under Soviet leadership. A single dogmatic ideology— Marxism-Leninism, as interpreted by one authorized interpreter—must prevail. There is one and only one path to socialism—the Soviet path. All countries moving towards socialism must take the course already traversed by Soviet socialism. Revolution elsewhere must follow the Soviet pattern. The sole organ of international communism—the Cominform—would serve as the vehicle of policy transmission, and if necessary, of chastisement of dissidence. This monistic view treated all communist states . . . as integral parts of an organic whole. Needless to say, ideological and organization bonds of solidarity were to be reinforced by others no less potent if not so much discussed military, economic, and political controls in the hands of the leading country of the bloc. . . . The Yugoslav view of communism was pluralistic, seeing it as "a house of many mansions," each independent of Soviet mastery, and each having its own design and style. The ideology of Marxism was common to all, but there could be variations on the common theme, with no one orthodox version enunciated by Moscow. Each communist state had the right to develop its own brand of socialism, or communism, according to its own needs and conditions. There were "many roads to socialism": there was no need for a rigid, centralized international organization such as the Cominform. Cooperation among equals was desirable and could be attained through institutions of looser voluntary coordination. Above all, any effort at military or economic subordination and exploitation of the weaker communist state was rejected as an expression of great power politics inappropriate to a communist world.[3]

With the Soviet Union determined to expel any Communist state that rejected its "vanguard" position, there was bound to be a conflict with the new China. Historically, the relationship between Czarist Russia and Imperial China had hardly been that of equals. During the nineteenth century, the Russians, who by then had already extended their domain to Siberia and the Pacific coast, expanded farther eastward and southward. In 1860, they founded Vladivostok ("Ruler of the East") on former Chinese territory, and in the last decade of the century, they began to con-

[3] H. Gordon Skilling, "Communism: National or International," in DeVere E. Pentony (ed.), *Red World in Tumult*, p. 8.

struct the Trans-Siberian Railroad. Taking advantage of the weakness of Imperial China, the Czarist Government gained the right to lay the track through Manchuria and to control the management and finance of the railway. The Chinese Eastern Railroad thereby became a principal instrument for the expansion of Russian influence in northern Manchuria. The Russians also penetrated China in Sinkiang and Outer Mongolia, and occupied the island of Sakhalin. In fact, Czarist Russia's territorial gains and concessions in China exceeded those won by Britain and France. At Yalta during World War II, the price Stalin demanded for Russian participation in the war against Japan was, interestingly enough, a guarantee of the *status quo* in Outer Mongolia and the restoration of the "former rights of Russia violated by the treacherous attack of Japan in 1904"—the return of the southern part of Sakhalin, the internationalization of the port of Dairen (where the Soviet's "pre-eminent interests" were to be safeguarded), the lease of Port Arthur as a Soviet naval base, and joint operation of the Chinese Eastern Railroad and the Southern Manchurian Railroad, which connects with Dairen, "by the establishment of a joint Soviet-Chinese Company, it being understood that the pre-eminent interests of the Soviet Union shall be safeguarded." Finally, the Soviet Union was to be given the Kurile Islands.[4]

The establishment of the Chinese People's Republic thus posed a serious problem for the Soviet Union. On the one hand, Stalin was determined to preserve Soviet leadership of the new Sino-Soviet bloc and would not accord equality to Communist China. And he had no intention of abandoning the Soviet positions in Manchuria, Sinkiang, or the (renamed) Mongolian People's Republic. On the other hand, Mao Tse-tung, the leader of the Chinese Communist Party, intended to unify China and, like Tito, he controlled his own Party and army. Even more than Tito, he had used both to achieve his victory over Chiang Kai-shek and the Kuomintang (Nationalists). What then, was the new China's place to be in the Communist state system? How was Stalin to preserve the Soviet Union's territorial rights in China without antagonizing the Chinese leaders and thereby risking a repeat of his experience with Tito? The Treaty of Friendship, Alliance, and Mutual Assistance was Stalin's answer. Its central clause provided Soviet protection to China against an American attack:

> Both High Contracting Parties undertake jointly to take all necessary measures at their disposal for the purpose of preventing a repetition of aggression and violation of peace on the part of Japan or any other State which should unite with Japan, directly or indirectly, in acts of aggression. In the event of one of the High Contracting Parties being attacked by Japan or States allied with it [the United States] and thus being involved

[4] See David Floyd, *Mao Against Khrushchev*, pp. 213–15, for the treaty provisions.

in a state of war, the other High Contracting Party will immediately render military and other assistance with all the means at its disposal.[5]

The two treaty partners also pledged that "Both High Contracting Parties will consult each other in regard to all important international problems affecting the common interests of the Soviet Union and China, being guided by the interests of the consolidation of peace and universal security."[6]

But Stalin's customary interpretation of the word "consult," as demonstrated by his "consultations" with the East European People's Democracies, was unilateral decision and declaration followed by automatic and full-fledged support from the other members of the Soviet bloc. The more specific clauses concerning the areas of traditional Chinese-Russian conflict showed that Stalin intended to preserve the Soviet position in China, although he did make some significant concessions. In Manchuria, the Soviets pledged to return the Chinese Changchun Railroad by 1952, rather than by 1975 as stated in the post-Yalta Soviet treaty with Chiang Kai-shek. This seemed to indicate that the Russians were willing to abandon Manchuria as a sphere of influence. Port Arthur was to be turned over to the Chinese by 1952, but the Chinese were to compensate the Russians for expenses incurred in the restoration and construction of installations since 1945. The future of Dairen was left open; its civilian administration, however, was to be taken over by the Chinese. The Soviets recognized Chinese sovereignty in Sinkiang, but gained China's agreement for the establishment of joint companies under the direction of Soviet experts for the exploitation of Sinkiang's oil and metal resources. It was these joint companies—there was to be an additional one in Dairen for shipbuilding and another for the development of passenger aviation between Russia and China—which had served as tools of Soviet control and exploitation in Eastern Europe. In Outer Mongolia, the Chinese had no alternative but to accept the "independent" status of the Mongolian People's Republic. Finally, the Soviet Union lent the Chinese $300 million ($60 million per year over a five-year period) at 1 per cent annual interest;[7] reportedly, Mao had requested a loan of almost $3 billion.[8] The size of the loan must have been a severe disappointment for Mao, who had his own plans for rapid industrialization. Certainly, it would slow down China's industrial development.

The Treaty did, however, assign thousands of Soviet advisers—soldiers, engineers, technicians, economists, and teachers—to help China modernize. While these advisers may also have served as Soviet agents to maintain checks on China, they were not able to achieve the kind of con-

[5] *Ibid.*, p. 213.
[6] *Ibid.*
[7] *Ibid.*, p. 214.
[8] David J. Dallin, *Soviet Foreign Policy After Stalin*, p. 83.

trol Soviet advisers had exercised in Eastern Europe. The informal controls did not—and could not—exist in China since Mao held the reins over his own political and military levers of power. The Soviet Union's protection and aid were, however, vital to China and therefore provided a strong incentive to Peking to preserve close, if not always harmonious, relations with Moscow. On the whole, one political analyst has concluded, the Sino-Soviet Treaty did not "signify an about-face in Sino-Soviet relations. Some leeway had to be granted to Mao's policies, and Stalin had to accede to a number of Chinese demands. But Moscow succeeded in temporizing and in delaying and conditioning the rise of China. Stalin had no reason to revise his basic views about his allies, about the structure of the Soviet bloc, or about his own role as the leader of that bloc."[9] China was assigned to the second rank in the Soviet bloc. But Sinkiang and Mongolia remained potentially divisive issues; and Stalin refused to return Port Arthur in 1952, using the Korean War as his pretext. Thus in Sino-Soviet relations, as in relations between the Soviet Union and Eastern Europe, there were clearly strains and tensions that someday would threaten the unity of the bloc.

They rose to the surface first in Eastern Europe. Stalin had left a legacy of popular resentment and hatred for Russia in the People's Democracies that confronted his successors—first Malenkov and then Khrushchev—with a serious dilemma. If they preserved the Stalinist conception of empire, they would only intensify the existing dissatisfaction, the opposition to Soviet exploitation and Soviet-imposed rapid industrialization, with its neglect of the people's standard of living and peasant agriculture and its attendant police terror. Indications of the trouble ahead came soon after Stalin's death in the form of a general strike and uprising in East Germany and East Berlin during June, 1953. The revolt was spearheaded, moreover, by the proletariat, to whose liberation from capitalist chains the Communists were supposedly dedicated. The chief victims of the rapid industrialization, they rebelled against the low wages, harsh discipline, and austerity. But their support came from the mass of the population: "Wage demands were only the starting point. Slogans voicing opposition to police oppression and dictatorship were added almost immediately. Expanding and reaching into the international field, the movements proclaimed their negative attitude toward Russian control and revealed a strong trend in favor of the West."[10] The use of Russian tanks and troops to quell the revolt, especially in Berlin, was hardly the way for the Soviets to impress on the world that Communism was the wave of the future because of its superior way of life. On the other hand, what if the Soviet leaders relaxed their grip on the satellites too much? Might not this stimulate further demands for concessions until

[9] *Ibid.*
[10] *Ibid.*, p. 170.

Soviet authority had been virtually whittled away? Could they thus safely eliminate the worst abuses and the most oppressive features of the Stalinist system without disintegrating the bloc? While suppression produced resentment, concessions might create popular defiance and self-confidence.

The East German uprising allowed the new Soviet leaders little time to consider these questions. A relaxation of the Soviet reins—"thaw," as it came to be called—was absolutely necessary. Exploitation of the satellites had to be abandoned; the joint companies were abolished. The satellite governments were to be allowed a greater degree of political authority in their domestic affairs. And the power of the Soviet-controlled secret police was curtailed and subjected to national Party control, thus decreasing Moscow's authority. Moscow's willingness to tolerate "different roads to socialism" was symbolized by Khrushchev's surprise visit to Belgrade in 1955 and his humble apology for Russia's anti-Yugoslav activities. This attempted *rapprochement* with Tito was intended to bring him back into the socialist camp and thus close the rift in world Communism.

The Soviet leaders acted upon the apparent conviction that

> . . . when stripped of its worst excesses, communism possessed enough historical truth and popular attraction to secure the devotion of even those who had suffered for years under its "errors." In the immemorial manner of politicians, the Soviet leaders assumed that they could have their cake and eat it, too; that the fundamental features of internal totalitarianism and essential control over the satellites could be preserved, and yet the removal of the worst abuses would procure them genuine loyalty, would release new creative impulses and ideological fervor among the Communists at home and abroad.[11]

This was one of the principal reasons for the attack on the dead Stalin. For by attacking the creator of many of these abuses and the symbol of the tyranny and injustice of Communist rule—the former master whom he had once praised so fulsomely—Khrushchev could suggest the removal of these abuses and the basic soundness of Communism. His portrait of the dead Russian dictator was even more terrifying than that drawn by the bitterest anti-Communist propaganda. Stalin was depicted as a mass murderer who abused his power and systematically purged his colleagues. Thus it was not Communism that was at fault. Stalin's terror was a perversion of Communism. Communism remained a vital ideology binding the socialist parties of the Soviet Union and the People's Democracies together in fraternal association.

This revived ideology was, however, to be supplemented by mutual economic interests. While each satellite Party was to be granted a degree of autonomy in directing its affairs, with a corresponding loosening of

[11] Adam B. Ulam, "Soviet Ideology and Soviet Foreign Policy," *World Politics*, January, 1959, p. 164.

Moscow's political strings, economics was to provide the uniting link. Eastern Europe was to be treated as a single economic unit within which each nation specialized in certain tasks. Poland would become the principal producer of bituminous coal; East Germany, lignite and chemicals; and Czechoslovakia, cars. In this way, the bloc was to become interdependent, with Comecon as its governing institution.

In a sense, then, the new shape of Soviet-Yugoslav relations was to serve as the pattern for relations between the Soviet Union and the other People's Democracies:

> Noting that, domestically, Tito had been a forceful Communist, the Soviet leadership appears to have assumed that an arrangement stressing common party bonds while accepting Tito's domestic autonomy would establish a pattern for similarly firm Communist regimes elsewhere. They would be bound together through the rigorous party dictatorships run on similar doctrinal assumptions, reinforced by integrated economic processes.[12]

This economic unity was to be strengthened further by Soviet military power. In 1955, the Soviet Union signed the twenty-year Warsaw Pact with Albania, Bulgaria, Czechoslovakia, East Germany, Hungary, Poland, and Romania. Ostensibly the Communist version of NATO, this Pact in fact "represented the single most important formal commitment binding the states to the U.S.S.R., officially limiting their scope of independent action, and legalizing the presence (and hence the political influence) of the Soviet troops stationed in some of them.[13]

But by relaxing its former tight grip, Moscow stimulated the demand for even greater independence; the Soviet-controlled thaw soon became an uncontrolled flood. The first sign of trouble was the workers' strike in the Polish city of Poznan in June, 1956. Starting as a demand for better economic conditions, the strike quickly turned into a political revolt. Conflicts with the police and army ensued. There was a period of general unrest and then, in October, came the dramatic climax. The Polish Communists announced their intention to elect Gomulka as First Secretary of the Party and to dismiss Soviet Marshal Rokossovsky. That these significant decisions had been taken without any prior consultation with Moscow was tantamount to a revolt. When the Russians learned what was about to occur, they requested that the Poles come to Moscow to talk matters over. The Poles refused. The Russian reaction was to order Red Army units in Poland to move toward Warsaw and other cities; and troops in East Germany were sent to the Polish border. Khrushchev and several colleagues flew to Warsaw and there uttered some harsh and threatening words, calling Gomulka a traitor and demanding that

---

[12] Brzezinski, op. cit., p. 173.
[13] Ibid., p. 171.

Rokossovsky be reinstated. The answer given by the Poles was that they would not even talk to Khrushchev unless he stopped all Russian troop movements. This was the decisive moment. The Polish Internal Security forces were controlled by the Poles, and the loyalty of the Polish Army to the Soviets was unreliable. A war in Poland would cut East Germany off—and perhaps spark a renewed East German revolt. The Polish situation thus held the seeds of a revolt throughout the satellite area, threatening to undermine the entire Soviet position in Europe. Khrushchev therefore called off his troops. And the "Polish October" ended safely. Khrushchev realized that the Polish Communist Party was in control of the country and that Gomulka remained loyal to the bloc. Thus he could grant Gomulka's request for a degree of internal autonomy to carry out some domestic reforms.

In Hungary, however, Khrushchev did use force. Hungary's "time of troubles" started with a mass demonstration calling for freedom, proclaiming Polish-Hungarian friendship and solidarity, demanding restoration of the Kossuth emblem on the national flag, and urging the Russians to go home. The demonstrators converged on Radio Budapest and demanded that the radio be given to the people; in the ensuing melee, the security police began firing into the mob. Workers soon joined the fighting against the police, who were subsequently reinforced by Soviet tanks. Order was restored, but the Stalinist Premier was replaced by Imre Nagy. His supporter, Janos Kadar, was named First Secretary of the Party. Nagy negotiated a cease-fire, and Soviet troops began to pull out of Budapest. But Nagy insisted that they withdraw from all of Hungary. If they refused, he informed the Russians, Hungary would denounce the Warsaw Treaty and assume a neutral course. It was this decision to quit the Soviet bloc, plus Nagy's restoration of a genuine multiparty government, including the peasant and social-democratic parties, which triggered Soviet military intervention. Unlike Poland, Hungary had tried to defect; and again unlike Poland, the Communist Party had lost its monopoly of power. The Kremlin was not willing to tolerate either condition. If it did, the Soviet empire in Eastern Europe would "wither away." The Red Army therefore squashed the rebellion. But the Hungarian Revolution had offered dramatic proof once more that in the final analysis the Soviet empire rested on naked force. And it demonstrated to the Soviets that if force was not to be used frequently, the reins on satellite freedom had to be tightened again.

The third period (first there had been the long Stalinist period, then the relatively short-lived thaw) in Soviet-satellite relations was officially proclaimed by the 1957 Moscow Conference of Communist Parties. Its stress on the unity of the socialist camp seemed to represent a return to the Stalinist system. The Soviet experience was once more emphasized as being applicable to all Communist states:

The experience of the Soviet Union and the other socialist countries has fully borne out the correctness of the Marxist-Leninist proposition that the processes of the socialist revolution and the building of socialism are governed by a number of basic laws applicable in all countries embarking on a socialist course. . . . These laws are: guidance of the working masses by the working class, the core of which is the Marxist-Leninist Party; in effecting a proletarian revolution in one form or another and establishing one form or other of the dictatorship of the proletariat; the alliance of the working class and the bulk of the peasantry and other sections of the working people; the abolition of capitalist ownership and the establishment of public ownership of the basic means of production; gradual socialist reconstruction of agriculture; planned development of the national economy aimed at building socialism and communism, at raising the standard of living of the working people; the carrying out of socialist revolution in the sphere of ideology and culture and the creation of a numerous intelligentsia devoted to the working class, the working people and the cause of socialism; the abolition of national oppression and the establishment of equality and fraternal friendship between the peoples; defence of the achievements of socialism against attacks by internal enemies; solidarity of the working class of the country in question with the working class of other countries, that is proletarian internationalism.[14]

But this apparent shift back to Stalinism was far from complete. Nor could it have been without generating the kind of conditions that had led to explosions in East Germany, Poland, and Hungary. Thus, it was made clear that while there were certain "basic laws" of socialist construction, there were also

. . . a great variety of historic national peculiarities and traditions which must by all means be taken into account. . . . Marxism-Leninism calls for a creative application of the general principles of the socialist revolution and socialist construction depending on the concrete conditions of each country, and rejects mechanical imitation of the policies and tactics of the Communist Parties of other countries. Lenin repeatedly called attention to the necessity of correctly applying the basic principles of communism, in keeping with the specific features of the nation, of the national state concerned. Disregard of national peculiarities by the proletarian party inevitably leads to its divorce from reality, from the masses, and is bound to prejudice the cause of socialism.[15]

The conclusion seemed clear: While national circumstances were not to be ignored, "exaggeration of the role of these peculiarities or departure, under the pretext of national peculiarities, from the universal Marxist-Leninist truth on the socialist revolution and socialist construction is just as harmful to the socialist cause."[16] This was exactly what the

[14] Quoted in G. F. Hudson, Richard Lowenthal, and Roderick MacFarquhar (eds.), *The Sino-Soviet Dispute*, p. 51.
[15] *Ibid.*, pp. 51–52.
[16] *Ibid.*, p. 52.

Yugoslavs, who were now once more isolated, had done. "National Communism" was unacceptable to the Soviet Union. Completely independent Communist states, such as Yugoslavia, would destroy the unity of the Communist bloc and undermine Soviet leadership. National Communism was criticized as "revisionism," a term of vigorous condemnation carrying with it a reminder of the "betrayal" of orthodox Marxism by European social democrats at the turn of the century. In short, the Soviets were prepared to accept national "adaptations" of the basic laws of socialist construction, but only so long as the resulting diversity presented no challenge to their dominant role in the international Communist movement. Communist states could experiment internally, but only within certain limitations: recognition of the Soviet Union as the leader of the socialist camp; retention of the dictatorship of the proletariat—that is, the Communist one-party state; acceptance of the basic irreconcilability of the capitalist and socialist worlds; and finally, rejection of an independent, or "neutral," foreign policy. Yugoslavia's refusal to accept any of these conditions except the second one was the reason for her new isolation and the bitter Soviet attack against all reformist efforts in Eastern Europe. Violation of any of the conditions by a satellite, it was implied, might precipitate Soviet military intervention.

Thus, while the concept of "different roads to socialism" was not eliminated, the main emphasis was placed upon the "great commonwealth of socialist nations." As if to re-emphasize their determination to hold the bloc together, the Soviets began a partial rehabilitation of Stalin. Certain of Stalin's policies had, of course, never been completely rejected—for example, collectivization and industrialization, with their fearsome toll in excessive discipline, deprivation, and actual human lives. Nor had his execution or exile of the Old Bolshevik revolutionaries who had purportedly sought to lead the Party and nation from the true Leninist path been denounced. Stalin's crimes were said to have been committed only after 1934, when he had begun to use terror on an extensive scale to establish and preserve his personal dictatorship. The Soviets now declared that the fight against the Stalinist "cult of personality" would continue, but that this campaign had no bearing on the fight against Western imperialism—which had, according to the official Soviet line, provoked the "counterrevolutions" in East Germany and Hungary. So, only ten months after his withering denunciation of Stalin, Khrushchev said: "If it is a question of fighting against imperialism we can state with conviction that we are all Stalinists in fact. We can be proud that we have taken part in the fight for the advance of our great cause against our enemies. From that point of view I am proud that we are Stalinists." Shortly thereafter, Khrushchev reaffirmed this when he explained that "Stalinism, like Stalin himself, is inseparable from communism. Where it was a question of the revolution, of the defence of the class interests of the proletariat in the fight against the enemies of our class, Stalin defended the cause of Marxism-Leninism bravely and unyieldingly." While admitting that Stalin had committed errors, Khrushchev pointed out that he had been convinced that his policies were necessary for the defense of the interests of the working class against hostile plots and attacks by the imperialists. In such fundamental matters, Khrushchev concluded, "God grant, as the saying goes, that every communist may fight as Stalin fought."[17] In this manner, the People's Democracies of Eastern Europe were informed that there were definite limits to the diversity the Soviets were willing to tolerate within the bloc and that the Kremlin intended to preserve its hegemony in the Communist world. To dramatize the point, Imre Nagy and several other leaders of the Hungarian revolt were executed. Moscow would tolerate "Autonomy of action, yes, but within the intimate voluntary solidarity of the bloc; differences of policy, yes, within certain strict bounds of common action; reforms in communism, yes, but only within the framework of the system itself. The limits within which this diversity should operate would be set by Moscow; outside those narrow and arbitrarily movable limits, strict uniformity of policy and of ideology would be required."[18] The Moscow-Peking conflict of the next decade would, however, further undermine Moscow's authority over the People's Democracies and increase the scope of their independence from the Kremlin.

The Sino-Soviet Conflict of "Revolutionary Interests"

The issue of Soviet hegemony was exactly the one on which the Sino-Soviet conflict, which broke out into the open in 1956–57, was to revolve. China considered itself the Soviet Union's equal and potentially one of the world's great powers. Furthermore, it possessed an independent Party and army. China could hardly therefore be transformed into a satellite. Indeed, Communist China's first objective—although ultimately not its most important—was to restore its own unity, status, and strength. For much of the 2,000 years preceding the Communist takeover, China as an imperial power had exercised hegemony over large areas of the Far East, Central Asia, and Southeast Asia. China was the "Middle Kingdom," receiving tribute from the surrounding states. The Chinese have always been convinced of their primacy in Asia—as well as their cultural superiority. Non-Chinese were regarded as "barbarians." Such an attitude naturally bred a sense of superiority and condescension toward other nations —similar to that generally harbored by the West toward the non-Western (formerly colonial) peoples. But China's goal in its determination to be a great power was not limited to playing a pre-eminent role in Asia;

---

[17] Quoted in Wolfgang Leonhard, *The Kremlin Since Stalin*, p. 232.
[18] Skilling, in Pentony (ed.), *op. cit.*, p. 11.

the new China's second aim was to play a major role in determining the bloc's over-all policies.

The question this posed for the Soviets, and for the future of the Sino-Soviet alliance, was whether they should permit China to *share* the leadership of the bloc. Aware that tensions with Peking already existed, Stalin's successors sought to relieve them by immediately granting China and Mao greater status within the Communist movement. Symbolically, Chou En-lai as the representative of the Chinese Communist Party at Stalin's funeral walked side by side with Malenkov and Khrushchev behind the carriage bearing the Soviet dictator's body; and he stood among the Soviet leaders on the balcony of Lenin's tomb, from which the eulogies were delivered, rather than with the other foreign Communist leaders. Moreover, a Soviet delegation visited Peking on the fifth anniversary of the Chinese regime, in 1954; the Russians promised to withdraw from Port Arthur by mid-1955, agreed to the abolition of the remaining joint companies, and relinquished control of Sinkiang to the Chinese. Thus, with the exception of Mongolia, China had recovered control of all her border areas where the Soviets had encroached. Finally, the Russians agreed to increase their total economic aid funds to help in the industrial development of China.

But if the Soviet Union was willing to accord the new China greater status within the Communist world, it soon became apparent that the Kremlin had no intention of sharing its dominant position. Ironically, it was Khrushchev's attack on Stalin in 1956 that precipitated the Sino-Soviet conflict. The Chinese considered the attack a blunder. Not that they bore any great love for Stalin's memory, but they apparently saw the implications of this drastic step more clearly than Khrushchev himself. Partly, no doubt, they were embarrassed by the implications of Khrushchev's denunciation of Stalin, having themselves publicly praised Stalin for years. The revelation of Stalin's real personality and methods of ruling Russia made the Chinese look foolish. Moreover, the attack on the cult of the individual might be considered applicable as well to the organized adulation for Mao Tse-tung. Even worse, Khrushchev's denunciation had raised the fundamental question as to whether Stalinism was the product of the late dictator's personality or of the nature of Communist society. Khrushchev had clearly blamed the former and sought to exonerate the latter. But such critics as the leaders of the Italian and American Communist parties continued to assert that Stalinism was a reflection of the Soviet system. Could they not properly contend that a repetition of Stalin's crimes could be avoided only by placing some checks on the exercise of totalitarian power? And could such checks be accepted without an undermining of the Party's monopoly of authority? Had Khrushchev, indeed, not placed the legitimacy of the Communist system in jeopardy by his denunciation of the man who for three decades had been depicted by Communist propaganda as the wise and humane successor to Lenin and the legitimate ruler of world Communism? Furthermore, had he not gravely weakened the international movement by dethroning Stalin? For his criticisms were bound to set in motion centrifugal pressures within the bloc, since he had in fact undermined Moscow's authority as the infallible interpreter of Marxist-Leninist doctrine. After Khrushchev's revelations, who could again trust Moscow's leadership? This raised the danger of polycentrism—that is, "the removal of the CPSU from the center of the international Communist movement, and for a new arrangement in which all the Communist parties would be equal and would have bilateral relations, one with another, rather than being collectively subordinated to Moscow. The absence of unilateral dictation by Moscow would thus inhibit any desires on the part of more powerful parties to dictate to weaker parties. Polycentrism would also mean much greater independence for Communist parties throughout the world to establish policies in accord with local conditions."[19] But the emergence of several independent Communist centers of authority would severely weaken the bloc's ideological and political unity, required for effective action against the capitalist enemy. It was just this kind of reaction that the Chinese purportedly anticipated.[20]

Finally, the Chinese questioned not only the wisdom of Khrushchev's action but also the manner. The paradox, as the Chinese saw it, was that on the one hand Khrushchev was denouncing Stalin for the way in which he had exercised his absolute power, but on the other hand, Khrushchev expected all Communist parties to accept Moscow's unilateral decision to downgrade Stalin. The new Soviet leader was thus behaving in a characteristically Stalinist manner. Since the destruction of the Stalin myth discredited not only Russian Communism but the entire international movement, the Chinese felt that they should have been consulted before Khrushchev made his decision—and they were all the more bitter because he had actually consulted Tito. In the aftermath of Poland and Hungary, the Chinese therefore asserted their claim to share in the Soviet Union's monopoly of decision-making authority for the entire socialist camp by intervening in Eastern Europe to preserve socialist unity. In both cases, Khrushchev's judgment had clearly been poor, and the results disastrous.

What was significant about this Chinese intervention was that they intervened at all. The states of Eastern Europe were, after all, Russia's satellites, and previously they had been a matter solely for Moscow's concern. But China now asserted the right to a voice in Moscow's relationships with Warsaw, Budapest, and Belgrade. In early 1957, China sent Chou En-lai as a mediator on a visit to the Soviet Union, Poland, and

[19] Donald S. Zagoria, *The Sino-Soviet Conflict, 1956–1961*, p. 54.
[20] Edward Crankshaw, *The New Cold War: Moscow v. Peking*, pp. 53–54.

Hungary, to help restore the unity of the bloc under Soviet leadership. China's aid at the time was welcome to the Kremlin. Given the continuing dissension over the events of 1956 within the Soviet leadership, and the damaged prestige of Moscow, Chou's mediation helped the Soviet Union to survive a humiliating situation and recover from a weakened stance. But the importance of China's intervention in Eastern Europe should not be underestimated. For Peking was in fact claiming that any "counterrevolution" in a Communist-ruled state or conflict among Communist states was the concern of *all* Communist states—or, at least, of the two largest Communist states. As the Chinese told the Soviets:

> Stalin displayed certain great-nation chauvinist tendencies in relations with brother parties and countries. The essence of such tendencies lies in being unmindful of the independent and equal status of the Communist parties of various lands and that of the socialist countries within the framework of international bond of union. There are certain historical reasons for such tendencies. The time-worn habits of big countries in their relations with small countries continue to make their influence felt in certain ways, while a series of victories achieved by a party or a country in its revolutionary cause is apt to give rise to a sense of superiority. . . . If the Communist parties maintain relations of equality among themselves and reach common understanding and take concerted action through genuine, and not nominal, exchange of views, their unity will be strengthened. Conversely, if, in their mutual relations, one party imposes its views upon others, or if the parties use the method of interference in each other's internal affairs instead of comradely suggestions and criticism, their unity will be impaired.[21]

In short, the Chinese wished to preserve a united bloc in which they would be the equals of the Russians. As the strongest Communist power, the Soviet Union was the bloc's obvious "center," but China was claiming co-leadership. In effect, the Chinese were seeking the establishment of a Sino-Soviet high command that would wage an effective *coalition* campaign against the capitalist enemy.

If the principal issue between the Chinese and Soviets was the nature of the decision-making process within the bloc, this issue was clearly related to the problem of the "correct strategy" to be pursued toward the West and the underdeveloped nations. The difficulty was that the Chinese disagreed with Soviet strategy, and the Kremlin refused to budge. As the historical source of authority and policy, Moscow considered its position the right one and consequently continued to assert its authority to speak for the international Communist movement while strongly attacking the Chinese views on global strategy. This ensured that the Sino-Soviet "debate" would become embittered and, in turn, intensify the

[21] *The People's Daily*, December 29, 1956; quoted in Floyd, *op. cit.*, p. 246.

struggle for leadership. For China, too, was confident that its strategy was the correct one.

One of the basic issues on which they disagreed was the issue of war and peace, which came to the fore in late 1957 after the successful Soviet firsts with an ICBM and two earth satellites. Khrushchev interpreted these events as significantly changing the balance of power between socialism and capitalism, but he did not claim that the Soviet Union, or the Sino-Soviet bloc, had become predominant. The principal effect of the ICBM and Sputniks, in the Soviet view, was to ensure the Soviet capacity to deter a U.S. attack. As the Soviet missile force grew, it would gain increased ability to inflict a catastrophic counterblow on America if she attacked the Soviet Union. The resulting mutual capacity for massive retaliation would make a nuclear war between the two powers unthinkable. Implicitly, the Soviets were thus admitting that nuclear war could upset the laws of history and forestall the final emergence of socialism. Lenin's view that this emergence would be preceded by a number of wars with the capitalists would therefore have to be revised.

The Soviet view now indicated the need for a strategy of peaceful coexistence. Mao, however, appraised the post-Sputnik situation somewhat differently. The East wind, he said, now prevailed over the West wind. Thus the Soviet Union should exploit its new superiority to pursue a more militant course. Nuclear arms did not, in any case, change Lenin's view that since wars were the outgrowth of capitalism they were still possible while capitalism continued to exist. In an article significantly entitled "Long Live Leninism," *Red Flag*, the theoretical journal of the Chinese Communist Party, explained:

> In the past few years, the achievements of the Soviet Union in science and technology have been foremost in the world. These Soviet achievements are products of the Great October Revolution. These outstanding achievements mark a new era in man's conquest of nature and at the same time play a very important role in defending world peace. But, in the new conditions brought about by the development of modern technology, has the ideological system of Marxism-Leninism been shaken, as Tito [also read, Khrushchev] says, by the rocket on the moon, atomic bombs and the great technical progress which Marx and Lenin "did not predict"? Can it be said that the Marxist-Leninist world outlook, social-historical outlook, moral outlook and other basic concepts have therefore become what they call stale "dogmas" and that the law of class struggle henceforth no longer holds good? . . .
>
> Marxist-Leninists have always maintained that in world history it is not technique but man, the masses of people, that determine the fate of mankind. There was a theory current for a time . . . which was known as the "weapons-mean-everything theory." . . . [But] Comrade Mao Tse-tung pointed out that the most abundant source of strength in war lay in the masses, and that . . . an awakened people will always find new ways to

counteract a reactionary superiority in arms and win victory for themselves. This was so in past history, it is so at present, and it will still be so in the future.

Of course, whether or not the imperialists will unleash a war is not determined by us; we are, after all, not chiefs-of-staff to the imperialists. . . . [But] if the U.S. or other imperialists . . . should dare to fly in the face of the will of all humanity by launching a war using atomic and nuclear weapons, the result will be the very speedy destruction of these monsters encircled by the peoples of the world, and the result will certainly not be the annihilation of mankind. We consistently oppose the launching of criminal wars by imperialism, because imperialist war would impose enormous sacrifices upon the peoples of various countries (including the peoples of the United States and other imperialist countries). But should the imperialists impose such sacrifices on the peoples of various countries, we believe that, just as the experience of the Russian revolution and the Chinese revolution shows, those sacrifices would be repaid. On the debris of a dead imperialism, the victorious people would create very swiftly a civilisation thousands of times higher than the capitalist system and a truly beautiful future for themselves. The conclusion can only be this: whichever way you look at it, none of the new techniques like atomic energy, rocketry and so on has changed, as alleged by the modern revisionists [what the Chinese were now calling Khrushchev], the basic characteristics of the epoch of imperialism and proletarian revolution pointed out by Lenin. . . . We believe in the absolute correctness of Lenin's thinking: War is an inevitable outcome of systems of exploitation and the source of modern wars is the imperialist system. Until the imperialist system and the exploiting classes come to an end, wars of one kind or another will always occur.[22]

Khrushchev, calling the Chinese "dogmatists" for their literal interpretation of Lenin, bluntly commented on the Chinese position:

Today some people who call themselves Marxist-Leninists allege that the defence of peace and the struggle against the war danger are contrary to the spirit of Marxism-Leninism and hamper the progress of the revolutionary movement. . . .

If the Communists were to be guided by a "theory" such as that, this would repel the masses instead of attracting them. This "theory" is all the more repellent in this rocket and nuclear age. . . . Foreign scientists and military experts estimate that the United States now has roughly 40,000 hydrogen bombs and warheads. Everyone knows that the Soviet Union, too, has more than enough of this stuff.

What would happen if all these nuclear weapons were brought down on people? Scientists estimate that the first blow alone would take a toll of 700 to 800 million human lives. All the big cities would be wiped out or destroyed—not only in the two leading nuclear countries, the United

[22] *Red Flag*, April 16, 1960; quoted in Floyd, *op. cit.*, pp. 267–68.

States and the U.S.S.R., but in France, Britain, Germany, Italy, China, Japan and many other countries of the world. The effects of a nuclear war would continue to tell through the lifetime of many generations, causing disease and death and the worst deformities in the development of people. I am not saying these things to frighten anyone. I am simply citing data at the disposal of science. These data cannot but be reckoned with.

There can be no doubt that a world nuclear war, if started by the imperialist maniacs, would inevitably result in the downfall of the capitalist system, a system breeding wars. But would the socialist countries and the cause of socialism all over the world benefit from a world nuclear disaster? Only people who deliberately shut their eyes to the facts can think so. As for Marxist-Leninists, they cannot propose to establish a Communist civilisation on the ruins of centres of world culture, on land laid waste and contaminated by nuclear fall-out. We need hardly add that in the case of many peoples, the question of socialism would be eliminated altogether, because they would have disappeared bodily from our planet.[23]

And later, Khrushchev made these further comments on the Chinese position:

We would like to ask the Chinese comrades, who suggest building a bright future on the ruins of the old world destroyed by a thermonuclear war, whether they consulted the working class of the countries where imperialism dominates? The working class of the capitalist countries would be sure to tell them: Do we ask you to trigger off a war and destroy our countries while annihilating imperialists? Is it not a fact that the monopolists and the imperialists are only a comparatively small group, while the bulk of the population of the capitalist countries consists of the working class, working peasantry and working intelligentsia? The atomic bomb does not distinguish between imperialists and working people. It hits big areas, and therefore millions of workers would be destroyed for each monopolist. The working class, the working people, will ask such "revolutionaries": What right have you to settle for us the questions of our existence and our class struggle?—we, too, are in favour of socialism, but we want to gain it through the class struggle and not by unleashing a world war.

Such a posing of the question by the Chinese comrades may engender well-justified suspicions that this is no longer a class approach in the struggle for the abolition of capitalism, but some entirely different aim. If both the exploiters and the exploited are buried under the ruins of the old world, who will build the "bright future"?

In this connexion it is impossible not to note the fact that instead of the class internationalist approach expressed in the call "Workers of the World, Unite" the Chinese comrades stubbornly propagate the slogan deprived of any class meaning: "The Wind from the East prevails over the Wind from the West."[24]

[23] Khrushchev's address to the Sixth Congress of the East German Communist Party, January 16, 1963; quoted in Floyd, *op. cit.*, pp. 353–54.
[24] *Pravda*, July 14, 1963; quoted in Floyd, *op. cit.*, p. 436.

For the Chinese, then, the class struggle was supposedly subordinated to the military struggle.

But these exchanges could hardly be interpreted to mean that the Soviets were for "peace" and the Chinese for "war." To be sure, this was how Khrushchev presented the issue in order to consolidate the Soviet position in the Communist movement and isolate the Chinese. But the issue of war or peace was not that simple. Only a few years earlier, in his power struggle with Malenkov, Khrushchev had himself taken the "hard" line now identified with Peking. Malenkov, successor to Stalin as Prime Minister, had stated that a nuclear war would destroy "world civilization"—i.e., both the capitalist and the Communist countries. Denying this, Khrushchev had said that while the Communist states would suffer heavy damage, they would not be destroyed; only the capitalist countries would be eliminated. The thesis that nuclear war would cause the destruction of world civilization was denounced as a capitalist trick to lull the masses into a false sense of security and to allow the capitalists to pose as saviors of peace while they really pursued an aggressive course.[25] Not until after Khrushchev—successor to Stalin's other and more powerful position as First Secretary of the Party—had toppled Malenkov, in 1955, did he reverse himself and adopt Malenkov's earlier position at the Twentieth Party Congress, in 1956. All of a sudden, he contended that nuclear war threatened the destruction of the Soviet Union. Ironically, it had been the Chinese, now accused by Khrushchev of being warmongers, who had first enunciated the principles of "peaceful coexistence," in 1954: mutual respect for each other's territorial integrity and sovereignty, nonaggression, noninterference in each other's internal affairs, equality, and mutual benefit. Peaceful coexistence was for the Chinese, as it was for the Russians, of course, a tactic designed to advance Communist purposes by exploiting such widely and intensely felt emotions as anticolonialism and anti-Westernism, the desire to remain uninvolved in the struggles of the great powers and concentrate on urgent domestic problems, a strong desire for peace, a conviction that military alliance and bases increased rather than diminished the chances of conflict, and a feeling that Asians have common bonds that set them apart from the West.[26]

When one examines actual behavior, it becomes even more difficult to analyze the Sino-Soviet debate in terms of the simple war-peace dichotomy. For despite all the talk of peaceful coexistence, it was Khrushchev who could not refrain from brandishing his Sputniks and ICBM's and making them "pay off" politically and psychologically. It was Khrushchev who violated the moratorium on nuclear testing in 1961; it was his

[25] The Malenkov-Khrushchev dispute over nuclear weapons is analyzed in Herbert S. Dinerstein, *War and the Soviet Union*, pp. 65–77.
[26] See A. Doak Barnett, *Communist China and Asia*, pp. 100, 101.

nuclear blackmail tactics that on several occasions brought the world to the brink of war; and it was he who repeatedly threatened America's allies that he would turn their countries into "cemeteries." Finally, it was Khrushchev who in the name of peaceful coexistence had occasioned the dangerous Cuban confrontation by seeking to gain a strategic superiority over the U.S. In turn, this attempt suggested that Khrushchev's concept of peaceful coexistence was less a matter of choice than a matter of necessity for the strategically inferior Soviet Union. Had he been able to place his missiles in Cuba, he might in fact have been able to treat the American "imperialists" as the "paper tigers" the Chinese alleged they were.[27]

By contrast, Chinese actions hardly matched their militant words. It may be true that the Chinese believe a "truly beautiful future" awaits the world after a nuclear war; and Mao is reported to have stated that even if China lost 300 million people in a nuclear war, she would—unlike the Soviet Union and the United States—still have 300 million people left and would therefore emerge as the world's strongest power. But the Chinese have shown little desire to become involved in a major war with the United States. They probably are quite aware that the nuclear destruction of China's food supplies and cities, however few and however primitively industrialized, would wreck the control system by which the totalitarian government in Peking maintains itself in power. In any case, the Chinese record when it has confronted American power is not one of recklessness but of caution. In the Korean conflict, the Chinese warned that an advance into North Korea would compel them to enter the war, just as the Communist invasion of South Korea had forced the United States to fight. Both sides intervened for the same defensive reason—to prevent the "Korean dagger" from being aimed, and thrust, into their hearts. The first Chinese intervention, in late October, 1950, was a limited one and was broken off in early November. Then there was no contact for three weeks—until the Chinese counterattack to MacArthur's "home by Christmas" offensive during late November. And once they were fully committed, the Chinese sought to ensure the "limitation" of the war by refraining from such measures as air attacks on the forces in the field or the supply ports. Several years later, in their two attempts to capture the offshore islands of Quemoy and Matsu in the Formosa Straits, the Chinese broke off the action when they realized the American determination to support the Nationalist troops on the islands. Thus American supply ships, just outside the 3-mile territorial limit, were not fired upon by Chinese shore batteries—even though Peking claimed a 12-mile limit. The Chinese attack on the northeast frontier of India in late 1962 was also carefully limited, in part perhaps because of the American and British fighter squadrons sent to India to deter the Chinese from

[27] Floyd, *op. cit.*, p. 67.

bombing Indian cities. These fighters, and the subsequent arms shipments, were symbolic of the American commitment to India's defense
in an emergency. Indeed, American Air Force cargo planes even carried
Indian forces and supplies to the mountainous areas where there was
fighting. The Chinese were actually so cautious that Khrushchev, whom
the Chinese were at this time accusing of having become "timid as a
mouse," taunted Mao: Pointing to the colony of Macao off the coast of
China, controlled by the Portuguese for centuries, and to the British
colony of Hong Kong, just below Canton, Khrushchev wondered why, if
the Chinese pursued the militant policy they were preaching and trying
to foist on the Russians, they did not simply march into Macao and
Hong Kong.[28] Surely they were not fearful of a war with Portugal or Britain. But that was precisely the point. Although NATO would no more
come to Portugal's aid in Macao than it had when the Indian Army took
over Goa, China was not prepared to risk any open conflict with the
West. Since Korea, China had resorted to arms only against weaker nations—Tibet and India. In short, the Chinese were acting just like the
Russians. When Mao was the responsible policy-maker instead of the irresponsible critic, he, too, was a "revisionist." No one, Khrushchev
said,

> . . . will denounce the Chinese People's Republic for leaving intact these
> fragments of colonialism. It would be wrong to prod China into any kind
> of action which she considers untimely. If the government of the Chinese
> People's Republic tolerates Macao and Hong Kong, it clearly has good
> reasons for doing so. Therefore, it would be ridiculous to level against it
> the accusation that this is a concession to Britain and Portuguese colonial-
> ists, that this is appeasement.
>
> But maybe this is a retreat from Marxism-Leninism? Nothing of the
> kind. It means that the government of the Chinese People's Republic
> takes into account the realities, the actual possibilities. And this is by no
> means because the Chinese are less sensitive to colonialism than the In-
> dians, or that they are more tolerant towards Salazar than is India. No;
> our Chinese friends hate colonialism, just as every revolutionary does. But
> they clearly proceed from their conditions and act on their own under-
> standing, and display patience. But does that mean that we must con-
> demn them for it, or contend that they have retreated from Marxism-
> Leninism? No, it does not. That would be foolish.
>
> In the consequence of a number of circumstances one sometimes has to
> live not among fragrant roses but amidst thorns, and sometimes even in
> close proximity to the colonialists' latrine.[29]

Khrushchev might well have continued by pointing out that Mao's
fame, on the basis of both his writings and his actions, has been built

[28] See *ibid.*, p. 328.
[29] Quoted in *ibid.*, pp. 328–29.

upon his concept of protracted warfare. His formula has always been to "strategically despise the enemy, tactically take them seriously." Translated into common-sense terms, this means that the opponent may be weak, a "paper tiger," a "giant with feet of clay," but in specific conflicts one must carefully reckon the balance of forces and proceed cautiously. As Mao has himself explained:

> Strategically we take the eating of a meal lightly: we know we can finish it. But when actually eating, we do it a mouthful at a time. It would be impossible to swallow the entire feast in a single mouthful. This is called a piecemeal solution. And in military literature, it is called smashing the enemy bit by bit.[30]

In the final analysis, these arguments over peaceful coexistence were somewhat misleading anyway. Lenin's statement that wars were inevitable while capitalism existed had *not* suggested that the Communists should attack the capitalist countries. Lenin had feared that the capitalists would seek to eliminate Communism in order to try to forestall their own doom. Khrushchev was merely saying that the Soviet Union now possessed the power to deter such an attack. Nor was Mao trying to prod the Soviet Union to launch an all-out war on the United States. The Russians and the Chinese have always been "militarily conservative." Military power has never been their principal tool of policy. The Communist concept of the international class struggle is couched in social and economic terms. Admittedly, both subscribe to Mao's dictum that "Power grows out a barrel of a gun." But this does not mean the gun has to be fired. Both have usually employed force politically and psychologically—to threaten, blackmail, harry, weaken, and isolate enemies—in a variety of situations ranging from nuclear blackmail to guerrilla warfare.

Thus one can hardly generalize about the Sino-Soviet conflict to say that the Chinese oppose peaceful coexistence while the Soviets support it. The issue between them is not one of principle, but one of emphasis or degree—more specifically, the degree of pressure that in individual challenges can be brought to bear on the West without precipitating nuclear war. How far can the West be pressured in particular crises before the nuclear threshold is crossed? To what extent can nuclear-blackmail tactics be employed to attain certain political and psychological objectives? It is this issue that divides the Chinese and the Russians—just as, no doubt, it divides policy-makers within both the Chinese and Soviet governments. The issue of whether to take a "hard" or "soft" stand[31] has on most occasions certainly divided the NATO allies, as well as policy-mak-

[30] Quoted in Allen S. Whiting, "The Logic of Communist China's Policy: The First Decade," in Pentony (ed.), *China, the Emerging Red Giant*, p. 71.

[31] The value judgments implicit in these terms can easily be reversed by calling them "inflexible" and "flexible" stands; the former then implies an obduracy that risks war, while the latter suggests a relaxation of tensions and preservation of peace.

ers within each of the NATO governments. Probably in every major international crisis since the end of World War II (when Churchill was calling for a tougher attitude toward the Russians), policy-makers on both sides of the Iron Curtain have divided in this way. And this issue, while it can be simply stated, is in reality a complex one. Whether the policy decided upon is a "hard" or "soft" one, it will in most cases have both advantages and liabilities. There is usually no clear-cut policy offering opportunities without simultaneously creating risks. The challenging or challenged party must always ask at what point the opponent is likely to resist with force and on what scale. These questions obviously require considerable and most careful calculation. And it is on these calculations regarding the level of risks that should be run that Moscow and Peking have differed.

Soviet strategy, despite intermittent tests of Western stamina, has been, on the whole, to minimize the risks of war and to assure the worldwide victory of socialism by patiently exploiting the nationalist and neutralist tendencies of the underdeveloped nations, holding up Russia as an example of a nation that modernized and industrialized itself in a relatively short time, and manipulating the aspirations for peace, fears of war, and national ambitions to weaken, if not disintegrate, the Western alliance. Even on the issue of "wars of national liberation," which Khrushchev said were unavoidable because the "colonialists do not grant independence voluntarily," the Soviet position was not unqualified. Despite vows of Soviet support, Khrushchev in fact suggested "that while the U.S.S.R. would render to liberation movements assistance of a scope and kind which would depend on the circumstances, it would not intervene directly with its own military forces unless the West did so. This, of course, left open the question as to what the Soviet leadership would do if the West did intervene in a war of 'liberation.' "[32] This was particularly true because the Soviets feared the possibility of a rapid escalation in any conflict with American forces.

The Chinese, on the other hand, have pressed for a more activist and militant policy because they are more convinced than their Soviet colleagues that the capitalist world can be made to retreat. The logical policy conclusion is therefore to keep up the pressure on the West, especially on the United States. The Chinese view may derive, in part, from experiences with the United States. In Korea, China felt "victorious" because it had fought to a standstill the most powerful country in the world. Its belief that the United States was merely a "paper tiger" was reaffirmed by the Eisenhower Administration's loud threats in 1954 to intervene in Indochina and its later inaction. And in 1962, during the Laotian crisis, the Kennedy Administration went through much the same motions. Chinese confidence in pressure tactics may thus have been en-

[32] Zagoria, *op. cit.*, pp. 353–54.

couraged by American actions and inactions. In any case, the Chinese were apprehensive lest the Soviet Union's fear of war was so great that it would shrink from challenging the West and, in the process, lose its revolutionary fervor. For if the use of violence, in the form of threats and wars of national liberation, were foresworn because of anxiety that any spark might ignite a global conflagration, attempts to change the *status quo* by pressure tactics would also be reduced.

The Chinese were thus pointing toward the basic paradox of the Soviet position. If the Soviet leaders constantly talked of total war as suicidal, why would the West be intimidated and offer concessions to call off a threat of an all-out war or to avoid escalation of a limited conflict? Their continued references to war as "insane" in effect deprived their threats of any credibility.[33] Churchill had said shortly after World War II that the Russians did not want war, only the fruits of war. That is, they wanted to acquire gains without paying the requisite price. The Chinese pointed out that the Soviets could hardly expect results if the West did not believe the "nuclear gun," so to speak, was loaded and might go off. For China, as a nation, this meant that until the distant future when it had acquired a sizable nuclear stockpile and effective delivery system of its own, it could not gain possession of Formosa. And perhaps it could not even hope to recapture the offshore islands, whose continued Nationalist occupation was a humiliation to the Chinese. As a revolutionary power, China viewed the Soviet policy as portending a serious retardation, if not a virtually complete halt, of the Communist bloc's expansion. Since the United States had repeatedly shown its weakness, it would be "un-Communist" not to exploit the situation with more resolute policies. Indeed, it would be a "betrayal" of the Communist cause to forfeit any opportunities to defeat the "imperialists" because of a lack of nerve. Such cowardice was, in the language of American partisan politics, tantamount to accepting a "no-win" policy; in terms of Peking's polemics, it was tantamount to American-Russian cooperation to isolate and contain China! What particularly incensed the Chinese in these circumstances was that the Soviets' fear of nuclear war was not reduced by the fact that China's global strategy emphasized the role of guerrilla warfare, in which nuclear weapons were useless. Just as Mao's formula for success in "people's wars" was to win control of the countryside and then encircle the cities, so his strategy for universal success stressed the capture of the countryside of Asia, Africa, and Latin America, and then the strangulation of the world's cities—the United States and Europe. Even if the United States should seek to stop the gradual disintegration of the West's global position, through intervention in such

[33] See G. F. Hudson, "Russia and China: The Dilemmas of Power," in Philip E. Mosely (ed.), *The Soviet Union, 1922–1962* (New York: Frederick A. Praeger, 1963), pp. 421–24.

wars, full-scale escalation need not occur, according to Peking. The United States, too, wished to avoid a major war, let alone a nuclear war. To prove their point, the Chinese cited history:

> In recent years, certain persons have been spreading the argument that a single spark from a war of national liberation or from a revolutionary people's war will lead to a world conflagration destroying the whole of mankind. What are the facts? Contrary to what these persons say, [such wars] . . . that have occurred since World War II have not led to world war. The victory of these revolutionary wars has directly weakened the forces of imperialism and greatly strengthened the forces which prevent the imperialists from launching a world war and which defend world peace. Do not the facts demonstrate the absurdity of this argument?[34]

Sino-Soviet differences over the pressure to be exerted on the West through threats of violence or actual violence in the form of limited conventional or guerrilla warfare were not confined to the degree of risk involved. These differences spilled over into the issue of who would provide the leadership of the revolutions throughout the underdeveloped areas.

Peking has no reservations in asserting that it, and not the Soviet Union, is the model for the revolution in Asia, Africa, and Latin America. This assertion is based on Mao's claim that it was his Party that successfully completed the first socialist revolution in an underdeveloped country; in turn, this success was due to Mao's adaptation of Marxism-Leninism to the conditions of pre-industrial societies. This provides the Soviets with a fundamental challenge. Mao obviously places himself on a par with Marx and Lenin as one of the founding fathers of world Communism. In adapting Marxist theory to Asian conditions, he was an Asian Marx. In completing the Chinese revolution, he played the role of an Asian Lenin. It was China, a non-European and nonwhite nation, itself a victim of colonialism, that had chartered the path to power for the people in all underdeveloped countries. As one Chinese leader said:

> Mao Tse-tung's great accomplishment has been to change Marxism from a European to an Asiatic form. Marx and Lenin were Europeans; they wrote in European languages about European histories and problems, seldom discussing Asia or China. The basic principles of Marxism are undoubtedly adaptable to all countries, but to apply their general truth to concrete revolutionary practices in China is a difficult task. Mao Tse-tung is Chinese; he analyzes Chinese problems and guides the Chinese people in their struggle to victory. He uses Marxist-Leninist principles to explain Chinese history and the practical problems of China. He is the first that has succeeded in doing so. Not only has he applied Marxist methods to solve the problems of 450 million people, but he has thus popularized Marxism among the Chinese people as a weapon for them to use. On every kind of problem—the nation, the peasants, strategy, the construction of

[34] Quoted in Floyd, *op. cit.*, p. 412.

the party, literature and culture, military affairs, finance and economy, methods of work, philosophy—Mao has not only applied Marxism to new conditions but has given it a new development. He has created a Chinese or Asiatic form of Marxism. China is a semi-feudal, semi-colonial country in which vast numbers of people live at the edge of starvation, tilling small bits of soil. Its economy is agricultural, backward, and dispersed. In attempting the transition to a more industrialized economy, China faces the competition and the pressures—economic, political, and military—of advanced industrial lands. This is the basic situation that affects both the relations of social classes and the methods of struggle towards any such goal as national independence and a better, freer life for the Chinese. There are similar conditions in other lands of southeast Asia. The courses chosen by China will influence them all.[35]

To bolster its claim to serve as the model for the Communist revolution in underdeveloped areas, China even experimented with a new form of "socialist construction." The immediate cause was that in 1957, China was suffering an economic crisis in agriculture as a result of great difficulties brought about by collectivization. If China was to increase its food production and continue its program of industrialization, it appeared necessary to permit the peasants a greater degree of freedom and provide them with incentives to work in the form of higher wages and more consumer goods. But in turn, this diversion of badly needed funds to consumer industries would slow down the development of heavy industry. The missing capital might, of course, come from the Soviet Union, but after the explosion in Eastern Europe, massive Soviet aid did not seem likely. Before 1956, the Russians had exploited their satellites' economies; now they had to invest in them to help raise living standards and stem the rising tide of popular dissatisfaction. Thus, China's alternative was to tighten control over the peasants and squeeze the savings for rapid industrialization out of them.

It was at this point apparently that the Chinese decided that the Soviet model of modernization was inadequate for an underdeveloped nation with little machinery and skilled labor, a rapidly growing population, and a static agriculture. China should therefore solve its economic problems by the intensive use of the one resource it possessed in overabundance—its manpower. Modern machinery and skills would be supplanted by huge labor armies which could build dams and reservoirs, irrigation ditches, and other projects needed to make agriculture more modern, efficient, and productive. The political organization through which the Party would control these large rural labor forces was to be the People's Communes. The aims of the People's Communes were not, however, limited to vast agricultural and public-works projects; they were also to help develop industry. Small backyard furnaces were to produce sizable

[35] Quoted in Zagoria, op. cit., pp. 14–15.

quantities of steel; other small-scale industries were to be established for machine tools, power generation, textiles, and food processing. In both agriculture and industry, China would take a "Great Leap Forward" in production. Through their communal dining halls, nurseries, and homes for older people, the Communes would finally also change the peasants' traditional way of life. Women would thus be released for production, and the old ties of family life would be de-emphasized. Furthermore, there would be universal military training. A typical Commune slogan was "Organize along military lines, work as if fighting a battle, and live the collective way!"[36]

The Commune policy, launched in 1958, was to be the Chinese model for "building socialism" in an underdeveloped nation in one "great leap." The challenge to Soviet leadership of the world Communist movement was obvious. Just to make sure that the Russians would not miss it, the Chinese claimed that the Communes would "accelerate socialist construction, complete the building of socialism ahead of time, and carry out the gradual transition to Communism."[37] The Chinese were, in other words, asserting that they had reached a more advanced state of socialism than the Soviet Union. The communal living, mess halls, labor teams, combined industrial-agricultural production, and abolition of private property were all said to be characteristic of the Communist way of life. The transition from socialism to Communism, according to doctrine, could be made when production was sufficiently plenty to provide abundantly for everyone.[38] The Soviets, as might be expected, dismissed the Chinese claim and insisted that Moscow remained the vanguard. The other countries of the socialist camp were still "laying the foundations of socialism, and some of them have already entered the period of construction of a developed socialist society." But

> The Communist and workers' parties unanimously declare that the Communist Party of the Soviet Union has been, and remains, the universally recognized vanguard of the world Communist movement, being the most experienced and steeled contingent of the international Communist movement. The experience which the Communist Party of the Soviet Union has gained in the struggle for the victory of the working class, in Socialist construction and in the full-scale construction of communism, is of fundamental significance for the whole of the world Communist movement. . . . The role of the Soviet Union does not lie in its leading the other socialist countries, but in its being the first to blaze the trail to socialism, in its being the most powerful country in the socialist world system, in its having accumulated vast positive experience in building socialism, and

[36] Hugh Seton-Watson, *From Lenin to Khruschchev*, p. 370.
[37] Floyd, *op. cit.*, p. 63.
[38] Franz Michael, "Khrushchev's Disloyal Opposition: Structural Change and Power Struggle in the Communist Bloc," *Orbis*, Spring, 1963, p. 63; the dispute over the Communes is analyzed in great detail in Zagoria, *op. cit.*, pp. 77–141.

being the first to embark on the full-scale building of communism. It is stressed in the statement that the Communist Party of the Soviet Union has been and remains the universally recognized vanguard of the world Communist movement, being its most experienced and steeled contingent.[39]

In one sense, this dispute was soon settled. For it was not long before the Chinese Communists realized that they had been in error, that the peasants would not cooperate. Within a few months, therefore, a partial retreat began. Family living, payment according to work, and the restoration of some private property signaled this retreat. But the long-run significance of the Communes lay not in whether they would really provide the answer to China's economic backwardness but in the implicit Chinese challenge of the Soviet Union's leadership of the Communist world.

This challenge soon became apparent in Peking's dispute with Moscow over the achievement of the socialist revolution in the underdeveloped nations. The Soviet approach, as we have seen, was to cooperate with the national bourgeoisie during their anti-imperialist phase and thus cut the links—especially economic—between the ex-colony and the ex-mother country. The new nation was to be made as economically dependent upon the socialist camp as possible. Its traditional ruling class was to be destroyed through land reform. All industry was to be nationalized. And the Communist Party was to organize the working class and peasantry under its leadership. The new nation would then be entering its second, or "national democratic," phase. With its members placed in strategic political, military, and economic positions, the Party would increase its influence within the government to the point, finally, where it could assume leadership and capture state power. Thus the Communist takeover would be gradual and peaceful. The alternative of violent revolution would be self-defeating as it would only frighten the bourgeoisie and drive them to suppress the Communists.

The Chinese dissented from the Soviet emphasis on national democracy. On the basis of their own experience during the Stalinist period, they denied that cooperation with the national bourgeoisie would merely be a transitional phase to socialism. In the 1920's, Stalin had ordered the Chinese Communists to join a coalition with the Kuomintang, which, as a nationalist party, sought to unify China by destroying the local warlords and ejecting the colonial powers. The Soviet Union's view was that a united China would serve Soviet interests because it would divert Japanese pressure from Siberia. In addition, Moscow saw an opportunity to transform its coalition with the "national bourgeoisie" into a spearhead of revolution by infiltrating the Kuomintang and organizing the workers in the cities. Thus the Communist participation in the Kuomintang

---

[39] *Two Communist Manifestoes*, pp. 24, 25, 101, 103.

would enable the proletariat to achieve hegemony in a national bourgeois revolution, bringing about the socialist revolution more quickly. The alliance with the Communists also proved useful to the Nationalists. Among other things, the Russian emissaries taught the Chinese Nationalist leaders how to organize their party according to Communist lines. But the alliance proved to be only temporary. In 1927, Chiang Kai-shek turned on the Communists in Shanghai and shattered the coalition and Stalin's policy. The idea of basing the Communist Party upon the proletariat died at the same time.

In early 1928, Mao Tse-tung began to organize the Party with the peasants, rather than the proletariat, as the revolutionary vanguard—hardly an orthodox approach. Mao has consequently been called a heretic, but in fact he was merely adapting Leninist strategy for the conquest of power to China's conditions. Lenin himself had, after all, not been averse to exploiting peasant unrest and dissatisfaction to undermine the Czarist regime and its moderate successor. Mao simply went a step further in organizing the peasants into a guerrilla force to fight against the Nationalists. The principal attraction to the peasants was the Communist policy of land reform: to confiscate the land of the landowners and redistribute it to the poor peasants. Thus the Communists *posed* as "agrarian reformers": "The Chinese communist movement was a movement of peasants, but not a peasant movement. . . . The communists had to get peasant good-will, as Lenin in 1917 and 1918 had had to get peasant good-will. The only way, for Mao as for Lenin, was to give the peasants what they wanted—the use, on more favourable terms, of the land. But in the 'liberated territories' the political and military hierarchy was firmly controlled by communists."[40]

The Chinese civil war between the Communists and the Kuomintang was interrupted by the Japanese seizure of Manchuria in 1931 and much later by the large-scale Japanese attacks on China in 1937. Stalin, interested in seeing that China continued to fight—lest a powerful Japan that had conquered much or all of China establish itself on Russia's Asian borders—ordered the Chinese Communist Party to form a united front with Chiang. But this united front soon collapsed, and the civil war was resumed and fought throughout the rest of the Sino-Japanese war. After Japan's defeat by the Allies in 1945, Stalin again intervened. This time, he reportedly told Mao that he was still too weak to defeat Chiang and that he should therefore join a coalition government and "bore from within." Mao is supposed to have nodded his assent, but he then went on to disregard Stalin's advice. He resumed his war against Chiang—and ultimately won.

The Chinese learned several important lessons from their experience. First, they questioned the wisdom of the Soviet leadership and gained

[40] Seton-Watson, *op. cit.*, p. 153.

new confidence in their own (superior) ability to judge political situations and the balance of forces correctly. Their victory in spite of Soviet advice was testimony to Moscow's fallibility and poor political judgment. Second, they concluded that Communist cooperation with the national bourgeois could only be short-term at best. For the bourgeoisie would, sooner or later, when it no longer needed the Communists, turn upon them. Thus Communist cooperation could only strengthen the nationalists' power and grip on the government. Lengthy cooperation with the national bourgeoisie was therefore *not* the road to travel toward socialism. Consequently, "national democracy" was rejected as a transition phase between the bourgeois nationalist and the socialist periods. The third conclusion the Chinese drew from their experience followed logically. The bourgeoisie might assume the leadership of the nationalist revolution, but once it had successfully accomplished this stage, the Communists had to take over the leadership of this united front. An underdeveloped country could not overnight become a socialist state—and the Commune experiment apparently reinforced this obvious lesson. The Communists could share power with other parties until the transition to socialism became possible, but they had to control the levers of power. In order to compel the nationalist leaders to let them enter their governments, the Chinese argued, the Communists would have to exert pressure. Presumably, where conditions were ripe, an insurrection, or war of national liberation, would also be launched. In brief, the Chinese argued in favor of violent revolution.

To the Russians, such a policy only spelled disaster for it would ensure that the bourgeoisie would quickly be driven back into the arms of the Western capitalists and colonialists. By the same token, the Communists would lose a great opportunity to identify themselves, through the bourgeoisie, with the nationalist and social revolution, to place men in key positions, and in general to strengthen their position and appeal and at the same time chip at the West's influence. Yet, as in the issue of war and peace, these Sino-Soviet differences were often more apparent than real. Both Russia and China remained committed to the world revolution and the vital role of the front in the ex-colonial world. Neither was prepared to accept a permanently neutral "third world." Even the Soviets considered such an acceptance as a temporary tactic—that is, as a means of exploiting the anti-Western nationalism and the neutralism of the underdeveloped countries to shift the global balance of power against the West. Khrushchev had not really sounded very different from the Chinese when he had said: "The breakdown of the system of colonial slavery under the impact of the national-liberation movement is a development ranking second in historic importance only to the formation of the world socialist system. . . . The national-liberation movement is striking telling blows at imperialism, strengthening peace and accelerating social progress. At present, Asia, Africa, and Latin America are the most important centers of the revolutionary struggle against imperialism."[41] And while the Chinese may have charged that the Russians did more talking about wars of national liberation than participating in them, it was the Russians who sent supplies and arms to the Congo to help the anti-Western Lumumba Government in 1960–61 and to the rebels in 1964–65, and the Russians flew arm into Laos to help the Communist Pathet Lao in 1962. The Chinese, after their takeover of the mainland, naturally supported the Viet-Minh and then later the Viet-Cong in Indochina. Furthermore, for all their skepticism regarding the political reliability of the national bourgeoisie, the Chinese have never hesitated to give political support, and even economic aid, to underdeveloped countries—particularly in Africa—wherever they thought it would be advantageous. Thus it would be hard to disagree with the following conclusion:

> Whatever the internal relations between Soviet and Communist strategies in any of these ventures may have been, it is evident that both policies, that of direct aggression and subversion and that of diplomatic support and aid to neutral governments, have been used by both the Soviets and the Chinese Communists. It would be impossible, in principle, to distinguish between the basis of Soviet or Chinese Communist policy, describing one as more conciliatory and the other as more aggressive. Their respective stance depends entirely on the time and place.[42]

In any case, by the early 1960's the Sino-Soviet conflict had become intense. Two of the principal objectives of Chinese foreign policy—to augment China's power and to increase its participation in the determination of over-all bloc policy—had failed. Its "socialist construction" had not made any spectacular headway, and Soviet policy had impeded China's efforts to strengthen itself. The Soviets had cut off their aid and called home their technicians. Also, after having promised—apparently in 1957, when Khrushchev had sought Chinese support in his domestic intra-Party struggles—to help China become a nuclear power, two years later they had abruptly ended the program. The suspension of both economic and nuclear aid was a reprisal against the increasing Chinese opposition to the general line and tone of bloc policy as determined by Moscow. China's opposition only made the Kremlin firmer in its de-termination not to share its authority in the formulation of the bloc's foreign policy.

In turn, Chinese anger and distrust of Moscow had been thoroughly aroused. Perhaps nothing more dramatically revealed the gap—and cross-

[41] *Two Communist Manifestoes*, p. 66.

[42] Michael, "Communist China and the Non-Committed Countries: Motives and Purposes of Communist China's Foreign Policy," in Kurt London (ed.), *New Nations in a Divided World*, p. 253.

purposes—between China and Russia than Sino-Soviet differences over India. As the largest and most influential neutral, India represented a test case for the Soviet policy of support for a bourgeois nationalist government. In 1959, the Chinese attacked India's northern boundaries to claim the Indian frontier territories that they alleged rightfully belonged to China. It seemed apparent that, by defeating the Indians, the Chinese also sought to demonstrate to the nations of Asia precisely who the most powerful Asian nation was.

The Soviets refused to take a position. "One cannot fail to express regret at the fact that the incident on the Sino-Indian frontier took place," said Moscow in a bit of understatement. "The Soviet Union is in friendly relations both with the Chinese People's Republic and the Republic of India. The Chinese and Soviet people are linked by indestructible bonds of fraternal friendship, based on the great principles of socialist internationalism. Friendly collaboration between the USSR and India is developing successfully in accordance with the ideas of peaceful coexistence."[43] The Chinese charged the Russians with betrayal for not condemning "reactionary and capitalist" India and for refusing to support a fraternal socialist country.

The Chinese resumed their attacks in 1962 and badly defeated the Indian forces. India, which already had American and British support, now asked the Soviet Union for aid as well. The Russians, the Indians said, had promised deliveries of Soviet jet fighters and even to build a plant in India to manufacture them. The Indian request naturally placed the Soviets in an awkward position. Open support for India would have lined them up with the "imperialists" against a fellow socialist state. Nor could they completely dissociate themselves without endangering the type of relationship they were cultivating with nationalist governments in underdeveloped societies—which was precisely China's goal. Meekly, the Soviets sought a way out by arguing for a "peaceful solution" of the dispute. Only after a cease-fire did the Indians state that the Soviet fighters were being delivered. But Soviet economic aid had continued during this period. Later, the Soviet Union did offer India guided missiles and other military equipment needed for defense against China. (The United States, too, drew up a program to increase the effectiveness of Indian forces.) In any case, the Soviets preserved their amicable relationship with India, as well as their general policy of support for the national bourgeoisie in the emerging nations. But the Chinese had also made their point—namely, that while Moscow might refuse to share its authority in the formulation of policy for the Communist world, it could not prevent China from attempting to upset its policies or pursuing their own policies.

[43] Tass statement, September 9, 1959; quoted in Floyd, *op. cit.*, pp. 261–62.

The central point about the Sino-Soviet dispute is by now clear: namely, that it is a conflict of "revolutionary interests."[44] Both China's and Russia's "national interest" is identified with the ultimate Communist goal of world revolution. China does not see its national interests merely in terms of expanding to the limits of Imperial China. It certainly holds such ambitions, but *Communist* China, like *Communist* Russia, has goals beyond those traditionally associated with the old empire. Both Communist powers see their respective revolutions as an integral part of the world revolution. Admittedly, both are concerned with such historic goals of states as status and power, but these goals are shared by all nation-states. Any state, whether it is Communist or national, will seek to protect itself and enlarge its power. The more powerful it is, the greater its ability to accomplish its purposes, especially the goal of "national security." But this term means quite another thing to a Communist state than it does to a non-Communist one because it is defined in offensive terms—that is, until the destruction of the capitalist enemy is achieved, there can be no real or lasting "security." The nation-state is in fact condemned as a "reactionary bourgeois" phenomenon whose national and cultural traditions, allegedly the offspring of its old class structure, the Communists attempt to destroy as they seek to reshape the society according to Communist values and norms. In neither China nor Russia does Communism represent the cultural tradition; indeed, it is "at war" with this tradition. All loyalty is claimed by the Party, not the state. And it is the Party that defines Soviet or Chinese foreign policy. To attribute Communist objectives to the state rather than to the Party is to omit the principal motivation that defines this "national interest"—the ideological motivation, which is the distinguishing mark of the Communist state. Both the Chinese and Soviet Communist parties are members of the world Communist movement, and both implement the Communist revolution domestically and internationally.

It is precisely because the two parties do not represent the traditional type of "national interest"—which would define the nation's interest in the context of its geopolitical situation—that the Sino-Soviet conflict is so fierce. In each case, the national interest is identified with the world revolution, and the struggle is between the Chinese and Soviet leaders and parties for influence and authority in determining the strategy that

---

[44] "I speak of 'revolutionary interests' rather than 'national interests' because, although the latter concept is not irrelevant to an explanation of conflict between the two, it is not wholly adequate. It fails to take account of the urge to expedite the revolutionary process so central to both Russian and Chinese actions. While the pursuit of this goal is influenced by national viewpoints, the goal of international revolution itself goes beyond such traditional goals of nation states as security and survival. In the perspective of both Russia and China, the world is in revolutionary ferment and ultimately destined to become Communist. But in the process of hastening this process, differences of priority, of sectionalism, and of timing arise." (Zagoria, *op. cit.*, p. 19.)

serves this common and ultimate aim.[45] It is in this sense that the struggle is essentially an ideological one. Both parties, to be sure, view reality in terms of the same *Weltanschäuung*. Both see U.S. "imperialism" as blocking the path to national, "democratic," "socialist" revolutions—that is, to the assumption of power by Communist parties. Both see the "inherent antagonism" between the capitalist powers and their colonies or ex-colonies, as well as the revolutionary potential of the peasantry in the backward areas. They see, in the West European capitalist powers, the same sharpening bourgeois-proletariat class conflict and the possibilities of encouraging fears of war and anti-Americanism. More fundamentally, they have the same view of history and of their historically appointed task to speed it along toward its "inevitable" end—the doom of capitalism and its replacement by socialism, the proletarian revolution and the establishment of the dictatorship of the proletariat, the alliance of the proletariat with the peasantry, rapid industrialization and the public ownership of all the means of production, the socialization of agriculture, and the planning of the entire economy in order to proceed with "socialist construction" and move nearer to the ultimate transition to a Communist society.

Although the basic Sino-Soviet dispute is thus argued within this common doctrinal framework, the difficulty arises from the fact that the Soviet Union is no longer the only powerful Communist state and that its monopoly on enunciation of the "truth"—that is, on decision-making—has been challenged. In part, Moscow has only itself to blame for the undermining of its authority. One of the functions of Communist ideology, as was noted earlier, is to legitimize those who hold authority. Communist ideology therefore legitimized the Soviet leaders both as the rulers of the Soviet Union and—when the Soviet Union was the only socialist state—as the leaders of the international Communist movement. Just as there can be only one Pope, there can be only one source of ideological pronouncements in a secular movement like Communism. Moscow was this infallible source. But paradoxically, its authority was undercut by Khrushchev's own de-Stalinization campaign. If Stalin had been a man of such character and committed such terrifying excesses, why should other parties continue to follow the Soviet leaders? Thus, regrettably for the Soviet party, the very sequence of first quietly correcting and then publicly denouncing the Stalinist legacy undermined its international moral authority at precisely the time when, because of the increasingly obvious limitations of its operative power within the socialist camp, it needed to be maximised."[46] Another, and even more fundamental cause,

---

[45] *Ibid.*, p. 244.
[46] Melvin Croan, "Communist International Relations," in Walter Laqueur and Leopold Labedz (eds.), *Polycentrism: The New Factor in International Communism* (New York: Frederick A. Praeger, 1962), p. 16.

of the challenge to Moscow's papal authority was the rise of Communist countries not controlled by Moscow. Yugoslavia was the first. But it was China, Russia's equal (if not ultimately superior) in power, which could most effectively challenge the Soviet Union's monopoly of political wisdom and authority. The resulting inter-Party conflict was bound to resemble past intra-Party conflict with each contender claiming to possess the correct interpretation of history and to be the true interpreter of the Party theology. Thus each has to denounce the other for heresy.

Khrushchev, for instance, called the Chinese "dogmatists" for their literal interpretation of Leninism:

> It should not be forgotten that Lenin's propositions on imperialism were advanced and developed decades ago, when many factors that are now decisive for historical development, for the entire international situation, were not present. . . . One cannot repeat mechanically now on this question what Vladimir Ilyich Lenin said many decades ago about imperialism, and go on asserting that imperialist wars are inevitable until socialism triumphs throughout the world. . . . One cannot ignore the specific situation, the changes in the correlation of forces in the world and repeat what the great Lenin said in quite different historical conditions. . . . We live in a time when we have neither Marx, nor Engels, nor Lenin with us. If we act like children who, studying the alphabet, compile words from letters, we shall not go very far. Marx, Engels and Lenin created their immortal works which will not fade away in centuries. They indicated to mankind the road to Communism. And we confidently follow this road. On the basis of the teaching of Marxism-Leninism we must think ourselves, profoundly study life, analyse the present situation and draw the conclusions which benefit the common cause of Communism.
>
> One must not only be able to read but also to understand correctly what one has read and apply it in the specific conditions of the time in which we live, taking into consideration the existing situation, and the real balance of forces. A political leader acting in this manner shows that he not only can read but can also creatively apply the revolutionary teaching. If he does not do this, he resembles a man about whom people say: "He looks into a book, but sees nothing!"[47]

The Chinese, in their turn, attacked the Soviet leader as a "deviationist," a man who had "forsaken the faith of his fathers"—in brief, a heretic. They were the fundamentalists, the Chinese claimed; they remained true to the Marxist-Leninist bible. This line of attack was deliberate, for if the Chinese could show that the First Secretary of the CPSU was betraying the principles for which not only Stalin but also Lenin had stood, that he had committed heresy, then the very basis of his domestic and international authority would be undermined, and at the very mini-

[47] Khrushchev's address to the Romanian Congress, June, 1960; quoted in Floyd, *op. cit.*, pp. 279–80.

mum he would have to compromise with the purists of Peking in order to save himself from the anathema.[48] Moscow, the Communist Rome, and Khrushchev, the Communist Pope, thus had to be challenged by Mao Tse-tung's Eastern Orthodox Church on the theology and its interpretation. Ominously, Peking declared that it would refuse to recognize the majority rule of the Soviet Union and its followers in the international Communist movement. It cited the fact that Lenin had not allowed himself to be outvoted by the revisionist Social Democrats, or Mensheviks. Instead, he had split the Party and formed his own Bolshevik faction. Drawing the parallel, Peking said: "The leaders of the CPSU have themselves undermined the basis of the unity of the international Communist movement and created the present grave danger of a split by betraying Marxism-Leninism and proletarian internationalism and pushing their revisionist and divisive line. . . . The revisionists are the greatest and vilest splitters and sectarians in the Communist movement."[49] How could China possibly follow a nation whose Communism was "phony," whose revisionist domestic policies were "rapidly swelling the forces of capitalism" inside Russia,[50] and whose foreign policy was aligning itself with the U.S. against China?[51]

The basic problem, of which this struggle for leadership is a symptom, is the absence within the socialist camp of some supranational organ of consultation and decision. The large and unwieldy inter-Party conferences, which include parties that do not control state power, are useless for this purpose. A political procedure through which bloc decisions on foreign policy can be arranged, particularly between Russia and China, has still to be decided upon and institutionalized. This is not simply a matter of establishing an appropriate organ. The real issue is whether the two Communist powers can work out a relationship between them that would recognize that, in order to preserve a united front against the West, they must compromise their differing interests and points of view,

---

[48] Hudson, Lowenthal, and MacFarquhar (eds.), *op. cit.*, p. 6.

[49] Quoted in *The New York Times*, February 7, 1964. The whole argument over revisionism is doctrinally rather absurd. For what Khrushchev defended as the "creative application" of Marxism to changing circumstances is precisely what Mao did when he fitted Marxism to Chinese conditions. And Mao's great mentor was Lenin, claimed by Mao to be the great orthodox teacher of Communism. "Lenin took liberties with Marxist ideas, preconceptions, and practices, so that his adversaries in the movement could accuse him of having broken with Marxism. . . . Still, Lenin defended every innovation he introduced as a thoroughly Marxist measure, claiming that Marxism was no fixed dogma but a 'guide to action,' that it should be regarded as an orientation, a framework of ideas and attitudes, within which the utmost concreteness of analysis and action would contribute to understanding and success, rather than to the destruction of the framework itself. Concreteness should be integrated, so that the most diverse situations, the most contradictory practices, would be part of a larger scheme of development." (Alfred G. Meyer, *Leninism*, pp. 12–13.)

[50] *The New York Times*, July 14, 1964.

[51] *Ibid.*, February 6, 1966.

since neither can impose its will upon the other or suppress these interests and points of view. The difficulty is, this kind of compromise within the Communist bloc may present an insuperable obstacle. In matters of doctrine, where the purity of the theology is at stake, will a policy of give and take not contaminate that purity? How can mutual adjustments be made between members of a movement in which differences of emphasis become issues of loyalty to the faith? How can Moscow's primacy, the Kremlin's infallibility, and its doctrinal purity be made compatible with Peking's desire for co-primacy, Maoist infallibility, and ideological fundamentalism? The Western allies, themselves pluralistic societies, can cope with pluralism and diversity. But the Communist states cannot because domestically their parties impose a uniform pattern in accordance with their ideological interpretation. Each is a totalitarian society precisely because the Party claims that it is the bearer of the revealed "truth." This truth is to be imposed upon the society because "the truth will make man free." Conversely, all heresy must be ruthlessly eliminated. How then can two such states, each convinced that its interpretation of the truth is the only correct one, coexist? Nonrevolutionary great powers at least share a degree of toleration. And they could, so to speak, divide the world between them. However, the self-righteous—for the righteous in arguments always tend to become self-righteous—exhibit no such tolerance. When ideology is so intimately linked with power as it is in Communist policy and decision-making, then there can only be one "correct" answer. Divergent policies cannot therefore be compromised. The essence of any give and take is thus blocked by the insistence on doctrinal purity. One "correct" answer demands a single center of political authority and ideological orthodoxy. *Any relationship between Communist states must therefore be hierarchical in nature; it cannot be one of equality.* Either Moscow or Peking must be the source of Communist theological interpretation. But the Soviet Union is one of the world's two great nuclear powers, and its governing Party was the first to win power in any country. Consequently, it will not surrender its claim to leadership of the Communist bloc. Nor will China subordinate itself to the Kremlin. The latter may have the support of the majority of Communist parties throughout the world, but, as the Chinese have stated the issue, "anyone with a little common sense knows that the question of who is right and who is wrong, and who represents the truth, cannot be determined by the majority or minority at any given moment."[52] In short, the very Marxism-Leninism that the Soviet and Chinese leadership have always stressed as the binding link of "proletarian internationalism" may prove to be the disruptive factor that will irreparably shatter the unity of the socialist camp.

It is of course conceivable that this very point may be a restraining fac-

[52] *People's Daily*, December 15, 1962; quoted in Floyd, *op. cit.*, p. 337.

tor. An irretrievable break would weaken each nation against the West—particularly Communist China, since she does not yet possess an effective nuclear deterrent; for Russia, it would mean greater insecurity of her southern and eastern borders. The Chinese have on several occasions since the eruption of their quarrel with the Russians talked of "unjust demarcations" along some sections of the Sino-Soviet border. Indeed, the Chinese once pointedly stated:

> In the hundred years or so prior to the victory of the Chinese revolution, the imperialist and colonial powers—the United States, Britain, France, Tsarist Russia, Germany, Japan, Italy, Austria, Belgium, the Netherlands, Spain and Portugal—carried out unbridled aggression against China. They compelled the governments of old China to sign a large number of unequal treaties. . . . By virtue of these unequal treaties, they annexed Chinese territory in the north, south, east and west and held leased territories on the seaboard and in the hinterland of China. Some seized Taiwan and the Penghu Islands, some occupied Hongkong and forcibly leased Kowloon, some put Macao under perpetual occupation, etc., etc. At the time the People's Republic of China was inaugurated, our government declared that it would examine the treaties concluded by previous Chinese governments with foreign governments, treaties that had been left over by history and would recognize, abrogate, revise or renegotiate them according to their respective contents.[53]

The Russians have however warned the Chinese that "the artificial creation of any territorial problems in our times, especially between Socialist countries would be tantamount to embarking on a very dangerous path."[54] For both Communist powers, furthermore, a break would restrain the momentum of the Communist movement. The schisms in many, if not most, Communist parties would be devastating to their vitality. Since the Chinese believe that their strategy is the correct one, they are already trying to gain control of most of the world's Communist parties in order to implement their policies. This has led to intense and bitter infighting within Communist parties outside Europe; the European parties, except for Albania, continue to give solid support to the Soviet side of the argument. Many other parties throughout the underdeveloped world are sharply divided between the Chinese and Soviet factions. Perhaps the more radical Chinese line, with its emphasis on direct revolutionary action, may increase in appeal to some Communist leaders the longer their bid for power is postponed by Soviet cooperation with their nationalist governments. But the existing divisions within the various Communist parties are already tending to render them increasingly useless as they spend much of their energies on internal factionalism.

[53] *People's Daily*, March 8, 1963; quoted in Floyd, *op. cit.*, pp. 388–89.
[54] Quoted in *The New York Times*, September 23, 1963.

Certainly, the image of Communism as the irresistible "wave of the future"—created by its postwar expansion to Poland, Hungary, Bulgaria, Romania, Czechoslovakia, Yugoslavia, Albania, China, Korea, Indochina, and Tibet—and the corresponding image of a decaying and disintegrating capitalism being swept into the "dustbin of history" has been increasingly marred by the Sino-Soviet split. Both Russia and China may thus share a vested interest in preserving at least some semblance of bloc unity.

Even if this should occur, there can be no doubt that the monolithic nature of the Communist bloc has been exposed as fraudulent. Three conclusions stand out. One is that this conflict is not primarily a matter of personalities. Khrushchev's removal from power in late 1964 clearly demonstrated that point. Calling his dismissal "a very good thing," the Chinese warned that they would continue their "unceasing struggle" against "revisionism"—that is, "Khrushchevism without Khrushchev." The Soviet leader, they said, had "betrayed Leninism, betrayed proletarian internationalism, betrayed the path of the October Revolution and betrayed the interests of the Soviet people." If Khrushchev's successors followed his policies, Peking warned, they too would meet the same fate. "Anyone who runs counter to Leninism, to proletarian internationalism, to the path of the October Revolution and to the interests of the people will inevitably, sooner or later, be spurned by the people. This was so in the past, is so in the present and will be so in the future." The Chinese left no doubt that bloc unity could be restored only if the Soviet Union made the necessary concessions. The quarrel between the two powers, they said, was due not to any "fault of ours" but to the Soviet Communist Party.[55] Yet Khrushchev's successors are unlikely to change Soviet foreign policies in any fundamental sense in order to placate the Chinese. For to do so would mean exposing themselves to a greater risk of war and nuclear destruction—something they are unlikely to do. The concessions, if any, will have to come from the Chinese—and this is more likely to be a long-run possibility, if it is a possibility at all. The fallen Humpty Dumpty of a world Communist movement led by one center will not, in any case, be put together again very soon, if ever.

The second conclusion is that there can be little doubt that the socialist camp has experienced a great transformation and that in the long run this will have a profound impact on the bloc and on Communism as an ideology. The Sino-Soviet conflict has given the smaller Communist states room for maneuver without being expelled, as Tito had been, as heretics. After 1956, the Soviet Union was willing to allow the satellite leaderships some freedom to travel their own roads to socialism so long as they remained loyal to the Soviet bloc and supported Russia in its struggle with China. The fact that the Soviet Union on the one hand

[55] Quoted in *The New York Times*, November 8, 1964.

sought to avoid more Hungaries and on the other hand needed satellite support in order to maintain its leadership of the Socialist bloc left it no choice but to grant the formerly Soviet-controlled Communist governments of Eastern Europe a greater measure of independence and accept a reduction of Soviet authority throughout the area.

It was Romania that most strongly asserted itself against Moscow and Peking. It boldly declared that all bloc members should control their own economic lives and suggested that the presence of Soviet troops on the soil of Warsaw Pact members was no longer justified. The Romanians' exercise of their greater independence began with their opposition to the Comecon division of labor in which they were assigned the production of oil, petrochemicals, textiles, and farm products. Heavy industry and machinery production was to be left to the more developed countries— the Soviet Union, Czechoslovakia, and East Germany. The Romanians, equating modernization with heavy industry, however, refused to scrap their sizable investments in steel and machinery. In any event the Romanians were tired of paying high prices for Czech machinery of poor quality. Thus they opposed the economic integration of Comecon. At the same time, they were importing machinery from Western Europe, and their behavior also opened up trade possibilities with the United States, since it would be good propaganda for the United States to reward Romania for thwarting Moscow (and by implication, such a deal was open to any East European nation that chose the same independent course). The Peking-Moscow conflict enabled Bucharest to demonstrate some "independence" and, in a sense, to pay Washington's political price by reducing Russian cultural influence, asserting the equality of all Communist parties and states, ending the jamming of Western propaganda broadcasts, and allowing Western cultural attractions to appear. The American purpose is, of course, to encourage all forms of self-assertion by the "satellites" and to intensify the centrifugal forces in Eastern Europe.

How much Moscow's former omnipotence over the People's Democracies—as well as some of the Communist parties in Western Europe—has diminished is clear from two incidents. The first was in connection with the Soviet desire for a meeting of world Communist parties in 1965 to discuss the Sino-Soviet quarrel. When the Chinese opposed such a meeting because they knew that Moscow could line up a majority of parties in support of its position, the Russians decided to go ahead even if the Chinese and their supporters did not attend. The Kremlin thereupon called a preliminary conference of twenty-six parties loyal to Moscow for December, 1964, at which it would seek the establishment of an association of world Communist parties to discuss and coordinate joint policies. This association, looser in organization than the previously more disciplined and Moscow-controlled Comintern and Cominform, was to be a sort of consultative body. But its purpose was clear. As the Czech Party newspaper stated the issue, the principle of Party autonomy did not mean that "each party answers only to itself and can ignore the common interests of the movement or even disrupt it." Central direction was no longer necessary. "But nothing releases the Communist parties of their international duty and obligation to insure unity of action in the joint struggle against imperialism, against the international forces of war and reaction."[56] For the parties of the People's Democracies and Western Europe, this seemed to suggest that Moscow was trying to reassert its former control over them. They therefore opposed the calling of the preliminary meeting. While backing Moscow in its conflict with Peking, they nevertheless balked at reading the Chinese out of the movement and the establishment of a new Moscow-dominated Communist international that would have the power of formal excommunication, could make binding majority decisions, and would not tolerate different points of view. The Poles were opposed. The Romanians were opposed. And the Italian and French Communist parties, the largest two in Western Europe, were opposed. The Italians vigorously supported the independence of all national Communist parties; the French proclaimed that "there are no dominant parties" and "subordinate parties." All Communist parties are "independent and equal in rights and they frame policy by applying the principles of Marxism-Leninism according to the basic conditions in their countries. The interference of one party in the affairs of another is a violation of these rules and cannot be permitted."[57] Such open opposition would have been inconceivable in Stalin's time—and that it could have been a factor leading to Stalin's dismissal would have been even more incredible. Yet, for Khrushchev, who had staked his prestige on this meeting, it was one of the factors that led to his displacement. And with his dismissal came the end of any plan to condemn the Chinese and split the international Communist movement. Instead, his successors called for a conference of all Communist leaders to seek a settlement of their differences. But only nineteen of the twenty-six parties invited to the preliminary conference attended, and the world Communist conference was postponed indefinitely. It now seems unlikely that China will be excommunicated unless its militancy alienates virtually every other Communist Party.

The second, and even more dramatic, example of Moscow's reduced authority over the parties it had once ruled completely came after Khrushchev's dismissal. A change in a nation's leadership is generally considered a matter only for that nation. Even in the international Communist movement, there is no precedent for Moscow's accountability to other parties. Yet this was precisely what some of these parties demanded after the fall of Khrushchev. As much as they may have opposed the Soviet leader's determination to censure the Chinese, they had not wanted him removed from power. For he had given them a greater de-

[56] *Ibid.*, September 13, 1964.
[57] *Ibid.*, September 5, 1964.

gree of independence from Moscow than they had ever known. The French Communist Party therefore publicly called upon the new Soviet leaders to explain why and how Khrushchev had been removed. And it announced that a delegation from the French Party would fly to Moscow to receive the explanation! One can just imagine what would have happened to that delegation in Moscow—and the French party leaders who sent them—during Stalin's rule. But by late 1964, the Italian and Austrian parties also announced that they would send delegations. Within the Eastern bloc, there was also a generally negative reaction to Khrushchev's removal. The East Germans and Czechs were unhappy, the Poles and Romanians expressed their concern, and the Hungarians openly praised the fallen leader. In this unique situation, Moscow had to explain why it had deposed Khrushchev. Apparently, the Soviet Party could no longer change leaders without justifying such a change to its "satellite" countries and parties—at least not without a considerable amount of grumbling and at the cost of further impairing its shaky authority and status.

It is doubtful, in fact, whether the term "satellite" is still properly descriptive. As Secretary of State Dean Rusk has said: "The Communist world is no longer a single flock of sheep following blindly behind one leader."[58] All the East European countries are, in fact, increasing their trade with the West, and most of them have made clear their desire to improve relations with the West. The countries remain Communist, of course. This is a matter of faith and political survival—and the ruling Communist parties in Eastern Europe are interested in their survival. They do not represent majority wills, and in the final analysis it is the Red Army that guarantees their power. Their link to Moscow is thus essential. But their regimes gain a measure of popularity by adapting Communism to the particular national conditions of the various People's Democracies and relaxing the pressures on their peoples somewhat. After Hungary, furthermore, this relaxation is not likely to boil over the limits prescribed by the Soviet Union, although Moscow has relaxed its grip on the reins holding Eastern Europe. But while it still holds the reins, it, too, finds itself in a quandary. Short of reimposing Stalinist controls, with all the dangers this would imply, or outright military intervention as in Hungary, Moscow really has no means of counteracting the growing trend toward greater independence. The outer bounds to this freedom are thus set by the necessity to remain loyal to Moscow. The Soviet leadership may not react if the countries of Eastern Europe open links to the West, but it is unlikely to permit them to substitute these links for their ties with the Soviet Union, and certainly, anti-Soviet policies will not be tolerated. The Kremlin does, however, appear willing to accept its reduction of status and authority and deal with its former satellites on the basis of a limited give and take.

[58] *Ibid.*, February 26, 1964.

The third, and most devastating, conclusion is that this increasing fragmentation within the Sino-Soviet bloc may weaken, and perhaps erode, the ideological foundation of the international Communist movement because it is bound to *relativize* what was formerly considered an absolute and exclusive ideology. Lacking a single center of infallible definition and interpretation, the ideology will embrace the varying situations and political perspectives of each ruling Party. Fraternal parties with the same general perception of reality will reach different conclusions.

> Even today, one should increasingly speak not of Communist ideology but of Soviet Communist ideology, Chinese Communist ideology, Yugoslav Communist ideology, etc. And since it was the Marxist-Leninist ideology's claim to universality that originally stimulated such intense Soviet involvement not only in the domination of its neighbors but particularly in directing the character of their domestic transformation, the increasing diversity in ideological emphases threatens the universal validity of even the Soviet ideology itself and thereby undermines one of the factors that shape the Soviet approach to the world.[59]

The basic question is whether such a relativization of ideology will someday deprive the Soviet and Chinese governments of their legitimacy? And if that should be the case, in view of the organic relationship between the missionary ideology and the totalitarian organization, will this not in turn undermine their political systems? Indeed, has this ideology—at least in Russia—not already been partially eroded by the increasing industrialization since the death of Stalin?

Soviet Totalitarianism and Economic Development: Political Erosion or Hopeful Illusion?

It has become commonplace to say that by the time the Soviet dictator died, industrialization and the nature of Soviet totalitarianism were becoming increasingly incompatible. Totalitarianism had certainly been effective in spurring Soviet industrialization. Communism, as a technique of political organization—that is, of bringing all the resources of the community together and focusing them on one task, industrialization—had transformed Russia into the second most powerful country in the world. But the cost was enormous—not only in terms of human lives, but also in terms of the vitality of the economy and its ability to function effectively and efficiently. Stalin's rule had become highly personal and extremely arbitrary. The pillars of Stalin's totalitarianism had been the Party, the technical-managerial personnel spawned by the industrialization and administering it, the secret police, and the army. Stalin had, however, ruled primarily through the secret police and the widespread

[59] Brzezinski, *Ideology and Power in Soviet Politics*, p. 126.

use of terror. Even the Party had become subordinated to the police, the principal instrument with which Stalin had eliminated all opposition to himself in the Party in the 1920's. It had been the secret police that Stalin had used to carry out his collectivization of the peasantry and vast program of industrialization during the 1930's, as well as the extensive purges in 1936–38 of the top personnel in the Party, the economic apparatus, the army, and even the secret police itself. But by the time of Stalin's death, this police-directed system was in serious trouble. In order to achieve rapid industrialization, the workers had been compelled to work hard at low wages. Although there were actual forced-labor camps into which millions of Russians were thrown, mostly for political reasons, the Soviet Union was really one massive forced-labor camp where workers had no right of protest, where they were subjected to excessive labor discipline and speedups, and where they lived in austerity and fear. The peasants who had not been removed from the land to the factory were equally harshly treated; in fact, Stalin tried to squeeze even more savings out of them than he did out of the workers. But this pervasive police supervision, the arbitrary power of arrest, and the fear of "being sent to Siberia," if not executed, had by the early 1950's brought the Soviet Union to an economic point of diminishing returns.

Fear is a potent incentive. Beyond a certain point, though, it tends to paralyze the system. Fear may have made Stalin feel secure since no one would dare to oppose him, but it could not stimulate the initiative, creativity, and imagination needed to direct large-scale industrial and scientific efforts. How could industry be expected to increase its productivity when there was such fear and the standard of living was so low that even threats of increased terror and of exile to Siberia were no longer effective? How could science—particularly nuclear physics—flourish in an atmosphere that discouraged critical inquiry and innovation? Popular dissatisfaction, ideological disillusionment, and a pervasive fear of assuming responsibility were thus the principal results of the use of terror. But no industrialized society could function effectively in this manner. As Napoleon is alleged to have said, one can do everything with a bayonet but sit on it. Or as one analyst of Soviet affairs has expressed it, the system

. . . established by Stalin and his followers in the late 1920's and early 1930's, had as its primary purpose the industrialization of the country by coercion and terror, and the transformation of Soviet society from a backward agrarian country into a modern industrial state. But the more advances were made in accomplishing this task and the nearer the USSR drew to this goal, the more the system became incompatible with the conditions and requirements of an emerging industrial society. Stalinist methods—police terror, the slave labor camps, the periodic decimation of the ruling elite through arrests and executions, and the clumsy centralized bureaucratic regulation of all areas of life—proved uneconomical and politically ineffectual in promoting the growth of Soviet society.

Toward the end of the Stalin era, and even before in some particular realms, the Soviet Union had reached a level of industrial and social development that required sophisticated methods of government as well as men and women capable of initiative and personally motivated to cope with complex new problems. It was essential to free the party and state bureaucracy, the officer corps, the intelligentsia, as well as workers and Kolkhoz farmers, from the fear that was crippling them, and give them at least some measure of personal security and a chance for personal initiative, if Soviet society was to progress.[60]

Thus, ironically, the Soviet system was itself the victim of the "inherent contradictions" that Soviet political leaders, quoting Marx, were so fond of seeing within the capitalist economy. Moreover, it was a typically Marxian contradiction—between the industrial-economic substructure and the political-social superstructure. Stalinism, in short, seemed to have become outmoded by the very industrialization it had fostered.

A mature industrial society cannot be ruled by terror. Rather, a developed society like the Soviet Union makes demands of its own, and the Party as the ruling elite must meet them. The first imperative for the Party is that in order to encourage productivity, it must grant workers higher pay and an opportunity to improve their living conditions. In a nation that has concentrated its energies on industrialization through decades of enforced self-denial and constant toil, it is natural that there would be an intense popular desire for better working conditions, shorter hours, more pay, better housing, and consumer products. And this material demand of the masses also has a nonmaterial corollary that expresses itself in a desire for a life that is less arbitrary, with fewer restrictions, some opportunity for changing jobs, more freedom to travel, and toleration of a certain degree of nonconformity. In short, in order to enlist people's willingness to work and to encourage the initiative and creativity needed for the operation of a complex economy, the political system must offer some material incentives as well as a degree of personal security and freedom.

The second imperative for the Party is to enlist the support of the growing "middle class" produced by industrialization. This class, composed by and large of the scientists, engineers, industrial managers, and technicians, is indispensable for the operational efficiency of the economy. As experts in various fields of competence, its members are the managers. If one were to compare the sociopolitical structure of the Soviet Union with an American corporation, it might be said that it shares the divorce of ownership and management characteristic of American industry: The Party represents the board of directors; it owns the corporation because it holds most of the shares—in fact, all the shares. The managers are the salaried employees responsible for the daily operations

[60] Leonhard, "Internal Developments: A Balance Sheet," *Problems of Communism*, March–April, 1963, p. 7.

of the corporation. Their reward is a high salary, social standing, and authority to achieve their economic targets, be it a certain quantity of goods or profit ratios. Their tenure is judged in terms of their successful accomplishment of these targets. In the Soviet Union, these functional experts also wish to improve their living conditions, acquire more leisure time, and gain some degree of autonomy and a guarantee against a return of the police state.

Finally, the third imperative for the Party is that it must educate its subjects. Illiterates cannot man machines—or become scientists or industrial executives. Industry increasingly demands trained manpower rather than unskilled labor. Education is thus a fundamental prerequisite of an urbanized and modernized society.

The question was whether implementation of the three imperatives would not gradually erode the foundations of the Soviet totalitarian state. (Eventually, of course, this question will apply to the Chinese state as well.) First, would an increasingly affluent population not threaten the future of the Party itself? If one of the major reasons for the Party's claim to power was that it could quickly industrialize the nation and provide its citizens with a better life, what justification would it have for staying in power once that industrialization had been accomplished? What need would there be for the Party to espouse Communist ideology and talk of world revolution in a mass-consumption society? An industrialized and urbanized society in which the populace has a reasonably high standard of living is less concerned with ideology than with its own well-being, along with the protection of political rights against the arbitrary acts of the government—at least if the Western experience of affluence *and* democracy can serve as any guide. And once some economic and political concessions had been granted, the pressure for even more concessions would only gather momentum.

Second, does not the functional specialization of the various Soviet elites destroy the monolithic nature of the Soviet "power elite"? The division of labor inherent in a sophisticated and advanced economy creates a number of elites, each with its own interests; these, in turn, will be reflected in the emergence of various factions within the Communist Party, in which most of the leading members of these "interest groups" are enrolled. The pluralistic nature of industrial society thus emerges within the power structure in the totalitarian Party. And there these elites work toward achieving sufficient freedom to practice their professions without political and ideological interference.

The Soviet military provides a good example. Nowhere had the stultifying impact of Stalinist terror been more noticeable than on military thinking and doctrine, which, after World War II, stressed that the so-called "permanently operating factors"—the stability of the rear, the morale of the army, the quantity and quality of divisions, the armament of the army, the organizational ability of the army commanders—would decide the outcome of a war. This formulation was, of course, truistic and largely meaningless since a nation with superior morale, armed forces, and economy would obviously be the victor. Yet it took no account at all of the impact of nuclear technology. If the permanently operating factors were decisive, then the possibility of a surprise atomic attack was obviously merely a transitory and nondecisive factor. To write off the effects of a surprise attack in an age of nuclear weapons and delivery vehicles of great speed was to enshrine Soviet *pre*-nuclear experience as a permanent guide to action in the nuclear age. At best, according to Stalin, a surprise attack could gain only temporary success. Had not the experience of the German surprise attack on the Soviet Union in 1941 "proven" its futility? Stalin's interpretation, in fact, claimed that Soviet World War II strategy would be the winning strategy in future full-scale wars.

While the Soviets developed nuclear arms, this did not mean they fully understood the revolutionary impact of the new technology. There was little discussion in Soviet military journals of the radically changed strategic posture. World War II experience was hardly relevant to the new challenge posed by the United States. Soviet military doctrine simply failed to develop an *inter*continental strategy that included in its formulation a realization of the innovative nature of nuclear weapons. The Soviets merely criticized the American evaluation of the decisive importance of surprise attack and nuclear bombs. Not until after Stalin's death did they re-evaluate their own strategic doctrine. And only then did Soviet military strategists admit that World War II did not provide a model for future wars and that a surprise nuclear attack could be decisive. For the first time, Soviet officers talked of "the laws of war as armed conflict." Armed conflict was to be discussed *per se*, independently of the Party's teachings on the causes of wars. The same laws of war applied to all participants in combat. The hydrogen bomb obviously had the same impact on a Communist target as on a capitalist one. In short, once the Stalinist mold was broken, Soviet military doctrine could adjust itself to "reality" without being "blinded" by ideology.

This represented a significant breakthrough. The laws of war, like the laws of chemistry or engineering or industrial management, were recognized as being the same for all industrial societies. It followed from this that if the experts were to apply their expertise in a professionally competent manner, ideological and political control had to be minimized. The multiplicity of interest groups would, indeed, radically change the role of the political leadership. Before industrialization had begun, the Party had been the only organized group and its word was law. The economy's "drive to maturity," however, created new groups who also possessed interests. In such circumstances, the Party loses its monopoly of authority and is compelled to share it; indeed, increasingly it must judge among the groups' conflicting interests and competing claims—whether for larger military forces or more investments in heavy or light industry—and play a mediating role. In short, this pluralism creates under the totalitarian form the substance of a Western-type system of checks and balances between professional and bureaucratic interest groups. In this context the Party, like Western democratic governments, must act primarily as the "honest broker."

If affluence undermines ideology, and pluralism the one-party state, does not education administer the final blow? Once a man is encouraged to "think for himself" as an engineer or scientist, will this not become a habit in ideological and political matters, too? As Allen Dulles, former Director of the Central Intelligence Agency, has said:

> Knowledge is not an inert substance. It has a way of seeping across lines and into adjacent compartments of learning. The Soviet leaders . . . cannot illuminate their scientific lecture halls and laboratories without also letting the light of truth into their history and economics classrooms. Students cannot be conditioned to turning off their analytical processes when the instructor changes a topic. . . . [Consequently] men and women who have their critical faculties sharpened are beginning to question why the Russian people canot be freed from rigid Communist Party and police-state discipline, given a greater economic share of the fruit of their labors, and allowed to participate—at least by an effective expression of consent—in their own governing.[61]

The implications of this theory of economic development are thus clear. A society, once it has "taken off" and "driven to maturity," emerges as a pluralistic, democratic, affluent or "high mass-consumption" society. An economically mature society, in other words, is a democratic society —and a relatively peaceful one. Even while the development process is eroding the missionary ideology and totalitarian political structure, the nation's foreign policy becomes increasingly cautious and circumscribed. If the popular demand for material improvement is to be met, the huge capital outlays that must be invested in consumer items detract capital from investment in heavy industry, arms production, and anything like a space race. Furthermore, if the new managerial "middle class" wishes to preserve its privileged social status and material perquisites, it is compelled to act as a restraining force opposing an adventurous foreign policy which might jeopardize its position. The masses and the new ruling class have gained a vested interest in their new prosperity; and in turn this wealth makes them conservative. The "have-nots" have become the "haves," and they wish to keep their gains. And with the end of the one-

[61] Allen W. Dulles, "The Communists Also Have Their Problems," speech delivered on September 19, 1957.

party ideological state, the refusal to recognize the right of other states of a different social and political persuasion to exist also ends. Soviet foreign policy once more becomes Russian foreign policy; and the Soviet Union's revolutionary aims and expansionism, having been "de-ideologized," return to more traditional Russian national interests and more limited objectives.

The hopeful conclusion drawn from this interpretation of industrial development and the nature of industrial society has been challenged however.

The fact that Khrushchev and his successors have recognized that they must come to terms with the Soviet Union's own revolution of rising expectations, it is asserted, does not mean that the rise in the Soviet standard of living since Stalin's death was granted as a reluctant concession by the Party to "democratic" popular pressure. From the Party's point of view, this move and others ranging from the closing of the labor camps to the granting of a modicum of freedom to the intellectuals to express themselves were intended only to rationalize and modernize Soviet life, and to increase its efficiency and productivity by stimulating initiative and a degree of dedication at all levels. These moves have not in any way reduced the Party's power. Rather, the relaxation of police controls and the gradual improvement of living conditions have served to bring the regime a larger measure of popular support, and thereby enhanced its ability to mobilize popular energy and loyalty behind its domestic and foreign policies. The Party has thus strengthened its grip on Soviet society, it is argued. One political analyst has emphasized that the post-Stalin reforms barely constitute the first faltering step toward the rule of law, let alone democracy or liberalism—"terms that anybody writing about the Soviet Union for the next generation or so would be wise to avoid." The reforms primarily reveal, he says, the conviction of the leaders that they can afford and must practice a "sane" totalitarianism, as distinct from the "morbid" totalitarianism of Stalin.[62] In brief, Stalin's successors eliminated some of the worst abuses and excesses of Stalinist totalitarianism. But the nature of Soviet totalitarianism cannot be attributed to Stalin; it is rooted in the views and methods of Communism. The new leaders placed a "new face" on it, but they kept the totalitarian structure intact.

Besides raising the standard of living, the Soviet regime has used three additional methods to control its people and enlist their support. First, it has sought to impose its values on the Soviet people with greater determination than ever before, with indoctrination substituted for terror. The mass media—newspapers, radio, and television—and the arts, literature,

[62] Ulam, *The Unfinished Revolution*, p. 270. See also Ulam, *The New Face of Soviet Totalitarianism*; and Mosely, "Soviet Myths and Realities," *Foreign Affairs*, April, 1961, pp. 341–54.

and other forms of entertainment are used to transmit the Party's values and point of view to the masses. Second, social conformity is used to enforce "correct" behavior and to regulate the attitudes of the people. In any society, of course, social pressure tends to compel the individual to conform. In the Soviet Union, however, such persuasion is thought of as a deliberately controlled government-sponsored force to secure conformity to the Party's purposes—a kind of nationally directed vigilantism to enforce the right Communist behavior. For example, labor discipline is enforced by the "comrades' courts,"[63] which are established in each place of work as well as in residential areas. The courts deal with minor violations of the law, but they can also concern themselves with such violations as absenteeism and sloppy work. They can impose public reprimands, fines, job demotions, and even five years of compulsory labor at a specified place of banishment. Such courts and Komsomol volunteer detachments can also deal with problems of juvenile delinquency, drunkenness, and rowdiness. But their purpose is less to punish than to focus social pressure on offenders and teach them proper "Communist morality": "The Comrades' Courts and the Citizens' Militia, staffed by narrow-minded and intolerant low-level activists, are forms of organized mass coercion designed to stifle politically dangerous individualism that might threaten the pattern of positive indoctrination. For that purpose, the potential of political terror in the background and organized social intolerance in the forefront is sufficient. A voluntarist totalitarianism can be far more effective than a terrorist one."[64] Finally, the Soviet regime seeks to link its indoctrination with its achievements. The benefits of Communism are associated with the gradually rising standard of living, a relaxation of police control, a degree of personal security, and the stature and success of the Soviet Union in international affairs—as the world's second greatest power, feared and respected by all nations, equipped with the most modern weapons, and proud achiever of a string of spectacular space achievements. There is, in any case, no alternative for the Soviet citizen. The system "works," and he has no choice but to live within it. Thus the Party retains its control—although it exercises this control with moderation—while the de-Stalinization (that is, the de-terrorization) has won the regime confidence and cooperation. The former hostility between the Party and society has therefore been diminished. Whatever dissent exists can be contained by a certain degree of relaxation of the controls, plus such more obvious measures as controlling job and educational opportunities. As the only employer and educator, the Party provides a strong incentive for self-restraint.

[63] See John A. Armstrong, *Ideology, Politics, and Government in the Soviet Union*, pp. 93–95; see also Paul Zinner, "Soviet Society Since Stalin: Changes and Continuities," in William Petersen (ed.), *The Realities of World Communism* (Englewood Cliffs, N.J.: Prentice-Hall, 1963), pp. 97–99.

[64] Brzezinski, *Ideology and Power in Soviet Politics*, pp. 81–82.

Nor has the "managerial revolution" threatened the Party's authority and supremacy. The Party retains its monopoly of control over all phases of Soviet life—political, economic, social, cultural, scientific, and even spiritual. Its authority has not only not been diminished, but has actually increased. The Party has, in fact, reasserted the primacy it had lost under Stalin. After Beria's attempted *coup d'état*, it established its control over the police. Next, Khrushchev decentralized industry by abolishing most of the central industrial ministries, who all had their headquarters in Moscow. These were virtual empires—the Minister of Steel, for example, controlled an enterprise and production far larger than that of U.S. Steel—and such highly central control by a top-heavy bureaucracy was inefficient. (This concentration of the top industrial managers in Moscow had also provided Malenkov, the representative of the new managerial class, with his base of power.) Khrushchev thus broke up these industrial empires by placing their direction in the hands of regional councils. Economic planning, though, remained in Moscow, which preserved central control. But in each region it was the first secretary of the provincial committee of the Party who was in charge. Decentralization thus ensured that the power of the technical-managerial elite would remain subordinated to the Party by strengthening the Party's grip over the industrial executives. Finally, the Party exerted its authority over the army. In the years following Stalin's death, the army's influence had greatly increased. The "collective leadership" that succeeded Stalin needed the army as protection against the threat of Beria and the secret police. Later, in his struggle to gain leadership, Khrushchev found his principal source of support in the army, whose backing he won by advocating further investments in heavy industry rather than consumer products. In turn, the army sought to reduce the influence of the political commissars, who kept a watchful eye open for signs of disloyalty and opposition, and the rehabilitation of some of the senior military officers purged by Stalin during the 1930's. The crucial point for the security of the Party was, however, the fact that the army had played such a decisive role in the post-Stalin struggles for succession. The authority of the secret police had been sheared, and that of the economic bureaucracy had become diffused. In these circumstances, the only possible challenger of the Party's supremacy was the military. The Party could scarcely afford to become dependent upon the army's support. It accordingly strengthened its control over the army by dismissing the most popular military figure, Marshal Zhukov, the hero of Stalingrad and Berlin during World War II. Party supremacy was thereby restored and the totalitarian structure preserved intact.

The Party's ability to impose its control on the other interest groups was hardly surprising, however. A multiplicity of experts is inherent in any urbanized and industrialized society, but this is not the same thing as a genuine social pluralism. The latter is a result not of industrialization *per se*, but of *political* development:

> In the Soviet Union, a primitive society was industrialized and relatively modernized through total social mobilization effected by violent, terroristic means wielded by a highly disciplined and motivated political élite. The very nature of this process is inimical to the emergence of a separate managerial class (not to speak of the even more amorphous concept of a "middle class"), which would be a first step in the direction of a limitation of the Party's power. Furthermore, a society developed under total political direction has a need for continued political integration on a national scale, since the liquidation of both the private economy sector and all informal leadership groups creates a vacuum that must be filled. In such conditions, the Party—its discipline, morale, and zeal—remains the determinant of change.[65]

Thus, it is unlikely that the new managerial "middle class" will soon throw off the political control of the Party as the commercial bourgeoisie in Western Europe once threw off the shackles of monarchism. Indeed, in the West industrialization occurred in societies that were already pluralistic. Even in the age of royal absolutism, more than one center of power existed in the state: the nobility, the Church, and the burghers. The monarch's need for support from one or more of these groups led him to grant concessions ranging from the Magna Carta for the nobility to charters for towns. He was therefore anything but absolute. In reality, he was checked and his authority, although great, was limited. The evolution of constitutional monarchies and democracies was thus, in a sense, inevitable. It was in this context that Western industrialization occurred. In addition, the role of private enterprise in this industrialization was politically significant. If Western economies had continued to be state-directed, as they were in the beginning, then the bourgeoisie could never have become an independent center of power. The state would then have concentrated all political and economic power in its own hands—as in Soviet Russia—and been able to forestall the emergence of the bourgeoisie as an independent social class. In Russia, the so-called managerial middle class has gained neither economic independence nor political self-confidence. In fact, even before the 1917 Revolution, Russia had not known a pluralistic tradition. The nobility and the Church had been strictly controlled by the Czar.

It is even more doubtful that education will undermine the foundations of Soviet totalitarianism. The Soviet student, to be sure, has many complaints. As an American observer has expressed it, the student "Sasha,"

> . . . has plenty of complaints, and if you have his confidence, he will show you that he is not an unquestioning robot regulated automatically by sig-

[65] *Ibid.*, pp. 88–89.

nals from above. He scorns his obligatory courses in political economy, dialectic materialism and the history of the Communist party, and he is annoyed by the propaganda campaigns that bombard him. ("Turn off that damned nonsense!" he would say when I listened to a radio editorial.)

He is irritated by corruption and heavy-handedness in high places, and saddened by the personal poverty everywhere else. "Soviet life is still ugly in many areas—you don't know the half of it. People in the countryside live like subhumans!" He knows very well that his standard of living is dismally low, that there are not enough consumer goods to satisfy even an underpaid population. He craves jazz, motor scooters, stylish clothes, a room of his own and everything else that he knows is far more available to his counterparts in the West. He longs to read the literature of the world, from the Bible to *Lolita* (the *Zhivago* affair wounded and humiliated him). And most of all, he yearns to travel—abroad.

Sasha and his friends are impatient with the militarization, drabness and restrictiveness of their lives. They wish for a state of "normalcy" in which they will be able to buy what they need without standing in line and discuss what they choose without the fear that what is permissible today may not be tomorrow.

Yet, in spite of these manifestations of dissatisfaction, it would be the greatest mistake to picture Sasha in a state of revolt, or even of anger against a "police state." He laughed when I read him articles from the Western press describing him as "seriously questioning the basic tenets of the creed forced on him," and "impatient to break the bonds of Communist tyranny." Sasha is very far from that. . . . The principal reason is that Sasha feels that the policies and arrangements of his leaders are essentially those needed for the welfare of the nation. Although at first I was struck by his dissatisfactions, I came to realize that these represent rather little compared to his sense of commitment. Could such measurements be expressed arithmetically, I would estimate that Sasha is 80 per cent satisfied.

For he is convinced that capitalism is *basically* bad and destined for disaster, and that socialism is *basically* good; basically progressive, fair and desirable. On what he considers the fundamental issues, he has no argument with the socialist system or even the Communist party; he is certain that the advantages of Soviet society far outweigh its disadvantages.

What advantages? For Sasha, they concern more than free medical care and education, full employment, rapid economic growth, expanding welfare programs and a promising personal future—for which he is grateful to his regime. To him, the real criterion of the good society is ownership of property; the Soviet Union has socialism, therefore the Soviet Union is fundamentally sound.

Politics, literature, the standard of living—all these questions are secondary to the question of who owns the means of production. If they are in private hands, subordinate (he feels) to the profit motive, society is unhealthy. However much Sasha wants things Western, he does not want what seems to him its essence: capitalism. "Free enterprise" is only an ugly phrase connoting greed, class war and exploitation, and Sasha is delighted that the Soviet Union has "left this stage."

In this way, Sasha is not unlike his Columbia University counterpart who, although impatient with America's faults and eager for reform, is convinced that the foundation for improvement—constitutionalism, a free press, the democratic process—is well laid. So, too, Sasha: the foundation—common ownership of the means of production—is secure, and if there is much yet which is unjust and undone, this implies the improvement of the Soviet system, certainly not its replacement. "You cannot have a free people and real progress toward a perfect society unless you have socialism."

This basic issue settled, everything else falls into place. It is unfortunate that individual liberties are sometimes sacrificed in the fight to build Communism and repel imperialism; it is a shame that a good pair of shoes costs a worker a week's wages, and that his diet is so starchy; it is inexcusable that thousands of loyal Soviet citizens were shot during the purges; and too bad that the truth must sometimes be manipulated in order to protect the still-unenlightened masses against the temptations and disortions of capitalism. But these are peripheral problems. The mistakes will be corrected in time, the shortcomings overcome. Nothing in them is so deep-rooted as are the evils and contradictions of capitalist society. . . .

Sasha is clearly a Marxist. He has been raised, literally since nursery school, on Marxist philosophy—and Marxist philosophy alone—with a persistence that staggered my imagination, and now its basic propositions, at least, seem to him beyond question—"natural," "logical," "obvious" and "plain common sense." I cannot do more than mention these beliefs: they concern the primacy of economics, the dialectic and the class struggle, the movement of history along a prescribed path, the inevitable triumph of Communism. These categories have become *his* way of looking at the world, and like anyone else, he is not inclined to change patterns of thought because of the frustrations of daily life. . . .

He believes, for example, that the present world conflict is inevitable: the laws of history require that capitalism and socialism struggle (though not militarily) to the death—of capitalism, of course. For he has no doubt about the outcome. "In the end, the more rational and progressive always wins. The new replaces the old—that is just natural." Nor has he any doubt about the cause of the conflict. "Of course the imperialists are guilty. They are not going to give up their profits all over the world without resistance."[66]

This illuminating account of the Russian student's beliefs does not indicate that Communist ideology is about to "wither away." Indeed, if Sasha attains a responsible position in the Soviet government, it means that the economic and ideological struggle will continue. As he himself

[66] George Feifer, "Sasha's Creed: 'Russia Right or Wrong,'" *The New York Times Magazine*, April 28, 1963.

said, "No matter what happens in the dispute with China, our countries will not become friends in our lifetime. . . . We are too far apart in everything basic for that." It is equally significant, however, that the fundamental values of Communism are apparently accepted as "natural" in Soviet society and that whatever criticisms the intellectuals make, they are made within the framework of Communist ideology. Even then, the Party defines the limits of tolerable criticism. It will not permit such criticism to extend to either the leaders or the ideology which legitimizes their rule. But the fact that the Party is willing to tolerate criticism at all is a sign of the regime's self-confidence and the Party's belief that it can assume the fundamental allegiance of the population—without the use of terror.

The final question is which of these two interpretations of the evolution of the Soviet political system is correct. The system has not been eroded; but neither is it the same system as under Stalin. An evolution has clearly occurred, and what seems to be emerging is a state that is both more stable and less arbitrary. But the state continues to be governed by a single and all-powerful Party which is unlikely to surrender its sovereign position. Similarly, the foreign policy of the Soviet Union continues to be revolutionary in its ambitions. The degree of militancy with which it pursues these ambitions is, however, likely to vary according to the problems the Soviet leaders confront at home, within the Communist bloc, and in the international system as a whole.

X

The Ambiguity of Reality

The State System and the Three Revolutions

Now that we have concluded the analysis of the three principal revolutions of our time, what remains to be done is to examine their impact upon the state system, assess the utility of analyzing international politics in terms of external *and* internal determinants, and determine the predictions one can make about the future course of international politics. But before we can make these assessments, it is necessary to see to what extent the state system—that is, the system's distribution of power (which has been essentially bipolar in the postwar period)—has shaped the behavior of the principal actors. For if it is true that the state system seeks to stabilize itself by counteracting any shift in power and re-establishing an equilibrium, the system will define each nation's security objective.

The collapse of Europe in the wake of World War II and the rise of an expansionist Soviet Union left Washington with no choice but to react and to contain Soviet expansionism. The confrontation between the two superpowers was direct and simple. Moreover, the United States was the only non-Communist nation that possessed sufficient strength to meet the challenge. Necessity, in short, compelled America to counteract Soviet—and later, Chinese—attempts to extend the Communist orbit. As a result, the Cold War has been a matter of drawing lines, or "frontiers," between the two blocs—first in the eastern Mediterranean, then along the Elbe River and in West Berlin, and finally along the coast of China at Quemoy and Matsu, at the 38th Parallel in Korea, and at the

17th Parallel in Vietnam. Those frontiers have to be drawn clearly and "obviously" so that the enemy will not miscalculate and attack, as the North Koreans did when they thought that the United States was not committed to the defense of South Korea.

The bipolar division of power has, furthermore, compelled each of the superpowers to be particularly concerned with the protection of its own bloc from "defection" or, where that has already occurred, to overthrow the alleged hostile regime. Thus, for example, the United States helped (through the CIA) to overthrow what it deemed to be a pro-Communist government in Guatemala; sent troops to prevent the victory of alleged pro-Castro, pro-Communist elements in the Dominican Republic; sought unsuccessfully to topple Castro's regime in Cuba; and has often "interfered" in European and other elections to the extent of making it clear which party (obviously the pro-American one) it favored. It even supported South Vietnam's refusal to participate in the 1956 country-wide election stipulated by the 1954 Geneva Agreements because it feared that the election would go to Ho Chi Minh's North Vietnamese regime rather than the American supported Diem regime. On the other side, the Soviets seized power in Czechoslovakia to "fill out" their Eastern zone; suppressed the East German revolt; threatened to crush the Polish uprising; and did crush the Hungarian revolution. Similarly, they have refused to allow the East Germans to express their views on the issue of a reunification with West Germany through free elections; and the Yalta obligation to permit free elections, with all parties represented (except those which collaborated with Nazi Germany), has been ignored. And when U.S. forces advanced into North Korea during the Korean conflict, China intervened—both to guard its security and to preserve a Communist regime.

Both superpowers have been extremely sensitive, in short, about where frontier lines would be drawn and the protection of their blocs because in a bipolar system all such issues become a matter of an advance or a retreat. The payoff for one is the other's loss, and since a loss cannot be tolerated, attempts to encroach upon one's sphere must be resisted (except in special instances, such as Cuba, for the areas "belonging" to the United States are not always as easily discernible and definable as the nations controlled by Russia or China). Every "tug of war" in these circumstances has become a test of will which, if not met, especially by the defending power, would have a detrimental effect in both the contested area as well as in other areas of confrontation. All parts of the bloc must be defended; if a particular frontier seems distant from the principal bloc power—and most are bound to be distant—disengagement may appear more attractive than becoming involved in costly hostilities far away. But what makes one area more vital and worth defending than other areas? Yielding one frontier would certainly tempt the opponent to compel further retreats, for he knows that the bloc can be protected only if the will to do so exists at the "center"; if that will is lacking or weak with regard to one area, it may be so elsewhere as well. The protection of the bloc has thus become a matter of vital interest to the security of the United States and the Soviet Union, and any efforts to change the status of any part of these areas is taken at the risk of war. Even if the initial challenge is one of nuclear blackmail, or limited war, the danger of escalation is never completely eliminated. The demarcation and guardianship of the respective blocs has therefore created intermittent periods of tension and danger, a continuing concern with the development of new weapons, and on occasion "frontier wars."

There have been three additional consequences of this bipolar distribution of power. The first was the search for allies. It has frequently been charged that the United States suffers from the disease of "pactomania" —that it indiscriminately collects allies, whether they are powerful or not, strategically located or not, developed or underdeveloped. This "pactomania" developed because of the bipolarity and the consequent demands it imposed upon the power seeking to contain the expansion of the Heartland powers. Because the confrontation was global, the United States became involved with NATO in Europe, METO in the Middle East, SEATO in Southeast Asia, and ANZUS (Australia and New Zealand), plus treaties of defense with Nationalist China and Japan in the Far East. Indeed, in our bipolar world, both aligned *and* nonaligned states attacked by members of one bloc or the other are protected. The Soviets threatened to intervene in Suez and the United States did intervene as far as furnishing aid to India in her fight against China. The Warsaw Pact and the Sino-Soviet alliance (prior to the schism) indicate that the Soviet Union has also been concerned with forming alliances. But as the expansionist power, she has not needed to be as concerned with collecting allies as have the defending nations.

Second, bipolarity compelled the two superpowers to extend their competition to the new nations in the developing areas, as well as to the older developing nations of Latin America. For the addition of these nations' strategic position, manpower, and natural resources to one side or the other could shift the balance. The maximum objective of the United States and the Soviet Union here has been to win allies; their minimum aim, to deny such allies to the opponent. The Soviets' chief hope for long-term success was to impress the new states with Communism as the key to nation-building—witness Russia's own rise to great-power status—thereby gradually drawing them into the Soviet sphere of influence and, finally, through the establishment of "national democracies," leading them to accept the hegemony of the Communist Party. More immediately, the Soviet Union tended to support any new regime that sought to reduce or eliminate Western influence in its area. American hopes in the "third world" were based primarily upon helping the new nations' "drive to maturity," which, hopefully, would strengthen their bonds of national unity, raise their standards of living, and derevolutionize the masses; these conditions would provide good breeding grounds for open societies and modern political systems, which would be jealous guardians of national independence. The only allies the United States gained among the new states were several bordering on the Sino-Soviet periphery; because these countries formed alliances with the United States largely for reasons of regional prestige or security against a local neighbor, the immediate result was usually increased tensions and anti-American feelings in the area.

Significantly, amid this search for allies and competition for the new states' allegiance between the United States and the Soviet Union, the "New Europe" (whose great-power status had vanished with their empires) and the new China (which sought great-power status) led "revolts" in NATO and the Sino-Soviet bloc respectively. Each had the choice of accepting a subordinate, if not passive, role within its particular alliance and state system, or of reasserting itself and demanding an equal role in the protector's decision-making process. France, West Germany, Italy, and the Benelux countries therefore began to work toward a greater economic unity in the expectation of one day creating a politically unified continental power (by then, hopefully, Britain would be included). Because of the U.S. nuclear monopoly and because of the U.S. opposition to the diffusion of national deterrents within NATO (except for Britain's, which tended to be American-controlled), the Europeans' revolt took the form of a critique of American strategic doctrine with its triple prongs of a damage-limiting strategy, adamant opposition to any independent national deterrents, and emphasis on conventional (i.e., nontactical nuclear weapons) defense of Europe. The Chinese took an even broader form of attack: against Russia's entire conduct of foreign policy, particularly toward the "imperialist" world and the "national bourgeoisie" in the underdeveloped areas. In asserting itself, China sought its own allies within the Communist bloc; tried to establish control over a number of Communist parties in non-Communist countries, particularly in Asia; and organized Chinese factions in many states where the Soviets retained control of the Party. China also made wide use of the race issue among the new nations, pointing to itself, a non-European and nonwhite country, as the proper leader against the colonial West. The Chinese even tried to identify the Soviets with this colonialism by raising the issue of the Sino-Soviet borderlands, which, they claimed, Czarist Russia had carved up in its favor and Soviet Russia had preserved. But it was not Peking alone that resisted Moscow's dominance; the East European People's Democracies also pressed—successfully—for greater autonomy in their internal affairs and, in Romania's case, in foreign policy.

Similarly, with the Russians and the Americans competing for friends and allies in the developing areas, most of the new nations adopted a policy of nonalignment. Thus they were able to preserve their national freedom; on some occasions they swung Eastward to reduce Western influence, and on other occasions they swung Westward to limit Soviet influence. Their "in-between" position also meant that their affluent superpower suitors would each woo them with money.

This example, and the previous ones, illustrate that the state system tends to define for its actors, both great and small, their behavior—their goals and therefore the amount of power required to achieve these goals, as well as how they should achieve them—as, for instance, by alignment or nonalignment. In fact, one writer has maintained that "international politics take place within the type of environment which leaves states no real choice as to whether or not they should pursue balance of power policies."[1] Perhaps this lack of choice—or conversely, the emphasis on the dictates of necessity—has been exaggerated. Yet the essential truth of the environmental impact cannot be doubted.

Indeed, it is clearly illustrated by one consequence of the global nature of the bipolar balance and the world-wide confrontation: the great cost of noninvolvement. The examples are both positive and negative. On the positive side, the U.S. intervention in Korea was required not merely by balance-of-power considerations in the Far East, but, even more important, by the need to preserve NATO and solidify it as a cohesive alliance. Not to have responded in 1950 to North Korea's attack upon the Republic of Korea would have undermined the possibility of an alliance with Japan and driven NATO into neutralism. Similarly, in South Vietnam in the early 1960's, the increasing American intervention grew out of Washington's fear that nonresistance to the Viet-Cong, who were aided and abetted by North Vietnam and Communist China, would lead to the fall of the other "dominoes" in Southeast Asia. In brief, all frontiers must be defended because they are interdependent. Even such strategically unimportant areas as West Berlin or Quemoy and Matsu thus become important. For the test in each instance is the same: Does the United States possess the will to defend its bloc? On the negative side, America's failure to help the East German population in 1953 and the Hungarian people in 1956 lowered its prestige among the countries of Eastern Europe, whom the United States had promised to "liberate" despite their status as part of the Soviet core area (which was, of course, precisely why the United States did not intervene militarily). And the failure of the Cuban invasion in 1961 presented an image of the United States as impotent and indecisive in her own backyard—not only to the Latin Americans but also to Moscow, which subsequently attempted to exploit this posture by the placement of missiles in Cuba. Similarly, if

[1] Fred A. Sonderman, "The Linkage between Foreign Policy and International Politics," in James N. Rosenau (ed.), *International Politics and Foreign Policy*, p. 13.

the Soviet Union had refused to act in East Germany or Hungary, it would have aroused the scorn of the Chinese and the other People's Democracies by such demonstrations of weakness and "un-Communist" behavior, and its claim to the leadership of the international Communist movement would have been challenged. Indeed, when Khrushchev backed down in the Cuban missile crisis in 1962, Peking charged Moscow with "adventurism" on the one hand and "capitulation" on the other; and four years later, China charged that the Soviet Union's alleged lack of support for Hanoi and failure to exert pressure on the United States in Western Europe showed not only a lack of concern for a fellow socialist state but tacit Soviet-American cooperation to isolate and contain China.[2]

It is at this point that we can see the impact of the nuclear revolution. For the restraint of both superpowers is primarily due to their mutual fear of nuclear war. Admittedly, it has been argued that the bipolar distribution of power is responsible for this caution in crises:

> crises also occur in a multipower world, but the dangers are diffused, responsibilities unclear, and definition of vital interests easily obscured. The skillful foreign policy, where many states are in balance, is designed to gain an advantage over one state without antagonizing others and frightening them into united action. Often in modern Europe, possible gains have seemed greater than likely losses. Statesmen could thus hope in crises to push an issue to the limit without causing all the potential opponents to unite. When possible enemies are several in number, unity of action among states is difficult to secure. One could therefore think—or hope desperately as did Bethmann Hollweg and Adolph Hitler—that no united opposition would form. In a bipolar world, on the other hand, attention is focused on crises by both of the major competitors, and especially by the defensive state. . . . One's motto may still be "push to the limit," but *limit* must be emphasized as heavily as *push*. Caution, moderation, and the management of crisis come to be of great and obvious importance.[3]

It may certainly be true that the bipolar distribution of power in the atomic age has contributed to the two superpowers' restraint. It is doubtful that either the United States or the Soviet Union has wanted to become involved in a long and costly total war fought like World War II. But if either power has entertained any thoughts of defeating its opponent by an all-out strike, or of "raising the ante" dangerously high in crises, or of realizing such grandiose objectives as world revolution or liberation in one quick blow, the temptation has been eliminated by the bomb. For the principal danger that in the past resulted in war was that one power underestimated its opponent's strength and will. Nuclear

---

[2] *The New York Times*, February 6, 1966.
[3] Kenneth W. Waltz, "The Stability of a Bipolar World," *Daedalus*, Summer, 1964, pp. 883–84.

weapons, however, have enhanced the deterrent value of the balancing process. Indeed, the more a nuclear power overestimates the relative capacity of the other side, the greater the possibility that both will refrain from using their power. "Even a megalomaniac would not easily discount enemy nuclear retaliatory power, provided he has the slightest reason to believe that his opponent might use that power to counter his moves."[4]

The crucial issue for the two nuclear giants has thus been not their ability to mobilize the power they needed, but their ability to discipline that power and use it with restraint. The record of the postwar years speaks for itself. The principal characteristic of the Cold War has been the high degree of caution exercised by the United States and the Soviet Union in their direct confrontations, as in Berlin and Cuba, as well as in their indirect confrontations on the fringes of the Cold War zones, as in Korea (where the North Korean and Chinese armies served as Soviet proxies), Suez, Lebanon, and the Congo. Their anxiety to avoid a holocaust has been reflected in a series of both tacit and formal arms-control arrangements. The anxiety of each superpower's respective allies concerning their protector's increasing caution is reflected by their apprehensions that their vital interests, as they define them, will not be defended and might even be sacrificed to avoid the risk of war. As regional powers with essentially regional interests (China, to be sure, has universal objectives, but her most immediate interests lie in Asia), they have all already experienced some concern on this score. Thus China has felt betrayed because the Soviet Union would not use its nuclear might to persuade the United States to abandon Formosa, or even the offshore islands; and the Chinese have frequently accused Moscow of insufficient support for the war of national liberation in South Vietnam. In short, the Chinese charge that the Russians are too fearful of precipitating a nuclear war and therefore fail to exploit the West's own fear of such a war to advance the cause of Communism. Similarly, Britain and France felt betrayed when the United States, apprehensive about Soviet intervention, failed to support them in the Suez invasion; and West Germany has feared, and continues to fear, that Washington might one day exchange West Berlin for the continued safety of its own cities. The fact that Britain and France have built their own small deterrents, and that West Germany seeks some voice regarding the use of the American deterrent, testifies to their doubts about the protection they can expect in future crises; their worry is that the United States will be too intimidated by the risk of war to preserve the *status quo* against future Soviet nuclear blackmail efforts. In short, similar situations exist in both blocs: China on one side and Britain and France on the other feel that their interests have become increasingly subordinated to the strategic caution of their

---

[4] Arnold Wolfers, *Discord and Collaboration*, p. 129.

respective superpower. These apprehensions provide clear evidence that bipolarity *plus* the bomb have proved to be effective stabilizers of the state system.

As a result, it can be said that the principal consequence of the nuclear revolution has been to change the management of international conflict. Instead of resolving their differences in a traditional war, the two superpowers have conducted their conflict as a Cold War; this change would have been necessary even if one of the two contestants had not been a revolutionary power committed to a strategy of international civil war. The principal function of their nuclear forces has been deterrence, and the eruption of a total war would have constituted a failure of military policy. Nuclear power has been used only in nuclear blackmail situations, as in the Soviet attempts to move the West out of West Berlin from 1958 to 1962; to prevent an unfavorable shift in the balance, as in the American confrontation of the Soviet Union in the 1962 Cuban missile crisis; and to limit actual hostilities that occur, as in Korea and South Vietnam. Pressure, limited conventional and guerrilla war, and psychological and economic warfare have been the typical instruments of the Cold War.

The second impact of nuclear technology has been to shift—although not completely—the area of conflict from Europe to the underdeveloped countries, where there are no clear dividing lines between the "peace zone" and the "war zone" and the two powers do not directly confront each other. In the Far Eastern conflicts, the Soviets have abstained from direct participation, although China has been directly involved twice. In the Middle East, the Soviets used local nationalist forces to reduce Western presence and influence. On the one occasion, in Lebanon in 1958, when the United States landed its forces to prevent a further expansion of the tactical anti-Western alliance of Russia and Egypt, the Soviet Union was careful not to do more than carry out war maneuvers in the Caucasus, despite threats to send volunteers and intervene if the West sent its troops into Iraq (which it did not intend to do). The Soviet Union has sought to exploit—and will no doubt continue to exploit—crises in Africa, such as that in the Congo; in Latin America, it can operate through Cuba. But the possibilities of the actual use of the Soviet Army in these areas and a resultant clash with American forces is extremely remote. Above all, the conflict in the developing areas is a political one fought with social, economic, and cultural "weapons." As the former "reservoirs of capitalism," these areas are—in both Soviet and Chinese views—the targets that must be captured next if the West is to be outflanked and defeated.

A third consequence of nuclear arms has been to enhance the role of the new nations within the United Nations. The attempt of both the superpowers to win over the new nations, and the latter's desire to remain independent and nonaligned, has led the new nations to use the international organization to prevent the extension of the Cold War into their areas. Where the end of colonialism has produced conflict with the West, the Soviet Union has inevitably sought to exploit the situation, and the United States has just as inevitably reacted. Because the resultant conflict threatened their new statehood, the new nations have supported peace-keeping forces to keep local belligerents apart or to resolve the situation that stimulated Soviet-American intervention. Since such intervention could spark a larger conflagration, the United Nations has, in fact, performed a vital arms-control function in the "in-between areas," the "Balkans" of the second half of the twentieth century.

(4)   The fourth and final significant effect of the nuclear revolution is that the bipolar distribution of nuclear power has compelled the allies of each nuclear giant to seek control over its deterrent or to build their own. Either way, they feel that they would share in the prestige and status nuclear arms confer upon their possessors and at the same time ensure the defense of their interests even in the absence of Soviet or American help. But since it is unlikely that either the Soviet Union or the United States will permit itself to be triggered into an all-out war by one of its allies, the actual result of the diffusion of nuclear weapons within each alliance system might be to loosen its bonds, if not to disintegrate it (quite apart from the effect of any other factor, such as ideology, which might cause a schism in its own right). The alternative solution is some greater political confederation in which the partners ensure that nuclear arms will be used only for commonly agreed-upon purposes, and that no member will unilaterally involve his colleagues in a war. Since this would require a profound political transformation even among partners who already share common interests and values, it is a solution that is not likely to be implemented easily or soon.

If the behavior of both the great powers and the new nations in the postwar state system has thus been determined largely by the distribution of power and nuclear technology, it has also been shaped by the presence of revolutionary powers within that system. For the effect has been to stamp international politics with a total character. The issue at stake in the resulting revolutionary system is, as we have seen throughout this book, how the system itself *and* the domestic order of its member states ought to be organized. The secular missionary purpose of the revolutionary state compelled it to seek the elimination of the *ancien régime*; the resulting conflict, because it is assumed to be "normal," continues, despite occasional truces, until the final victory is won. Thus the struggle has been both total and protracted. Even if the distribution of power within the system were not bipolar, the member states that are the objects of the revolutionary power's aggression (not for what they have done but for what they are) would be compelled to meet the latter's

thrusts wherever these occurred. For every challenge would still be regarded as a test of will which, if unmet, would have immediate repercus-
sions along the entire front. Thus, merely to preserve the balance, the
defenders of the traditional system have had to draw lines around their
bloc and defend it. In short, the requirements of a revolutionary system
and bipolarity have reinforced one another.

Yet, despite the revolutionary state's total aims, its tactic has been to
pose only limited challenges. This has been based in part on a determination to safeguard the bases of its power from a catastrophic blow—Communist states know how to advance without precipitating war *and* how
to retreat to avoid a showdown—and partly on a desire to exploit the
traditional power's preconceptions against it to advance its own purposes.
The extent to which the nature of the state system has affected the behavior of its members can indeed be no more vividly demonstrated than
in the difference between the traditional power's and the revolutionary
power's approaches to conflict and diplomacy.

In the traditional state system, in which all members recognized the
right of all other members to exist, conflict was of a limited nature. Since
coexistence was accepted, the real issue was the terms of coexistence. Precisely because the elimination of an opponent was not considered a legitimate objective, when conflicts were settled peacefully, they were resolved
by mutual concessions. Diplomacy was thus an instrument of compromise, and the Western approach to conflict was a pragmatic one. The resolution of differences of interest being assumed, the important matter was
to discover how the differences among the parties to the dispute could
be "split." It was strictly a question of bargaining, not of being doctrinaire and inflexible but of being empirical and willing to grant concessions in order to entice concessions from the other side.

A pragmatic or instrumental approach to world problems typifies the
Western policy-maker. Not theoretical conceptions enabling him to relate
policy to the general trends of events, but know-*how* in the face of concrete
problem-situations is what he typically emphasizes. He wants to "solve"
the immediate, given concrete problem that is causing "trouble," and be
done with it. Accordingly, diplomatic experience—always of great importance, of course—is exalted as the supreme qualification for leadership in
foreign policy. For experience is the royal road to know-how. It teaches the
statesman how to negotiate with the Russians, how to coordinate policy
with the allies, how to respond to emergencies, and so on.

In facing foreign-policy problems it is not the Western habit to attempt
first of all to form a valid general picture of the world-setting events in
which the problems have arisen. The tendency is rather to isolate the
given problem-situation from the larger movement of history and ask:
What can and should we *do* about it?[5]

[5] Robert C. Tucker, *The Soviet Political Mind*, pp. 181–82.

It is precisely this "normal" use of the technique of diplomacy that the revolutionary power seeks to exploit, particularly in the early stages of its existence when the principal issue confronting it is survival. Although it has announced its goal, destruction of the traditional states, and these states might accordingly, for self-protection, be tempted to strangle the revolutionary state in its infancy, this does not occur. The revolutionary state avoids this end by behaving as if it were a traditional power; to paralyze the will of its opponents, it issues only limited and ambiguous challenges, phrased in the language and principles of the traditional state system. Its grandiose verbal claims then tend to be dismissed by its potential victims as intended only for domestic consumption.

In a world in which each crisis could spark a nuclear holocaust, this tactic continues to be profitable even after the revolutionary power's survival is assured. For the very fear of war that a reaction to a specific challenge may entail is likely to increase the debate among the defenders of the *status quo* as to whether that challenge constitutes aggression or whether it is the product of legitimate grievances or misunderstanding and is thus soluble through conciliation and good will. In short, by using diplomacy as an instrument of compromise in a revolutionary system, the traditional powers put themselves at a disadvantage when they are challenged; conversely, by presenting its challenges as if it were a traditional power, the revolutionary state may be able to attain its goals. A diplomacy that seeks to conciliate differences can function only in a state system where each state recognizes the other's right to exist; compromise with a totalitarian state that is committed to the conversion of mankind to an absolute truth and the elimination of "heresy" appears as weakness and an invitation to further demands and "compromises." Thus diplomacy cannot resolve this type of conflict, although the traditional powers continue to hope that the revolutionary power can be reintegrated into the old state system. They will either meet some of its demands in the expectation that this will satisfy the revolutionary power and thereby derevolutionize it—as did Britain and France in the 1930's, and the United States during World War II—or hope that internal developments within the revolutionary power will eventually transform it so that a *modus vivendi* will become possible. But in the absence of either eventuality, the conflict will continue to be total and protracted, and it will be fought in terms of limited challenges.

Perhaps the most important reason why diplomacy cannot resolve the basic conflict in a revolutionary system—and confines itself largely to dealing with problems of arms control, preventing actual hostilities, or limiting and ending them as soon as possible—is that the conflict is one of international civil war.

Internal Determinants of State Behavior

In the traditional view, international politics is the result of interaction among states. The state system determines the behavior of all member actors, regardless of their social structure, economy, or political culture. Foreign policy begins where domestic politics leaves off; the two are seen basically as mutually exclusive categories. But while such a division might be acceptable in a stable, traditional system, it is not feasible in a system containing revolutionary powers:

> The challenge of the Soviet Union is not the same as that once presented by the rising young nation-states of Germany and Italy to the British balance-of-power system on the continent of Europe. Soviet dynamism includes, but is more than, the bursting energy of a nation-state entering upon a virile stage of its development.
>
> The essential characteristic of Soviet dynamism is that it transcends the plane of nation-state relations, and is closely bound to anticipated changes within the social systems it is dealing with. The central conception of Soviet policy, and the distinctive source of its dynamism, is that the world is in a process of transition; that our social order is no longer effective in the changing environment, and is therefore in a process of disintegration and replacement. . . .
>
> Behind the familiar multi-colored representation of two-dimensional territorial divisions on a conventional map, it is now necessary to visualize a third dimension, projecting—in depth—images of the seething interplay of political and social forces particular to the areas involved. To this must be added a fourth dimension, representing the changes, with the passage of time, within these states and societies, and in their relations with each other. . . .
>
> This is not to say that Soviet policy moves according to a precise timetable, or that it is always predetermined and foresighted. But only if we fully appreciate that Soviet policy is deeply rooted in a commitment to what Moscow regards as an inevitable process of social change, can we understand that relations with Russia resist stabilization in territorial terms.[6]

Since history has already determined the direction of this social change, the task of Communism is to hurry history along a bit—and ensure that it moves toward its predestined end! Quite apart from the fact that this "horizontal" approach to international politics is well suited to minimizing the risks of "vertical" interstate conflict in a nuclear age, it also reminds us that the state system cannot explain all state behavior. Even when states act as they should, the system can explain their actions only when they react to a shift in distribution of power and seek to re-estab-

---

[6] Marshall Shulman, "The Real Nature of the Soviet Challenge," *The New York Times Magazine,* July 16, 1961, p. 42.

lish an equilibrium; such actions are taken to preserve their individual security and the stability of the system. The system cannot, however, explain why a state may seek to expand in the first place, or how domestic factors affect its international behavior. It is the *Weltanschauung* of the Soviet leaders that determines their over-all objectives. Capitalism is alleged to be the source of all evil, of domestic injustice and international war. Thus, only when private property and profit have been eliminated, and man no longer exploits his fellow man, will human brotherhood, individual liberty, and the dignity of man be realized. The Soviet Union assumes this obligation to free man from his capitalist chains and ensure his secular salvation. But the Communist ideology does more than posit the ultimate objectives. It also provides a framework within which the political and social forces in the world are analyzed, and therefore defines the strategy and tactics of Soviet foreign policy in a particular "historical era," such as the contemporary era of the disintegration of the European-centered world order. To say therefore that Soviet leaders, like non-Communist statesmen, make their decisions on a pragmatic or power-politics basis is not quite correct. For *Realpolitik* does not mean a politics devoid of ideological orientation; foreign-policy decisions, however pragmatically each one is arrived at, are taken within the over-all ideological framework.

If proof is needed of the impact of ideology on foreign-policy behavior, the Sino-Soviet conflict provides it. This conflict and the resulting schism, hardly foreseen when the Sino-Soviet alliance was established, stemmed from the very fact that the two powers share a common revolutionary ideology and ultimate objective. It is for this reason that the conflict over the issue of authority in the bloc and the strategy and tactics toward the West and the new nations has become so intense and divisive. For an ideology that claims to represent the truth can have only a single source of authority and interpretation. An alliance committed to a monopolistic secular theology can therefore only be hierarchically organized, even if its principal members are approximately equal in strength. Thus the Sino-Soviet split is not likely to be resolved soon for the conflict is over control of the international Communist movement and eventually, after the demise of capitalism, the Communist world. Both Moscow and Peking see their conflict with one another, in brief, in the same manner as each sees its conflict with the West—as a struggle for global dominance and the elimination of heresy (defined as capitalism for both Communist powers and revisionism for the self-styled orthodox Marxist-Leninists of Peking). In any case, it should be clear by now that Soviet and Chinese foreign policy can no more be explained in terms of external determinants than the Soviet and Chinese leaders would explain the behavior of capitalist states in these terms.

Not ideology but the problem of nation-building defines the international actions of those new states whose behavior is not affected by an attack upon their territory. Even if the power distribution within the state system were not bipolar, the new states would follow a policy of nonalignment. For after gaining national independence, their lack of national cohesion and the slow progress of their political and economic development require an external source against whom to direct their frustration. Another factor that intensifies this requirement is the need for the Westernized leaders to identify themselves with the tradition-bound rural masses in whose name they exercise their authority. Hence the new states must be very nationalistic for internal reasons. And since the only nationalism the people of these countries ever knew was their common hatred for the former foreign ruler, the newly emerged states continue to rebel against their colonial "father" and, more broadly, against all "outsiders," Communist and Western.

But it is not only in these instances where states seek to change the *status quo* that internal factors seem to be of primary importance. It is equally true for those states interested in preserving the *status quo*. The two clearest examples we have seen of this were the failure of Britain and France to react as they should have to the Nazis' piecemeal moves in the 1930's, and the failure of the United States to commit itself to the European balance of power during the interwar period. Similarly, American policy during World War II hardly concerned itself with the postwar balance of power. And in the postwar period, the most dramatic example was the 1954 Indochina crisis. In terms of the balance of power, the area was clearly vital to American interests, as President Eisenhower himself stated when he defined Indochina as of "transcendent importance" to American security. But because another Korea would be unpopular and Eisenhower had actually been elected in the expectation that he could end the Korean War, he could hardly commit American forces to another land war on the Asian continent.

Internal factors also affect the amount and type of power a nation can mobilize. In wartime, for example, a democracy can arm itself fully to achieve victory, but in a time of peace—even a Cold War "peace" marked by intermittent crises—the nation may not be able to mobilize sufficient strength. If the nation's leadership or public opinion is pacifically inclined, is economy-minded, or fails to understand the importance of a particular instrument—such as economic aid in contrast to military strength, the need for which is so obviously related to national security— then the country's potential strength will not be converted into the right kind of strength in the needed amounts. The deeper issue raised is, of course, whether a democracy can meet the challenges of a totalitarian society, which can, within the limits of its capabilities, harness the resources it needs to achieve its objectives and pursue these objectives with the required flexibility or consistency to be successful.

Finally, internal factors also influence the use of power. The traditional American approach to war was hardly conducive to dealing with the limited challenges of a revolutionary power or compatible with nuclear technology once war erupted. The Korean War clearly demonstrated the unpopularity of limited war and the American preference for a clear-cut choice—either abstaining from the use of force or fighting an all-out war in order to achieve a "victory." The Eisenhower "massive retaliation" strategy fitted this mood. It rejected the concept of limited wars and reasserted the older way of either a complete abstinence from violence or a total commitment to punish any power that provoked the United States. Yet such an all-or-nothing strategy could provide only one answer to less than total challenges: inaction and defeat on the installment plan. This realization compelled the United States, in the early 1960's, to mobilize a limited-war capacity. But the crucial question was whether the United States would employ this capacity, if it became necessary, with proper restraint. On the one hand, Americans would continue to be reluctant to fight more Koreas; on the other hand, once committed, they were unlikely to tolerate a long war which seemed to sacrifice American men for limited objectives. American public opinion seemed too addicted to the apparent truth of General MacArthur's famous dictum that "there is no substitute for victory." The result was a dilemma: Either the United States would not respond to limited challenges and would therefore suffer piecemeal setbacks, or it would fight and seek a total victory, thereby possibly escalating the conflict into a major regional, if not global, war.

In contrast to this American emphasis on the quantitative, military aspects of power and the resulting tendency to see the Cold War as a unidimensional struggle—as if the Communist challenge were largely a matter of military expansion—the Soviets have stressed the qualitative, political aspects of power. Because Communist ideology emphasizes the cause-and-effect relationship between the internal dynamics of a state and its external behavior, the threat has not been Russia's great military strength but the relationship of Soviet military and economic power to such phenomena as the intense and widespread political, economic, and social crises in the developing areas of the world. In this instance, the "revolution of rising expectations" and the nationalism of the new states have acted as "multipliers" of Soviet Power.

International Politics in the Future

If we analyze state behavior in terms of both external and internal determinants, we must do the same in order to predict the future of international politics in the state system. Examining the external elements first, it would seem that, according to the traditional view, the "de-bipolarization" of the world—resulting from the "de-satellization" of Russia's former East European satellites, the Sino-Soviet split, the NATO disharmony, and the increasing international role of some of the developing nations—would re-introduce flexibility into the state system, and thereby decrease international tensions and enhance the possibilities of preserving peace. But will it? In the first place, we have already seen that the allegedly "rigid" post–World War II bipolar distribution of power was not necessarily an unstable condition. Second, it is doubtful that a fully flexible multipolar system, as in the classic European system, can be restored. China and the "New Europe" are not yet superpowers, China because she is not yet industrialized and Europe because it is not yet politically integrated. It would indeed be a grave error to overestimate the degree of de-bipolarization that has taken place so far. Furthermore, there cannot be a great deal of flexibility in an ideologically divided world. Russia or China is no more likely to align itself with the United States against the other than Europe or the United States would align itself with one Communist power against the other. While the two Communist giants may be involved in a deadly fratricidal struggle of their own, both are still anti-capitalist, and the United States remains *the* enemy. Their fight is for the leadership of the international Communist movement—i.e., who is to make the decisions on its behalf, particularly on the issues of the strategy and tactics to be pursued against the West. An alliance between a traditional and a revolutionary power which does not even recognize the former's right to exist—the very prerequisite for any balance-of-power system whose purpose is to protect the independence of all member states, not to eliminate them—is hardly feasible.

The question that remains, however, is whether some flexibility cannot be restored by the nonaligned nations, who can thereby help to lower international tensions. We have already seen that their middle position in the still essentially bipolar system does confer upon them a certain amount of bargaining power. Consequently, they have generally been successful in securing economic aid from both blocs and gaining support for anticolonial resolutions in the United Nations. Can they not then also moderate the positions of both superpowers, just as the independent voters in the United States moderate the positions of the two parties competing for their votes? The answer is negative, primarily because no single nonaligned nation or group of nations is sufficiently powerful to play a mediating role. The economic development of the new states is simply too slow. Furthermore, the nonaligned states do not act as a single unit; their differences—even among the states of a single area, such as sub-Sahara Africa—are too great. Their principal and most useful role has been to try to confine the Cold War to the "Cold War zone." But even this "preventive diplomacy," exercised through the United Nations, has depended on the tacit support of the two superpowers for its effectiveness.

Yet, if restoration of a fully flexible multipolar system is unlikely, there can be no doubt that the bipolar balance of the immediate postwar period has become "loosened" and that this promises to have a beneficial effect on international politics. The relaxing of control by Moscow and Washington over their Warsaw Pact and NATO allies is symbolic of this trend. In each alliance, the authority of the center has been reduced, and common policies are increasingly being decided on a give-and-take basis. The impact of this intra-alliance bargaining upon each superpower —at least, when it has been unwilling to act unilaterally (as the United States under President Johnson has acted in Vietnam)—has been to moderate its policies. Tiny Albania can today defy Russia and Gaullist France can oppose the United States; Soviet leaders fly to Bucharest to gain the consent, or to minimize the opposition, of Romania's leadership to Russian policies, and American leaders court West German leaders to gain their support of American policies. A price for such cooperation must be paid. Furthermore, the loosening of each bloc's cohesiveness grants each superpower an opportunity to exploit the opposing bloc's fissures and further weaken it (and its allies an additional opportunity to gain more leverage against it by establishing closer relations with the superpower of the other side).

Secretary of State Rusk has explained American policy in this respect as follows:

> The smaller Communist countries of Eastern Europe have increasingly, although in varying degree, asserted their own policies. We have always considered it unnatural for the diverse peoples of Eastern Europe, with their own talents and proud traditions, to be submerged in a monolithic bloc.
>
> We have wanted these peoples, while living in friendship with their Russian and other neighbors, to develop in accordance with their own national aspirations and genius. And they seem to feel a strong nostalgia for their traditional ties with the West. Most of them are increasing their trade and other contacts with Western Europe and, to some extent, with us. . . .
>
> Our capacity to influence events and trends within the Communist world is very limited. But it is our policy to do what we can to encourage evolution in the Communist world toward national independence and open societies. We favor more contacts between the peoples behind the Iron Curtain and our own peoples. . . .
>
> When Yugoslavia challenged Stalin's centralized control of Communist affairs in 1948, we gave that country military and economic assistance. . . . Its success in defending its independence made other peoples in Eastern Europe wonder why they could not do likewise.
>
> For some years, we have treated Poland somewhat differently from

other Soviet-bloc states. A good deal of the national autonomy and domestic liberalization which the Poles won in 1956 persists. Most of Polish agriculture remains in private hands; religion is strong; Poland has developed a broad range of relations and exchanges with the West. Poland has historic ties with the West. . . .

Recently Romania has asserted a more independent attitude and has expanded its trade and other contacts with the West. It has taken steps to improve its relations with the United States. We are responding accordingly.

Hungary has turned to a more permissive policy of national conciliation. We of course welcome any tendencies promising to ease the lot of the Hungarian people. We will do what we can to encourage them.

In Czechoslovakia and Bulgaria there are some signs of movement away from earlier and harsher policies. We are watching these developments with close attention.[7]

Similarly, the Soviet Union seeks to weaken NATO by exploiting its inner differences, especially those between France and the United States. Even more remarkable than these Russian and American efforts are the attempts by each of their allies to establish closer relations with the other side's allies—e.g., the visits by Polish and Romanian leaders to Paris.

Nevertheless, despite this increasing contemporary polycentrism within each major Cold War alliance, and the undoubtedly increasing multipolarity within the state system in the next decade or two, there remains a question as to whether the effects of such a balance will be as beneficial as they might have been in the days before competition between revolutionary powers, nuclear diffusion, and third-world weakness and disunity. Let us examine only two examples. The first is the Sino-Soviet schism. Clearly, the fewer the number of crises that have to be weathered in the future, the safer the world will be. The breakup of this Communist alliance should therefore be a safety feature because of its moderating consequences upon the capacity of the two powers to pursue their revolutionary and expansionist aims. The disharmony between China and Russia, their lack of a unified strategy, their failure to pool their strengths cannot but weaken their drive for world revolution and thereby reduce tensions. In the years immediately after it had gained power, Communist China could exploit the Soviet Union's strength, including her growing nuclear stockpile, for its own purposes. The Chinese could thus intervene in Korea in 1950 without suffering a retaliatory attack because the United States was anxious to avoid a total war with Russia. An American attack on China, it was feared, would provoke Soviet intervention. In Indochina four years later, the Chinese could again intervene with impunity for the same reason. In other words, China operated under the protective umbrella of Soviet power. At no time could American policy-makers exclude

[7] Quoted in *The New York Times*, February 26, 1964.

the Soviet Union from their calculations when they considered counter-moves to Chinese aggression. By contrast, once the Sino-Soviet quarrel had erupted, the Chinese could no longer count upon automatic Soviet protection—e.g., in the Quemoy-Matsu crisis of 1958. Therefore it seems that the centrifugal trends within the Sino-Soviet bloc would reduce tensions and calm the international situation.

But is this the only conclusion one can draw from observing the conflict between the two large Communist powers? Could one not argue, for instance, that the loosening of their bonds would raise international tensions because it would generate competition between Russia and China to prove which one was the *true* champion of the Communist cause? Furthermore, in this competition, is it not likely that the more militant power—China—would compel the Soviet Union to prove its equal, or greater, devotion to Communism by becoming at least as militant? Thus, in Vietnam, for instance, the Soviets are presumed to fear an escalation of the war and therefore to be in favor of negotiating an end to the hostilities. But China's adamant opposition has compelled Moscow to be equally rigid in its attitude for it could not afford to take a "no win" position and appear less militant than Peking. Clearly, the Sino-Soviet conflict could also have a destabilizing effect on the state system.[8]

Whatever the outcome of the Sino-Soviet conflict, however, instability in a future polycentric state system may be produced in another way: by the dispersion of nuclear weapons. That such a dispersion will occur seems inevitable; at issue are only the scope and speed of the dispersion. In 1960, one study based its prediction of nuclear diffusion on the basis

[8] American policy will clearly affect this outcome. If it succeeds in containing Chinese expansion it will, as one expert has noted

. . . give the Soviets an opportunity to meddle in Chinese internal politics while barring the Chinese from a similar opportunity. Soviet opportunities for exploiting differences in Chinese ranks would be enhanced by the failure of the Chinese hard-liners to demonstrate success over the next decade in terms either of direct C.P.R. victories or the seizure of power by national liberation movements instigated and supported by the Chinese. Moreover, their problem would be compounded if their failure on either count were clearly due to U.S. action. Thus, the U.S. can weaken the hard-liners' hand in an internal struggle by forcefully resisting any direct challenge, whether over Taiwan, the offshore islands, or elsewhere in Southeast Asia. If the U.S. stymied the Chinese after they acquired nuclear arms, it would demonstrate pointedly that these weapons had produced no greater direct gains for the C.P.R. than they did for the Soviets. Moreover, the United States would thereby underscore than the C.P.R.'s chances of successfully blackmailing the U.S. into concessions were even smaller than those of the Soviets. The C.P.R. could not hope to succeed when the Soviets failed with a much more powerful nuclear arsenal than the C.P.R. would have for some time to come. At the same time, if Chinese-backed national liberation movements had failed to seize power and U.S. military capabilities had deterred overt C.P.R. intervention, then it would be evident that the Chinese policy had been as barren as the Soviet policy which the C.P.R. had been attacking.

(John. R. Thomas, "Sino-Soviet Relations after Khrushchev and Mao," *Orbis*, Fall, 1963, pp. 548–49.)

of various nations' capacity to manufacture atomic weapons. Twelve countries—Belgium, Canada, China, Czechoslovakia, France, West Germany, East Germany, India, Italy, Japan, Sweden, and Switzerland— were considered "able to embark on a successful nuclear weapons program in the near future. Most of these countries are highly industrialized and either have operation reactors, or have already made plans and arrangements for obtaining reactors." Eight countries—Australia, Austria, Denmark, Finland, Hungary, the Netherlands, Poland, and Yugoslavia —were rated as "economically capable, fairly competent technically, although perhaps somewhat more limited in scientific manpower than the countries in Group (1)." Finally, six more countries—Argentina, Brazil, Mexico, Norway, Spain, and South Africa—were listed as "probably economically capable, although more limited in industrial resources and scientific manpower. It is not too likely that any of these countries could presently achieve a successful nuclear weapons program within five years."[9]

This quantitative estimate is open to question, however. For one thing, a few bombs constitute neither an effective deterrent nor a credible retaliatory force. In addition, the extremely high cost of the crucial factor, the delivery system, was not estimated. The United States could afford to go through the four stages from subsonic bombers to supersonic bombers to stationary missiles (liquid and solid fuels) and finally to mobile missiles. But Britain could not. Whether other nations will in the future abandon their desire for a nuclear arsenal and delivery system because of the immense cost remains to be seen. This cost could be reduced, of course, by basing national deterrents on missiles from the start; and the cost could be even further reduced if, as may happen, the rate of technological change in delivery systems slows down somewhat. But in the final analysis, much will depend on political factors.[10] How much will nations aspiring to great-power status be tempted to enter the nuclear arms race, determined to obtain a credible nuclear deterrent? How many nations will feel that a nuclear force, however expensive it may be to develop, is still cheaper than the preservation of large standing conventional forces? How many states will, moreover, believe that nuclear weapons are the sole deterrent against another nuclear armed power— particularly, if they are not protected by one of the nuclear superpowers or feel that in a crisis the superpower cannot be depended upon? How many nations, great or small, will believe that nuclear arms will enhance

[9] *The Nth Country Problem and Arms Control* (Washington, D.C.: National Planning Association, 1960).

[10] See Leonard Beaton and John Maddox, *The Spread of Nuclear Weapons* (New York: Frederick A. Praeger, 1962); Beaton, *Must the Bomb Spread?* (Baltimore, Md.: Penguin Books, 1966); Raymond Aron, "The Spread of Nuclear Weapons," *The Atlantic Monthly*, January, 1965, pp. 44–50; George Liska, *Nations in Alliance* (Baltimore, Md.: The Johns Hopkins Press, 1962), pp. 269–84.

their bargaining power and therefore their influence on the global or regional level?

Although the number of nuclear powers may not reach twenty-nine—the United States, the Soviet Union, Britain, and the twenty-six other countries estimated above—there is little doubt that it will exceed the original three plus France and China. In terms of security: Will the Chinese bomb not at some time in the future compel Japan, Indonesia, and India to produce their own bombs for security? Will Pakistan, in turn, not seek the bomb when India acquires hers? If Israel acquires a bomb, will Egypt not follow suit? And in terms of prestige, can West Germany and Italy really afford *not* to build nuclear weapons without a loss of status if Switzerland or Sweden ever build their own? What is likely to be the impact if at least a dozen nations should become nuclear powers? Will it destabilize or stabilize the situation? Statistically, of course, nuclear proliferation will tend to be a destabilizing factor. The more nations that possess the bomb, the greater the possibility that an accident, miscalculation, or deliberate attack by an irresponsible national leader will touch off a local war in which the nuclear giants may become involved. In the words of President Kennedy:

> I ask you to stop and think for a moment what it would mean to have nuclear weapons in many hands—in the hands of countries large and small, stable and unstable, responsible and irresponsible, scattered throughout the world. There would be no rest for anyone then, no stability, no real security, and no chance of effective disarmament. There would only be increased chances of accidental war, and an increased necessity for the great powers to involve themselves in otherwise local conflicts.[11]

There is also an additional danger, not cited by President Kennedy—namely, the possibility of a catalytic war in which a third power, say, China or Cuba, launches a few missiles against one of the two nuclear giants. The latter, presuming the attack came from its chief opponent, strikes a retaliatory blow. As a result, the United States and Russia devastate each other while the third party emerges unharmed and in a stronger position.

Perhaps these dangers are more speculative than real. It is unlikely that a small nuclear power would dare to attack either one of the giants with their virtually invulnerable missile systems. An attack would be tempting fate, since either Russia or the United States could wipe out the aggressor—even after absorbing a first strike. With invulnerable retaliatory systems, neither of the two nuclear superpowers would have to retaliate immediately; each would have time in which to ascertain whether its opponent had in fact launched the attack and, if not, who had done so.

[11] Quoted in *The New York Times*, July 27, 1963.

It would hardly be worth running the risk of being discovered. Nor is there any reason why the two superpowers should become involved if two small nuclear powers, such as Israel and Egypt, should engage in a nuclear war. Both would indeed have every reason to dissociate themselves from the belligerents. It seems quite apparent that neither the United States nor Russia will permit any other country to involve it in a conflict that risks its survival. Furthermore, it is certain that the impact of nuclear diffusion will not be symmetrical. If Switzerland or Sweden acquired nuclear arms, it would be within the context of a genuinely neutral foreign policy; a nuclear Switzerland or Sweden is hardly likely to increase the instability of the state system, for neither is really active on the international scene. But even if they were, the pattern of deterrence between the two nuclear giants might be reproduced between the smaller nuclear states. When their leaders realize the awesome destructive power of the atom, they, too, may learn to think of nuclear arms in terms of deterrent strategy. Or they might even be frightened into nuclear disarmament:

> So far as long-run world stability is concerned, the Nth country tends to think of the problem as beginning with N plus 1. The original irony intended by the label, "Nth power problem," was seated precisely in the fact that the United States and the Soviet Union thought of the trouble as the third-power problem, Great Britain thought of it as the fourth-power problem, France as the fifth-power problem, and so on. Each new or prospective nuclear power thinks of the problem as that of stopping the next country after itself. This is the N-plus-1-country problem . . . one might suppose that unanimity for nuclear disarmament may be achieved by distributing bombs to everybody.[12]

The *Pax Atomica* might yet, then, provide eternal secular peace. This conclusion will, no doubt, be regarded by many with a great deal of skepticism. But nuclear disarmament or not, only the future will tell whether a multinuclear world will be more or less stable than an essentially duopolistic one.

Whether the issue of bipolarity or multipolarity will in the final analysis be crucial is in itself a question. The stability or instability of the state system may depend less on the diffusion of power than on the ability of the new nations to modernize. For it is their inability to resolve their domestic problems that tempts them to turn to adventurous foreign policies for relief—with destabilizing results for the entire state system. These domestic problems, stemming from the frustration of the intelligentsia and the poverty of the masses in underdeveloped countries, also provide the social roots of Communism. Communism appeals to the West-

[12] Albert Wohlstetter, "Nuclear Sharing: NATO and the N+1 Country," *Foreign Affairs*, April, 1961, pp. 357–58.

ernized intelligentsia because it combines a hostility toward the West and capitalism with a penchant for nation-building, industrialization, and socialism—plus the added justification for the stewardship of the intelligentsia. To the needy and displaced peasant-worker, forced off the land and into the factory and urban slum, the resentment expressed by Marxism against the machine and the capital-accumulating state seems to express his own feelings. But Marxism does more than articulate the sense of alienation and loss of status and role experienced by the masses during the transitional period between the traditional, rural society and the urban-industrial society. It also gives voice to the hope that industrialization, once achieved, will free man for all time from the elemental struggle for the bare necessities of life; the machine is to be the provider of the abundant life. One political analyst has stressed the point that Marxism, itself the product of an industrializing society, is therefore the *natural* ideology of a developing community. Every society has to pass through a transitional, or "Marxist stage," of development, and it will consequently be during this phase that its direction—Communist or otherwise (but not necessarily capitalist)—will be determined. The Cold War thus becomes basically a struggle of techniques of modernization, of social and economic statesmanship on a global scale.[13] For the West, the problem is to shorten this "Marxist period" once the initial development has broken what Walter Bagehot once called "the cake of custom" of the traditional society and launched the nation on its drive to maturity. If an international Marxist revolution is to be avoided, the very minimum requirement will be a major redistribution of income in the international system akin to the redistribution of income which within Western nations staved off the proletarian revolution during the nineteenth century. For the Communists, the task is to demonstrate that Communism is to the last half of the twentieth century what capitalism was to the nineteenth century—the most effective means of modernizing nations. Whatever the results, it is clear that the state system's stability in the coming decades may well be decided by the new nations' ability to consolidate their tenuous unity, speed their modernization, and adjust themselves psychologically and socially to industrial culture.

The most significant relationship and one that will largely determine the issue of war or peace, then, may be that between economic and political development. As nations pass through the various stages of economic growth and finally mature as consumer-oriented societies, will they also become pluralistic and democratic? Are affluent societies also more peaceful than authoritarian or totalitarian states? The problem is that we do not know the answers to these questions. The few attempts at building theories of development have been based largely upon Western experience, and they have smacked either of a non-Marxist economic determinism or a simple positing of the United States and England as the

model of a modern political system.[14] Most Western societies were traditional monarchies before their modernization; as urban-industrial nations
today, they are democratic. Hence, it is concluded, by passing through a
series of stages of economic growth, nations will evolve into pluralistic,
politically competitive, open—and peaceful—societies. We certainly know
that only among "people of plenty," where the "plenty" is equitably distributed among the various classes of society, can democracy flourish; the
lack of a middle class and a social imbalance between the privileged few
and the deprived majority provide ideal breeding grounds for political
instability and revolution. Yet we also know by the examples of Germany
and Russia that economic development does not by itself produce political democracy. In the United States, we still refer to "grass-roots" democracy—that is, to its agrarian origins; industrialization strengthened this
democratic order, but did not produce it. In fact, we know all too little
about the political development of those Western nations where democracy has securely established itself to apply any generalizations about
economic growth and political evolution with great confidence to non-
Western societies, about whom we know even less—or, for that matter, to
totalitarian regimes.

When we were analyzing Soviet totalitarianism, for instance, we saw
that the post-Stalinist changes could be interpreted in two completely
contradictory ways. The first interpretation maintained that industrialization had resulted in a change of the Soviet social structure by producing a managerial elite comprised of bureaucrats, military officers, technicians, scientists, artists, and writers. This elite has sought security in a
predictable political order, more material advantages, and fewer restrictions on life in general. The reforms of the secret police and the greater
emphasis on consumption were thus all indications of a fundamental
transformation of the Soviet system, not just a tactical maneuver. Furthermore, since the internal structure of the system determined its foreign policy, it could only be concluded that the objectives of this
"conservative managerial state"—that is, a state in which the managers,
concerned with the preservation of their social status and economic privileges, opposed foreign "adventures"—were being moderated by being cut
back from world revolution to Russian "national interest."

The opposing view held that industrialization led to the rationalization
and streamlining of Soviet totalitarianism by raising the standard of liv-

[13] Adam B. Ulam, *The Unfinished Revolution*, pp. 285–86.
[14] See particularly W. W. Rostow, *Stages of Economic Growth*; A. F. K. Organski,
The Stages of Political Development; and Gabriel A. Almond and James S. Coleman,
The Politics of the Developing Areas, pp. 3–64, 532–76.
For excellent critiques of these general theories, see Alexander Gerschenkron, *Economic Backwardness in Historical Perspective*; and Henry A. Kissinger, *The Necessity for Choice*, pp. 287–308. For an evaluation of these theories as applied to Soviet
totalitarianism, see Zbigniew K. Brzezinski and Samuel P. Huntington, *Political
Power: USA/USSR*.

ing and eliminating the harsher and more arbitrary features of Soviet life. By reducing the tensions between the political leaders and the masses through these means, the leaders gained a measure of popular support and were more able to mobilize the population for their purposes. At the same time, they consolidated the Party's control over the secret police, the managerial elite, and the officer corps. Thus Soviet global objectives remained unchanged. The Kremlin's theme of "peaceful coexistence" only meant that it wished to avoid risking its survival; it did not mean that Moscow accepted permanent coexistence and that its policies were only to consolidate the postwar *status quo*. A world-wide victory was still expected, but the tactics had changed greatly.

The difficulty of predicting on the basis of a theory of economic development is even further complicated and confused by the fact that each one of these two interpretations can also result in an opposite conclusion. It has been argued that even if the Soviet Union is becoming more of an affluent society and thereby increasingly rendering both Marxism and totalitarianism—which helped speed up its process of industrialization—irrelevant to the problems of Soviet society, the Soviet leaders' continued need to legitimatize their authority can only be preserved through a continuing assertion in foreign policy:

> Communist ideology now has but little relevance insofar as domestic problems of the Soviet Union are concerned. Were the USSR to cease being a one-party state equipped with totalitarian paraphernalia, the process of industrialization and modernization would go on under the aegis of another ideology and another political system. There has been no change or reform in the social or economic field in the last six years which might not have been effected in the USSR for purely pragmatic reasons. If the ideology is to remain demonstrably important to the Soviet citizen, and demonstrably correct to the Party members, and the perpetuation of the Communist Party rule rests in the long run upon these assumptions, then there must be another dimension than the domestic one in which Communist ideology does make a difference. Succesful proselytizing becomes an important factor in the preservation of the faith. Foreign successes, the preservation and expansion of collaboration within the Communist bloc, become important insofar as the preservation of the present pattern of communism in the USSR is concerned.

If this hypothesis is correct, then there is little foundation in the hope often expressed in the West that the growth and maturity of the USSR as a modern industrial state will necessarily be reflected in more peaceful and less expansive policies . . . in the measure that the Communist movement achieves its objectives, it becomes increasingly difficult to preserve the totalitarian system, to continue to exact sacrifices and deny basic freedoms and amenities of life. The program of ideological revival devised by the despot's [Stalin's] successors has aimed at preventing communism from "withering away," and thus at preserving the rationale of Soviet totalitarianism. An increasingly great part in this revival has been played by the renewed missionary character of communism. Thus the success of communism as a self-proclaimed world-wide liberation and peace movement, and as a tenable basis for the association of Communist states, becomes increasingly important to the continuance of the present form of the Communist regime in the USSR.[15]

Soviet militancy in Berlin and Cuba from 1958 to 1962, and indeed the large-scale Soviet effort to win friends and influence nations throughout the underdeveloped nations after Stalin's death, may well fit this interpretation. So might the post-Cuba American-Soviet *détente*. For Cuba had proved that unless the Soviet Union was strategically superior, she could not face the United States down in a crisis. The Soviets had been first with the ICBM, but were unable to exploit their lead because of their inferior economy; in contrast, the United States because of its far greater economic strength was able to catch up and surpass Russia in the production of missiles. Thus Moscow needed an extended period of relaxation to hurry its economic growth so that she could better match the United States in strategic capability.

Finally, it can be argued that even if those skeptical of Soviet "liberalization" are correct, modifications in Soviet foreign-policy objectives may occur—if Soviet expectations about the future are disappointed. The Soviets anticipate that the European nations—which they classify as "capitalist"—will suffer an economic decline. Now that these bourgeois states' colonial "super-profits" have been eliminated, the class struggle within each state will reassert itself and bring about the long-postponed proletarian revolution. The European nations are also expected to quarrel among each other as they struggle and compete for markets. A second Soviet expectation is that the underdeveloped countries will fail in their development efforts and that as the gap between popular aspirations for a better life and governmental fulfillment grows, the national bourgeoisie will be overthrown and the people will install a socialist government. Thus, if the nations of Europe should continue to integrate economically and politically, and their internal class struggle declines as each class obtains a greater share of an ever-growing economic pie, the Soviets must wonder why their projections, which stemmed from their analysis of the social and economic forces in Europe, turned out to be so wrong. Could it be that their way of looking at the world—at "reality"—was faulty? Furthermore, if the new nations do develop without turning to totalitarian techniques, the Soviet leadership must wonder even more why the predicted result was not realized. Could the ideological framework be the reason? In short, at some point in the future, the Kremlin may, by the repeated frustration of its expectations, be compelled to reconsider

[15] Ulam, "Soviet Ideology and Soviet Foreign Policy," *World Politics*, January, 1959, pp. 170–71.

the validity of its ideological premises. Persistent failure in foreign policy rather than internal change may in this instance lead to a reassessment of the ideology. If the decision is that the failures resulted from a faulty conceptual framework, then the Soviet leaders may re-examine their mode of analysis and the dynamics of what they call capitalist society. If that occurs—and if the Chinese leaders should someday make a similar reassessment—the world might yet see the end of the Cold War. (On the other hand, a new Lenin could appear on the scene to explain, as Lenin once did, that the reason the expected goals had not yet been realized was not because of a faulty analysis but because of unforeseen capitalist efforts to stave off the inevitable revolution; these efforts could not, however, change the predestined course of historical change, and capitalism was therefore still doomed. Thus, by adding a new theory—e.g., the theory of imperialism—to the already existing body of theory, the true believers can retain faith in their ideological framework and in the certainly of the future secular salvation for mankind.)

The point that becomes clear from these different conclusions is that our knowledge is still inadequate on this most crucial issue of the relationship of economic development to various political stages of growth. Only time will validate or invalidate some of our hypotheses concerning, on the one hand, the interrelationships between industrialization and political structure and, on the other hand, between mature economic societies and international behavior. In short, we possess at best some conceptual tools with which we can analyze the present and speculate about the future. Some of these, like the balance of power, are time-honored because they have served as useful tools for analyzing international politics and predicting state behavior; they have even been useful for the analysis of domestic politics for, as we have seen, a state in which economic wealth and political power are distributed unequally does not provide a firm basis for a democratic society. But many of the concepts needed for a study of contemporary international politics are still young —for instance, those concerning totalitarianism, economic development, regional integration, and deterrence. To understand the new world in which we live, the social scientist has been compelled to grope for such new concepts. Even our language is sometimes new, reflecting the inadequacy of older terminology in dealing with some of the unique problems of our time. Thus our military vocabulary now includes terms virtually unknown before World War II: nuclear exchange and stalemate; mutual deterrence; credibility; "soft" and "hard" weapons; passive and active defenses; pre-emptive, first, and second strikes; assured destruction; countervalue, counterforce, and damage-limiting strategy; spasm, accidental, and limited wars; escalation; Nth-country problem; nuclear proliferation; arms control; tacit agreement; nuclear blackmail; crisis management; nuclear threshold; and overkill. This intellectual ferment is likely to continue and to help us broaden and deepen our insight into our environment as our conceptual tools become more refined and sophisticated.

Yet it remains a vain hope to expect our future increase of knowledge to yield any simple, easy, or quick answers—an illusion to which Americans are particularly prone. It is perhaps not very surprising that Americans nurture such an illusion since we have, after all, been successful in all our endeavors—expanding across a continent, urbanizing and industralizing, and defeating every enemy from Britain through Germany and Japan; we therefore feel confident that no problem is too big for us to solve. The fact that no one has yet found the foreign policy to end all foreign policy is thus frustrating. Are we not the strongest nation on earth? Why can't we win the Cold War? Our cause being just, why do we not prevail? Unfortunately, in the real world, problems are rarely solved. More often, they are compromised, isolated, contained, conciliated. Indeed, the art of surviving in the nuclear age may well be the ability to learn to live *with* problems, however unpleasant or dangerous they may be. For we live in an age of paradox: Man has never possessed greater power, but because he can use this power only at the risk of suicide, he has never been more impotent. In the past, a nation could on occasion build up superior strength and then use that strength to resolve some of the issues confronting it; in the contemporary world, the principal issue is how to restrain power and use the available strength in a disciplined fashion so that the cost of conflict will not be totally disproportionate to the value of the objectives sought. Consequently, most conflicts have been perpetuated, not reconciled. As one observer has wisely noted:

> In some cases, the realistic ideal may be not to achieve the permanent settlement of a dispute, but to persuade the parties to settle down permanently with the dispute. The agendas of the Security Council and the General Assembly are liberally sprinkled with items that are beginning to seem like permanent fixtures, quarrels which the United Nations has managed to subject to peaceful perpetuation rather than peaceful settlement. This is not a cynical comment; many of life's problems are meant to be lived with rather than solved, and the urge to have a showdown, to settle the matter one way or the other, is often an unwise impulse in both personal and international affairs.[16]

Our generation is called upon—or condemned—to live with an ambiguous reality and to forswear both cynicism and illusion in defining it. To do this is to live dangerously. We must simultaneously avoid a seduc-

---

[16] Inis L. Claude, Jr., *Swords Into Plowshares*, pp. 216–17.

tive but futile escape into nostalgia for the past and an imperious rage at a world that will not conform to our vision. Instead, we must adjust ourselves to living in a world where the constant is neither war nor peace, where the millennium remains a distant dream and where the threat of a nuclear Armageddon is an ever-present fear. In short, we must accept and live in the most difficult of all worlds—the *real* one.

A Selective Bibliography

Introduction to International Politics

HERZ, JOHN H. *International Politics in the Atomic Age.** New York: Columbia University Press, 1962.

HOFFMAN, STANLEY. *Contemporary Theory in International Relations.* Englewood Cliffs, N.J.: Prentice-Hall, 1960.

————. *The State of War: Essays in the Theory and Practice of International Politics.** New York: Frederick A. Praeger, 1965.

KAPLAN, MORTON A. *System and Process in International Politics.** New York: John Wiley and Sons, 1964.

MORGENTHAU, HANS J. *Politics Among Nations.* 4th ed.; New York: Alfred A. Knopf, 1967.

NEUMANN, SIGMUND. *Permanent Revolution: Totalitarianism in the Age of International Civil War.** 2d ed.; New York: Frederick A. Praeger, 1965.

ROSECRANCE, RICHARD. *Action and Reaction in World Politics.* Boston: Little, Brown and Co., 1963.

ROSENAU, JAMES N. (ed.). *International Politics and Foreign Policy.* New York: Free Press of Glencoe, 1961.

WALTZ, KENNETH N. *Man, the State, and War.** New York: Columbia University Press, 1959.

WOLFERS, ARNOLD. *Discord and Collaboration: Essays on International Politics.** Baltimore, Md.: The Johns Hopkins Press, 1965.

Deterrence and Conventional Limited War

ABSHIRE, DAVID M., and ALLEN, RICHARD V. (eds.). *National Security: Political, Military, and Economic Strategies in the Decade Ahead.* New York: Frederick A. Praeger, 1963.

ATOMIC ENERGY COMMISSION. *The Effects of Nuclear Weapons.* Rev. ed.; Washington, D.C.: Government Printing Office, 1962.

BRODIE, BERNARD. *Strategy in the Missile Age.** Princeton, N.J.: Princeton University Press, 1959.

* Titles thus asterisked are available in paperback editions.

FRYKLUND, RICHARD. *100 Million Lives.* New York: The Macmillan Co., 1962.

HALPERIN, MORTON H. *Limited War in the Nuclear Age.** New York: John Wiley and Sons, 1963.

HIGGINS, TRUMBULL. *Korea and the Fall of MacArthur.* London and New York: Oxford University Press, 1960.

KAHN, HERMAN. *On Thermonuclear War.* Princeton, N.J.: Princeton University Press, 1960.

———. *Thinking About the Unthinkable.** New York: Horizon Press, 1962.

KAUFMANN, WILLIAM W. *The McNamara Strategy.* New York: Harper & Row, 1964.

——— (ed.). *Military Policy and National Security.* Princeton, N.J.: Princeton University Press, 1956.

KISSINGER, HENRY A. *The Necessity for Choice.** New York: Harper & Row, 1961.

———. *Nuclear Weapons and Foreign Policy.** New York: Harper & Brothers, 1957.

KNORR, KLAUS, and READ, THORNTON (eds.). *Limited Strategic War: Essays on Nuclear Strategy.* Chicago: University of Chicago Press, 1957.

LAPP, RALPH E. *Kill and Overkill.* New York: Basic Books, 1962.

MORGENSTERN, OSKAR. *The Question of National Defense.** New York: Random House, 1959.

OSGOOD, ROBERT E. *Limited War: The Challenge to American Strategy.* Chicago: University of Chicago Press, 1957.

SCHELLING, THOMAS C. *Strategy of Conflict.** Cambridge, Mass.: Harvard University Press, 1960.

SNYDER, GLENN H. *Deterrence and Defence.* Princeton, N.J.: Princeton University Press, 1961.

SPANIER, JOHN W. *The Truman-MacArthur Controversy and the Korean War.** Cambridge, Mass.: Harvard University Press, 1959. Rev. paperback ed.; New York: W. W. Norton, 1965.

TAYLOR, MAXWELL D. *The Uncertain Trumpet.* New York: Harper & Brothers, 1960.

TURNER, GORDON B., and CHALLENER, RICHARD D. (eds.). *National Security in the Nuclear Age: Basic Facts and Theories.** New York: Frederick A. Praeger, 1960.

WHITING, ALLEN S. *China Crosses the Yalu: The Decision to Enter the Korean War.* New York: The Macmillan Co., 1960.

Arms Control and Disarmament

BARNET, RICHARD J. *Who Wants Disarmament?** Boston: Beacon Press, 1960.

BRENNAN, DONALD G. (ed.). *Arms Control, Disarmament, and National Security.* New York: George Braziller, 1961.

BULL, HEDLEY. *The Control of the Arms Race: Disarmament and Arms Control in the Missile Age.** 2d ed.; New York: Frederick A. Praeger, 1965.

ETZIONI, AMITAI. *The Hard Way to Peace.** New York: Crowell-Collier, 1962.

———. *Winning Without War.** New York: Doubleday & Co., 1964.

FROMM, ERICH. *May Man Prevail?** New York: Doubleday & Co., 1961.

GILPIN, ROBERT. *American Scientists and Nuclear Weapons Policy.** Princeton, N.J.: Princeton University Press, 1962.

HADLEY, ARTHUR T. *The Nation's Safety and Arms Control.* New York: Viking Press, 1961.

HENKIN, LOUIS (ed.). *Arms Control and Inspection in American Law.** New York: Columbia University Press, 1958.

HUNTINGTON, SAMUEL P. "Arms Races: Prerequisites and Results," in CARL J. FRIEDRICH and SEYMOUR E. HARRIS (eds.), *Public Policy: A Yearbook of the Graduate School of Public Administration, Harvard University.* Cambridge, Mass.: Graduate School of Public Administration, Harvard University, 1958.

LEFEVER, ERNEST W. (ed.). *Arms and Arms Control.** New York: Frederick A. Praeger, 1962.

LEVINE, ROBERT A. *The Arms Debate.* Cambridge, Mass.: Harvard University Press, 1963.

MADARIAGA, SALVADOR DE. *Disarmament.* New York: Coward-McCann, 1929.

MELMAN, SEYMOUR (ed.). *No Place To Hide.** New York: Grove Press, 1962.

MILLIS, WALTER, *et al. World Without War.** New York: Washington Square Press, 1961.

NOEL-BAKER, PHILIP. *The Arms Race: A Program for World Disarmament.** Dobbs Ferry, N.Y.: Oceana Publications, 1959.

NOGEE, JOSEPH L. *Soviet Policy Toward the International Control of Atomic Energy.* Notre Dame, Ind.: University of Notre Dame Press, 1961.

OSGOOD, CHARLES E. *An Alternative to War or Surrender.** Urbana, Ill.: University of Illinois Press, 1962.

ROOSEVELT, JAMES (ed.). *The Liberal Papers.** New York: Doubleday & Co., 1962.

RUSSELL, BERTRAND. *Common Sense and Nuclear Warfare.** New York: Simon and Schuster, 1959.

———. *Unarmed Victory.** New York: Simon and Schuster, 1963.

SCHELLING, THOMAS C., and HALPERIN, MORTON H. *Strategy and Arms Control.** New York: Twentieth Century Fund, 1961.

SPANIER, JOHN W., and NOGEE, JOSEPH L. *The Politics of Disarmament: A Study in Soviet-American Gamesmanship.** New York: Frederick A. Praeger, 1962.

TATE, MERZE. *The United States and Armaments.* Cambridge, Mass.: Harvard University Press, 1948.

WASKOW, ARTHUR. *The Limits of Defense.* New York: Doubleday & Co., 1962.

Guerrilla and Unconventional Warfare

FALL, BERNARD B. *Street Without Joy: Insurgency in Indochina, 1946–1963.* 3d rev. ed.; Harrisburg, Pa.: The Stackpole Co., 1963.

———. *The Two Viet-Nams: A Political and Military Analysis.* 2d rev. ed.; New York: Frederick A. Praeger, 1967.

GALULA, DAVID. *Counterinsurgency Warfare: Theory and Practice.* New York: Frederick A. Praeger, 1964.

GREENE, T. N. (ed.). *The Guerrilla—And How to Fight Him: Selections from the Marine Corps Gazette.** New York: Frederick A. Praeger, 1962.

HEILBRUNN, OTTO. *Partisan Warfare.* New York: Frederick A. Praeger, 1962.

HUNTINGTON, SAMUEL P. (ed.). *Changing Patterns of Military Politics*. New York: Free Press of Glencoe, 1962.

Mao Tse-tung on Guerrilla Warfare. Translated and with an Introduction by SAMUEL B. GRIFFITH. New York: Frederick A. Praeger, 1961.

PARET, PETER. *French Revolutionary Warfare from Indochina to Algeria: The Analysis of a Political and Military Doctrine*. New York: Frederick A. Praeger, 1961.

PARET, PETER, and SHY, JOHN W. *Guerrillas in the 1960's.** Rev. ed.; New York: Frederick A. Praeger, 1962.

PYE, LUCIAN. *Guerrilla Communism in Malaya*. Princeton, N.J.: Princeton University Press, 1956.

SZULC, TAD, and MEYER, KARL E. *The Cuban Invasion.** New York: Frederick A. Praeger, 1962.

TANHAM, GEORGE K. *Communist Revolutionary Warfare: The Vietminh in Indochina*. New York: Frederick A. Praeger, 1961.

THAYER, CHARLES W. *Guerrilla.** New York: Harper & Row, 1963.

TRINQUIER, ROBERT. *Modern Warfare: A French View of Counterinsurgency*. New York: Frederick A. Praeger, 1964.

NATO and European Unification

BELOFF, NORA. *The General Says No.** Baltimore, Md.: Penguin Books, 1964.

BENOIT, EMILE. *Europe at Sixes and Sevens: The Common Market, the Free Trade Association, and the United States.** New York: Columbia University Press, 1961.

BUCHAN, ALASTAIR. *NATO in the 1960's: The Implications of Interdependence.** Rev. ed.; New York: Frederick A. Praeger, 1963.

COTTRELL, ALVIN J., and DOUGHERTY, JAMES. *The Politics of the Atlantic Alliance.** New York: Frederick A. Praeger, 1964.

DEUTSCH, KARL W., et al. *Political Community and the North Atlantic Area*. Princeton, N.J.: Princeton University Press, 1957.

HAAS, ERNST B. *The Uniting of Europe: Political, Social, and Economic Forces, 1950–1957*. Stanford, Calif.: Stanford University Press, 1958.

KISSINGER, HENRY A. *The Troubled Partnership: A Re-Appraisal of the Atlantic Alliance.** New York: McGraw-Hill, 1965.

KITZINGER, U. W. *The Politics and Economics of European Integration: Britain, Europe, and the United States.** New York: Frederick A. Praeger, 1963.

KLEIMAN, ROBERT. *Atlantic Crisis.** New York: W. W. Norton & Co., 1964.

KNORR, KLAUS (ed.). *NATO and American Security*. Princeton, N.J.: Princeton University Press, 1959.

KRAFT, JOSEPH. *The Grand Design*. New York: Harper & Row, 1962.

LICHTHEIM, GEORGE. *The New Europe: Today—And Tomorrow.** New York: Frederick A. Praeger, 1963.

OSGOOD, ROBERT E. *NATO: The Entangling Alliance*. Chicago: University of Chicago Press, 1962.

SHANKS, MICHAEL, and LAMBERT, JOHN. *The Common Market Today—And Tomorrow.** New York: Frederick A. Praeger, 1963.

STEEL, RONALD. *The End of Alliance: America and the Future of Europe*. New York: Viking Press, 1962.

WHITE, THEODORE H. *Fire in the Ashes: Europe in Mid-Century*. New York: William Sloane Associates, 1953.

WILCOX, FRANCIS O., and HAVILAND, H. FIELD, JR. (eds.). *The Atlantic Community: Progress and Prospects.** New York: Frederick A. Praeger, 1963.

Communism

BOBER, M. M. *Karl Marx's Interpretation of History.** New York: W. W. Norton & Co., 1965.
DANIELS, ROBERT V. *The Nature of Communism.** New York: Random House, 1962.
HUNT, R. N. CAREW. *The Theory and Practice of Communism.** Rev. ed.; Baltimore, Md.: Penguin Books, 1963.
LICHTHEIM, GEORGE. *Marxism: An Historical and Critical Study.** 2d ed.; New York: Frederick A. Praeger, 1965.
MARCUSE, HERBERT. *Soviet Marxism.** New York: Columbia University Press, 1958.
MENDEL, ARTHUR P. (ed.). *The Essential Works of Marxism.** New York: Bantam Books, 1961.
MEYER, ALFRED G. *Leninism.** Cambridge, Mass.: Harvard University Press, 1957. Paperback ed.; New York: Frederick A. Praeger, 1957.
————. *Marxism: The Unity of Theory and Practice: A Critical Essay.* Cambridge, Mass.: Harvard University Press, 1954.
POPPER, KARL R. *The Open Society and Its Enemies.** Vol. II: *High Tide of Prophecy.* Princeton, N.J.: Princeton University Press, 1950.
WILSON, EDMUND. *To the Finland Station: A Study in the Writing and Acting of History.** New York: Harcourt, Brace & Co., 1940.

Soviet Political System

ARMSTRONG, JOHN A. *Ideology, Politics, and Government in the Soviet Union: An Introduction.** New York: Frederick A. Praeger, 1962.
BRUMBERG, ABRAHAM (ed.). *Russia Under Khrushchev: An Anthology from Problems of Communism.** New York: Frederick A. Praeger, 1962.
BRZEZINSKI, ZBIGNIEW K., and HUNTINGTON, SAMUEL P. *Political Power: USA/USSR.** New York: Viking Press, 1964.
CRANKSHAW, EDWARD. *Khrushchev's Russia.** Rev. ed.; Baltimore, Md.: Penguin Books, 1962.
DEUTSCHER, ISAAC. *Stalin: A Political Biography.** London and New York: Oxford University Press, 1949.
DJILAS, MILOVAN. *The New Class: An Analysis of the Communist System.** New York: Frederick A. Praeger, 1957.
EBENSTEIN, WILLIAM. *Totalitarianism.** New York: Holt, Rinehart and Winston, 1962.
FAINSOD, MERLE. *How Russia Is Ruled.* Rev. ed.; Cambridge, Mass.: Harvard University Press, 1963.
FRIEDRICH, CARL J., and BRZEZINSKI, ZBIGNIEW K. *Totalitarian Dictatorship and Autocracy.** 2d ed. rev. by CARL J. FRIEDRICH. Cambridge, Mass.: Harvard University Press, 1965. Paperback ed.; New York: Frederick A. Praeger, 1966.
LEONHARD, WOLFGANG. *The Kremlin Since Stalin.** Translated by Elizabeth Wiskemann and Marian Jackson. New York: Frederick A. Praeger, 1962.

MEYER, ALFRED G. *The Soviet Political System.* New York: Random House, 1965.

MOORE, BARRINGTON, JR. *Soviet Politics—The Dilemma of Power: The Role of Ideas in Social Change.** Cambridge, Mass.: Harvard University Press, 1950.

SCHAPIRO, LEONARD. *The Communist Party of the Soviet Union.** New York: Random House, 1960.

SETON-WATSON, HUGH. *From Lenin to Khrushchev: The History of World Communism.** New York: Frederick A. Praeger, 1960.

TUCKER, ROBERT C. *The Soviet Political Mind: Studies in Stalinism and Post-Stalin Change.** New York: Frederick A. Praeger, 1963.

ULAM, ADAM B. *The New Face of Soviet Totalitarianism.** Cambridge, Mass.: Harvard University Press, 1963. Paperback ed.; New York: Frederick A. Praeger, 1965.

———. *The Unfinished Revolution.** New York: Random House, 1960.

Soviet Foreign Policy

BRZEZINSKI, ZBIGNIEW K. *Ideology and Power in Soviet Politics.** New York: Frederick A. Praeger, 1962.

DALLIN, DAVID J. *Soviet Foreign Policy After Stalin.* Philadelphia: J. B. Lippincott Co., 1961.

DINERSTEIN, HERBERT S. *War and the Soviet Union: Nuclear Weapons and the Revolution in Soviet Military and Political Thinking.** Rev. ed.; New York: Frederick A. Praeger, 1962.

GARTHOFF, RAYMOND L. *Soviet Military Policy: A Historical Analysis.* New York: Frederick A. Praeger, 1966.

———. *Soviet Strategy in the Nuclear Age.** Rev. ed.; New York: Frederick A. Praeger, 1962.

KENNAN, GEORGE F. *American Diplomacy, 1900–1950.** Chicago: University of Chicago Press, 1951.

———. *Russia and the West Under Lenin and Stalin.** Boston: Little, Brown and Co., 1961.

LEDERER, IVO J. (ed.). *Russian Foreign Policy: Essays in Historical Perspective.** New Haven, Conn.: Yale University Press, 1962.

LEITES, NATHAN. *The Operational Code of the Politburo.* New York: McGraw-Hill, 1951.

———. *A Study of Bolshevism.* Chicago: The Free Press, 1953.

MOSELY, PHILIP E. *The Kremlin and World Politics.** New York: Random House, 1960.

PENTONY, DEVERE E. (ed.). *Soviet Behavior in World Affairs.** San Francisco: Chandler Publishing Co., 1962.

SHULMAN, MARSHALL D. *Beyond the Cold War.** New Haven, Conn.: Yale University Press, 1965.

———. *Stalin's Foreign Policy Reappraised.** New York: Atheneum Publishers, 1965.

SOKOLOVSKY, V. D. (ed.). *Military Strategy: Soviet Doctrine and Concepts.** New York: Frederick A. Praeger, 1963.

STRAUSZ-HUPÉ, ROBERT, et al. *Protracted Conflict.** New York: Harper & Brothers, 1959.

Von Laue, Theodore. *Why Lenin? Why Stalin? A Reappraisal of the Russian Revolution, 1900–1930.** Philadelphia: J. B. Lippincott Co., 1964.
Washington Center of Foreign Policy Research. *Two Communist Manfestoes.** Washington, D.C., 1961.

The Communist Bloc

Barnett, A. Doak. *Communist China and Asia: Challenge to American Policy.** New York: Harper & Brothers, 1960.
————. (ed.). *Communist Strategies in Asia: A Comparative Analysis of Governments and Parties.** New York: Frederick A. Praeger, 1963.
Bromke, Adam (ed.). *The Communist States at the Crossroads: Between Moscow and Peking.** New York: Frederick A. Praeger, 1965.
Brzezinski, Zbigniew K. *The Soviet Bloc: Unity and Conflict.** Rev. ed.; New York: Frederick A. Praeger, 1961.
Crankshaw, Edward. *The New Cold War: Moscow v. Peking.** Baltimore, Md.: Penguin Books, 1963.
Floyd, David. *Mao Against Khrushchev: A Short History of the Sino-Soviet Conflict.** New York: Frederick A. Praeger, 1964.
Hudson, G. F.; Lowenthal, Richard; and MacFarquhar, Roderick (eds.). *The Sino-Soviet Dispute.**New York: Frederick A. Praeger, 1961.
Ionescu, Ghita. *The Break-Up of the Soviet Empire in Eastern Europe.** Baltimore, Md.: Penguin Books, 1965.
Mehnert, Klaus. *Peking and Moscow.** New York: G. P. Putnam's Sons, 1963.
Pentony, DeVere E. (ed.). *China, the Emerging Red Giant.** San Francisco: Chandler Publishing Co., 1962.
———— (ed.). *Red World in Tumult.** San Francisco: Chandler Publishing Co., 1962.
Skilling, H. Gordon. *The Governments of Communist Eastern Europe.** New York: Thomas Y. Crowell Co., 1966.
Wint, Guy. *Communist China's Crusade: Mao's Road to Power and the New Campaign for World Revolution.** New York: Frederick A. Praeger, 1965.
Zagoria, Donald S. *The Sino-Soviet Conflict, 1956–1961.* Princeton, N.J.: Princeton University Press, 1962.

Underdeveloped Countries

Almond, Gabriel A., and Coleman, James S. *The Politics of the Developing Areas.* Princeton, N.J.: Princeton University Press, 1960.
Berliner, Joseph S. *Soviet Economic Aid: A New Policy of Aid and Trade in Underdeveloped Countries.* New York: Frederick A. Praeger, 1958.
Black, Eugene R. *The Diplomacy of Economic Development.** New York: Atheneum Publishers, 1963.
Burke, Fred G. *Africa's Quest for Order.** Englewood Cliffs, N.J.: Prentice-Hall, 1963.
Campbell, John C. *Defense of the Middle East: Problems of American Policy.** Rev. ed.; New York: Frederick A. Praeger, 1961.

CHAMBERS, WILLIAM N. *Political Parties in a New Nation: The American Experience, 1776–1809.** London and New York: Oxford University Press, 1963.

CREMEANS, CHARLES D. *The Arabs and the World: Nasser's Arab Nationalist Policy.** New York: Frederick A. Praeger, 1963.

DEUTSCH, KARL W., and FOLTZ, WILLIAM J. (eds.). *Nation-Building.* New York: Atherton Press, 1963.

EMERSON, RUPERT. *From Empire to Nation.** Cambridge, Mass.: Harvard University Press, 1960.

FINER, S. E. *The Man on Horseback: The Role of the Military in Politics.* New York: Frederick A. Praeger, 1962.

GEERTZ, CLIFFORD (ed.). *Old Societies and New States.* New York: The Free Press of Glencoe, 1963.

GERSCHENKRON, ALEXANDER. *Economic Backwardness in Historical Perspective: A Book of Essays.** Cambridge, Mass.: Harvard University Press, 1962. Paperback ed.; New York: Frederick A. Praeger, 1965.

GOLDSCHMIDT, WALTER (ed.). *The United States and Africa.** Rev. ed.; New York: Frederick A. Praeger, 1963.

HEILBRONER, ROBERT L. *The Great Ascent.** New York: Harper & Row, 1963.

———. *The Making of Economic Society.** Englewood Cliffs, N.J.: Prentice-Hall, 1962.

HODGKIN, THOMAS. *African Political Parties.** Harmondsworth: Penguin Books, 1961.

JANOWITZ, MORRIS. *The Military in the Political Development of New Nations.** Chicago: University of Chicago Press, 1964.

JOHNSON, JOHN J. (ed.). *The Role of the Military in Underdeveloped Countries.* Princeton, N.J.: Princeton University Press, 1962.

KAUTSKY, JOHN H. (ed.). *Political Change in Underdeveloped Countries: Nationalism and Communism.** New York: John Wiley and Sons, 1962.

LEGUM, COLIN. *Pan-Africanism: A Short Political Guide.** Rev. ed.; New York: Frederick A. Praeger, 1965.

LIEUWEN, EDWIN. *Arms and Politics in Latin America.** Rev. ed.; New York: Frederick A. Praeger, 1961.

LIPSET, SEYMOUR M. *The First New Nation.* New York: Basic Books, 1963.

LISKA, GEORGE. *The New Statecraft: Foreign Aid in American Foreign Policy.* Chicago: University of Chicago Press, 1960.

LONDON, KURT (ed.). *New Nations in a Divided World: The International Relations of the Afro-Asian States.** New York: Frederick A. Praeger, 1964.

MARTIN, LAURENCE W. (ed.). *Neutralism and Nonalignment: The New States in World Affairs.** New York: Frederick A. Praeger, 1962.

McCORD, WILLIAM. *The Springtime of Freedom.** London and New York: Oxford University Press, 1965.

MILLIKIN, MAX F., and BLACKMER, DONALD L. M. (eds.). *The Emerging Nations: Their Growth and the U.S. Policy.** Boston: Little, Brown and Co., 1961.

ORGANSKI, A. F. K. *The Stages of Political Development.* New York: Alfred A. Knopf, 1965.

ROSTOW, W. W. *Stages of Economic Growth: A Non-Communist Manifesto.** London and New York: Cambridge University Press, 1960.

SCHMITT, KARL M., and BURKS, DAVID D. *Evolution or Chaos: Dynamics of*

Latin American Government and Politics.* New York: Frederick A. Praeger, 1963.

SHILS, EDWARD A. *Political Development in the New States.** 's-Gravenhage, The Netherlands: Marten and Co., 1962.

SIGMUND, PAUL E., JR. (ed.). *The Ideologies of the Developing Nations.** Rev. ed.; New York: Frederick A. Praeger, 1967.

STALEY, EUGENE. *The Future of Underdeveloped Countries: Political Implications of Economic Development.** Rev. ed.; New York: Frederick A. Praeger, 1961.

SZULC, TAD. *The Winds of Revolution: Latin America Today—And Tomorrow.** Rev. ed.; New York: Frederick A. Praeger, 1965.

VON DER MEHDEN, FRED R. *Politics of the Developing Nations.** Englewood Cliffs, N.J.: Prentice-Hall, 1964.

WALLERSTEIN, IMMANUEL. *Africa: The Politics of Independence.** New York: Vintage Books, 1961.

WARD, BARBARA. *Five Ideas That Change the World.** New York: W. W. Norton & Co., 1959.

————. *The Rich Nations and the Poor Nations.** New York: W. W. Norton & Co., 1962.

ZARTMAN, I. WILLIAM. *International Relations in the New Africa.** Englewood Cliffs, N.J.: Prentice-Hall, 1966.

International Organization

BAILEY, SYDNEY D. *The United Nations: A Short Political Guide.** New York: Frederick A. Praeger, 1963.

BLOOMFIELD, LINCOLN P. *The United Nations and U.S. Foreign Policy.** Boston: Little, Brown and Co., 1960.

————, et al. *International Military Forces.** Boston: Little, Brown and Co., 1964.

BOYD, ANDREW. *United Nations: Piety, Myth and Truth.** Baltimore, Md.: Penguin Books, 1963.

BURNS, ARTHUR LEE, and HEATHCOTE, NINA. *Peace-keeping by U.N. Forces: From Suez to the Congo.* New York: Frederick A. Praeger, 1963.

CALVOCORESSI, PETER. *World Order and New States: Problems of Keeping the Peace.* New York: Frederick A. Praeger, 1962.

CLAUDE, INIS L., JR. *Power and International Relations.* New York: Random House, 1964.

————. *Swords into Plowshares.* Rev. ed.; New York: Random House, 1964.

DALLIN, ALEXANDER. *The Soviet Union at the United Nations: An Inquiry into Soviet Motives and Objectives.** New York: Frederick A. Praeger, 1962.

FRYE, WILLIAM R. *A United Nations Peace Force.* Dobbs Ferry, N.Y.: Oceana Publications, 1957.

HAMMARSKJÖLD, DAG. *Servant of Peace: A Selection of the Speeches and Statements of Dag Hammarskjöld.* Edited by Wilder Foote. New York: Harper & Row, 1963.

LASH, JOSEPH P. *Dag Hammarskjöld: Custodian of the Brushfire Peace.* Garden City, N.Y.: Doubleday & Co., 1961.

MILLER, RICHARD. *Dag Hammarskjöld and Crisis Diplomacy.* Dobbs Ferry, N.Y.: Oceana Publications, 1961.

NICHOLAS, HERBERT G. *The United Nations as a Political Institution.** 2d ed.; London and New York: Oxford University Press, 1962.

WILCOX, FRANCIS O., and HAVILAND, H. FIELD, JR. (eds.). *The U.S. and the U.N.* For The Johns Hopkins University, School of Advanced Studies, Washington, D.C. Baltimore, Md.: The Johns Hopkins Press, 1961.

Index

JX 1906 W7

P.

International
Political
Community-
an anthology
Anchor Books

$2.25